Job Creation in Urban Informal Sector in India: Issues and Policy Options

Job Creation in Urban Informal Sector in India: Issues and Policy Options

Papers and Proceedings of the National Workshop on
Strategic Approach to
Job Creation in the Urban Informal Sector
17-19 February 2000, Surajkund

Edited by

A. S. Oberai and G. K. Chadha

South Asia Multidisciplinary Advisory Team (SAAT)
International Labour Organization
New Delhi - India

June 2001

ISBN : 92-2-111904-1

Published 2001

ILO Publications can be obtained through major booksellers or ILO local offices in many countries, or direct from ILO Publications, International Labour Office, CH-1211 Geneva 22, Switzerland. Catalogues or lists of new publications are available free of charge from the above address.

Printed in India.

Contents

Page No.

Preface

Ever since the presentation of the Director-General's Report, on the Dilemma of the Informal Sector, before the International Labour Conference in 1991, the ILO has continued to show a profound concern about the working and living conditions of people engaged in the informal sector of the developing economies. The ILO's concern has manifested itself in many different ways, most ostensibly in building consensus among its tripartite partners (the employers, the workers and governments) about the urgency of restoring economic health to the sector, developing and implementing technical cooperation programmes, and through intermittent launching of systematic studies to understand and interpret the ground realities in this sector. The Director-General's personal commitment to carry the cause of this sector to its logical end, has been expressed, on numerous occasions, in different national and international meetings. To quote from one of his speeches:

> Some believe that it is better for people to have their noses above the water than to be drowning, so let us not care too much about the working conditions provided there is employment. That may be true for a moment, but, in the long run, we all know that this is not sustainable. So, if we are talking about the informal economy, right from the start we have to have the perspective, even if it is not immediate, of making it a part of the formal economy, in order to defend rights and assure protection. How can we make sure it moves in the right direction, even if there is first a period of time in which it stays at a certain level? The only sustainable process would be one in which the working conditions and the processes in small and informal enterprises become part of a much wider framework of economic growth, social stability and recognition of social protection.

In pursuance of its continuing concern for improving the working conditions, productivity and earning levels of the workers engaged in the informal sector, especially after its most recent declaration on 'Decent Work', made by the Director-General, Juan Somavia, before the 87th Session of the International Labour Conference in 1999, the ILO took the initiative of commissioning a number of studies on the urban informal sector in India. Among policy-makers and development specialists in India, there has also been a growing realisation that informal sector stands out as a major source of future employment creation particularly since formal sector has failed to generate adequate employment opportunities for the growing labour force. To ensure that the underlying realities are brought to the surface, five field-based studies (covering such dynamic sub-sectors as khadi textiles, food processing, leather and leather products, software and tourism) dealing with different aspects of the working of the urban informal sector including its potential for job creation were commissioned. The five sub-sectors were studied for purposes of illustration, and it was considered that based on the experience gained, issues in other sectors could be addressed later. The sub-sectors were selected based on their dynamic behaviour, characterised by growth in employment, expansion of market, increase in sales in recent years and the extent to which the sub-sector has vertical linkages. A sufficient concentration of sub-sector in one particular geographical location was also viewed as an important criterion for being able to make an impact through strategic intervention. The ultimate aim has been to better understand the specific problems of each sub-sector and to explore new ways and opportunities to deal with them. In addition to the field-based studies, four status papers reflecting the realities in the States of Assam, Gujarat, Uttar Pradesh and West Bengal were invited from individual scholars. One paper each on the role of employers' and workers' organisations and on training needs of the informal sector was also commissioned. Finally, two other papers, one on macro-economic policy issues and the other on trends and policy perspectives were also invited. The focus of all these studies was to examine the scope for additional job creation and for improving the quality of employment in the urban informal sector in India.

For discussing the numerous issues raised by these papers, and to evolve an action plan of its own, the ILO, in collaboration with the Ministry of Labour, Government of India, and the IFCI-sponsored Institute of Labour Development, Jaipur, and with the active support of employers and trade unions, organised a three-day national workshop on 'Strategic Approach to Job Creation in the Urban Informal Sector in India' at Surajkund in Haryana during February 17-19, 2000. The workshop was attended by over 100 delegates, representing a cross-section of the community — academic and research institutions, workers' and employers' organisations, central, state and local governments, donors and international development agencies. Besides, the presence of Mr. Juan Somavia, Director-General of the ILO, Dr. Manmohan Singh, former Secretary General of the South Commission and former Finance Minister of India, Dr. S.N. Jatiya, Union Minister of Labour, Mr. S.S.Dhindsa, Union Minister of Urban Employment and Poverty Alleviation, Mr. I.P. Anand, Member, ILO Governing Body and Dr. L. Mishra, Secretary Labour, Government of India, among others, in the inaugural session of the workshop, clearly demonstrated the importance that the ILO and the Government of India attach to the problems and prospects of the urban informal sector.

The present volume puts together the thoroughly revised and edited versions of the 15 papers presented at the National Workshop in order to make them available to a wider readership. It also includes an overview, proceedings of the inaugural session and major highlights of the discussion during the various sessions of the workshop. The papers cover issues related to a wide range of production and service activities in the informal sector that adequately inform the reader about the working conditions, employment status, wage levels, market performance and the future prospects of the informal sector enterprises in India. The individual papers are grouped under six broad areas which include: (1) Analytical and Policy Issues, (2) Sectoral Issues, (3) Regional Perspective, (4) Training and Skills Development, (5) Role of Social Partners, and (6) Decent Work Perspective.

Many people in addition to the authors of the papers have contributed to this volume. It is difficult to single out individuals, but a large number of resource persons, senior government officials, representatives of workers' and employers' organisations and eminent scholars who acted as Chairpersons have contributed to the technical discussions. We are indebted to all of them. A number of ILO colleagues and Headquarters technical units have also provided useful inputs in planning and preparation of the background studies. In particular, we would like to thank Mr. Samir Radwan, Mr. Rizwanul Islam, Ms. Andrea Singh, Mr. F. Fluitman, Ms. Leyla Tegmo-Reddy, Ms. Mary Johnson and Mr. S. Acharya. We are also grateful to Mr. I.P. Anand, Member, ILO Governing Body for providing advice and encouragement in the preparation of this volume and for chairing the meetings of the Advisory Committee which was established to guide and monitor the Work Programme. Technical support for preparation of background studies was provided by Senior Specialists in the South Asia Multidisciplinary Advisory Team (SAAT). The administrative support throughout the period was provided by the ILO Area Office, New Delhi. The present volume is therefore the product of joint efforts of ILO-SAAT and the ILO Area Office, New Delhi. Mr. M.L. Nandrajog, ILO consultant, coordinated the work of the Workshop. The work of preparation of the manuscript for publication was handled by Ms. Amrita Mehrotra, Ms. Jolly Dawar, Ms. Pushpinder Seera and Mr. Gopi Krishna. We gratefully acknowledge their assistance.

Needless to say, the views and opinions expressed in this volume reflect those of the individual authors, and not necessarily those of the ILO or the Government of India.

A.S. OBERAI
Director
South Asia Multidisciplinary Advisory Team (SAAT)
International Labour Organisation

New Delhi
June 2001.

An Overview of Urban Informal Sector in India

A.S.Oberai and G.K.Chadha

Understanding the Urban Informal Sector

The dualistic nature of developing economies is characterized by the existence of a modern capitalist sector, side by side with a traditional subsistence sector. The two are variously described as the 'formal' and the 'informal' sectors. The formal-informal dichotomy is particularly sharp in the urban areas.

The most common perception of the informal sector is that it comprises very small-scale units producing and distributing goods and services, and consists largely of independent, self-employed producers in urban areas. Most of them employ family labour and operate with very little capital. They utilise a low level of technology and skills and end up with low level of productivity which, in turn, provides very low and irregular incomes and highly unstable employment.They are informal in the sense that they are for the most part unregistered. Generally, they tend to have little or no access to organised markets, to credit institutions, to formal education and training institutions, or to many public services and amenities. They are often compelled by circumstances to operate outside the framework of the law, and even where they are registered and respect certain aspects of the law, they are almost invariably beyond the pale of social protection, labour legislation and protective measures at the workplace. Informal sector producers and workers are generally unorganised, and in most cases, beyond the scope of action of trade unions and employers' organisations although as we shall discuss below there have been some recent attempts at formation of self-help groups, and trade and welfare associations in certain sectors and States in India.

Beyond the generalisations given above, two other characteristics of the urban informal sector need to be underlined. First, the sector is highly heterogeneous from within. At one end of the spectrum is the group of relatively thriving small-scale modern manufacturing and service enterprises while, at the other end, are street vendors, shoe-shiners, junk collectors, and domestic servants. In between are a whole range of (primary service) activities such as informal transport services, small trading and commercial establishments, repair shops, etc. In terms of persons employed, the variation goes from a single-worker self-employing household enterprises to a total of 5 or 6 workers including some hired workers. Heterogeneities are equally glaring in terms of capital invested, technology-in-use, management practices adopted, productivity levels realised, and net earnings raised. It is these very heterogeneities, and the consequent mingle of a small but vibrant and a large but languishing section of the informal sector, which suggest the potential of the former becoming a significant contributor to the national economy. From the point of view of human welfare, it is, however, the weaker segment of the informal sector that deserves more attention and support. It needs to be underlined that a preponderant majority of the urban poor belong to this segment. Policy orientation therefore needs to take note of the specific problems of the two distinct segments of the informal sector.

Second, a very high proportion of the informal sector enterprises suffer a high degree of vulnerability. It arises largely due to the fact that they have to rely on self-supporting and 'informal' institutional arrangement. Having little access to the modern capital market, informal sector enterprises have to obtain credit from informal sources, usually friends and relatives, and non-banking financial agencies, often on highly unfavourable terms. Lacking access to formal training institutions, they acquire skills through their own informal, apprenticeship schemes. Lacking access to official social security schemes, they have to rely on family or group solidarity or on non-governmental organisations.

The vulnerability of the informal sector enterprises is due also to the fact that many among them operate beyond the law, and receive little or no legal protection including the right to appeal in a court of law. Their existence on the fringes of the law has often led public authorities to interpret them as unauthorized activities which often invite harassment and repression to the people engaged in them.

Urban Informal Sector in India

The size of the informal sector in India is large. The available data suggest that more than 90 per cent of the total work force of 380 million is engaged in the informal sector. In the urban areas this figure is close to 65-70 per cent. Not all of these workers are poor but crude estimates suggest that close to half this number is in dire need of occupational up-scaling. The truly dynamic segments, it is believed, may constitute less than one-third of the total size of the informal sector.

The large size of the informal sector in India has prompted some analysts to describe it as an 'informal economy' rather than an 'informal sector'. Both because the urban formal sector has never been a big source of employment in India, especially to people with low educational and training background, and because agriculture too could not accommodate, on an enduring basis, more than a small proportion of the incremental labour force, the urban informal sector has proved to be a refuge for a large majority of job seekers not getting absorbed elsewhere. Since there are no barriers to entry, and capital required to start an enterprise is highly flexible, and usually within the affordable limits of the prospective 'entrepreneurs', and, more importantly, since alternative sources of employment are not around, growth of employment in India's urban informal sector has simply been phenomenal. In fact, most of the recent employment accretion (97 per cent) has been in this segment alone.

The available evidence suggests that a sizeable proportion of the workers engaged in the urban informal sector are rural migrants. With their poor educational, training and skill background, they land up in low-paying, semi-skilled or unskilled jobs, and lend themselves to a high degree of exploitation. The productivity and earning levels in most of the urban informal sector enterprises are low; many of those working in this sector are under-employed. The working environment is often poor; working hours are very long; most pre-requisites of a decent employment (paid leave, pension and bonus, medical support and health insurance, maternity leave benefits, compensation against accident, etc.) are nearly conspicuous by their absence.

In India, as in most other developing economies, macro-economic policy biases against the informal sector have persisted for a long time. Import-substituting industrialisation strategies, restrictive trade practices, and the skewed allocation of resources have somehow worked to the disadvantage of the informal sector. Moreover, it is commonly believed that stringent labour laws, rigidities in the labour market and growing international competition have encouraged the use of capital-intensive technology which have restricted the growth of employment in the formal sector, forcing the informal sector to absorb most of the additional job aspirants.

A very sizeable part of the informal sector has continued to be discriminated against by public institutions. The most vocal instances come from credit, educational and training institutions. For a large part of their credit requirements, the informal sector enterprises have still to fall back upon the informal credit sources such as the usurious money lenders or friends and relatives; most of the people employed in the informal sector get only on-the-job training, since the formal training institutions either do not take them or else, they do not have any appeal for them. The local government authorities, including the civic agencies and the police, have also generally looked at the informal sector with disfavour, if not with disdain.

Until recently, government policy has given very little attention to the informal sector, primarily because the policy-makers believed it to be a transient phenomenon which would ultimately fade away or get integrated, even if gradually, into the mainstream of the economy. It was considered that, with economic growth, the formal sector would witness a sizeable expansion and that most of the surplus labour would be absorbed by it. Nonetheless, in spite of a reasonably strong growth of 5 to 6 per cent over many years, this has not happened. On the contrary, the informal sector has continued to grow, along with worsening employment and living conditions. This has raised serious doubts about the functioning of the 'trickle-down' process. An important reason for the failure of this process is that access to opportunities, opened up by growth, is rarely equal in a society such as India, where the initial distribution of income and wealth is highly unequal. The capital and labour markets are both far from 'perfect', and often work to the detriment of the poorer sections of society. Access to education, health and other social amenities is also highly inequitable. Further, access to information is both restricted and too costly for the poor. Consequently, the benefits of growth accrue more to the relatively well-off in the formal sector.

In sharp contrast to the implicit faith in the 'trickle-down' thesis, once held by policy makers and development specialists, it is now widely recognised that the informal sector is a living reality that will endure itself for decades to come, and would embrace a sizeable segment of the labour force. It is essential, therefore, that national policy on labour should now be redirected towards the informal sector, rectifying the policy biases that have somehow persisted against it, so that it emerges as a growing and more productive source of employment and incomes for India's growing labour force.

Thus, the informal sector now stands out 'as a potential provider of employment and incomes to millions of people who would otherwise lack the means of survival' or 'as a breeding ground for entrepreneurship on a mass scale'. It is now increasingly realised that the informal sector can significantly improve itself, practically in each aspect of its functioning, if only the past policy biases and the currently hostile policy environment, under which it is denied access to the advantages (e.g., the availability of credit, foreign exchange, and tax concessions) offered to the formal sector, are removed. A healthy growth of the urban informal sector could provide an impetus to growth of the urban and the overall economy. In the current economic environment, the proverbial argument of low capital intensity, and cost advantage, lends considerable strength to the case for greater allocation of resources to the informal sector. Further, by providing access to training and apprenticeship at substantially lower costs than that provided by formal institutions and the formal sector, the informal sector can play an important role in human capital formation.

As the pace of globalisation and economic liberalisation picks up in the coming years, and the formal sector jobs become more education-, training- and skill-intensive, it is the informal sector that can emerge as a saviour of the unskilled and semi-skilled job aspirants whose supply is increasing. It is again in the context of the increasing degree of globalisation that a sizeable part of the urban informal sector can be groomed to act as an adjunct to the formal sector, now that success stories about sub-contracting, ancillarisation, and out-sourcing abound from many parts of the Indian economy; the mutual interest of the two sectors is more than evident now. Finally, to reiterate the traditional argument, promotion of the informal sector would ensure an increased share of the benefits of development to the poor, many among whom are concentrated in the urban informal sector, and a more even regional spread of employment, earnings and better-living.

To make this a reality, a multi-pronged strategy has to be put into operation, both to rectify the domestic policy gaps of the past and to initiate new measures to the requirement of the changing external scenario. Undoubtedly, a selective approach is required, as it is unrealistic to expect that the whole of the urban informal sector could undergo a full-scale structural or technological transformation in the near future. Some segments, especially those which can potentially be associated with the formal sector through a chain of technological, production and marketing links, clearly have a bright future and must, therefore, be promoted in the interest of creating decent jobs, including higher earnings and improved standards of living. Another section of the informal sector, engaged especially in manufacturing, can clearly benefit from modern methods of production, management and marketing, but institutional handicaps (e.g., lack of access to institutional credit and training) stand in the way of its growth and progress.

Although the informal sector has provided almost all additional employment in recent years, and is now India's major hope for future employment generation, it has never achieved such desirable economic targets as high growth, technological breakthrough, productivity improvement or substantial income propagation; over years, the sector has displayed a contrasting mingle of strengths and weaknesses. Its failures need to be understood and dealt with, at the institutional, market and individual levels. Perhaps, questions need to be put more pointedly and answers sought, some through demand-side and some through supply-side interventions that have already established their efficacy in different sectors and sub-sectors of the informal sector.

Macro-Economic Issues

The cause of up-scaling the informal economy in the urban areas assumes particular importance because the formal sector has failed to generate adequate employment opportunities for the growing labour force in India. The syndrome of jobless growth in the formal sector leaves little choice but to make efforts to raise the potential of the informal sector, to create jobs for newer entrants to the labour force (7-8 million per year), not necessarily possessing adequate skills or financial resources.

But this does not mean that the informal sector can grow in isolation. It has important linkages with the formal sector. The formal sector depends on the informal sector for economical inputs and a variety of wage goods for its workers. The informal sector, in turn, depends to a large extent on the growth of the formal sector for its market and income; and also obtains a variety of raw materials for sustaining its own production.

There is thus no merit in concentrating all policy attention on the informal sector alone, just as the economy today is precariously poised between a buoyant formal sector and a sluggish informal sector due to the past neglect of the latter, or the exclusive pre-occupation with the former. There is a real possibility for the two sectors to co-exist and grow to their mutual benefit.

The informal sector today offers jobs in a highly flexible labour market, which permits the semi-skilled and the unskilled to gain access to work, albeit at low earnings and often under insecure and unwholesome working conditions. Jobs created are increasingly bereft of labour standards and social protection. This provides for survival but does not necessarily help in creating decent jobs. The real challenge is, therefore, to straighten out the policy kinks that have kept the informal sector in a state of deprivation. This is, by no means, an easy job but improving productivity levels, conditions of work and earnings of the informal sector workers, should now become an integral part of the overall development strategy.

The two papers in the volume dealing with macro-economic issues are optimistic that the informal sector can transform itself from its present status of a stagnant, low-productivity, and worker-unfriendly sector to a house of dynamic, market-savvy and worker-friendly enterprises. A number of interventions, both on the supply and demand side, are urgently called for. On the demand side, accelerating and sustaining a rapid pace of economic growth, promoting linkages with the formal sector, boosting exports from the informal sector, and stimulating internal demand, are the major interventions needed. On the supply side, major interventions suggested include: eliminating biases in macro-economic policies that have persisted against the informal sector, defining an appropriate regulatory framework for micro-enterprises, removing constraints on the growth of small scale and tiny enterprises, increasing access to credit, preferably within a participatory framework, granting of land titles and registration with public authorities, substituting selective assistance to the informal sector entrepreneurs in terms of provision of technical guidance, subsidized credit, scarce raw materials and marketing support in place of the present system of general subsidization and regulatory control, enhancing productivity through training and skills development, and regulating the flow of migration from rural areas.

Sectoral Issues

Field-based studies carried out in five dynamic sub-sectors (textiles, tourism, food processing, leather, computer software) provide useful information on sector specific issues. Almost all the studies found evidence that questioned the stereotyped notion of the 'informal sector'; empirically, it was difficult to find a dividing line between the formal and the informal enterprises in the continuum of economic activities. What was especially striking was the prevalence of the informal labour markets and hiring practices along formal lines.

The studies threw up a mixture of similarities and dis-similarities. A few common features identified are: (1) almost all the responding enterprises are characterized by low capital inputs and rudimentary techniques of production or service provision; (2) many employers engage migrant labour which permits them to extend the working hours as well as keep wages and earnings at low levels; this is especially true of jobs that entail relatively low skills and mundane and repetitive operations; (3) a preponderant majority of workers have self-acquired skills; workers with formal institutional training were relatively few; (4) pro-worker inspections, monitoring and enforcements of regulations of any kind by government officials were usually non-existent; (5) most workers are engaged for long, indefinite and unpaid working hours when there is rush of business; in some cases, this does not exclude the self-employing entrepreneurs; (6) in most cases, the net earnings are low; this is especially so in the case of wage-paid workers; (7) there is virtually no social protection, other than that provided through family, kinship and community links; (8) the working conditions and the work environment in some of the informal sector activities are poor; the bakeries, fish processing, and leather industry are the typical examples; (9) most workers at the lower end of the job hierarchy are first generation migrants or first time workers; being nearly totally illiterate, and untrained, they lend themselves to extreme types of exploitation by their urban employers; and (10) in some industries, and in some operations, (e.g., tanning, leather processing), there is some caste and religion specificity in the deployment of workers.

The dis-similarities too were numerous. Some of the more glaring ones are: (1) internal heterogeneities are rather strong in some sectors and activities. For example, making and vending of bread or rickshaw plying present fairly simple production or service chains, beginning and ending with just 1-2 activities There are many others that have complicated production processes, starting with humble origins and winding through complicated labyrinths into an international division of labour. Leather products provide a typical example; (2) software industry stands apart because of its high-skill/high demand syndrome. While many workers in this sector are transient and graduate to the formal sector in relatively short periods, the sector as such is expanding fast and provides chance and space to many job seekers who have otherwise lost out in the admissions race to formal engineering or technical institutions; (3) demand fluctuations can severely affect workers in industries such as khadi, leather or tourism. Such demand cycles are, however, not found in food-related industries; (4) in industries such as leather and fish processing, the removal or relative isolation of workers from the actual market place considerably retards their bargaining capacity; (5) in industries such as tourism, there are relatively high overhead costs and low value-addition, because tourists in general, and domestic tourists in particular, spend too little in contrast to the overhead costs; and (6) the deployment of child labour was observed only in some of the sectors studied. This was particularly seen in low-skill jobs such as cleaning restaurant tables and utensils, and in fish processing. There is gender specificity here; the girl child is the worst placed.

A range of recommendations follow from field based studies and the follow-up discussions. It is emphasized, for example, that there is a crucial need to give legal recognition to the existence of the informal sector in general, and some of its activities in particular. In the absence of such a legal recognition, the up-scaling of such activities, through legal channels and institutional interventions would be difficult. Government laws and regulations should also be realistic and inclusive, and the licensing system should be simple. An important issue is that of land rights, since the initial recognition of any activity emerges from legal access to land. Freeing the informal sector enterprises from the clutches of the usurious money lenders, and the increasing role that credit institutions have to play in this regard, are emphasized with equal vehemence. The cluster approach, on the lines of the recommendation of the Abid Hussain Committee, is also pleaded for. Social protection, skills development and transfer of technologies are other areas that need much more attention, and effective support. Finally, attempts need to be made for organizing the informal sector entrepreneurs, the self-employed and the workers since social organization helps in collective bargaining *vis-à-vis* the formal sector.

Not all the recommendations apply to all sectors, industries and locales; a uniform transfer of skills, resources and credit across sectors and locales would not be very productive. The heterogeneity of the informal sector is stoutly revealed, for example, by the credit needs of the software units, which often go as high as Rs. 1,00,000, and for a relatively longer period, while street vendors or fisher-folk may require only Rs. 500, usually on a daily production-sale cycle basis. In some activities, the absence of new technology is critically holding up the improvement in productivity while in others, occupational safety and health issues demand a much higher priority. Accordingly, some policy and institutional initiatives need to be taken at the 'broad sectoral level', others at the local or 'neighbourhood level', clearly distinguishing between the scale of operations in each segment of the informal sector. The adoption of a differentiated approach to address micro entrepreneurs, the self-employed and wage workers, would also be meaningful.

Regional Perspectives/State Efforts

Four papers on regional perspectives prepared by senior State civil servants put fourth their perception of the problems and highlight the efforts being made to address them, in each State.

Each of the States perceived the problems to be gigantic. The census and other survey data presented show that the labour force has been growing rapidly and the organised sector is hardly creating jobs anywhere. Consequently, workers find refuge in the informal economy where the conditions of work and earnings are often poor. The report on Uttar Pradesh found that most of the informal sector enterpreneurs are no better in their socio-economic conditions than the depressed working class elsewhere. Their interests too are often close to those put forward by wage earners. Public utilities such as health services are not readily available, child labour is widely prevalent, market interest rates on credit are hefty and the morbidity and mortality of the micro and small enterprises is high. Similarly, in West Bengal, the system of employment outside the organised sectors is characterized as exploitative. Labor contracts are heavily loaded against the working class; the wages are low, the poor are exploited and child labour is widespread.

None of the States has a specific strategy for the informal sector *per se,* instead, each aims to address poverty and unemployment as part of the general development problem. To achieve these goals, the State authorities implement strategies for employment creation, training and social assistance. Among the programmes that are in place are those for small and cottage industries, anti-poverty schemes and training modules for different vocations. Services offered to different (small and micro) businesses are in the areas of marketing and technology transfer. Priority sector lending and establishment of industrial areas are the other facilitating means. In some cases, the approaches are 'sector-oriented' as well. Specialized institutions have been set up for this purpose. All admit, however, that the size of the effort is no match to the size of the problem.

Attention can be drawn to some contrasting observations such as the courses on information technology and computer training initiated by Assam in the North-East region where 486 computer centres with 2,000 computing machines, have been set up, particularly to combat the problem of unemployment among the educated youth. Gujarat on the other hand, has concentrated on promoting a range of traditional industries like textiles, diamond polishing, garments, waste recycle and bookbinding. Gujarat has also created schemes to reach out to home-based workers and has extended some social protection to the hitherto unprotected workers.

Almost all the approaches adopted by the State Governments can be characterized as supply-led and delivered through a top-down bureaucratic channel which is hardly conducive to promoting efficiency.

Policies towards the Informal Sector

The above analysis suggests that the task of decent job creation must assume top priority in a country like India where a very large proportion of the work force is underemployed and works in marginal work environments in the informal sector. This task has both macro and micro dimensions. At the macro level, a policy framework conducive to employment creation should be drawn up. Such a policy framework should address issues relating to existing labour laws, capital-intensity in modern sector enterprises, regulatory environment for promoting small businesses and institutions that aid the growth of self-employment. At the micro level, efforts should be made to prepare the youth to establish businesses through entrepreneurship development and training programmes. Keeping in view the established gender gap in access to job opportunities in the country, specific efforts must be made to reach out to the female youth.

While an important part of the long-term solution to the employment problem is to restore higher rates of growth in the modern-sector, there are nevertheless undeniable benefits in promoting the informal sector. Many of its activities are labour-intensive. The informal sector therefore provides an easy way to create and expand employment. By supporting and interacting with the formal sector, informal activities are not only a "sponge" for extra labour but also an alternative source of rapid growth. It is therefore important for policy makers to actively support the growth of such activities.

The labour productivity and returns to the sector must be increased without reducing its labour absorptive capacity. This will increase the output, raising returns to the sector, reversing its involution, and its generation of poverty and inequality. However, policy for the informal sector in India must be cognisant of some of the key parameters that have emerged from the analysis in this volume.

Given the immense size of the informal sector, micro interventions, be they micro credit, micro skilling, or micro output marketing, cannot have a macro impact on the sector. If the macro conditions of the sector are to be transformed significantly in such areas as access to capital, capital labour ratios, technology and skill levels, labour productivity, wage rates and returns, higher valued added products, a more diversified product range, higher prices for its products, and demand linkages to the formal and export sectors, then macro interventions will also be needed.

Macro interventions will require a significant re-allocation of resources towards the informal sector, which would mean a reversal of existing policy. Existing policy allocates resources predominantly towards the formal sector on the rationale that it produces 40 per cent of the output. Re-allocation of some share of the resources currently going towards the formal sector has to be based on the rationale that while the informal sector provides employment to more than 90 per cent of the labour force, it receives highly inadequate returns, largely because of low labour productivity. Informal sector policy has to be re-prioritised in terms of resource allocation to improve productivity and income of the overwhelming majority of the labour force.

As the field studies included in this volume suggest, the informal sector is vast and extremely heterogeneous; it consists of a large number of very diverse activities, each characterised by a certain techno-economic competence and market access. There cannot thus be a uniform policy for all the activities in the informal economy. Certain segments are, to an extent, already linked to, or with some effort can be linked to, the larger markets and thereby yield/can yield, higher productivity and better working and living conditions for workers engaged in them. At the other end, there are activities that can only be served through social welfare and anti-poverty programmes. To begin with, it is more practical to adopt a 'piece-by-piece' approach of intervention for up-scaling activities in the informal economy. It would be meaningful to concentrate on certain 'promising' economic activities, i.e. those activities which, with some minimal input(s), can readily be up-scaled and linked to the larger markets. To pursue such an approach, an integrated policy package can be developed. As regards, 'promising economic activities', participants at the workshop have suggested a number of areas such as tourism, I.T. services, entertainment goods, construction activities, infrastructure development, food processing and handicrafts which have significant potential for growth and job creation.

There are also some recommendations on specific topics which follow from the background papers and discussions in the working-group sessions. Some of these are briefly discussed below:

Policy and Regulatory Environment

This should include action to resolve unnecessary regulatory obstacles to enterprise formation and growth, and measures to improve access to credit. In many situations, the official regulations often present a considerable handicap for the sector by requiring complex administrative procedures and excessively high standards of products and processes, and by limiting location. Such regulations encourage the development of illegal activities that damage the informal sector's operations. The appropriate policy response is to bestow secure property rights to the land, squatter housing and other productive assets assembled by the poor, and to remove administrative obstacles and controls that prevent the growth of micro-enterprises and small-scale businesses.

The removal of regulatory obstacles must, however, be accompanied by the protection of the basic rights, health and safety of workers and the progressive improvements of overall working conditions, together with the strengthening of efforts to make some enterprises part of the formal sector.

The policy focus has to be first on recognition of informal sector units as economic entities and partners in development. There should be a proper registration system that provides valid documents to entrepreneurs to engage in business. The legal and regulatory framework should be transparent and simple, with a facility for 'single window' clearance.

Micro Finance

There is a major challenge to divert resources from the established banking system to small borrowers. While it is now accepted that small producers can be credible borrowers, the financial institutions are presently not equipped to lend and manage thinly spread small loans with fast turnovers. For enabling this, both legal and institutional changes will have to be made. Attitudinal changes among bankers must be effected. As the studies in this volume suggest, the present government schemes merit better implementation through improved monitoring, more flexibility in the lending portfolio, taking evaluation reports more seriously and emulating best practices in the field. The financial system should be decentralised and capacities should be built at the local level in disbursement of funds, client identification, monitoring, etc. Credit should be extended only for activities that possess a market. Feasibility studies here can be of help.

It is important to promote both the existing initiatives and encourage newer ones. The NGOs involved in credit delivery systems should network, and some of them should become nodal agencies. They should be exposed to training in entrepreneurship development programmes. As of today, the most successful experiments of micro finance are the ones managed by women associations. It would be most useful and instructive to ensure maximum involvement of such associations and also to learn from their experience in this area.

It is widely agreed that access to credit rather than the cost of the credit is the bottleneck for small-scale enterprises. Very small enterprises face special problems because of a lack of collateral. So, successful credit schemes must by-pass normal collateral requirements and substitute alternatives such as group guarantees, as has been done so successfully in Bangladesh under the Grameen Bank Programme.

Technology, Training and Skills Development

Upgrading technologies to meet the demands of larger markets is paramount. The extent of product specific 'necessity' should first be established, and then institutional mechanisms should be set up to satisfy it. In this regard, it is essential to create a dialogue with different institutions for enabling technology transfers.

But it must be recognised that technology dissemination is not gender neutral; under the present conditions, any technology upgradation will essentially benefit the men, thus further widening the knowledge gap and hence the earnings capacity between the males and females. It may therefore be necessary to be sensitive to this aspect while addressing the technology transfer question.

Keeping in view the fact that most workers in the informal economy are self-taught - they have not benefited from formal schooling and training systems - it is important that institutional mechanisms be established to upgrade workers' skills on an on-going basis. Reorientation of the skills of self-employed and bare foot entrepreneurs is called for. Answers to questions such as, how the existing institutions and schemes can accommodate the training needs of the informal economy, too need to be sought. Once again, the concern mentioned above about the differential access of male and female workers to knowledge will need to be addressed.

Training is a critical input for up-scaling the informal sector activities. This is highlighted in the papers presented at the workshop. The papers touch upon issues such as extending training to workers who are not necessarily educated, are scattered over wide geographic locales, without easy access to stipulated centres of training and not necessarily able to pay for it.

It is difficult to address the issue of training in the conventional training framework, given the broad band of activities in the informal economy. Most studies suggest that there is very little training available for informal sector activities, and whatever is available, is not necessarily relevant or effective. Some characteristics of a successful approach to training were identified at the workshop. These include: (1) the design of effective training programmes requires knowledge of labour markets; (2) the whole training approach should be demand-driven and job-linked, so as to minimize skill mis-match; (3) multi-skilling should be a part of the training process; (4) effort should be made to ensure that training is skill oriented and therefore cuts across occupational specificity; (5) training, as a matter of principle, should be of relatively short duration; if possible, it should be field based and cost effective and there should be stakeholder participation in the design of training schemes; and (6) training for the informal sector work should not be linked to degrees or diplomas; the aim should be to identify effective users of skills.

There is no necessity to establish new training institutions or to allocate new budgets for training. It should instead be possible to create space for informal sector training in the existing institutions and their present budgets should be reoriented to accommodate the new training needs. Some innovative approaches for cost-effective skill transfers can be attempted through a 're-discovery' of hereditary learning processes, wherever applicable, in view of their proven performance. But it must be remembered that many hereditary learning processes begin at a fairly early age in the life of the informal sector workers. There should, therefore, be a conscious attempt not to put children to arduous work.

Identification of the right agencies forms a critical component in successful training. These institutions should be flexible and trainers should be genuinely committed to the cause of the trainees. A decentralized extension training system should be emphasized. Training should be a package, consisting of credit and backup service in addition to skill transfer, so that its effectiveness is maximized. A typical non-material package could consist of knowledge, skills and attitude.

Effort should be made to provide basic education and numerical knowledge as a part of the training system in view of the fact that a large section of the working population in the informal economy as yet is illiterate. Targeting people at work or taking skills to people rather than making trainees to come to notified centres can be a useful approach. Training should be sensitive to the needs of different groups — the micro-enterprise owners, self-employed and paid workers.

Extending Social Protection/Social Security

Considering the fact that there is very little social protection available to workers outside the formal sector, there is a need to extend some form of cover against a number of contingencies and uncertainties. This does not have to be only for social welfare considerations; it has been demonstrated that it is possible to establish viable systems of protection for small contributors. It is a major challenge to multiply these experiments on a large scale. In the same vein, it needs to be mentioned that occupational health and safety and working conditions, not adequately addressed in the informal sector so far, too obligate regulation. Workers' protection against multiple health risks need to be dealt with on priority basis as exposures to dangerous chemicals are widespread in the informal economy and workers are poorly protected and educated to understand dangers arising out of their work. Improvements in working conditions will result in workers' better protection and working capacity and increased productivity.

All this will require to compile best practices and low cost solutions on work improvements in small-scale undertakings. Special attention to female workers, who to a great extent are 'invisible' because they are marginal or home based, must be made, in both social security and occupational health and safety issues. Some successful schemes of extending social protection to informal sector workers are already noticeable even though there are sometimes questions about their high administrative costs and sustainability in the long-term. These include: the Kerala Welfare Funds, the Bidi Workers' Welfare Fund, group insurance schemes of the Life Insurance Corporation of India, the SEWA insurance scheme, the Maharashtra Mathadi Workers' Scheme and the different welfare systems operated by Tamil Nadu Government. Special attention needs to be given to methods of financing, replicability and the degree to which such schemes respect the initially laid down objectives. A review of the existing legislation and its applicability to the informal sector or creation of new laws that may help extend social security in the informal sector, too are tasks which need to be undertaken.

At the 'programme level', a cluster approach is suggested, which would involve development of pilot projects in specific locales. With reference to social protection, it would be necessary to identify organisations through which action programmes can be developed, for example, co-operatives, trade-based guilds, trade unions (including the smaller ones) and self-help groups.

Role of Social Partners

The representatives of employers' and workers' organisations at the workshop highlighted a common view concerning the increased informalisation of work in the economy. It was argued that a dualistic model of growth, wherein one sector increasingly shuns employment promotion and the other presents a picture of rising deprivation, is non-sustainable. Among other problems, it leads to the gradual shrinking of markets and thereby to an overall slowdown of the economy, harming the big and small alike. In this regard, upscaling of activities and improving working conditions in the informal sector can help reduce the widening gap between the formal and informal segments of the economy. While the representatives of employers' organisations put more emphasis on developing production support mechanisms, the representatives of workers' organisations were more concerned with extending social protection/social security, including basic education to informal sector workers as well as their social organisation. It was also proposed that irrespective of the initiatives undertaken by private agencies or NGOs, the state should affirm its responsibility for universal enforcement of minimum wages and provision of housing, basic education and health services. The need to cover home-based workers under the ambit of law, was specifically emphasised.

There was a general consensus at the workshop that social dialogue among workers, employers and the government on important issues such as wage setting, occupational health and safety, social security, labour legislation, gender equity, labour market flexibility and even on broad areas of economic reforms is an important process to achieve participation, equity and sustainability. Such a process will not only help in consensus building on major issues, it will also commit and obtain the support of different social partners for pursuing development goals. Some mechanisms of social dialogue for workers and employers in the informal sector need to be developed and promoted irrespective of whether they are home-based or in part-time jobs. Some limited initiatives and experiences already exist in this field. It is imperative to put them together for wider application. Participation of women in social dialogue can help in achieving a gender balance.

Conclusions

Overall, the above analysis suggests that the informal sector needs to be given legitimacy, recognition and policy support. It provides employment to the majority of the labour force which would otherwise lack the means of survival. The informal sector also holds the potential for additional job creation and a strong capacity to contribute to economic growth. The focus of economic policy-making should therefore shift to the informal sector. But this does not mean that the formal sector should now be neglected. In fact, it is the growth in the formal sector which is likely to pull the informal sector. The real challenge is therefore to promote the linkages between the two sectors so that they can support each other and grow together to their mutual advantage.

There are a number of important issues which need urgent policy response. These include: removal of regulatory constraints which prohibit the growth of informal sector enterprises; improvement of access to markets, credit, training and technology; elimination of policy biases against the informal sector; and extension of social protection and social security to informal sector workers.

A major challenge is to organise workers and small entrepreneurs in the informal sector with a view to raising their voice. It is only through their own organised efforts and group solidarity that informal sector workers and producers can hope to achieve lasting improvements in their situation. Anther challenge is to create conditions for the progressive application of labour standards in the informal sector. The imperative of promoting decent work conditions and higher productivity in the informal sector will contribute to faster employment growth since rising labour productivity contributes to expansion of business activities and job creation.

While the supply side interventions in terms of credit availability, training, skills development, education are all needed to promote productivity and income in the informal sector, greater efforts are needed to enhance the demand for informal sector products. This would require forging and strengthening linkages with the export sector as well as between small and large enterprises. It may also require promotion of investment in such sectors as housing and infrastructure development which have not only significant employment potential but also have strong forward and backward linkages with the informal sector enterprises. The overall impetus for growth in the demand for informal sector products can of course come only from high and sustained economic growth.

Job Creation in Urban Informal Sector in India: Some Macro-Economic Policy Issues

A.S.Oberai and G.K. Chadha

1. Introduction

1.1 Job Situation on the Eve of Ninth Plan

One of the most daunting challenges facing the policy makers in India is to provide employment not only for those newly entering the labour force but also to reduce the backlog of unemployment carried over from the previous plans. On the basis of the age and sex structure of the population, and the anticipated labour force participation rates, the labour force in India is projected to increase by nearly 53 million during the Ninth Five Year Plan (1997-2002) (Govt. of India, 1999: 187). By any objective reckoning, it is a tremendous task to create employment for so many people during a single plan. The task seems all the greater, in the light of India's own past record of employment creation and of the emerging domestic and international compulsions under which new production regimes and competitive technologies have to be positioned in certain strategic sectors of the economy.

However, the task would become still more daunting if the under-employed were added to those openly unemployed. Rough estimates suggest that around 25 per cent of the employed persons in the informal sector are seriously under-employed. It is not only important to provide work to those who have none but also to improve the productivity and income levels of those who subsist on such low-earning jobs that they are simply unable to rid themselves of poverty and deprivation. The real challenge, therefore, is twofold: first, to devise strategies for creating jobs for those who are without them, and second, to identify ways and means to improve the quality of jobs for those who are already working, but who earn inadequate incomes or face difficult employment and working conditions.

What are the options open to Indian policy makers? In a situation of supply demand imbalance in the labour market, as has typically been the case in India, the usual approach is to turn to labour-intensive techniques of production; more jobs must be created per unit of capital invested. However, lack of labour market flexibility and the pressures of international competitiveness sometimes encourage the use of capital-intensive technology; as a result, employment elasticity with respect to output goes on declining. In India, employment elasticity with respect to

GDP has consistently been declining from 0.59 over the period 1972-73/77-78 to 0.53 during 1977-78/1983, and to 0.40 in the most recent period, 1983/93-94. According to the Planning Commission, this figure is likely to decline further to 0.38 during the Ninth Plan (*ibid:* 189). Moreover, in recent years, incremental capital:output ratio has also been steadily increasing and that too has added, indirectly, to the difficulty of expanding employment at a fast pace (RBI, 1999: III-10). Thus, GDP growth, even at the projected rate of around 6.5 per cent, cannot be relied upon as the only source of job creation. Efforts at the level of individual economic sectors must, therefore, be intensified.

In order to provide some idea about the quantity as well as the quality of employment generated over the years, the Indian economy, like most in the developing world, may be divided (for the purpose of discussion) into two broad sectors: organised and unorganised. There is no single or universally accepted definition of the term "unorganised sector". The organised-unorganised dichotomy is often used interchangeably with formal-informal, registered-unregistered or modern-traditional. The present paper does not deal with the finer nuance of each dichotomy although a broad description of the informal sector is briefly provided in the Appendix. In the Indian context, 'unorganised sector', 'unregistered sector' or 'traditional sector' can all be used as a proxy for the 'informal sector'.

The available data suggest that the organised sector of the Indian economy has never in fact succeeded in generating employment on a very large scale. For example, during the five year period 1972-73/1977-78, employment in the organised sector grew annually by 2.45 per cent against 2.75 per cent for the economy as a whole; over the next five years by 2.48 per cent against 2.36 per cent, by 1.38 per cent against 1.77 per cent during 1983/1987-88, over the next five years (1987-88/1993-94) by only 1.05 per cent against 2.37 per cent (Govt. of India, 1999A: 147), and by 0.87 per cent against 1.53 per cent during 1993-97 (Govt. of India: 2000: 326). Given the overwhelming weight of the unorganised sector in employment (about 92.0 per cent in the mid-nineties; Table 1), it is absolutely clear that employment growth in the unorganised sector has consistently been of a much higher order than that in the organised sector. Not only has the rate of growth of employment been much lower in the organised sector, it has been declining almost continuously during the past three decades or so. The consistently declining pace of labour absorption in the organised sector seems to have reached its nadir during the early nineties, when it is estimated that 98 per cent of the incremental employment that accrued in the Indian economy was in the unorganised sector (see Table 2).

To Indian policy makers, the unorganised sector thus stands out as the one major source of future employment expansion. However, although it has provided almost all additional employment in recent years, and even now is India's major hope for future employment generation, the unorganised sector has never achieved such desirable economic targets as high growth, technological breakthrough, productivity improvement or substantial income propagation. Over many years, the sector has displayed sharply contrasting strengths and weaknesses. On the positive side, the sector is variously described "as a provider of employment and

TABLE 1 : **Share of Unorganised Sector in Employment and Value Added: All India**

(per cent)

Year	Share of Unorganised in	
	Employment	Value Added
1	**2**	**3**
1977-78	92.2	68.1
1982-83	92.1	66.4
1987-88	92.0	63.0
1990-91	92.2	63.8
1993-94	92.6	63.1
1997-98	-	60.5

Source : 1. IAMR, Manpower Profile yearbook, 1999, New Delhi, 1999, pp. 264-65, 371.
2. Govt. of India, National Accounts Statistics 1970-71/1982-83, CSO, Jan. 1985, p. 139.
3. ___________, National Accounts Statistics 1998, CSO, June 1998, p. 193.
4. ___________, National Accounts Statistics 2000, CSO, July 2000, p.xl.

TABLE 2 : **Share of Unorganised Sector in Incremental Net Domestic Product (at Current Prices) and Employment in India: 1972-73/1995-96**

Period	Share of Unorganised Sector in Incremental (per cent)	
	Net Domestic Product	Employment
1	**2**	**3**
1972-73/77-78	64.5	93.0
1977-78/82-83	65.0	91.0
1982-83/87-88	71.0	91.0
1987-88/90-91	58.0	95.0
1990-91/93-94	59.0	98.0
1993-94/97-98	57.0	-

Source : 1. Govt. of India, National Accounts Statistics, (for various years), CSO, New Delhi.
2. IAMR 1999, Manpower Profile Yearbook, 1999, New Delhi. pp. 264-65.

incomes to millions of people who would otherwise lack the means of survival" or is romanticised "as a breeding ground of entrepreneurship which could flourish if only it were not encumbered with a network of unnecessary regulation and bureaucracy" (ILO, 1991: 1). On the negative side, it is interpreted as that "segment of society that escapes regulation" and is "condemned as a vast sea of backwardness, poverty, crime and insanitary conditions" (ILO, *ibid*).

1.2 Additional and Decent Jobs in the Urban Informal Sector

The present paper takes the view that there is a considerable scope for additional job creation, and for improving the quality of employment in the informal sector. In particular, the urban informal sector has some promising segments where technological improvement and labour absorption can move in tandem through effective policy interventions, improvement in productivity and earning levels can take place through suitable institutional and market adjustments, and where working conditions can improve and decent job creation can become a definite reality. It needs to be said at the outset that in the fiercely competitive economic regime that has already taken root in the Indian economy, and is likely to become fiercer in the near future, the informal sector can no more operate in the manner that it has been doing so far. The policy approach to the informal sector must undergo a drastic reformulation; instead of looking at the sector as an economic drag on the rest of the economy, government must put in place some strategic macro-economic policy measures to promote growth in the sector, which in turn, will enhance its working efficiency and ultimately lead on to the goal of improving the quality of employment and the earnings of people engaged in the sector.

Undoubtedly, a selective approach is required, as it is unrealistic to expect that the whole of the urban informal sector could undergo a full-scale structural or technological transformation in the near future. Some segments, especially those which can potentially be associated with the formal sector through a chain of technological, production and marketing links, clearly have a bright future and must, therefore, be promoted in the interest of better job environments, including higher earnings and improved standards of living. Another section of the informal sector, engaged especially in manufacturing, can clearly benefit from modern methods of production, management and marketing, but institutional handicaps (e.g., lack of access to institutional credit and training) stand in the way of its growth and progress. Finally, the informal sector includes a large number of workers operating at the very lowest economic levels, many of whom are self-employed, notably in trade and services. Many of them survive in distressing conditions. This component of the informal sector indeed poses difficult supply as well as demand side policy options, firstly because the type of workers involved in such jobs are poorly educated (or uneducated), and unskilled or inadequately trained, and secondly, because the demand for goods and services offered by these sub-sectors comes largely through the unstable earnings of the poorer sections of urban society.

1.3 Purpose and Scope of the Paper

The purpose of this paper is not to provide a detailed empirical analysis of the informal sector but to raise certain issues which, in our view, deserve serious policy attention in the interest of the sector's steady and healthy growth. As such, the paper poses a number of questions. For example:

- Why do we need to focus on the informal sector for job creation?
- Is there really a potential now for creating many more jobs in the informal sector?
- How do we raise the productivity and employment-generating capacity of the informal sector?
- What should be the policy stance towards the informal sector? Should it be welfare or growth-oriented?
- Can the informal sector be considered in isolation or should it be considered in the context of the overall growth of the economy?
- Would diverting promotional resources towards the low-productivity informal sector reduce overall economic growth?
- Are micro interventions adequate or do we need to change the overall policy environment to one which is conducive for the growth of the informal sector?
- How do we organise workers and producers in the informal sector? Can trade unions and employers' organisations help in these efforts?

After a brief introduction in this section, Section 2 discusses major reasons for focusing on the informal sector for decent job creation. Section 3 brings out the policy dilemmas in promoting job opportunities in the informal sector, particularly in view of its discomforting record of low labour protection. Section 4 briefly discusses the policy stance that needs to be adopted towards the urban informal sector. Section 5 reminds the policy makers about the complementarity between the informal and the formal sectors; in particular, it suggests that a healthy and steadily expanding formal sector is a necessary pre-requisite for the growth of the informal sector itself. Section 6 highlights the major problems and constraints facing the urban informal sector which reduce its capacity to provide decent jobs. Section 7 examines policy options for promoting decent jobs in the urban informal sector, focusing on both demand and supply side interventions. It also discusses a wide range of special measures and institutional reforms needed to overcome certain inherent weaknesses of the informal sector and to strengthen the productive capacity of the informal sector units. And finally, Section 8 provides concluding observations and highlights some major policy challenges for strengthening the employment-generating capacity of the informal sector and for integrating this sector into the mainstream of the economy.

2. Why Focus on the Urban Informal Sector

Until recently, government policy paid very little attention to the informal sector, primarily because the policy-makers believed it to be a transient phenomenon which would ultimately fade away or merge, even if gradually, into the mainstream of the economy. It was considered that, with economic growth, the formal sector would witness a sizeable expansion and that most of the surplus labour would be absorbed by it. Nonetheless, in spite of a reasonably strong growth over the years, this has not happened. On the contrary, the informal sector has continued to grow, along with worsening employment and living conditions. This has raised serious doubts about the functioning of the "trickle-down" process. A major reason for the failure of this process is that access to opportunities opened up by growth is rarely equal in a society such as India, where the initial distribution of income and wealth is vastly unequal. The capital and labour markets are both far from "perfect", and work very much to the detriment of the poorer sections of society. Access to education, health and other social amenities is also highly inequitable. Further, access to information is both restricted and too costly for the poor. Consequently, the benefits of growth accrue disproportionately to the relatively well-off in the formal sector.

Thus, in sharp contrast to the implicit faith in the "trickle-down" thesis once held by policy makers and development specialists, it is now recognised that the informal sector will be a living reality for many years, perhaps decades, to come embracing a sizeable segment of the labour force. Presently, it represents more than 90 per cent of India's workforce. It is essential, therefore, that national policy on labour should now be redirected towards the informal sector, rectifying the bias that has somehow persisted against it, so that it emerges as a growing and more productive source of employment and incomes for the growing urban labour force in India.

2.1 The Formal Sector Cannot do it all

An equally important reason for focusing attention on the informal sector is the inability of the formal sector to generate adequate employment opportunities. In India, the labour force is growing much faster than employment opportunities in the formal sector. The formal sector alone, therefore, cannot solve the problems of rising urban unemployment and under-employment. The organised sector in India has never provided a very large employment base; for nearly three decades now, the unorganised sector has continued to absorb more than 90 per cent of workers (Table 2). Moreover, the organized sector employment has hardly grown at all in recent years; during the 1990s, it recorded a dismal growth of 0.81 per cent per annum (Table 3). Most of the additional jobs which have accrued in the Indian economy in recent years have been in the unorganised sector (Table 2). Workers employed on an unorganised basis now predominate in such sectors as agriculture, manufacturing, construction, trade (including hotels and restaurants) and transport (including storage and communications; Table 4). Not only that the proportion of the informal sector workers is very high in many sectors its share in factor income is also high, ranging from 36.6 per cent in the secondary sector to 49.6 per cent in the tertiary sector and to as high as 96.4 per cent in the primary sector (Table 5). An important point that testitfies to the internal dynamism of the informal sector is that, compared with the formal sector, it is relatively more widely spread over the three major sectors of the economy; the formal sector is nearly totally absent form the primary sector (Table 5; Cols. 4 and 5). This clearly hints towards a much bigger potential for flexible choices of production/service facilities available to the informal sector, compared with the formal sector.

Finally, the substantial position of the informal segment can be seen even in the manufacturing sector (Tables 6 and 7); it contributes no less than 36 per cent of net and 33 per cent of gross domestic product originating in the manufacturing sector.

The fact that, within the organized sector itself, public sector accounts for as high as 70 per cent of the organized sector employment clearly points to the inadvisability of relying on it as a future source of employment; during the 1990s, public sector employment in the organized segment of the Indian economy grew by 0.11 per cent per annum against 2.1 per cent per annum in the private sector (Table 3). It hardly needs to be emphasized that employment expansion in the organized sector would he highly constrained, first, because in the changing world of international competitiveness, private enterprises are most likely to follow highly selective (albeit education- and skill-intensive) recruitment policies, and second, because public sector itself is, and would be, under squeeze.

The low capacity of the formal sector to absorb additional labour has arisen for two main reasons: (1) import-substituting growth strategies in the past emphasised the growth of industrial sectors with low labour-intensity; and (2) labour policies which have given rise to rigidities in the organised labour market have provided an incentive to adopt capital-intensive technology. While the labour market has lacked flexibility, employers have often devised other means of restructuring their production processes; one of the most common has been the decentralisation of production through sub-contracting. Most sub-contractors

TABLE 3 : **Employment in the Organised Sector during the 1990s**

(Numbers in Lakh)

As on	Employment in Organized Sector			Annual Percentage Change		
	Public	Private	Total	Public	Private	Total
1	**2**	**3**	**4**	**5**	**6**	**7**
March 91	190.60(71.3)	76.80(28.7)	267.40(100.0)	1.52	1.24	1.44
March 92	192.10(71.0)	78.50(29.0)	270.60(100.0)	0.80	2.21	1.21
March 93	193.30(71.1)	78.50(28.9)	271.80(100.0)	0.60	0.06	0.44
March 94	194.50(71.0)	79.30(29.0)	273.80(100.0)	0.62	1.01	0.76
March 95	194.66(70.7)	80.58(29.3)	275.24(100.0)	0.11	1.63	0.55
March 96	194.29(69.5)	85.12(30.5)	279.41(100.0)	-0.19	5.62	1.51
March 97	195.59(69.3)	86.85(30.7)	282.44(100.0)	0.67	2.04	1.09
March 98	195.40(69.0)	88.35(31.0)	283.75(100.0)	-0.09	1.72	0.46

Note: In columns 2-4, the figures in parentheses are percentage shares.

Source: 1. Govt. of India, Economic Survey, 1999-2000, Feb. 2001, p. 168.

2. RBI, Handbook of Statistics on Indian Economy, 1999, p. 20.

TABLE 4 : **Share of Unorganised Sector in Employment and Net Domestic Product by Economic Activity : All India**

(per cent)

Economic Activity	Share of Unorganised Segment in				
	Net Domestic Product			Employment	
	1990-91	1993-94	1997-98	1991	1993-94
1	**2**	**3**	**4**	**5**	**6**
Agriculture Forestry and Fishing	96.2	96.5	96.4	99.2	99.4
Mining and Quarrying	7.7	7.3	6.1	35.3	59.0
Manufacturing and Utilities	37.3	34.3	34.0	74.3	82.1*
Construction	55.5	51.2	53.5	77.8	89.9
Trade, Hotels and Restautrants	91.9	88.8	83.1	97.6	89.6
Transport, Storage and Communication	52.3	42.7	48.2	60.8	71.1
Financing, Insurance and Real Estate	40.6	50.7	43.0	57.2	-
Community, Social and Personal Services	19.6	19.0	18.2	-	66.1
All Sectors	63.9	63.1	60.5	91.2	91.1

Note: 1. Employment estimates for 1991, are not strictly comparable to those for 1995-94, the two being drawn from different sources.

2. *does not include utilities, as under the 1991 employment estimates; instead it includes repair services.

Source: 1. For col. 2, Govt. of India, National Accounts Statistics 1995, CSO, May 1995, pp. 208-211.

2. For cols. 3 and 4, Govt. of India, National Accounts Statistics 2000, CSO, July 2000, pp. 172-175.

3. For col. 5, Kulshreshtha, A.C., and Singh, Gulab, "Contribution of Unorganised Sector in the Indian Economy", Manpower Journal, October-December, 1998, p 62.

4. For col. 6, S. Mahendra Dev, "Economic Liberalization and Employment in South Asia-I", Economic and Political Weekly, Nos. 1 and 2, Jan. 8-14, 2000, p. 48.

TABLE 5 : **Structure of the Informal Sector in the Indian Economy: Net Domestic Product Originating in Organised and Unorganised Sectors by Broad Industry Groups**

Sector	Distribution of NDP by Broad Industry Groups in Organised and Unorganised Sectors				Share of Factor Incomes by Organised and Unorganised Sectors by Broad Industry Groups			
	1993-94		1997-98		1993-94		1997-98	
	Org.	Unorg.	Org.	Unorg.	Org.	Unorg.	Org.	Unorg.
1	**2**	**3**	**4**	**6**	**7**	**8**	**9**	**10**
Agriculture, Forestry, Fishing	3.1	50.3	2.7	47.7	3.5	96.5	3.6	96.4
Mining-Quarrying, Manufacturing, Utilities and Construction	41.5	13.5	38.7	14.6	64.2	35.8	63.4	36.6
Services	55.4	36.1	58.6	37.7	47.3	52.7	50.4	49.6
Total	100.0	100.0	100.0	100.0	36.9	63.1	39.5	60.6

Note: Org. = Organised, Unorg. = Unorganised.
Source: Govt. of India, National Accounts Statistics 2000, CSO, July 2000, pp. xl-xli.

TABLE 6 : **Level and Growth of Employment in Organised and Unorganised Manufacturing: All India**

Sector	Level of Employment (in Lakh)			Annual Compound Growth Rate of Employment (%)		
	1984-85	1989-90	1994-95	1984-85/89-90	1989-90/94-95	1984-85/94-95
1	2	3	4	5	6	7
Organised	60.91 (14.2)	63.26 (15.1)	69.70 (17.4)	0.76	1.96	1.36
Unorganised	369.50 (85.8)	354.74 (84.9)	332.02 (82.6)	-0.81	-1.32	-1.06
Total	430.39 (100.0)	418.00 (100.0)	401.72 (100.0)	-0.58	-0.79	-0.69

Note: Figures in parentheses are percentage shares.
Source: 1. Govt. of India, Annual Survey of Industries, Summary Results for Factory Sector, 1984-85 and 1994-95, CSO, Ministry of Planning.
2. ________, Unorganised Manufacturing Sector in India : Its Size, Employment and some Key Estimates, Report No-433, NSSO, August 1998.
3. ________, Directory Manufacturing Establishment Survey, 1984-85, CSO.
4. ________, Survey of Unorganised Manufacture: Non-Directory Establishment and Own-Account Enterprises, NSSO, June, 1989.

TABLE 7 : **Share of Unregistered Manufacturing in Gross and Net Domestic Product Generated by the Manufacturing Sector of the Indian Economy**

Year	Unregistered Segment's Share in Gross and Net Domestic Product Contributed by Manufacturing Sector	
	Gross Domestic Product	Net Domestic Product
1	**2**	**3**
1993-94	34.8	36.6
1994-95	33.3	34.8
1995-96	32.9	34.2
1996-97	32.8	34.4
1997-98	33.2	35.4
1998-99	33.0	36.0

Source : Govt. of India, National Accounts Statistics 2000. CSO, July 2000, pp. 145, 147.

operate in the unorganised sector. This results naturally in a trend towards deregulation and casualisation of work which was formerly performed by the 'core' workers in formal sector enterprises. The overall result of the labour market rigidities faced by formal sector employers has thus been an increase in the quantum of employment in the informal sector and a decline in the general quality of employment.

The situation is likely to become much more serious in the near future for several reasons. First, the slumbering pace of investment expansion in recent years has been a very unhappy and employment-unfriendly episode in the Indian economy. For example, gross fixed capital formation (at 1993-94 prices) grew negligibly from Rs. 25, 37,430 million in 1995-96 to Rs. 25, 99, 350 million in 1998-98 while net fixed capital formation witnessed a decline from Rs. 15,53,450 million to Rs. 13,87,950 million during the same period; in other words, consumption of fixed capital as a proportion of gross fixed capital formation has increased substantially from 38.8 per cent to 46.6 per cent (Govt. of India, July 2000: 37-47). Second, the rising levels of capital:labour or capital:output ratios, partly necessitated by the pressure of global competition, first unleashed by economic reforms of 1991 and then by WTO's membership since 1995, have further restricted the employment generation capabilities of the near-stationary levels of investment. The rising levels of capital:labour and capital:output ratios seem to be the reality of the 1990s, in a wide array of organized manufacturing industries, most notably food products, textiles, leather, rubber and plastic products, repair services, etc. (Chadha, 1999: 45).

The continuing stream of such technological changes is bound to slow down the growth of employment in general, and regular wage-employment in particular. Finally, the pace of privatisation in India is gaining momentum. Experience shows that the process of privatisation and industrial restructuring usually involves a substantial loss of jobs, primarily through retrenchment.

2.2 The Potential of the Informal Sector

While the formal sector can be expected to provide only limited growth of job opportunities in the future, the informal sector can be seen to hold very great potential for job creation, and accordingly, a strong capacity to contribute to economic growth. Particular segments of the urban informal sector can be identified as having exceptional potential for growth, but may depend on the creation of a more favourable policy environment than the one that exists now. A recent ILO study estimates that around 500,000 jobs have been created in the informal sector in the software and related services industry in recent years. By and large, these meet the criteria of "decent work" in terms of wages and income, though not in terms of social protection. With the likely expansion of this industry in the next few years, it is expected that more than a million new jobs would be created.

An important role played by urban informal sector and micro enterprises in India has been to absorb surplus labour from rural areas, and so to help in alleviating poverty, mainly through the promotion of self-employment. Table 8 provides some broad information on the process of transfer of surplus rural labour to the urban informal sector as self-employed workers. During 1990-98, the number of own-account enterprises grew by 1.5 per cent per annum in rural areas, compared with a rate as high as 2.4 per cent per annum in the urban areas.

The case for promoting the urban informal sector includes several other strong arguments. First, although the surveys have been irregular and the evidence is scattered, yet it is clear that some segments of the informal sector (most conspicuously, the larger manufacturing establishments in it) do generate surpluses even under the currently unfavourable policy environment. Potentially, a more favourable policy climate should further enhance the profitability of this sector and so in turn, stimulate the growth of the urban economy. Second, because of its low-capital intensity, only a fraction of the capital needed in the formal sector is required to create a comparable number of new jobs in the informal sector, and this represents a more economical approach, particularly at a time when there is an overall shortage of investment resources. And third, the informal sector plays an important role in the recycling of waste materials, engaging for example, in the collection of goods ranging from scrap metals to cigarette butts, many of which find their way to the industrial sector or provide basic commodities for the poor.

TABLE 8 : **Proliferation of Informal Economic Enterprises in India during the 1990s: Economic Census Data**

Nature of Enterprises	Year	No. of Non-Agricultural Economic Enterprises (00')			Annual Compound Growth Rate (per cent) 1990-98		
		Rural	Urban	Total	Rural	Urban	Total
Own Account Enterprises	1990	94735 (60.52)	61791 (39.48)	156526 (100.00)	1.46	2.42	1.84
	1998	106364 (58.71)	74807 (41.29)	181171 (100.00)			
Other Enterprises	1990	31517 (44.91)	38657 (39.48)	70174 (100.00)	2.24	2.69	2.49
	1998	37616 (44.03)	47816 (55.97)	85432 (100.00)			
All Enterprises	1990	126252 (55.69)	100448 (44.31)	226700 (100.00)	1.66	2.52	2.05
	1998	143980 (54.01)	122623 (45.99)	266603 (100.00)			

Note: Figures exclude Jammu and Kashmir. Figures in parentheses are percentages shares of rural and urban areas, respectively.

Source: 1. For 1990, Govt. of India, Economic Census, 1990, All India, Report, CSO, March 1995, p 9.

2. For 1998, Govt. of India, Fourth Economic Census: Provisional Results, CSO, June 1999b, Table 1.

2.3 Improving Welfare of the Urban Working Class

For the urban informal sector, by and large, regulatory controls are fewer and largely ineffective. Productivity levels are extremely low, working conditions are frequently appalling and the abuse of child and women workers is common. In many cases, minimum wages are not paid, there is little or no recognition of the principles of occupational and gender equality in either earnings or hiring practices, and the use of child labour is still widely prevalent. Such wide-ranging issues cannot remain neglected. The welfare of more than 90 per cent of workers is at stake. On the other hand, the positive aspect of the urban informal sector lies in its very considerable potential, still largely untapped, to generate growth of production, income and exports and to reduce poverty.

An issue of major concern to national planners, urban development authorities and other public institutions has been the effect on the environment of a highly concentrated informal sector in the urban areas. Many informal sector activities cause pollution, congestion or inconvenience to urban dwellers. Conditions, already poor, for those living in slums and low-income neighbourhoods, are worsened by increasing densities coupled with poor urban services. These problems are particularly acute in the metropolitan cities of Mumbai, Delhi, Kolkata and Chennai, and the stress of life may be exacerbated in areas where migrant workers, engaged in numerous but irregular informal sector activities, are now threatening to over-take the local urban population. These slums have become breeding grounds for urban unemployment and poverty, accompanied by a diverse variety of social abuses of which those relating to children and women are of special concern.

There is therefore an urgent need to eliminate, progressively, the worst aspects of exploitation and to improve the living and working environment of the urban poor. This is needed, not for reasons of welfare alone, but also for raising their productivity and incomes. It is difficult to envisage an economy in which dualism persists to the extent that a small segment continues to enjoy the gains from high technology, social protection and preferential access to markets, while the majority subsists in a state of deprivation. The sheer rise in the numbers of the deprived, resulting from social and economic neglect, will be a serious threat to the sustenance of the social fabric. The need to intensify productive activities in the informal sector, and thus assure a better quality of life for those engaged in them, is therefore of fundamental importance.

3. Policy Dilemmas of the Informal Sector

A new level of attention to the informal sector poses several policy dilemmas. First, if lack of labour market flexibility in the formal sector is an important contributory factor for rapid expansion of the informal sector, should then the focus of policy be not on providing such flexibility in the formal sector; employment might then grow more in the formal rather than the informal sector, with the attendant problems of raising productivity and improving conditions of work. Second, since the formal sector is more productive, it is questionable whether scarce development resources should at all be diverted to the low-productivity informal sector, which may reduce the overall efficiency and growth in the economy. And third, the policy-makers must decide whether the informal sector should be assisted and allowed to continue to expand outside the framework of formal rules, regulations and institutions governing social and economic life, and thus to provide a convenient, low-cost way of absorbing labour that cannot be employed elsewhere. Or whether attempts should be made to bring this sector within the legal and institutional framework, with the possible risk of impairing its capacity to absorb labour?

It may be argued, in the interest of equity, that promotional resources need to be diverted to the informal sector which now provides employment to an overwhelming majority of the working population. But critics would say that the efficiency costs of such a policy shift will be high. The result will be to waste scarce capital resources and thereby slow down the rate of economic growth. These critics would also argue that the benefits of investing more public resources in the informal sector are likely to be small, particularly since the sector will contribute very little in return to the state exchequer by way of taxation, or otherwise. The nature of informal sector is such that most enterprises continue to operate outside the tax net. Efforts to raise resources for infrastructure investment in the economy would be undermined, thereby further constraining the prospects of higher growth. In the long run, the country will thus be even less able to redistribute income and remedy the problems of poverty. The conclusion of this line of argument is that, if a high rate of economic growth is to be achieved, the concentration of resources on the development of formal sector is essential.

However, such a view is not uncontroversial. It may be argued that higher productivity in the formal sector is achieved, to some extent, at the cost of lower productivity in micro and small enterprises in the informal sector. If the equivalent social and economic infrastructure (access to institutional credit, training, subsidies, etc.) were available to informal sector enterprises then the productivity of these enterprises would also rise.

Leaving other considerations aside, the issue still remains as to whether informal sector can be neglected, inasmuch as it provides employment and incomes to a vast majority of the population which would otherwise lack the means of survival. In the short run, we may achieve the objective of growth and efficiency by focusing greater attention on the formal sector, but in the long run, the result may well be large-scale deprivation, increasing inequalities, urban discontent and social unrest. Higher growth itself will not be sustainable in such a situation.

Most observers also believe that the two objectives of labour absorption and regulation can be reconciled if measures are taken simultaneously to enhance the employment generating capacity of the informal sector and to improve the legal and social protection of the informal sector workers, with a view to more fully integrating the sector into the mainstream of the economy. Regulating the informal sector or enforcing measures aimed at applying laws and regulations with which enterprises and workers in this sector could not comply, would only serve to increase the vulnerability and the poverty of those engaged in informal-sector activities.

4. Policy Stance towards Informal Sector

There is a growing recognition that informal sector makes an invaluable contribution to job creation and overall development. Accordingly, the most crucial policy issue is to identify ways to promote its growth. The issue cannot, however, be prejudged in this way. We need to begin by asking what exactly it is that we seek to influence through macro-economic policies. Put this way, we face the fundamental issue of the optimal size of the informal sector. If the informal sector is too large in relation to this optimum, promotional policies would not be warranted. There seems to be no prior way of determining the desirable size of the informal sector; it is an empirical question that has to be resolved in each specific context. The optimal size of the informal sector can be defined, for instance, by reference to efficiency criteria in the allocation of capital and labour. It might be considered too large in terms of the labour-allocation criterion if labour has flowed into it beyond the point where marginal returns have become lower than in alternative sectors. Excessive rural-urban migration tends to suggest an informal sector which is too large. Conversely, an informal sector may be considered too small if there is evidence of misallocation of capital, such as is the case where capital-labour ratios are very high in the modern sector, and an excessive proportion of total capital resources of the economy is concentrated in this sector.

It should be noted, however, that the issue of optimal-size cannot be settled simply by static, cross-sectional analysis. Ideally, we also need to build upon the dynamics of the growth of the informal sector, which provides information on why and how the informal sector has grown. Such an analysis will not only provide answers to the optimal-size issue, but, more importantly, will yield insights into the specific form that overall policies towards the informal sector need to take.

There has been a basic divide as regards interpretation of the growth of the informal sector between those who see such growth as the manifestation of an involutionary process and those who see the process as evolutionary. According to the involutionary view, the growth of the informal sector is seen as essentially pathological, fuelled by the influx of migrants pushed out of the rural areas by lack of employment and income opportunities, highly unequal agrarian structures, and labour-saving technical change in agricultural production. This process is usually exacerbated by barriers to entry into the modern sector arising from the oligopolistic industrial structures, capital-market distortions, labour-market segmentations, and unfair employment practices. Informal sector growth does not therefore reflect any normal response to economic incentives but is merely symptomatic of a deep malaise in the economic structure and growth process. The way forward would not be to try to ameliorate production conditions in the informal sector, since this does not represent a productive growth strategy. Rather, the best solution would be to tackle the problem at its roots, that is, to reduce the excessive movement of labour from the rural sector and to remove barriers to labour absorption in the modern sector. Such a strategy would raise growth rates in the economy as well as reduce inequality in the distribution of income.

The opposite view of the informal sector would tend to see it as being at or below its optimum size. This evolutionary view focuses on the economic virtues of the informal sector itself. It is depicted as a system of production which is appropriate to the factor and resource endowments of a labour-surplus, low-income country. It is also seen as a reservoir of entrepreneurship and innovativeness which uses resources efficiently and competitively and which would grow apace, given the right institutional and policy environment. According to this view, the growth of the informal sector can be promoted through a combination of policies such as the forging of regulatory linkages between it and the formal sector and the removal of regulatory restrictions and disincentives. These regulations either forbid particular activities (for example street trading) or impose onerous regulatory conditions which increase start-up and operating costs (for example standards of construction, environmental regulations, licence fees, taxes, etc.)

These two opposing views have been presented in order to illustrate the complexities involved in deciding overall policies towards the informal sector. There is no basis for assuming that one or the other view must necessarily prevail. Given the heterogeneity and complexity of the informal sector, elements of both views will be present, but it is nonetheless important to have some calibration of the relative proportions involved. This is important not only to avoid the error of framing policies on the assumption that the informal sector conforms entirely to one or the other outfit, but also to emphasise the need to search for a differentiated set of policies to deal with different facets of the informal sector.

One can think of a basic division in types of policy on the basis of whether we are dealing with the 'growth potential' or involutionary aspects of the informal sector. The former would be directed at promoting the growth of potentially viable micro- and small enterprises through removal of unwarranted market and institutional handicaps as well as through subsidies justified on the basis of infant industry-type arguments. In contrast, policies designed to deal with the informal sector as a symptom of involutionary growth would not look for solutions within the sector, but in economy-wide structural changes which could reduce the pressures resulting in the expansion of the informal sector. These would be directed at issues relating to equitable growth in agriculture and the possibilities for rapid, labour-intensive industrialisation. The policy stance towards this part of the informal sector might still be to assist it, but this would be motivated more by welfare considerations and social pressures than under weight of economic rationale or considerations of growth potential and job creation.

Thus, instead of proceeding from the assumption that informal-sector activities across the board are worthy of promotion, it would be more effective to carry out assessments of the competitive and growth potential of specific activities or sub-sectors, and to concentrate promotional resources on those with the highest likelihood of survival and success.

5. Complementarity between Informal and Formal Sectors

As we have discussed above, there is an urgent need to focus attention on the informal sector as the main engine for job creation. This does not mean that the informal sector can grow in isolation. It has important linkages with the formal sector within the framework of the growth process. The formal sector depends on the informal sector for economical inputs and a variety of wage goods for its workers. The informal sector, in turn, depends in large measure on the growth of the formal sector for its market and income; and also obtains a variety of raw materials for sustaining its own production. The fundamental policy question, therefore, is how the two can grow in tandem. In what ways, can each one complement and strengthen the growth effort of the other?

5.1 The Formal Sector is More Productive

Although not more than 8-9 per cent of the total employment in the economy is now located in the organised sector, its share of value added or net domestic product is no less than 40 per cent (Table 4). Among the major sectors, the organised sector's share in net domestic product is highest in community, social and personal services (82 per cent in 1997-98), followed by manufacturing and utilities (64 per cent), transport, storage and communications (52 per cent), and construction (around 46 per cent). In contrast, the overall contribution to net domestic product from the unorganised sector is only 60 per cent, even though it employs more than 90 per cent of the labour force (Table 4).

The need to increase productivity levels in the unorganised sector is therefore compelling, but there is a good reason to promote the organised sector in addition. On the strength of its superior productivity (Table 9) and faster output growth

TABLE 9 : **Rate of Total Factor Productivity Growth in the Organised and Unorganised Manufacturing Sectors : 1973-74 / 1993-94**

(per cent)

Period	Organised Manufacturing	Unorganised Manufacturing
1	**2**	**3**
1973-74 / 77-78	0.43	-4.10
1977-78 / 83-84	2.48	-2.21
1983-84 / 87-88	2.33	1.06
1987-88 / 93-94	1.47	-0.88

Source: Goldar, B.N., and Mitra, Arup, "Productivity Growth in Informal Manufacturing Sector in India", Paper read at Workshop in Measurement of Productivity in India, July 9-10, 1999, Institute of Human Development, New Delhi.

alone, the formal sector must continue to receive support; this will be to the benefit of the whole economy including the informal sector itself, through the assured and regular availability of raw materials at acceptable reasonable prices, and the formal sector's demand for goods and services supplied by the informal sector.

5.2 Outsourcing and Sub-contracting

In recent years, partly because of the labour market rigidities faced by the formal sector and partly because of other trends of technological, economic and management change, decentralisation of production through subcontracting is now commonly resorted to by the formal sector enterprises. In the process of subcontracting, a number of operations are passed on to sub-contractors or vendors and sub-vendors, a large majority of whom are located in the informal sector. This provides greater opportunities for employment, and for higher incomes, to the small enterprises of the informal sector. In addition, knowledge of improved techniques is also transmitted from the formal to the informal sector, either because of the specific stipulations of the subcontract itself or else because an expanding, and technologically-conscious, group of sub-contractors is emerging independently in the Indian industrial sector.

5.3 The Informal Sector Cannot Take Care of Everything

In spite of its proliferation into diverse production and service activities, the informal sector has not, and is unlikely to develop, the capacity to enter into certain fields, notably those where large capital investments and relatively long gestation periods are involved. In particular, the complete absence of informal sector firms from the infrastructure sectors is evident in Table 10 (Cols. 2 and 3). Considerations including economies of scale, capital requirements and long gestation periods, especially in such sectors as electricity, gas, water, road, railway and air transport would dictate that infrastructural development necessarily remains in the domain of the formal sector. Until recently, even the private segment of the organised sector could not be relied upon for certain areas of infrastructural development, all of which remained the responsibility of the public sector alone. It is only in recent years that private capital, both from within the country and abroad, has penetrated into a few such areas. Many other industries such as chemicals and petrochemicals, steel, cement, automobiles and heavy electrical equipment/instruments, will certainly remain in the formal sector.

With the emergence of new production and distribution regimes, notably in the form of public and private sector partnerships, in different segments of the infrastructures sector, the organised sector's efficiency should improve. These developments hold the potential to relieve some critical infrastructure bottlenecks that bear most heavily on the informal sector enterprises. All this, in turn, may well improve productivity and profitability of the informal sector itself.

6. Problems Facing the Informal Sector

As discussed above, some segments of the informal sector have the potential to transform themselves into vibrant growing sectors of the modern economy. Table 11 shows, for example, that within the unorganised manufacturing, productivity levels vary markedly between tiny enterprises (OAMEs) and the better organised segment of DMEs, in most branches of production. Clearly we cannot think of making every segment of the informal sector equally vibrant, market-savy and commercially viable. There are some severe constraints to this: the policy and regulatory environment is often not conducive; the skill levels, technology and management are generally inadequate to induce growth; and access to market, credit and other resources, as well as information, is usually restricted.

Most workers in the informal sector are also not covered by any form of social protection. They neither enjoy social security (retirement benefits, pensions, health insurance, etc.) nor do they benefit from any programmes relating to safety at work. Use of dangerous tools, handling of hazardous substances, exposure to transmittable diseases, lack of ergonomically correct equipment and furniture, poor lighting and ventilation etc. are all common to workers in the informal sector.

Aside from issues of equity and human rights, lack of social protection is closely linked to low productivity in the informal sector. Work days lost due to poor health, accident or injury combined with related medical costs are a major contributor to poverty in this sector.

The public and private social security schemes, designed for the formal sector workers, cannot be easily extended to cover informal sector workers. In many cases, informal sector workers are themselves unable or unwilling to contribute, particularly to long-term programmes such as pension schemes. Most workers earn so little that their capacity to pay contributions to the existing schemes is limited, while many others can pay, but not regularly as required by the rules. Many among the self-employed, who can pay regularly, are often not aware of different options. Employers' contributions to workers' benefits are also extremely limited. There are two reasons for this. First, the law does not require such contributions. Second, many workers are employed on a temporary basis and worker turnover is often too high for the development and implementation of viable social security schemes.

There is also a general lack of institutional mechanism for collecting small-scale contributions, which poor workers (including housewives and home

TABLE 10 : **Level and Growth of Per Worker Productivity and Employment in the Manufacturing Sector: All India**

Manufacturing Group	Per Worker Productivity in Organised Manufacturing (Rs. '000)		Per Worker Productivity in Unorganised Manufacturing (Rs.)		Ratio of Productivity in Org. to Unorg. Manufacturing		Annual Growth Rate of Productivity (84-85/94-95) (%)		Annual Growth Rate of Employment (84-85/94-95) (%)	
	1984-85	1994-95	1984-85	1994-95	1984-85	1994-95	Organised	Unorganised	Organised	Unorganised
1	**2**	**3**	**4**	**5**	**6**	**7**	**8**	**9**	**10**	**11**
Food Products (20+21)	18.51	35.57	2950.96	3239.71	6.27	10.98	6.75	0.94	1.97	-1.53
Beverages (22)	12.81	14.50	1654.11	1486.08	7.75	9.76	1.25	-1.07	5.51	0.91
Cotton Textiles (23)	14.25	27.51	1744.02	2843.09	8.17	9.68	6.80	5.01	-2.06	-10.03
Wool, Synthetic, --(24)	27.54	71.42	3594.09	6557.66	7.66	10.89	10.00	6.20	1.39	4.01
Jute, Mesta, --(25)	6.46	11.85	1202.25	1406.49	5.37	8.42	6.25	1.58	-4.22	6.22
Textile Products (26)	25.91	38.98	2630.64	2838.37	9.85	13.73	4.17	0.76	11.48	-5.89
Wood/Paper Products 27-28	22.36	37.81	2524.12	2058.78	8.86	18.37	5.40	-2.02	0.37	1.08
Leather/Products (29)	20.02	29.14	4243.87	5098.10	4.75	5.72	3.82	1.85	6.46	-4.02
Chemicals/Products (30)	63.70	151.68	8101.75	4718.40	7.86	32.15	9.06	-5.26	12.40	6.26
Rubber, Plastic, Coal, Pet (31)	62.30	159.75	4389.42	11993.19	14.19	13.32	9.87	10.57	-4.26	-1.07
Non-Met. Min. Prodts. (32)	20.89	38.71	1677.09	2534.59	12.45	15.27	6.37	4.22	0.40	-0.06
Basic Metal (33)	28.61	75.13	7425.72	8758.57	3.85	8.58	10.14	1.66	-0.46	1.42
Metal Products (34)	25.42	40.81	5546.24	5155.33	4.58	7.92	4.85	-0.73	1.64	1.04
Machine Tools Etc. (35+36)	53.48	93.65	9020.34	9800.55	5.93	9.56	5.76	0.83	0.75	-0.92
Transport Equip. (37)	33.92	65.53	40542.89	10407.77	0.84	6.30	6.81	-12.71	0.12	1.27
Other Manufacturing Ind. (38)	49.16	96.81	3721.52	6429.08	13.21	15.06	7.01	5.62	5.68	7.38
Electricity (40)	44.65	136.45							1.18	
Gas & Steam Generation (41)	46.98	293.25							7.68	
Water Works & Supply (42)	23.10	57.62							4.57	
Storage & WH Services (74)	17.35	38.34							4.62	
Repair Services (97)	20.99	54.94							-11.66	
All Sectors	21.57	57.92	2828.08	3616.24	7.63	16.02	10.38	2.49	-1.35	-1.06

Note: Per worker productivity figures for 1984-85 and 1994-95 are at constant (1981-82) prices; all commodities wholesale price index has been used for converting figures at current prices to those in constant prices:

Source: 1. Govt. of India, Annual Survey of Industries, Summary Results for Factory Sector, 1984-85 and 1994-95, CSO, Ministry of Planning.

2. Govt. of India, *Unorganised Manufacturing Sector in India: Its Size, Employment and Some Key Estimates,* Report No-433, NSSO, August 1998.

3. Govt. of India, *Directory Manufacturing Establishment Survey, 1984-85, CSO.*

4. Govt. of India, Survey of Unorganised Manufacture: Non-Directory Establishment and Own-Account Enterprises, NSSO, June, 1989.

TABLE 11 : **Per Worker Labour Productivity (Rs. at Constant: 1981-82 Prices) for the Three Layers of Unorganised Manufacturing in Urban India : 1984-85 and 1994-95**

Manufacturing Group	1984-85			1994-95			Productivity Gap between			
							NDME and OAME		DME and OAME	
	OAME	NDME	DME	OAME	NDME	DME	1984-85	1994-95	1984-85	1994-95
1	**2**	**3**	**4**	**5**	**6**	**7**	**8 = 3/2**	**9 = 6/5**	**10 = 4/2**	**11 = 7/5**
Food Products (20+21)	4309.50	8898.87	10523.65	4593.35	6933.09	8722.37	2.06	1.51	2.44	1.90
Beverages (22)	1485.54	4297.98	7462.59	1969.01	3544.29	3543.41	2.89	1.80	5.02	1.80
Cotton Textiles (23)	1959.61	7923.62	4580.19	1944.66	6197.59	7210.36	4.04	3.19	2.34	3.71
Wool, Synthetic, --(24)	1948 67	4693.81	10202.85	4368.48	11001.18	11765.40	2.41	2.52	5.24	2.69
Jute, Mesta, --(25)	593.35	1029.93	5256.86	1206.17	4996.29	1926.61	1.74	4.14	8.86	1.60
Textile Products (26)	2835.85	5041.26	6276.43	2411.68	5230.93	9639.18	1.78	2.17	2.21	3.17
Wood/Products 27	2335.09	6206.04	6903.34	2179.33	6185.04	6376.96	2.66	2.84	2.96	2.93
Paper/Products (28)	1898.43	7572.07	7285.52	3138.10	6131.74	9669.59	3.99	1.95	3.84	2.44
Leather/Products (29)	2698.83	5859.06	11361.80	2307.87	5599.31	7672.65	2.17	1.05	4.21	1.45
Chemicals/Products (30)	3406.85	7099.30	14631.12	2214.96	7139.72	11722.70	2.08	3.22	4.29	5.29
Rubber, Plastic, Coal, Pet. (31)	1239.70	17004.21	6339.97	6263.21	12851.45	14036.89	13.72	2.05	5.11	2.24
Non-Met. Min. Prodts (32)	2909.48	5130.75	3006.93	2478.06	4706.57	4759.88	1.76	1.90	1.03	1.92
Basic Metal (33)	3712.97	6019.19	11019.71	6574.47	7401.46	12671.78	1.62	1.13	2.97	1.93
Metal Products (34)	5012.73	8837.71	14818.10	4206.50	6510.83	8153.92	1.76	1.55	2.96	1.94
Machine tools Etc. (35)	4774.39	9163.70	10246.51	6562.29	9116.67	12638.31	1.92	1.39	2.15	1.93
Machine Tools Non-Elect. (36)	9048.47	16646.32	37286.89	4271.85	8776.67	18388.91	1.84	2.05	4.12	4.30
Transpot Equip. (37)	8315.65	188220.90	37037.53	4993.29	13423.06	12220.96	22.63	2.69	4.45	2.45
Other Manufacuring Ind. (38)	3960.12	6355.93	7110.70	9311.03	10717.90	16720.92	1.60	1.15	1.80	1.80
Repair of Capital Goods (39)	5600.17	5630.66	6252.97	5892.69	5948.25	18315.45	1.01	1.01	1.12	3.11
All Sectors	3034.62	7330.59	8503.11	4119.42	6942.71	9284.97	2.42	1.69	2.80	2.25

Note: 1. OAME: Own-Account Manufacturing Enterprises.
NDME: Non-Directory Manufacturing Establishments.
DME: Directory Manufacturing Establishments.
2. For definition of OAME, NDME and DME see Government of India, Unorganised Manufacturing Sector in India: Its Size, Employment and Some Key Estimates, NSSO, August 1998.

Source: Same as in Table 10.

workers) might be able to put aside on a daily or weekly basis. The existing social security institutions are usually large, centralised and bureaucratic entities, governed by archaic rules and regulations. They possess little flexibility and are ill-equipped to deal with large numbers of small-scale contributors. They also find the transaction costs too high in the present administrative set-up. As such, they restrict their services to larger clients, mostly operating in the formal sector. Small-scale savers need easily accessible savings institutions. They should also be able to place absolute trust in the integrity of those who do collect money from them. Few such vehicles exist at present, and many workers fall back upon whatever social protection they can derive from traditional networks of caste and kinship. To the extent that they can save money, this may well be in the form of gold or other unproductive assets. This is both financially inefficient and, in today's context, can expose the poor to exploitative practices

Likewise, lack of safety at the work place has received too little attention. One reason is that there are few, if any, institutions with the necessary outreach to the widely spread informal sector. Tools and machines of the quality which might promote safety are often unaffordable, and even when they are installed, many workers lack the skill and knowledge to use them safely. As a result, accidents at work are frequent, and legal sanctions, including the payment of compensation for injuries sustained are - notwithstanding the protection notionally offered to all workers by the Workmen's Compensation Act - rarely enforced.

The promotion of social protection and safety at work also depend heavily on the establishment of effective institutional structures which would include labour and factory inspection systems and appropriate social security schemes. In India, such institutions have been in place for many years. Although they may rely on cadres of well-trained, experienced and highly professional staff, both their numbers and administrative resources are grossly inadequate. As a result, their effectiveness is seriously hampered. In the case of social security organisations, this is ostensibly reflected in a low degree of confidence among the public, and even amongst their own contributors, who feel a lack of effective representation in the supervisory structures. To some extent, the reduced effectiveness of these institutions stems from the fact that the laws under which they operate have not been updated to correspond with the fast changing work practices.

The practice of hiring contract and casual labour is widespread in India. One example of this is the case of migrant contract workers in the construction sector who often cross the provincial boundaries for work under the same or different contractors, and for various reasons, do not get any assistance from local unions or labour officials. The problem is further compounded by the fact that many state governments within India have different labour market practices and regulations.

This poses a major challenge to the national trade unions as also the government in improving the working conditions of migrant contract workers.

The low productivity of the informal sector is primarily due to the capital constraint and low levels of skills of the workers. Very few workers in the informal sector acquire their skills through formal training institutions; in a recent study, Chadha finds that 88 per cent of workers engaged in India's urban informal manufacturing enterprises learn them on the job by working as apprentices or wage paid helpers in informal enterprises (Chadha, 2001a: 173). Some acquire their skills through wage employment in the formal sector. The findings of most empirical studies the world over suggest that it is difficult for them to improve their physical and human capital base because they cannot access formal institutions for either credit or training, or indeed any other resources.

Studies of technology adaptation in the informal sector suggest that though many seek to innovate and improve the technology, and even succeed on occasions, it is rarely easy. Technology is often embodied in machinery and equipment. Improvement in technology implies acquisition of capital equipment which in turn depends on access to financial capital. Technology upgrading depends on the availability of capital goods as well as their suitability to small-scale operation. To adapt and to innovate requires substantial expenditure on R&D, technical skills and access to information which, in most cases, bypass enterprises in the informal sector (Chadha, 2000).

The difficulties that informal sector producers face in obtaining credit on terms applicable to modern enterprises constitute one of the main obstacles to their growth. Since many of the informal sector enterprises cannot fulfil those terms, they are not able to obtain credit from the banks. They have no collateral to offer as a guarantee when asking for loans since they operate on land or property which is seldom registered or owned by them. As a result, they are obliged to resort to borrowing from money-lenders or from other informal sources of finance, on highly unfavourable terms.

A major handicap suffered by the informal sector is that it generally lacks basic facilities and amenities. Informal sector enterprises often operate in makeshift premises, from which they may be forced to move at any time, without access to electricity, clean water or sanitation facilities, all of which discourage investment. This is, of course, the result of years of neglect by state and municipal authorities, or their inability to cope with the pace of urbanisation. But it is difficult to see how the informal sector can be "integrated" into the rest of the economy unless there is a radical shift in priorities for public spending, and in the overall approach to urban planning.

7. Strategies for Creating Decent Jobs

Policies and programmes to support the informal sector will have to be multi-faceted. The major thrust of such policies and programmes should be to provide a more conducive macro-economic environment for the growth of the informal sector. Some specific measures are also needed to raise the productivity and employment-generating capacity of this sector. Such measures should aim at enhancing the demand for informal sector products as well as strengthening its supply-side capacities. More targeted interventions will also be needed for improving employment and working conditions and for promoting the welfare of informal sector workers.

7.1 Demand-side Interventions

Potential sources of demand for the products of the informal sector can be placed in three broad categories: the domestic formal sector, the export sector and internal demand from within the informal sector. A major impetus to raising aggregate demand and expansion of markets is provided by high and sustained economic growth.

7.1.1 Accelerating and Sustaining Rapid Economic Growth

Demand for labour is a derived demand and hence, would change, other things remaining the same, in the same direction and to the same extent as output. One can increase the elasticity of employment with respect to output by changing the composition of output. A radical change in output, which invariably implies a substantial redistribution of income and wealth, is politically difficult to accomplish. Even when accomplished, the effect of a change in the composition of output is a one-off effect. For employment to increase then output must grow. Economic growth is unlikely to be a zero-sum game for the formal and the informal sectors and therefore would contribute to the increase in the demand for the latter.

While economic growth is necessary to promote employment and higher incomes, it may not be sufficient to substantially reduce poverty in the informal sector. High economic growth can coexist with both unemployment and underemployment. A major challenge therefore will be to make growth employment-intensive and to ensure that the benefits of growth percolate down to the workers in the unorganised sector. Another challenge will be to develop social and labour legislation that protects employment and working conditions but does not promote rigidities in the labour market and thus hamper economic growth and employment.

The experience of East Asian and South East Asian economies shows that sustained high rates of growth increased incomes and reduced poverty and underemployment within a generation. The projections made for India's Ninth Five Year Plan (1997-2002) suggest that the growth rate of the labour force will exceed 2.2 per cent per annum for the next decade and more. At the present levels of elasticity of employment, the economy will need to grow at over 7 per cent per annum to absorb the new entrants to the labour force. Acceleration of growth will thus be necessary.

But how to promote employment-friendly growth? The experience of East and South-East Asian countries suggests that outward-oriented growth strategies, macro-economic stability, flexible labour markets and emphasis on human resource development are the basic ingredients of a strategy of employment-intensive growth in a globalised world. Thus, to achieve the goal of higher growth, government should strive to ensure a certain level of political and social stability, to implement policies that encourage high savings and to provide strong and stable incentives to both local and foreign investors. Volatile government policies - and arbitrary changes in policies - increase risk and hamper investment whereas stable policies and a credible policy regime, by reducing uncertainty, create a more favourable economic environment and can help to stimulate private investment and growth. In order to maximise the impact on employment creation, incentives could be provided for investments to enter activities that are employment-intensive, areas that suffer from high unemployment, and to promote technologies that are compatible with the skill levels available in the country.

It must be recognised that without macro-economic stability, economic reform policies cannot be carried out successfully. To this end, it is necessary to reduce unsustainable fiscal and balance-of-payments deficits.This process has, however, to be carefully managed. By cutting back on all current public expenditure, the stabilisation policies could lead to excessive contraction of output and loss of jobs. Instead of overly concentrating on reducing current deficits, government should strive to increase domestic savings and investment to build a strong fiscal capacity to deal with macro-economic shocks. This would inspire greater confidence among investors and facilitate the adherence to a stable growth path.

7.1.2 Promoting Linkages with the Formal Sector

India has a small, though strong, organised sector with which informal sector can strengthen linkages given a conducive environment. Such linkages can be promoted in both production and marketing, and can be mutually beneficial. The advantages flow from the fact that most small enterprises operate with low labour and overhead costs. At times, the formal sector markets its products through the informal sector to save on marketing overheads. The linkages might be backward or forward in direction. The formal sector would have a forward linkage with the informal sector if its output was used as an input by the informal sector. It would have a backward linkage with the informal sector if an increase in the demand for its output led to an increase in demand for inputs supplied to it by the informal sector.

The dynamism of small enterprises usually derives from such linkages as large enterprises in the formal sector can provide them with an important stimulus for technological innovations and skills development. The Japanese small-scale sector is the example par excellence of being based on supply links to the formal sector's large, export-based corporations. The informal sectors in the Republic of Korea and Taiwan China are also characterised as being strongly based on similar links to the formal sectors in their countries. The clustering of small-scale enterprises in Northern Italy is attributed largely to the collective efficiency of location, in producing for mainstream markets.

There is virtually no data available on the demand linkages of the informal sector to the formal sector in India although several studies indicate that such linkages do exist at low levels. Nevertheless, there is already some evidence that a number of small enterprises in India that were successful in establishing linkages with larger enterprises, have benefited from them. In a recent study of the tiny and small unorganised manufacturing enterprises that operate as sub-contractors to large enterprises, Chadha reports the benefit of an assured market for an overwhelming majority of them, technological links for nearly one-third of them, the facility of raw material supply by the parent company for more than 50 per cent of them, and soon (Chadha, 2001b).

There is thus considerable scope for further strengthening the access of informal sector enterprises to the markets of the modern sector through the development of subcontracting. But the huge differences in economic power between large modern enterprises and the small operators of the informal sector tend to place the latter at a great disadvantage. The most disturbing fall-out is a delayed release of payments by the parent company to its sub-contractors which occasionally force some of the informal manufacturing units to close down. Subcontracting under these potentially exploitative conditions is hardly conducive to the growth of informal sector enterprises, or even in the longer-term interests of modern enterprises which need to encourage reliable suppliers. Happily, a suitable legislation, i.e. Interest on Delayed Payments to Small Scale and Ancillary Industrial Undertakings Act has already been enacted to secure timely payments to small-scale industries; under this Act, it is now compulsory that the payments to such industrial units be made within 120 days after which penal interest would be imposed (Chadha, 2001b).

7.1.3 Boosting Exports from the Informal Sector

India must jettison its traditional inward-oriented approach in favour of the outward-oriented strategy that has produced such dramatic improvements in East Asia and many other regions. Due to the path of insularity which it had chosen, India has seen its share of world exports drop from 2.5 per cent in 1950 to 0.6 per cent now, whereas China has experienced precisely the opposite result and achieved a double-digit expansion of exports for many years now.

Export growth for formal sector products is limited in scope because of the growing competition. Greater attention has therefore to be given to exports from the informal sector for products such as processed food, leather goods, handicrafts, software development, flowers, etc.

Despite the fact that, in the new paradigm of development, the state is expected to intervene minimally in economic activities, there still are facilities (particularly under an employment protection/promotion clause in the WTO agreements) that permit the government to accord infant industry status to small units, particularly those that hold special promise in the export markets. The most crucial requirement will be an improvement in the quality of the products to meet international standards.

Besides technological up-grading to achieve international standards, a more conducive policy environment is needed to encourage export growth from informal sector enterprises. In particular, the foreign exchange regime, multiple taxation practices and administrative procedures require simplification. Suitable methods of subsidy transfer that would help strengthen small units on a sustained basis would also go a long way in establishing a place for them in international markets.

While linkages of small enterprises to export markets need to be encouraged, such linkages also need to be developed for the domestic market. No country can afford to depend solely on export markets since volatility in international markets can be severely disruptive. It needs hardly to be emphasized that such volatilities are too costly for the informal sector enterprises to absorb on their own.

7.1.4 Stimulating Internal Demand

Increased investment in housing and the development of other infrastructure sectors (irrigation, transport, telecommunication, power, education, health, etc.) would benefit the informal sector most strongly. There is a significant direct employment potential in these sectors as well as indirect multiplier employment effects through a chain of backward and forward linkages with the informal sector.

The present state of infrastructure development in India is very poor. Some recent estimates suggest that there is a shortage of electricity to the extent of 20-30 per cent of the current demand, and the proper development of roads requires an additional investment of Rs. 800 billion. In fact, the success of the economic reform programme in India is likely to depend critically on the quantity and quality of the available social and physical infrastructure.

A particularly strong boost to internal demand can come from the housing sector. There is an acute shortage of housing, and yet the supply is limited, due to legal restrictions on land-use, inadequate access to finance by housing development companies and lack of easy mortgage schemes available for home owners. In fact the housing market, despite its size, is seriously underdeveloped. Investment in housing generally represents less than 1 per cent of GDP in most urban areas. A policy that would permit housing to become a full-fledged industry, would lift the house-building activity considerably from its present low level, thereby raising aggregate demand leading to scaling up of the informal sector. Increased investment in housing would not only address the housing shortage but also generate increased employment. There is ample evidence that investment in housing has a much greater employment multiplier effect than investment in most other sectors.

The one sector that has exhibited significant promise is software development (that registered a 40-50 per cent annual growth since mid-nineties), and the evidence suggests that many firms in this sector started their operations with a humble beginning. But this industry appears to be reaching its limits for want of efficient telecommunications support. The telecommunications sector itself has the potential to grow in areas such as entertainment. The government presently controls this sector, and private initiative has been restricted to small segments only. The laws regulating the communication sector are archaic and stifling. An opening up of this sector should unleash the private sector's potential, using its own funds, which in turn can contribute significantly to economic growth. Since this sector is inextricably linked with most other sectors, its growth would herald a high level of overall growth in the economy. Again, with growth in aggregate demand (as well as through direct activity promotion), informal sector activities would receive an impetus to grow.

To a fairly large extent, the demand for informal sector products comes from within the informal sector itself, and indeed this sector plays an important role in satisfying the basic needs of the urban poor. However, in view of the extremely low, and often fluctuating, incomes and purchasing power of those who work in the sector, this is an inadequate base for growth. A large proportion of the informal sector output is consumed by individuals and households who derive their income from the modern and the public sectors. Nevertheless, if demand for its output is to grow significantly, it is necessary to strengthen market linkages with the rest of the economy.

An important role can be played in this respect by the government as a major purchaser of goods, services and buildings. Rarely, however, are informal sector enterprises in a position to participate in the bidding process for government procurement, or to secure contracts for road maintenance or school buildings. This may be due to the inability of these enterprises to meet the quality standards required by governments or to their lack of information about the existence of such possibilities; it could also be due to the nature of procurement procedures or other stipulations. The latter can, for instance, discriminate against the informal sector because the bids are in such large batches that small informal sector producers are unable to supply the quantity required within the deadline. Restrictions such as these could be eliminated without unduly complicating the bidding and procurement process, or alternatively producers could be encouraged to join together in bidding.

7.2 Supply-side Interventions

There are certain specific supply side areas where interventions could help create conditions for the development of a more dynamic and better protected informal sector and for its progressive integration into the economy at large. These interventions should include broad-based policy and institutional reforms in addition to programmes of direct assistance. A particular challenge will be to eliminate biases in public policy which operate to the disadvantage of the informal sector.

7.2.1 Eliminating Policy Biases against the Informal Sector

In the past, import-substituting industrialisation strategies, restrictive trade practices, regulatory industrial policies and the administrative allocation of resources had created a highly-protected and inefficient industrial sector in India. The priority accorded to heavy and capital goods industries and an overvalued exchange rate increased capital intensity across industries. Capital intensity was higher in industries which enjoyed a higher effective protection and lower in those in which the effective protection was lower. The informal sector was doubly disadvantaged. It lacked access to influential bureaucrats and ministers who allocated foreign exchange and domestic resources, permits and licenses, often for a consideration. Large-scale industry reaped high "quasi rents" created by the "licence permit raj". No wonder, workers employed in large-scale industry demanded and succeeded in chipping off a fairly big share in these rents through collective bargaining. As if this were not enough, the government's labour policy granted workers in the formal sector many non-wage benefits through labour legislation. The effect of collective bargaining, labour legislation and increased capital-intensity restricted the growth of employment in the formal sector, forcing the informal sector to absorb most of the additional job seekers entering the labour force.

There is thus an urgent need for progressively removing some of the biases in public policy which continue to operate to the disadvantage of the informal sector. Such distortions may take several forms and operate against small labour-intensive enterprises. They can take the form of tax exemptions, tariff protection and other forms of direct or indirect subsidies to large, and sometimes unprofitable, public sector enterprises, whereas potentially viable, but much smaller-scale, informal sector enterprises are deprived of any such support. Biases can also take the form of preferential access which large firms may enjoy to capital, foreign exchange and imported inputs, or of pricing policies which favour production technologies and capital goods used by large enterprises. Or they can take the form of unnecessary (and excessively lengthy and costly) legal, bureaucratic and administrative obstacles to starting up or operating a business. These are impossible for informal sector operators, with few resources and limited education, to overcome. All these, and many other, biases in public policy and institutions combine to perpetuate low productivity, marginalisation, and poverty, among a large section of the urban population.

7.2.2 Workable Regulatory Framework for Micro-enterprises

Most micro-enterprises in the informal sector operate in an environment where the regulatory framework is very poorly defined. While some micro-enterprises face over-regulation, others have to depend on the whims of local authorities (for example, in matters of taxes or access to business premises), and face serious problems of access to markets, technology and credit. Close attention needs to be paid to defining an appropriate regulatory framework which assists rather than obstructs the growth of micro-enterprises.

More 'friendly' laws and regulations would also encourage informal sector enterprises to operate within the framework of the law. The progressive 'legalisation' of the informal sector is clearly an essential requirement for its integration into society. But it is more likely to take place in a positive environment where the obstacles to legitimisation are reduced to a minimum, where the costs of gaining legality are not prohibitive, and where there are clear benefits - i.e., where the public authorities are known (and seen) to be supporting rather than harassing the informal sector.

Obstacles to gain legality can take many forms. They can take the form of excessive bureaucratic requirements for clearances, registration, land-use conditionalities, etc. The high costs of registration can also be an obstacle to informal sector operators with few resources and very low profits. Sometimes, the way in which taxes are levied on enterprises discourages employment creation, since the hiring of additional workers can result in a large increase in the tax to be paid by the employer.

Problems such as these should be relatively simple to overcome, provided the government is prepared to streamline the bureaucratic procedures, and to reduce registration fees to a nominal amount (or even abolish them altogether) for informal sector enterprises. The establishment of a tax system which is progressive, simple to administer and to understand, and beyond corruption would also be an important step towards removing the stigma of 'illegality' that surrounds most of the informal sector enterprises.

Far more complex problems are, however, presented by government regulations designed to protect the general interests of the community. Here, it would seem important to identify regulations that are less essential and place unnecessary obstacles to the functioning of the informal sector units. It would, for instance, be difficult to justify relaxing or failing to enforce regulations governing the safety and maintenance of vehicles used for public transport in order that informal sector operators may more easily obtain licences to provide such services. On the other hand, regulations which give a monopoly to public companies, or which fix the tariffs to be charged on public transport, may well prevent informal sector operators from competing to provide a much needed public service.

At the same time, certain regulations or procedures which are justified could be applied with some flexibility. In the case of housing, for instance, the rigorous enforcement of zoning regulations and building standards results in enormous hardship to those unable to comply with them and obliges the informal sector to operate at great distances from its potential markets.

The general point to be made here is that some laws, regulations and administrative procedures are essential to the functioning of the society while others are not, or could be applied with some flexibility to the informal sector without prejudicing or harming public interest. A greater sensitivity to the situation and the needs of the informal sector is essential if the sector is to be brought progressively into the regulatory framework of the society at large. What is needed is a democratic process, typically characterized by quick decision-making, appropriate land-use policies and simple and transparent laws.

7.2.3 Removing Constraints on the Growth of Small-scale Industry

In India, a system of "reservation" of specified industrial items for small-scale industries (SSIs) was instituted to protect them from undue competition. For example, the number of items reserved for exclusive manufacture in the small-scale sector, which was 47 only in April 1967, gradually rose to 836 in July 1991

(Hussain, 1997: 102-03). Although, because of political expediency involved, especially the anticipated employment stakes, the number has summarily remained the same since 1991, yet for a variety of reasons, most noticeably the forceful plea for de-reservation made in 1997 by the Abid Hussain Committee, the product reservation policy seems to be on its way-out. In more recent years, the WTO-inspired free trade regime seems to have hastened the process of de-reservation. The de-reservation in the garments sector has already been announced (The Economic Times, November 3, 2000:5); it may follow soon for other sectors. Thanks to numerous fundamental flaws in the policy of product reservation, in spite of the overarching umbrella of protection, technological obsolescence of both products and processes, managerial, financial and marketing weaknesses, cumbersome rules, regulations and procedural hassles, etc. could not be tided over. Most importantly, it has restricted exports and has done little to promote small-scale industries, most ostensibly because a fairly big proportion of the items reserved for the small scale sector have never been produced by it (Chadha, 2001b).

The firms in the small-scale sector often benefit from certain concessions in terms of tax rebates or subsidies. In the event that they grow beyond a certain ceiling, they not only forfeit the concessions, but may also lose the right to manufacture the reserved item(s). This law acts as a natural barrier for firms to grow or acquire technological prowess; many larger firms split into smaller units to gain access to concessions but then lose out on acquiring or sustaining competitiveness. In the process, the potential of the industry to grow through its own strength is seriously diminished. It is often stated, albeit anecdotally, that the advantage gained by such reservations is small compared to the price paid by the society, in terms of stifling growth.

There are also some indications that the production of more than 200 items on the reserved list has ceased since their production calls for investment which cannot be realised. This suggests that these items are now being imported, thereby creating employment opportunities abroad rather than in India. One possible solution, short of de-reservation, as some observers have suggested, would be to develop the concept of a 'deemed small-scale industry', analogous to the concept of 'deemed exports' currently being applied by the Ministry of Commerce. This concept enables certain items, even though they are not exported physically, to enjoy the benefits of actual exports. In the same vein, the concept of a 'deemed small-scale industry' would imply that small firms can exceed the investment limit but still qualify for concessions available to those which actually fall within the limit.

7.2.4 Increasing Access to Credit

As already discussed, small businesses and individuals generally access unorganised capital markets which operate along traditional trade/money-lending lines. Some estimates suggest that private money-lenders meet as much as 80 per cent of the credit needs of the informal sector. Small entrepreneurs also pay a far higher interest rate - as much as 3 times that prevailing in the organised market. Most of these loans are serviced. This may suggest that small entrepreneurs are demonstrating an ability to make better use of capital than many in the organised sector. Thus, the problem with the credit market in India appears not to be one of a "high" real interest rate but inadequate penetration of organised credit to benefit large parts of the economy.

The Small Industries Development Bank of India (SIDBI) provides loans to "modern" small industries. Some commercial banks too have schemes for the modern small-scale sector, and some (very restricted) governmental support is available to handloom/ khadi/ village industries. In general, most micro-enterprises are not eligible to obtain loans from institutional sources, unless they are able to provide collateral. In recent years, an initiative has been launched by some non-governmental organisations (NGOs) engaged in development finance, which has been backed, to an extent, by commercial banks, the National Bank for Agriculture and Rural Development (NABARD) and the SIDBI. Two successful examples are of Hyderabad-based BASIX and SHARE organisations getting involved in micro credit lending. The SIDBI is perhaps the most progressive among all agencies; it has created a Micro Finance Foundation with a capital base of Rs. one billion which provides loans to credit groups through NGOs. The mode of lending nonetheless continues to be promotional rather than of mainstreaming the credit requirements.

Recent experiments, however, reveal that while small operators may not individually qualify for credit within the stipulated banking norms, their credit worthiness rises if they work in groups. Credit groups composed of small borrowers often begin as savings groups, and while they establish their credibility as savers, they also qualify to apply for group loans - in quantities that banks can administer with reasonable efficiency - and then distribute the amounts among themselves according to each member's needs. There are usually no concessions on interest rates or on terms of payback. The interest rates are often at par with prime bank lending rates or somewhat higher. The loan repayment rate is generally in the range 90 per cent and above, which is comparable with, if not better than, the repayment rate of the formal sector clients. However, an important challenge in this direction is to institutionalise this effort at the national level. This may perhaps require strengthening of local governments - the third tier of governance - to take up the task.

A high powered committee, set up by the Reserve Bank of India (RBI) in 1998, for improving credit delivery system to SSIs and simplification of procedures thereof, made as many as 126 recommendations. Many of its recommendations have been accepted by the RBI. These include enhancement in limit of composite loan from Rs. 2 lakh to Rs. 5 lakh, delegation of more powers to branch managers for granting ad hoc facilities to the extent of 20 per cent of sanctioned limit, strengthening of recovery mechanism, opening of more SSI bank branches in localised neighbourhoods in the private sector, and so on (Govt. of India, 1999: 110; SIDBI, 1999: 101-02). The major hurdle that the authorities perceive is the difficulty of safe-keeping of money with such "small" unit banks. Issues are also raised concerning the credit worthiness of small borrowers. While the 'group-approach' may be acceptable, subject to the group having to establish itself in accordance with the established banking norms, the issue of developing an appropriate regulatory framework for supervising the administration of small loans on a very large scale still remains.

The problem of inadequate credit will not be fully overcome unless informal sector enterprises gain adequate access to modern financial institutions. But then, the banks cannot be expected to lend money without some form of guarantee; moreover, the relative cost of processing small loans is high. Attempts to get around this problem by means, for instance, of subsidised interest rates for micro-enterprises have not proved successful in the past, since they have only discouraged banks from lending to micro-enterprises. Some other agency is needed to provide a guarantee to the banks and to assist them in drawing up requests for loans. Finally, due expertise is required to distinguish the good risks from the bad.

Assessing the credit worthiness of micro-enterprises would require that such enterprises be accredited. There are few, if any, tools, techniques and experiences that can be drawn upon for assigning credit ratings to micro-enterprises. The banking/financial sector is simply not conversant with this issue. The lack of a suitable concept of accreditation in the informal sector is a major problem.

The rating of small banks and similar financial institutions is also an outstanding issue. The RBI is still debating on what standards to set for monitoring the proposed small unit banks that are expected to be fairly evenly distributed over vast geographical areas. The high-powered committee mentioned above has proposed that a self-regulatory mechanism, in which a number of these banks could associate together to decide norms for themselves, be one possible approach. But this idea has its own risks: on what basis can a central bank permit experimentation with people's deposits?

The real challenge is therefore to develop innovative credit delivery systems. Commercial banks are singularly ill equipped to deal with small borrowers.

Alternatives have to be found which combine the flexibility of the trader/money-lender relationship, with access to institutionalised credit. Lessons can be drawn from the creative refinancing being carried out by truck manufacturers in recent times.

Not only are alternative banking systems/delivery mechanisms needed, but funds must also be steered from the formal banking sector into micro finance, since it is the formal (commercial) banking sector which is presently the custodian of almost all the savings and deposits in the country. It is not uncommon for the government or the banking system to siphon off the savings of the poor to finance housing programmes or other facilities for the relatively well-off.

7.2.5 Enhancing Productivity through Training and Skill Development

Improving productivity and incomes in the informal sector requires greater emphasis on human resource development in India. A major challenge is to ensure "trainability" of the entire labour force. This requires the universalization of primary and secondary education to ensure people's basic capacity to learn new skills, particularly those working in the informal sector. Despite repeated commitments made by the government to raise expenditure on education and skills development to 6 per cent of GNP, it has so far not been able to reach even half this figure (IAMR, 1999: 158). In contrast, in many South East Asian countries, expenditure on education has been more than 7 per cent of GNP. It is hardly surprising, therefore, that India ranks poorly, behind 127 countries, on the ranking of nations according to the Human Development Index (HDI) (UNDP: 2000: 159).

Most informal sector workers lack access to formal training institutions. Lack of managerial and marketing skills on the one hand, and the low and outdated technical skills of workers on the other, are major problems for the informal sector entrepreneurs. If the general policy aim is to bring about a progressive integration of the informal sector into the formal sector by improving its level of productivity and technology, there needs to be a greater interaction between formal training and that provided in the informal sector.

In order for this to be achieved, it may be necessary to adapt and re-orient the formal training systems. For example, in order to permit informal sector workers, or potential workers, to benefit from the training offered by formal establishments, it may be necessary to lower entry requirements by placing less emphasis on diplomas or other educational attainments, which very few informal sector workers will have achieved, and put more emphasis on practical aptitudes and experience.

An improvement or upgrading of the technologies used in the informal sector must clearly be an important objective of any new approach to training, since this is a key requirement if the sector is to break out of its disadvantaged position in the economy. It is equally important to be aware of the remarkable ingenuity and capacity to innovate and improvise that usually exists in the informal sector. Indeed, such ingenuity is the result of years of learning how to survive in a hostile environment. It is important that, whatever approach is followed to training for the informal sector, it should build on, and not smother, these qualities of the informal sector.

Large modern laboratories and research institutions essentially support the interests of organised sector industries. There is a need to create centralised product development/R&D facilities or to establish and strengthen centres for transfer of technology to the informal sector. Besides technology transfer, there is a need to extend business support and information services to this sector.

A particularly critical need is to provide training for micro-entrepreneurs in the informal sector in basic techniques of book-keeping, marketing, production organisation, costing, pricing, etc. Without such a knowledge, they are and will remain at a great disadvantage in relation to modern sector enterprises. Some initiatives to promote skill development have been taken by NGOs such as Resource and Support Centre, Mumbai and Development Alternatives, New Delhi, but much more needs to be done, especially in the backward regions.

In some countries, efforts have been made to consolidate skills in the informal sector through the provision of mobile training units or through the establishment of training schools near the workplace. Since few informal sector workers have the resources or the time for learning new skills, some innovative approaches to training are necessary, such as the provision of training in the evenings after working hours.

It may also be more advantageous to develop community based training. Unless such initiatives are taken to extend education, research and training to the larger masses, it is difficult to envisage that informal sector will break out of its low productivity status. In other words, there is a strong case for re-orienting education, research and training priorities to meet the express needs of the informal sector enterprises which, in any case, accommodate more than 90 per cent of India's workforce.

7.2.6 Reducing the Flow of Migration from Rural Areas

To make macro-economic policies more effective in improving productivity and working conditions in the urban informal sector, a number of additional measures will need to be adopted. One such set of measures obviously involves structural reforms aimed at slowing down the excessive expansion of the urban informal sector. As already discussed, the persistence and growth of the urban informal sector in India has often been due to an unbalanced approach to development, which has bypassed a sizeable section of the population in the rural areas. This has induced millions of rural workers to take refuge in the urban informal sector as the only means of survival for themselves and their families. It is clear that the problems presented by a large and growing urban informal sector can be effectively tackled only if there is a more favourable environment of growth and employment creation in rural areas, and if efforts are made to redress the rural-urban imbalances in general development policy. The latter would include much greater emphasis on the revitalisation of rural areas and equitable policies for rural development, which are essential prerequisites for stemming migration to the already inflated urban informal sector.

7.3 Improving Employment and Working Conditions

Since discriminatory policies and practices have been allowed to persist to the disadvantage of the informal sector, measures to improve its productive potential are unlikely to succeed or result in improved employment and working conditions unless social protection is extended to informal sector workers and those engaged in informal sector activities are better organised to protect their own interests. It is therefore important to examine alternative approaches for extending social protection to informal sector workers and to consider ways and means of organising workers and producers in this sector.

7.3.1 Promoting Social Protection and Social Security

As already discussed, most workers in the informal sector generally lack any kind of formal social protection or access to social security. Of particular concern to the ILO is, of course, the non-compliance of the informal sector with labour legislation and core labour standards. To a large extent, such a non-compliance is due to the fact that a majority of the informal sector workers are self-employed or unpaid family workers who are not subject to many legal obligations of this nature. In the case of informal sector enterprises which do hire labour, compliance with the full range of labour regulations; including those governing hours of work, weekly rest, holidays with pay, minimum wages and social security contributions would more than fully absorb the very low profits made by such enterprises and may drive many of them out of business altogether. But another reason is to be found in the manner in which such enterprises operate. Labour relations are not subject to explicit and enforceable contracts; no job security is enjoyed or expected by informal sector workers; working hours are flexible (and often very long indeed) and wages are paid irregularly. In the absence of trade unions in micro-enterprises or generally in the informal sector at all, labour relations tend to be paternalistic, with the owner of the enterprise working alongside his employees and apprentices. Moreover, the incorporation of such units into contributory social security systems scarcely seems feasible in view of the instability of the employment relationship.

The non-observance of labour legislation is therefore linked with the precarious existence of most informal sector enterprises, and the problem will not be entirely overcome until such enterprises are able to operate profitably in a more stable environment. In fact, there is some evidence that in many East and South-East Asian countries, the growth of the more successful informal sector firms has resulted in improved standards for their employees, including paid holidays and the payment of bonuses. The progressive extension of labour legislation and social protection to informal sector workers is perhaps the only feasible option. Another solution that may be proposed is the deregulation of social protection in the formal sector so as to enable the informal sector to meet the lowered requirements. But this form of deregulation is to be resisted as it would signal the consolidation of the "informal sector" and perpetuation of the sub-standard conditions in which it operates.

It must also be recognised that the inability of the informal sector to comply with certain aspects of labour legislation is not necessarily an indication of defects in the legislation itself; it should rather be taken as a reflection of the highly unsatisfactory conditions in which the informal sector has to operate. Deregulation of the labour market would do little, if anything, to improve those conditions. The general approach should therefore be to regard the basic standards and provisions of labour legislations as non-negotiable goals to be attained progressively in the informal sector - and to establish the needed institutions to promote their attainment rather than to regard the precarious and unregulated nature of work in the informal sector as the norm for the rest of the society.

The progressive application of labour standards does not necessarily have to wait until the informal sector starts to "catch up" with the modern sector. There are certain core standards that are so fundamental that their non-observance should not be tolerated. For example, fundamental human rights at work (freedom of association, abolition of forced labour and child labour, non-discrimination in occupation and employment) are not the luxuries reserved for one economic sector alone; they are fundamental to human dignity, and indeed to the success of efforts to integrate the informal sector into the rest of the economy. Freedom of association is particularly important in this respect, because it is only through forming and joining organisations of their own choosing that those employed in the informal sector will be able to generate sufficient pressure to bring about the necessary changes in policies, attitudes and procedures that hamper the development of the sector and the improvement of working conditions in it. In the case of child labour, high priority needs to be given to eliminating the worst forms of child labour, such as their involvement in hazardous work. Law enforcement must be accompanied by measures to extend and improve facilities for education - formal and non-formal - and by income-generating measures for parents.

Another area which deserves priority attention is occupational safety and health. While it may not be possible for informal sector enterprises to comply with the full range of government safety and health regulations, there is no reason why they should not be able to benefit from information and guidance on the often simple and inexpensive measures that can be taken to reduce risks or from occupational health and safety counselling provided through community-based programmes, perhaps supported by NGOs.

The same factors which inhibit the application of labour standards in the informal sector also prevent the development of social security schemes which might provide protection against loss of income or which would meet the costs of health care services. In particular, the low incomes of the informal sector workers make such provisions difficult. But the difficulties are compounded by the absence of any framework within which participation can be organised, contingencies and entitlements defined, benefits established and contributions levied. In addition, the instability of many informal sector enterprises mitigates against long-term commitments, such as those underlying old-age or invalidity pensions. And although, at least a moderate degree of social protection might be feasible if some means could be found of spreading the burden equitably across all active members of the sector, some degree of compulsion would be an essential ingredient: no single entrepreneur (or employee) can afford to absorb the additional costs of social security if his competitor can obtain a commercial advantage by opting out of the scheme.

Nevertheless, there is an urgent need for a large-scale extension of social protection, beyond the small fraction - less than 10 per cent - of the labour force, almost entirely confined to the organised sector, who presently enjoy social security coverage. To begin with, the well-established social security schemes of the formal sector could be extended to the informal sector, wherever a suitable framework can be found, such as in the case of more developed micro-enterprises. For this reason, the Union Government should strengthen the national social security institutions, and, hopefully, the public's confidence in them. It should also encourage, and where possible, assist the state governments to strengthen locally-based institutions. The involvement of groups from civil society is essential in order to reach out to widely-spread workers in the informal sector/rural areas. Group-based solidarity schemes, though usually small in scale and coverage, are often attractive to informal sector workers. Some such schemes could be directly governed by associations or organisations of the informal sector workers themselves (e.g., producer and employers' organisations, cooperatives and credit associations), or they could use intermediate carriers such as trade unions and non-governmental organisations. Some states, notably but by no means only Kerala, have significantly extended social protection to workers in the unorganised/agricultural sectors. Social security and welfare schemes are also operating somewhat successfully for manual and construction workers in Tamil Nadu and for Mathadi workers in Maharashtra. And a number of NGOs such as Annapoorna Mahila Mandal (AMM), Self-Employed Womens' Association (SEWA), Asian Centre for Organisation, Research and Development (ACORD) and CDF have developed successful schemes providing at least basic social security benefits at the "grassroots" level. Such initiatives and experiences need to be documented and replicated.

7.3.2 Organising Informal Sector Workers and Producers

A major challenge facing trade unions and employers' organisations in India is to organise workers and small entrepreneurs in the informal sector. It is only through their own organised efforts and through group solidarity that informal sector workers and producers will achieve lasting improvements in their situation. It is largely because of the absence of pressure from within the informal sector that the various discriminatory policies and practices against the sector have endured themselves for so long. Those working in the informal sector continue to be harassed and exploited, and enjoy little or no protection at all.

In the past, trade unions and employers' organisations have generally ignored this problem under the commonly held belief that, with development, the informal sector would eventually be absorbed by the modern sector, and that those who worked in it could therefore eventually be embraced by the trade union movement. In fact, at present the reverse is happening. As already discussed, the informal sector has been incessantly growing and the modern sector has failed to take on additional working hands during the nineties. Thus, more workers than ever before are lodged in the informal sector, who are nearly completely deprived of protection.

To some extent, lack of organisation is due to the very heterogeneity of the informal sector itself. The artisans, street-vendors, transport operators, small producers and wage earners found therein, all have very diverse interests, priorities and involvements. Moreover, competition within these groups for very small markets may often be an obstacle to group solidarity. Nevertheless, there are numerous examples of small local organisations that have been created within the informal sector. Most of the hawkers on the streets of Mumbai are members of some trade unions or associations. In certain cities of Gujarat, they are members of trade associations. Taxi drivers and truck operators have also formed loose federations that protect their interests. Two remarkably successful and very well-known women's movements in India - the Working Women's Forum (WWF) and the Self-employed Women's Association (SEWA) - which started out as cooperative-type movements have succeeded in developing numerous services for an ever-growing number of members. These are now registered as trade unions.

Generally, however, and with few exceptions, such organisations have been too limited in scope or too localised in their operation. Moreover, operating as they do with inadequate resources, expecting them to achieve any major change in the environment in which the informal sector operates or in its relationships with the institutions and enterprises of the modern sector or with the public authorities, would not be realistic.

In the past, trade unions have experienced difficulty in organising informal sector workers because they are often difficult to contact and because their needs are usually different from workers in the formal sector. Moreover, informal sector workers are mostly self-employed, from amongst whom the trade unions have traditionally recruited few members. Those who are not self-employed, usually work in very small units, often family units, where labour relations are conducted on a very different basis compared with modern sector enterprises, and to which trade unions rarely have access besides offering little appeal to workers involved.

Nevertheless, there is a growing realisation that the trade union movement has to adopt a longer term perspective and recognise that organising the informal sector is critical if the movement is to have a wide membership base and retain the capacity to protect all kinds of workers. It is also increasingly realised that a "community-based" approach to organising, in conjunction with other proven "shop-floor" organising methods, might be more effective in reaching workers in informal activities, particularly when organisers, howsoever determined they may be, are denied access to the workplace or cannot locate the workplace, as is often the case with home workers or domestic workers.

However, to successfully organise unorganised workers today, unions must do more to accommodate their needs through specially tailored programmes. At the heart of the struggle to organise is the ability of trade unions to deliver tangible benefits and increased protection to workers in informal activities.

A comparable challenge is faced by employers' organisations whose members have, until now, largely been the owners of modern enterprises, and whose activities have therefore quite naturally focussed on promoting and protecting the interests of the modern sector. The extent to which they can be expected to enlarge the scope of their activities to cover informal sector entrepreneurs will naturally depend very much on whether their members perceive it to be in their interests to do so.

The micro enterprises of the informal sector should be viewed by employers not so much as "unfair competitors" to the formal sector, or as the providers of inputs produced in highly exploitative conditions, but rather as potential partners whose growth could result in more dynamic interchanges between the formal and the informal sector from which all could benefit. The informal sector, if it had the opportunity to develop, could become a far more important market for the goods produced by the modern sector and at the same time a more efficient source of a broader range of high-quality inputs required by the modern sector.

Employers' organisations have therefore a critical role to play in promoting self-employment through spreading entrepreneurial culture and assisting the informal sector to emerge from its marginalized and segmented place in society and the economy. They could act as a pressure group for the removal of many of the constraints which at present impede the growth of the informal sector. They could also, and probably more effectively than most other institutions can do, provide the informal sector with access to improved technology and with the improved skills necessary to operate that technology. And they could help small entrepreneurs by educating them about simple management concepts of successfully running an enterprise. Obviously, the teaching has to be done in the vernacular medium and the examples kept simple so that entrepreneurs in tiny and small enterprises can understand the cash flow cycle and other functional areas of management.

8. Concluding Remarks

The worsening overall employment situation in India and the limited scope for employment generation in the formal sector require that job creation in the informal sector must be a priority item on the National Policy Agenda. While economic growth will be a necessary condition for employment generation, the problems faced by informal sector workers and producers will not be overcome merely through stimulating economic growth or through a more favourable climate for employment creation. Specific measures are also required to help the informal sector improve its productive capacity, break out of its marginalized, vulnerable and semi-legal position in society and overcome the obstacles to ultimate integration into the rest of the economy.

The specific interventions, most often recommended and applied, are those directed at providing credit, market and extension services to micro and small enterprises in the informal sector. A related set of measures sometimes deals with start-up assistance and entrepreneurship training to encourage the setting up of new enterprises and other forms of self-employment. It is more unusual, however, to see small-industry promotion measures of this kind being supported by wider policies aimed at changing the overall institutional and policy environment affecting the growth potential of small enterprises. There are few attempts, for instance, to redress the fiscal and other policy biases that have somehow persisted in favour of large modern-sector enterprises, to shift the pattern of income distribution so as to increase the demand for the informal sector products, or to forge greater technological and commercial linkages between small and large enterprises.

Thus if the overall conditions of the informal sector are to be transformed in aspects such as improving its access to credit, technology and skills levels, enhancing labour productivity, shifting to higher value added products and a more diversified product range, gaining higher prices for its products, and strengthening demand linkages to the formal and export sectors, then macro policy interventions are needed. Such interventions will require a significant re-allocation of resources towards the informal sector. This would mean a reversal or re-orientation of existing policy which allocates resources predominantly towards the formal sector.

There are also a number of other difficult problems which must be addressed in specific terms. These include the removal of gender-based discrimination from employment, the need to widen women's access to productive resources and skill enhancement, the elimination of child labour and the extension of proper employment rights and protection to contract and home-based workers. The goal of employment policy should not be just the creation of jobs but creation of jobs of acceptable quality. A coherent policy should try to integrate concerns about employment generation, social protection and social organisation. This may imply that society would have to accept some core labour standards.

Given the decentralised nature of the informal sector it would be futile to expect that labour standards could be enforced legally by the state. Laws may help but much would depend on the voluntary acceptance of the standards. Progress may, however, require the involvement of agencies that have gained acceptance and credibility among the participants in the informal sector. Such agencies alone can exercise their moral pressure to secure acceptance of standards. Cooperation among social partners and civil society groups to promote decent work conditions will be of utmost importance in encouraging gradual application of labour standards and mainstreaming informal sector workers socially and economically. The issue then is to identify the type of linkages and alliances which could be established between informal sector organisations and employers' and workers' organisations to their mutual advantage.

There are clearly numerous challenges as well as advantages for conventional workers' and employers' organisations in organising and representing informal sector workers and producers. Whether employers' organisations and trade unions will in fact be able to bring about this somewhat radical shift in the scope and range of their activities remains to be seen. Nonetheless, unless they do so, and unless they cease to be seen to be engaged primarily in the protection of the interests of a highly privileged few, the prospects of integrating the informal sector into the mainstream of economic life are decidedly poor.

Bibliography

Chadha, G.K., 1999. "Non-farm Sector in Rural India: Past Experience and Future Strategies", paper read at IFPRI-Washington Seminar, Chandigarh, November 9-11.

____, 2000. Development of Small and Medium Enterprises in the Developing Economies: Learning from Chinese and Indian Experiences, Stockholm School of Economics-JNU Collaborative Project (on-going).

____, 2001a. "Education, Skills, and Working Environments of Workers in India's Rural Industry", International Journal of Occupational and Environmental Health, 7/3, April-June.

____, 2001b. Rural Industry in India: Policy Perspectives, Past Performance and Future Options, (mimeo.), ILO-SAAT, New Delhi.

Dev, Mahendra S., 2000. "Economic Liberalisation and Employment in South Asia-I", Economic and Political Weekly, Nos. 1 & 2, January 8-14.

Goldar B.N. and Mitra Arup, 1999. "Productivity Growth in Informal Manufacturing Sector in India", Paper read at Workshop on Measurement of Productivity in India, IHD New Delhi, July 9-10.

Govt. of India, 1985. National Accounts Statistics, 1970-71/1982-83, CSO.

____, 1986. Directory Manufacturing Establishment Survey, 1984-85,CSO.

____, 1989. Survey of Unorganised Manufacture: Non-Directory Establishments and Own-Account Enterprises, NSSO, June.

____, 1995. Economic Census, 1990, All India Report, CSO, March.

____, 1998. National Accounts Statistics,1998, CSO, June.

____, 1998. Fourth Economic Census: Provisional Results, CSO, June.

____, 1998. Unorganised Manufacturing Sector in India: Its Size, Employment and Some Key Estimates, Report No. 433, NSSO, August.

____, Annual Survey of Industries: Summary Results for Factor Sector (for various years), CSO, Ministry of Planning.

____, 1999. Ninth Five Year Plan 1997-2002, Vol. I: Development Goals, Strategy and Policies, Planning Commission.

____, 1999a. Economic Survey 1998-99, Ministry of Finance.

____, 1999b. Fourth Economic Census: Provisional Results, CSO, July.

Govt. of India, 2000. National Accounts Statistics 2000, CSO, July.

____, 2001. Economic Survey 1999-2000, Ministry of Finance.

Hussain, A., 1997. Report of the Expert Committee on Small Enterprises, July.

IAMR, 1999. Manpower Profile Yearbook, 1999, New Delhi.

ILO, 1991. The Dilemma of the Informal Sector, Report of the Director-General, (Part I), International Labour Conference, 78th Session 1991, ILO,Geneva.

Kulshreshtha, A.C. and Singh, Gulab, 1998. "Contribution of Unorganised Sector in the Indian Economy", Manpower Journal, October-December.

Reserve Bank of India, 1999. Handbook of Statistics on Indian Economy.

Shah, Amita, 1998. "Scalar Linkages in Industries: Implications for Productivity and Employment", Indian Journal of Labour Economics, 41/3, July - September.

SIDBI, 1999. SIDBI Report on Small Scale Industries Sector, Lucknow.

The Economic Times, 2000. New Delhi, November 3.

UNDP, 2000. Human Development Report.

Informal Sector in India's Urban Economy: Macro Trends and Policy Perspectives

Amitabh Kundu[1]

1. Introduction

There has been an upsurge of interest on urban informal sector, in India in recent years. A number of studies have been commissioned, books and articles published, and seminars and workshops conducted, focussing both on its theoretical as well as operational aspects. The substantial increase in the volume of person days of employment, percentage of subsidiary and casual workers in the early nineties, after the formal launching of the programmes of structural adjustment, has given a boost to informal sector studies since much of this incremental employment has been generated within this sector. There has, however, been a hiatus between conceptualization of the informal sector in theory and its practical application in empirical research.

Theoretical research on the development dynamics in India as also in other developing countries has stipulated several characteristics of the informal sector in terms of technology, production relations, conditions of work and workers, among others. It also envisages certain types of relationship between the formal and informal sectors. Unfortunately, empirical studies analyzing the pattern of growth of the informal sector at the national or state level have generally used a single criterion such as the number of workers, capital employed, use of electricity or registration with certain public agencies, as the basis for identification of the informal sector (Mathur, 1993). This is mainly due to limited availability of data from secondary sources and problems of temporal comparability therein.

Understandably, development economists have found this approach, based on limited indicators, inadequate and unsatisfactory for capturing the whole gamut of informal sector activities (Bromley, 1994; Breman, 1995; Nurul Amin, 1996; Nagamine 1996). They have argued that some of the crucial characteristics of the

---

[1] The paper was published earlier in 1999, as Discussion Paper No. 25, by Development Policies Department of the International Labour Office, Geneva. The author thanks Dr. Shalini Gupta and Mr. Sant Lal Arora for their help in the preparation of the draft and development of arguments in the paper, Ms. Debolina Kundu for help in data analysis and review of literature, and Mr. Steven Miller, Dr. Ajit K. Ghose and Ms. Andrea Singh for their extensive comments on an earlier draft which helped in redesigning the structure of the paper as also for changng the thrust of several arguments.

informal sector pertaining to labour relations, producer-trader nexus, linkage with the government and other formal agencies, considered important in the theoretical literature, have been ignored in macro level analysis based on secondary data.

Several scholars have gone in for a more rigorous identification of this sector using complex and multifarious indicators. This could only be done based on survey data. Understandably, they could conduct such detailed analysis only at the settlement level. Enthusiasm for this approach has, however, been somewhat overwhelming in recent years. Voluminous literature has come out comprising case studies of industries, towns/cities and localities (Papola, 1981; Bhattacharya and Dey, 1991; Subrahmanian, Veena and Bhanumati, 1982; Lall, Hazra and Sharma, 1988; Von der Loop, 1988). There is, however, one major drawback in this approach. As individual researchers have come up with their own set of indicators for identifying informal activities, comparability of the results across industries, urban areas and over time has become the major casualty. Sometimes, the results have even been contradictory and, consequently, provided little assistance in policy formulation (Kundu, 1993).

Faced with the hiatus between theoretical and empirical research, on the one hand, and non-comparability of the results of different micro-level investigations, on the other, scholars have questioned the relevance of informal sector studies, describing these as mere academic exercises. Some have even dismissed the boundary between the formal and informal activities as theoretically tenuous and empirically non-testable (Richardson, 1985). Admitting the difficulties of assessing the macro dimensions of this sector and of making generalizations about its socio-economic characteristics, some scholars have argued that we can know the informal sector only when we see it. There has thus developed a general criticism among many researchers and policy makers who have come to believe that conclusions of the informal sector studies are highly subjective, depending almost totally on the subjective judgement of the researchers. Consequently, these studies have not been considered useful for providing inputs in policy formulation or developing a support system for informal activities.

In view of this scepticism regarding the theoretical validity of the distinction between the formal and informal sectors and, more importantly, usability of micro-level studies in policy formulation, it would be worthwhile to begin this paper with a critical review of this existing studies, focussing on their approaches and data-bases, for assessing the dimensions of the informal sector in India. The Population Census, Economic Census, National Sample Survey (NSS) and other periodic surveys conducted by the Central Statistical Organization (CSO), Government of India, generate very useful information that can be used to identify the broad trends and characteristics of the informal sector. An attempt has, therefore, been made here to critically analyze the problems of comparability in the data-base and assess the trends and patterns of growth of the informal sector at the national level, using these data. The literature surveyed here comprises books and articles, proceedings of seminars, workshops and meetings, and government declarations, having a bearing on this sector. The review covers studies using both secondary as well as primary data. Strengthening of administrative and institutional support systems for the healthy and sustainable development of the informal sector has been a major concern in this paper.

The second section of the paper discusses the various approaches for assessing the broad dimensions of the informal manufacturing sector in India, using the available secondary data. In the third section, an attempt is made to identify trends and patterns in the informal sector at the national level, based on secondary data drawn from diverse sources and research studies; despite the problems due to differences and discrepancies in definitions and coverage by different sources, trends and patterns at the macro-level emerge quite clearly. The fourth section overviews the micro-level studies following a thematic approach, classifying these in three categories viz.: (a) industry-specific studies, (b) locale-specific studies, and (c) studies on the urban poor and slum populations. The last sub-section also overviews the studies pertaining to institutional interventions for organizing informal sector activities. The fifth section makes a critical evaluation of the programmes and policies designed to strengthen the informal sector and overviews the studies analyzing their impact. The sixth and final section presents generalizations and conclusions and analyses their policy implications for the future growth of the sector.

2. Trends and Characteristics of the Informal Sector: A Macro View

The importance of field based studies cannot be exaggerated in the present era of economic liberalisation which has brought forth political decentralisation as a concomitant necessity[2]. Nonetheless, it is necessary to have a macro perspective for creating the right kind of policy environment and identifying the parameters of support system that can promote sustainable and spatially balanced growth of the informal sector. Furthermore, it can be argued that the data available from secondary sources have not been fully exploited. Keeping these in view, an overview of the secondary data sources analysing their scope, coverage and problems of

[2] The process of liberalisation has been associated with reduction of functions and consequently budgetary expenditures on various services by the federal government. For filling in the vacuum, thus created, it has become necessary to stipulate that the government will take up these functions.

temporal and cross-sectional comparability have been presented below. It may be useful for the readers to broadly familiarise themselves with these issues to appreciate the relevance and limitation of the framework presented in this section and of the results discussed in the subsequent sections.

2.1 Data Sources for the Economy and the Organised Sector

Detailed data on the workforce structure for the total economy are available from Population Census, Economic Census and National Sample Survey (NSS); the Population Census data give information on employment structure on a decadal basis. The General Economic Tables of the Census give information on the number of workers in various industrial and occupational categories at a very high level of spatial dis-aggregation, viz., settlement and even ward level for class I cities. The information is collected through a schedule canvassing households and individuals.

The other source of information for the total economy is the Establishment Tables, which is a by-product of the House-listing Operation for the Population Census of 1961 and 1971, conducted during the year preceding the Census. Here, one gets information on the establishments as well as workers therein at about the same level of dis-aggregation as the Population Census. It was decided in the year 1976 to launch country-wide Economic Census at regular intervals, followed by surveys to ascertain the structure, activity and performance of not only the total non-agriculture economy but also to assess the distribution pattern of organised and unorganised segments. Consequently, the first Economic Census was conducted during October-December 1977 by the Central Statistical Organisation (CSO), restricting its coverage to non-agricultural enterprises employing at least one hired worker on a regular basis. It, thus, excluded the own account enterprises (OAEs) from its purview. The second Economic Census, was undertaken in conjunction with the House-listing Operation for the Population Census of 1981. This time, OAEs units were also covered. The third Economic Census was also conducted along with the house-listing operation of 1991 Population Census and provides information similar to that in the Second Economic Census. The last Economic Census was carried out in 1998, and its detailed report is yet to be released.

The third important source of statistics on workforce structure for the total economy are the NSS rounds pertaining to Employment/Consumer Expenditure. Data on workforce structure by National Industrial Classification (NIC) categories are available along with the nature of their involvement in work viz. regular, casual and self-employed, on a quinquennial basis. Importantly, since 45th round (1989-90), information on employment/expenditure are available on an annual basis also, although the information is less detailed and is at a higher level of aggregation. Further, the sample size for these annual rounds is very thin, resulting in lesser reliability, particularly of the state level estimates.

Two major sources of data for the organised or formal sector are Annual Survey of Industries (ASI) and Employment Market Information (EMI). ASI provides information on manufacturing, processing and repairing units registered under section 2m (i) and 2m (ii) of the Indian Factories Act, 1948, on an annual basis, with certain time lag. The units covered are all those that employ 20 or more workers without the use of power or 10 to 20 workers using power. The data permit a comprehensive analysis of the technology, factor shares, changing production conditions etc. in different industries at the state level.

In the Employment Market Information (EMI) scheme, employment exchanges gather data on secondary and tertiary units in the private sector employing 10 or more persons and all public sector units. Private establishments employing 25 or more persons are obliged to provide this information under the Employment Exchanges (Compulsory Notification of Vacancies) Act, 1959. Information from the remaining private enterprises, employing 10 to 24 workers, are collected voluntarily from the employers. There are some inaccuracies in the figures due to non-response of some units, but that is not very serious. The real problem arises because the figures for the establishments are provided by local employment officers on the basis of the data furnished for previous quarters. Further, the EMI data do not provide rural-urban break-up.

2.2 Data Sources for Different Components of the Informal Sector

The data on the informal sector, comprising the units not covered by ASI or EMI, are collected neither regularly nor systematically. Different agencies cover different segments of this sector but due to their using different concepts, sampling frames etc., temporal comparability of the data is extremely difficult.

Information on workers in household manufacturing units are available from Population Census/Economic Census. There are problems of temporal comparability in the data, but trends can be assessed using this data after making appropriate adjustments. Unfortunately, such data are not available for household tertiary activities.

Further NSS gives comprehensive data on household industries since its 14th round held in 1958-1959. Subsequently, the 23rd, 29th, 33rd and 40th rounds of the survey have brought out information at the state level. The data, however, are not strictly comparable over time, even after making adjustments, because of the differences in coverage, changes in the criteria of identification pertaining to (1) the number of hired or family labour, (2) location of the units (within or outside the house), (3) type of ownership, and (4) sampling frame, in different rounds.

In the enterprise surveys, NSS provides information on OAE that can be compared with that of household industries of Population Census/Economic Census, as mentioned above. OAEs are defined as enterprises "run without any hired worker employed on a fairly regular basis". Further, the NSS surveys cover units employing five or less workers including the household workers, described as Non-Directory Establishments (NDEs). In the 33rd round for 1978-79, NDE units engaged in manufacturing (NDMEs) were covered. NDMEs comprised the units that, besides satisfying the employment criterion noted above, also had an annual turnover not exceeding rupees one hundred thousand per year. In the subsequent rounds, conducted in 1984-85, 1998-90 and 1994-95, the output criterion has been dropped and an NDME has been defined only in terms of the size of employment. Also, the units employing six or more workers - categorised as Directory Establishments (DEs) - have also been covered in these surveys, except in the early eighties, when a separate survey was conducted for this segment by the CSO. Importantly, the DEs do not include the organised sector, which in the case of manufacturing, would imply exclusion of the units covered under Annual Survey of Industries (ASI). All these periodic surveys use the framework of the Economic Census and together are supposed to cover the entire gamut of unregistered enterprises, on a regular basis.

The NSS Organisation conducted the first ever nation-wide survey on informal sector non-agricultural enterprises during 55th round (July 1999-June 2000). The survey covered all unincorporated proprietary and partnership enterprises. This definition of informal sector, thus, differs from that of the unorganised sector used in National Accounts Statistics since the latter, in addition to the unincorporated proprietary or partnership enterprises, also covers those run by co-operative societies, trusts, private and public limited companies that are not part of ASI. Informal sector is, therefore, considered a subset of the unorganised sector.

Data on household-based manufacturing workers are available at district and even settlement/urban ward level from the Population Census. The information is disaggregated as per the NIC. Unfortunately, the scope and coverage of these national level agencies are not strictly comparable. More disturbing is the fact that the concepts and coverage of the Census and NSS have not been kept uniform over time.

Yet another source of data is the Census of Small Scale Industries, conducted for the first time by its Development Commissioner in 1973-74. The coverage was restricted to units registered with the Directorate of Industries and thus excluded those falling within the purview of specialised Boards or Agencies. The information from the second census of SSI conducted during 1978-88, has a similar coverage. Finally, a sample survey of SSI was also conducted in 1993-94 but, for many reasons, the information is not entirely comparable with the 1987-88 census data.

2.3 Assessing Dimensions of the Informal Sector

Researchers analysing the structure of the informal sector at the macro-level have mostly considered it to be a *residual category*. There are sources like the Population Census, Economic Census and NSS, that give information on the number of workers, establishments etc. for the total economy, classified as per the NIC. Similarly, information on the organised sector is collected and brought out on a fairly regular basis by national level agencies, specially created for the purpose, as per certain statutory requirement or well established conventions. The researchers, have, therefore, found it convenient to deduct the figures for organised sector from the total figures and obtain the data for informal or unorganised activities. Understandably, following this residual category approach, information on the informal sector can be computed only for a limited number of variables for which the figures are available for the total economy. This information is, therefore, not as detailed as that for the organised or formal sector gathered by the national agencies as discussed above.

Two alternative ways of estimating the number of workers in the informal sector, based on the residual approach discussed above, are presented below:

1) The units registered under the Factories Act, 1948, for which data are tabulated systematically by the Annual Survey of Industries (ASI) may be taken to constitute the formal manufacturing sector. The estimates for the informal manufacturing can, therefore, be obtained by subtracting the ASI (factory sector) figures from that of total manufacturing workers, available from Population Census, Economic Census or NSS. It is important to note that the national income from the unorganised manufacturing activities is obtained by multiplying the productivity estimates by the corresponding number of workers. The figures for the later for many industries are obtained by taking the difference between the number of workers from Population Census and ASI.

2) The units covered under the EMI scheme may be considered as belonging to the formal sector. The unorganised sector may then be obtained as a residual of the Population Census or NSS figures by subtracting the formal sector figures as reported by the EMI figures. In activities, like trade, hotels and restaurants, storage and warehousing services etc., it is mostly the public enterprises that get registered and provide information on a regular

basis, due to their administrative requirements. Consequently, the entire private sector is taken to "constitute the unorganised segment, on consideration of non-availability of regular accounts of their activity" (Sardana, 1989).

Those in the private sector rarely comply with the requirement of providing this information. This approach is followed by CSO[3] in computing the employment figures used in the estimation of income for the unorganised tertiary activities.

The residual approach discussed above has serious limitations as one can get information basically on the number of units and employment only. Also, one would not be very happy to treat all non-public sector enterprises outside manufacturing, including large business and transport houses, as a part of the informal sector simply because these are not providing information under the EMI network. Besides, the figures for some establishments covered under EMI are of previous years. As a consequence, several scholars have recently attempted to estimate the figures for the informal sector at the macro level directly (Kundu and Lalitha, 1998; Shah, 1997; Duraisamy, 1997).

Direct identification of the informal sector at the micro level using a large number of criteria is possible when the data are generated through surveys. However, if one is interested in identifying the informal sector on the basis of a simple criterion like employment size, use of only family labour or use of electricity, employment as also certain other broad characteristics at the national or state level can be obtained through available secondary data .

One can, for example, define the informal sector, in a rather narrow sense, as comprising the enterprises carried out within the household, employing only family labour. This has been presented under (a) in the following sub-section. There are, however, other approaches that can be used for determining the size of the informal or unorganised activities directly at the macro level, in a somewhat broad-based manner. Despite the anomalies and discrepancies in the data, it is possible to assess the broad trends at national and state levels by using the approaches, described below:

(a) The household-based activities as identified by the Population Census and the NSS or the OAEs given by NSS and the Economic Census, may be taken to comprise the informal sector.

---

[3] As per the official methodology, CSO computes the workforce in unorganised tertiary sector by subtracting the EMI figures from those of the Population Census. The income generated is then worked out by multiplying the workforce figures by value added per worker, estimated through surveys of CSO, as in case of the unorganised industries.

(b) OAEs and NDEs, as defined by NSS and CSO, may be taken to constitute this sector. Together, these would cover all units employing less than 6 workers.

(c) Informal sector can be defined by combining DEs with OAEs and NDEs, as given by NSS and CSO.

(d) Small-scale industries may be taken as constituting the informal manufacturing sector as covered by the Development Commissioner of Small Scale Industries (DCSSI).

The temporal profile of informal manufacturing activities has been assessed at the national level in the following section based on an analysis of the secondary data and a review of literature. In analysing the macro level data, the first three approaches described above have been used. It has not been considered appropriate to take the small scale industries as constituting the informal sector since several among these are registered under the Factory Act and other Acts. It may, however, be pointed out that the insistence of a fixed premise for the household industries and establishments by all the national level data gathering agencies mentioned above tends to underestimate the unorganized sector. By their very definition, these exclude the hawkers, vendors etc. that may be an important component in the repair and maintenance activities of the informal sector.

3. Informal Manufacturing in Urban Areas

It would be worthwhile to overview the developments within the manufacturing sector in urban areas before narrowing down the focus on the informal sector. There seems to be a weakening of manufacturing base in the urban centres with the percentage share of workers going down systematically during the seventies and the eighties (Table 1). The decline is quite sharp in the case of non-household manufacturing, coming down from 26.0 per cent in 1981 to 23.2 per cent in 1991 for males, as per the Population Census[4]. A similar decrease by 1.7 percentage points, from 4.2 per cent in 1981, may be noted in the case of employment in household manufacturing. The decline in the case of the share of female manufacturing workers to total female workforce is also significant but somewhat less than their male counterparts.

---

[4] The data on women workers from Population Census has serious anomalies making temporal comparison extremely tenuous. The problem exists, although to a lesser extent, in the case of NSS data as well. Consequently, the analysis in this section has largely been restricted to male workforce only, both for Census as well as NSS data.

TABLE 1 : **Sectoral Distribution of Urban Main Workers as per Population Census**

(percentages)

Sector	Male			Female		
	1971	1981	1991	1971	1981	1991
Cultivators	5.2	5.2	4.9	4.1	4.6	5.1
Agricultural Labourers	4.7	4.7	5.4	17.7	16.7	15.6
Forestry, Fishing etc.	1.6	1.8	1.7	2.0	1.8	1.5
Mining & Quarrying	1.0	1.1	1.2	1.0	0.7	0.7
Manufacturing (Household)	4.4	4.2	2.5	10.0	10.4	7.5
Manufacturing (Non Household)	24.3	26.0	23.2	13.0	14.6	14.1
Construction	3.5	4.3	5.3	2.9	3.1	3.3
Trade & Commerce	21.4	21.3	23.7	8.2	8.9	10.0
Transport	10.7	10.0	9.2	3.2	2.2	1.9
Other Services	23.3	21.4	22.8	37.9	37.0	40.1

Source: Census of India (1971, 1981 and 1993).

Information from Economic Census, too, confirms that the share of manufacturing sector in employment is decreasing over time (Kundu and Lalitha,1998). The percentage of manufacturing and repair workers (comprising those in all establishments and own account enterprises) to the total workforce in urban areas is 28.3 per cent in 1990 which was as high as 35.6 per cent in 1980. The share of manufacturing in total employment in "establishments" of the Economic Census has also declined from 35.7 per cent to 30.0 per cent during this period. Expectedly, the decadal increase in manufacturing employment during 1980-90 is low viz. 5.5 per cent only, which is less than that in population or total employment.

The annual growth rates of enterprises and employment for all the industrial groups combined have been observed to decrease during the period 1990-98 in comparison to that for the period 1980-90. It is evident from Table 2 that, as per the Economic Census, annual growth rates of the number of enterprises and employment in urban areas were 4.1 per cent and 2.8 per cent, respectively, during the period 1980-90. These rates have decreased significantly to 2.2 per cent and 1.2 per cent respectively during the period 1990-98. In the case of number of enterprises, the decrease was much higher for establishments in comparison to own account enterprises (OAMEs)[5].

Sectoral break-up of information from the Economic Census of 1998 has been released so far only for a few states viz. Uttar Pradesh, Gujarat, Delhi,

[5] NSS defines own account enterprises (OAEs) as those that are run primarily by family labour as discussed later. OAME stands for own account manufacturing sector.

Himachal pradesh, Haryana, Nagaland and Mizoram. It may be observed from this limited data that the share of manufacturing to all non-agricultural enterprises has decreased significantly. This implies that the growth rates in the number of manufacturing enterprises have been relatively low, both for OAEs as well as establishments during the entire period 1980-98. In the case of employment in manufacturing, there appears to be a marginal improvement in the share during 1990-98 after a significant fall during 1980-90. The growth rates of employment for the period 1990-98 was higher in comparison to the rates for the period 1980-90, going up from 1.1 per cent to 2.7 per cent (See Kundu, Lalitha and Arora, 2001). One must, however, add that this acceleration is due primarily to Delhi whose growth rate has jumped from 3.7 per cent to 11.1 per cent. The rate would come down drastically, much below that of the eighties, if Delhi is excluded.

TABLE 2 : **Units and Employment in Urban Non-agricultural Enterprises: 1980, 1990 and 1998**

(in 000s)

Type of Enterprise	1980	1990	1998
(A) Number of Enterprises			
i) Own Account Enterprises	3530.2	5069.2 (3.7)	6166.2 (2.5)
ii) Establishments	1995.5	3199.5 (4.8)	3623.0 (1.6)
Total (A)	5525.7	8268.7 (4.1)	9151.2 (2.2)
(B) Employment	23710.0	31317.2 (2.8)	34162.0 (1.2)

Note: (i) Figures in brackets give the annual compound growth rater for the period from the last Economic Census.

(ii) Due to non availability of data for certain years, the figures for Jammu & Kashmir, Assam, Andhra Pradesh and West Bengal have been excluded for all the years to make them temporally comparable.

A similar picture emerges from sectoral distribution of the data in different NSS Rounds relating to employment and unemployment. Considering only the usually employed persons as per principal and subsidiary status (Kundu and Lalitha, 1998), the share of male workers in the manufacturing sector has come down from 27.7 per cent in 1977-78 to 25.8 per cent in 1987-88 (Table 3). It has further declined to 23.5 per cent in 1993-94 and to 22.4 per cent in 1999-2000. A corresponding decline is noted for female workers as well, the percentage figure for manufacturing going down from 29.4 in 1977-78 to 24.0 in 1999-00.

TABLE 3 : **Sectoral Distribution of Usually Employed Persons (Principal and Subsidiary Status) in Urban Areas as per NSS**

(percentages)

Sector	Male					Female				
	1977 -78	1983	1987 -88	1993 -94	1999 -00	1977 -78	1983	1987 -88	1993 94	1999 00
Agriculture(0)	10.2	10.3	9.1	9.0	6.6	25.1	32.0	29.4	24.7	17.7
Mining & Quarrying (1)	0.9	1.3	1.3	1.3	0.9	0.6	0.8	0.8	0.6	0.4
Manufacturing (2&3)	27.7	27.0	25.7	23.5	22.4	29.4	27.1	27.0	24.1	24.0
Electricity(4)	1.1	1.1	1.2	1.2	0.8	0.1	-	0.2	0.3	0.2
Construction (5)	4.2	5.2	5.8	6.9	8.7	2.6	3.3	3.7	4.1	4.8
Wholesale/Retail Trade (6)	21.6	20.2	22.0	21.9	29.4	9.8	9.0	10.0	10.0	16.9
Transport, Stroage etc. (7)	9.9	9.9	9.7	9.7	10.4	1.2	1.6	0.9	1.3	1.8
Financial, Ins. Serv. (8)	3.0	3.5	3.5	3.8	4.5	0.7	0.4	1.2	1.9	2.5
Community Services etc. (9)	21.5	21.4	21.7	22.6	16.5	30.4	25.8	26.6	33.1	31.7

Source: NSSO (1986, 1990, 1997 and 2000a).

Another significant phenomenon is that there has been a decline in the number of workers and units in the unorganised manufacturing, going by both the Population Census as well as the Economic Census, until at least the early nineties. In case the household-based activities are taken to constitute the unorganised or informal sector, the Primary Census Abstract of the Population Census suggests a decline in absolute number of the unorganised manufacturing workers from 2.4 million in 1981 to 2.0 million in 1991 (Table 4). Data from the Economic Census indicate that when informal sector is taken to comprise the OAME, there has been a decrease in units from 1.36 million in 1980 to 1.02 million in 1990. Employment here has decreased from 2.40 million to 1.93 million during this period. The share of informal manufacturing sector employment (OAMEs) to total manufacturing employment (OAEs) has decreased drastically from 35 per cent to 22 per cent. Similarly, the combined number of units in OAMEs and NDMEs in rural and urban areas has decreased from 5.58 million in 1980 to 4.82 million in 1990 (Table 4).

The NSS data relating to the follow-up surveys on unorganised manufacturing sector in 33rd, 40th, 45th, 51st and 55th rounds further confirm the above facts because the growth rates of units and employment within the informal manufacturing segment have been low/negative during the eighties and the nineties (Table 5). It is observed here that the number of OAME units has more than doubled during the period 1978-79 to 1984-85 (hereafter referred to as the first period). Between 1984-85 to 1989-90 and 1989-90 to 1994-95 (henceforth second and third period, respectively), however, the number has decreased by 22.6 and 3.8 per cent, respectively. Correspondingly, the employment in OAMEs has increased by 121.7

TABLE 4 : **Units and Workers in Manufacturing and Repair Activities in the Informal Sector**

(in million)

Sources		Units			Workers		
		Rural	Urban	Total	Rural	Urban	Total
Population Census, 1971							
I Primary Census Abstract		-	-	-	4.8	1.6	6.4
II Establishment Tables	(a)	1.69	0.39	2.08	2.93	0.87	3.80
	(b)	2.15	1.04	3.19	3.57	2.11	5.68
	(c)	2.23	1.16	3.39	4.20	3.00	7.20
Economic Census, 1980	(a)	3.28	1.36	4.65	5.70	2.40	8.11
	(b)	3.67	1.91	5.58	6.60	3.97	10.57
	(c)	-	-	-	-	-	-
Economic Census, 1990	(a)	2.78	1.02	3.80	5.08	1.93	7.01
	(b)	-	-	4.82	-	-	-
	(c)	-	-	5.08	-	-	-
Population Census, 1981							
I Primary Census Abstract		-	-	-	5.5 (6.5)	2.4 (2.8)	7.9 (9.3)
Population Census, 1991							
I Primary Census Abstract		-	-	-	4.8	2.0	6.8
National Sample Survey							
14th Round 1958-59		10.83	2.17	13.00	12.63	4.21	16.84
23rd Round 1968-69		6.57	2.00	8.57	9.99	3.93	13.92
29th Round 1974-75		6.49	2.32	8.81	10.27	4.64	14.91
33rd Round 1978-79	(a)	5.72	1.45	7.17	9.22	2.40	11.62
	(b)	6.22	1.90	8.12	10.62	3.78	14.40
	(c)	6.39	2.10	8.49	12.50	5.71	18.21
40th Round 1984-85	(a)	13.44	3.65	7.09	21.90	15.32	27.23
	(b)	14.47	4.78	19.25	24.27	7.98	32.25
	(c)	14.64	5.08	19.72	26.26	10.68	36.94
45th Round 1989-90	(a)	11.28	2.82	13.10	9.53	4.98	24.51
	(b)	12.02	3.71	15.73	21.70	7.93	29.63
	(c)	12.24	4.05	16.29	24.46	11.02	35.48
51th Round 1994-95	(a)	9.53	2.71	12.24	17.84	4.82	22.66
	(b)	10.20	3.64	13.84	19.69	7.88	27.57
	(c)	10.50	4.01	14.51	22.13	11.08	33.21

Notes·

1 The all India figure for the year 1991 from the Population Census include the estimated value for Jammu and Kashmir where census could not be conduced. The same has been done in case of the census estimate of 1981 for Assam.

2. The figures within brackets for 1981 include marginal workers. The 1961 and 1971 census did not canvass the concept of main and marginal workers.

3. The figures given from the Primary Census Abstract of different population censuses pertain to household industries. Under "Establishment Tables" three estimates have been given for the year 1971. The estimate (a) includes only those units, which are household industries. Estimate (b) has been obtained by adding the figure of unregistered establishments (industries), having four or less workers, with that of (a). Similarly (c) has been obtained by adding the figure of all unregistered establishments (industries) having more than four workers with that of (b).

4. Economic Census and NSS data also give three estimates of informal sector that are somewhat comparable to those obtained from the Establishment Tables. The estimate (a) includes only the "own account enterprises" and may therefore be conceptually comparable with that of household industries. The estimate (b) has been obtained by adding the figure of non-directory manufacturing units with those of own account enterprises. The estimate (c) has been obtained by adding the figures of directory manufacturing units with those of OAME and NDME in case of NSSO. In case of Economic Census, all units with less than 10 workers have been taken to comprise (c).

TABLE 5 : **Units and Employment in OAME, NDME and DME in Urban India**

(Figures are in million)

Year	OAME		NDME		DME		Total	
	Units	Emp.	Units	Emp.	Units	Emp.	Units	Emp.
78-79	1.45	2.40	0.45	1.38	0.19	1.93	2.10	5.71
		(1.65)		(3.05)		(10.16)		
84-85	3.65	5.32	1.13	2.66	0.29	2.70	5.08	10.68
		(1.46)		(2.35)		(9.31)		
89-90	2.82	4.99	0.89	2.94	0.34	3.09	4.05	11.02
		(1.77)		(3.30)		(9.02)		
94-95	2.71	4.82	0.93	3.06	0.36	3.20	4.00	11.07
		(1.77)		(3.28)		(8.89)		
99-00	3.35	5.57	-	-	-	-	4.66	11.97
		(1.66)						
78-84	16.6*	14.2*	16.6*	11.6*	7.3*	5.8*	15.9*	11.0*
84-89	-5.0*	-1.3*	-4.7*	2.0*	3.2*	2.7*	-4.4*	0.6*
89-94	-0.8*	-0.7*	0.9*	0.8*	1.1*	0.7*	-0.3*	0.1*
94-2000	4.3*	2.9*	-	-	-	-	3.1*	1.6*

Notes: 1. Emp. denotes employment.

2. Figures in parentheses are employment per enterprise.

3. Figures with stars(*) are the annual compound growth rates during that period.

per cent in the first period but during the second and third periods, it has gone down marginally by 6.2 and 3.4 per cent, respectively. However, between 1994-95 and 1999-2000, one notices an increase in the number of enterprises as well as employment but that is much less than what was noted during the first period.

A similar picture emerges for the NDMEs as well. The number of NDME units has more than doubled and employment therein increased by 92.7 per cent during the first period. This may be attributed only marginally to the modification in the definition of NDME viz. dropping off of the output condition in 1984-85, noted above. Indeed, the number of units producing goods of over rupees one hundred thousand per year, excluded as per the definition in 1978-79, is unlikely to be very large. In the second period, however, the number of NDME units has decreased by 21.2 per cent although employment has increased by 10.5 per cent. In the third period, both the units as well as employment have increased but only by 4.5 per cent and 4.1 per cent, respectively.

Unlike OAMEs or NDMEs, within the DME segment in urban areas, both units and employment increased in all the three periods though at a decreasing rate.

To elaborate, the number of units increased by 52.6, 17.2 and 5.9 per cent while employment has increased by 39.9, 14.4 and 3.6 per cent, respectively, in the three periods. As a consequence of the fast growth in the number of units during the first period, employment per enterprise (EME) has gone down from 1.65 to 1.46 for OAMEs. In the case of NDMEs, the decline is sharper, from 3.05 to 2.35. During the second period, however, EME has increased for both the categories. For, OAMEs, it has moved up from 1.46 to 1.77 due to a larger decline in the number of units compared to that in employment. In the case of NDMEs, the number of units has declined while that of workers has gone up. As a consequence, EME increased significantly from 2.35 to 3.30. As against this, the EME within DMEs has gone down consistently from 10.16 to 8.89 during the entire period, despite the fact that the latter is the only category where both units and employment have increased in all the three periods. This is due to a slower growth in employment than in the number of units.

Based on the above overview, one would argue that the share of employment in the manufacturing industries is going down significantly in the urban areas. This is so despite the fact that income in this sector grew very rapidly viz., by over 7.0 per cent annually. Further, informal manufacturing sector in the urban areas has also been on a decline in recent years.

The number of units and employment in some of the informal industries have, however, gone up despite a decrease in value added in the late eighties (Kundu, Lalitha and Arora, 2001) which appears to be an enigma. Why should the entrepreneurs go into industries or employ additional workers in activities that are doing badly in terms of productivity? This could partly be attributed to under-reporting of value added/earnings due to administrative and legal constraints. Other deficiencies in the database can also provide partial explanation to this queer phenomenon. What, however, seems more likely is that people are continuing in their traditional or family occupations irrespective of considerations of per capita levels of earning or value added.

It is important to mention here that employment in the informal manufacturing, despite a deceleration, has increased over the years in relation to that in the formal sector. This is because growth of employment in organised manufacturing has been negligible - indeed negative for a few years - during the late eighties and the early nineties. Further, the data suggest that the informal sector comprising both manufacturing as well as tertiary activities as a whole, has gone up significantly in urban areas. This can also be inferred from the NSS data in the latest five quinquennial employment surveys, as discussed below.

The data on total workers by different definitions viz., usual, weekly and daily status, their classification into different categories viz., regular, casual and self-employed, corroborate the above proposition. The growth rate of employment by usual status has been low during 1977-93, reflected in a stability or slight decrease in workforce participation rate (WPR)[6], including the subsidiary status workers, for the adult (age group 15-59) population (Kundu and Lalitha, 1998)[7]. Surprisingly, however, WPRs by current (weekly and daily) status have gone up significantly during this period (Table 6). This is valid not only for the males but also for the females. It is, thus, evident that the period 1977-78 to 1993-94 is characterised by opposing tendencies in the labour market. While the usual status employment rate has declined, those by current status moved up. All these reflect an increase in the volume of casual and part time work, which may reflect casualisation of manufacturing and tertiary sectors.

TABLE 6 : **Percentages of Workers in Different NSS Rounds by Current Weekly and Current Daily Status**

Years	Urban Male			Urban Female		
	Usual Status	Weekly Status	Daily Status	Usual Status	Weekly Status	Daily Status
All Ages						
1977-78	50.8	49.0	47.2	15.6	12.5	10.9
1983	51.2	49.2	47.3	15.1	11.8	10.6
1987-88	50.6	49.2	47.7	15.2	11.9	11.0
1993-94	52.0	51.1	49.8	15.4	13.9	12.0
1999-00	51.8	50.9	49.0	13.9	12.8	11.1
Age Group 15-59						
1977-78	81.0	78.6	75.7	24.6	19.6	17.1
1983	81.0	78.3	75.2	23.4	18.4	165
1987-88	79.3	77.3	75.1	23.5	18.5	17.0
1993-94	79.7	78.2	76.0	23.4	20.9	18.1
1999-00	78.5	77.1	74.4	20.9	19.1	16.7

Note: Usual status includes principal and subsidiary.
Source: NSSO (1986, 1990, 1997 and 2000a).

[6] Population Census data also indicates a declining WPR for men during the period 1981-91. For women, however, Census reports an increase in WPR which, at least partially, can be attributed to a better coverage of women workers in the 1991 Census.

[7] When we consider the period 1987-93 only, there seems to be an increase in WPR for total population as also for the adult age group. The severe drought in 1987-88 would explain the low WPR, both for males and females, in the urban areas as many activities here are linked to agriculture. A rise in WPR during 1987-93 can, therefore, be attributed, at least partially, to the drought situation in the base year.

The recent (1999-2000) data, from the 55th round of NSS, give further insights into the growth of informal employment in urban India. The percentage of workers by usual status (principal plus subsidiary employment) has declined slightly from 79.7 to 78.5 among adult men during 1993-99 (Table 6). For women, the two figures are 23.4 and 20.9. This is in line with what was observed during the eighties and the early nineties. However, in sharp contrast to the pattern noted during this period, the WPR by weekly as well as daily status has gone down during 1993-99, both for men and women. This could be indicative of a process of slowing down of growth of the informal sector as a whole, during the later half of the nineties.

The percentage of unemployed persons (person days) to the total labour force (labour days), however, has gone down until 1993-94 (Kundu & Lalitha, 1998). This emerges clearly by all the three concepts of employment, canvassed by NSS. The decline, nonetheless, is relatively high by weekly and daily status compared to the usual status. This, once again, is a clear indication of an increase in part time and short duration work for the labour force, reflecting informalisation of the urban economy. One may infer that, in recent years, a number of households have been forced into poverty and are sending more of their members to seek or create employment for themselves as a part of their survival strategy. One must, nonetheless, note that the trend has altered in the late nineties. The unemployment rate has registered a significant increase for all categories of workers except for urban women during 1993-99. This could be due to the informal sector having reached a saturation point in terms of its absorptive capacity.

There have been changes in the urban workforce structure also, during recent decades. A clear declining trend in the share is observed in the case of regular/salaried workers as a proportion of total male workforce during the entire period. It is the shares of the casual and the self-employed that have gone up (Table 7). In contrast, the share of regular workers has gone up only among females. It can be argued that the current system of sub-contracting of work in the urban economy is such that a large number of female workers, including the domestic help, are not being reported as self-employed or casual workers. They are getting work - whatever may be the wage rate or working conditions - more or less on a regular basis. This reflects a significant change in the organisation of work and growing incidence of sub-contracting of jobs to the informal sector. This, to a certain extent, is true for the males as well but here the process of casualisation and growth of the self-employed is strong so as to offset any increase in regular workers due to this sub-contracting arrangement, as noted above.

The volume of work for the usually employed persons in urban areas gives further insight into the functioning of the labour market. Out of every 100 usually

TABLE 7 : **Percentage of Usually Employed Persons by Type of Employment**

Year	Usually Employed					
	Principal Status			Principal + Subsidiary Status		
	Self Employed	Regular Employees	Casual Labour	Self Employed	Regular Employees	Casual Labour
Males						
1977-78	39.9	47.2	13.9	40.4	46.4	13.2
1983	40.2	44.5	15.3	40.9	43.7	15.4
1987-88	41.0	44.4	14.6	41.7	43.7	14.6
1993-94	41.1	42.7	16.2	41.7	42.1	16.2
1999-00	41.2	41.9	16.9	41.5	41.7	16.8
Females						
1977-78	42.2	30.8	27.0	49.5	24.9	25.6
1983	37.3	31.8	30.9	45.8	25.8	28.4
1987-88	39.3	34.2	26.5	47.1	27.5	25.4
1993-94	36.4	35.5	28.1	45.4	28.6	26.0
1999-00	38.4	38.5	23.1	45.3	33.3	21.4

Source: NSSO (1986, 1997 and 2000a).

employed males, only 96 were employed by weekly status in 1983 (Table 8). The figure has gone up to 98 in 1993-94. For females the increase is much sharper - from 77 to 88. Correspondingly, the percentage of unemployed by weekly status (to all usually employed persons) has declined from 1.7 to 1.1 for males. For females, the decline is from 1.5 to 0.9. Similarly, the number of employed persons by daily status among 100 usually employed persons has gone up from 92 to 95 among males (Table 9), although the figure has come down a bit in 1999-00. For females, once again, it has moved up very sharply - from 70 to 77. It went up

TABLE 8 : **Percentage Distribution of Usually Employed Persons (by Principal and Subsidiary Status) as per their Current Weekly Status in Urban India**

	Male			Female		
Weekly Status	1983	1987-88	1993-94	1983	1987-88	1993-94
Employed	95.8	96.7	97.6	76.7	76.8	88.4
Unemployed	1.7	1.7	1.1	1.5	1.7	0.9
Not in Labour Force	2.6	1.6	1.2	21.8	21.5	10.7
All	100	100	100	100	100	100

Source: NSSO (1986, 1990 and 1997).

TABLE 9 : **Percentage Distribution of Persons-Days of Usually Employed Persons (by Principal and Subsidiary Status) as per their Current Daily Status in Urban India**

Daily Status	Male			Female		
	1983	1987-88	1993-94	1983	1987-88	1993-94
Employed	92.1	93.8	94.9	70.2	76.6	79.1
Unemployed	4.1	3.7	2.7	3.8	2.4	2.2
Not in Labour Force	3.8	2.5	2.5	26.1	21.0	18.7
All	100	100	100	100	100	100

Source: As in Table 6.

further to 79 in 1999-2000. The percentage of the unemployed as also those not in the labour force (by daily status) among the usually employed women has correspondingly gone down. All these changes tend to suggest that the volume of work available to usually employed women on daily basis has increased substantially in recent years. This, however, is not necessarily the case for males.

Increase in the share of regular/salaried workers for adult women, in their volume of work, decline in their unemployment rate, etc., in urban areas, must be interpreted with caution. One should not be enthusiastic in welcoming these as indications of growing capacity of the urban economy to absorb women labourers or a reduction of gender bias. Such generalisations, without an in-depth analysis of the dynamics of development can be misleading. The mere fact that an increasing proportion of female workforce now belongs to a regular category is not a matter of great satisfaction. Indeed, employment growth for women during the eighties and the early nineties has taken place in sectors with low productivity and low wage rates (Kundu, 1993). Indeed, in quite a few of the urban sectors, regular female workers are paid about the same as the male casual workers.

The wage rates at current prices for regular and casual workers reflect a sharp disparity across sectors and between males and females (*ibid*). Importantly, the real wages for both salaried as well as casual workers have gone up during 1983-87 as well as 1987-93 in most of the urban economic sectors. The annual growth rate in real wages of all regular workers, however, is much less during the second period compared to the first, both for males and females (Table 10). The increase for male salaried workers is 1.3 per cent per year during 1987-93 while the figure for 1983-87 was as high as 6.3 per cent. For females, the corresponding figures are 0.6 and 9.2 per cent. An identical pattern emerges for casual workers as well. Strikingly, the percentage growth rates for wages of casual workers are 1.6 and 2.9 only for males and females during the second period. These are much less than those noted for the first period. One would, therefore, infer that the growth in average earnings has decelerated substantially during the second period which may partly be attributed to the programmes of structural adjustment.

It may be observed in Table 10 that there are sectors wherein the wages for the casual workers have gone down in real terms during 1987-93. For males, the

TABLE 10 : **Annual Compound Growth Rates of Real Wages for Adult (15-59 Age Group) Regular/Salaried and Casual Workers in Different Sectors)**

Sector	Regular/Salaried Workers		Casual Workers	
	1983-87	1987-93	1983-87	1987-93
MALES				
Agriculture	11.4	1.2	3.1	2.0
Mining and Quarrying	7.6	2.8	-0.2	-0.4
Manufacturing				
Div. 2	2.8	1.6	4.7	1.4
Div. 3	5.3	0.5	-1.5	1.5
Electricity etc.	5.8	2.5	3.2	5.0
Construction	5.6	0.7	3.3	1.8
Trade	3.1	1.8	3.7	1.2
Transport	5.8	0.6	3.4	2.1
Other Services				
Div. 8	4.7	2.6	3.8	-0.9
Div. 9	7.6	1.4	7.8	-0.9
All	6.3	1.3	3.3	1.6
FEMALES				
Agriculture	8.5	6.0	2.8	3.9
Mining and Quarrying	9.9	2.6	10.7	1.9
Manufacturing				
Div. 2	4.4	4.9	5.3	1.9
Div. 3	0.4	0.3	9.5	0.9
Electricity etc.	2.6	2.8		4.0
Construction	4.8	-3.7	5.0	3.2
Trade	-1.3	5.2	1.0	6.2
Transport	10.2	-1.0	6.7	-4.4
Other Services				
Div. 8	6.0	2.1	22.2	-0.4
Div. 9	9.8	0.1	5.9	2.9
All	9.2	0.6	5.3	2.9

Source: 1. NSSO (1986, 1990, 1997).

decline is significant viz. about one per cent per year for "other services" (viz., Divisions 8 and 9 of NIC) and less than half a per cent for mining and quarrying. In the case of trade and manufacturing, the growth rates are positive but very low. For the regular (male) workers, the real wages have not gone down in any sector, although the growth rates in the second period are substantially below those of the first. A sharp decline in the growth rate of real wages is discernible in trade, transport, construction and even manufacturing. This can possibly be explained in terms of greater heterogeneity among workers due to the sub-contracting of jobs and lower wages being paid to (regular) sub-contracted workers in the nineties.

The decline in real wages for casual female workers is reported for Division 8 of other services (as in the case of males) during 1987-93. A more substantial fall, however, is in the transport sector viz. 4.4 per cent per year. Surprisingly, the decline is not restricted to casual workers only, as far as women workers are concerned. The real wages for regular/salaried workers had gone down in trade during 1983-87 while in the subsequent period, such a decline was observed in construction and transport and storage.

Notably, the gap between the wages of regular and casual workers, at current as well as constant prices, was noted to have increased during 1983-87, both for males and females (Kundu, 1993). This can be explained in terms of casual work being generated at a low wage rate due to excess supply of labour. Importantly, however, the gap has declined significantly during 1987-93 for the females. For males, the decline is only marginal. This is primarily due to the fact that the increase in the wages of regular/salaried workers has been low in real terms during 1987-93. The most significant phenomenon is that the growth in real wages for regular female workers is about half percentage point only, as mentioned above. One can attribute all these to a large part of regular employment being generated within the informal sector at a low wage rate, particularly for females.

The specific features of employment growth during 1987-93, as discussed above, were noted by scholars analysing data for the period 1983 to 1987-88 as well. The WPR by usual status was observed to have declined while that by current status had gone up. Further, there was a distinct increase in the amount of work available to usually working persons. All these were attributed to a slower growth in jobs available on a regular basis in the informal sector and an increase in part-time or casual work in informal activities (Planning Commission, 1991).

Alarmed by these trends, the Planning Commission (1991) had pleaded for "the adoption of an employment oriented strategy" in the Eighth Plan. Acceleration in the growth rate of employment was put forward as the prime concern for the economy. Unluckily, the depressing employment trend continued during the nineties; in the opinion of some, the employment situation deteriorated rather alarmingly. The absorptive capacity of the informal sector seems to have declined due to various policy measures. It is a bit surprising that no word of caution has been expressed by the planners officially with regard to the pursuance of the present strategy of development in the Tenth Plan and its employment implications. What is needed is a shift in the thrust of development in favour of the informal sector activities, at a reasonable level of productivity, during the transitory period of structural adjustment.

4. A Thematic Overview of Micro-Level Studies

In recent years, there has been an upsurge of interest in micro-level studies on the urban informal sector. These are mostly carried out at the level of a city or a segment of it, covering a sample of industrial establishments, household-based enterprises, or activities with no fixed locale. It is believed that identification of the informal sector units, at the micro-level, using multiple criteria, based on Census or NSS data, is an impossible task. Further, any assessment of the size of the informal sector directly through the enterprise surveys of NSS or CSO, covering OAEs, NDEs and DEs, would be a gross- underestimation, at any level. This has prompted researchers to go in for primary surveys. Scholars have argued that it is only through household-based surveys that one can hope to capture the entire gamut of informal activities (Datar, 1986; Singh, 1990). Importantly, some of the informal sector workers are employed by formal enterprises (through sub-contracting) who can only be captured through these household surveys (Unni,1997).

There are serious problems with regard to the micro-level studies as well. The concepts, coverage and framework of these studies, being determined by individual researchers or their sponsoring agencies, it is difficult to compare the results and draw macro-level inferences regarding the emerging pattern. It would, nonetheless, be worthwhile to review these studies to develop some, *albeit* rough, idea about the nature, changing characteristics and socioeconomic correlates of the informal sector since one cannot get such a perspective from studies based on secondary data.

Another important point is that while the analysis of secondary data in the macro analysis had to be confined to the manufacturing sector alone, the overview of research at micro-level has a larger canvas, covering a number of tertiary sector studies as well. This discrepancy can be explained in terms of the nature of the database and available research studies. The information on informal activities within the tertiary sector, particularly from NSS, are highly unreliable and have been built up using definitions that do not find general acceptability. These problems, however, do not exist for field level studies. The keen interest in tertiary activities within the informal sector at this level is due largely to its massive growth in recent years, as noted above. This can also be explained in terms of tertiary activities being perceived by a section of researchers and policy makers as a nuisance due to their proliferation in residential areas, including the posh colonies. On the other hand, many consider these as providing a lifeline for urban living and advocate subsidizing it indirectly. In any case, the tertiary informal sector has been considered to be of immense importance for future urbanization in the country.

In the present overview, the studies have been grouped into three categories. Those pertaining to a specific industry or occupation have been put in the first category. Those covering all informal activities in a city or a locality belong to the second. The third category comprises research, not directly focussed on the informal activities, that looks into the conditions of the urban poor and the slum dwellers. The last category is considered to be important for this overview since many of the studies on the urban poor give considerable emphasis to their economic activities that mostly belong to the informal sector. The last sub-section overviews the general conclusions emerging from the studies, focussing on the institutional interventions launched for assisting the informal activities in the recent decades.

4.1 Industry/Occupation Specific Studies

An overview of the existing literature suggests that certain activities have attracted the researchers much more than others, owing to their low productivity, low capital stock, exploitative labour relations, etc. These are (1) building construction, (2) *rickshaw* pulling, (3) *hawking* and vending, (4) textile and garment related activities, (5) carpet making, (6) *beedi* making and (7) garbage collection.

These studies generally attempt to locate the place of work and residence and often present a rough distribution of enterprises engaged in the concerned activity within the city. The nature of production or servicing units, ownership pattern, number of hired workers, if any, capital invested, etc., are also analyzed in some detail. Except textile and transport industries, wherein the initial capital investment is high (and so is the percentage of workers not owning their "enterprises"), capital requirements are very small and the workers are mostly self-employed in informal activities (Bhattacharya and Dey, 1991).

Researchers have enquired into the issues pertaining to seasonality of employment and earnings per day/month, in a somewhat approximate manner. Low productivity, and uncertainty and irregularity of employment are the major problems identified in this sector. The studies reveal that employment is often limited to much smaller number of days than that for which the work is sought. The strong competition among hawkers, vendors, garbage collectors, transport operators (*rickshaw* pullers), etc., brings down their earnings, often below the statutory minimum wage (AMDA and CMDA, 1995). Non-availability of marketing facilities to the producers (Kale, 1985) and absence of bargaining capacity through unions among the wage earners have been noted as important reasons for their low "efficiency". However, in the metro cities like Mumbai, Delhi, Ahmedabad, etc., researchers have reported household earnings above the poverty line, even for hawkers, vendors and rickshaw pullers (Deshpande, 1983; TCPO, 1983).

The studies have often looked into the age-sex composition and migratory behaviour of the workers (Arunachalam and Azad, 1985; Banerjee, 1983). It is argued that a large number of current or short duration migrants find employment in the informal sector (Das, 1994). Also, the workforce in this sector is very young, dominated by people in the age group 15-35 years. Most occupations are selective of adult males except vending, beedi- and garment-making. However, in recent years, there has been an increase in job opportunities for females in several activities. This helps to explain the increase in the female-male ratio in urban areas in the eighties and the nineties. Unfortunately, these activities tend to be highly exploitative of the work-force employed in them.

The level of literacy or skills among workers in most of the activities is reported to be very low. This is true for both migrant as well as non-migrant workers. Surprisingly, however, several studies show that formal training does not increase the income generating capacity of workers (Von der Loop, 1988). Rather, it is the on-the-job training and the number of years spent in a specific activity that makes a real difference to income.

There are not many Non-Governmental Organizations (NGOs) or Community Based Organizations (CBOs) to make them aware of their rights and privileges (Ghosh, 1988; Sanyal, 1991). This reduces their accessibility to institutional support of any kind. Except in activities or localities wherein the involvement of these organizations is significant, the availability of institutional finance has been negligible.

In some of the activities, however, there is a healthy process of skill formation leading to improvement in the earnings and living conditions of the workers. Some scholars have identified certain informal activities as dynamic - opting for modern technology, high rate of capital formation, etc., resulting in a marked increase in labour productivity. These may have linkages with the formal manufacturing sector, often catering to regional and national markets (Ribeiro, 1993; Singh, 1997). It is, however, difficult to distinguish these dynamic units which are showing distinct signs of improvement over the years, from ancillary units, established by large enterprises. The share of these units in the total informal sector in terms of the number of units or employment would be very small. Nevertheless, the studies do indicate that there is a considerable heterogeneity within the informal sector.

Most of the studies report unhygienic working and living conditions of the informal sector workers. Their access to basic amenities is extremely poor. The government programmes designed for their betterment, unfortunately, seem to have bypassed a large majority of them. The conditions have deteriorated further in recent years with the increasing segmentation of the cities into formal and informal settlements. Some scholars have explained it in terms of the withdrawal of the state and a sizeable decline in public expenditure on social sectors.

Drawing inferences and making generalizations based on the results of the micro-level studies could be hazardous. For example, one can mention the case of sport goods industry in Meerut, a class I city[8] in Uttar Pradesh. A study conducted in the late seventies found that capital investment per unit was Rs. 70,000. (Sharma and Singh, 1980). The corresponding figure in the mid-eighties, however, was Rs. 8,000 (Lall, Hazra and Sharma, 1988). Evidently, this is due to differences in the concepts and coverage which is difficult to resolve without having access to the unpublished information regarding the questionnaire, sampling frame, etc.

4.2 City/Locality Specific Studies

Several scholars have chosen to focus on a city or a locality and to cover all the informal activities located therein, hence covering a wide range of commodities and services. The cities/localities selected are generally those having a large concentration or rapid growth of informal activities. Simple criteria such as the number of employees or registration with a local or state authority have usually been used in determining the coverage or size of the universe (Mazumdar, 1990; Buch and Pathak, 1985).

These studies have taken up most of the issues raised above regarding industry specific research (Mathur and Moser, 1984). The conclusions, too, have been similar. However, as these studies covered activities in two or more industries, it has been possible to make inte-ractivity or inter-industry comparisons of the working and living conditions, organizational structure, migratory behaviour, age-sex composition, etc., of the work-force (Papola, 1981). In addition, certain dimensions such as linkages among informal activities or between formal and informal units have also been investigated. Dupont (1995), for example, has highlighted the segmentation of the labour market based largely on non-economic criteria and highly exploitative conditions for certain categories of workers in Jetpur town. These studies tend to suggest that a number of informal manufacturing units owe their existence to sub-contracting of jobs by formal industries, usually on a piece-meal basis (Nagraj, 1984; Venkata Ratnam, 1997). The informal units, it is argued, thus complement and subsidize the formal sector of the economy (Subrahmanian, Veena and Bhanumati, 1982). This is basically due to informal sector workers undercutting

[8] Urban Centres having population of one hundred thousand or more are classified as class I cities by the Population Census of India.

their wages and supplying their products and services at extremely low rates, owing to their excess supply in a fragmented labour market (Breman, 1995). Thus, by accepting wages below subsistence requirements, they are "forced to subsidize" formal enterprises[9]. Another study of Bhadohi town by Singh (1990) substantiates the above proposition. The study shows that the traditional carpet industry is organized by merchant-manufacturers as putting-out work to domestic weavers on highly unfavourable terms. Similarly, in the *beedi* industry of Mysore, there has been a changeover from workshops to a (home-based) putting-out system to avoid labour problems, especially a possible strike by the workers.

4.3 Studies on the Urban Poor

Studies on the urban poor or slum dwellers constitute the third category in this section. These are not focussed on the informal sector *per se*. Nonetheless, they raise broader socioeconomic issues and look into diverse aspects such as employment generation, earnings, conditions of work, etc., of the sample households. A few of these have been sponsored by government agencies before launching certain schemes or for evaluating the impact of schemes already in progress or recently completed[10]. Besides these, several individuals/institutions have taken up research on poverty or slums that have provided additional useful insights into the functioning of informal activities.

Most of these studies highlight the low income levels and the non-availability of basic amenities and infrastructural facilities to the production units set up by the urban poor (Banerjee, 1982; Alam, Alikhan and Bhattacharji, 1987). Some studies show how public agencies and government programmes have by-passed such units. The production units often do not have access to these programmes since they are not registered with any public agency and hence cannot satisfy the prescribed administrative and legal requirements (Kundu, 1993). The need to legalize or

---

[9] Breman (1996) argues that piece-work is a manner of contracting under which the employer persuades, or in effect forces the labourers to determine their own input and to vary it in length and intensity according to their working ability.

[10] The programmes for Small and Medium Towns Development (SMTD) and Integrated Development of Small and Medium Towns (IDSMT), for example, include schemes for strengthening the urban economic base. For implementing these programmes, studies have been sponsored by the government (undertaken by the Town and Country Planning Organization, National Institute of Urban Affairs and other research organizations) for analyzing the nature of economic activities in the towns. Besides, there are programmes like Urban Community Development, Urban Basic Services, Environmental Improvement of Urban Slums, etc., designed to provide certain basic amenities and social inputs to the poor; largely through community participation. Studies undertaken in connection with these programmes have also investigated working conditions, income and consumption patterns of the economically underprivileged households.

legitimize many of the activities of the poor, for example, by authenticating land lease or land tenure, subsidized finance and critical raw materials, etc., has been duly emphasized by several scholars and activists (Bhatt, 1988 and 1989). New legislation, unionization and provision of institutional support to organize marketing of their products, etc., have also been recommended to tackle the problem of labour exploitation (Harriss, 1982; Nambiar, 1995).

4.4 Organizing Informal Sector Activities

One general conclusion, emerging from the micro-level studies in the three categories discussed above, is that the poor have the capability to organize their enterprises or businesses in such a manner as to earn a rate of return higher than the market interest rate (Chatterjee, 1995; Singh, 1997). All that is needed is to extend institutional credit to them, within a participatory framework, preferably through NGOs or CBOs. Once this perspective is accepted, the task of upgrading the informal sector, and through that, of poverty alleviation, should become easy. However, there are also a few studies that reveal that the growth process in India is characterized by a high degree of uncertainty even for organized enterprises of which many face problems in gaining access to critical inputs and marketing facilities (Jagannathan, 1987). The success of informal enterprises may not, therefore, be contingent on credit availability alone.

In many of the celebrated programmes for supporting informal activities of the poor through the provision of credit facilities - often cited as success stories - the overhead costs, particularly those incurred by the organizers/motivators, are not taken into consideration. Indeed, many of the organizers do not charge their salary to the organization; their 'earnings' are really in terms of recognition at national and international levels. The crucial question which is now being asked is whether or not the poor entrepreneurs are able to face free market conditions independently and make their units viable if only institutional credit is brought to their doorsteps without any other organizational support from government or non-governmental organizations. And, if such support is essential, the question is how do we do its proper costing?

Unfortunately, the available success stories do not provide a clear-cut answer to this question. The case studies on different programmes suggest that the answer is situation-specific and varies from region to region. Many of these, however, reveal that a participatory approach involving NGOs and CBOs reduces the establishment and supervision costs. Also, it ensures greater compliance to norms and repayment of loans. Nonetheless, the implicit cost of building up the umbrella organization and the sacrifices made by a few committed individuals in the process cannot possibly be measured in monetary terms. These, therefore, do not enter the accounting framework for most of the nationally known programmes and consequently, no proper cost-benefit analysis can be carried out. This is the reason why it has not been possible to multiply the success stories and to pursue this as an alternative approach to development (Kundu, 1993).

Admittedly, certain support systems (not in terms of finance alone) have become available to these programmes from outside the organization, but these may not be available in future years. If the objective is to multiply the experience of these few well-known experiments in the whole country, these organizational tasks and the costs of the support system cannot be ignored. The studies reveal that to have a few successful projects is one thing; to multiply them on a national or international scale is another.

Finally, researchers have expressed concern with regard to the stringent controls imposed by public agencies on the informal sector, on the one hand, and the absence of positive incentives to it, on the other. Many have urged the government to design a framework for protecting the informal sector workers from an exploitative nexus in the market and providing a support system to improve their working and living conditions (Pillai, 1997). It is further argued that the details of such a system in a particular town/settlement or industry can be designed only through micro-level studies (Sunderam 1995; Tripathy and Dash, 1995).

5. Policies for Promoting the Informal Sector

An analysis of the policies and programmes for the informal sector can be attempted, based on plan and policy documents along with evaluation reports of governmental schemes, among others. Importantly, the absence or inadequacy of an administrative and institutional support system has been considered responsible for the slow growth of this sector. A number of specific recommendations are made below for creating and/or strengthening this support system.

A number of studies have looked into the incentive system for promoting industrial growth in the country, like tax holidays and income tax rebates for new undertakings, allowances on investment in plants and machinery and on export, capital subsidy in backward areas, etc. (Tulsi, 1980; Sanyal, 1996). Many of these studies have tried to assess the extent to which benefits have reached the unorganized sector. Further, industries belonging to SSS, namely those having investments in plant and machinery up to Rs. 10 million for ancillary and other units[11] enjoy special concessions and incentives12, as discussed below. Here again, the scholars have enquired, how many of the informal sector units could register with the Development Commissioner for Small Scale Industries (DCSSI) and take advantage of these concessions?

SSS units producing any of the 72 specified items are exempt from central excise duty up to the output level of Rs. 0.5 million per year, provided their production is below a certain threshold. On other items, the exemption limit is Rs. 1.5 million if

[11] An ancillary unit is one which is generally set up by a larger parental unit for the purpose of getting regular supply of certain inputs or for processing a specific output.

the output (in the preceding year) has not exceeded Rs. 3 million. For SSS units having obtained clearances in the preceding financial year and whose turnover is not exceeding Rs. 30 million, the rate of excise duty is levied on the basis of modified value added tax credit (Modvat Credit). This benefit is allowed at the rate of 100 per cent of all the duties paid on inputs purchased, including capital goods. Besides reduced excise duty, other incentives like reduction in sales tax, product subsidies, input quotas, subsidies on power, etc., are also extended to small-scale industries (SSIs). The price paid by the central government and public undertakings in purchasing the products from SSS is 15 per cent higher than those from medium or large scale industries. SSIs units get a similar price preference in the purchases made by certain state governments as well. In addition, a subsidy of 15 per cent on the capital invested in new units or on expansion and diversification of old units is available from the Central Government. Capital subsidies are also given by the states, although the amount is small. Finally, units located in backward regions, identified by the central government, can get an income tax rebate of up to 20 per cent on their profits (Sandesara, 1988). Many of these concessions are, however, being withdrawn with liberalization and structural adjustments catching up in the Indian economy.

Besides these fiscal and financial measures, certain administrative stipulations are in operation that indirectly help small entrepreneurs. There are, for example, restrictions on the expansion of production by the large and medium scale units for over 800 commodity groups. This is a kind of reservation which helps small entrepreneurs in industries where significant economies of scale exist that can be enjoyed only by large units. Entrepreneurs producing chemical products, rubber, light engineering goods, paper and wood products, textiles and so forth, have been the major beneficiaries of this policy. The growth of small scale and informal activities in these industries may partially be attributed to this. On the recommendation of the Abid Hussain Committee, these items are now under threat of de-reservation (Hussain, 1997). The Committee has proposed Rs. 5 billion per year to be given as equity support and interest concession for upgrading technology in the SSS units, affected by de-reservation, over a period of five years.

Besides the fiscal and financial concessions, administrative guidelines, etc., discussed above, various infrastructural facilities and services are also provided, both by the central as well as state governments. Industrial development corporations in different states provide developed land, water, sanitation, local roads, electricity, etc., to the units located in their designated industrial estates. The former also help the entrepreneurs in obtaining subsidized finance and critical raw materials. Moreover, central and state level industrial finance corporations (refinanced by central level organizations like the Industrial Development Bank of India, commercial banks, etc.) provide loans to SSIs at concessional rates of interest.

The crucial question one may now ask is whether these benefits meant for SSIs have indeed reached the informal manufacturing units? Studies on this subject clearly give a negative answer. For example, reduction in excise duties has failed to benefit the handloom sector. Power-looms also gained at the expense of handlooms when purchase of hank yarn intended for handlooms was appropriated by the Power-looms (Jain, 1983). It is important that registration with the DCSSI, for that matter, with any specialized commission or board (e.g., Khadi and Village Industries Commission/Board for silk and coir industries), is optional. Only the units that have a legal status and have obtained necessary clearances from the local government (e.g., its health and planning departments, pollution control boards, etc.) can apply for registration entitling them to the concessions and subsidies. This automatically debars almost all informal manufacturing units from enjoying the available benefits.

Studies show that many units within the SSS that are benefiting from governmental programmes belong to the organized sector (registered under the Factories Act). These programmes have emphasized the importance of SSIS, but benefited largely the relatively modem units. These units are noted to be fairly capital intensive and operate at a high level of technology (Ghosh, 1988a). Scholars have, therefore, questioned the postulate that the small scale units, encouraged through government programmes, are labour intensive and can promote balanced regional development (Sandesara, 1991 and 1992).

Researchers, probing into the distributional aspects within the SSS, have identified a new category, namely the "tiny sector", comprising units having investment in plant and machinery up to Rs. 2.5 million. It has been shown that this sector has an extremely small share in the governmental subsidies. Scholars like Kurien (1978) and Goldar (1988) have pointed out that if the objectives are employment generation and an optimal use of capital resources, it is difficult to justify the promotion of modem capital intensive industries through state sponsorship, as has been the case so far. The informal sector, that should get very high priority in terms of both the objectives, has unfortunately been left out of nearly the whole lot of promotional programmes.

Needless to say, connection and corruption have played an important role in the disbursement of incentives and subsidized capital among small-scale units. This has continued even though the economy has moved from a regime of control to that dictated by the market, with drastic reduction in the volume of subsidies. As a consequence, a handful of industrialists are cornering much of the benefits, mostly under a false identity. Although there is no lower limit on fixed capital for registration with the DCSSI or other boards and commissions, the informal sector entrepreneurs have generally remained outside the system, largely due to legal and bureaucratic hassles. Even when registered with the DCSSI, they do not curry favour with the banks or other public agencies because of their lack of economic and social status or because of doubts regarding their credit worthiness. Procedural requirements of pledging adequate physical and financial assets have often disqualified them, in the very first instance. It has, therefore, been argued that, even without corruption, the existing legal structure, norms and administrative stipulations are such that the workers/entrepreneurs in the informal activities can rarely gain access to the benefits attached with promotional schemes.

A liberal policy for sanctioning institutional loans and government grants has often been proposed as a remedy to the situation. The proposal, however, has both positive and negative implications. It has been pointed out that sanctioning of credit without insisting on elaborate procedures and regulatory norms would theoretically increase the access of the poor and tiny sector entrepreneurs to the formal financing system. However, given the present resource scarcity and the power structure in the country, credit liberalization is likely to benefit the modem capital intensive sector only as it has greater capacity to manipulate the procedures or show more demonstrative benefits. It might also increase the default rate in repayment of loans, increasing thereby the burden on the public exchequer.

Similarly, deregulation and decontrol of the process of entry and exit and the day-to-day functioning of private enterprise may help the existing power groups and vested interests within the industrial sector because of their dominant position. Deregulation may help the industrialists to cut down on real wages and the facilities provided to the workers, and increase their own profitability. A few studies have shown that the genuine informal sector entrepreneurs, operating with a low level of skills, technology and productivity are not able to compete with others in an environment of market-led economic liberalization (Duraisamy and Narasimhan, 1997).

The other important point emerging from the overview in this section is that the incentive system in the country has been designed primarily for the manufacturing sector. Much of the institutional finance provided at a subsidized rate are meant for industries. However, keeping in view the objective of employment generation, one should assign a far more important role to the service sector than industries in the nineties. This is because the employment elasticity in manufacturing is low and decreasing over time. The opposite is the case in the service sector.

Indeed, designing a support system for promoting tertiary activities has not been given a serious consideration so far. In view of the fact that the responsibility of labour absorption in the next few years will fall squarely on the services sector, it would be important to develop certain institutional support systems, specifically for this sector or bring it under the existing system created for industries, with appropriate modifications.

The decentralization of planning and administrative functions by rejuvenating and transferring powers to local bodies would go a long way in supporting service activities. So far, the local bodies have been looking at the informal service sector largely from a negative viewpoint. This sector has generally been viewed as a civic nuisance and health hazard and consequently, attempts have generally been made to control, rather than promote, it through various acts. The local administration can be encouraged to play a positive role in future years and to support the service activities. It should shoulder the responsibility of creating an appropriate economic and administrative environment in which the urban poor can find productive employment for themselves.

In the light of the above, it can be argued that the incentives and regulatory system in the country should not be abandoned in a hurry. There is a need to redesign these with the specific objective of facilitating the growth of tiny or informal sector units. Importantly, the Ninth Plan envisages a four per cent growth in employment. Given the magnitude of employment elasticities, currently operating in the economy, achieving this would mean more than twelve per cent growth in organized industries which is beyond the limit of feasibility. This can, however, be achieved through a sustained development of informal activities - both manufacturing and services - wherein it is possible to increase the employment elasticities through an appropriate support system.

It has proven difficult to provide institutional loans and capital subsidies to informal sector entrepreneurs, specially those engaged in petty services. This has become even more difficult in a period of structural adjustment wherein the emphasis has been on economic recovery. Similarly, relaxation in the laws pertaining to labour welfare, and environmental protection (or lack of seriousness in their implementation) are likely to have an adverse impact on the welfare of workers in this sector. Further, the legal system presently covers, by and large, only the manufacturing sector and there has been a systematic reduction in its coverage. The analysis in the paper, however, suggests that even tertiary activities need to be brought effectively under the system. The government cannot abdicate its responsibility of safeguarding the interests of the entrepreneurs/workers engaged in informal tertiary activities. A purposeful and definitive intervention, therefore, seems to be the need of the hour and not a state sponsored resignation to laissezfaire.

6. Need to Develop a Support System

The overview of the existing database for the unorganized industry clearly brings out serious gaps, anomalies and discrepancies. The data even from national sources like Population Census, Economic Census and NSS suffer from problems of comparability. Owing to changes in the scope and coverage, assessing the trends or making generalizations about the pattern becomes difficult, even when using data from the same source. It is, therefore, important that agencies like the Census and NSSO standardize their methods of data collection and tabulation to permit cross-sectional and temporal comparability. The ILO has played an important role in building up comparable statistical systems across countries by lobbying for standardization and comparability at various international fora. It can certainly play a crucial role in generating temporally and cross- sectionally comparable data on the informal sector by recommending certain systems of data compilation to national level agencies in India.

Notwithstanding the problems in the database, it is observed that much more can be said about the changing character of the informal sector, its problems and possibilities for its future development than has been done in the past. These inferences and generalizations would be extremely important for designing the right kind of policy environment at the macro-level and launching specific schemes at the micro-level.

The overview of the macro data reveals that there has been a decline in the share of informal manufacturing employment which must be understood in the context of the declining industrial base in the urban areas. The changing nature of production relations, sub-contracting of jobs and ambiguity of contracts, growth of self-employed and casual workers, etc., have carried many of the activities out of the realm of manufacturing and placed them under the tertiary sector. As a consequence of this subcontracting, the workers stand exposed to more serious exploitation as there are fewer institutions and labour laws to protect subcontracted tertiary sector workers. The basic factor responsible for the growth of these activities is excess supply in the informal labour market. Further, there are indications that the absorptive capacity of informal manufacturing activities are reaching saturation limits, which is further reflected in a decline in rural to urban migration.

It is often stipulated that informal manufacturing activities would generate employment to compensate for the reduction in organized employment during the period of structural adjustment. Some of the recent studies, however, question this proposition, keeping the recent economic trends in view. Scholars have pointed out that a large number of informal sector units belonging to the OAME, NDME and DME categories have shown a significant decline in the growth of urban workforce during the late eighties. This can be explained partly in terms of the increasing incidence of subcontracting jobs, and partly in terms of this sector losing out to large capital intensive units. All these developments point towards a low productivity syndrome for the unorganized workers in the urban areas. These are likely to slow down the growth of employment in the manufacturing sector and adversely affect the rate of rural to urban migration and urbanization itself, in future years.

A large part of the informal sector seems to be surviving at a low level of productivity as a consequence of its low technology, very little capital assets and adverse market conditions. Further, the enterprises in the sector generally do not have much liquid cash for maintaining inventories. Still more important, they also face serious difficulties in getting adequate and regular supplies of a variety of raw materials. In general, the sector does not quickly respond to economic stimuli or the demand factors. As a consequence, the increase or decrease in the number of units or employment in many informal sector enterprises takes place without a corresponding increase in value added per worker or per enterprise. For them, being in business is more a matter of survival rather than making profits.

A small segment of entrepreneurs in the informal sector, however, is linked with the market, has access to credit facilities and quickly responds to productivity increases. It seems that institutional credit is a crucial factor for these enterprises for purchasing or hiring capital assets. Importantly, ownership of land increases access to credit. One may, therefore, argue that giving land titles to households would go a long way in strengthening informal enterprises. Finally, registration with public agencies makes a significant difference in access to land, fixed and working capital. Providing the protective cover of public agencies, thus, emerges as yet another critical factor for the success of informal enterprises in the urban areas.

The survey of micro-level studies indicates that low productivity, low wage rates, underemployment, poor working and living conditions, absence of skill formation, etc., are the major problems facing the informal sector. Insecurity and uncertainty also characterize this sector. These are, therefore, the major hurdles in developing an institutional support system, including provision of credit. A large majority of entrepreneurs struggle for subsistence without any hope of vertical mobility while only a few, that too in select occupations, manage to climb up the ladder. The fluctuations in the global or national market and changes in government policies threaten the growth, and even sheer continuance, of many of the activities in this sector. Individual entrepreneurs are in no position to safeguard themselves against these risks. Absence of formal registration with the local government or any other public agency is responsible for non-availability of adequate infrastructural facilities to them. More importantly, many engaged in this sector face harassment at the hands of police and local government functionaries.

Availability of credit, land titles and registration with public authorities emerge as important factors for the success of informal micro-enterprises. Studies based on secondary as well as primary data underline the importance of these factors in improving the nature of technology and capital investment per worker that lead to higher productivity and profitability. Concern has also been expressed regarding the unrestrained competition among micro-enterprises in the input and product market. Regulating such unhealthy competition, establishing norms and practices for business, standardizing the products and services, and providing market information have been advocated as important components of a support system at the micro-level.

The review of policies and programmes for promoting industrial growth suggests that the "tiny units" with investment in plant and machinery up to Rs. 2.5 million and informal units with an investment of a few thousand or hundred rupees that generally do not get registered with any public agency, receive virtually no support. This corroborates the findings of the micro-level studies. Most of the benefits go to the modern capital intensive "small scale industries". The "dynamism" shown by the informal sector, therefore, is not because of the government support, but is in spite of the constraints and controls imposed by the public authorities. In many branches of its activities, its continuance and growth can be explained in terms of undercutting of wages by its workers in their sheer struggle for survival.

Significant measures have been proposed to modify the present organizational structure and the modus operandi of the public agencies with the objective of increasing their accessibility to informal entrepreneurs. Researchers have also tried to identify the possible areas of public/collective control to ensure that the entrepreneurs do not exploit the poor workers. Defining the role and strategies for intervention by the central, state and local governments, for the efficient functioning of informal activities and protection of the workers therein, thus, emerges as a critical area for future research.

One proposition gaining currency among policy makers at the national and international levels is that the people engaged in informal activities can achieve reasonable rates of return and conduct their business profitably, provided institutional credit is extended to them within a participatory framework. It may, nonetheless, be pointed out that generalizations based on a few successful programmes can be grossly misleading. Often, these success stories do not consider the overhead cost of setting up the NGOs or CBOs responsible for the implementation of the project.

Based on the present overview, a case can be made for selective assistance to the informal sector entrepreneurs in terms of provision of technical guidance, subsidized credit, scarce raw materials and marketing support in place of the present system of general subsidization and regulatory control. Economic liberalization in the nineties does not seem to have made any positive impact on the profitability and growth of informal enterprises. Steps would, therefore, have to be taken to channel these benefits to the tiny/informal sector units that seem to have been marginalised in the present administrative environment. The allotment of scarce raw materials must be linked to re-sale of their output. Co-operatives created for this specific purpose, if organized properly, can help reduce the bureaucratic procedures in identifying and providing support to their members as well as non-members. The units attached to or created by the large industries/industrial houses are, however, not in a great need of the technical or marketing support. Targeting of the benefits should, therefore, be the central concern of the support system for promoting the informal sector along the desired lines.

Bibliography

Alam, S.M., Alikhan, F. and Bhattacharji, M. (1987). "Slums in Metropolitan Hyderabad - A Profile", in S.M. Alam and F. Alikhan (eds.): Poverty in Metropolitan Cities, Concept, New Delhi.

Association of Metropolitan Development Authorities and Kolkata Metropolitan Development Authority (1995). "Potential and Durable Employment Generation for Slum Women of Kolkata", (mimeo.), AMDA,New Delhi.

Arunachalam, J. and Azad, N. (1985). "Role of Women and Children in the Informal Sector", Productivity, Vol. 26, No. 3.

Banerjee, B, (1983). "The Role of Informal Sector in Migratory Process: A Test of Probabilistic Migratory Model and Labour Market Segmentation for India", Oxford Economic Papers, Vol. 35, No. 3.

Banerjee, N. (1982). "The Weakest Link", in Helen Safa (ed.): Towards a Political Economy of Urbanization in Third World Countries, Oxford University Press, New Delhi.

Bhattacharya, K. P. and Dey, P. (1991). " Problems of Hawkers in Kolkata: A Case Study ", Indian Journal of Social Science, Vol. 4, No. 2.

Breman, J. (1996). Footloose Labour Working in India's Informal Economy, Cambridge University Press, Cambridge.

Bromley, R. (1994). "Informality de Soto Style: From Concept to Policy", in Cathy A. Rakowski (ed.): Contrapunto: The Informal Sector Debate in Latin America, State University of New York Press, Albany.

Buch, M.N. and Pathak, P. (1985). "The Role of Informal Sector in Development of Small and Intermediate Cities of India: A Survey", Paper Presented at the Round Table Conference on Informal Sector in the Economy of Small Cities, (mimeo.), National Institute of Urban Affairs, New Delhi.

Census of India (1971). General Economic Tables, Government of India, New Delhi.

____ (1981). General Economic Tables, Government of India, New Delhi.

____ (1993). Final Population Totals, Government of India, New Delhi.

Charmes, J. (1996). "Progress in Measurement of Informal Sector Paradigm: Analytical Contributions and Development Role", Regional Development Dialogue, Vol. 17, No. 1.

Chatterjee, S. (1995). "Organising the Unorganised Workers: A Study of CITU's Role in West Bengal", Indian Journal of Labour Economics, Vol. 38, No. 4.

Central Statistical Organization, (1989). Statistical Abstract, Chapter 24 on Labour, Government of India, New Delhi.

Das, B. (1994). Socio-Economic Study of Slums in Surat City, Centre for Social Studies, Surat.

Datar, C. (1986). "Organizing of Women Tobacco and Bidi Workers in Nipani in a Historical Perspective", Paper Presented at the Third National Conference on Women's Studies.

Deshpande, L.K. (1983). "Urban Labour Market - Problems and Policies", in Employment Policies in a Developing Country.- A Case Study of India, Vol. I, Macmillan.

Dupont, V. (1995). Decentralized Industrialization and Urban Dynamics: The Case of Jaipur in West India, Sage Publications, New Delhi.

Duraisamy, M. (1997). "Structure, Productivity and Employment in the Unorganised Manufacturing Sector in India", Paper presented IAMR-IHD Seminar, New Delhi.

Duraisamy, P. and Narasinhan, S. (1997). "Migration, Wages and Wage Discrimination in Urban Informal Sector - A case Study of Chennai Metropolitan Area", Paper presented at IAMR-IHD Seminar, New Delhi.

Ghosh, A. K. (1997). "Should There be a National Minimum Wage in India", Indian Journal of Labour Economics, Vol. 40, No. 4.

Ghosh, B. (1988). Organising Unorganised Workers.- A Sociological Study of Trade Unionism in the Leather and Book-Binding Industries in Kolkata, Thesis submitted to the Jawaharlal Nehru University, 1988.

Ghosh, A. (1988a). "Government Policies Concerning Small Scale Industries - An Appraisal", in K.B. Suri (ed): Small Scale Enterprises in Industrial Development: The Indian Experience, Sage Publications, New Delhi.

Goldar, B. (1988). "Relative Efficiency of Modern Small Scale Industries in India", in K.B. Suri (ed.): Small Scale Enterprises in Industrial Development: The Indian Experience, Sage Publications, New Delhi.

Government of Tamil Nadu (1986). Tamil Nadu Urban Development Project, Housing and Urban Development, Madras.

Harriss, J. (1982). "Character of an Urban Economy: Small Scale Production and Labour Markets in Coimbatore ", Economic and Political Weekly, Vol. 17, No. 23.

Hussain, Abid (1997). Report of the Expert Committee on Small Enterprises, Ministry of Industry, Government of India, New Delhi.

Jagannathan N.V. (1987). Informal Markets in Developing Countries, Oxford University Press, New York, Oxford.

Jain, L.C. (1983). "Handlooms Face Liquidation: Powerlooms Mock at Yojana Bhawan", Economic and Political Weekly, Aug. 27. Development, Vol. 17, No. 1.

Kundu, A., (1993). In the Name of Urban Poor: Access to Basic Amenities", Sage Publications, New Delhi.

Kundu, A. and Lalitha, N, (1988). "Informal Manufacturing Sector in Urban India: Sectoral Trends and Interdependencies", Indian Journal of Labour Economics, 43/3.

Kundu, A., Lalitha, N. and Arora, Sant Lal (2001). "Growth Dynamics of Informal Manufacturing Sector in Urban India: An Analysis of Interdependencies", in Amitabh Kundu and Alakh N. Sharma (eds), Informal Sector in India: Perspective and Policies, Institute of Human Development, New Delhi.

Kurien, C.T. (1988). "Small Scale Sector in New Industrial Policy", Economic and Political Weekly, March.

Lall, V.D, Hazra, S. and Shrama S.C. (1988). Informal Sector and Development Strategy : Meerut and Panipat, Society for Development Studies, New Delhi.

Mathur, O.P. (1993). "Managing the Urban Informal Sector : A New Challenge for Developing Countries", in Shabbir G. Cheema (ed.): Urban Management Policies and Innovations in Developing Countries, Praeger, Westport.

Mathur, O.P. and Moser, C.O.N. (1984). "The Urban Informal Sector: An Agenda for Future Research", Regional Development Dialogue, Vol. 5, No. 2.

Mazumdar, S. (1990). Industrial Development in India since the Mid Seventies (Doctoral Thesis), Centre for Economic Studies and Planning, JNU, New Delhi.

Nagamine, H. (1996). "Planning for Employment in the Urban Informal Sector", Regional Development Dialogue, Vol. 17, No. 1.

Nagraj, R. (1984). "Subcontracting in Indian Manufacturing Industries: Analysis, Evidence and Issues", Economic and Political Weekly, Vol. 19, No. 3.

Nambiar, A.C.K. (1995). "Unorganised Labour Unionism: The Case of Headload Workers in Kerala", Indian Journal of Labour Economics, Vol. 38, No. 4.

National Sample Survey Organisation (1986). " Key Results of Last Three Quinquennial NSS Enquiries on Employment and Unemployment, Sarvekshana, 9(4), Department of Statistics, Government of India, New Delhi.

____ (1990). "Results of the Fourth Quinquennial NSS Survey on Employment and Unemployment", Sarvekshana, 9(4), Department of Statistics, Govt.of India, New Delhi

____ (1997). Employment and Unemployment in India, 1993-94, Fiftieth Round,Department of Statistics, New Delhi.

____ (2000a). Employment and Unemployment in India 1999-2000, Key Results, NSS 55th Round, Department of Statistics, Government of India, New Delhi.

____ (2000b). Non-Agricultural Enterprises in the Informal Sector in India 1999-2000, Key Results, NSS 55th Round, Department of Statistics, Govt.of India, New Delhi.

Nurul Amin, A.T.M. (1996). "The Informal Sector Paradigm: Analytical Contributions and Development Role", Regional Development Dialogue, Vol. 17, No. 1.

Papola, T. S. (1981). Urban Informal Sector in a Developing Country, Vikas Publishing House, New Delhi.

Pillai, M. (1997). "Social Security of Unorganised Sector: An Alternate Approach to Poverty Eradication", Paper Presented at IAMR-IHD Seminar, New Delhi.

Planning Commission (1991). Employment: Past Trends and Prospects for 1990s, Working Paper, Government of India, New Delhi.

Ribeiro, E.F.N. (1993). "Informal Sector in India- A Case Study of Anand Parbat", in Readings in Urban Informal Sector, Society for Development Studies, New Delhi.

Richardson, H. W. (1 985). " The Role of Informal Sector: An Overview ", in The Role of Informal Sector in Developing Countries, UNCHS, Nairobi.

Sandesara, J.C. (1992). Industrial Policy and Planning, 1947-91: Tendencies, Interpretation and Issues, Sage Publications, New Delhi.

____ (1991). "New Industrial Policy - Questions of Efficient Growth and Social Objectives", Economic and Political Weekly, August 3 - 1 0.

____ (1988). "Small Industry Development Programme in India: Efficacy, Explanations and Lessons: Some Field Studies", in K.B. Suri (ed.), Small Scale Enterprises in Industrial Development: The Indian Experience, Sage Publications, New Delhi.

Sanyal, B. (1996). "Intention and Outcome - Formalisation and Its Consequences", Regional Development Dialogue.

____ (1991). "Organising the Self-Employed: The Politics of the Urban Informal Sector", International Labour Review, Vol. 130.

Sardana, M.G. (1989). "Statistics of Unorganized Segments of Non-Agricultural Sector of Indian Economy", in Proceedings of the Meeting, International Statistical Institute, 47th Session, Paris.

Shah, A. (1997). "Scalar Linkages in Industries: Implications for Productivity and Employment", Indian Journal of Labour Economics, Vol. 41, No. 3, New Delhi.

Sharma, K.L. and Singh, M. (1980). Entrepreneurial Growth and Development Programme in Northern India: A Comparison of Sports Goods Industry in Jalandar and Meerut.

Singh, B. (1997). "Generation of Self Employment via Organised Industry - An Assessment of Subcontracting Model", Paper Presented at IAMR-IHD Seminar, New Delhi.

Singh, S. (1997). "The Informal Sector: Some Linkages and Credit Issues", Paper Presented at IAMR-IHD Seminar, New Delhi.

Singh, M. (I 990). The Political Economy of Unorganised Industry: A Study of the Labour Process, Sage Publications, New Delhi.

Subrahmanian,K.K., Veena, D.R. and Bhanumati, K. P. (1982). Construction in Labour Market - A Study in Ahmedabad, Concept, New Delhi.

Sunderam, S.K.G. (1995). "Organising the Unorganised Urban Labour: Case Studies from Maharashtra", Indian Journal of Labour Economics, Vol. 38, No. 4.

TCPO (Town and Country Planning Organisation) (1983). Informal Sector in a Metropolis - A Case Study of Anand Parbat, TCPO, New Delhi.

Tripathy, S.K and Dash, A. (1995). "Organising the Unorganised Tendu Leaf Workers in Orissa", Indian Journal of Labour Economics, Vol. 38, No. 4.

Tulsi, S.K. (1980). Incentives for Small Scale Industries: An Evaluation, Kunj Publishing House, Delhi.

Unni, J. (1997). "Distinguishing Employment and Enterprise in the Informal Sector", Paper Presented at IAMR-IHD Seminar, New Delhi.

Venkata Ratnam, C.S. (1997). "Formal informal Sector Linkages: Role of Social Partners", Paper Presented at IAMR-IHD Seminar, New Delhi.

Visaria, P. and Minhas, B.S. (1996). "Evolving an Employment Policy for the Nineties: What do the Data Tell Us?", Economic and Political Weekly, April 13.

Von der Loop, T. (1988). Structure of Building Sector in a Medium Sized City: Contractors, Jobbers and Hutmakers in Vellore (Tamil Nadu), Work document, Center for Asian Studies, Amsterdam.

Informal Sector in the Indian Economy: A Case Study of Khadi Textiles

G.K.Chadha

1. Introduction

Khadi is defined as any cloth woven on handlooms in India from cotton, silk or woollen yarn, handspun or from a mixture of any two or all of such yarns. Khadi, which was conceived in the twenties as a promoter of Swadeshi movement and an instrument of self-reliance in the rural areas, owes its origin and expansion to Mahatma Gandhi who firmly believed that the destiny of the Indian Nation in general, and rural India in particular, depended on the loom. The first cloth woven out of hand spun yarn at Sabarmati Ashram in 1918 was named khadi after the word Sowbagyam. In 1923, All-India Khadi Board was set up with branches all over the provinces while in 1925, an independent organization known as All-India Spinners' Association was created to further propagate khadi. Ever thereafter, many developments took place, from time to time, in the Indian economy which directly or indirectly aimed at ameliorating the economic status of the vast army of spinners and weavers that constituted an overwhelming proportion of rural artisans.

Other rural industries could not stay behind. In 1934, All-India Village Industries Association came into existence for specific development of village industries, which in a way, triggered the process of rural industrialisation in a modest form. Khadi and village industries that were once an integral part of and an acknowledged source of prosperity in rural India, but were systematically destroyed during the British rule, thus became synonymous with freedom movement and a hope for rejuvenation of the rural economy. Gandhi's vision of such industries and activities becoming a potent source of rural peoples' employment, earnings and well-being was well-received inside and outside the political circles, during and after the freedom struggle. No wonder, therefore, soon after gaining political Independence, when the era of planned economic development ensued in 1951, khadi and village industries were adopted as a part of the national development plan.

In 1953, All-India Khadi and Village Industries Board was established which was, a little later in 1957, converted into Khadi and Village Industries Commission (KVIC). The Commission was entrusted with bigger responsibilities for planning, organising and implementing diverse programmes for the development of khadi (and rural industries whose list expanded substantially over the years). Since then, there was no looking back. Between 1957 and now, the KVIC has many milestones, most ostensibly improvements in technology-in-use, training of artisans and marketing network, to its credit. To take note of some of the major developments, in 1957 itself, an improved spinning wheel (known as AMBAR CHARKHA) was introduced; in 1962-63, renovation of AMBAR CHARKHA was initiated; in 1966-67, New Model Charkha with 6 spindles was introduced; in 1972-73, muslin khadi (a refined version of cotton khadi) production programme was introduced; in 1976-77, a four-tier system of training the artisans was adopted; in 1985-86, it was decided to set up two central silver plants, one at Rae Bareilly for the New Model Charkha and Polyvastra, and the other at Trichur for muslin khadi; in 1989-90, government's decision to opt for polyvastra uniform for its 'D' category employees, gave boost to the khadi sector, and so on. Procedural improvements in lending financial support to Khadi institutions, individual artisans and other prospective entrepreneurs, most notably the introduction of the Margin Money Scheme in 1995-96, and a change-over from weaving subsidy to sales rebate, were other notable steps for their wider impact.

All has, however, not been well with the khadi sector. In spite of the state patronage or support, spanning as it did well over four decades, the khadi has not come off age. Most strikingly, the price of khadi items has been going up and the intending purchasers invariably wait for the months (usually October to December every year) during which substantial rebates are available on khadi cloth and other khadi products. There is a wide-spread belief among the khadi institutions, officials and workers that khadi production is sustaining itself only on the strength of augmented sales at reduced seasonal prices; otherwise, khadi products are tending to become rich men's prerogative. The very fear that forced Gandhi to do something for the rural artisans is looming large in India's rural economy, especially after the introduction of new economic reforms in 1991.

It is widely feared that under the new economic dispensations, khadi faces a bleak future, and with that, the employment prospects of a fairly big chunk of rural workers and artisans engaged in this sector, also hang in uncertainty. Their low educational background and traditional outlook, and consequently, their unwillingness to switch over to alternative jobs, etc. clearly stand in their way. Moreover, there is a wide spread feeling that the working conditions of the on-going workforce engaged in khadi textiles is anything but pleasing. That they suffer from low productivity and earning levels; that their working conditions are highly unpleasing; that they operate under many inhibitions; that discrimination against female workers is rampant; that child labour is abused, etc, are the commonly heard complaints, keeping aside the allegation that a very big proportion of the khadi institutions are bogus and are floated by a few influential people, largely to corner the financial and other support forthcoming under the KVIC schemes and programmes.

This study attempts to look into the working of the Khadi Textile Sector in the Indian economy. The study is spread over seven sections. Section 1 introduces the Khadi Textile Sector. Section 2 looks at the Khadi Sector in relation to other industries which together are officially designated as Village and Small Industries (VSI). Clearly, at this level of aggregation, Khadi Sector does not seem to fare very well in comparison to other industries under VSI, especially the set of modern small scale industries. Section 3 looks at the status of Khadi as a part of the total textile industry. Section 4 sketches out the temporal profile of the Khadi Sector, in terms of its four components: viz.: cotton, woollen, silk and muslin, from 1953-57 to 1998-99. Certain weaknesses on the production and employment fronts, in respect of the various components of the Khadi Sector come up in bold relief. Section 5 describes the usual set of problems that workers are believed to face in the Khadi Sector, especially the two most dominant categories of artisans involved in the sector, viz.: spinners and weavers. Section 6 gives an analytical account of their working conditions, earnings, level of living, future prospects, as gathered through a small field survey. Finally, Section 7 ventures to make a few concluding observations.

2. Khadi in the VSI Sector

In official documents, khadi and village industries are clubbed with handlooms, sericulture, handicrafts and coir under the group of industries called traditional industries. There is the other component of modern industries that comprises powerloom and small-scale industries. Both the traditional and modern components put together constitute the group of Village and Small Industries (VSI). To begin with, it is essential to see how the khadi has been faring in relation to the other components included under the VSI sector. This is what we do in this chapter.

The time-series data on the VSI sector is difficult to deal with. First, the series begins only from 1973-74 onwards. But then, there are many information gaps: no data either on production or employment for the years 1974-75 to 1978-79; no information on employment for the years 1980-81, 1981-82, 1982-83. Such gaps do undermine the quality of data. Second, production figures at current prices are oddly mixed up with those at constant prices, sometimes even for the same year; a uniform series either at current or constant prices is not available. The best that one can do is to construct three production series, at 1979-80, 1984-85 and

1993-94 prices, respectively. Towards this end, certain adjustments/assumptions have to be made which may not be the best to go by. To quote a few examples, for some years, production data for a specific sector available only in physical terms were converted into monetary terms, using the 'implicit unit price' prevailing in the base year. Obviously, no regard is paid to the changing composition of output within that sector. Again, the available data for the post 1990-91 years are largely available at current prices only, and one could put them at constant prices using price index with 1993-94 as the base. The resultant production figures (at 1993-94 prices) are not completely free of price deflator bias, especially for the years 1990-91, 1991-92 and 1992-93 when the deflator works in the opposite direction. Value of output in the handicrafts sub-sector is available only up to 1996-97; for 1997-98 and 1998-99, we go by extrapolated figures. In spite of these problems, it is worthwhile looking at the khadi sub-sector in conjunction with the other seven constituents of the VSI sector. As far khadi itself, happily, none of these difficulties are encountered when we derive value of output in each of the four khadi sub-sectors in Section 4 below.

Third, for a number of reasons, there is really no way of arriving at comparable per worker productivity figures for individual segments of the VSI sector. Firstly, except for the group of small scale industries, part-time employment is reported, in varying form and content, practically by all other constituents of the VSI sector, and there is no way of arriving at the standard full-time equivalent labour units, without indulging in 'blind guesses'. Secondly, the ratio between part- and full-time workers varies fairly substantially among individual segments of the khadi sector itself (see Table 4.2 below). Thirdly, again for the khadi workers themselves, although the part- and full-time workers' division is available, yet the daily work duration of part-time workers/artisans is not known. Fourthly, part- and full-time workers' division is not given for other industries, as is given for khadi workers. Fifthly, for some sectors (e.g., sericulture), employment for some years includes the connected-work in agriculture while for others, no such mention is made. In total terms, we can neither ignore the reality of part-time employment nor can we convert part-time workers into full-time workers. Accordingly, estimating figures of per worker productivity, without getting involved into the intractable problems set out above, would be highly misleading, especially if the intention is to compare the productivity levels among the eight sub-sectors. The advisable course, at this stage of our analysis, is to compare the performance profile of the individual VSI sub-sectors with reference to output and employment only; some idea on productivity in the khadi sub-sectors comes forth later in Section 4 when we look at net earning per full- and part-time worker (see, e.g., Table 4.8 below).

Building a temporal profile for employment too is not free of blemishes, for reasons which are partially set out in the preceding paragraph. Nonetheless, since the division between part- and full-time workers in the khadi sector does not seem to have changed much over time, most markedly during the recent decade, growth rates for employment in this sector built on the given series of khadi workers, would not distort the reality. Employment growth rates for the other VSI sub-sectors would suffer much less distortions since the proportion of part-time workers is possibly much lower and, like khadi sub-sectors, has not changed much over time (Chadha, 1996: 60).

Lastly, the (compound) growth rates are computed on point- to-point basis for the sub-periods 1973-74 to 1984-85 (Series I) and 1984-85 to 1989-90 (Series II) and through fitting of semi-log functions for the period 1990-91 to 1998-99 (Series III); in the case of Series I and II, the number of available observations is too small to justify a semi-log function. We know that our growth rates under Series I and II are highly sensitive to base- or end-year variations and are not, therefore, completely reliable yet they do capture the uneven pace of output and employment expansion, across the sectors and across the three sub-periods devised by us. Most surely, the declining or slumbering 'spots' stand out as contrasts to their expanding counterparts. In brief, the time-series data for VSI Sector do have their serious limitations, yet for fixing ideas of temporal changes, these are the only sources to go by.

The VSI sector consists of eight sub-sectors (Table 2.1). Location-wise, five sub-sectors (i.e. Khadi, Village Industries, Handloom, Sericulture and Coir are preponderantly rural, handicrafts are largely divided between rural and semi-urban locales while small-scale and powerloom sub-sectors are spread over rural, semi-urban and urban locations. In other words, looking across the six industrial groups under the traditional sector, one is really comparing one industry group with the other largely within the rural areas while the modern sector delivers ideas on a mix of rural-urban industries. Moreover, the intra-group heterogeneity in terms of the size of operation, persons employed, technology-use, market coverage, etc., are bound to be far greater among the group of small-scale industries which are indeed a heterogeneous mix of enterprises ranging from tiny, cottage, household-based activities on one end and modern factory-based enterprises, on the other. These observations may be kept in mind while inter- group or rural-urban comparisons are made from Table 2.1.

Table 2.1 (split into two parts: Sub-Table 2.1A gives production expansion while Sub-Table 2.1B takes care of employment) throws up a few disturbing features for the traditional sub-sector in general and khadi and handloom in particular. First, all along, output in real terms has shown impressive expansion in the modern sector compared with the traditional sector. A growth rate of 10.9 per cent per annum

TABLE 2.1A : **Output Expansion in Village and Small Industries (VSI) in India: 1973-74/1998-99 (Rs. in Crores)**

Year	TRADITIONAL SECTOR (TS)							MODERN SECTOR (MS)			Total VSI Sector
	Khadi	Village Industries	Hand-loom	Sericulture	Handicrafts	Coir	Total TS	Small Scale Industries	Power-loom	Total MS	
1	2	3	4	5	6	7	8	9	10	11	12
Series - I (1979-80 Prices)											
1973-74	50.7	187.4	1290.2	96 8	1635.8	92.2	3353.1	11059.2	3041.3	14100.5	17453.6
1979-80	92.0	348.0	1740.0	131.0	2050.0	86 0	4447.0	21635.0	3250.0	24885.0	29332.0
1984-85	115.9	517.3	1964.2	215.9	2387.0	68 5	5268.9	34454.6	4244.1	38698.7	43967.5
Series - II (1984-85 Prices)											
1984-85	170.0	758.6	2880.0	316.6	3500.0	100.5	7725.7	50520.0	6423 0	56943 0	64668.7
1985-86	164 6	900.4	2589.0	370.0	4100 0	139.5	8263 5	57100.0	7668.5	64768.5	73032 0
1986-87	167.0	1034 0	2759.2	417.0	5100.0	141 0	9618.2	64500.0	8106.3	72606.3	82224 5
1987-88	178 3	1265.2	2806.0	445.0	6150.0	148.7	10993.2	72880.0	8394.0	81274.0	92267.2
1988-89	187 0	1473 8	2773.1	490 0	8250.0	153.2	13327.1	73125 0	9092.0	82217.0	95544.1
1989-90	203 0	1101.0	3377.0	493 0	7067 0	128.0	12369.0	92080.0	9865.0	101945.0	114314.0
Series - III (1993-94 Prices)											
1990-91	349 4	2705.6	3973 2	1011 5	15366.4	161.0	23567.0	210773.4	16073.3	226846.7	250413.7
1991-92	355 8	2698 5	3351.4	925.2	15804.5	167.8	23303.1	190669.8	20961.5	211631.4	234934.5
1992-93	336 5	2733 5	4242.3	1095.4	16847.2	174.7	25429.6	183055.3	23224.6	206279.9	231709.5
1993-94	346 2	3232 0	4421 9	1197.5	18250.0	183.1	27630.7	241650.0	24079.3	265729.3	293360.0
1994-95	301 2	2904 1	5023.4	1185.6	19054.2	186.9	28655.5	261092.4	26187.3	287279.6	315935.1
1995-96	336 5	2881 6	5854 1	1096 1	20723 7	200.7	31092.7	292938 3	22410.3	315348.6	346441.3
1996-97	355.8	3058.2	6060.6	1113.2	23270 4	210.6	34068.8	324399.4	25212.7	349612.1	383680.9
1997-98	334 0	3226.7	6180 1	1200.7	23585.4	225.8	34752.6	350279.4	27296 0	377575 4	412328.0
1998-99	363.1	3180 5	5520 9	1224.9	24408.8	239.6	34937.9	374964.5	26956.0	401920.4	436858.3
Compound Growth Rate											
1973-85	7 8	9 7	3 9	7.6	3 5	-2 7	4 2	10.9	3.1	9.6	8.8
1984-90	3 6	7.7	3 2	9 3	15 1	5.0	9.9	12.8	9.0	12.4	12.1
1990-99*	0.1	2 2	7.2	2.5	6.6	5.0	6.0	9.5	5.0	9.2	8 9

Note Output figures (values in crores of rupees) under Series-I, Series-II and Series-III are at constant prices with Base 1979-80, 1984-85 and 1993-94, respectively; * Growth Rate has been computed through semi-log curve.

Source. 1. Govt. of India, Seventh Five Year Plan, 1985-90, Vol.II, p.99 (for figures under Series-I at 1979-80 prices).

2. ________, Annual Plan for 1986-87 (p.151), 1987-88 (p.180), 1988-89 (p.202), 1989-90 (pp.188, 190), 1990-91 (p.180), 1991-92 (p.188), for figures under Series-II at 1984-85 prices.

3. ________, Annual Plan for 1993-94 (pp.290-91), for figures under Series- III at 1993-94 prices.

4. ________, Indian Planning Experience: A Statistical Profile, January 2001.

5. ________, Annual Plan for 1999-2000 (pp 424-25), for figures under Series- III at 1993-94 prices.

6. ________, Annual Plan for 2000-01 (pp 378-79), for figures under Series- III at 1993-94 prices.

7. ________, Economic Survey 2000-01, for All Commodity Wholesale Price Index.

TABLE 2.1B : **Employment Expansion in VSI Sector : 1973-74/1998-99**

Year	TRADITIONAL SECTOR (TS)							MODERN SECTOR (MS)			Total VSI
	Khadi	Village Indus-tries	Hand-loom	Seri-culture	Handi-crafts	Coir	Total TS	Small Scale Industries	Power-loom	Total MS	
1	2	3	4	5	6	7	8	9	10	11	12
1973-74	8.8	9 3	52.1	12 0	15.0	5.0	102.2	39.7	10.0	49.7	151.9
1979-80	11.2	16 1	61.5	16.0	20 3	5 6	130 7	67.0	11.0	78.0	208.7
1984-85	14.6	22.4	74 7	20.0	27.4	5.9	165.0	90.0	32.2	122.2	287.1
1987-88	14 0	27 8	74.8	57.7	34.9	5 5	214.7	107 0	42.1	149.1	363.8
1989-90	14.1	32.1	76.0	50.0	42 2	5.5	216.9	119 6	45.0	164.6	381.5
1990-91	14.2	34.4	96.9	52.0	43 8	5.5	246 7	124 3	55.0	179.3	426.0
1991-92	14 3	35.4	106.0	54 5	48.3	5.5	263.9	126.0	55.0	181 0	444 9
1992-93	14 5	36.6	106.0	54 8	53 1	5 5	270.4	128.3	60.0	188 3	458 7
1993-94	14.5	39 4	110 0	56 0	58.3	5.0	283.2	139.4	56.0	195.4	478.6
1994-95	15 5	42 0	112 0	60.0	64.0	5.0	298 5	145.0	65.0	210.0	508.5
1995-96	16.7	40.3	128 0	60 0	66 0	5.5	316.1	153.0	68.6	221.0	537.1
1996-97	16 0	45.0	149 0	59 6	70.8	5.5	347 2	160.0	70 8	228.0	575.2
1997-98	14.0	42 5	135 0	60 6	73.0	5 2	330.3	167.0	72.0	239 0	569.3
1998-99	13 9	44.4	160.0	61 4	65.0	5 0	349.7	171.6	70.0	241.6	591.3
Compound Growth Rate											
1973-85	4.7	8.3	3 3	4.8	5.6	1.5	4.5	7.7	11.2	8.5	6.0
1984-90	-0 7	7 5	0 3	3 0	9.0	-1.4	5.6	5.9	6.9	6.1	5.9
1990-99*	0.3	3.4	6.1	2 1	6.0	-0.8	4.6	4.6	3.9	4.4	4.5

Note: Employment Figures are in Persons in Lakhs;
* Growth Rate has been computed through semi-log curve.

Source: Same as in Table 2.1A.

among the small scale industries, during 1973-74/1984-85, compared with 4.2 per cent among the traditional industries, testifies to the relative dynamism of the former, partly facilitated by comparative size and location advantages and partly by more buoyant demand conditions. The Khadi Sector also grew rather impressively (@ 7.8 per cent per annum) during this period. During the subsequent period 1984-85/1989-90, output growth rate improved among many traditional groups but the modern sector fared much better so that the gaps between the two got widened. For example, the growth rate in the small scale sector climbed up to a high of 12.8 per cent compared with just 3.6 per cent only for the Khadi. In fact, khadi/handloom output growth rate was the lowest among the traditional set of industries, let alone in relation to small-scale modern industries and the powerloom. In plain terms, a big decline in output growth was faced by the khadi sub-sector during the post-1984 years.

The first 3 years or so beginning 1990-91 showed a slack, in real output expansion, in most of the traditional sectors, most visibly in the Khadi and Handloom segments, compared with the Powerloom Sector. Even the small-scale industries could not insulate themselves from the general recession that plagued the industrial sector as a whole since the closing part of the 1980s. In particular, the poor performance in the small scale sector during those early years of the 1990s could possibly be attributed to import compression measures, credit squeeze, high cost of credit, etc. operating during the two-three years since the introduction of new economic policies in 1991 (Annual Plan, 1993-94:276). Happily, the situation was redeemed since 1993-94; output expanded significantly from 1993-94 onwards in small-scale industries, and a few of the traditional sub-sectors. For the whole period 1990-91/98-99, output grew fairly impressively at a rate of 9.5 per cent in the modern small-scale industries. In contrast, in the traditional sector as a whole, the corresponding increase in output growth was only 6.0 per cent, although in some of the traditional sub-sectors (e.g., village industries, sericulture, handicrafts, etc.), rate of growth of output fell by sizeable margins during sub-period III compared with sub-period II. *Khadi fared the worst; the growth rate of output was a mere 0.1 per cent during 1990-91/1998-99 compared with 3.6 per cent during 1984-85/1989-90.*

Second, throughout the post-1973 years, employment expanded at fairly high rates in many of the VSI sub-sectors. Of course, the level and pattern of employment growth did vary markedly among individual sectors, from one sub-period to the other. In general, employment expansion was relatively sluggish in khadi and coir sub-sectors. On the other hand, powerloom and small-scale industries under the modern sector and handicrafts and village industries under the traditional sector threw up, *almost dutifully,* impressive employment growth rates, in each sub-period. The handloom sector too performed well except during 1984-85/1989-90. On the whole, the picture on employment expansion has not been too bad, except for khadi ever since we stepped into the mid-eighties. As a matter of fact, employment in the Khadi sector stopped expanding from 1984-85 onwards, and most distressingly, against fairly impressive employment growth rates witnessed during the nineties by handicrafts, handloom, village industries among the traditional segment and small scale industries and powerloom in the modern segment, employment in the khadi sub-sector grew sheepishly by 0.30 per cent only. This would lead any public analyst to declare that, during the past decade and a half, the Khadi sub-sector failed miserably even on the employment front. The distress gets magnified if we remind ourselves that nearly 70.0 per cent of the Khadi workers are only part-time workers.

Third, contrary to the usual perception, employment growth in the modern sub-sectors has usually been higher than that in their traditional counterparts. For example, during 1973-74/84-85, it was 8.5 per cent per annum in the modern sector against 4.5 per cent in the traditional sector and only 4.7 per cent in Khadi; 6.1 per cent against 5.6 per cent and -0.7 in the three sectors during 984-85/89-90; and 4.4 per cent against 4.6 per cent and 0.3 per cent, again for the three sectors, during 1990-91/98-99, and so on. Given the fact that an overwhelming proportion of khadi workers are engaged only a on part-time basis (see Section 4 below), in net terms, the employment profile of the Khadi sector really pales into insignificance, especially in relation to the modern small scale industrial activities, for the post-1984 years. In other words, the most avowed objective of (non-farm) employment generation for the rural masses, through khadi and handloom sub-sectors, seems to have been fulfilled only partially; in an accounting sense, the number of people employed in the khadi sector has certainly been increasing, *albeit very moderately at times*, yet the economic content of this employment has not been much since a preponderant majority of khadi workers have been part-time workers only. For most of such part-time workers, especially the female workers engaged in spinning, the usual work-time does not go beyond 3 hours or so per day. Their earnings are thus ridiculously low, as indeed we see later in Section 4.

Fourth, the uneven output and employment growth performance of individual industry groups readily convinces us that the absolute level of productivity in khadi and other traditional rural industries should be many times lower than that in the modern sectors. Still more important is the fact that over time, the ratio between the high-productivity sector (small-scale industries) and low-productivity sector (say, khadi) has been expanding, almost on a continuing basis. From this point of view, *modern small-scale industry must be looked upon as a hope for the future.* If mere expansion of numbers is to be taken as an index of employment, most of the VSI segments, except Khadi, have acquitted themselves well. However, if productivity level and its growth are the basic criteria for viability, sustainability and growth of industrial units, including their long-run capability to take on more and more of working hands, only small-scale industrial units seem to fill the bill. In most other sectors, employment expansion without much regard for productivity and earning levels seem to have guided the course of events. Khadi undoubtedly failed on both fronts; undoubtedly, it is the declining or sagging levels of productivity that must have been responsible for cutting into its employment capabilities since 1984-85. In recent years, employment in the Khadi sub-sector has indeed been the most distressing spot in the VSI sector.

To feel sure that our assertion of sluggish or negative growth of output in the Khadi sub-sector is not a monetary illusion, we constructed Table 2.2 in terms of physical quantities. Without any doubt, the picture in Table 2.1 gets authenticated. For example, during 1984-85/1989-90, output in khadi grew negatively (by 1.3 per cent) compared with very impressive growth rates registered by handloom,

TABLE 2.2 : **Output Expansion in Physical Terms in Selected Sub-Sectors of the VSI Sector: 1973-74/1998-99**

Year	TRADITIONAL SECTOR (TS)				MODERN SECTOR
	Khadi (Million Sq.Mts.)	Handloom (Million Sq. Mts.)	Sericulture (Lakh Kgs. of Raw Silk)	Coir (Lakh Tonnes of Fibre)	Powerloom (Million Sq.Mts.)
1	**2**	**3**	**4**	**5**	**6**
1973-74	56.00	2100	29.00	1.50	2400
1979-80	82.00	2900	48.00	1.85	3450
1980-81	91.01	3100	50.41	1.59	3440
1981-82	96.42	3136	52.49	1.70	3797
1982-83	107.91	3253	57.00	1.74	3871
1983-84	127.29	3400	64.23	1.75	4432
1984-85	127.82	3600	76.70	1.64	4930
1985-86	108.58	3236	78.97	1.83	5886
1986-87	106.42	3449	89.00	1.85	6222
1987-88	114.68	3508	94.98	1.95	6457
1988-89	108.53	3466	106.53	1.90	7008
1989-90	107.47	4155	120.16	2.02	9788
1990-91	109.00	4888	128.36	2.11	12337
1991-92	111.00	4123	117.40	2.20	16089
1992-93	105.00	5219	139.00	2.29	17826
1993-94	108.00	5440	151.96	2.40	18482
1994-95	94.00	6180	150.45	2.45	20100
1995-96	105.00	7202	139.09	2.63	17201
1996-97	111.00	7456	141.26	2.76	19352
1997-98	104.20	7603	152.36	2.96	20951
1998-99	113.30	6792	155.44	3.14	20690
Compound Growth Rate (per cent)					
1973-85	7.8	5.0	9.2	0.8	6.8
1984-90	-1.3	4.3	9.6	2.8	8.9
1990-99*	0.1	7.2	2.5	5.0	5.0

Note: 1. Compound Growth Rates have been computed on point-to-point basis and are rough indicators of the changing magnitudes.

2. * Growth Rate has been computed through semi-log curve.

Source: Same as in Table 2.1A.

sericulture and coir in the traditional sector, and powerloom in the modern sector. The Khadi could not recover its verve during the nineties as well; the relative stagnation shown by the Khadi during 1984-85/1989-90 got further intensified during the nineties. In fact, Khadi was the only sub-sector that staged a backward march, on year-to-year basis, ever since we entered into the later half of the eighties. It was a clear signal of its sufferance on the productivity front inasmuch as the growth rate of employment too behaved bearishly during all these years. In net terms, Khadi is the only visible worry spot, most distressingly because it is no more able to take on additional hands, even on part-time basis.

Let us revert to Table 2.1. A striking contrast between the traditional and modern sub-sectors is that unlike in the earlier two decades, during the 1990s, the gap between the output and employment growth rates has tended to narrow down relatively much more in the case of the former, while it has tended to widen in respect of the modern small scale industries sub-sector. It is not surprising, therefore, that in the case of the small scale modern industries, growth rate of productivity/ worker increased from 2.9 per cent in 1973-74/84-85 to a high of 6.5 per cent in 1984-85/89-90, and to a all-time high of 11.9 per cent during 1990-91/98-99. For khadi, the corresponding figures were 3.0, 4.3 and a low of 2.5 per cent per annum.

The close correspondence between growth of output and employment, in the case of some of the traditional sub-sectors, was due presumably to the compulsions of taking on additional working hands from within the family; alternative employment opportunities are not so easy to come by, especially for workers engaged for long spells in the traditional industries, especially khadi, handloom, village industries, sericulture, etc. For them, alternative skills and education are big constraints.

Table 2.1 also shows the changing relative importance of individual segments of the VSI sector (Cols. 2 to 11 as a percentage of Col.12, both in Sub-Tables 2.1A and 2.1B). As is expected, the modern sector accounts for a lion's share of output while the bulk of employment is offered by the traditional sector. In the modern sector, both output and employment shares have expanded while the opposite has happened with the traditional sector. It seems that the traditional sector is being pushed to a corner as far as its share in output is concerned; in 1998-99, it had to contend with a mere 8.00 per cent share in output against as high as a 59.14 per cent share in employment; way back in 1993-74, the two figures were 19.21 per cent and 67.28 per cent, respectively. The implications towards productivity levels should thus be clear. *Over time, the traditional rural industries have steadily lost their ground to modern small-scale industries, whether located in the rural or urban areas.* Interestingly, the powerloom sub-sector seems to have been an absorber of many additional working hands even while losing tremendously in its share in output. Thus, as said earlier, in de facto terms, productivity/worker profile in the powerloom sub-sector has put it more in the league of traditional sub-sectors rather than modern small-scale industries.

An especially distressing picture emerges for the handloom sector where in 1998-99, a mere 1.26 per cent share in output was accompanied by as high as a 27.06 per cent share in VSI employment; in 1973-74, the two shares were 7.39 per cent and 34.30 per cent, respectively. This sub-sector seems to serve as a dumping ground for a lot of additional labour force, presumably because alternative employment opportunities are not available to those already engaged in it, especially to those weavers who have been in the craft for a long time and primarily due to lack of education and alternative skills, cannot shift to other jobs. What explains the weakening of this sub-sector during the past decade or so?

The khadi sector has been losing its ground even more precipitously, and that too, both from output and employment angles. For example, in 1973-74, it had as small a share in VSI output as 0.29 per cent only, against a 5.79 per cent share in employment; in 1990-91, the output share declined to a negligible level of 0.14 per cent, against 3.33 per cent share in employment; and finally, in 1998-99, the output share was a ridiculously small figure of 0.08 per cent, against a 2.35 per cent share of employment. From the above figures, the decline in khadi's share of employment does not look terrifying, but taking account of the fact that nearly 70.0 per cent of the khadi workers are part-time workers only, the real decline would indeed be steeper still if full-time equivalent of part-time workers could somehow be ascertained.

While the inherent weaknesses of the handloom sector cannot be wished away, the economic tug of wag incessantly going on since the 1960s between the handloom and powerloom sectors has played a decisive role in the secular decline of the former. The history of textile industry points to a number of policy slants, especially those connected with price of yarn and chemical dyes, working against the handloom sector; the mill-sector lobby, working in league with powerloom lobby, on the one hand, and, the lackadaisical and disinterested administrative responses, on the other hand, have brought about the gradual squeeze of the handloom sector. Its future seems equally grim because, *inter alia*, it suffers from technological and commercial weaknesses of its own and because the handloom weavers are not an organized forum with a significant reckoning (Srinivasulu, 1994:2332-33).

In total terms, looking back to the past three decades, it is fairly obvious that, by and large, the traditional rural industries have acquitted themselves well in fulfilling their avowed objective of providing employment to the expanding army of rural labour-force. In the context of wide-spread rural poverty, especially that occasioned by the rising incidence of rural landlessness and marginalization of land holdings, on the one hand, and under- (if not un-) employment of a big mass of rural workforce, on the other, it has not been a trivial development. Yet, from the point of view rural poverty, a more lucrative employment status, most essentially in terms of high productivity and earning levels, is an inescapable pre-condition. Unluckily, expansion in productivity nowhere seems to have been in sight, either during 1973-74/1984-85 or during 1990- 91/1998-99. This was largely so because employment growth closely chased, and in some sub-sectors (most notably, the khadi sub-sector) exceeded, output growth, during the 1990s. The periodic up- and down-swings in production has been another noticeable feature of some among the traditional industry groups including khadi. The modern sector offers a contrast. The picture about the small scale industries is fairly satisfactory in the sense that production and employment grew at satisfying rates, practically during each of the three sub-periods, a two- year slack during 1991-92 and 1992-93 notwithstanding; improving levels of productivity clearly followed here which, unfortunately, was not at all the case for most of the traditional sub-sectors, most certainly the khadi textile segment.

In sum, it is clear that, of late, the khadi sector has not been doing well; other traditional sub-sectors such as handloom, sericulture and other village industries (except handicrafts) too have been posing problems, most notably the decline in the level of per worker productivity. All these sub-sectors, including khadi, pale into insignificance in the matter of labour absorption, output growth, productivity expansion, etc., in comparison with modern small-scale industries. The house of khadi thus poses questions about its future survivability, especially in the context of the liberalized market regime that has been operating since 1991. Perhaps, more firm ideas about the status of employment of people engaged in the khadi sector, and the future employment prospects that await them in the near future, could be framed if we look at khadi's position and its relative strengths and weaknesses vis-a-vis its competitive counterpart, namely the textile industry as such. This follows next in Section 3.

3. Khadi in the Textile Industry

Textile industry in India is both important and complex. Nearly 20.0 per cent of the value added in the manufacturing sector is contributed by the textile sector alone. The sector contributes 4-5 per cent to G.D.P. and about one-third to total export earnings. It provides employment to millions of skilled and semi-skilled workers, a sizeable proportion of whom are from rural areas. The complexity of the sector arises due to a wide diversity of production scale, technological outfits, market linkages, discernible all along the production continuum. There are four major sub-sectors that constitute the production continuum. These are (a) textile mills, (b) powerlooms, (c) handlooms, and (d) khadi. Down the production line, there are millions of spinners, weavers, artisans and farmers. Amongst the four sub-sectors, only mills and khadi segments are engaged in spinning operations; the other two segments perform only weaving activity after purchasing yarn produced by the mill sector. In respect of the fibre specific configuration, the product range comprises cotton, jute, wool, silk, and other man-made fibres. The khadi sector is largely engaged in cotton textiles although silk and woollens have also been the other noticeable product lines. Since the early eighties, a refined version of cotton textile, called muslin, has also come into existence.

The technologies employed by textile mills and by the khadi sector are not comparable in speed and output. Nonetheless, apart from other technological improvements effected in the khadi sector, from time to time, the most noticeable has been the introduction of the improved spinning wheels (called New Amber/ Model Charkhas with varying numbers of spindles). For the production of textiles in general, there is an intricate interplay of the processes which include ginning, reeling, spinning, weaving and garment manufacture. Expressly, for the production of khadi textiles, the processes vary from product to product. For example, the production of cotton khadi involves pre-spinning, spinning, pre-weaving, weaving and post-weaving operations. There has been a change in the character of employment provided by the khadi over the years, mainly due to the introduction of new technologies, the general preference for a workshed type of organisation and the growing importance of post-weaving activities such as dyeing, printing and finishing.

It is thus clear that the khadi sector is one of the (rather small) segments of the textile industry. From all conceivable angles, the khadi sector has never been a challenge to the rest of the partners in the industry. On the contrary, it has steadfastly tried to maintain a small production and marketing niche for itself, largely for relieving the economic stress caused by un- and under- employment of millions of rural artisans and other unskilled or semi-skilled workers. Let us look into the relative position of the major partners involved in fabric production during the nineties.

3.1 Khadi and Other Sectors in Fabrics Production

Table 3.1 clearly shows that the mill sector has witnessed a continuous decline during the nineties. On the contrary, powerlooms and handlooms sectors have grown fairly impressively since 1991-92; a growth rate of fabric production to the tune of 9-10 per cent per annum, for the nineties, is not a trivial development. But then, the khadi sector has hardly witnessed any progress in its production graph; its production grew merely by 0.25 per cent per annum during 1991-92/1997-98. By all reckoning, it has been a dismal performance.

The varying pattern of output growth among the textile sectors has been responsible for changing their relative share in output. For example, the output share of the mill sector has shrunk from 10.3 per cent in 1991-92 to as low as 5.2 per cent in 1997-98 while the share of the powerloom sector, which was already as high as 69.9 per cent in 1991-92, rose further to 73.0 per cent by 1997-98. Likewise, the output share of the handloom sector too went up from 17.9 per cent in 1991-92 to 20.3 per cent in 1997-98. Germane to our study is the disturbing trend of khadi's steeply declining share in total production of fabrics; it had a mere 0.47 per cent share in 1991-92 which got reduced to 0.28 per cent only 1997-98. The situation does not improve if we add khadi's share of output to that of wool and silk (the latter two are categorized as **'others'** in Table 3.1). The decline is equally persistent for the three of them put together, from 1.86 per cent in 1991-92 to 1.44 per cent in 1997-98.

TABLE 3.1 : **Production of Fabrics in India : 1991-92/97-98**

Year	Production (in million sq. mts.)					
	Mills	Powerlooms	Handlooms	Khadi	Others	Total
1	**2**	**3**	**4**	**5**	**6**	**7**
1991-92	2367	16089	4123	109	320	23008
1992-93	2000	17826	5219	105	325	25475
1993-94	1990	19631	5851	98	328	27898
1994-95	2271	197 24	6180	91	340	28606
1995-96	2019	22239	7202	105	393	31958
1996-97	1967	24885	7456	112	428	34848
1997-98	1948	27344	7604	104	436	37436
Growth Rate (%)						
1991-92/97-98*	-2.03	9.02	10.10	0.25	5.93	8.04
Share in Output (%)						
1991-92	10.29	69.93	17.92	0.47	1.39	100.0
1992-93	7.85	69.97	20.49	0.41	1.28	100.0
1993-94	7.13	70.37	-20.97	0.35	1.18	100.0
1994-95	7.94	68.95	21.60	0.32	1.19	100.0
1995-96	6.32	69.59	22.54	0.33	1.23	100.0
1996-97	5.64	71.41	21.40	0.32	1.23	100.0
1997-98	5.20	73.04	20.31	0.28	1.16	100.0

Note: * Growth Rate has been computed through semi-log curve.

Source: 1. Govt. of India, Economice Survey, Ministry of Finance, 1998-99, p. 109.
2. KVIC, Statistical Abstract, Directorate of Economic Research, Mumbai, 1998. pp. 84-85.

It may look ironical that some of the problems that have been plaguing the mill sector have also been at work in the khadi sector. For example, product quality and cost efficiency are reported to be the two most baffling problems of the textile industry, especially after the onset of the open trade and liberalised economic regime in 1991. The khadi sector has been facing the cost and pricing problem almost on a perpetual basis. Ironically again, while the government is taking some initiatives, for example, Cotton Technology Mission to improve productivity and quality of cotton, and Technology Upgradation Fund to address the problem of technology obsolescence, particularly in the weaving and processing sectors of the industry, specific policy initiatives to redress the problems of the khadi sector are not in sight (Govt. of India, 1999: 108).

3.2 Cotton Khadi in Cotton Textile Industry

Cotton khadi constitutes an overwhelming proportion of total khadi production and provides employment to a pre-ponderant majority of khadi workers. It may be worthwhile looking at the position of cotton khadi also in the cotton textile industry as such. Table 3.2 again poses some disturbing elements in respect of the khadi segment just as it does for the mill sector.

Growth rate of production, which picked up very well from a negligible of 0.12 per cent per annum during the sixties to 4.82 per cent per annum during the seventies, slumped down to just 1.14 per cent per annum during the eighties, and slumped down further to a negative of 0.78 per cent per annum during the nineties. By all reckoning, it has been a highly unsatisfactory performance, especially during the nineties. The mill sector has shared the same trend, although more distressing in terms of sharper declines and nominal recoveries. In sharp contrast, the decentralized sector (that largely comprises the powerloom and the handloom segments) has been doing remarkably better, most noticeably during the eighties.

The most striking feature is the remarkable restructuring that has been going on in the cotton textile industry since the sixties. Its most convincing characteristic is the steeply declining share of output contributed by the mill and khadi segments and the steeply increasing share of the decentralized sector. In 1960-61, the mill sector had a commanding share of 69.0 per cent in the total output which gradually went on declining in the subsequent years, ultimately reaching such as low as 9.74 per cent in 1997-98. Likewise, the khadi sector too lost heavily in its share of output. And, as in the case of total textile production (Table 3.1 above), the decentralized sector witnessed a phenomenal increase in its share of the output from 31.0 per cent in 1960-61 to as high as 90.3 per cent in 1997-98. It would not be wrong to say that, at present, it is the decentralized sector which sums up the beginning and the end of the cotton as well as the total textile industry in the Indian economy. The khadi sector is indeed a meek partner, both in the cotton sub-sector as well as in the textile production as a whole. Should this prompt us to dismiss khadi as an irrelevant entity in the textile regime? Our reply is in the negative, for reasons of employment, if not of output. The khadi sector is a big provider of employment.

TABLE 3.2 : **Production of Cotton Cloth in India (Million Sq. Mts.)**

Year	Mill Sector	Decentralized Sector		Total
		Total	Khadi	
1	**2**	**3**	**4**	**5**
1960-61	4649	2089	49.06	6738
1970-71	4055	3547	49.63	7602
1980-81	3434	4934	79.48	8368
1985-86	2716	9751	87.04	12467
1990-91	1859	13572	89	15431
1991-92	1651	12996	89.77	14647
1992-93	1453	11601	85.36	13054
1993-94	1990	15800	80.82	17790
1994-95	2271	14748	73.8	17019
1995-96	2019	16881	84.97	18900
1996-97	1957	17884	89.08	19841
1997-98	1948	18044	84.24	19992
Annual Compound Growth Rate (%)				
1960-61/70-71	-1.36	5.44	0.12	1.21
1970-71/80-81	-1.65	3.36	4.82	0.96
1980-81/90-91	-5.95	10.65	1.14	6.31
1990-91/97-98*	0.67	4.15	-0.78	3.77
Share of the Sector in Total Production				
1960-61	69.00	31.00	0.73	100.00
1970-71	53.34	46.66	0.65	100.00
1980-81	41.04	58.96	0.95	100.00
1990-91	12.05	87.95	0.58	100.00
1997-98	9.74	90.26	0.42	100.00

Note: * Growth Rate has been computed through semi-log curve.

Source: 1. Govt. of India, Economice Survey, Ministry of Finance, 1998-99, p. S-35.

2. KVIC, Statistical Abstract, Directorate of Economic Research, Mumbai, 1998, pp. 85-85.

3.3 Khadi Employment against Total Employment in the Textile Industry

Table 3.3 gives us some clues about the magnitude of employment in the mill sector against that in the khadi sector, both under cotton textiles, and, wool and silk fabrics. It is interesting to see that the khadi sector has been showing a matching performance in providing employment, most conspicuously in the wool and silk sector during the seventies, eighties and the first few years of the nineties.

In the cotton sector too, its performance has improved steadily over time. In plain terms, it is interesting to see that while the khadi's share in output, in total textile production or in sector-wise production, has been declining steadily (Table 3.2), its share in employment has been improving steadily over time (Table 3.3). The khadi sector almost looks like a residual sector where employment can expand just around the time that other sectors put up 'no entry signals' to the expanding army of rural workers and artisans. It is, however, a different matter that a preponderant majority of khadi workers are engaged on part-time basis only, and accordingly, to their share, a very small proportion of the industry-wise earnings would accrue. Poverty and low-level of living are thus the endemic characteristics of their existence. We have concrete empirical evidence, in Section 4 below, to show extremely low levels of productivity and earnings in respect of the part-time khadi workers.

TABLE 3.3 : **Employment in Cotton, Wool and Silk Textiles by Production Sector : 1971/93**

(Persons in Lakhs)

Year	Cotton Textiles			Wool and Silk		
	Mill Sector	Khadi Sector	K:M Ratio	Mill Sector	Khadi Sector	K:M Ratio
1	**2**	**3**	**4**	**5**	**6**	**7**
1971	9.44	7.94	0.84	1.47	1.48	1.00
1981	11.88	9.72	0.82	1.92	2.34	1.22
1991	10.75	10.65	0.99	2.53	2.81	1.11
1992	10.75	10.67	0.99	2.74	2.85	1.04
1993	10.66	10.76	1.01	2.75	3.00	1.09
Annual Compound Growth Rate (%)						
1971/81	2.33	2.04		2.71	4.69	
1981/93	-0.99	0.92		2.80	1.85	
1971/93	0.00	0.02		0.80	0.14	

Note: K= Khadi Sector, M= Mill Sector.

Source: 1. Govt. of India, Statistical Abstract India, CSO, 1997, Dec. 1997, pp. 389-90.
2. KVIC, Statistical Abstract, Directorate of Economic Research, July 1998, pp. 170-176.

4. Khadi by Production Sectors

As noted above, the khadi sector consists of four product lines, viz., cotton, silk, woolen, and muslin. The oldest among the four product lines is cotton-khadi for which we have the production profile right from 1953-54 onwards; silk- and woollen-khadi joined cotton-khadi around mid-sixties while muslin, a refined version of cotton-khadi was introduced only in 1982.

Production and employment in the four sectors have had their own vicissitudes. There have been periods of high growth rate of production and/or employment followed by periods of slow-down and subsequent recoveries. The recent years seem to have been rather hard on most of them; the opening up of the Indian economy to world production, trade and technology systems, firstly under the aegis of the 1991 economic reforms and then under the WTO regime since 1995, seems to be affecting, *albeit indirectly,* the khadi sector just as it is bringing in more formidable changes in many other production lines, and so on. The present section looks at the temporal profile of production and employment of each of the four khadi sectors; the stresses of the recent years come up neat and bold.

4.1 Changing Composition of the Khadi Sector

Table 4.1 shows the relative position of each sector. While sector-wise output figures are available right from 1953-54 onwards, employment figures are available for cotton, wool and silk together till 1966-67 whereafter these are published separately for each product line. Then, to have a more firm (and stable) view of the changing composition, three-yearly averages have been taken for various time-points, beginning with 1953-54 and ending with 1998-99. Table 4.1 throws up two interesting features.

First, cotton-khadi was summarily the beginning and the end of the total khadi sector. during the fifties; woollen and silk were marginal entities while muslin was conspicuous by its absence. Gradually, woollen- and silk-khadi gained more eminence in the khadi sector. Among the newly emerging areas for woollen-khadi, the major locales were Rajasthan, Uttar Pradesh, Punjab, Jammu-Kashmir and Maharashtra, while for the silk-khadi, such major locales were West Bengal, Tamil Nadu, Bihar, Karnataka and Assam. Of course, cotton-khadi continued to dominate in each area. Consequently, cotton-khadi is still the most dominant component, both from production and employment points of view. Because of its over-bearing position in the khadi sector, cotton-khadi has been the major source of policy attention by the KVIC, although silk- and woollen-khadi too have been engaging more rigorous and region-specific policy attention and support during the past two decades or so (KVIC, 1998: 15-21).

Second, looking at the output and employment shares, one may be tempted to concluded that, among the four production segments, cotton is relatively less labour-intensive; woollen-khadi appears to be the most labour-intensive. That may well be the case but a more firm judgement of the kind can be framed only when the division between the full-time and part-time workers is known in terms of precise work-hours per day. This information is just not available. Instead, what is

TABLE 4.1 : **Share of Each Khadi Sub-Sector on the Basis of Value of Production and Employment (%)**

Period	Item	Cotton	Woollen	Silk	Muslin	Total Khadi
1	2	3	4	5	6	7
1953-56	O	94.73	3.77	1.63	-	100.00
	E	-	-	-	-	-
1959-62	O	91.77	6.15	2.08	-	100.00
	E	-	-	-	-	-
1969-72	O	87.04	10.01	2.95	-	100.00
	E	85.49	11.45	2.16	-	100.00
1979-82	O	86.22	10.35	3.42	-	100.00
	E	78.47	17.14	4.39	-	100.00
1989-92	O	81.96	9.94	4.73	3.37	100.00
	E	75.14	17.78	4.87	2.21	100.00
1996-99	O	80.42	9.77	6.90	2.19	100.00
	E	75.56	16.71	5.72	1.94	100.00

Note: O= Output, E= Employment.
Source: KVIC, Statistical Abstract, Directorate of Economic Research, Mumbai, 1998.

known (see Table 4.2 below) is the division between full-time and part-time workers which varies substantially among the four segments. Our view about the differing level of labour intensity among the four segments is, therefore, not more than a mere conjecture.

4.2 Composition of Khadi Employment

Table 4.2 gives a few important insights about the composition of employment in the khadi sector. First, in each of the four segments, the share of the part-time workers is fairly substantial. In woollen-khadi, the proportion of part-time workers was as high as 85.1 per cent in 1998-99, followed by 68.1 per cent in cotton-khadi and 57.6 per cent in silk-khadi; in muslin-khadi, part-time workers are totally absent. The very high incidence of part-time employment is the real hall-mark of the khadi sector where people are encouraged to take up specific production tasks to their living abodes, on contract or piece wage rate basis, so that some bit of supplementary employment and earnings accrue to them at their very door step. The most conspicuous example of part-time employment is provided by

TABLE 4.2 : **Composition of Employment in Khadi Sector : 1998-99**

Item Description	Production Sector				
	Cotton	Muslin	Woollen	Silk	Total
1	**2**	**3**	**4**	**5**	**6**
1. Employment (Persons in Lakhs)					
a) Full Time	3.33	0.27	0.34	0.34	4.30
	(31.9)	(100.0)	(14.9)	(42.4)	(31.0)
b) Part Time	7.12	-	1.94	0.49	9.55
	(68.1)	-	(85.1)	(57.6)	(69.0)
c) Total	10.45	0.27	2.28	0.85	13.85
	(100.0)	(100.0)	(100.0)	(100.0)	(100.0)
2. % of Schedule Castes/ Tribes Employed	24.67	7.40	30.10	22.37	25.12
3. % of Women Employees (in Spinning)	75.14	63.0	39.47	58.47	70.16

Note: Figures in parentheses are percentage shares.
Source: KVIC, Annual Report 1998-99, Directorate of Economic Research, pp. 9-14.

female workers who are overwhelmingly engaged in the spinning operation in each sector; more than three-fourths of spinning workers engaged in cotton-khadi are women. The proportion of women workers is much lower in the woollen-khadi sector.

Second, typical of the Gandhian tradition of helping the under-privileged in the rural society, quite a sizeable proportion of workers belonging to scheduled castes and scheduled tribe households are also engaged in the khadi sectors; their presence is rather marginal in the muslin sector.

4.3 Output and Employment Growth in Khadi

To portray the long temporal profiles of khadi production and khadi employment respectively, we drew graphs (not reproduced here) for each of the four khadi segments. We discover that alternating phases of expanding and contracting trends have been at work. For example, keeping aside the year-to-year ups and downs, production of cotton- and total-khadi clearly showed an expanding phase from 1953-54 to the middle of sixties, a contracting trend thereafter till the middle of the seventies, again a phase of expanding trend till we reach the late 1980s and finally a declining trend during the nineties. In contrast, the wollen-khadi, starting from a very low base in 1953-54, grew impressively till the early sixties, and put up alternating trends in the subsequent periods. The same is more or less true of silk-khadi while muslin-khadi hardly picked up since 1982-83.

Likewise, the employment profile shows its own phases, most demonstrably in respect of cotton-khadi and total-khadi. Interestingly, there is no one-to-one correspondence between the delineated expanding/contracting phases on the production side with those on the employment side; for example, for some years, production in a sector was falling while employment was not. We thought it advisable, therefore, to look at the growth rates for employment in two different ways: once for the same sub-periods as for production, and once in terms of the delineated phases from the graphs. Table 4.3 thus gives us two sets of growth rates for employment against one for production. Let us look at the expanding and contracting phases for production and employment. First, a look on the production side.

Till about the mid-sixties, production expanded rather impressively in cotton-, woollen- and silk-khadi sectors. But then, a reverse trend set in and lasted till about mid-seventies in respect of cotton-khadi and silk-khadi, and till about the close of sixties in respect of woollen-khadi. Cotton-khadi looked up again during the period 1975-76/1987-88, woollen-khadi during the period 1968-69/1986-87 and silk-khadi during the period 1975-76/1997-98. Muslin-khadi registered a modest growth rate of 1.58 per cent per annum in its production for the lone period 1982-83/1998-99. And then, production of cotton-khadi and woollen-khadi faced a decline, albeit small, during the decade ending 1998-99.

With hardly any exception, the phases of expanding output do have their counterparts on the employment side, and vice versa for phases of declining output. This is true whether we look at employment growth rates for the same sub-periods as for output growth, or, for slightly differing sub-periods. In any case, it is absolutely clear that the recent decade or so has witnessed no employment growth, in cotton-khadi, woollen-khadi, muslin-khadi and total-khadi, primarily because the production scenario too has been rather depressing. The two major khadi sectors viz. cotton and woollen, clearly stand out as worry spots.

4.4 Employment and Earnings in Khadi Sectors

As pointed out above, production estimates for individual khadi sectors are available right from 1953-54 onwards, while employment estimates are available only since 1967-68. Unluckily, comparable sector-wise information on earnings is available only from 1989-90 onwards. We can thus build production-employment-earnings profile for individual khadi sectors only for a decade or so, commencing 1989-90. This is attempted in this sub-section. Production figures in each of the khadi sectors are expressed both in physical terms (quantity in lakh sq. mts.) and

TABLE 4.3 : **Growth of Output and Employment in Khadi Sector (%)**

Output		Employment			
Period	Growth Rate*	Period	Growth Rate*	Period	Growth Rate*
1	**2**	**3**	**4**	**5**	**6**
Cotton					
1953-54/1965-66	15.99				
1965-66/1975-76	-4.02	1965-66/1975-76	6.94	1967-68/1975-76	-6.94
1975-76/1987-88	5.86	1975-76/1987-88	4.55	1975-76/1987-88	4.55
1987-88/1998-99	-1.23	1987-88/1998-99	-0.03	1987-88/1998-99	-0.03
Woollen					
1953-54/1963-64	30.99				
1963-64/1968-69	-10.98				
1968-69/1986-87	5.03	1968-69/1986-87	5.91	1967-68/1979-80	9.41
1986-87/1998-99	-0.88	1986-87/1998-99	-0.39	1979-80/1998-99	0.88
Silk					
1953-54/1965-66	25.33				
1965-66/1975-76	-1.66			1967-68/1987-88	8.16
1975-76/1998-99	5.39	1975-76/1998-99	3.44	1987-88/1998-99	0.90
Muslin					
1982-83/1998-99	0.85	1982-83/1998-99	-0.26	1982-83/1998-99	-0.26
Total Khadi					
1953-54/1965-66	16.65	1953-54/1965-66	13.79	1953-54/1965-66	13.79
1965-66/1975-76	-3.40	1965-66/1975-76	-7.59	1965-66/1975-76	-7.59
1975-76/1987-88	6.00	1975-76/1987-88	4.72	1975-76/1987-88	4.72
1987-88/1998-99	-0.94	1987-88/1998-99	-0.08	1987-88/1998-99	-0.08

Note: * Growth Rate has been computed through semi-log curve.

Source: 1. KVIC, Statistical Abstract, Directorate of Economic Research, Mumbai, 1998.

2. KVIC, Annual Report, 1998-99, Directorate of Economic Research, Mumbai, 1999.

value terms (Rs. in lakhs, at constant 1981-82 prices, using All-India Index of Wholesale Prices for Khadi Cloth; Govt. of India, 1998: 453-54).

4.4.1 Employment and Earnings in Cotton-Khadi

Table 4.4 throws up many interesting features in respect of cotton-khadi. First, production in physical terms fell annually by 0.89 per cent during the decade 1989-90/1998-99. In value terms, it fell as steeply as 6.19 per cent per annum. It clearly points to a relatively higher movement of prices in respect of khadi products compared with, say, textile products in general, especially during the concluding 2-3 years of this decade which, by implication, would depress the value of output much more substantially when we switch over from current to constant prices. Higher levels of khadi prices is duly confirmed by the uneven movement of price indices for khadi cloth against textiles in general. For example, the Index Numbers of Wholesale Prices (Base: 1981-82=100) for Textiles stood at 114.8 in 1982-83, 119.5 in 1985-86, 294.6 in 1995-96 against 108.2, 148.4 and 439.1 for Khadi Cloth (Govt. of India, 1998: 454). In a broad sense, therefore, it is the higher levels of prices that clog the demand and production levels in khadi.

Second, employment of full-time workers increased meekly by 0.36 per cent per annum while there was no increase, whatsoever, in respect of the part-time workers. The past decade has thus been quite depressing as far as employment is concerned (see also Table 4.3 above).

Third, more depressing has been a steep decline in the level of real earnings (better call them 'wages') of both the full- and part-time workers. It is extraordinarily depressing to see the real earnings of full-time workers tumbling down by as much as 7.38 per cent per annum, and of part-time workers by as much as 10.57 per cent per annum. The per worker earnings of part-time workers are many times lower than those of their full-time counterparts understandably because of difference in work-hours. The earning differences, however, defy all limits of work-hour differences. In plain terms, employment of part-time workers engaged in cotton-khadi, a preponderant majority of whom comprise females very largely engaged in spinning, on piece wage basis, reflects **anything but decent employment.** It is not at all implied that full-time workers enjoy decent standards of employment; far from it. Our stress on the paltry earnings of the part-time workers is to suggest that cotton-khadi employment is availed of by as many as 70 improve their living standards. Poverty among them is thus bound to stay pretty high.

It is worth pointing out that the downswing commenced only in 1993-94. Until 1992-93, production in physical as well as (real) value terms, total as well as per worker earnings (or wages!), both for full- and part-time workers, looked up steadily, on year-to- year basis. It is only during the past 5-6 years since 1993-94 that everything seems to have gone out of hand. The precipitous decline in value of output and earnings need to be underlined in particular. It seems the arrival of new economic regime, open trade policy, squeeze on financial/budgetary support to the khadi sector, etc. have been the events that have worked together to cause an all-round decline.

4.4.2 Employment and Earnings in Woollen-Khadi

Table 4.5 unfolds the story of woollen-khadi, precisely on the lines of what Table 4.4 did earlier for cotton-khadi. In a broad qualitative sense, it is the same story for woollen-khadi, as we have seen above (Section 4.4.1) for cotton-khadi. In fact, here the employment of part-time workers declined by 1.45 per cent per annum during 1989-90/98-99 while under cotton-khadi, employment witnessed no change for the above period. It is equally disappointing here, as it was under cotton-khadi, to see a substantial decline in total as well as per worker earnings of not only part-time but also of full-time workers. Again, the story of the steadily declining fortune of woollen-khadi since 1993-94, in tersm of (real) value of output as well as earnings, against a steady expansion till 1992-93, is commonly shared with cotton-khadi. Perhaps, the only comfort, if it could indeed be so termed , is that the level of per worker earnings, on a more firm and comparable basis in respect of full-time workers, is slightly higher in woollen-khadi than in cotton-khadi; the abysmally low levels in both cannot, however, escape anybody's notice.

4.4.3 Employment and Earnings in Khadi-Silk

The post-1989 details for silk-khadi are given in Table 4.6. Silk-khadi throws up a mixture of similarities and dissimilarities with cotton-khadi (Table 4.4) and woollen-khadi (Table 4.5). On the side of similarities, value of output as well as total and per worker earnings witnessed a varying degree of decline during the period 1989-90/1998-99. Again, as in cotton- and woollen-khadi, the decline in the real earnings of the part-time workers was far too higher than that witnessed for full-time workers. Yet again, the steady expansion till 1992-93, and a steady decline thereafter in real value of output, and total as well as per worker earnings (both for full- and part-time workers), is equally discernible for silk-khadi.

On the side of dissimilarities, first, compared with cotton-khadi and woollen-khadi, the decline in real value of output as well as total and per worker earnings, was milder here; the difference in terms of the value of output needs to be underlined in particular. Second, unlike the decline in employment, both in cotton- and woollen-khadi, silk-khadi registered a sizeable growth (4.35 per cent per annum) of employment for full-time workers, and a moderate growth (1.18 per cent per annum) for part-time workers. Third, the level of per worker earnings, both for full-time and part-time workers, has been higher than their respective counterparts in cotton and woollen-khadi; during the 1990s, the differences between silk-khadi and cotton/woollen-khadi have, however, narrowed. For example, for the average of 1989-92, the ratio of per worker earnings, in respect of full- time workers, in silk-khadi to that in cotton-khadi was 1.32:1.00 which, for the average of 1995-99, declined to 1.22:1.00; similar ratios between silk-khadi and woollen-khadi were 1.20:1.00 and 1.02:1.00.

TABLE 4.4 : **Production, Employment and Earnings of Cotton Khadi in India : 1989-90/98-99**

Year	Production		Employment (in lakhs)			Earning (in Rs. Lakhs, at 1981-82 Prices)			Earnings Per Worker (Rs.)		Share of Full Time Workers in (%)	
	Quantity (lakhs sq. mts.)	Value (in Rs. lakhs)	Full Time	Part Time	Total	Full Time	Part Time	Total	Full Time	Part Time	Employ-ment	Earnings
1	**2**	**3**	**4**	**5**	**6**	**7**	**8**	**9**	**10**	**11**	**12**	**13**
1989-90	879.65	10080 90	3 09	7.50	10.59	5487.99	896.43	6384.41	1776.05	119.52	29.18	85.96
1990-91	890.04	11163.46	3.41	7.24	10 65	6058.19	775.20	6833.39	1776.60	107.07	32.02	88.66
1991-92	897.73	12938.61	3.32	7.35	10 67	6788.26	1065.27	7853.53	2044.66	144.93	31.12	86.44
1992-93	853.56	13711.92	3.37	7.39	10.76	7176.58	1133.02	8309.60	2129.55	153.32	31.32	86.36
1993-94	808.18	10803.87	3.19	7.19	10.38	5979.61	836.64	6816.25	1874.48	116.36	30.73	87.73
1994-95	738.00	6466.80	3.18	6.83	10 01	3498 15	476.23	3974.38	1100.05	69.73	31.77	88.02
1995-96	849.70	6808.39	3.33	7.28	10.61	3321.57	477.11	3798.68	997.47	65.54	31.39	87.44
1996-97	890.80	7704 53	3.49	7.69	11 18	3538.94	539.16	4078.10	1014.02	70.11	31.22	86.78
1997-98	842.40	7707.66	3.27	7.35	10.62	3739.44	518.07	4257.51	1143.56	70.49	30.79	87.83
1998-99	791.20	7438.09	3.33	7.12	10.45	3856.75	328.11	4184.86	1158.18	46.08	31.87	92.16
Rate of Growth (%)												
1989-90/92-93*	-1.00	10.80	2.93	-0.49	0.53	9.35	8.12	9.18	6.24	8.65		
1992-93/98-99*	-1.26	-9.69	-0.20	-0.62	-0.49	-9.83	-18.66	-10.80	-9.65	-18.16		
1989-90/98-99**	-0.89	-6.19	0.36	-0.14	0.01	-7.38	-10.57	-7.73	-7.72	-10.44		

Note: * Growth rate has been estimated on point to point basis; ** Growth rate has been computed through semi-log curve.

Source:
1. KVIC, Annual Report, 1990-91, Dec. 1991, p. 5.
2. KVIC, Annual Report, 1992-93, Dec. 1992, pp. 69-73.
3. KVIC, Annual Report, 1993-94, Dec. 1994, pp. 78-81.
4. KVIC, Annual Report, 1994-95, Dec. 1995, pp. 78-84.
5. KVIC, Annual Report, 1996-97, Dec. 1997, pp. 5-9.
6. KVIC, Annual Report, 1997-98, Dec 1998, pp. 7-11.
7. KVIC, Annual Report, 1998-99, Dec. 1999.
8. Govt. of India, Statistical Abstract, CSO, 1998, p. 33.

TABLE 4.5 : **Production, Employment and Earnings of Khadi Wool in India : 1989-90/98-99**

Year	Production		Employment (in lakhs)			Earning (in Rs. Lakhs, at 1981-82 Prices)			Earnings Per Worker (Rs.)		Share of Full Time Workers in (%)	
	Quantity (lakhs sq. mts.)	Value (in Rs. lakhs)	Full Time	Part Time	Total	Full Time	Part Time	Total	Full Time	Part Time	Employ-ment	Earnings
1	**2**	**3**	**4**	**5**	**6**	**7**	**8**	**9**	**10**	**11**	**12**	**13**
1989-90	107.20	3474.31	0.33	2.20	2.53	635 38	408.15	1043.52	1925 39	185.52	13.04	60.89
1990-91	109.07	3806.08	0.36	2.14	2.50	643 69	514.27	1157.96	1788.04	240.31	14 40	55.59
1991-92	107.11	4348.46	0.30	2.22	2.52	721.71	566.85	1288.56	2405.71	255.34	11.90	56.01
1992-93	106.10	4457.02	0.35	2.30	2.65	909.76	567.09	1476.85	2599.33	246.56	13.21	61.60
1993-94	92.28	3398.29	0 34	2.17	2 51	793.15	484.21	1277.36	2332.79	223.14	13.55	62.09
1994-95	82.70	1844.32	0.33	1.88	2.21	439.80	235.41	675.21	1332.71	125.22	14 93	65.13
1995-96	95.80	1992.03	0 37	1 92	2 29	418.58	226.60	645.18	1131.31	118.02	16.16	64.88
1996-97	109.90	2457.60	0.38	2.11	2.49	519.25	273.23	792.48	1366.44	129.49	15.26	65.52
1997-98	98.60	2407.27	0.32	2.04	2.36	400.09	349.80	749.89	1250.27	171.47	13.56	53.35
1998-99	98.10	2537.80	0.34	1.94	2.28	446.35	348.04	794.39	1312.79	179.40	14.91	56.19
Rate of Growth (%)												
1989-90/92-93*	-0.34	8.66	1.98	1.49	1.56	12.71	11.59	12.27	10.52	9.95		
1992-93/98-99*	-1.21	-9.76	-1.48	-1.98	-1.91	-12.80	-7.74	-10.68	-11.48	-5.87		
1989-90/98-99**	-1.08	-6.97	0.46	-1.45	-1.18	-6.49	-6.59	-6.48	-6.92	-5.22		

Note: * Growth rate has been estimated on point to point basis; ** Growth rate has been computed through semi-log curve.

Source: Same as in Table 4.4.

TABLE 4.6 : **Production, Employment and Earnings of Khadi Wool in India : 1989-90/98-99**

Year	Production		Employment (in lakhs)			Earning (in Rs. Lakhs, at 1981-82 Prices)			Earnings Per Worker (Rs.)		Share of Full Time Workers in (%)	
	Quantity (lakhs sq. mts.)	Value (in Rs. lakhs)	Full Time	Part Time	Total	Full Time	Part Time	Total	Full Time	Part Time	Employ-ment	Earnings
1	2	3	4	5	6	7	8	9	10	11	12	13
1989-90	50.67	3088.48	0.23	0.47	0.70	526.58	216.52	743.09	2289.46	460.67	32.86	70.86
1990-91	53.27	3478.63	0.24	0.45	0.69	581.41	221.61	803.02	2422.53	492.47	34.78	72.40
1991-92	49.97	3915.55	0.24	0.44	0.68	636.56	232.36	868.92	2652.35	528.09	35.29	73.26
1992-93	54.33	4571.39	0.24	0.45	0.69	727.16	257.22	984.38	3029.83	571.60	34.78	73.87
1993-94	53.80	3548.92	0.24	0.41	0.65	621.91	187.86	809.78	2591.30	458.21	36.92	76.80
1994-95	57.60	2365.35	0.26	0.42	0.68	419.02	128.66	547.68	1611.60	306.35	38.24	76.51
1995-96	70.30	2640.95	0.29	0.49	0.78	398.77	134.14	532.91	1375.07	273.75	37.18	74.83
1996-97	79.40	3217.44	0.31	0.52	0.83	507.30	172.57	679.87	1636.45	331.86	37.35	74.62
1997-98	68.80	3016.98	0.28	0.48	0.76	510.67	170.66	681.32	1823.81	355.54	36.84	74.95
1998-99	68.3	3215.89	0.36	0.49	0.85	588.35	174.13	762.48	1634.30	355.36	42.35	77.16
Rate of Growth (%)												
1989-90/92-93*	2.35	13.96	1.43	-1 44	-0.48	11.36	5.91	9.83	9.79	7.46		
1992-93/98-99*	3.89	-5.69	6.99	1.43	3.54	-3.47	-6.30	-4.17	-9.78	-7.62		
1989-90/97-98**	4.73	-2.20	4.35	1.18	2.35	-1.95	-4.51	-2.62	-6.04	-5.62		

Note: * Growth rate has been estimated on point to point basis; ** Growth rate has been computed through semi-log curve.

Source: Same as in Table 4.4.

4..4.4 Employment and Earnings in Muslin-Khadi

Muslin-khadi is a very small segment of the khadi sector; in 1998-99, real value of output of muslin-khadi constituted just about 3.3 per cent of the total khadi output. It is important, however, to note that we have no part-time employment in this segment.

Table 4.7 shows an extremely displeasing scenario for this segment. Unlike the other three segments, employment (of full-time workers) has fared more poorly. The real disappointment, however, comes from the precipitous decline in real earnings (11.03 per cent per annum) and earnings per worker (9.26 per cent per annum). Equally disappointing is the level of per worker earning which is the lowest among all the four khadi segments.

4.4.5 Employment and Earnings in Total Khadi

Both in qualitative as well as quantitative terms, Table 4.8 portray the picture for total khadi almost identical with what Table 4.4 did earlier for cotton-

TABLE 4.7 : **Production, Employment and Earnings of Muslin Khadi in India : 1989-90/98-99**

Year	Production		Employment (in Lakhs) Full Time	Earnings (in Rs. Lakhs at 1981-82 Prices) Full Time	Earnings Per Worker (Rs.)
	Quantity (lakhs sq. mts)	Value (in Rs. Lakhs at 81-82 Prices)			
1	2	3	4	5	6
1989-90	37.17	733.43	0.30	423.42	1411.41
1990-91	36.47	820.71	0.31	420.03	1354.93
1991-92	36.13	942.46	0.33	500.54	1516.79
1992-93	38.64	999.75	0.35	515.14	1471.84
1993-94	29.98	722.53	0.33	368.53	1116.75
1994-95	30.10	417.02	0.29	213.49	736.18
1995-96	35.20	451.85	0.29	215.90	744.47
1996-97	34.80	478.91	0.29	216.15	745.35
1997-98	32.20	453.20	0.27	205.27	760.25
1998-99	24.40	427.29	0.27	196.40	727.41
Rate of Growth (%)					
1989-90/92-93*	1.30	10.88	5.27	6.75	1.41
1992-93/98-99*	-7.38	-13.21	-4.23	-14.85	-11.08
1989-90/98-99**	-3.056	-8.874	-1.953	-11.027	-9.256

Note: * Growth has been estimated on point to point basis.

** Growth rate has been computed through semi-log curve.

Source: Same as in Table 4.4.

khadi. Because of its over-bearing relative position, cotton-khadi's performance gets re-produced under total-khadi; all growth rates, especially those of earnings under total-khadi are remarkably closer to those for cotton-khadi. The decline that set in since 1993-94, for each khadi segment, naturally get more vociferously re-echoed in total khadi. In brief, khadi-sector has become an acute worry-spot in recent years, partly because of the lack of internal dynamism that once characterised the output and employment performance of this sector, and partly because of exogenous circumstances following the open-door policies of the early 1990s.

5. Problems of Khadi Workers / Industry

In a broad sense, the economic interests of khadi workers are expected to be looked after well, through the auspices of the Khadi and Village Industries Commission (KVIC) at the national level, or Khadi and Village Industries Boards (KVIBs) at the state level. Their wage levels, as also the unit cost of production, are institutionally fixed, after taking due cognizance of the increasing cost of living, prices of raw material and other associated elements, from time to time. Their employment, spread as it is throughout the length and breadth of rural India, is largely located in khadi institutions (usually called khadi centres). Such centres, operating in varying form and size at the grass-roots level, are primarily cooperative associations/bodies which come into existence only after the KVIC/KVIB certifies the genuineness of their interest, especially their commitment to promote rural craft/industry, employment and earnings among the lower strata of the rural society, in conformity with the Gandhian economic ideology (KVIC, 1998: 2-3). The pre-conditions of providing for Artisans Benefit Fund, Consumers Benefit Fund, Price Fluctuation Fund, Artisan Welfare Fund, Establishment Margin, etc. speak well for the good intentions behind the khadi programme (*ibid: 2*). The promoters of such cooperative ventures are expected to be public-spirited people whose heart 'bleeds for the poor' and whose 'energies are addressed to rural betterment'.

The KVIC and KVIBs have their own wide-ranging institutional network that operates throughout the length and breadth of the country, and seeks to promote khadi and village industries through a series of institutional interventions/supports. For example, a number of steps have been taken, from time to time, to upgrade production technology and thereby enabling productivity of khadi workers to improve. The introduction of a continuing stream of improved spinning wheels (from Desi Charkha to Amber Charkha, with varying spindlage provisions, etc.) is a well acknowledged landmark in technology improvement (see Section I for details).

TABLE 4.8 : **Production, Employment and Earnings of Khadi Wool in India : 1989-90/98-99**

Year	Production		Employment (in lakhs)			Earning (in Rs. Lakhs, at 1981-82 Prices)			Earnings Per Worker (Rs.)		Share of Full Time Workers in (%)	
	Quantity (lakhs sq. mts.)	Value (in Rs. lakhs)	Full Time	Part Time	Total	Full Time	Part Time	Total	Full Time	Part Time	Employ-ment	Earnings
1	**2**	**3**	**4**	**5**	**6**	**7**	**8**	**9**	**10**	**11**	**12**	**13**
1989-90	1074.69	17377.12	3.95	10.17	14.12	7073.36	1521.09	8594 45	1790.72	149.57	27.97	82.30
1990-91	1088.85	19268.87	4.32	9.83	14.15	7703.32	1511.07	9214.39	1783.18	153.72	30.53	83.60
1991-92	1091.12	22145.08	4.19	10.01	14.20	8647.08	1864 47	10511.55	2063.74	186.26	29.51	82.26
1992-93	1052.63	23740.09	4.31	10.14	14.45	9328.65	1957.33	11285.98	2164.42	193.03	29.83	82.66
1993-94	984.27	18473.61	4.10	9.77	13.87	7763.20	1508.77	9271.96	1893.46	154.43	29 56	83.73
1994-95	908.40	11093.48	4.06	9.13	13.19	4570.45	840.31	5410.76	1125.73	92.04	30.78	84.47
1995-96	1051.00	11893.22	4.28	9.69	13.97	4354.82	837.85	5192.67	1017.48	86.47	30.64	83.86
1996-97	1114.90	13858.47	4.47	10.32	14.79	4781.64	988.94	5770.58	1069.72	95.83	30.22	82.86
1997-98	1042.00	13585.11	4.14	9.87	14.01	4855.46	1038.53	5893.99	1172.82	105.22	29.55	82.38
1998-99	982.00	13619.40	4.30	9.55	13.85	5088.03	850.29	5938.32	1183.26	89.04	31.05	85.68
Rate of Growth (%)												
1989-90/92-93*	-0.69	10.96	2.95	-0.10	0.77	9.66	8.77	9.51	6.52	8.88		
1992-93/98-99*	-1.15	-8.85	-0.04	-0.99	-0.70	-9.61	-12.97	-10.15	-9.57	-12.10		
1989-90/98-99**	-0.66	-5.63	046	-0.36	-0.12	-7.00	-8.22	-7.20	-7.43	-7.90		

Note: * Growth rate has been estimated on point to point basis; ** Growth rate has been computed through semi-log curve.

Source: Same as in Table 4.4.

On the marketing side, many strategic changes have been effected from time to time. Examples are change-over from sales rebate of 20.0 per cent into production subsidy equivalent to weaving charges on cotton khadi in 1964-65, change-over from weaving subsidy to sales rebate in 1975-76, extension of the special rebate period for cotton-khadi to 90 working days in a year instead of 30 days, making government opt for polyvastra uniform for 'D' category of its employees in 1989-90, introduction of margin money scheme in 1995-96, and so on.

Initiatives to improve access to finance, especially for the khadi centres located in the backward regions, was another area of effective intervention. The introduction of working fund system and of the imprest system in 1964-65, introduction of a scheme of direct financing of individual artisans in 1974-75, a comprehensive scheme for providing interest subsidy to the KVIC in respect of loans raised from the financial institutions in 1977-78, roping in NABARD's financial support in respect of numerous bankable schemes in 1991-92, setting up of a consortium of banks and adoption of project approach in place of financial assistance for schemes exceeding Rs. 1 lakh, and introduction of margin money scheme for the upcoming projects in 1995-96, are examples of policy changes in the area of finance.

A number of Evaluation and Review Committees were instituted, from time to time, to suggest ways and means for improving the khadi (and village industries) sector. Khadi Evaluation Committee 1959, Khadi Marketing Committee 1962, Khadi and Village Industries Committee 1968, Khadi and Village Industries Review Committee 1984, High Power Committee 1994, etc. made numerous suggestions to improve the working of the khadi sector in general, and of the working and earning conditions of khadi workers in particular. A few specially commissioned studies, such as Finmark India Management Services' Report on KVIC's cotton purchasing function, Venkataraman Committee Report on working capital for silk khadi, etc. looked into problems of individual khadi sectors. And then, Padmanabhan Committee Report, appointed by the KVIC itself, for framing model service rules for workers in KVI institutions was another landmark in KVIC's history of institutional intervention towards improvement of working conditions.

One cannot but be impressed with the long chain of concerns, interventions and policy initiatives, shown by the KVIC right from the days of its inception, for improving the working of khadi institutions and khadi workers. Perhaps, working conditions of khadi workers, especially looking back to their own past, have improved a lot. Possibly, the degree of their technology consciousness has grown apace. Perhaps, the number of people migrating from private sector employment to the khadi network has increased over years. Most certainly, the barter economic culture of the weavers of yester- years now resides only in history. Ostensibly, the living conditions of spinners and weavers have been improving, just as it has been so with other segments of the rural society. All these developments do make a happy reading.

But then, somebody has to unfold the unhappy part of the story as well. To begin with, it somehow appears that the huge institutional interventions and policy changes effected by the KVIC/KVIBs, from time to time, have conferred much less improvements on the working and living conditions of khadi artisans and other grass-roots workers, although improvement of khadi institutions and the 'upper layer of khadi employees' cannot be doubted. There are still numerous inhibitions, handicaps and disadvantages under which the khadi artisans/workers have to work, and carry on the weight of their living close to poverty and unsecured future. One is bound to discover a mixture of improved working and living conditions side by side with some unhappy elements. The present section seeks to unfold this mixture.

5.1 Characteristics of Cotton-Khadi Production

It may be in the fitness of things to take note of the distinct characteristics and problems that are typically associated with production in the most dominant segment of the khadi sector, viz. cotton-khadi. For this purpose, we extensively draw upon the 1987 Report of the Khadi and Village Industries Review Committee. Analytically, it is essential to go by the five different stages of production viz., (1) pre-spinning; (2) spinning; (3) pre-weaving; (4) weaving; and (5) post-weaving.

5.1.1 Pre-Spinning

Pre-spinning process under cotton-khadi includes opening and carding of cotton, drawing, sliver making and preparation of rovings. The quality and cost of the hand-spun yarn depends largely on the quality and cost of slivers and rovings. There is a need for adopting the most modern technology in the preparation of slivers and rovings which, in turn, will have the twin advantage of improving the quality of cotton yarn and reducing the cost of production. Often, relatively better and costlier varieties of cotton are used for manufacture of coarse and medium varieties of cotton-khadi. Naturally, this pushes up the cost of production which, in turn, affects the demand for cotton-khadi. It is, therefore, generally felt that any technology which enables less costly varieties of cotton to come up through proper blending, will reduce the cost of production of cotton-khadi. There is, therefore, considerable scope for the KVIC to improve pre-spinning operation, partly through forging cooperation with the private sector for supply of ready-made slivers, and partly through introduction of machines (say, Simplex type) for preparation of rovings.

5.1.2 Spinning

The KVIC has evolved an improved version of spinning equipment, viz., New Model Charkha (NMC)fitted with six and twelve spindles. The NMC is trouble free and has the capability of providing expanded employment at reasonable wages/earnings. Common village people, both males and females, can operate the NMC after a short spell of training. Unluckily, for various reasons (which need to be fully ascertained), there are areas where the NMC has not made its presence felt in a sizeable way; the possibility of increasing the earnings of spinners, therefore, remain unexplored.

As regards coarse count of spinning, i.e. below 33 metric, which is largely used in weaving non-wearable varieties such as chaddars, carpets, towels, durries, etc., the KVIC does not have many concrete technological improvements to claim. Even today, the most traditional charkha (one-spindle type) is widely used. It has very low productivity at 2 or 3 hanks for every 8 hours of labour. Further, the quality of yarn produced is poor and unacceptable to the weaver, in spite of the fact that the cotton used may be of superior and costly variety. No wonder, therefore, the cotton-khadi activity pursued on such out-dated charkhas requires relatively more of working capital than the NMC. It is indeed paradoxical that rural areas having high per capita income (e.g., Punjab, Haryana, Western Uttar Pradesh, etc.), the traditional charkha is still used as a supplementary source of income. In other words, for a commodity which has an assured market, the production technology continues to be traditional.

5.1.3 Pre-weaving

The most crucial aspect of the pre-weaving operation is its standardization. Not much has been done with regard to pre-weaving standardization. That is perhaps the reason that, until recently, the semi-automatic Nepali loom has not become popular since the warps coming out under the existing pre-weaving technology are not suited to the high speed of the shuttle. It is because of the present system of defective sizing and the unsatisfactory drying arrangements for the warps that the Nepali loom does not lend itself to smooth weaving. In the opinion of experts, it would be advisable to go in for the mill technology, both in sizing and drying for preparing long warps, which can be attached both to the ordinary frame-looms and the semi-automatic Nepali looms. Perhaps, in due course of time, the KVIC can develop its own centralized units for warp preparation.

In many cases, child labour is involved in winding the bobbins pirns. Winding of bobbins for the creel and pirn winding are strenuous processes. It is suggested that child labour can be spared of the extra drudgery and stress if a suitable attachment to the six-spindle and twelve-spindle charkha could be devised for preparing bobbins and pirns.

5.1.4 Weaving

Most of cotton-khadi continues to be woven on the traditional looms because the efforts of KVIC to popularize improved looms have not been much of a success. It is only the new entrants to the weaving profession that have shown interest in the use of improved looms. Quite often, weavers from the traditional handloom families are reluctant to use the semi-automatic looms (say, the Nepali models) due to some operational difficulties or constraints on their freedom. The failure of the khadi institutions to supply ready warps may also have contributed to the reluctance of the traditional weavers to switch over to improved looms.

Nonetheless, in design weaving, the traditional loom plays an important role. One of the reasons for the preference enjoyed by khadi furnishing fabrics is their intricate and attractive designs, dished out on traditional looms; these are higher value varieties. In this behalf, the introduction of a jacquard loom with the accessories for pre-preparation of popular designs, was a suggestion that did not go much beyond the experimental stage.

5.1.5 Post-weaving Processing

This is an area where sufficient ground is yet to be explored. In the past, a few khadi institutions used to maintain their own processing facilities, with the financial support of the KVIC. Some of them exist no more. Now, several khadi institutions get their khadi cloth processed in the organised mill sector or through private processing agencies. In some cases, the khadi fabrics are transported over long distances for the purpose of processing and, as a consequence, their prices get escalated. The problem still stands.

We have, by now, a fairly wide view of the problems confronting cotton-khadi, including the technological challenges that are still to be answered. We do not wish to prepare similar accounts for woollen- and silk-khadi; many problems are common. Inasmuch as the cotton-khadi is the most domineering component of the khadi sector, we would like to pursue matters connected with working conditions, earning and living levels of workers engaged in cotton-khadi alone.

6. Working Conditions and Earnings: Evidence from the Field Survey

A brief field survey to throw bare the realities operating at the level of khadi workers themselves was in or around Ghaziabad (Uttar Pradesh) and Panipat (Haryana), based on semi-structured/unstructured group interviews. In Ghaziabad, we surveyed Sushila Gramodyog Sansthan (hereafter SGS) while in Panipat, we surveyed two production centers: Krishanpura Khadi Production Cooperative Industrial Society (hereafter KCS) and National Khadi Wool Production Cooperative

Industrial Society (hereafter NCS). The NCS and KCS are 25-year and 12-year old khadi centres, respectively having their catchment areas deep into the distant rural areas of Districts Panipat, Karnal and Kurukshetra. On the other hand, the SGS is a 10-year old khadi centre which has its own catchment area going deep into district Ghaziabad. The three khadi centres surveyed by us have practically everything to educate us about the working and living conditions of khadi workers, who come from different rural backgrounds, who possess varying varieties of skills, and who share varying perceptions about the future of khadi workers, most especially the spinners and weavers. It is in the fitness of things to gain an introduction to the three khadi centres. Inasmuch as the KCS is a small but quite similar to the NCS, in what follows, we give introductory information only on the two major khadi centres, viz: NCS from Panipat and SGS from Ghaziabad; this adequately informs us about the similarities and dissimilarities of two major khadi production centres as also the two different product lines pursued by them.

6.1 Introduction to NCS and SGS

NCS was established in 1963 while SGS was set up in 1989. These are primarily cooperative industrial societies, registered with the respective government agencies, and carrying out their production and marketing programmes in conformity with the guidelines stipulated by the KVIC/KVIB. Moreover, the wage rates for each specific job operation as also the cost/price for each product/item are determined in conformity with cost charts, primarily given out, and revised, by the KVIC/KVIB from time to time. Most importantly, while individual khadi centres may have some discretion, depending upon the local market conditions and the centre's own capabilities of internally providing for all stages and ingredients of production requirements, the centres are not generally allowed to use mill-spun yarn or indulge in other labour-saving production devices. Primarily, all khadi centres are founded on Gandhiji's original idea of harmonizing the interests of rural spinners, rural weavers and rural consumers while, at the same time, keeping the expansion of employment for the rural artisans as their avowed objective.

Four major categories of workers are employed in SGS for the on-site production. These are 50 weavers, 35 spinners, 15 fabricators and 25 helpers. In all categories, we have a mix of people from local and nearby areas as also those from distant (rural) areas. Spinning is done nearly exclusively by female workers. In addition, SGS has nearly 150 workers who work, usually on part-time basis, within their own household premises, under piece rate system. Nearly 80.0 per cent of them are women, and a very small proportion of children, scattered over a few villages deep inside district Ghaziabad. A big majority of workers are Muslims; among the spinners, female workers are in a preponderant majority, although a small proportion of them are occasionally involved in weaving and other operations also. *No child labour was reported to be in regular employment of SGS;* some child labour is, however, discernible in spinning and weaving, mostly as an occasional short-duration help to parents who sometimes work under a family-contract arrangement.

In NCS, we have three major categories of workers, viz: spinners (including twisters), weavers and winders. Here, weavers, numbering 16, and winders, numbering 10, are the on-spot workers while spinners, numbering more than a thousand, are home-based workers, nearly the whole lot of whom are females, engaged in spinning on part-time basis. Unlike SGS, finishing of the product is got done through outside private sources. As in SGS, *no child labour is employed by NCS either;* only occasional help is forthcoming from children in the household, either in spinning or in weaving or in both, or in other odd jobs.

NCS is primarily engaged in the production of woollen blankets, shawls and 'lois'; cotton textiles are nearly totally absent. On the other hand, SGS is primarily engaged in the production of cotton textiles; nearly 90.0 per cent of its production is cotton-khadi, with woollen-khadi constituting only 3.0 per cent and polyvastra another 7.0 per cent. The major raw material used by NCS is raw wool. Raw wool consists of two types: clipped wool and pulled wool. It is obtained through local private traders, and quite often, imported from Russia, Pakistan and Argentina. On the other hand, the major raw materials used by SGS are raw cotton, and raw wool, obtained from local and outside marketing centres. Apart from direct supply to government against pre-booked orders, sale through khadi bhandars, is a major means of marketing their products; *exports are non-existent.* The sales are heavily concentrated (nearly 70.0 per cent) in October-December each year, when a 30.0 per cent rebate (financed by Central and State Governments) is offered on normal prices; only about 30.0 per cent of the sale takes place during the remaining nine months. While NCS is engaged in the production of three woollen items alone, and has no subsidiary production system of its own, SGS produces handmade paper and ready-made garments in addition to its main activity of producing cotton-khadi.

As is the case with most khadi production centres, *both NCS and SGS operate with a mixture of improved and traditional technologies.* Between the two, however, SGS reflects a much better and improved technological outfit. For example, SGS reports a stock of 2200 traditional charkhas, largely obtained through local artisans, the oldest being 5 years and the newest being one year old, simultaneously with 50 New 6-Spindle Model Charkhas, obtained from KVIC's Rajkot and Coimbatore production centres, the oldest being 5 years and the newest being 3 years old and 200 New 8-Spindle Charkhas, obtained only one year back, and so on. NCS is a strict adherent of the 'labour friendly' technology with their total stock of traditional charkhas. Then, while SGS operates with 60 improved looms, the oldest being 6 years and the newest being 1 year old, NCS's stock of 20 looms is totally of the traditional variety. Further, while SGS's stock of 15 sewing machines is largely traditional, ranging from one to 7 years in life, NCS's stock of two "Tana Machines" is a mixture of one improved (with bearing) and one traditional (without bearing). Yet again, while NCS does not have a carding machine of its own since carding of raw wool is got done through private sources out in the open market, SGS has a stock of two warping machines, two welders and one carding machine, representing a semi-improved stock of capital equipment. Finally, improvement of looms is the avowed goal of SGS; its plan is to get 25.0 per cent additional stock of still-better looms during the next one year while NCS does not have any such plan.

But then, there are noticeable differences in many other respects. First, SGS has its own production premises inside which a reasonably livable, and rent free, residential complex is also built for the workers. Telephone, electricity, drinking water, and other basic minimum facilities are available inside the premises themselves. On the other hand, NCS does have its own production premises but no residential complex for the workers is provided for. Other facilities too are not available on the same scale as in SGS.

Both in NCS and SGS, workers report varying levels of work experience, ranging from as small as one year and as long as 25 years. Many among the present lot of workers came over from private employment; most of them reported the present job to be in line with their ancestral occupation; some of the workers in SGS did receive short-term training from KVIC/KVIB centres, were given Charkhas (on concessional pay-back basis), and were then ushered into the occupation while in NCS, none of them received institutional training of the kind given to SGS workers, or Charkhas by the KVIC. *It is interesting nonetheless to see an occasional shift of workers from khadi production centres to private production centres, and vice versa, largely depending upon the fluctuating demand and production schedules in the khadi sector.* In general, a mixture of facilitating and repulsive factors were at work to 'push them into this occupation'. While charkhas and training provided by the KVIC centre, as also the latent flexibility in combining household work with spinning/weaving, etc. facilitated their entry, typified in our case by SGS, lack of alternative employment, especially with their extremely low or nil educational attainments pushed them on to this occupation, as was reported both in SGS and NCS.

6.2 Workers Reponses and Perceptions

The field survey was organised at two levels: inside the khadi production centres and out in the villages attached to the respective khadi centres. First, for the first type of survey, ten, seven and five group-interviews/discussions were held in SGS, NCS and KCS production premises, respectively, in late October and early November, 1999. A semi-structured questionnaire was used for this purpose. For analytical convenience, we call workers interviewed in the production centres as *on-site workers*. Given the nature of our inquiry, as also the composition of workers in the three khadi centres, we chose to concentrate on three categories of workers: *spinners, weavers and others* (which comprised fabricators in the case of SGS and winders/wrappers,etc. in the case of NCS). In what follows, some rough but fairly understandable generalizations are provided, in respect of the three categories of workers, largely on the basis of our semi-structured group-interviews, but also on the basis of visual impressions gathered by the survey team.

Again, using a different semi-structured questionnaire, six and five group-interviews/discussions were held in Village Nahal of district Ghaziabad and Village Katlihari of district Karnal, to ascertain the views and perceptions of cotton and wool spinners, respectively; these are mostly women who work for SGS/NCS/KCS on putting-out basis, for a few hours a day as and when they are given some raw material for spinning. Again, for convenience, we call them *home-based* (piece-rate) *workers.*

6.2.1 On-site Workers

As comes out clearly in Table 6.1, a mixed picture emerges as regards the literacy standards and work arrangements in the three khadi centres. In general, weavers are relatively better educated in comparison to spinners and other categories of khadi workers; in a way, this points to better educational attainments of male khadi workers (mostly weavers) compared with their female counterparts (nearly exclusively engaged in spinning). The position varies among the three centres. Among the weavers, a very big majority has middle-level schooling in SGS and KCS while in NCS, they stay below at primary level only. Among the spinners, who are mostly rural women, engaged on this activity on part-time basis, a preponderant majority is illiterate in SGS and NCS while in KCS, most of them have primary level schooling to their credit. In total terms, SGS has a band of relatively better educated workers, and among the different categories of khadi workers, weavers alone have the background of middle level schooling. In other words, for a majority of khadi workers, most noticeably the spinners, lack of education is undoubtedly stands out as their Achilles' heel.

Skill formation too offers a mixed picture. The art of spinning was learnt, by most of the spinners, partly through family's occupational background and partly through contract work for the centre. However, weavers acquired their skills mostly

TABLE 6.1 : **Literacy Standards, Work Arrangement and Other Introductry Information on On-Site Khadi Workers**

Items	Spinners			Weaver			Others *
	Sushila (SGS)	Krishanpura (KCS)	National Khadi (NCS)	Sushila (SGS)	Krishanpura (KCS)	National Khadi (NCS)	Sushila (SGS)
Literacy Standard #	Illiterate	Primary	Illiterate	Middle	Middle	Primary	Middle
Skill Formation @	Mixed	Mixed	Mixed	Family	Family	Outside	Outside
Training	KVIC	NA	Centre	Mixed	NA	Centre	Mixed
Work Arrangement	Contract	Contract	Contract	Contract	Contract	Contract	Contract
Nature of Job	Fulltime	Fulltime	Fulltime	Fulltime	Fulltime	Fulltime	Fulltime

* Others include a variety of workers i.e., fabricators and workers engaged in wrapping, dusting etc. confirmed to SGS alone.

Primary means illiterate to primary and middle means illiterate to middle.

@ Mixed implies training from both production centre and outside.

through family's own occupational background. Only in NCS, weavers reported to have acquired their skill through outside training centres. And finally, other khadi workers such as fabricators, acquired their occupational skill through formal training from the open market. In plain terms, there is no fixed source for skill acquisition; different areas report different arrangements.

Diverse arrangements are reported in respect of sources of training also. For example, SGS spinners were trained mostly by KVIC centres while NCS spinners picked up the craft at the production centre itself. Similarly, a mixed pattern is reported by weavers and other khadi workers.

A uniformly common feature about all categories of khadi workers and all varieties of khadi production centres is that the work is organised on contract basis. The employment is mostly on piece-rate basis. Often, the whole family is involved including the occasional help that comes from the children. It is this nature of work arrangement that makes one khadi worker relatively 'more efficient' or 'better earner' than the other. Yet one more uniform feature across khadi centres and khadi workers is that all employment in the centres (on-site) is on full-time basis. An 8-hour per day work norm was uniformly reported not only by the management at the centres but by workers themselves in each of the many group interviews.

Let us now look at the *working conditions* of the khadi workers, as ascertained through group discussions as also through the interviewees' perception and assessment. First, we look at the *physical aspects of the working conditions.* Table 6.2 (upper portion) shows that there was no complaint about undue scrutiny and questioning at the work place, or about irregular/untimely payment of wages, or about undue deductions and under-payment, or of harsh treatment or of stress of work. Usually, an 8-hour per day work norm is followed; 'untimely' work was occasionally asked for, only against over-time payment which is usually much higher than the usual wage rate. Regular payment of wages, on monthly basis in SGS and fortnightly basis in KCS and NCS, is the rule rather than the exception. In total terms, in all the three production centres, the workers were rather unanimous in reporting the accommodating nature of the manager and other supervisory staff.

Some contrasts about *the monetary aspects of the working conditions* exits among the three production centres, as also among individual monetary compensations (lower portion, Table 6.2). By any reckoning, SGS would appear to be better employers. For example, the facility of paid-leave duly exists here; Sundays and all important festivals days are paid-days, in conformity with the KVIC directions. Then, provision for maternity leave also exists for which the period of leave was reported to vary from two to two-and-a-half months. Workers are paid bonus also, again in terms of KVIC guidelines. Occasionally, financial support is extended for medical treatment. Most importantly, housing facility is also available right within the SGS campus, perhaps for a preponderant majority of workers. On all these counts, SGS is way ahead of the two other khadi centres.

Certain facilities that are commonly available in all the three centres are as follows. Interest-free loans, for meeting unforeseen emergencies, are provided on request; its frequency is nonetheless very limited. Some compensation could be available in case of an accident although it was extremely difficult for the workers to recall of any major accident in the recent past. Gifts on festivals are also given to the workers, their monetary worth notwithstanding.

A few other items are conspicuous by their absence in all the three centres. For example, there is no provision for provident fund and pension, in any of the three khadi institutions. Again, provision for insurance cover just does not exist.

The *working environment* too was a mixture of many good points and a few negative ones (Table 6.3). For example, electricity, drinking water and toilet facilities are available to the workers in each of the three khadi centres. This was also the response about adequacy of working space. But then, differences exist about the availability of other facilities. For example, the facility of working under an electric fan is available in SGS and KCS while it is not available in NCS. A telephone facility exists in SGS while it is not available to workers in NCS and KCS.

In each of the three centres, there is no regular heating system, during the cold winter months; only cow-dung cakes are allowed for heating purposes. Occupational hazards such as an accident at the workplace, fire or electric shocks

TABLE 6.2 : **Working Condition of On-site Khadi Workers**

I. Physical Aspects	Sushila	Krishanpura	National Khadi
1. Mode of Payment	Monthly	Fortnightly	Fortnightly
2. Stress of Work	No	No	No
3. Undue Scrutiny	No	No	No
4. Irregular Payment	No	No	No
5. Harsh Treatment	No	No	No
II. Monetary Aspects			
1. Undue deduction	No	No	No
2. Paid Leave	Yes	No	Yes
3. Bonus	Yes	No	No
4. Provident Fund	No	No	No
5. Pensions	No	No	No
6. Medical Support	Yes	No	No
7. Maternity Leave	Yes	NA	Yes
10. Compensation for Accident	Yes	No	No
11. Insurance Policy	No	No	No
12. Gifts on Festivals	Yes	Yes	Yes

TABLE 6.3 : **Working Environment for On-site Khadi Workers**

Items	Sushila	Krishanpura	National Khadi
1. Electric Fan	Yes	Yes	No
2. Heating System	No	No	No
3. Telephone Facility	Yes	No	No
4. Adequate Working Space	Yes	Yes	Yes
5. Toilet Facility	Yes	Yes	Yes
6. Drinking Water	Yes	Yes	Yes
7. Occupational Hazards	No	No	No

are also nearly totally absent in each of the three centres. We may as well look into the reality of *social and legal protection,* if any, enjoyed by khadi workers (Table 6.4). Trade unionism among khadi workers is completely absent in each of the three production centres. Whether this is the reality of khadi workers in general is, however, difficult for us to say. Khadi institutions/centres are under a legal compulsion to observe all labour laws; there is, however, some deviation between the *de jure* and *de facto* positions. Consequently, it would be na‹ve to believe that such workers enjoy legal security of a substantial nature, in case some dispute

TABLE 6.4 : **Social Protection for On-site Khadi Workers**

Items	Sushila	Krishanpura	National khadi
Trade Union	No	No	No
Legal Security	No	No	No
Application of Labour Laws:			
i) De jure	Yes	Yes	Yes
ii) De facto	No	No	No
Social Organisation			
i) Social Partnership	Yes	Yes	Yes
ii) Self-help Group	Yes	Yes	Yes
iii) Mutual Help	Yes	Yes	Yes

arises or dismissals are resorted to, or re-employment claims are lodged, and so on

Happily, however, the deficiency on the legal side is more than made up through forging mutually beneficial *social organizations.* For example, khadi workers in each of the three production centres did report the existence of social partnership not only among workers themselves but also, *albeit occasionally,* between workers and management. And then, self-help and mutual help groups are commonly reported from all the three production centres. Perhaps, economic strain gets somewhat diluted when such social groups and partnerships are around.

Let us now look at the work effort and earnings of each category of on-site workers (Table 6.5). We begin with *spinners.* This activity is nearly completely monopolized by female workers; occasionally, child labour comes to help parents. The work schedule is unevenly distributed over the months. In SGS, during the 'peak season' that usually consists of 3 months (October to December), they work for a maximum of 12 hours a day while during the lean season (partly coinciding with the rainy season) and the rest of the year, they work for 8 hours a day, as is the usual practice in all decent employment avenues; in contrast, NCS does not report inter-seasonal variation in work intensity. With this year-round composition of employment, a typical on-site spinner in SGS earns an average of Rs. 21,314.58 per annum while her counterpart in NCS earns Rs. 21,600.00. Unlike the piece-rate contract workers, there are usually no inter-person variations in earnings; to spinners under its regular employment, SGS and NCS pay the same wage rate irrespective of whether a particular worker does a bit less of work on a day or a bit more on another.

Contrasted to spinners, *weavers* are largely males although, of late, an increasing proportion of females are also taking up this activity. In general, no child labour is involved; only an occasional help to parents is reported. Weaving is

TABLE 6.5 : **Employment and Earning Patterns of On-site Khadi Workers**

Category	Sushila	Krishanpura	National Khadi
I. Spinners			
1. Working Hours / day			
a. Peak Season	8-12 hrs		8 hrs
b. Remaining	8 hrs		8 hrs
2. Earning / day			
a. Peak Season	Rs. 93.3		Rs. 69
b. Remaining	Rs. 46.6		Rs. 69
3. Earning / year	Rs. 21314		Rs. 21600
II. Weavers (Individual)			
a. Peak Season	8 - 12 hrs	10 hrs	10 - 12 hrs
b. Remaining	8 hrs	8 hrs	8 hrs
2. Earning / day			
a. Peak Season	Rs. 124.5 - 166.0	Rs. 100-110	Rs. 120-150
b. Remaining	Rs. 83.0 - 124.5	Rs. 80 - 90	Rs. 90 - 100
3. Earning / year	Rs. 29133 - 42081	Rs. 26520 - 28860	Rs. 30420 - 35100
III. Weavers (Family)			
1. Working Hours			
a. Peak Season	8 - 12 hrs	NA	NA
b. Ramaining	8 hrs		
2. Earning / day			
a. Peak Season	Rs. 253.6 - 295.1		
b. Remaining	Rs. 170.6 - 212.1		
3. Earning / year	Rs. 59718 - 72666		
IV. Fabricators			
1. Working Hours			
a. Peak Season	8 - 12 hrs	NA	NA
b. Remaining	8 hrs		
2. Earning / day			
a. Peak Season	Rs. 200 - 215		
b. Remaining	Rs. 125		
3. Earning / year	Rs. 44850 - 46020		

undertaken usually on contract basis. In some cases, the contract involves the *whole family* of weavers comprising the husband, wife and children whose number goes up to 3 in some cases; in any case, the involvement of child labour is only occasional. Usually, the wife spins, the husband weaves and the children come in occasionally for both activities. In other cases, the contract is with *individual workers,* mostly males, who then work on piece rate basis. For analytical convenience, we term these two arrangements as *family-contract weaving and individual-contract weaving.* As is evident from Table 6.5, the system of family-contract weaving is prevalent only at SGS.

Like in spinning, the peak season roughly goes for three (October to December) during which the weaving-team works for a maximum of 12 hours (and a minimum of 8 hours) a day. For the remaining 9 months, the norm of 8 hours a day is usually followed, although occasional deviations are also reported. Quite often, during the peak season, some extra work comes in (e.g., dusting or sewing work, within the SGS premises, roughly twice a week, entailing a payment of Rs. 40-45 per day for work involving 4-8 hours, and another Rs. 20-25 per day for meals).

During the peak season (comprising 3 months in the year), the *family-contract earning per day* varies from Rs. 253.65 to Rs. 295.15. During the remaining months, the per day earning varies from Rs. 170.65 to Rs. 212.15. On the above basis, the total yearly earning under the *family-contract weaving* ranges from a minimum of Rs. 59718 to a maximum of Rs. 72,666, which comes to Rs. 4976.50 and Rs. 6055.50 per month.

The inter-centre comparison is forthcoming only in respect of *individual contract* weaving. In each of the three centres, work intensity goes up beyond the normal 8 hours a day norm but during the rest of the time, it stays at 8 hours a day. The peak season earning per day is relatively higher in SGS (ranging from Rs. 124.50 to Rs. 166.00) and is the lowest in KCS (Rs. 100-110). Similarly, inter-centre variations are discernible for the remaining months of the year. On this basis, the total yearly earning varies from Rs. 29133 to Rs. 42,081 in SGS, from Rs. 30420 to 35,100 in NCS, and from Rs. 26,520 to Rs. 28,860 in KCS. These are the estimates of monetary rewards; the inter-centre variations would grow a lot if we add the imputed value of the house rent which workers at SGS do not have to pay, and other 'saved expenditure' which they do not have to incur by staying and working within the same premises. In total terms, therefore, the total yearly earnings of workers at SGS is really much higher than what the above figures reveal.

Finally, let us look at the group of fabricators working inside SGS; a small number of fabricators work from outside also, on contract basis. Inside the SGS premises, only males work as fabricators; outside, they are a mixture of males and females. Some evidence of child labour as a part of contract (from outside) work , carried out at home, is also reported. Generally, the working hours inside the SGS production premises are from 9.00 am to 5.00 pm but almost all of them work over-time for 1 to 3 hours a day, almost for the whole year. Again, during the peak season, they work for a maximum of 12 hours and a minimum of 8 hours per day. For the remaining months, the usual norm of 8 hours a day is followed.

During the peak season, their average per day earning varies from Rs. 200 to Rs. 215 while during the remaining months, it comes to Rs. 125. On this basis, their annual earning comes to a minimum of Rs. 44,850 and a maximum of Rs. 460,20 or on monthly basis, it varies from Rs. 3737.50 to 3835.00.

Before we close our discussion of on-site workers, let us have a hurried look at their *living conditions*. Table 6.6 takes a *qualitative note* of some of the important items of their consumption basket which easily convinces us that 'all is not lost on the consumption front'. For example, all categories of workers, in each of the three production centres, report consumption of milk and milk products, purchase of new clothing once or twice a year, availability of electricity for household use, access to drinking water, and toilet facilities, and so on. Most of the on-site workers at SGS report occasional consumption of meat, egg and fish to the extent they can afford; workers in the other two centres generally eat vegetarian meals, as a social practice. The incidence of houselessness is nearly conspicuous by its absence. Appropriate means of entertainment, such as a television, radio or transistor, are also reported to be available to most of the families. Some among the weavers have their means of transport also, such as a scooter or a bicycle. An extremely important feature that distinguishes one set of workers (say, Muslims) from the other (say, Hindus) is their approach towards child education. In SGS, child education is the least important item on their living agenda while in the other two production centres, the Hindu khadi workers do send their children to school, and would strive to improve upon their performance in this regard if ever their resources and earnings permit them to do so. *The Hindu-Muslim gap is all the more glaring in the context of education of female children.* Thus, even our sketchy household survey convinces us that social development is not necessarily tagged to better economic earnings. The inter-centre gap in approach to child welfare similarly needs to be interpreted in the vein of Hindu-Muslim perceptional gaps.

6.2.2 Home-Based Work

The most important among the home-based khadi workers are *spinners*. They are nearly exclusively the female workers who undertake to do spinning inside their own dwellings, on behalf of khadi centres to which they are attached under KVIC/KVIB directives. In real effect, the work is done on contract basis.

As stated earlier, our group-interviews for spinners were held in two villages: Nahal (District Ghaziabad in Uttar Pradesh; attached to SGS) and Katlihari (District Karnal in Haryana; attached to NCS). A brief socio-economic profile of such workers in the two villages is set out in Table 6.7. It is hardly surprising that most of the female-spinners are illiterate (Village Nahal) or have had low level of schooling (Vill. Katlihari). While the spinners in Katlihari did not receive training outside the family, their counterparts in Nahal received short-term training in spinning from KVIC/SGS sources. The training was essential for those who worked on New Model (six- or eight-spindle) Charkhas.

The spinning is done on contract basis. Again, it is done only on part-time basis where every female member who can spin, and has some time to spare for it,

TABLE 6.6 : **Living Condition of On-site Khadi Workers**

Items	Spinners			Weaver			Others @
	Sushila	Krishanpura	National Khadi	Sushila	Krishanpura	National Khadi	Sushila
Food							
1 Milk & Products	Yes	Yes	Yes	Yes	Yes	Yes	Yes
2 Meat, fish egg, etc.	Yes	No	No	Yes	No	No	Yes
Clothing	Two/yr.	One/yr.	One/yr.	Two/yr.	One/yr.	One/yr.	Two/yr.
Housing	Free	Own	Own	Free	Mixed*	Mixed*	Free
Entertainment	NA	Yes	Yes	NA	Yes	Yes	NA
Electricity	Yes	Yes	Yes	Yes	Yes	Yes	Yes
Drinking Water	Yes	Yes	Yes	Yes	Yes	Yes	Yes
Toilet	Yes	Yes	Yes	Yes	Yes	Yes	Yes
Transport	No	No	No	No	Yes	Yes	No
Child Education	No	Yes	Yes	No	Yes	Yes	No
Child Welfare	No	Yes	Yes	No	Yes	Yes	No

* Denotes both own house and rented.

@ Others include a variety of workers i.e., fabricators and workers engaged in wrapping, dusting, etc.

is involved. Their work pattern and involvement in spinning depend exclusively on the quantum of raw material delivered by the concerned khadi centre and time at which the spun yarn is requisitioned back; the khadi centre assigns a kind of 'work permit' to each registered spinner. During normal times, on an average, they work for five days a week, and on each day that they spin, the duration of work varies from 3 to 5 hours. These are the hours contributed by the whole family, usually dominated by the mother and occasionally assisted by her daughter(s). In Village Nahal, the home-based female spinners reported a mixture of different types of Charkhas while in Katlihari, we had only the traditional charkhas in operation. Incidentally, the most common complaint was that the payment was made irregularly by the production centre just as the raw material was delivered most erratically. In plain terms, there was no regular pattern or quantum of employment for the spinners, and the earnings that came through this source were at best interpreted as a meek supplementation to the total household income a major chunk of which comes through agriculture and allied on-farm activities.

TABLE 6.7 : **Socio-economic Profile of Home-based Spinners**

Items	Nahal	Katlihari
1. Literacy Standard	Illiterate	Upto Primary
2. Skill Formation	Outside	Family
3. Training	KVIC / SGS	No
4. Work Arrangement	Contract	Contract
5. Nature of Job	Part Time	Part Time
6. Mode of Payment	On the delivery of Yarn	On the delivery of Yarn
7. Stress of Work	No	No
8. Undue Scrutiny	No	No
9. Irregular Payment	Yes	Yes
10. Harsh Treatment	No	No
11. Undue Deductions	No	No

* Payment is made in kind and cash.

The level of earnings largely depends on the type of technology under which a particular person works. The two villages differ starkly in this regard (Table 6.8). In Village Nahal, we have three layers of spinning technology: layer I, representing the old/traditional technology and encapsulated by a one-spindle charkha, gives an average output of one kg. for every 12 hours of labour put in; *layer II,* representing a more efficient technology and proxied by a six-spindle charkha, gives an average

TABLE 6.8 : **Employment and Earning Patterns of Home-based Khadi Spinners**

Category	Nahal		Katlihari*	
	Layer I	Layer II	Layer III	Layer I
1. Productivity	12 hrs / kg.	6 hrs / kg.	4 hrs / kg.	10-12 hrs /kg.
2. Earning / year				
a) Actual	Rs. 8149	Rs. 16369	Rs. 16848	Rs. 3600
b) Potential	Rs. 8149	Rs. 16848	Rs. 24570	Rs. 3600

Note: Layer I refer to Charkha used with one spindle.
Layer II refer to Charkha used with six spindles.
Layer III refer to Charkha used with eight spindles.

* Payments are made both in kind and cash.

output of 2 kgs. of yarn for every 12 hours of labour put in; and *layer III*, representing a still better technology that is based on a eight-spindle charkha, gives an average of 3 kgs. of output for every 12 hours of work put in. On this basis, the average annual potential earning of a spinner, operating with layer-I level of technology roughly comes to Rs. 8149; for those operating under layer-II, it comes to Rs. 16,848 ; and finally for those working with eight-spindle charkhas, it works out to Rs. 24,570 per annum. However, the potential is not fully realized by the workers, especially those working on an eight-spindle charkha since it involves tremendous human effort entailing body-ache, shoulder-pain and eye-strain. Thus, the gap between the actual and the potential earning goes on increasing as we move from layer-I to layer-II and further on to layer-III type of technology. For layer-I, the actual and potential are the same (Rs. 8149 per annum); for layer-II, the actual is Rs. 16,369 against the potential earning of Rs. 16848; and finally, for layer-III, the actual and the potential earnings are Rs. 16369 and Rs. 24,570, respectively. It is important to point out that the above estimates of earnings are in respect of only the part-time work of spinning which the female folk of the household undertake in addition to other activities, including wage employment in agriculture and non-farm jobs. In sharp contrast, it is a petty earning of about Rs. 3600.00 per annum that is reported from Katlihari.

It is not advisable to look into the living conditions of such workers through the window of earnings from spinning. As pointed out above, these earnings are at best a part of total household earnings, coming as they do largely through farming and allied on-farm activities. It is essentially the latter earnings that determine the pattern of consumer expenditure and the quest for improving the living standards. This is remarkably true in Katlihari, where the irregular and erratic earnings from spinning makes a highly negligible fraction of the total household income.

Taking a composite view of the categories of workers, the types of activities involved, the seasonal intensity of work, the per day or per month level of earnings in cash accompanied by housing and other facilities, etc., we are persuaded to believe that in respect of the *on-site khadi workers*, things are not so bad, as is generally given out to be. It is not advisable to make assertive statements about their present standard of living, or the future prospects of their profession, or the possibility for them to migrate to other occupations, just on the basis of a limited number of one-shot group-interviews conducted with a handful of respondents. For more firm insights, a full-fledged survey, perhaps involving a few hundred spinners, weavers and other khadi workers may be in order. Nevertheless, even the limited survey impressions do lead us to believe that most of the on-site khadi workers are far above the level of economic destitution. For example, even a sketchy peep into their consumption basket tells many good things. But then, social development is nearly conspicuous by its absence among the SGS workers; they have no interest whatsoever in education; for them, every child is 'an earning machine' and the family welfare lies in 'producing more and more of working hands'. The shrinking per capita living space is no consideration. KCS/NCS are healthy contrasts in this regard.

Practically nothing exists for them in the name of social protection; perhaps none of the khadi workers have an insurance cover for their life, much less for their property. *Collective bargaining and artisans' associations are totally absent in the case of khadi workers interviewed by us.*

In sum, our survey of the three khadi centres gives the impression that the quality of employment of khadi workers may not compare well with workers employed in the organised manufacturing sector but it is no worse than that of rural workers in general and agricultural labour in particular. In the ultimate analysis, the quality of employment in an industry and net earnings attached to it do necessarily depend on the level of education, skill and training background of the workers much the same way that the buoyancy of demand that an employing industry can cultivate depends on the kind and depth of technological, marketing and managerial strategies followed by it. In the case of khadi, one is confronted with a mixture of successes and failures on all these counts. There have been technological changes, and yet much more needs to be done; and whatever technological improvements have been thrown upon for use, are not widely accepted, for reasons which are partly attributable to workers' own stubborn choices. What can otherwise explain the continuing use of the most traditional (nay, ancient!) spinning wheel (one-spindle charkha) in larger parts of rural India. Most crucially, whatever technological upgradation policies have been pursued by the KVIC/KVIBs have been nearly the in-door activities; no serious effort has ever been made to integrate them with the general strides on the technology front. Similarly, marketing strategies have generally been pursued on extra-commercial considerations; very little cognizance has been taken of the changing tastes of the consumers or of the spade of competitive impulses that unleashed themselves in recent years. Naturally, therefore, an all-round decline followed.

7. Concluding Observations

The khadi sector accounts for a big proportion of employment in the textile sector although its share of output is very small. Since the early fifties, it has seen many vicissitudes in its output and employment graphs. In recent years, every thing seems to have gone out of hand; real value of output, employment, and earnings have witnessed varying degree of decline during the past 5-6 years, in each segment of the khadi sector. This has indeed become a source of concern, most certainly for reasons of declining employment, if for none else.

The khadi sector is institutionally regulated by the KVIC at the Centre and KVIB at the state level. Individual production centres are registered with the KVIC/KVIB, in conformity with a well-articulated set of rules. The employment of artisans/workers is, however, the prerogative of the centres. Production, including product specialization, marketing and artisans' welfare is their responsibility. Raw materials, i.e. raw cotton, wool and silk, are generally bought by these centres from the open market, through a chain of working arrangements, including imported supplies to the intending khadi production centres by designated private suppliers. Generally, these centres do not face much problem in getting raw materials; however, credit is often a big bottleneck. In a preponderant majority of khadi centres, production is carried on all the year round but the sale is heavily concentrated during the three months of rebate; quite naturally, a lot of money get blocked for many months. Information flow from KVIC downwards to the khadi centre level takes considerable time; re-attuning to market and technological requirements often is a long, and lagged process.

From the viewpoint of khadi centres, dealing with semi-literate artisans poses difficulties of their own kind. Such workers are not easily amenable to change. Moreover, they would abstain for long intervals, that often proves highly detrimental to production, especially during the peak season.

The khadi sector sails on its own. There is no formal relationship between the organised section of the textile industry and the khadi sector; even the closer-to-the-door segments, viz. handloom and powerloom segments, are not consulted for matters relating to information, technology and market intelligence. The khadi sector has its own network, which regulates cost and price matters, technology improvement, skill upgradation, sales promotion and so on. The pulse of the market is, therefore, felt rather feebly; the kind of demand buoyancy experienced by growing industries is hardly felt by this sector. Most importantly, the relatively higher cost of production and prices, determined as they are through a long chain of pre-production, production and post-production circumstances, not always favourable in the case of khadi textiles, are big hurdles in the way of sale expansion.

In our opinion, and in the opinion of some of the management interviewees that we met during the field survey at Panipat, it is clear that some specified production linkages with the modern textile mill sector can bring in a lot of benefits to the khadi sector itself. Besides lending greater access to the market, better and more market-savvy technological improvements and skill upgradations, and enduring product improvements, these formal linkages would ensure a more prolonged cycle of production for the whole year. By implication, employment would expand not only in terms of sheer man-days of work but also through substantial increase in productivity and earning levels. Somehow, there has been a dogged historical insistence on using hand-spun yarn by the khadi production centres. It is now openly conceded, and confidentially agreed to by many of the khadi functionaries, that if instead of hand-spun yarn, mill-made sliver or tape is allowed to be used, it will considerably improve the quality of the product, will reduce the unit cost of production and, by the same token, lower the level of sale-price which may, in turn, give a boost to the level of sales, and so on. Most importantly, the use of hand-spun yarn is responsible for as high as 50-60 per cent wastage under the present dispensation. Undoubtedly, these changes should bring forth concrete improvement in the quality of employment and the level of earnings of the khadi workers; nothing else would be more gratifying to Gandhiji himself.

To put the issue of price disadvantage in a comparative commercial perspective, let us look into the price structure of the three major products of National Khadi Wool Primary Cooperative Industrial Society (NCS; one of the three centres surveyed by us) vis-a-vis other competitors in the market. Table 7.1 gives two sets of prices for the khadi sector: one before the discount and the second after the (30.0 per cent seasonal discount) has been allowed for. The table unmistakably shows the relative price disadvantage suffered by the khadi sector. One can imagine the decline in sales that would accrue if the discount of 30.0 per cent were not available during the three designated months of each year; in fact, it is precisely because of this high rate of discount that sales are concentrated in these three months while sales during the remaining nine months constitute a very small proportion of total yearly sales. While the khadi people believe that khadi-wool items enjoy a high degree of reliability in the market, yet, in terms of finish, smoothness and sturdiness, the khadi claims are not always vindicated. There is no hesitation on the part of many public-spirited people, including some well-meaning and enlightened functionaries at the level of khadi production centres as also among the KVIC/KVIB officials, to say that the khadi sales are sustained largely because of concessional/subsidized prices offered during three months every year; and, a very big majority of public analysts do acknowledge that the quantum of budget support on account of khadi subsidies is becoming a big question mark with every passing years.

Most importantly, the usual claim of the informal sector that the demand for its products comes mostly through the lower strata of the consuming public does not seem to apply to the khadi sector, as can be seen through khadi's sale pattern. For example, again going by the information gathered at the NCS-Panipat, people belonging to the weaker sections of the society constitute hardly 20.0 per cent of their customers; even the discounted khadi prices (available only during the peak

TABLE 7.1 : **Price Differentials for Three Major Woollen Products among Different Sources of Production (Rs.)**

Item Description	Khadi Sector	Handloom Sector	Powerloom Sector	Automatic Mill Sector
1	**2**	**3**	**4**	**5**
Blanket	213.00 (153.00)	140.00	125.00	100.00
Shawl	260.00 (182.00)	165.00	150.00	130.00
Loi	470.00 (330.00)	300.00	290.00	275.00

Note: In the column 2, the figure in parenthesis is the discounted price; a 30.0 per cent is allowed on all the three items.

Source: Information gathered at the National Khadi Wook Primary Cooperative Industrial Sociey, Panipat, during the field survey.

TABLE 7.2 : **Sales of Khadi Textiles in Recent Years at Current and Constant (1981-82 Prices) (Rs. in Crores)**

Year	Khadi Cotton		Khadi Woollen		Khadi Silk		Khadi Total	
	Current Prices	Constant Prices	Current Prices	Constant Prices	Current Prices	Constant Prices	Current Prices	Constant Prices
1	**2**	**3**	**4**	**5**	**6**	**7**	**8**	**9**
1989-90	199.65	134.54	54.08	36.44	37.53	25.29	291.26	196.27
1990-91	201.62	135.86	58.10	39.15	36.46	24.57	296.18	199.58
1991-92	249.44	168.09	66.99	45.14	52.54	35.40	368.97	248.63
1992-93	252.25	169.41	75.40	50.64	59.48	39.95	387.13	259.99
1993-94	261.85	135.39	78.12	40.39	69.27	35.82	409.24	211.60
1994-95	314.30	89.47	91.74	26.11	83.45	23.75	489.49	139.34
1995-96	359.03	81.76	105.82	24.10	96.91	22.07	561.76	127.93
1996-97	353.19	78.14	116.30	25.73	108.56	24.02	578.05	127.89
1997-98	416.40	90.64	135.41	29.48	191.78	41.75	743.59	161.86
Annual Compound Growth Rate								
1989-90/92-93	8.11	7.99	11.72	11.59	16.59	16.46	9.95	9.83
1992-93/97-98	10.54	-11.76	12.42	-10.26	26.38	0.89	13.95	-9.04

Note: All-India Wholesales Price Index Numbers for Khadi Cloth (under Textiles) with base 1981-82 has been used to convert figures from current to constant prices.

Source: 1. KVIC, Annual Report for various years.
2. Govt. of India, Statistical Abstract of India 1998, CSO, 1999, p. 336.

sale months) are beyond the reach of such people. On the other hand, ironically, nearly 60.0 per cent of the khadi customers belong to the well-to-do sections of the society.

Be that as it may, khadi sales, whether to open general public or to government departments and agencies, have not been a happy episode in recent years. Let us first look at the open sales. Table 7.2 undoubtedly lends itself to a dual interpretation; it reveals a myopic illusion when looked at in terms of current prices, and it can be a source of drooping when constant prices replace the prism of current prices. As we saw earlier (Section IV) in the case of production under individual khadi sectors, sales too under each of the three major khadi sectors grew rather impressively till about 1992-93; most happily, this was true whether sales were measured in current or constant prices. Perhaps, a little surprisingly, sales both at current and constant prices grew annually, more or less, at the same rate, primarily because the wholesale index of khadi cloth prices also remained constant. But then, the myopic illusion could not hold on for long; in the post 1992-93 years, sale proceeds at constant prices, for each of the khadi sectors fell sizably, on year to year basis, although the monetary value of sales at current prices continued to grow a little more robustly in the post 1992-93 years. Admittedly, 1997-98 seems to have put some life back into khadi sales although production-wise (and presumably, sales-wise), the following year 1998-99 again posed a halting scenario; if, therefore, we exclude 1997-98 from Table 7.2, the post 1992-93 scenario would look all the more disappointing. But then, the sagging fortune of khadi textiles during the past 5-6 years should not be seen independent of the decline witnessed by the textile industry in general; during the nineties, the textile industry has been a source of great worry, most pointedly from the point of view of employment.

The reality of dwindling levels of sales was duly confirmed by the khadi centres visited by us during the field survey. For example, the annual sales of the National Khadi Wool Primary Cooperative Industrial Society Ltd., Panipat (NCS) witnessed a precipitous fall from Rs. 90 lakhs in 1997-98 to Rs. 20 lakhs in 1998-99. This was attributed both to a decline in the purchasing power of the common people as also to the on-going recession in the economy. Khadi cannot operate in an isolated compartment; all major developments in the economy encompass all production sectors including khadi. Moreover, there is a sort of general impression that prices are inflated in the first instance and then a publicly declared rebate does not attract expanded sales to the extent that it should; variously, it is interpreted as a spurious rebate. Still further, certain internal elements in the functioning of the KVIC, for example, stoppage of advance payment of rebate by the KVIC or delayed disbursal of the 25.0 per cent rebate payment to the khadi centres (say, March/ April of the next year against November/December of the previous year) extraordinarily by the KVIC or extraordinarily late payment of 5.0 per cent rebate payment by the KVIB, have also been responsible for making inroads into the level of annual sales. In total terms, the disharmony between the khadi institutions at the apex level and those at the grass-roots levels, seems to be growing apace. It should not, therefore, be surprising that the khadi production centres are least enthusiastic about their present production environment, much less about the commercial prospects for expanding their enterprise.

Sales to government departments/agencies could hardly compensate for the sagging demand among the public in general. For example, sales of 24 khadi items to government departments including railways under the auspices of the Accepted Tenders (AT) supply arrangements showed a highly irregular profile, punctuated by expansions and contractions, almost on year to year basis. For example, the sale of cotton khadi (Rs. in crores) was of the order of 2.80 in 1991-92 which expanded to 3.24 in 1992-93 and fell to 1.12 in 1993-94, and then again rose to 3.93 in 1994-95 and to 4.64 in 1995-96. A much more disappointing profile is discernible for woollen khadi sales to government. In plain terms, in spite of the KVIC's best efforts, including strengthening of its Accepted Tenders Supply Directorate and vigorous negotiations with government agencies, around mid-1990s, sales under A.T. arrangements ranged between 1.25 to 1.30 per cent of total sales of khadi under the cotton sector and between 0.20 to 0.25 per cent under the woollen sector. So much for the sales to government!

There is indeed tremendous scope for raising productivity. Unluckily, the khadi sector appears to have been extremely slow in putting through the available technological changes, even in the most crucial segment of the production chain, namely spinning, for example. Our own field survey shows that production efficiency grows apace if the artisans switch over from the one-spindle charkha to six- or eight-spindle new model charkha. It is a sad reading of the khadi sector that the spread of the new model charkha has been extraordinarily uneven among various regions, sometimes among closely located pockets within the same area. We discovered, in our field survey, that even within the same village (Nahal, district Ghaziabad in Uttar Pradesh), three types of charkhas, viz. one-, six- and eight-spindle charkhas, were in operation. We could see the remarkable improvement in production efficiency of those working on the eight-spindle charkha compared with those working on a six-spindle one, and many times more compared with those working on a one-spindle charkha. Many regions in the country have not gone beyond the eight-spindle charkhas although technologically much advanced versions are available. But then, there are regions (typified by village Katlihari, district Karnal in Haryana) where the spinners have not given up their age-old, least-efficient, one-spindle charkha; here, the scope for productivity improvement is anybody's guess. Apart from technological upgradation of the kind mentioned above, there is tremendous scope as well as need for product standardization and specialization. The pulse of the market needs to be felt with a perfectly open mind, and changes in production patterns including the use of new types of raw materials, or throwing up new designs or newer varieties, etc., must be made without the conventional hesitation.

Following its June 1998 Declaration on Fundamental Principles and Rights at Work, the ILO has been keenly working towards elimination of all forms of forced or compulsory labour, the effective abolition of child labour, and the effective recognition of the right to collective bargaining, and so on. The khadi sector offers a mixed picture about the precincts of the ILO Declaration. As is typical of most industries, the working conditions of workers engaged in the khadi sector also vary from region to region. In our own field study, we discovered a pleasing mixture of strong and weak elements. In total terms, the workers did work under reasonably good working conditions, and earned a level of income which was slightly better than what might be available to agricultural labourers or rural labourers as such. Perhaps, in relation to workers in the organised segment of the textile industry, they may be getting much less but then, their earnings cannot be out of proportion to their educational, skill and training backgrounds. *Happily, problems of gender segregation and prevalence of child labour were not discovered by us;* perhaps, in the khadi sector, these problems are summarily non-existent in the sense that these are frequently reported from other industrial and work environments.

But then, it is a pity that the khadi workers do not have social protection of the kind enjoyed by the organised segment of the workforce. The khadi workers are not unionized; generally, they do not have insurance cover for life or property, principally because they cannot afford to pay for it. Social organizations such as self-help groups are rather conspicuous by their absence. Social development has so far evaded them, undoubtedly for a bunch of economic reasons, but also because of their obsessive pre-occupation with traditional moorings and family occupations. Lack of education in respect of a preponderant majority of such workers stand in their way. And most unhappily, their attitude towards education of their children, leaves much to be desired. In sum, there is much ground to be covered.

Our study persuades us to believe that the avowed goal of providing employment to the rural artisans, through the auspices of khadi production centres, seems to be losing ground, in recent years. Not only that productivity per worker has been presenting a very unhappy scenario, employment too has been on the decline in recent years. Our brief field survey (more pointedly in KCS and NCS at Panipat) convinced us that *year-round employment in khadi production centres is a thing of the past.* One can imagine a far more depressing state of employment for the khadi workers, perhaps commonly with textile workers in general, that may emerge when international trade in textiles grows apace following further implementation of the WTO conditionalities. In respect of khadi textiles, exports are not a major issue in the liberalized trade regime inasmuch as khadi exports, although stretched over quite a few items under silk, cotton and muslin khadi, do not make a noticeable proportion even of KVIC exports (in 1998-99, it was 0.01 per cent) much less of the total textiles export from India. It is the increasing volume of textile imports anticipated in the years ahead that constitute the real source of policy concern. Perhaps, the khadi sector can stand its ground if it thoroughly revamps its house, most pointedly from the points of view of technology upgradation, quality improvement and price competitiveness.

Happily, the issue of revamping is currently in the priority zone of government's attention. Three recent reports, all commissioned by government itself, have some, *albeit* diverse, suggestions to make. For example, the Planning Commission March 2001 report suggests that the entire business of marketing and product development be left to the private sector while the semi-processed goods may continue to be produced by khadi units under the guidance and supervison of KVIC (Government of India, 2001:79). The Anderson Consultancy report goes a step further and insists on a private sector model for KVIC. It advocates marketing and advertising to boost national as well as international demand for khadi products; as a consequence, four khadi shops are planned to be launched at Delhi and Mumbai international airports (Walia, 2001:7). The third report by Tata Institute of Social Sciences recommends that khadi rebates should be stopped (*ibid:7*). It is the marketing strategy that has been picked up for the time being. A few selected sale outlets in Delhi are getting refurbished, at a fairly high cost to be borne by the central government, presumably to rope in the upper segment of the capital's population. One is not quite sure how this top-down marketing strategy will succeed in a substantial expansion of demand among the masses.

Bibliography

Chadha, G.K., The Industrialisation Strategy and Growth of Rural Industry in India, Working Paper, ILO-SAAT, New Delhi, June1996.

Govt. of India, Report of High Power Committee on Khadi and Village Industries, Dept. of Small Scale Industries, Ministry of Industry, New Delhi, July 1994.

____, Report of the Khadi Village Industries Review Committee (KAVIRC), Dept. of Industrial Development, Ministry of Industry, New Delhi, Feb. 1987.

____, Annual Report 1998-99. Ministry of Textiles, New Delhi.

____, Statistical Abstract, 1998. CSO, Ministry of Planning, New Delhi.

____, Annual Plan (for various years), Planning Commission, New Delhi.

____, Seventh, Eighth and Ninth Five Year Plans, Planning Commission, New Delhi.

____, Reports of the Commission for Agricultural Costs and Prices for Crops Sown in 1993-94 Season, Ministry of Agriculture, 1994.

____, Draft Mid-Term Appraisal of the Eighth Five Year Plan, 1992-97. Planning Commission, 1996.

____, Economic Survey, 1998-99. Ministry of Finance, New Delhi, 1999.

____, Evaluation Study on Khadi and Village Industries Programme, Planning Commission, March 2001.

ILO, Declaration of Fundamental Principles and Rights at Work and its Follow-up, ILO Geneva, June 1998.

KVIC, Khadi Certification Rules, Directorate of Khadi Coordination, KVIC, Mumbai, Sept, 1998.

____, Statistical Abstract, Directorate of Economic Research, KVIC, Mumbai, Sept. 1998.

____, Annual Report for various years.

____, Report of the Venkataraman Committee on Working Capital for Silk Khadi, 1996.

Singh, Ajit Kumar and Sasikumar S.K., (eds) Restructuring of the Textile Sector in India, Vikas Publishing House, New Delhi, Nov. 1999.

Singh Surjit, Khadi Spinners and Weavers: Do They Have any Future? IDS Working Paper No. 96, Jaipur, November 1997.

Walia, Nona, "Ten Outfits and Three Bags: All for a Khadi Makeover", The Sunday Times of India, June 3, 2001.

Unorganized Food Processing Industry in Mumbai: A Study of Bakery, Savouries and Fish Processing

Ritu Dewan

1. Introduction

The economic development of India, as of several other third world nations, seems to be counter to the historical growth patterns experienced by 'developed' countries. This is true of particularly two simultaneous processes especially since the unleashing of the policies of globalisation and 're-structuring' - that of the proportion of workers as well as of manufacturing activities in the informal/unorganised sector actually increasing rather than the reverse. It is, however, a pity that the 'new economic policy' in India has left out of its ambit practically the entire informal sector, thus negating the existence of the major source of both output and employment. Research in this field of economics thus assumes a special significance, especially in view of the fact that the nature and focus of these policies are not likely to change in the near future. The present study of the informal food-manufacturing sector in India attempts to incorporate these components, additionally and necessarily integrating the gender based division of labour into analysis.

The presentation is carried out in separate sections as each sub sector presents a distinct scenario. We begin with the macro level analysis of the food-manufacturing sector in Section 2, without visiting the debate on the formal-informal dichotomy or demarcation and on the appropriateness of data to capture their realities. This has been deliberately done for two reasons - one, enough general data at the all-India level are already available; two, the examination of three sub sectors within such a short span of time demands that more attention be focussed on specificities rather than generalities.

Section 3 situates food manufacturing in relation to all industry divisions based on the 2 digit data available for both formal and informal sectors, focusing on employment, output and value added. The bakeries sub sector is dealt with in Section 4 which gives a five stage linkage analysis between the macro, meso and micro segments and, based on field survey data, throws up many valuable insights on wages and wage mechanisms, conditions of work and degree of exploitation of labour, health, hygiene and product quality, and production and marketing patterns. Section 6 on fish processing is divided into four major sub-sections beginning with an examination of linkages between the macro, meso and micro regimes. The aspects covered on the basis of field survey data are demographic and occupational patterns of the area of research, types of fishing boats and catch, processing and preservation of fish and crustecea, workers and work conditions, and sales and marketing.

Each sub sector is deliberately not concluded with a typical summary. We feel it makes for better analytical, conceptual and theoretical sense to integrate all aspects of convergence and divergence in the conclusion along with policy recommendations and issues for further debate.

Both published (e.g., NSS Survey Reports on Unorganized Manufacturing, Economic Census and Survey of Maharashtra, Annual Survey of Industries Reports, etc.) and unpublished (e.g., Reports on Unorganised Manufacturing in Maharashtra, Maharashtra Department of Fisheries, Ward Level Shops and Establishments Records, etc.) have been used. Besides, enterprise-level data were gathered through a field survey for selected sub-sectors in the district of Greater Mumbai, through group discussions and interviews with office bearers of manufacturers' associations, union activists, export companies in the formal sector, export agents, suppliers, consumers, vendors, and government officials.

2. Macro Level Analysis of Food Manufacturing

The study focuses on three sub sectors within the overall category of food processing - bakery products, savouries and fish processing. In this section we give a short overview of the food-processing sector based on 2 digit data. A 3 - and 4 - digit analysis is carried out later.

While food processing is categorised, under Code Nos. 20-21 of the 1987 NIC 2-digit classification, as 'manufacture of food products', bakeries and fish processing come under 20. Savouries sub-sector is, however, not identified anywhere, not even in the 5 digit NIC categorisation of 1998 (see Appendix II: 4 Digit 1987 and 5 Digit 1998 NIC Codes for Food Processing). After detailed discussions, all senior directors of the Directorate of Economics and Statistics, Government of Maharashtra, advised us not to use any secondary data whatsoever for this sub sector, not even 'manufacture of food items not elsewhere classified' (3 digit Code 219), as it would distort analysis and lead to, in their words, 'incorrect conclusions and policy recommendations'.

Table 2.1 presents basic information at the all-India level relating to the number of units and employment generated under category 20 in relation to the total of all industries. For lack of more detailed break up, we have, for the present, assumed the informal sector to comprise of Own Account Manufacturing Establishments (OAME) and Non Directory Manufacturing Establishments (NDME). OAMEs are defined as pure self-employment. An 'establishment' is defined as one 'with at least one hired worker', further divided into NDME with

TABLE 2.1 : **Informal Food Manufacturing Units and Labour Emplyed, All-India (2-digit)**

(percentages in parenthesis)

Sr. No.	Category	OAME		NDME	
		Units	Workers	Units	Workers
1.	20	196348 (7.0)	367720 (7.4)	97392 (11.0)	387322 (9.8)
2.	All Industry	2822112 (100.0)	4985218 (100.0)	889430 (100.0)	2937381 (100.0)

Source: Calculations based on : 1. ASI, Vol. II 1993-94, Table 1, p.2050 - I - 001.
2. NSS, 45th Round 1990, Sarvekshana, Statement 13.

TABLE 2.2 : **Selected Indicators of Informal Food Manufacturing Units, All-India (2-digit)**

Sr. No.	Category	OAME		NDME	
		20	All Industry	20	All Industry
1.	Value added as proportion of output	0.47	0.56	0.30	0.41
2.	Output as % of input	1.88	2.28	1.43	1.69
3.	Value added per worker (Rs.)	10910	5386	11370	11998

Source: Calculations based on NSS 45th Round 1990, Sarvekshana, Statement 6.7.

'5 or less than 5 workers', and Directory Manufacturing Establishments (DME) with '6 or more than 6 workers', irrespective of power used.

As many as 1,96,348 establishments employing 3,67,720 workers have been identified as OAME's in code 20, accounting for 66.8 per cent of the informal sector. At the all-industries level, however, the proportion is much higher at 76 per cent. The remaining 33.2 per cent in code 20 are NDME's totaling 97,392 units and employing 2,87,322 workers. It is interesting to note that the proportions of OAME food manufacturing units and labour employed are almost identical at 7 per cent and 7.4 per cent respectively of all-industry OAME's. The two proportions are, however, quite different for NDME's, implying that there is more employment generation in the self-employed sector.

A few selected characteristics presented in Table 2.2. compare the food-manufacturing sector to the all industries division in the informal sector. The most significant fact that emerges is that while both value added as proportion of output as well as output as percentage of input are lower in OAME food manufacturing units as compared to all industries, the value added per worker is almost double. The productivity differentials are rather negligible for NDME segment.

We will now try and trace the same connections for the state of Maharashtra, keeping in mind the major data limitation that there is only a general category of 'establishments' (employing at least 1 hired worker) which includes NDME. It can be seen from Table 2.3 that the proportion of OAME's to total food-manufacturing units is 66.6per cent, exactly the same as at the national level.

The major difference between the state and the national level picture arises in relation to the fact that although the food manufacturing OAME units account for 21.6 per cent of all OAMEs at the state level, they employ a lower proportion of labour at 16.6 per cent. The respective proportions for code 20 establishments are 17 per cent and 9.8 per cent. However, these contradistinctions are not surprising considering the fact that Maharashtra is the most industrially developed state, that it has a relatively advanced level of technology in the food-manufacturing sector, and that labor productivity is amongst the highest.

TABLE 2.3 : **Food Manufacturing Units and Labour Employed (2-digit)**

(percentage in parenthesis)

Sr. No.	Category	Units		Labour Employed	
		20	All Industry	20	All Industry
1.	OAME	63892 (21.6)	295768 (100.0)	78547 (16.6)	472746 (100.0)
2.	Establishments	32025 (17.0)	188183 (100.0)	213903 (9.8)	2179527 (100.0)

Source: Calculations based on NSS 45th Round 1990, Sarvekshana, Statement 6.7.

3. Bakery Establishments

3.1 Introduction

The analysis of the bakeries sector is divided into various sub-sections. Each sub-section requires a different method of analysis often necessitating varied styles of presentation. We begin with tracing every linkage possible, starting from the location of 3 digit data at both the national and regional levels, and 4 digit data at the three levels of the state of Maharashtra, the district of Greater Mumbai and the Ward the field samples fall into, right up to the geographical area of research.

The subsequent sub sections based on field analysis relate to, in that order, identification and details of bakeries establishments; ownership structure;

production design including the types of products manufactured and the processing of each; the nature and extent of division of labour, prevailing wage patterns and wage mechanisms; conditions of work including the application of relevant laws, health, hygiene and quality; marketing and costs of production wherein an attempt is made to calculate the rate of exploitation of labour.

3.2 Linkage Between Macro, Meso, and Micro Realities

The five level linkage analysis presented here draws upon upon published data sources, unpublished data collected from various directorates and offices, and material obtained from the relevant local Ward office. We begin with the location of the state in the macro perspective as presented in Table 3.1. As 3 digit information is not available for DME's at the national level, only OAME's and NDME's have been taken.

TABLE 3.1 : **Number of Bakery Units and Labour Employed (Code 205), All India and Maharashtra**

(in actuals)

Sr. No.	Type of Units	All India		Maharashtra	
		Units	Workers	Units	Workers
1.	Factories	775 (100.0)	32112 (100.0)	123 (15.9)	5422 (16.9)
2.	OAME	9647 (100.0)	31497 (100.0)	2715 (100.0)	6884 (100.0)
3.	NDME	10946 (100.0)	41811 (100.0)	1582 (100.0)	1128 (100.0)
4.	Total	21368 (100.0)	105420 (100.0)	4420 (100.0)	23434 (100.0)

(percentages in parenthesis)

Source: Calculations based on

1. ASI, Vol. II 1993-94, Table 1, pp. 2050-I-001; 2050-III-001; 2050-III-003.
2. NSS 45th Round 1990, Sarvekshana, S-13.
3. NSS 51st Round 1994-95, unpublished data.

The results are indeed amazing. Maharashtra accounts for over 28 per cent of all OAME bakeries in the entire country, employing more than one-fifth of total labour. Also, if OAME's and NDME's are assumed to constitute the informal sector, then over one-fifth (20.9 per cent) of all bakeries employing almost one-quarter (24.6 per cent) of India's unorganised bakery workers are concentrated in the state of Maharashtra.

A significant deviation from the national picture at 2-digit level (see Table 2.3) is that NDME's in Maharashtra are more labour intensive, employing 26.6 per cent of all-India unorganised bakery workers. This obviously implies that bakeries constitute what is probably the largest sub sector within the general category of informal 'food manufacturing'. This is exactly the reason why we felt it necessary to analyse secondary data in the greatest detail possible as tracing linkages at every level - in this case comparing 2 digit and 3 digit data - brings out unsuspected nuances.

It would be interesting to note at this stage that even in the formal sector, the state of Maharashtra operates the largest number - almost 16 per cent - of all bakeries, employing nearly 17 per cent of all formal bakery workers in India. Maharashtra additionally reports the second highest number of average working days at 309 (ASI, Vol.II 1993-94: 2050-I-001). This aspect is supported even at the city level. Of all the industries in Greater Mumbai, food processing was one of the only two sectors reporting a positive annual compound growth rate of 4.02 per cent over the entire decade 1981-1991 (MMRDA Development Plan 1995:142).

Table 3.2 deepens our analysis further with more detailed unpublished data from the 51st Round of the NSS. In the informal sector, which we assume to be the combination of OAMEs and NDMEs, it is immediately apparent that self-employment accounts for 63.2 per cent of the units and an almost equal proportion of total workers at 61.9 per cent (Combined-I, Table 3.2). It is also obvious that few women participate in the informal bakeries sector; of the few who do, 99.3 per cent are self-employed.

TABLE 3.2 : **Number of Units and Gender-based Labour Employed in Bakeries: (Code 205), Maharashtra**

(in actuals)

Sr. No.	Type of Units	Number of Units	Total Males	Total Females	Total Children	All Workers
1.	OAME	2715	4024 (58.5)	679 (9.9)	2181 (31.7)	6884 (100.0)
2.	NDME	1582	2995 (70.6)	5 (0.1)	1244 (29.3)	4244 (100.0)
3.	Combined I	4297	7019 (63.1)	684 (6.2)	3425 (30.8)	11128 (100.0)
4.	DME	2087	12807 (88.8)	1260 (8.7)	359 (2.5)	14426 (100.0)
5.	Combined II	6384	19826 (77.6)	1944 (7.6)	3784 (14.8)	25554 (100.0)

(percentages to total workers in parenthesis)

Source: Calculations based on NSS, 51st Round 1994-95, unpublished data.

What is really amazing is the large number of child workers who constitute an astounding 30.8 per cent of the work force in the informal sector, outnumbering women at the ratio of 5 : 1.

Of the total of 3784 children employed, only 8 per cent (304) are girls. That the gender based division of labour permeates at all levels is apparent from the fact that all these girl children are recorded, similar to the majority of adult women, as 'unpaid household workers'.

Further, it is not surprising that while the formal sector represented by DME's accounts for 32.7 per cent of total bakeries in Maharashtra, it employs 56.5 per cent of the workforce. Accordingly, the degree of labour intensity follows a similar pattern. The average number of workers employed in OAME's is 2.5, in NDME's 2.7, and in DME's 6.9.

We now come to the third level of linkage tracing based on unpublished 4 digit data from the Economic Census of Maharashtra 1990 relating to the city of Mumbai. We had hoped to present a time series analysis, and were quite distressed to be informed that all the data of the 1980 Economic Census had been lost as the floppies had been corrupted and no hard copies retained. Also, 1998 data are still not open to public use.

The 3 digit code 205 relates to 'manufacture of bakery products'. The 4 digit codes we have chosen are 2051 ('bread making') and 2052 ('manufacture of biscuits, cakes and pastries'). The remaining code, 2059, relates to 'manufacturing of other bakery products not classified elsewhere'. This category, which reported a total of 32 units, has not been included as we were informed that it produces mainly sugar candy.

There are a total of 640 bakery manufacturing units, both formal and informal, in Greater Mumbai. While 95.3 per cent produce only bread (code 2051), these 610 units account for a lower proportion of total labour at 72.5 per cent The implication is obviously that cake and biscuit manufacture is much more labour-intensive, 4.7 per cent of total units employing 27.5 per cent of all workers.

Further, 91.9 per cent of all workers are hired by both categories of units taken together, merely 6 per cent of them women. This trend is obviously a carry over from the earlier levels of linkages analysed, thus reinforcing our assertion of a strong gender based division of labour in the bakeries sector. Additionally, this is true both for self-employment and for the labour market as the relative proportions are almost the same. Cake making, however, has a higher percentage of hired women workers, reportedly for the relatively 'delicate' task of packing.

TABLE 3.3 : **Bakery Manufacturing Units, (Codes 2051 and 2052), Greater Mumbai**

Sr. No.	Category	Bread Making		Biscuits / Cakes		Total Bakeries	
		No.	%	No.	%	No.	%
1.	Units	610	95.3	30	4.7	640	100.0
2.	Total power, of which	513	95.9	22	4.1	535	100.0
2.1	Non fire wood	245	94.2	15	5.8	260	100.0
2.2	Fire wood	268	97.5	7	2.5	275	100.0
3.	W/o power	97	92.4	8	7.6	105	100.0
4.	Social group, of which	610	95.3	30	4.7	640	100.0
4.1	S.C.	4	100.0	0	0.0	4	100.0
4.2	S.T.	1	100.0	0	0.0	1	100.0
4.3	Others	605	95.3	30	4.7	635	100.0
5.	Total workes, of which	6630	100.0	2512	100.0	9142	100.0
5.1	Males	6523	98.5	2070	82.4	8593	94.1
5.2	Females	107	1.6	442	17.6	549	6.0
6.	Total hired, of which	5919	100.0	2479	100.0	8398	100.0
6.1	Males	5830	98.5	2042	82.4	7872	93.7
6.2	Females	89	1.5	437	17.6	526	6.3
7	Total unpaid, of which	711	100.0	33	100.0	744	100.0
7.1	Males	693	97.5	28	84.8	721	96.9
7.2	Females	18	2.5	5	15.2	23	3.1

Note: Upto Sr. No. 4, the percentages are to be read horizontally, and beyond Sr. No. 5, these are to be read vertically downwards.

Source: Calculations based on Economic Census 1990, unpublished data.

A noticeable fact is the predominant use of firewood in the process of production. Although 84.1 per cent of bread making units use power, more than half use firewood, while only 31.8 per cent of the 22 cake and biscuit units with power do so. Additionally, socially 'backward' groups are almost totally absent, merely 5 bread making units being owned by them.

Let us look into bread-making and biscuit/cake manufacturing units a bit more in detail. Of the total 610 bread making units, 225 have 10 or more workers with power, while another 6 employ 20 or more workers without power. All these 231 units, 37.9 per cent of the total, are therefore in the formal sector. They together employ 4900 workers, merely 1.3 per cent of them being women.

The 379 units in the informal sector account for 62.1 per cent of all units, and employ a total of 1730 workers, i.e., 26.1 per cent of all workers in bread making. The 78 OAMEs constitute 20.6 per cent of informal sector units, and account for 145 workers (8.4 per cent), all obviously unpaid household labour, 93.8 per cent of them being men. The 161 NDMEs in bread making in Mumbai employ 547 workers, 98.7 per cent of them men. 78.6 per cent of all labour is hired, women accounting for merely 0.7 per cent.

It is somewhat confusing to give data for DMEs as they include the formal sector. We have therefore separately identified establishments using power in the process of production and with up to 9 workers. The 256 units together employ 1384 workers, 85 per cent of them hired. As usual, the proportion of women to total labour is almost non-existent at 2.5 per cent.

There are only 30 biscuit and cake making units reported for the entire city. Of these, 8 (27 per cent) are in the formal sector, employing an overwhelming 94.9 per cent of the total work force of 2512 (see Table 3.4). They also account for 96.8 per cent of all women workers. It would be interesting to point out that one single factory employs 1833 workers of which 375 are women. Another relatively smaller factory has 254 male workers. Thus, the remaining 6 factories, i.e. three-fourth of all formal units, employ 297 workers, merely 12.5 per cent of the formal labour force.

TABLE 3.4 : **Number of Units and Gender-based Labour Employed in Manufacturing Biscuits and Cakes (Code 2052), Greater Mumbai**

Sr. No.	Category	Total	Formal Sector	Informal Sector
1.	Units	30 (100.0)	8 (26.6)	22 (73.9)
2.	Total workers employed, of which	2515 (100.0)	1956 (94.8)	114 (5.2)
2.1	Males	2070 (100.0)	1956 (94.5)	114 (5.5)
2.2	Females	442 (100.0)	428 (96.8)	14 (3.2)

(percentages in parenthesis)

Source: Calculations based on Economic Census 1990, unpublished data.

Nine NDMEs employ only 28 workers, including one hired woman worker. There are 10 DMEs in the informal sector with 93 workers, 9 of them being women. The 3 OAMEs provide employment to 10 workers, interestingly half of them are women. Further, 22 of the total 30 units use power in the process of production, 7 using firewood and exactly half using electricity.

3.3 Field-based Analysis

3.3.1 Identification of Establishments

We now commence the final level of linkage analysis which integrates information from three sources - unpublished data from the Directorate of Economics and Statistics relating to the Economic Census of 1990, Ward records of the research area and actual field based survey conducted during August - October, 1999.

The area chosen for field survey is Kurla, a major suburb in the north east region of Mumbai. It is renowned both historically and currently for its large quantity and high quality production of bread and biscuits, generally being considered as one of the most important centers in the entire city. The 1990 Economic Census had identified a total of 640 units producing both bread and biscuits for the entire city, 397 of which we have been able to identify as being in the informal sector, that is, 62 per cent Records obtained from Ward 'L' in which Kurla is located show that while 101 bakery units and shops exist in this area, only 16 report manufacturing. However, the Ward Officer informed us that all shops with 4 or more workers are actually manufacturing units.

Two extremely significant issues emerge here. One, that unrecorded manufacturies exist, not a surprising discovery. This is borne out by our fieldwork as only 4 of the 9 units we selected for detailed analysis could be traced in the records. Second, that the very definition of NDME's needs to be debated as the existing differentiation with DME's exists on the basis of 6 workers and not 4, as seems to be in reality. Consequently, the number of bakery manufacturies increased from the registered 16 to 60 with the inclusion of 44 units which reported themselves as only shops but are actually involved in production. The number would be much higher as only 4 of our 9 case studies are registered under the Bombay Shops and Establishments Act which is applicable to this sector. Also, all our sample units have been in existence for at least three decades, implying that the gap of 9 years between the 1990 Economic Census and our fieldwork is not the reason for this difference.

Additionally, one of the four registered sample units is recorded as a shop with only one worker, whereas actually nine are employed. Another unit has registered only eight workers when 21 are employed in reality; the category of 'establishment' has thus changed from 'factory' to 'DME', enabling the owner to circumvent all laws applicable to the formal sector under the Factories Act.

As mentioned, nine bakery manufacturies have been taken for detailed analysis. According to existing industrial regulations and laws, seven of our nine sample units employ more than ten workers each and also use power in the process of production, thereby coming under Section 85 and Clause 'm' of Section 2 of the Factories Act, 1948 (LXIII of 1948). The four registered units reported only a maximum of seven workers each in Ward records, officially none of the total 60 in L ward hiring more than nine workers each. In no case in our field survey did we find workers less than the magic figure nine. The reason is obvious - circumvention of labour and other legislation applicable to the formal sector. These 9 bakeries employ a total of about 105 workers, the average working out much higher than the Ward level data which reported the 60 manufacturing units as having 364 workers, that is, an average of about 6 each.

Various forms of 'formal' and 'informal' methods were used for data collection. Owners were suspicious of our motives, generally uncooperative, at times rude, and kept asking us why we were interested in them when there were 'bigger fish' to catch. Discreet attempts to get information on sales and production met with dis-approval, if not scorn. Also, it was extremely difficult to meet workers individually as they are kept as virtual bonded labour on the premises. Nonetheless, in spite of these odds, we succeeded in collecting data that proved fairly sufficient for an in-depth investigation. It should be noted at this stage of analysis that there are several similarities between bakery and savoury establishments, especially in relation to the structure and nature of employment, conditions of work, sales and marketing,

3.3.2 Ownership Structure

Bakeries are classified by owners on the basis of land area irrespective of the number of ovens (*bhatti*) installed or in operation. Thus, a bakery is 'big' if the total area exceeds 2000 sq. ft., 'medium' if it is over 1000 and less than 2000 sq. ft., and 'small' if it is less than or equal to 1000 sq. ft. On the basis of these criteria, six of our nine sample units are thus small, two are medium and only one is big. All operate only two ovens each, except one medium manufactury which has three.

Interestingly, all the nine bakeries are owned by muslims from the northern state of Uttar Pradesh who migrated to Mumbai at least two generations ago. This pattern is reflected in the Ward data where we found that only about 6 per cent of owners are hindus, again all of them migrants from the same state. As we shall see later, these geographical and community patterns are replicated in the case of workers.

All the bakeries are run on a partnership basis, the number of partners ranging from a minimum of four to anything up to 20, although registration is generally done in an individual's name. Each partner has an 'interest' in at least four to five other units, not necessarily in Kurla itself, the share in profits being calculated on the basis of the initial amount of capital invested. One partner takes the responsibility of supervising and managing the accounts of at least one unit, as well as disbursing the share of profit to other partners. The other partners are what we have termed as 'absentee' owners. Interestingly, few owners live in the vicinity of their bakeries, most of them having purchased flats in more 'up-market' areas.

Bakery manufacturing is a trade inherited over generations, the present owners having 'transferred' their business from their 'native' region or having inherited it from their fathers. Our earlier assertion that bakery manufacturing is almost entirely male-oriented is borne out by the fact that only sons can inherit the business. We deliberately selected the one single bakery in the Ward records which reported a woman owner, only to find that her name had been registered for probably 'tax' purposes.

3.3.3 Production Design

All bakeries manufacture both bread and biscuits. The separate 4-digit coding of 2051 and 2052 is therefore somewhat questionable, the point of difference arising on the basis of production of cakes and up-market confectioneries. Every bakery produces the following items in two sizes, big and small - *pav* (a small non-sweetened plain bun), sweet and salty rusks called 'toast', and *khari* and butter biscuits. Six of the nine units also bake biscuits called *nankhatais*, while 4 additionally make *mawa* cakes. One unit, in fact, produces 35 varieties of biscuits. Interestingly, none manufactures buns or confectionery which are considered to be 'unsuited for normal Indian tastes'.

Bread, and what we have termed as 'basic' biscuits (toast, *khari* and butter), are manufactured in the same unit because both require identical levels of technology and skill, apart from sharing almost the same process of baking. The ovens are all made of a mix of clay, stone and cement. They are huge in size, at least 30 feet long, 10-12 feet deep and 4 feet in height, occupying one entire wall of the premises. As noted earlier, only firewood is used in the process of production.

3.3.4 Division of Labour, Wages and Wage Mechanisms

In general, the level of specialisation of labour is extremely high; each process is done almost exclusively by different categories of workers. At the top of the hierarchy, after the owner, is the manager who looks after sales, takes orders and deals directly with customers, apart from keeping accounts when the owner is absent. Then comes the supervisor (*mistry*) who controls workers and oversees the entire manufacturing process. Next below follow *munshi, bhattiwala, patrawala/tablewala, gheewala,* etc. with their respective areas of specialization. At the lowest rung are the cleaners who rinse the trays for the next lot of baking. They are also responsible for sweeping and cleaning. Generally boys in the early or mid teens are employed as cleaners, euphemistically termed by owners as 'apprentices learning the trade'.

Only one unit reported employing a separate category of shop assistants, sales normally being done by whoever is 'idle'.

Specialisation of labour is not always enforced. The flexibility is exercised not on the grounds of a worker's efficiency but by the exigency of work requirement that usually entails an extremely high degree of labour utilisation and exploitation. No worker, not even the highly skilled *bhattiwala*, is permitted to be idle. When not occupied by their assigned tasks, they have to compulsorily help in other jobs. A short-term and occasional work flexibility notwithstanding, a general upward mobility, both in the bakeries and savouries sub-sectors is not reported, most ostensibly because the rigidly prescribed division of labour keep workers confined to their respective job moorings.

There is great divergence between what the owners reported they were paying as wages, and what the workers had to tell. The owners said that supervisors and managers were paid Rs.100-125 per day; *munshis* Rs.90-100; *bhattiwalas* Rs.100; *gheewalas* Rs.90; *tablewalas* Rs.80-100; packers Rs.70, and cleaners Rs.50 per day. On a monthly basis, wages would thus range between Rs.3750 and Rs.1500.

As noted earlier, it was extremely difficult to meet individual workers in both bakeries and savouries sub-sectors. Not a single owner allowed us to ask them any question whatsoever. We therefore used various tactics such as pretending to inquire about their families and quickly slipping in relevant questions; diverting the owner's attention; following the worker when he stepped outside the premises even for a moment; urgently whispering questions when the owner was busy with customers; visiting the unit when the owner was away for lunch; and so on.

The workers told us that none of them, including the highest paid manager, receive monthly wages of more than Rs.1600, the lowest in the hierarchy getting less than Rs.900. The owners told that two shifts are employed, each worker being paid per shift of supposedly 8 hours. However, we found that only one shift exists, all workers without exception working for almost 19 hours a day. The process of baking starts at about 3.30 a.m. early morning when flour is kneaded. By the time the workers perform their morning ablutions, the dough has to be kneaded again, shaped and baked so as to catch the early morning buyers by 5 a.m. Production continues uninterrupted throughout the day, ending by about 10.30 p.m. The work hours therefore extend over 19 hours, exceeding the legally stipulated limit by 10 hours, an entire shift of workers being made redundant. Bakery owners are thus able to reduce the already low wage bill by more than half.

It is important to point out at this stage that bakeries are covered by the Minimum Wages Act, 1948 as well as by the Maharashtra Minimum Wages Rules of 1963. Further, the Government of Maharashtra revised the minimum wage rates applicable to bakery workers with effect from 18 August, 1994 (Government Notification No.MWA.5292/(7433)/Lab-7). The minimum wages legally applicable today are - Rs.1413 for skilled, Rs.1208 for semi-skilled and Rs.1090 for 'unskilled' workers. These wages are calculated on the basis of a nine-hour working day, as opposed to the reality of existence of the bakery workers who generally receive less than minimum wages and that too for more than double the hours of work.

Further, none of the stipulations, laid down in the Bombay Shops and Establishments Act of 1948 and the Maharashtra Shops and Establishments Rules of 1961 and amended up to 1999, are implemented. Units are open for business at 5 am and close only by about 11 pm, as against the 8.30 pm closure rule (Bombay Shops and Establishments Act, 1948, Chapter III, Section 11(b)). The number of working hours themselves are 19 hours, when the law stipulates that even the spread-over should not exceed 11 hours (Chapter III, Section 16).

No leave whatsoever is given, not even the stipulated weekly off with wages (Chapter III, Section 18(1-a) and Section 18(3)). The owners very categorically informed us that all workers are given a paid holiday every Friday when the market is closed. However, we specially visited the area on four consecutive Fridays and found the bakeries invariably functioning, the excuse given being the hackneyed one of 'too many orders today'. No leave of any kind is given, wages being deducted for any absence from duty, including illness. In fact, we found the entire section on benefits in our questionnaire to be almost redundant. As we see later, this is true of the savouries sub-sector as well.

The most important 'benefit' provided to the workers is 'letting' them sleep on the premises. We hasten to add that this 'benevolence' on the part of the owners is a clear reflection of their own 'self-interest'. All workers, without exception, are migrants, interestingly from the same community and the same districts of Uttar Pradesh as the owners. Most of the workers migrate through friends and family members who are already employed in bakeries, though not necessarily the same ones.

This meso level connection results in various simultaneous processes that prove extremely beneficial to owners. One, it allows for the emergence of a patron-client relationship, in which the migrants, who are generally from the landless and marginal farming households from 'backward' villages, are provided at least some employment by their 'benefactors', along with shelter in a 'crowded' and 'inhospitable' city. Two, owners are assured of relatively 'permanent' labour without giving any other benefits apart from shelter, as workers obviously hesitate to leave their jobs for fear of becoming homeless in a 'heartless' city. Three, 'allowing' workers to sleep in the bakery itself ensures the availability of and access to labour throughout the day and night. Moreover, the 'permission' granted to the workers to cook on the premises reinforces the dependency relationship by creating the mythical concept of a 'home away from home'. Further, being migrants without any immediate families and with few connections in the city, the workers rarely take leave; there is no one to take leave for, no household problems, no children, no births or deaths, no family gatherings, no festivals. And, finally, all these factors merge into the unabated exploitation of labour that adds further to the difficulty of organising the unorganised.

However, the patron does not ensure the most fundamental aspect of employment to his client - that of continuity of work, even if at such low wages for a 19-hour working day. The migrant workers go back to their villages for a month every summer for the agricultural season. There is no guarantee of them getting employment in the same bakery again. The turnover of workers is therefore fairly high, generally two to three years. Nor does working for the same employer for a number of years ensure increase in wages. We met a worker in his early seventies who has been employed in the same bakery for almost 30 years. Though he is the most 'trusted' employee and has been given full responsibility in running the bakery, he is paid exactly the same as a new worker with no additional benefits whatsoever. He is obviously bitter, but has no option.

A small part of the wage is taken by the worker every month for incidental expenses, the rest being left with the owner for 'safe-keeping'. Most of the workers being illiterate, the owner not only gets away with the fudging of accounts but derives an additional benefit by depositing the not-so-inconsiderable amount in either fixed deposits or loaning it out in the unorganised credit market on usurious rates of interest. The worker's dues are given when he returns to his village, obviously without any interest added.

The accommodation provided to workers is usually a low loft, built probably illegally, above the bakery. The buildings in which the bakeries are housed are old and quite dilapidated, the walls dark and dirty, the roof generally made of corrugated iron or asbestos sheets. There is little or no ventilation; only one unit has a ceiling fan. This, coupled with the intense heat of the ovens and the humidity in Mumbai, often gets unbearable. All workers share one single room. Under such conditions, it is obvious why women are not employed. Although most bakeries have a small bathroom, not a single unit, including one renovated just a few weeks ago, provides toilet facilities, all workers having to use public toilets. Everything else has to be purchased by the workers - sheets, buckets, vessels, stoves, toiletries, medicines, rations, etc. Only one owner claimed to give flour and sugar, although the workers later told us that they are charged for it, the amount being cut from their wages. Another owner complained that there was no need for giving provisions, since workers 'steal' them anyway, an accusation that upset the workers very much.

3.3.5 Work Conditions, Hygiene and Product Quality

The issues of product quality, health and hygiene cannot be separated from the work conditions. The two Acts applicable to bakeries specify 5 factors relating to health and safety. These are cleanliness, ventilation, sufficient lighting, precautions against fire, and the maintenance of a first aid box (Bombay Shops and Establishments Act, Chapter VIII, Sections 39-42). Only one bakery has a fire extinguisher, and that too not in a working condition. All units except the one recently renovated are dark and dimly lit, only one being fitted with an exhaust fan. None has a first aid box, the owners being quite amused when we asked about it.

Flour is never sieved. The water used for kneading is dirty and carried in unwashed slime-layered plastic buckets. The platform on which the dough is kneaded is rarely washed. Kneading is done with bare, obviously unclean hands. Dough balls sometimes fall on the floor when the over-stacked trays overturn; they are just picked up and replaced. The suffocating heat and smoke of the continuously burning ovens in a room which has little ventilation and a clogged chimney impacts both the quality of the product and the health of workers. In every bakery we visited we saw the kneader's sweat falling straight into the dough. All workers complained of eye, breathing and 'throat' problems; we ourselves could not bear the smoke for more than a few minutes. The workers spend a not negligible amount every month on eye drops, *kajal* and *netranjan,* as well as on tonics 'to make breathing easier'.

It is difficult to decide which is filthier, the floor or the sacks on which the products are dumped. Floors are merely swept, even though we had walked in with our shoes on; the sacks are sometimes dusted but never washed. The ovens have not been cleaned for years. The heat of the continuously operating ovens is so intense that it takes a full week for them to be cold enough for a human to enter; owners told us it was not 'economical' to clean ovens.

No worker is compensated for any injury at work; the Worker's Compensation Act does not apply to bakeries. Burnt and scarred hands and feet have to be tended by workers themselves. Also, as the workers sleep on the hot floor only on weed mats, they are continuously affected by insect bites and rashes, some even reporting rodent bites. The long hours of work, carried out while standing, result in backaches and varicose veins.

The issues of quality control and product standardisation thus seem somewhat irrelevant in the present situation; these will get improved upon only when working conditions are rectified.

3.3.6 Production, Marketing and Degree of Exploitation

The products produced, almost on daily basis, are *pav,* basic biscuits, *nankhatai* and *mawa* cakes We were not quite sure about the reliability of the information on costs of production given out by our respondents, especially for items not purchased on daily basis; the best that we could do was to work out some approximate estimates of the cost of production on the basis of daily expenses incurred by the enterprises. On such approximate basis, the daily expenditure for manufacturing bakery products (from 270 kgs. of flour consumed every day) totals Rs 8212. To this if we add the daily wage bill of Rs.330 (based on an average monthly wage of Rs.1100 for 9 workers), the total cost of production is Rs.8542. All raw materials are supplied by agents who deal exclusively with one single input, and delivered at the very doorstep of the manufacturer, the transportation cost is nil.

The share of wages in the total circulating capital thus works out to an astounding low of 3.86 per cent. Absolutely no details whatsoever are available on sales and production. It is therefore not possible to work out the rate of profit. Further, we believe that other components of constant capital should not be included in any calculations. The buildings in which the bakeries are housed are generally old and dilapidated; the iron trays which cost Rs. 60 each have gone way beyond the depreciation period, as have the ovens which are as old as the units and require little maintenance which in any case is done by the workers themselves. Also, the shelter provided by owners does not imply any extra expenditure. 'Shadow' costs which could be incorporated are bribes to labour inspectors and sales department officers, and cuts to electricity and water companies which provide illegal connections to specially unregistered units. As there is 'enough' demand for the products, no capital is wasted on advertising and marketing.

Pav is a highly perishable commodity as no preservatives are added. Although generally all output is sold, sometimes it does get spoilt. Spoilt *pav* is then sold to cattle owners as feed at the rate of Rs.3-4 per kilo. Broken biscuits are purchased at half price by mainly slum dwellers, while burnt remnants are put back into the oven as fuel.

All bakery products are sold directly from the manufacturing unit itself, each bakery having either a regular shop or a sales counter on its premises. Customers include direct consumers, small hotels and restaurants, professional caterers, department stores, roadside stalls, and vendors. Only *pav* is sold loose, at the rate of 75 paise per piece. All other products are priced differently and sold in plastic bags in packets of 200 grams and half a kilo, none of the packets carrying any brand names. We were told that often the products are opened and repacked in branded plastic bags by the larger purchasers, mainly department stores.

A significant proportion of *pav* and basic biscuits is purchased by vendors who then resell directly to customers at their homes at varying prices determined by the kind of locality. Normally the vendor earns one rupee on 6 *pavs* and about Rs.2 on every 200 gram packet of basic biscuits. The products are placed by vendors in huge cloth bags or iron trunks, and carried either on foot or bicycles. A unit generally has its own fixed vendors. No bargaining is conducted, as uniform prices are enforced by the Bakers' Association. Vendors do not have much capital and therefore are given credit, accounts compulsorily being settled the same day itself. This system ensures tying of vendors to particular bakeries, as well as the settlement and distribution of profits to all partners on a daily basis. Some owners complained about instances of vendors reneging; we found this to be generally untrue as they would then be boycotted by all bakeries.

4. Savouries Establishments

4.1 Introduction

It has been stated at the outset that savouries establishments do not exist in any NIC code, except at the broadest 2-digit level. Also, we were advised both by the Directorate of Economics and Statistics as well as the NSS not to include this category in 3- and 4-digit analysis as it would distort results and lead to wrong conclusions and policy recommendations. Additionally, several aspects of these establishments and consequently, the analysis relating to them, are somewhat similar to the bakeries sub- sector. The points of similarity and divergence unfold themselves as we proceed along.

The region selected for field survey is the suburb of Ghatkopar in the northeast part of the city of Mumbai, about 10 kms. up from Kurla. It is one of the three major centres in the city renowned for the manufacture of savouries (*farsan/chivda*). The ward office was not as cooperative as in the case of Kurla and therefore no local level data are available. Our analysis is hence based exclusively on field survey investigations.

The majority of the savouries establishments are located on a single narrow lane towards the eastern side of the local railway station. Only three owners of the six units in operation agreed to talk, though grudgingly. One of these three units manufactures only potato wafers, and is known throughout the city. The other two units produce a vast variety of items which will be listed later. In spite of the limitations, we did manage to collect sufficient information, though obviously not as detailed as we would have liked. As in the bakeries sub-sector, data on sales and production were not easily forthcoming; meeting all workers directly was not possible either.

4.2 Ownership Structure and Production Design

All savouries establishments are owned by individuals, the trade being passed on from the father to the son. One owner was earlier operating a cattle stable which he converted into the wafer unit about 40 years ago. The other manufacturies have been in existence for a relatively short period, one for about 20 years and the other 12 years, both being only shops earlier. Interestingly, as in the case of bakeries, owners are migrants from Uttar Pradesh, as are all the workers. The only point of divergence is that all owners and the majority of workers are hindus.

The wafer unit should technically be covered by the Factories Act and classified as a formal sector unit as it employs 12 workers and uses power in the process of production. When we pointed this out to the owner, he just laughed and began deriding the educational system that 'produces professors who cannot count', declaring that he employed only the magic figure of 9 workers.

The 2 savoury units produce a large variety of deep-fried items, all of them using the basic ingredient of gram flour (*besan*) mixed with other inputs. These items include *bhakarwadi, kachori*, spicy chick peas, *masala channa* (gram), gram flour chips, six types of pulses and peas, four types of peanuts, seven of *chivda*, six of *gathia,* nine of *sev*, four of *samosas*, and seven types of *farsan.*

All savoury establishments operate a single oven; one had two but the second was not in use. Only diesel is used, as deep-frying requires extremely powerful fuel. Depending on the specific item, various raw materials such as peanuts, are mixed in huge vats along with the necessary spices. The mixture is then poured into the ever- boiling oil, the vessel used being a huge *kadai* (wok). Only one *kadai* is used for all items, the residue of a specific variety of savoury being strained out through the perforated ladle. While one item is being fried, other varieties are prepared so that the heat of the oil is not lost. The savouries are then emptied out on large iron trays, similar to the ones used in bakeries. After cooling, the items are weighed and packed in unbranded plastic bags of 200 grams and one kilo, the packets being sealed with small electric machines. The sealed packets are then placed in their fixed spaces on roof-high shelves for sale.

The process of production in the wafer-manufacturing unit is almost fully mechanised. Four varieties of wafers are produced - plain salted, spiced, plain sliced (*salli*) and spiced s*alli*. The process of production and the machines used are the same, the difference arising in the type of cutting blade used.

Huge sacks of potatoes are emptied on the floor, from where they are shoveled in their unsorted state by a worker called 'washer' into the washing machine. After peeling, the potatoes go through certain other processes such as slicing, whitening, de-starching and drying and are finally poured into a massive *kadai* in which the oil is perpetually boiling. The frying process takes less than 10 minutes, after which the ready wafers are put into iron trays, cooled, mixed with salt and/or spices, weighed and then packed into plastic bags of 200 grams and one kilo. Interestingly, only the smaller plastic bags used are branded.

4.3 Division of Labour, Wages and Work Conditions

The division of labour is more intensive in savouries establishments, though not as layered. Each category of worker performs a task exclusively assigned to him. There is no need for having a supervisor or manager since the owner himself or his son is always present. He oversees the entire process of production, checks the raw materials, supervises weighing and packing, and conducts all sales personally. The *bhattiwala* who does the actual frying is the highest in the hierarchy of workers as only his job is considered 'skilled'. Below him is the *attawala* who mixes the various ingredients according to the variety of item currently being made. The lowest category is that of packers who weigh the products, pack and seal them, and then place them on the assigned shelves.

The division of labour in the wafer-manufacturing unit is determined by the kinds of machines used and the product design followed. At the highest rung of the hierarchy is the *kadaiwala* who does the actual frying, followed strictly in order by the 'dryer' who operates the drying machine, the 'cutter', the 'peeler' and finally the most 'unskilled' 'washer'. Packers have to perform several tasks - that of carrying and unloading the potato sacks, mixing the required spices in the cooled wafers under instructions from the *kadaiwala*, weighing and packing. All activities are carried out at a remarkably fast pace so that no machine or worker remains idle.

As in bakeries, the wage structure is determined by the division of labour. Owners, of course, reported the daily wages as being quite high : Rs.100-125 for *kadaiwalas*; Rs. 70 for dryers and cutters; Rs. 60 for *attawalas*; and Rs. 50 for peelers, washers and packers. Workers confided with us that the wages actually paid are at least Rs.10-20 less in every category.

The meso level analysis presented in the bakeries sub-section applies here too. Workers in savouries establishments are given a place to sleep in, as all are migrants. All workers are charged rent, a fact even the owners told us, at an approximate rate of Rs.150-200 every month. The conditions, however, differ in all the three units. In one, the workers are 'allowed' to stay in a suffocatingly small and unventilated room where sacks of raw materials are stored. The 'enlightened' owner of the other savoury establishment has rented a small room just behind the premises where all the six workers live. The wafer unit owner strangely said that none of his workers are given shelter, although we ourselves saw the room where the workers stayed.

All owners also claim that they provide two free meals and one tea every day to all their workers. This is blatantly untrue. The savoury units only allow the workers to cook their meals, as in the case of bakeries. The wafer unit owner does provide meals but deducts Rs.350 every month from the wages. The quality of the meals is pathetic - watery *dal* (pulse) and vegetable with rice; no *rotis* are ever given which is what the workers are used to in their villages in north India. There is no fixed time given off for meals; the worker grabs a few minutes whenever he can and therefore rests content with cold food.

Unlike the bakeries sub-sector, no laws apply to workers in savouries establishments. We counter-checked with government officials, labour lawyers and union activists, and studied in detail the Shops and Establishments Act and Regulations along with all the amendments and judgements up to 1999. There are no working hours; opening and closing timings are not specified; the savouries units begin work around 7 a.m. and continue up to 10.30 or eleven at night, implying a working day of about 15 hours, with little rest in between. The owners insisted that all workers are given a weekly off on Mondays when the market is supposed to be closed. We deliberately visited the area on three consecutive Mondays to discover that all units were functioning, the excuse once again being the usual one, that of ' working to clear too many orders'.

The only rule that applies to savouries establishments is Section 394 of the Bombay Municipal Corporation Act which states that a license would be given on the condition of installation of a fire extinguisher. Of course, not even a single unit has it. Several other conditions of work are similar to the bakeries sub-sector - no leave of any kind; no overtime; insect infested rooms to sleep in; no bedding; no toilets; no fans; no medical assistance; no compensation for injury or death, and so on.

The one major difference between bakeries and savouries establishments is that at least two of the latter have fairly good ventilation. Though there are no exhaust fans, the building is constructed in such a manner that the top 3 feet of one wall is not built up to the ceiling, thus leaving a big enough gap for air to circulate. There are, of course, no ceiling fans except where the owners themselves sit and work.

4.4 Health, Hygiene and Product Quality

We present the analysis of the three savouries establishments separately as health, hygiene and quality conditions differ significantly among the three.

The savoury establishment started about 12 years ago is relatively clean, partly because the construction is new and partly because the owner is a graduate and quite 'enlightened'. In fact, he was the only owner who was polite and somewhat responsive. The floors are swept regularly and washed once a week. The products are kept in trays and not dumped on gunnysacks; this, of course, may be partly due to the fact that savouries are tiny. The 'only' complaints of the workers in this unit related to heat in the manufactury and insects in the room they sleep in.

In contrast, the other savoury unit is utterly filthy. Rats and cockroaches scurry around even in the day; the chimney does not function; there is no exhaust fan; raw materials are stored in the sleeping area of the workers; the floors are rarely washed; the walls are black with dirt and grease; spider webs cover all corners; savouries are sometimes dumped on gunny sacks; split savouries are swept up and re-packed; the oil is re-used till it loses its original colour and taste; the list of unwholesome elements is rather large. The unit is located just next to open and overflowing drains which are covered with scum and layers of insects; the public toilet next door has probably not been cleaned for years and remains clogged leading to an unbearable stench. In contrast, the 'enlightened' owner whose unit too is near the open drains has covered them with cement slabs.

The filth and dirt in the wafer unit is shocking, enough to put us off from enjoying eating wafers ever again. Potatoes are dumped into the washing machine without even sorting; we could see a few worm-infested ones being thrown in. The peeled waste is spewed onto the floor and pushed with bare feet through a hole in the wall into the lane outside which is heavily over-crowded and teeming with playing children. While talking to us, the washer kept dipping his feet into the tub in which potatoes were soaking; his feet were full of boils and bleeding sores which he told us he got from having to push the worm-infested potato peels with his bare feet. The tub in which potato slices are soaked was so dark with dirt that we thought chemicals had been added.

The machines are rarely cleaned, rinsed only occasionally. The floor is always wet and slippery; every worker reported he had slipped at least once and injured himself. The machines become so hot that workers' hands are covered with burns and scars. The continuously bubbling oil spatters the *kadaiwala* and any other worker nearby. The *kadaiwala* is perched precariously on a plank as the wok is kept at a height; we were relieved to know that there had been no reported incident of anyone falling into the oil. The workers, 12 in all, reported suffering from backaches due to the continuous bending and lifting of heavy loads, varicose veins bulging from hours of standing, and eye and breathing problems due to the intense heat.

Fiddling in the weighing process is a foregone conclusion. We witnessed the entire process and saw that the needle never touched the 200 gram mark, and that often the weighing machine does not function and, more often than not, an 'approximated' amount is packed.

Product and quality standardisation thus seem somewhat irrelevant in the context of both bakeries and savouries establishments. And, as mentioned categorically earlier, no quality issue can be debated in isolation from improvement in work conditions.

4.5 Production Costs, Sales, Marketing and Share of Wages

It is difficult to calculate precisely the average costs of production of savouries partly because of the large variety of items produced and partly because of the total lack of response. What is, however, possible to calculate with some certainty is the value of daily sales. A minimum of 300 kilos of savouries are sold every day at the rate of Rs.50 per kilo. The turnover per day is thus Rs.15,000, an amazing amount by all standards particularly in the informal sector. During one of our several visits to the wafer unit we met a sales tax officer who informed us that the daily turnover is easily double of what owners told us; we have no reason to disbelieve her. Wafers are sold at Rs.67 per kilo; if the daily sales are 300 kgs. as the owner insisted, the turnover would be Rs.20,100, and if doubled according to the sales tax officer's advice, the amount would be Rs.40,200.

Even if we assume the costs of production to be as much as 50per cent including depreciation, the profit rate is remarkably high. In this context, it would be interesting to estimate at least approximately the share of wages. Taken at a monthly average of Rs.1200 per worker, somewhat on the higher side so as not to be accused of underestimation, the total for nine workers would come to Rs.10,800. For wafers, it would work out to be Rs.480, calculated again at an average wage of Rs.1200 per month for the 12 workers.

All products are sold from the premises themselves; no sale is done outside. Customers include individual consumers, caterers, small hotels and restaurants, supermarkets and department stores. We met a buyer from one of the most renowned department stores in South Mumbai; though he denied it, we were able to judge that the savouries are re-packed in branded plastic bags and sold as products manufactured 'exclusively' by the store. This is apparently a regular practice as far as savouries and wafers are concerned, a fact which even the owners duly confirmed.

Prices are fixed partly by the Savouries Association and partly by competition from other units located in the same lane. We purchased a few packets of similar products manufactured by the formal sector in order to calculate the price differential. The results are amazing. Savouries which are sold by the informal sector are priced at Rs.50 per kilo, while the branded formal sector products are priced three times higher at Rs.150. For wafers, the informal sector prices are Rs.67, while the multinational Uncle Chipps sells them for Rs. 200 per kilo.

Owners complained that although demand is 'steady', the growth rate is declining due to the entry of big business houses particularly multinationals into the food-manufacturing sector ever since 'India became a part of the world economic system'. They also blamed the media for hyping consumerism and 'foreign' values and products.

5. Fish Processing

5.1 Introduction

The analysis in this section is divided into four sub-sections. We start with 3- and 4-digit analysis at the macro level, tracing linkages from the all-India to the state level and then to the city of Greater Mumbai. Area analysis begins with the delineation of demographic and occupational patterns in the fishing village of Versova. Here, we present some basic information on the number and types of boats and nets as they are closely linked with processing and marketing. The section dealing with processing is further sub-divided into methods of preservation according to fish varieties. Patterns of employment, wages and working conditions are inter-linked with health, hygiene and quality. For marketing, a separate and detailed analysis is attempted since here, both formal and informal forms co-exist.

5.2 Linkage Analysis: Macro, Meso, and Micro Realities

Fish-processing falls under NIC code 20 (manufacture of food products), as do the other sectors of bakeries and savouries. The specific 3 digit code is 203, (processing, canning and preservation of fish, crustecea and similar foods). For detailed analysis, we have selected the 4 digit codes of 2031 (sun-drying of fish), 2034 (processing and canning of fish), and 2039 (processing and preserving of fish crustecea and similar foods not elsewhere classified).

The available secondary data, both for all-India and Maharashtra, are strangely quite incomplete and scattered in comparison to the bakeries sub sector. While formal sector information is available only for codes 2034 and 2039 at both levels, informal sector information exists only for all-India. Inexplicably, the unpublished data of the 51st Round of the NSS records no information whatsoever even for the 3 digit code for Maharashtra.

Although Maharashtra has the second highest number of formal sector fish processing plants among the 8 major coastal states of the country, it accounts for only 1.4 per cent of labour employed. This is not surprising considering the relatively higher level of technology that exists in the food-manufacturing sector in Maharashtra. However, the state also records the second highest number of average working days at 331 (ASI Vol. II 1993-94 : 2034-I-001).

TABLE 5.1 : **Formal Sector Processing, Canning and Preservation of Fish and Fish Crustacea (Codes 2034 and 2039), All India and Maharashtra**

Sr. No.	Category	All India		Maharashtra	
		Code 2034	Code 2039	Code 2034	Code 2039
1.	Number of factories	146	65	23 (15.6)	4 (6.2)
2.	Invested capital (Rs.)	3451537	428765	386482 (11.2)	20561 (4.8)
3.	Number of workers	16135	3471	2270 (1.4)	59 (1.7)

Source: Calculations based on ASI Vol. II 1993-94, p.2034 - I - 001 to 2039 - X - 001.

The scenario is somewhat different so far as fish crustecea is concerned, Maharashtra reporting only 4 units employing merely 59 workers. These data reveal an extremely high level of underestimation, as within our small area of research itself, at least 5 such units exist. The estimated marine fish catch of Maharashtra was 4.54 lakh tons in 1997-98, down 6per cent from the previous year. 2.8 lakh tons were used in fresh form and 0.10 were salted. Of the 1.64 lakh tons sun dried, 0.33 were used as manure (Economic Survey of Maharashtra, 1998-99 : 55).

TABLE 5.2 : **Number of Informal Fish Processing Units and Gender-based Labour Employed (Code 203), All India**

Sr. No.	Type of Units	No. of Units	Labour Employed		
			Males	Females	Total
1.	OAME	5548 (92.5)	5712 (39.5)	8735 (60.5)	14447 (100.0)
2.	NDME	452 (7.5)	39015 (93.3)	2799 (6.7)	41814 (100.0)
3.	Total Informal	6000 (100.0)	44727 (79.5)	11534 (20.5)	56261 (100.0)

(percentages in parenthesis)

Source: Calculations based on NSS 45th Round 1990, Sarvekshana, p. S.13.

The available all-India three-digit level data show that while 92.5 per cent of informal sector units are OAMEs, they account for only 25.7 per cent of workers, obviously all family labour. The NDMEs reveal an opposite trend, the respective percentages being 7.5 per cent and 74.3 per cent An interesting fact that emerges is that self-employment involves more women, OAMEs accounting for 61.0 per cent of all women workers. On the other hand, 93.3per cent of NDME workers are men.

The implication therefore could be that the participation of women declines when economic activity extends outside the home into the market.

Unpublished data from the Economic Census of Maharashtra gives fairly detailed information of fish processing relating to our three codes of 2031, 2034 and 2039 for the city of Mumbai. This is the only data source that includes sun drying. In any case, according to available records, only one other unit exists, that of code 2032 relating to artificial dehydration. This single unit employs merely 4 workers and hence falls in the informal sector. We present the basic information in Table 5.3.

TABLE 5.3 : **Drying, Processing and Preservation of Fish and Crustacea (Codes 2031, 2034 and 2039), Greater Mumbai**

Sr. No.	Category	2031	2034	2039	Total
1.	Units	10	3	1	14
2.	Without Power	10	1	0	11
3.	Total Workers, of which	30	76	10	116
3.1	Males	20	48	1	69
3.2	Females	10	28	9	47

(percentages in parenthesis)

Source: Calculations based on NSS 45th Round 1990, Sarvekshana, S. 13.

Only 14 fish processing units reportedly exist in Greater Mumbai, 71.4 per cent of them involved in sun drying. All these 10 are OAME units, employing an average of 3 workers each. The 4 processing units of fish and crustecea come under the formal sector, the single unit with no power having more than 20 workers. 43 per cent of the total 86 workers employed in the formal sector are women. That these figures relating to both units and employment are amazingly underestimated is borne out by the fact that in our sample village of Versova alone, at least a thousand women are involved in the processing and preservation of fish and crustecea. In the following section, we analyse the field reality. As we were able to get quite a vast amount of information and as fish processing is tightly inter related to fishing activity, the analysis has to be necessarily divided into various sub sections.

5.3 Field-based Analysis

5.3.1 Demographic and Occupational Patterns

Versova is one of the two most important fishing villages in Mumbai. With a coastline of 1.5 kms. and a shallow sandy beach, the main occupation for men is fishing, while most of the processing and marketing is done by women. The demographic and occupational data are given in Table 5.4.

TABLE 5.4 : **Demographic and Occupational Patterns, Versova, 1991**

Sr. No.	Category	Number
1.	No. of households	1127
2.	Total population, of which	5988
2.1	Adult males	1761
2.2	Adult females	1853
2.3	Children	2374
3.	Active fisherfolk	359
4.	Allied workers, of which	3917
4.1	Marketing	1427
4.2	Net making	1000
4.3	Processing / Curing	1082
4.4	Others	408

Source: Department of Fisheries, Government of Maharashtra, unpublished data.

It is a little puzzling that the number of workers exceeds total adult population. Perhaps, a large number of children are at work. This did not seem to be true of the sample village since we found most children going to school, and the standard of living in general to be fairly above the defined poverty line. But it is also a fact that child labour amongst the non-migrant residents is widespread, and is not accounted for in Census calculations.

An extremely significant fact that emerges is the high work participation of women. The historical tradition among the Koli community to which the fisher folk in Versova belong is that only men go out in boats for fishing and all on-shore activities. are conducted by women. They are almost solely responsible for marketing, and also curing and processing, while the only on-shore activity for men is making nets and building boats. This gender-based division of labour exists along the entire coast of Maharashtra.

It is also interesting to note that the sex ratio is fairly highly, especially in Mumbai which has more male migrants than any other city in the entire country.

5.3.2 Types of Fishing Boats and Fish Catch

It is necessary to give an overview of the number and types of boats in the selected sample village because the fish catch and hence, the extent of fish processing are determined primarily by the prevailing level of technology.

Table 5.5 shows that 57 per cent of the boats are mechanised, only about 26 per cent of them being trawlers. It was reported by experienced fisher folk that almost 98 per cent of the total catch is accounted for by mechanised boats. The level of technology is additionally determined by two other components - the tonnage and the length of the boats. Tonnage data are presented in Table 5.6 and length data in Table 5.7.

TABLE 5.5 : **Types of Fishing Boats According to Nets, Versova**

Sr. No.	Category	Number
1.	Total mechanised, of which	341
1.1	Trawlers	90
1.2	Gill nets	77
1.3	Bag nets	174
2.	Total non-mechanised boats	258
2.1	Plank built bag net boats	31
2.2	Dugout gill net canoes	98
2.3	Dugout bag net canoes	110
2.4	Other dugout canoes	19
3.	Total boats	599

Source: Census of Fishermen, Boats and Nets 1992, Department of Fisheries, Government of Maharashtra, unpublished data.

TABLE 5.6 : **Fishing Boats According to Tonnage, Versova**

Sr. No.	Tonnage Group	Mechanised	Non - mechanised	Total
1.	0 - 1	4	213	217
2.	1 - 3	77	16	93
3.	3 - 10	220	29	249
4.	10 - 20	32	0	32
5.	20 - 30	8	0	8
6.	Total	341	258	599

Source: Census of Fishermen, Boats and Nets 1992, Department of Fisheries, Government of Maharashtra, unpublished data.

Non-mechanised boats have a maximum tonnage of 10 and length of 17.5 meters. A very big majority (82.6 per cent) has merely a single ton capacity, and 98.0 per cent of them operate with boats having the minimum length of 7.5 m. Consequently, one of the main recommendations for the fish sector would be increased availability of easy credit for upgrading the technology and purchase of bigger boats.

Extensive interviews and group discussions with elders revealed that fish catch has been consistently declining in Versova. Whereas a few years ago, a single trawler could catch at least 35 to 40 tubs of fish in one landing, the number of tubs caught at present are merely 10 to 15, and that too during season. This was ratified by the Department of Fisheries which gave us data that is reproduced in Table 5.8. There has been a drastic decline in marine fish landing at Versova, both in relative and absolute terms. While the tonnage has fallen by 7,657, its proportion to the increasing Mumbai level stands reduced from 26.6 per cent to 18.7 per cent.

TABLE 5.7 : **Fishing Boats According to Length, Versova**

Sr. No.	Length of Boats (in mts.)	Mechanised	Non-mechanised	Total
1.	Upto 7.5	102	252	354
2.	7.6 - 10	146	5	151
3.	10.1 - 17.5	86	1	87
4.	More than 17.5	7	0	7
5.	Total	341	258	598

Source: Census of Fishermen, Boats and Nets 1992, Department of Fisheries, Government of Maharashtra, unpublished data.

TABLE 5.8 : **Marine Fish Landing, Versova and Mumbai (in Tonnes)**

Sr. No.	Year	Greater Mumbai	Versova
1.	1992 - 93	170276 (100.0)	45242 (26.6)
2.	1996 - 97	201121 (100.0)	37585 (18.7)

(percentages in parenthesis)

Source: Calculations based on Fish Production Report 1996 - 97] Chapter on Landings in Greater Mumbai, Department of Fisheries, Government of Maharashtra.

Several reasons have been identified for the drastic decline in catch, one of the more important ones being pollution of seawater. Just across the jetty are several large industrial estates and many chemical factories which discharge effluents into the sea with no pollution control whatsoever. The water at this corner of the village is black, oily and has an unbearably foul smell. Lead, mercury, arsenic and other pollutants have depleted the oxygen content of water. This results not only in decreasing fish catch and spawning, but also the rusting of boat-joints, leading to increased expenditure on repair and maintenance of boats themselves.

The original white sandy beach is also getting choked with sewage, garbage, plastic bags, immersion of religious idols, etc. Additionally, reclamation in the up market areas of Bandra, Worli and Nariman Point has resulted in massive erosion, silting and sandbars. Several representations have been made to the concerned authorities to rectify the situation but to no avail. The extent of erosion and pollution is so high that it is financially not possible for the local residents and their 3 cooperative societies to resolve the problem. Also, climatic changes have altered the peak season of different varieties of fish.

Another major reason for the decline in catch is the large number of foreign trawlers, what the local fisher folk call 'factory ships'. These massive trawlers, with their highly sophisticated technology, can go deep into the sea, process the fish on board itself, and take the products directly to their own countries. A nation wide agitation of fisher folk under the banner of the National Fish Workers Forum in 1997 led to cancellation of foreign traveller licenses, but some of these permissions are still valid.

Over-fishing is probably the single most important cause of depletion in fish catch. Local fisher folk are aware of this and have discussed the issue often enough, but few care to implement the ban imposed by the *Naqwa Mandal* (Association of Boat Owners). Over-fishing which began in the mid-1980s, with the entry of export companies into Versova, has now reached virtually unmanageable proportions. We ourselves witnessed this. It is traditionally accepted that no fishing should take place during the monsoon which is the main breeding season. Yet, it continues; boat landings take place twice every single day.

Apart from the decline in production, loss of species is also to be reckoned with. One of the most important and lucrative fish is the lobster that used to be found in abundance in Versova. Lobsters were processed through the boiling method before selling, and provided a substantial income; today, the few lobsters caught are sold directly without processing. Other endangered species include tiger prawns, squids, frogs, pomfret, *ghol* (jew fish), *titam, dhada,* eels, rays and salmon. The catch of cod fish is negligible now, whereas at one point of time it was quite substantial and was a rich source of liver oil.

Older fisher women told us that they also used to participate in catching fish in the creek and marsh before pollution set in and the dense mangroves disappeared. The species almost lost today include *nevti* (newts), small crabs, mysids and mud skippers which used to be caught earlier by women and young children in the creek.

5.4 Processing and Preservation of Fish and Crustecea, Workers and Work Conditions

5.4.1 Introduction

Although most of the processing is done on land, fisher folk have begun carrying out the minimum preservation procedure of putting fish in ice on the boat itself. Sometimes, sorting is also done according to species. Generally, huge cane baskets are used, now being increasingly replaced by longer-lasting plastic tubs. Thermacole boxes were tried out, but they failed because of greater spoilage.

Landing takes place twice a day, at about 3 a.m. in the early morning when the smaller boats come in and at 4 p.m. in the evening when the trawlers anchor. Almost the entire adult population of the village along with hundreds of buyers and workers await each landing. The fish baskets are taken out at great speed by fisher folk and handed down to male workers.

The catch of each boat is then placed in a pre-determined spot on the beach where the women family members of the owners are waiting. The women keep a strict check on the baskets, and with the help of hired women workers, immediately begin sorting and grading. Sales are conducted, at the first stage, right on the landing spot, the buyers primarily being the processors, again almost exclusively women. There are two kinds of processors, those dealing with crustacea and fish, and those who sun dry. We examine either category of processors separately and describe the method of preservation according to species. Many commonalities on the characteristics of the workers and their work conditions emerge nonetheless.

One of the major problems in the landing centre at Versova is the lack of infrastructure facilities. There are no lights even though boats land mainly in the dark, no market and sale centers, no toilet and garbage-colledction facilities people have to stand for hours as there are no sitting arrangements, no built path to carry the heavy loads, no communication facilities, and so on.

5.4.2 Sun Drying, Salting and Curing

Fifteen varieties of fish and fish crustacea are sun dried and salted. The eatable varieties are *wakti* (small croaker), *dhoma* (large croaker), *mandeli* (golden anchovy), *rawas* (small shear fish), pomfret, *bangda* (mackerel), ambari, bombil (bombay duck), small ribbon fish, jowla, and *tengli* (tiny shrimps). The non-eatable varieties are kuta and small trash fish used as fertilizers and for poultry feed, and eel and *ghol* (jew fish) used to make surgical threads and thermometers.

There are variations in the timings of landing (the most common being the evenings), timings, duration and procedure of salting (essential to prevent fly larvae), techniques and intensity of washing and post-washing handling of the stuff, sieving, drying, sorting, packing, and so on, the details for which need not be repeated. Most of the operations, especially the drying, salting and curing, are carried out largely by family members themselves, although occasional hiring of additional hands is a common practice. It is important, however, to mention that drying and salting are carried out almost exclusively by women 'suppliers' from Gujarat who migrated to Versova less than two decades ago. Earlier, the elderly fisher women from the resident Koli community used to do the processing, but as their income levels improved and no let-up occurred in the 'back breaking' nature of the work, they happily allowed the *kathiawadis* to take over. The majority of these migrants live in slums on the outskirts of the village; financially, they are not badly placed but the lack of 'free' space for residential purposes leaves them no alternative. Some amongst them, steadily after migrating and becoming suppliers, have been able to raise enough funds to build large houses in their 'native' place. It is mainly the hired workers who earn little, some of them even below the poverty line.

5.4.3 Freezing and Cleaning

Thirteen varieties of fish are only frozen without cleaning - big ribbon fish (*bagha*), shear fish, large mackerels, squids, lobsters, pomfrets, *rawas,* cat fish (*singhoda*), eels, rays, crabs, starfish and sharks. They are packed in huge plastic tubs in layers of crushed ice and transported early next morning. Sometimes the faster spoiling species are kept in the ice factory founded by the cooperative societies, the low payment made based on the number of tubs stored.

Large *dhoma* is the only variety, apart from prawns, that is cleaned before freezing. After removing the head, the scales are scrapped off by hand with a *kati.* The de-headed and de-scaled fish is then salted and iced before being sold next morning.

Versova is renowned for its quantity and quality of prawns. There are 6 varieties of prawns - jumbo tiger, medium brown, *pivdi* (yellow), *patta* (lined), and *kolbi* (small red). The tiniest of all, bushy, also called *tengli,* is directly dried.

Prawns and shrimps land mainly in the evenings. Processing starts immediately, nearly exclusively by girl children who come in search of work to the landing center. These 5 to 10 year-old girls, all migrants, are paid extremely poorly. Generally 2 or 3 girls, often sisters, share one basket of prawns which they manage to de-head in about two hours. The wages are not determined by size as larger prawns require the additional process of deveining.

About 90 per cent of prawns and shrimps are purchased by the 3 main 'suppliers' in Versova, who get the crustacea cleaned and then transported to the export companies they are linked with. All three suppliers are women. It is indeed fascinating to watch the women family members of boat owners and the suppliers bargaining at the landing center, each armed with a calculator. The existence of almost total control over marketing explains the relatively high level of literacy and full command over numeracy achieved by the Versova fisher women.

Crustacea are purchased mainly in the evening when the big trawlers land, and kept overnight in huge tubs layered with crushed ice. This task is performed by men, interestingly, as in the bakeries and savouries sub sectors, all migrants from Uttar Pradesh and Bihar who are employed on a monthly salary of about Rs.2000.

The fish are stored in sheds (*vakhar*) where the peeling is to be done next morning. The shed is a large single room measuring about 40' x 20', with a cemented floor, brick walls and an asbestos roof.

Before the hired women workers arrive at about 3.30 am to begin the process of de-heading, the male workers who live in the sheds drain out the melted ice in the tubs and pack in more prawns. These tubs are emptied out on the floor in front of women who come in hordes. All these male workers are migrants, mainly from southern regions like Andhra Pradesh, Kerala, Karnataka and Tamil Nadu, and a few from West Bengal too. Most of them are land less labourers from 'lower' castes and tribes, and are almost evenly spread over Budhist, Muslim and Christian communities . The women squat cramped together on the wet floor, a single shed accommodating between 150 to 200. The cleaner is generally accompanied by all her children, the older daughters helping their mothers and so learning the 'trade', and the babies playing nearby.

The working conditions are hopelessly poor. The only facility provided is drinking water. There is no toilet; no fan; little cross ventilation; small windows with dim lighting; no space for babies. Going by the size of their operation, all prawn processing units in Versova, should come under the Factories Act with the application of all formal sector laws and regulations. No benefits are given - no leave; no compensation for injury; no weekly off; no bonus or provident fund or pension; no security of job; no insurance schemes. Wages are calculated on a piece-rate basis, the cleaning of one tub containing at least 45 to 50 kgs. of prawns fetching Rs.80 during the off season and Rs.100 during the peak season. One woman, even if assisted by her daughter, can clean only about half a tub if the deadline of 10am is to be met. This deadline is determined both by the spoilage time and by the export company where the fish has to reach latest by noon. Thus, a woman receives only Rs.40 for the six and a half to seven hours she spends in de-heading half a tub of prawns.

Wages are not paid when the work is done, though calculations are made on a daily basis. Two reasons were given. One, which we disbelieve, is that as most women have drunkards for husbands, daily wages would be snatched away and the women would not be able to feed their children properly. The second reason is valid. Export companies make payments to the suppliers only after 8 days; wages too are therefore paid only on the ninth day. Each woman is given a printed slip of paper that testifies to the quantum of work put in every day. Cash payment is made on the 9th day on the basis of the number of slips returned. No payment is made if the slip is lost. Apparently this has happened several times, especially when the slums these women live in were demolished.

All work is on a daily casual basis, being given to whoever arrives first. However, the demand for labour is so high that the cleaners are rarely turned away, except, of course, if the catch is below expectations. During the off season about 250 to 300 women are employed to clean 3 tons of prawns in one unit. In the peak season the amount to be processed daily often exceeds 7 tons, the number of women employed thus more than doubling. However, we found the daily production figures to be grossly underestimated, as it implies that one woman cleans only 12 kgs. of prawns per day.

As in the earlier sector studies, here too health and hygiene are determined by the work conditions. As there are few sheds available, women have to sit out on the road in the heat of the morning sunlight. And when the catch exceeds expectations, cleaning is also carried out at night with little lighting provided.

The floors of the *vakhars* (sheds) are wet, dirty and slippery. Several women workers often slip and fall down, resulting in injuries which they themselves have to tend. Hours of fast-paced work, and that too continuously bending over fish that are placed on the floor, leads to permanent back aches. Lack of proper lighting, especially when the work involved is delicate, has led to deteriorating eyesight. Long hours without toilet facilities result in 'stomach ache', more so for pregnant women.

One of the most painful impacts of prawn cleaning is on the fingers. The sharp 'whiskers' of the fish penetrate the delicate skin, leading to ruptures and sores that bleed; the knife-sharp heads and pincers cause deep cuts; the ice-cold fish numbs the finger-pads and creates white patches of deadened skin. The women use the *ayurvedic balm* (*kailash jeevan*) which is diluted with coconut oil as the medicine is quite expensive. All women take anti-tetanus injections regularly, as the 'black poison' of prawns enters the cuts and inflames them. Consequently, a large number of clinics run by doctors and also quacks have sprung up in the vicinity.

While the cleaned fish are put into cane baskets, prawn heads are piled in heaps which are periodically swept away by men or dumped outside in the adjoining lane. These heads are so sharp that they cut the bare feet of women and also of the many children playing outside awaiting their mothers. The prawn heads are left piled up in the blazing sun, permeating the atmosphere with an unbearable stench, and are swept away only after the last consignment leaves. Younger fisher folk who are environmentally more conscious told us that these piles are thrown back into the sea, adding to the already high level of pollution; though biodegradable, they take several months to dissolve.

5.5 Sale and Marketing Patterns

Marketing and sale begin immediately on landing. Most of the fish, and almost all the prawns, are purchased from the landing spot itself mainly by the women suppliers, who represent different export companies. Export companies cannot directly enter the village for any marketing whatsoever; they have to function through local suppliers. Prices vary according to species, season and amount of catch, the demand being unlimited.

As in most other perishable commodities, for fish also, the modus operandi for effecting the actual sales differs among the specified layers of marketing channels and the types of sellers and buyers involved in each. Women members of boat owning families do not generally sell all their wet fish. Different varieties are kept overnight in ice and after grading is done early next morning, are transported to the major fish markets of Andheri, Bandra, Borivili, Matunga, Dadar, Mahalaxmi, Crawford Market, Palton Road and Sassoon Docks. If the quantity to be sold is large, several women get together and hire a truck from the nearby Cooperative Transport Society against fairly reasonable charges. Other not so well off women hire auto rickshaws to the nearest market and local railway station.

The remaining fish are taken to a designated spot a little away, along with that purchased by local women whose families do not own boats. At this second stage of marketing, prices are already up by about 10per cent. The main buyers are direct consumers, restaurant owners, caterers, and the gujarati women who deal in dry fish. Direct consumers come either individually or in groups of 3 to 4 families from surprisingly far-off localities. They come here because Versova prawns are of the best quality and also extremely cheap when compared to retail market prices. Stall owners and vendors too purchase wet fish from here, carrying away the fish in cane baskets. All stall owners are women who sell in retail at various outlets. The poorer women sit in several nearby markets starting right from the municipal market in the village itself up to localities a few kilometers away. Vending at a house-to-house level is done mainly by women, though a few male migrants too have entered the trade now.

Fish varieties to be dried and salted are purchased by the kathiawadi women suppliers directly from the boat owners. Most boat owners have a verbal contract with several suppliers, the number of suppliers depending on the boat size and tonnage. Fish are thus purchased 'in advance' at pre-determined prices. Two reasons were given for entering this contract. One, it ensures less 'headache' of long drawn out haggling. The second reason is extremely important. The two existing cooperative societies disburse loans mainly for purchase of boats. All operating expenses have to be borne by the boat owners. As the smaller owners normally do not have enough liquid capital to cover the expenses of diesel, ice, wages, etc., they take an advance from the suppliers. This method of borrowing is beneficial to both the borrower and the lender. No interest is charged; the fixed prices protect both parties from risk and uncertainty; the supplier is assured goods and the borrower is ensured returns.

Smaller suppliers and home based enterprises involved in drying and marketing fish generally enter the market during the second stage. All family members including children help in carrying the fish home where salting is started immediately. Although local traders do exist, they are not preferred as payments are rarely made on time.

Most of the dry fish is sold in Marol. This is the largest dry fish market in the entire city started by the municipal authorities. Selling space is provided at minimal rates. Sale takes place mainly on Fridays and women are the main suppliers arrive in Marol on Thursday night itself. Soon thereafter, the allotted space is occupied and bargaining begins at night itself as the purchase agents also move in at this time; the final settlement, however, is made only in the morning. These agents, most of them muslims, come from all over the country including various districts of Maharashtra, and the states of Andhra Pradesh, Karnataka, Uttar Pradesh, Bihar and Gujarat. It needs to be underlined that the agents derive fairly substantial gains through processing or value-adding in their home states. This is also true of dry fish suppliers who earn a minimum of 100 per cent rate of profit.

Export marketing is equally difficult to explore and understand. Suppliers linked to export companies were not so forthcoming about sales, costs of production and profit rates. Prawns are sold in two conditions - peeled and head-on (un-peeled). Export companies obviously prefer peeled prawns as they are then saved time, effort and capital.

Second, sale price is calculated in a complicated manner, both before the stuff reaches the export company and after. For the former set of calculations, more than one set of norms have to be followed, e.g., purchase of the raw stuff on per tub basis, cleaning and peeling on per kg. Basis, cost of ice on per pillar basis, wage rate on per month basis, rent for the shed on yearly basis, electricity charges on metered consumption basis, and so on.

The basis of calculation of sale price changes once again when the prawns reach the export company. Payment is made according to pairs and counts. 60 pairs are multiplied by 2 and then divided by a count of 0.2, that is, Rs.600. To this figure is added an amount of Rs.80, the total now being Rs.680. Count rates decrease by Rs.5 for every increase of 10 in the number of pairs.

We thought it advisable to visit a medium sized export company in Sassoon Docks in order to get a better understanding of the linkages between the formal and informal sectors. Although processing in the factory is highly mechanised, the most important tasks of sorting and grading are done additionally by hand. Even fish that have already been sorted and graded by machines are rechecked. The graders then pass on the fish to packers who rinse them under running water, weigh and pack them according to size and species in labeled plastic bags. These packets are then carried in huge trays by men who place them in the freezing machine. The owner was very categorical about quality checking; we found this to be true as there was a small laboratory within the factory itself with full time staff making a random check by de-freezing and scientifically testing each sample.

It may be worthwhile taking a quick look at the working conditions of the women in these formal sector units. The majority are migrants from Kerala, with a few local women who stay in their own homes. The rest, all young girls, are mostly unmarried. They are provided shelter in a low badly ventilated loft above the factory, all 30 of them sleeping on weed mats. Their meager belongings are kept in cardboard boxes bearing the company's name. Though toilet and bathing facilities are provided, no food is given. A full time cook is hired, each girl shelling out Rs.390 per month for rations. The food consists mainly of rice and pulses, vegetables being rarely cooked. Wages average approximately Rs.900, with another Rs.200-300 earned from overtime. The girls prefer to work as they have nothing else to do and no family to take leave for. The pattern and characteristics of migration, with all attendant benefits to employers, are common to all the sectors analysed. No gloves are used, as they prove 'cumbersome' and delay sorting and grading. Fingers are deeply, probably permanently, numbed by continuous work in ice. The employer provides them with B-tex, a balm which is extremely strong and deadens sensation. Other health complaints include backaches and varicose veins, the result of standing for hours. No benefits relating to formal sector legislation are given - no leave; no compensation; no medical benefits; no pension; no provident fund; no security of employment.

An amazingly large variety of fish is exported. We list these in detail, along with the countries exported to. All fish are exported for final consumption, except for Thailand which apparently practices switch trading. For example, three types of shrimps are exported to all countries around the world; eight varieties of cuttle fish and squids are exported mainly to China, Europe, the United States, Japan and South East Asian countries; whole cooked lobsters go to Japan, while lobster and sand lobster tails are exported to USA and Europe; the whole round fish largely go to Japan, Taiwan and China; seer fish goes to the United States; ribbon fish mainly serve the Chinese market, and finally, mackerel finds a market in Sri Lanka and Malaysia.

6. Convergence and Conclusions

6.1 Introduction

It is time we integrate the entire analysis. It is carried out through identification of aspects of convergence of the three sub sectors as well as the points of divergence. Policy recommendations based on theoretical components and empirical findings are integrated in the four sub sections which focus, in that order, on data sources; wages, labour legislation, skills and technology; working conditions, health, hygiene, quality and production; and characteristics of workers. And finally, an attempt is made to identify what we perceive to be additional issues for further debate.

6.2 Data Sources and Definitional Lacunae

One of the major problems that confronted us was the difficulty in obtaining secondary data, especially in relation to comparability. Here are a few features common to all sub-sectors studied that, in our view, need to be brought out in bold relief.

1. Much rich data do exist, but all are not published. We find this quite inexplicable, considering that easy availability would not only speed work but would also extend accessibility to a wider audience. It is a pity that government departments are often restricted by the conditions under which they function. For instance, the entire 3 digit and 4 digit data of the Economic Census conducted for every district and for all industry divisions in Maharashtra in 1980 stand lost simply because the floppies got corrupted and there was no space available to store the hard copies. Neither has the NSS 51st Round Survey on Unorganised Manufacturing carried out in 1994-95 ever been published because of 'lack of finance'. This also applies to the 3 and 4 digit data of the 1990 Economic Census of Maharashtra. One of our major recommendations is that such rich data be carefully preserved and be easily accessible in print.
2. Data are non-comparable at various levels because often the categories themselves are not comparable. For example, in several sources, the category of DME does not exist particularly at 2 and 3 digit levels. Also, the break-up of DME into less than or equal to 5 workers and those with 6 or more workers is not available; comparative analysis between formal and informal sectors thus becomes difficult.
3. It is indeed quite amazing how an important food manufacturing sub-sector such as savouries does not exist in any data source whatsoever. All concerned officials advised us not to use any secondary data, not even at the 3 digit level for this sub sector as it would lead to wrong conclusions

and incorrect policy recommendations. Understandably, this lapse has not been rectified even in the latest 5 digit NIC code of 1998.

4. The 51st Round of the NSS conducted in 1994-95 records no data at all in either 3 digit or 4 digit classification for fish preservation and processing in Maharashtra. It is plainly shameful that for a state which has a 720 kilometre coast line with lakhs of people, mostly women, dependent on it. It needs to be rectified in subsequent rounds.

5. The 4 digit NIC codes of 2051 and 2052 are incorrect. This categorical statement is made on the basis of our fairly extensive and detailed field survey. None of the bakery units combine production of biscuits with cakes or confectionery; in fact, all of them combine manufacture of *pav* and biscuits. This is because the production of bread and biscuits is based on identical technology, skill, product design and process of baking. We therefore suggest that the NIC codes of 2051 and 2052 be changed to 'bread and biscuit making' and 'cake and confectionery' instead of the existing break up of 'bread making' and 'biscuits, cakes and confectionery'.

6. Finally, an extremely important point which has an impact on the national level classification for all industry groups is that the differentiation between NDME's and DME's should be 4 workers rather than the existing 6. We found this to be true not only of the bakery sub-sector but of savouries establishments too.

6.3 Wages, Labour Legislation, Skills and Technology

Of the three sectors, only bakeries are governed by minimum wages as defined in the Bombay Shops and Establishments Act, along with specific hours of work, closing time and weekly off; of course, none of these rules are implemented. Savouries establishments are not recognised in any law or regulation except in relation to 'fire hazards'. And for the informal fish-processing sector, not even a single directive applies.

Workers in all the three sub-sectors face similar concerns relating to wages; whichever few labour laws exist are hardly implemented. There are no fixed working hours; overtime allowance, weekly offs, leave of any kind (earned, casual, sick or maternity) bonus, pension, gratuity, provident fund, medical support, insurance coverage, are all conspicuous by their absence; there is no compensation for injury; wages are cut for any absence from duty (see D'Souza 1994 : 1551-1554).

Not only in the informal sector enterprises, workers even in the single formal fish-processing factory studied by us generally do not get benefits under any of the applicable labour laws (see Desai and Gopalan, 1983; Dietrich, 1995). Most notoriously, employing young unmarried girls permits circumvention of maternity benefits, additionally assuring 'undiverted dedication' to the work. Fish processing is the only sector that hires women; both the bakeries and savouries sectors are totally male oriented (Savara 1990 : 73-74).

The average weekly working hours for a bakery employee is an astounding 133 hours, while for savouries workers it is 105 hours. The average of 49 hours for fish cleaners is not any less exploitative, as these workers are perceived as 'part timers' employed only for half the day.

The acceptance of such a low wage regime by these informal sectorworkers is based on the existence of an unlimited labour supply; lack of alternate employment opportunities specially since the initiation of the 'new' economic policy; The craft-fully maintained 'patron-client' relationship; the total lack of bargaining power. Compounding these various aspects is the intensification of 'push' factors in rural areas which compel urban-ward migration, especially of the landless and other assetless households.

The obvious issues which are already identified and, in fact, widely accepted concern the implementation and monitoring of applicable laws, and their extension to sectors that lie outside the ambit of legislation. Added to this is the fundamental aspect of debating the very pattern of the 'development' process that appears not only to by-pass the poor but even subsume them, both in the urban and the rural areas.

There are five specific additional recommendations we wish to make. One, that export companies in the formal sector be compelled to make payment immediately on receipt of goods from the informal sector. The 8-day delay in settling accounts results in a chain reaction. The fish suppliers have to wait for the payment and have thus to borrow from moneylenders, usually at usurious rates of interest, primarily to cover immediate expenses. The worst affected are the workers who are paid only after 9 days, their wages not being considered by the supplier as an 'immediate expense'.

Another urgent problem needing immediate attention is that the workers in each of the sub-sectors have any place to keep their wages and savings. This issue becomes desperately urgent, especially in the context of migrant workers who predominate in all sectors. With no direct families and with no time left after their hectic and long hours of work to nurture the few contacts they have, all wages are retained by the employers for 'safe-keeping'. There is no control over and no record maintained of how these wages are 'guarded'; no information available on the use to which these savings are put by the employers; And, of course, no interest is paid when the wages are handed over to the migrant workers once a year when they go home. The impact of creating micro-finance facilities relevant to the felt needs of informal workers would benefit not only them but also increase the savings rate at the macro level.

Three, the very basis of determination of 'minimum' wages needs to be re-examined, specially in the context of the long working hours in the informal sector which extend way beyond any humanly and humanely acceptable limits. Minimum wages should necessarily and compulsorily be linked to price rise, costs of living and inflation rates, and be upgraded regularly. The basis of wage determination should be re-defined specially in relation to the prevailing gender bias and the existence of child labour.

Four, an extremely important technological change that should be introduced is shift over from the use of fire wood in the process of production in bakery units. The resultant advantages would be increased efficiency of energy use, decline in pollution, improvement in work conditions and hence the health of bakery workers, saving of a scarce natural resource, utilisation of a more environmentally friendly energy source, and so on.

Finally, an aspect that has both theoretical and empirical ramifications is the concept of 'skill'. Repeatedly and without exception, various reports and laws as also the vast literature on the informal sector, pontificate about the 'low skills' and 'low productivity' of the urban informal worker. We find this not only totally untrue but also highly objectionable. It requires tremendous skill to perform the delicate task of packing fragile biscuits and dry fish packet after packet without letting much breakage to occur. All the three features of skill, appropriate use of technology and high productivity are reflected in the ability to dry and process fish so scientifically without any formal training whatsoever, not even basic literacy. Also, the tasks of de-scaling croaker fish and prawn peeling cannot be entrusted to machines. In the formal sector unit, grading and sorting are re-done by hand even though highly sophisticated machines exist, because 'the machine can make mistakes, the hands cannot'.

First of all, the basic premise of the definitions of skill and technology is itself incorrect as it is based on the typical, neo-classical concept of skill and technology perceived from the viewpoint of 'industrialised' and hence 'developed' economies.

Second, the concepts of skill, productivity and technology are viewed in total isolation from the historical forces that shape them in the context of the concrete societal-cultural conditions and traditions of specific nations, especially those that have a common 'developmental' experience of colonisation.

6.4 Work Conditions, Hygiene, Quality of Production

The detailed analysis of the three sectors reveals that work conditions, health, hygiene and product quality are tightly inter linked, each impacting and reinforcing the other. To this prevailing reality we add another common factor relating to all sectors, that of geographical concentration, and make the recommendation that informal manufacturing units be located in an industrial estate. There is enough government owned land available in the city of Mumbai in the same localities not yet fully encroached upon by the builders' lobby.

The re-location of the units in an industrial estate would lead to significant benefits. One, the architectural design could take into account the need for good lighting, ventilation, drainage and sewage facilities. Also, technology could be upgraded to provide clean water for kneading, mixing of savouries and cleaning of fish.

We wish to specifically state here that introduction of mechanisation in bakeries would not necessarily lead to increase in production. The only study apparently ever done in the last three decades on bakeries concludes that mechanisation in bakeries will reduce labour intensity, and that in any case, non-mechanised informal units are not more profitable than larger mechanised units if the price of the final product is kept uniform (Keddie and Cleghorn, 1980 : 41-220; Keplinsky, 1980 : 275-350).

Migrant workers would benefit from clean dormitories with proper sleeping arrangement on cots, bathing and toilet facilities, and clean drinking water. A common mess could take care of the problem of cooking food, particularly in the middle of a long and hectic working day. The provision of creche facilities would not only safe guard children but would also increase productivity even more. The industrial estate could have a dispensary to take care of the medical needs of workers, and a small savings bank for workers to deposit their wages and thereby earn interest. The method of work could be altered by making compulsory the use of tables and chairs in order to replace the existing compulsion of standing or crouching for hours.

Locating units and workers in one place would facilitate the application and strict enforcement of quality controls including cleanliness and product standardisation. Also, it would make it much easier to regularise 'illegal' units. It would thus become possible to monitor the implementation of laws, particularly those relating to child labour, regularisation of work hours, minimum wages and weekly offs. Customers would not be inconvenienced as sales would continue in the same locality.

The industrial estate could possibly be operated as a cooperative thus ensuring benefits not only to workers but also to owners. One of the major complaints of bakeries and savouries owners is the lack of an efficient infrastructure relating to supply of raw materials. Most purchase inputs from agents who obviously charge higher rates. This is because the government operated Agriculture Produce Market Committee is run not only inefficiently, but also the quality of raw material, particularly wheat, is unsatisfactory. Other complaints relate to cheating in weighing and adulteration especially in spices and clarified butter. The location of a branch office in the estate would resolve these issues.

A 'new' problem facing the bakeries and savouries establishments is that of increasing competition from big business houses, especially multinationals which have recently entered the field of food manufacturing. Several owners told us that the growth rate has declined, and that the potential for increased production has been negatively affected since 'the world has entered India'.

We strongly recommend a cooperative fish processing and export plant in Versova on the grounds of both increased production and the redistribution of wealth from what is essentially a common property resource. With full democratic control over processing and export, depletion of catch due to over fishing could be restrained and production increased in a sustainable manner. There are more than enough skilled, trained and knowledgeable fisher folk in Versova to take on this responsibility. This task is urgent in view of the fact the policies of liberalisation and privatisation unleashed in the last decade and a half have resulted in increased utilisation of the nation's marine wealth for developed countries, on the one hand, and marginalisation of large sections of people, on the other (Acharya and Acharya 1995 : 46-47; Kurien 1995; Pinto et al. 1995; Korakandy 1996; Shajahan 1996; Dewan 1997, 1999).

Technology could be upgraded in association with the existing cooperative societies by increasing mechanisation, tonnage and length of boats. Refrigerated vans would transport the fish directly to export outlets, and also reduce occurrence of spoilage. Technology could be upgraded in several other ways to increase value added, product quality, labour productivity and working conditions. The use of steel knives instead of the rusty iron *katis* currently used; hand gloves not only to protect workers' hands but also enhance quality; piped running water for washing fish instead of the polluted seawater; proper and sufficient arrangements for drying and hanging; good quality salt; introduction of new methods of processing; specially designed tables and chairs for workers - the list is endless.

However, it should be pointed that mechanisation is neither possible nor correct for all types of processing. For example, *dhoma* (large croaker) retains its shape and beauty only when de-scaled by hand. Also to be taken into account and carefully monitored is the existing conflict between owners of mechanised trawlers and non-mechanised boats.

Other significant impacts would be on prevailing pollution levels. With a strong cooperative, it would become that much easier to alter the existing system of releasing sewage and garbage into the sea. Pollution by dumping of prawn heads would be stopped, currently, these are being used to earn additional income by conversion into aqua and poultry feed. Also, dealing with authorities on problems concerned specifically with reclamation, erosion and encroachment by the builders' lobby would be possible with the stronger bargaining power a cooperative has.

Finally, the benefits of increased sustainable production would be dispersed over broader sections of people, with positive results for re-distribution of wealth. The demand for labour would not decrease in view of the projection of expansion of production and rise in value added. When we discussed these ideas with the people of Versova, they were initially inclined to dismiss it as utopian, but soon saw the potential and possibility and reacted extremely positively. The 'only' problem that remains is to convert the dream into a reality.

6.5 Migration and Migrant Workers

The problems of migrant workers need also to be underlined. The three sectors are characterized by an extremely high level of employment of migrants, all of them, except in fish processing, from the same community, religion and region as the employers.

Migration took place through friends and family members, and sometimes on assurances given by the owners. None of them came to Mumbai either on their own or with the hope of a 'secure' job in the formal sector. This finding is somewhat different from that of several studies on this issue (see, for example, Bannerjee 1991 : 350; Bannerjee and Bucci 1994 : 33-47). Also, the informal sector appears to be the major point of entry for fresh migrants. This finding again goes counter to several studies (see, for example, Mazumdar 1975b).

Employers in bakeries and savouries prefer to hire migrants as they are more 'hard-working' than the 'locals', and also because 'we must help our own people'. We find the reality to be quite different. Hiring workers from one's own region and community ensures various economic and extra-economic benefits to employers. One, it allows the emergence and reinforcement of a patron-client relationship that possibly extends from the 'native' place.

Two, employers are assured of relatively permanent labour without doling out any of the due benefits, as workers obviously hesitate to leave their jobs for fear of becomimg homeless in a 'heartless' city which has no traditional structures of solidarity to support them.

Three, 'permitting' workers to sleep in the premises ensures availability of and access to labour for the entire day and night, resulting in the 19 hour work day in bakeries and just a little less in savouries establishments.

Four, 'allowing' workers to cook on the premises reinforces the dependency relationship by creating the mythical concept of 'a home away from home'.

Five, most of the workers have migrated without their direct families. With no family and few connections which in any case they have little time to nurture, the workers rarely take leave. It is natural, therefore, that all these factors merge, along with the mai-baap myth so carefully nurtured by the employers, into the continuation of unabated exploitation of labour power, a low wage regime and insecurity of employment that hamper the urgent task of organising the unorganised.

6.6 Issues for Further Debate

A vigorous debate on the 'informal' sector in third world countries was initiated with the publication of Keith Hart's paper and ILO's popularisation of the concept. Since then various definitions have been put forth, each leading to more debate. We thus have the capitalist versus the peasant system of production; firm-centered versus bazaar type economy; upper and lower circuits; legal versus illegal; formal versus informal; organised versus the unorganised; protected versus the unprotected; recorded versus unrecorded; high versus low productivity; modern versus traditional; mechanised versus non-mechanised; advanced versus backward (see, for example, Geertz 1963; ILO 1972; Mazumdar 1975a, 1975b; Sethuraman 1976; Adams and Paul 1987; Sanyal 1991; World Bank 1991; World Development Report 1995; Breman 1996; Fidler and Webster 1996; Datt 1997).

The process of integration of theoretical components and the findings of our study reveals the following characteristics that we hope will enrich the on-going debate.

The informal food-manufacturing sector performs several crucial economic functions. Cheaper goods are supplied not only to those with low purchasing power but also to formal enterprises which include canning units, super markets, department stores, hotels and restaurants. The goods are obviously much cheaper than those produced in the formal sector as little capital is 'wasted' on wages and none at all on advertising and marketing. The low prices benefit not only the poor but even the middle class which is being increasingly marginalised by forces of globalisation and the resultant intensification and concentration of capital in the formal sector. Additionally, steady demand is determined and ensured by geographical concentration and inherited expertise and ownership in the informal sector, though it is being eroded by the entry of the formal sector. Employment is provided not only to direct workers but also to several 'indirect' categories such as vendors and traders who have no access whatsoever to formalised market channels. In this sense, informal and formal sector linkages already exist, and bring substantial benefits to both (see Hemmer and Manuel 1989).

Another significant result of our study is that the informal sector is not necessarily only a supply-led activity from those who command few 'skills'. It is equally a demand-led activity increasingly resorted to, both in terms of production and employment, by those who are being increasingly marginalised by the prevailing developmental processes. Added to this is the process of deliberate organised informalisation which proves economically beneficial to owners of micro enterprises (see Kundu 1997 : 450).

In this context, it is necessary to point out that none of the bakeries and savouries establishments fall in the category of 'own account'. This finding is opposed to that of several studies which state that most informal sector workers are self-employed (see, for example, Sanyal 1991 : 41). Breman, however, reports the same results as we do (Breman 1996 : 10). This is because these enterprises need a relatively large amount of initial capital investment and fairly big business premises. It thus makes economic sense to purchase the cheap and easily available food products and re-sell them as vendors rather than attempt to raise enough capital to enter production. In the fish processing sub-sector, where a few 'own account' units do exist, there is sufficient demand for the product as well as enough marketing outlets to make this activity possible.

The single most significant characteristic of our study is the co-existence of formalization of production and informalization of labour. Future research should, therefore, incorporate restructuring of both theoretical paradigms as well as empirical concepts. And, in the context of the economic reality of the existence of the many employed in this economically productive sector, the central issue, and consequently the strategy, must get shorn of all ideological fogging and intellectualization, fully de-mythicized and demystified, one of *facta non verba.*

Bibliography

Acharya, Sarthi and Niru Acharya 1995. 'Structural Adjustment and Small Producers: Reflections from Case Studies', Economic and Political Weekly, Vol. XXX, No. 1, January 7, pp. 45-52.

Adams, John and Linda Paul 1987. 'The Informal Sector in India: Work, Gender and Technology', in Bjorkman, James Warner (ed.) The Changing Division of Labour in South Asia, Manohar, New Delhi.

Govt. of India. Annual Survey of Industries 1993-94, Factory Sector, Vol. II, CSO, Ministry of Planning and Programme Implementation, Kolkata.

Banerjee, Biswajit 1991. 'The Determinants of Migrating with a Pre-arranged Job and of the Initial Duration of Urban Unemployment', Journal of Development Economics, No.36.

Banerjee, B & Gabriella A Bucci 1994. 'On the Job Search After Entering Urban Employment: An Analysis Based on Indian Migrants', Oxford Bulletin of Economics and Statistics, Volume 56.

Baron, Christopher G (ed.) 1980. Technology, Employment and Basic Needs in Food Processing in Developing Countries, Pergamon Press, Great Britain.

Bhowmik, Sharit Kumar 1994. "Workers Co-operatives in the Unorganised Sector: An Alternative Strategy", in Davala, Sarathi (ed.) Unprotected Labour in India: Issues and Concerns, Friedrich Ebert Stiftung, New Delhi.

Bombay Metropolitan Region Development Authority 1995. Draft Regional Plan for Extended Bombay Metropolitan Region 1996-2011, BMRDA, Bombay.

Bombay Shops and Establishments Act 1948 as amended up to 1999. Labour Law Agency, Mumbai.

Breman, Jan 1996. Footloose Labour: Working in India's Informal Economy, Cambridge University Press.

D'Souza, Radha 1994. "Informalisation of Work and the Legal Process", in Davala, Sarathi (ed.) Unprotected Labour in India: Issues and Concerns, Friedrich Ebert Stiftung, New Delhi.

Datt, Ruddar 1997. "Organising the Unorganised Workers", Indian Society of Labour Economics, Vikas Publishing House, New Delhi.

Desai, Neera and Prema Gopalan 1983. "Changes in the Food Processing Industry from Traditional to Modern Forms and its Impact on Women's Role and Status", ICSSR/ IDPAD, (mimeo).

Dewan Ritu 1997. Runways Across Villages: Critique of the Proposed New International Airport for the City of Mumbai, Himalaya Publishing House, Mumbai.

____, 1999. Of Development amidst Fragility: a Societal and Environmental Perspective on Vadhavan Port, Popular Prakashan, Mumbai.

Dietrich, Gabriele 1995. "Women's Struggle for Production of Life: Public Hearings of Women Workers in Informal Sector", Economic and Political Weekly, Vol. XXX, No. 26, July 1.

Govt. of Maharashtra, Economic Census 1990, A Report on Economic Census 1990, Maharashtra State, Part I and Part II, Directorate of Economics and Statistics.

____, Economic Survey of Maharashtra 1998-99. Directorate of Economics and Statistics.

Fidler, Peter and Leila Webster 1996. "The Informal Sectors of West Africa", in Webster,Leila and Peter Fidler The Informal Sector and Micro Finance Institutions in West Africa, World Bank, Washington.

Govt. of Maharashtra, Fish Production Report 1996-97. Department of Fisheries, Government of Maharashtra.

Geertz, Clifford 1963. Peddlers and Princes: Social Change and Economic Modernisation in two Indonesian Towns, University of Chicago.

Hemmer, Hans-R and C.Mannel 1989. "On the Economic Analysis of the Urban Informal Sector", World Development, Vol. 17, No.10.

ILO, 1972. Employment, Incomes and Equality: A Strategy for Increasing Productive Employment in Kenya', Geneva.

____, 1982. Small-scale Processing of Fish, Geneva.

Jetley, Surinder 1983. Women Workers in the Food Processing Industry: UP and Delhi, ICSSR, New Delhi.

Jhabvala, Renana 1998. "Minimum Wages Based on Workers Needs", Economic and Political Weekly, Vol. XXXIII, No. 10.

Kaplinsky, R 1980. "A Country Case Study: Food Processing in Kenya", in Baron, Christopher G (ed) Technology, Employment and Basic Needs in Food Processing in Developing Countries, Pergamon Press/ILO, Great Britain.

Keddie, J and W.H. Cleghoru 1980. "The Choice of Technology in Food Processing: Some Case Studies", in Baron, Christopher G, (ed) Technology, Employment and Basic Needs in Food Processing in Developing Countries, Pergamon Press / ILO.

Korakandy, Ramakrishnan 1996. "Managing World Fisheries: Third World's Loss", Economic and Political Weekly, Vol. XXXI, No. 34, August 24-31.

Kundu, Amitabh 1997. "Trends and Patterns of Female Employment in India: A Case of Organised Informalisation", Indian Journal of Labour Economics, Vol. 40, No. 3.

Kurien, John 1993. The Marine Fish Economics of India: The Assessment of Potentials and Performance, Ph.D. Thesis, Research Papers - Area I, Tata Institute of Social Sciences, Mumbai.

Kurien, John 1995. "Impact of Joint Ventures on Fish Economy", Economic and Political Weekly, Vol. XXX, No. 6, February 11.

Govt. of Maharashtra, Minimum Wages Rules 1963 as Amended upto 1999. Labour Law Agency, Mumbai.

Govt. of Maharashtra, Shops and Establishments Rules 1961 as Amended upto 1999. Labour Law Agency, Mumbai.

Mazumdar, Dipak, 1975a. The Theory of Urban Under Employment in Less Developed Countries, World Bank Staff Working Paper No. 198.

Mazumdar, Dipak 1975b. The Urban Informal Sector, World Bank Staff Working Paper No. 211.

Govt. of Maharashtra, Minimum Wages Act 1948 as Amended upto 1999. Labour Law Agency, Mumbai.

Govt. of India 1987. Census of India, 1991, Ministry of Home Affairs, New Delhi.

N.S.S.O. 1990, "A Note on Survey of Unorganised Manufacturing Sector (All-India)", Sarvekshana, 63rd Issue, Vol. XVIII, No. 4, April - June.

Pinto, Ambrose, Berin Leekas and Latha Radhakrishnan 1995. "No Fish to Eat: Impact of Liberalisation", Economic and Political Weekly, Vol. XXX, No. 4, January 28.

Rao, P.S., S.K..Pandey and G.K.Rao 1988. "Wages and Wage Structure of Fishing Operations: A Case Study of Versova Fishing Village", in M. Mohan Joseph (ed.) The First Indian Fisheries Forum Proceedings, Asian Fisheries Society, Indian Branch, Mangalore.

Rao P.S. and S.K..Pandey 1990. "Cost of Production of Various Types of Mechanised Fishing at Versova Landing Centre, Bombay", Second Indian Fisheries Forum Proceedings, Mangalore.

Sanyal, Bishwapriya 1991. "Organising the Self-employed: The Politics of the Urban Informal Sector", International Labour Review, Volume 130, Number 1.

Savara, Mira 1990. "Levels of Technology: Effect on Women's Employment in Food Processing: A Case Study from Bombay", in Pandey, Divya and Mira Savara (eds.) Between the Farm and Thali: Women and Food Processing, Research Centre for Women Studies, SNDT University, Bombay.

Sethuraman, S.V. 1976. "The Urban Informal Sector: Concept, Measurement and Policy", International Labour Review, Volume 114, No. 1, July-August.

Shajahan, K.M. 1996. "Deep Sea Fishing Policy: A Critique", Economic and Political Weekly, Vol. XXXI, No. 5, February 3.

Todaro, M.P. 1969. "A Model of Labour Migration and Urban Unemployment in Less Developed Countries", American Economic Review, Vol. 59.

Webster, Leila and Peter Fidler (eds) 1996. The Informal Sector and Micro Finance Institutions in West Africa, World Bank Regional and Sectoral Studies, Washington.

World Bank 1991. Gender and Poverty in India, Washington.

World Development Report 1995. Workers in an Integrating World, World Bank, Washington.

Informal Sector in Urban India: Case of Leather and Leather Products Industry

Sumangala Damodaran

1. Introduction

This paper attempts to document the role of the urban informal sector in the leather and leather products industry in India. It is proposed, through an explication of the nature and growth of the urban informal sector and an analysis of its links with the formal sector, to examine the necessity as well as the possibility of transformation of informal activities in the industry.

The leather and leather products industry is one of India's oldest manufacturing industries that catered to the international market right from the middle of the nineteenth century, the demand for its products being both domestic as well as international right from the beginning.[1] Also, the industry is a traditional one with strong links with the social structure through the caste system. Thus a large number of operators in the industry (entrepreneurs as well as workers) even today come from traditional leatherworking castes (usually the scheduled castes) and the muslim community.[2] Due to the age of the industry and its links with the social structure, the organizational structure that has emerged is a very complex one that contains within it elements of continuity with traditional structures as well as those that represent a break with them. In addition to these historical aspects of its evolution, the dynamic of the industry has been shaped, to a large extent, by government policies since the sixties. These policies put increased emphasis on export orientation and value addition, keeping in view the nature of markets catered to. The industry is overwhelmed by tiny units specializing in one part of the production process or performing traditional leather work side by side with large, integrated firms producing and exporting value added products, with a large variety of different kinds of units in between.

[1] A committee on Leather and leather goods set up by the Government of Madras in 1949 reproted that the export of tanned hides and skins from India had been taking place from the middel of the 19th century. However, trade picked up only in the early part of the twentieth century. Refer to P. Usha (1984).

[2] Socially traditional leather workers of all kinds flayers, tanners, cobblers belonged to communities which were considered among the lowest in the caste hierarchy, mostly from the chamars. There has also been the creation of subcastes within them, with the flayers considered the lowest in the hierarchy, followed by the tanners and the cobblers. In several parts of India, there has been and exodus away from flaying activities because of the social ostracism. During the British period, Muslims, who were engaged in the slaughter business and had no social taboo for leatherworking activities, entered the sector. Refer to SADC (1999).

Given this kind of structure, any enquiry into the degree of informalisation, kinds of informal processes and the links between the formal and the informal segments of the industry has to deal with the following vexed issues: First, it is extremely difficult to distinguish between formal and informal segments in the industry using standard criteria. While the term "informal sector" was coined by Hart (1971) it was launched as a major concept in economic policy making by the ILO's report titled "Employment, Income and Inequality" after its study of Kenya's employment situation as part of the World Employment Programme in 1972. These and several subsequent studies have used different criteria to characterise the informal sector[3]. In a survey of criteria used to identify the informal sector, Mead and Morrison (1996) note that three ideas seem central to the concept of the informal sector, legality (registration with official bodies, payment of taxes, regulation of working conditions for the labour force), enterprise size and capital intensity. In this industry, we find that classifying enterprises as informal based on a combination of these criteria gives a very limited idea of the degree of informalisation. There are many instances where a unit would classify as part of the formal/organized sector as far as its legal status, production process and size of capital employed are concerned, but could be considered part of the informal sector as far as employment, labour conditions and standards are concerned. These units would not be formally classified as informal sector enterprises but according to us represent and important facet of the informalisation of production in sector as a whole. The operations of such units, which border the formal and informal in some sense, as well as those that directly are part of the informal sector, would be violative of the conditions of "decent work" that are considered essential by the ILO. Second, published data of the kind that this study warrants is woefully scarce and what exists is also incomparable over time or across sectors. Available aggregative data sources like the Annual Survey of Industries or the National Sample Survey underestimate major magnitudes and do not give precise figures for aggregative magnitudes. Industry level data sources like surveys conducted by the Economics Research Unit of the Central Leather Research Institute, Madras, have been once-and-for-all exercises and do not permit comparisons over time. Third, while this study has been conducted for a specific purpose, and is therefore supposed to look at the role of the urban informal sector in the leather and leather products industry, merely looking at this and ignoring the rural or more formal segments in the industry (where these can be identified) will not permit a complete analysis of the dimensions of urban informal sector activity in the industry. This is because rural areas form a distinct link in the production chain in the sector as a

[3] For example, Hart (1971) described the informal sector as that part of the urban labour force that falls outside the organized labour market. The ILO, on the other hand, described the informal sector in terms of ease of entry, reliance on indigenous resources, family ownership of enterprises, small scale of operations, labour intensive technology, skills acquired outside the formal schooling system, and unregulated and competitive markets.

whole, and influence organisational structure to a large extent, as does the link between the formal and informal elements.

Keeping in mind the above, this study has tried to distinguish between formal and informal elements/segments in the industry as much as possible, although we also argue that this distinction is not possible across a significant spectrum of the industry. Very little of the information presented in this study has been culled out from available data sources, and is primarily based on our own fieldwork. And finally, since we emphasise that it is not possible to present the urban informal sector's features and problems without looking at the rural and formal elements in the industry, the study presents an integrated view of the industry with a special focus on the characteristics and problems of the urban informal sector.

Section 2 presents a broad macroeconomic view of the industry. In this section, a major lacuna in existing data sources on the industry is highlighted, i.e., their inability to precisely provide estimates of output, employment, the number of different types of enterprises in the industry, and so on. Since the extent of formal or informal activity cannot be judged in terms of these aggregative estimates, we therefore attempt to identify the different types of enterprises that are in existence in the industry, and within them, informal enterprises, This is done through the elaboration of the production chain in the sector as a whole, beginning from the collection of raw hides and skins till the ultimate marketing of leather products. Two major aspects that have contributed significantly to the evolution of the industry and have influenced the degree of informalisation are also discussed briefly, i.e., the nature of demand and markets catered to, and government policy.

Since most of the information presented in this report is based on field work, sections 3-6 are devoted exclusively to presenting the main results of the field study done in two major locations where the leather industry is concentrated, i.e., Madras and Kolkata. Section 3 briefly presents the salient features of the two clusters and attempts to outline the similarities and dissimilarities between them in terms of production processes, market orientation, ethnic composition and historical evolution. It also details the methodology that was used to obtain field level information which, to state it briefly, was based on semi-structured interviews with employees and entrepreneurs in different enterprises as well as with trade union representatives, representatives of industry and trade associations, etc. The selection of the units covered was random and based on the criterion that they represent typical units in their respective segments. Specifically the different kinds of units covered were: (i) small units in the tanning segment of the industry, including those that do traditional tanning as well as those that do more modern chemical tanning, (ii) small leather product producing units, encompassing independent household workshops set up by artisans, those that work on orders from exporters/domestic traders and tiny home based units, and (iii) larger tanneries and/or product making units which, though using relatively modern technology and operating in a factory mode, could be said to be employing informal labour processes.

Sections 4, 5 and 6 present the results of the field work which attempted to find answers to the following questions: To what extent does the informal sector play a role in the leather and leather products industry? In particular, is it more prevalent in some segments of the sector than others, like those catering to the lower end of the domestic market, as it is true for the urban informal sector in other industries and in many countries? What is the nature of informalisation where it exists, i.e., what is the nature of employment, what kinds of labour are employed, and what are the conditions of their employment and work? Is the process of informalisation a result of the continuation of traditional forms of economic organisation in this traditional industry, or has it been an integral part of the development of the sector as a whole? What have the links between the formal and informal segments been in this sector?

Section 7 sums up the main conclusions of the field study and tries to identify the major constraints faced by the industry as a whole and the informal sector in particular and also presents the major macro and micro level recommendations that are being made in this report. Both the constraints as swell as the recommendations have been grouped into three categories, i.e., those that obtain at a sectoral level, those that affect individual enterprises, and those that affect labour.

2. Macro Picture of the Industry and its Structure

This section provides an overview of the leather and leather products sector as a whole by looking at the activities that constitute it, the nature of demand for its products, output produced and numbers employed, and the policy environment in which the sector operates. It also presents a slightly detailed picture of the structure of the sector as a whole and tries to assess the degree of formal or informal activity in the industry.

2.1 General Estimates of the Size of the Sector and its Structure

The leather and leather products industry consists of the following activities : *carcass collection and flaying,* i.e., the process of acquiring the main raw material, raw hides and skins, their curing and elementary processing; *tanning*, with the conversion of raw hides and skins into semi-finished leather in the first stage and the processing of semi-finished leather into finished leather in the second, and *manufacture of leather products* i.e., footwear, garments and goods using finished leather.

Manufacture of leather and leather products is classified under code 29 in the National Industry Classification under the broad heading "Manufacture of Leather and Fur Products". Table 2.1 provides the 3-digit breakup of the various activities that constitute the sector. As can be seen, this encompasses only the "manufacturing" activities in the sector, beginning from the manufacture of leather from the main raw

TABLE 2.1 : **Main Activities in the Leather and Leather Products Industry**

NIC CODE	DESCRIPTION OF THE ACTIVITY
29	Manufacturing of leather and fur products (excluding repairs)
291	Tanning, currying, finishing, embossing, and japanning of leather.
292	Manufacture of leather except vulcanised or molded rubber or plastic.
293	Manufacture of wearing apparels like coats, gloves etc.
294	Manufacture of other leather consumer goods (other than apparel, footwear)
299	Manufacture of leather products not elsewhere classified.

295-298 cover fur products and haver therefore been excluded.
Source: Central Statistical Organisation, Annual Survey of Industries, Output, Employment and Number of Enterprises.

material, raw hides and skins. However, a major part of the industry consists of the set-up to procure, process and transport raw hides and skins. This is not included in the data sources based on the NIC, and the information on this had to be acquired from the data sources provided by research institutes and business associations in the industry.

Table 2.2 provides aggregate information on the number of units, output and employment under category 29 in both registered and unregistered manufacturing in urban areas. The table has combined information available in the Annual Survey of Industries (which covers all units registered under the Factories Act), representing the so called 'organised' sector, and the National Sample Survey (which covers unregistered manufacturing units), representing the so-called unorganized sector, in order to get an industry level picture of main macro aggregates. At the aggregative level, the table shows that the industry's total output from the urban segment amounted to about Rs. 50,610 million and it employed about 0.37 million people in 1994-95. If we include information from the NSS on the rural segment of the industry (given in Table 2.3), it is seen that rural enterprises of all types in the different segments contributed Rs. 3,100 million to output and 0.2 million to employment, taking the total output to Rs. 53,700 million and employment to 0.57 million. However, the Working Group on Leather and Leather Products for the IX Plan estimated that the industry employed 1.1 million people around the same time, and experts in the industry estimated that its output was worth around Rs. 72,000 million (Sahasranaman 1998). Another aggregative data source, the National Account Statistics published by the Central Statistical Organisation shows different figures in the time-series information presented in Table 2.4 below.

TABLE 2.2 : **Estimated Number of Enterprises, Employment and Output (in Rs. million) by Different Types of Enterprises at 3-digit Level for the Leather and Leather Products Industry (1994-95) (Urban)**

Type of Enterprise	NIC Codes					
	290	291	292	293	299	29
1. Unregistered Manufacturing						
Total No. of enterprises	4910	68000	2328	12135	1104	90212
Total output produced	2276	8286	290	1104	108.74	12297.9
Total Employment	11148	224750	14262	45305	5422	300887
1.1 *Own Account Enterprises*						
1.1.1 No. of enterprises	3654	436297	825	6260	845	55257
1.1.2 Output produced	405	3346.2	23.8	175.7	42.7	3993.8
1.1.3 Total Employment	5988	93874	1127	9697	1670	112401
1.2 Non-directory Establishments						
1.2.1 No. of enterprises	104.8	15193	248	3069	207	20610
1.2.2 Output produced	287	1897.5	41.53	300.8	15.4	2633.8
1.2.3 Employment	367.4	62791	1317	11388	3376	83389
1.3 Directory Establishments						
1.3.1 No. of enterprises	208	9180	1255	2806	52	14345
1.3.2 Output Produced	1584.5	3041.8	224.5	627.3	50.64	5670.3
1.3.3 Employment	1486	68085	11818	24220	376	111682
2. Registered Manufacturing						
No. of Factories	916	460	284	158	53	1338
Output Produced	23763.5	21202.1	6560.2	3552.8	770.9	38312.2
Employment	38172	32108	5622	15656	1084	7235
3. Total Urban Manufacting						
No. of Enterprises	5826	68460	2612	12293	1157	91550
Output produced	26039	29488	6850	4657	880	50610
Employment	49320	256858	19884	60961	6506	373242

Note: Own Account Manufacturing Establishments (OAMEs) are enterprises run without any hired workers on a regular basis. Non Directory Manufacturing Establishments (NDMEs) are establishments employing less than 6 workers (household and hired taken together) engaged in manufacturing or repairing activity. Directory Manufacturing Establishments (DMEs) are establishments employing more than 6 workers.

Source: (1) National Sample Survey, 51st Round (July 1994-June 1995)-Unorganised Manufacturing sector in India : Its size, employment and key estimates, August 1998.

(2) Annual Survey of Industries, Central Statistical Organisation, 1994-95.

TABLE 2.3 : **Estimated Number of Unregistered Enterprises, Employment and Output (in Rs. million) by Different Types of Enterprises at 3-digit Level for the Leather and Leather Products Industry (1994-95) (Rural)**

Type of Enterprise	NIC Codes					
	290	291	292	293	299	29
Own Account Manufacturing Establishments						
No. of Enterprises	20298	436297	1649	3286	3012	116549
Output Produced	591.9	2209	9.3	81.6	89	3000
Employment	28706	128751	1881	6564	NA	17353
Non Directory Manufacturing Establishments						
No. of Enterprises	704	2096	62	819	71	3960
Output Produced	329.8	200.7	5.9	119.6	2.0	670
Employment	2382	6476	144	3091	234	23745
Directory Manufacturing Establishments						
No. of enterprises	3	269	304	11	NA	592
Output Produced	0.3	217.3	NA	2.5	NA	290
Employment	17	2633	NA	1834	NA	4686

Source: National Sample Survey, 51st Round (July 1994 - June 1995) - Unorganised Manufacturing sector in India : its size, employment and key estimate, August 1998.

TABLE 2.4 : **Output Produced by the Leather and Leather Products Sector at 1995-96 prices**

(Rs. Million)

Year	Registered Manufacturing	Unregistered Manufacturing
1980-81	5280	2330
1990-91	3055	6180
1991-92	32230	6500
1992-93	35760	8220
1993-94	48940	9060
1994-95	57650	9820
1995-96	65440	10090

Source: CSO, National Accounts Statistics, Central Statistical Organisation, 1998.

These anomalies in available aggregate data only go to show how difficult it is to make precise macro statements about the industry. For example we cannot assume that information on unregistered manufacturing or specific categories within it would give us a realistic picture of informal sector presence because, apart from the fact that it is not only these that constitute informal establishments, clearly, all published information seems to be an underestimate of actual magnitudes. Aggregate published information of this kind, therefore, has been used only sparingly and with great caution for this study. A realistic picture of overall informal sector activity can only be going into the different forms of production organisation in the industry as a whole, which has been done in the subsequent sub-section.

To go back to Table 2.2, what can be said definitely about the sector is that it consists of a large number of enterprises that could very clearly be considered part of the informal sector in all activities under the relevant NIC code. The large number of enterprises constituting (OAMEs, in rural as well as urban areas, NDMEs and DMEs mostly in urban areas bears adequate testimony to this. If we were to take into consideration the NSS figures for rural areas (Table 2.3), we see that rural areas have large numbers of OAMEs (double the numbers in urban areas) and they dominate in the leather tanning and finishing segment, whereas urban areas have larger numbers of NDMEs and DMEs. In addition, the organised sector also contains within its fold several kinds of enterprises that can be considered part of the informal sector as the next sub-section will show.

The sector is also a major employer. According to the Ninth Plan Working Group on Leather and Leather Products, of a total of 1.7 million people employed in the sector as a whole, about 0.6 million are involved in collection and flaying of raw hides and skins, around 0.8 million are engaged in tanning and product making activities, 0.1 million in repair activities and more than 0.15 million people are indirectly employed in various segments, of which at least the employment figures provided by the NSS constitute those employed in the informal sector, apart from the informal work-force employed in the organized sector.

A distinct aspect of employment in this traditional industry is that, even in its modern segments, we can still find a distinct ethnic component to the identity of the entrepreneurs as well as workers. Thus, in each area in the country, where leather and leather product manufacturing is concentrated, the dominant businesses are still in the hands of traditional businessmen and the workforce still consists mostly of people who have traditionally been associated with leather work, i.e., those belonging to the Scheduled Castes[4]. This paper does not intend to discuss whether this ethnic component to production acts as a progressive or a retrogressive factor in the development of the industry. We only state that it has a major role to play in affecting skills, productivity, earnings, etc. Also, during the past decade or so, there have been changes in the composition of people involved in the industry, especially a significant entry of persons without any distinct family background in leather business into the industry, more pointedly in Madras.

[4] See Knorringa (1996) for the ethnic composition of those engaged in the sector in the Agra cluster, as an example.

Having gone over broad estimates of the size of the sector, we now go on to look at the production chain in the sector, in order to identify the kinds of enterprises, informal production and labour processes that exist in the industry.

2.1.1 Structure of the Industry: How Much Formal is it?

As already mentioned, the industry consists of the following activities: Carcass collection and flaying, tanning and manufacture of leather products. Of these, carcass collection and flaying are dispersed across rural and urban areas all over the country whereas tanning and product making which constitutes the manufacturing activities in the industry, has come to be concentrated mostly in urban centers, usually in the form of industrial clusters. In Figure 1, we have tried to trace the chain of production and trade from the village level flayers to the ultimate markets for the industry's value added products.

Carcass collection as an activity is strongly linked to traditional caste structure and most of it is done by people belonging to lower castes in rural areas, as part of caste-determined occupational structures. *Flaying* takes place as dispersed activities in rural areas as well as in dispersed units and slaughter houses in semi-urban and urban centers that are linked to markets for raw hides and skins. The raw hides and skins that are flayed undergo preliminary processing such as salting to preserve them and are mostly transported to raw hide and skin markets all over the country. Collection and trade in raw hides and skins is controlled heavily by traders and middlemen who take full advantage of caste factors in giving very low prices to flayers. Some raw hides and skins are consumed at village level itself, by tanners and cobblers, for making traditional leather and footwear but even they have to source most of their raw material from outside at high prices because the development of the urban clusters has led to the outflow of raw material from the rural to the urban areas.

This phenomenon of tanning and product making getting concentrated in the urban areas has resulted in (a) poor quality of raw material due to decay of hides and skins caused by delays in processing and high prices due to high transportation cost and a long chain of intermediaries involved in trade; (b) decline in rural tanning leading to unemployment among trade leather working communities and increased artisanal migration to urban and semi-urban areas; and (c) adverse terms of trade for rural tanners and product makers. Traditionally, producing leather was a part of the chain of processes in dispersed villages where the same artisans undertook flaying of animals, tanning as well as manufacturing and repairing of leather products. As a result of a complex set of forces including the conscious development of the urban clusters and the changing tastes of consumers in rural and urban areas that were not commensurate with the skills of the traditional artisans, rural tanning and product making declined drastically. The system of production got geared to the priorities of the urban clusters that produced both for the domestic as well as the international market.

FIGURE 1 : **Production Chain in the Leather and Leather Products Industry**

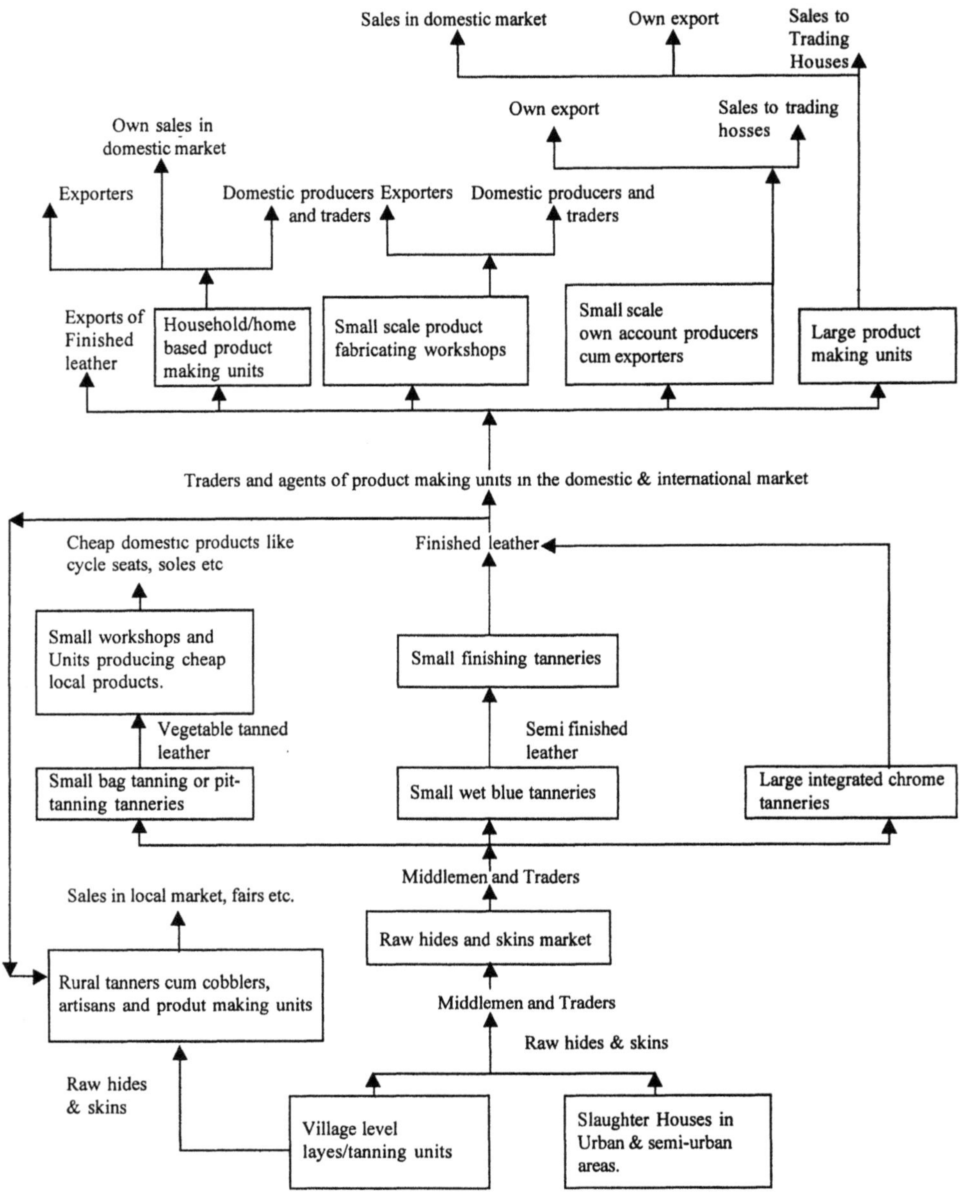

From the raw hide and skin markets, the raw material finds its way, through agents and traders, to different kinds of tanneries (that do either traditional vegetable tanning, wet-blue tanning or integrated tanning, as the figure shows).

Vegetable tanning is the traditional tanning method. It is of two types, bag tanning and pit tanning. In bag tanning, the carcass is sewn together and then tanned with amla or babool or myrabulan bark. In pit tanning, the same sequence is followed except that the open hide instead of being sewn into bags, is soaked in pits and tanned with the same vegetable substance. Traditional vegetable tanning is highly labour intensive and involves hard manual work in extremely difficult working conditions. The tanned leather made through either bag tanning or pit tanning processes is tough, reddish in colour and used for special products such as saddlery, and sports goods, and for shoe soles. One problem with vegetable tanning is that it is a fairly slow process; it takes nearly three weeks for the hide to be tanned, rendering it relatively less economic compared with chrome tanning. Improved methods for vegetable tanning have been developed by the Central Leather Research Institute (CLRI), Madras but these have not yet become popular. All over the country, those involved in traditional tanning come from leatherworking castes where skills have been handed down to them across generations. With the decline in rural tanning mentioned earlier as well as the relatively uneconomical process of production of vegetable tanned leather, a large number of these workers have remained unemployed in villages or migrated to towns and cities.

Chrome tanning is the more modern process of tanning using powdered chrome as the tanning substance. There are two stages to the chrome tanning process: wet blue tanning and leather finishing. Both these stages can be done in the same tannery (which we have called integrated tanneries) or can be divided between different tanneries.

Vegetable tanned leather that is made traditionally is used to produce cheap products such as cycle seats, etc. for the local market in semi-urban areas and the urban clusters, or to produce traditional items such as shoes and bags that are demanded in the national as well as the international markets. Finished chrome leather is produced either by integrated tanneries (which exist in different sizes and employ different production modes), or by finishing tanneries that acquire semi-finished leather from wet-blue tanneries. This finished leather has several uses. It is either exported directly to product makers in other countries, or goes into the production of leather products in a large variety of production outfits. For example, footwear production of the standardized variety is amenable to assembly line production and is also demanded in large batches and is, therefore, produced, to a large extent, by large domestic and multinational firms. At the same time, *a large chunk of footwear production is also decentralized, with the chain of subcontracting extending from large firms down to tiny household workshops.* Bags, wallets, and leather garments, on the other hand, require greater supervision for their production, are not amenable to assembly line production, and are consequently produced typically in small batches in small enterprises.

Having gone through the production chain for leather and leather products, a summary of the major characteristics of the different kinds of enterprises that exist in the tanning and the product making segments is provided in Tables 2.5 and 2.6. It is clear from these tables that of the 13 kinds of listed enterprises, 10 of whom exist in urban areas, as many as 11 are clearly small units. The degree of mechanization, markets catered to, type of output produced, employment size vary between the units, but all of them employ informal labour. The rural traditional tanneries, and traditional tanners-cum-cobblers, who are essentially self-employed and use only family labour, could be considered OAMEs, whereas the rural artisanal shoe making units (where seasonal hiring of labour does take place) and urban and semi urban artisanal units probably, need to be classified under NDMEs. These four types of enterprises, therefore, clearly are part of the unorganized and hence informal sector. The other seven kinds of units may or may not belong to the unorganized sector. In fact, of these, many small scale tanneries and product making units engaged in own production, as well as those that are part of larger groups could be considered part of the organized sector and are probably covered under ASI enumeration, but could still be considered part of the informal sector due to being dependent, to a great deal, on the informal sector for credit, recruitment, etc. Thus, apart from a handful of large integrated firms that undertake all activities from tanning to product making and operate fairly independently even as part of a cluster, most of the other kinds of units could be considered to be employing informal production processes or to be at least linked organically to the informal sector for employment, credit etc, which will become obvious when our field insights get unfolded. Thus, in this sector, the informal sector not only consists of units/enterprises in the unregistered manufacturing sector, but also many in the organised sector within the manufacturing sector. In addition, it consists of the entire set-up that exists around the procurement and preliminary processing of raw hide and skins.

Tanning is undertaken throughout the country, but the major units are concentrated in and around Madras and North Arcot District in Tamil Nadu, Kanpur and Kolkata. These centres account for nearly 85 per cent of India's tanning and finishing capacity. Product making from finished leather for sale in the export as well as the domestic market has also tended to get concentrated in these clusters as well as in Agra, Delhi and Bangalore.

TABLE 2.5 : **Kinds of Enterprises and their Characteristics in the Tannery Segment**

Kind of Enterprise	Technology / Degree of Mechanisation	Market Catered to	Nature of Labour Employed
Rural traditional vegetable tanneries	Traditional bag tanning or pit tanning mechanisation almost nil	Product sold to local cobblers selling in local market	Family labour, apprentices from the same community
Urban traditional vegetable tanneries	-do-	Product sold to cycle seat, saddlery and sole manufacturers in domestic market	Informal, caste based employment
Small tanning jobwork workshops	One or two machines doing simple tanning or fininshing jobs	Production on the basis of order from larger units	Informal employment
Small scale tanneries doing own production	Significant mechanization	Product sold to exporters or domestic manufacturers of leather products.	Some permanent workers and largely casual workers with no benefits
Small scale tanneries that are part of larger groups	-do-	Product made for other units that are part of the group	-do-
Medium scale and large integrated (diversified into product making units too)	Highly mechanized, sometimes automated	Direct exports of own finished leather and products, or sales to	Combination of casual and permanent employment depending upon demand informal labour market

TABLE 2.6 : **Kinds of Enterprises and their Characteristics in the Leather Product Making Segment**

Kind of Enterprise	Technology / Degree of Mechanisation	Market Catered to	Nature of Labour Employed
Rural artisanal units 1. Traditional tanners-cum-cobblers 2. Rural artisanal modern shoe producing units	Traditional handtools used - no mechanization -do-	Traditional products sold in the local market Modern shoes sold in the local market	Self employed artisan with at most one apprentice Combination of family and hired, casual labour recruited from the informal market
Urban and semi-urban artisanal units established mainly by migrated artisans	-do-	Premium arsanal products like kohlapuri chappals sold in the domestic and export markets, as well as modern shoes and chappals sold in the domestic market	Mostly self employed, sometimes hiring casual labour from the informal market
Jobwork units and fabricating units	Simple machines and handtools used	Produce and orders from larger units	Informal employment
Small scale product making units engaged own production	Significant mechanization	Mostly exported	Combination of casual and permanent employment depending upon demand. Strong links with the informal labour market
Small scale product making units that are of large groups	-do-	Mostly exported on behalf of group	-do-
Medium scale and large integrated product units with backwardly integrated tanneries	Highly mechanused, sometimes automated	Direct exports or domestic sales	Combination of permanent and casual casual employment depending on demand. Strong links with the informal labour market

2.2 Demand and the Nature of Markets

Demand for leather and leather products is almost equally distributed between domestic and export markets, with about 55 per cent of total production going to satisfy domestic demand and roughly 45 per cent exported. Table 2.7 provides information on estimated values of output, based on estimates of demand made for the Eighth Five Year Plan, which shows the relative weights of output domestically consumed and exported for different product categories. Figure 2 classifies the demand for various products produced by the sector and the kind of units that meet the same. It shows that domestic demand is restricted to conventional leather items such as footwear and bags, wallets, etc., whereas international demand includes, in addition, finished leather (which is used by product making units abroad to make leather products), footwear components (which consist of shoe uppers that are imported by shoe manufacturers abroad to save on labour intensive upper making operations), and leather garments for which India is turning to be a major exporter.

It can also be seen that it is the small scale enterprises that cater to most categories of demand, both in the domestic and the international markets. This stylized picture is based on information provided in various publications of the Central Leather Research Institute and our own field-work. What is notable about the demand for this sector's products is its segmented nature, whether it is for the export market or the domestic market. This means that due to large numbers of varieties of different products that exists and their differing product specifications, demand is specific and flexible. Small batch and small enterprise production with their inherent flexibility

TABLE 2.7 : **Value of Output of Leather and Leather Products**

(in Rs. million)

	1990-91			1994-96		
	Domestic +	Exports =	Total	Domestic +	Exports =	Total
Closed shoes	11400	2800	14200	17100	5800	22900
Chappals	8020	-	8020	13700	-	13700
Sandals	3360	2000	5360	6440	600	7040
Shoe Uppers	-	5860	5860	-	10250	10250
Footwear	22780	8860	31640	36240	16550	52790
Garments	-	1840	1840	-	3210	3210
Leather Goods	4620	3000	7620	7560	7320	14880
Finished Leather	-	6300	6300	-	7500	7500
Total	27400	20000	47400	43800	34580	78380
%	(58%)	(42%)	(100%)	(56%)	(44%)	(100%)

Source: Govt. of India, Report of the working group on leather and leather products for the VIIIth Five Year Plan, Ministry of Industry, 1990.

are suited to this sector and this has contributed to its structure. Demand for leather footwear, garments and accessories is also highly volatile, dependent as it is on changes in fashion and seasonal requirements; this has influenced the size of the units and the types of processes that take place in the industry.

Apart from the large integrated firms that produce exclusively for the export market and whose main demand segment is the medium price range in the international market, almost all other categories of enterprises, whether producing for the domestic or the export market, aim primarily at producing output at as low a cost as possible, primarily because they produce for the bottom segment in the international as well as the domestic market. In a highly volatile and segmented market, firms/units have evolved strategies that enable this cost cutting through keeping wage costs as low as possible by informal employment, extensive sub-contracting and job-working to cut down capital costs; very little innovation or technological development is discernible since this involves big capital cost that is usually beyond their means. Another major aspect of demand is that it gets mediated through a long chain of trade intermediaries; output produced passes through many hands before it reaches the final customers, in both the domestic and the international markets. Pressure from these intermediaries also forces enterprises to keep margins as low as possible[5].

These factors have necessitated the evolution of a production structure that has, built into it, a high degree of flexibility to cater to the kind of demand mentioned above. That almost half of the sector's output is exported has a lot to do with the fact that India has traditionally enjoyed certain advantages such as abundant raw material availability and low labour costs in an essentially labour-intensive industry[6].

2.3 Government Policy

Government policy towards the leather and leather products sector has been two pronged: the first aspect is that of reservation of a large number of processes for

---

[5] Refer to Knorringa (1996) for an explication of producer-trader relations in the Agra footwear cluster. He found that the conditions of production and employment in the cluster were set by the buyers of the products, both in national and international markets. A 1999 publication by the Swiss Agency for Development Cooperation (SADC) states that profit margins for small leather product traders are in the range of Rs. 10,000 to 20,000 per month, whereas it varies from Rs. 1.0 to Rs.1.2 lakh for the large trader in the domestic market. The report also notes that the wholesale hide traders operating in the urban markets are extremely powerful in terms of possessing capital and controlling entry and exit in the market.

[6] In terms of availability of raw material for the industry, India has the largest cattle and goat populations in the world, enough to sustain a much higher growth of output in the industry (See Central Leather Research Institute; Report of the All-India Survey of Raw Hides and Skins, 1987). However, this does not translate into actual offt-take rates due to various structural problems. As far as labour costs are concerned, whereas the average monthly wage rate for unskilled and semi-skilled labour in China and Indonesia (who are major competitors) would be US$ 50, in India it is much less, ranging between US $ 30 and 40.

the small scale sector, the second is that specific export promotion measures have been in force for the sector by virtue of the large amount of foreign exchange that it earns. The policy of reservation has been inspired by the fact that the sector has employed a large numbers of people who constitute the bottom of the economic and social hierarchy and that production based on small scale can be conducive to maximization of employment and harnessing of the available skills. *Conversion of raw hides and skins into semi-finished leather, and the manufacture of products using finished leather, are reserved for the small scale sector.* Larger firms can also enter into production in these categories if they undertake to export at least 75 per cent of their total production. The structure of the sector, heavily dominated as it is on small scale production, is due largely to this policy of reservation. Table 2.7 provides information on the share of different kinds of enterprises by size of production in different segments of the industry. Export promotion measures, ever since the sector was declared a thrust area for exports, have been characterized by several incentives for export production as well as an emphasis on the production and export of increasingly value-added items. The export incentives include duty free import of raw hides and skills, semi-finished and finished leather, low duties on import of chemicals used by the industry, duty drawback, value based advance licensing schemes, etc.

Table 2.8 shows the composition of India's leather and leather product exports over the years. It is clear that the nineties have seen significant increases in exports, particularly in products such as footwear, garments and leather goods. Export policies since 1991 have progressively banned the export of raw hides and skins and semi-finished leather, and those of finished leather have been discouraged strongly, in order to encourage the production and export of value added products, resulting in the farming out of several operations to job-work units and household workshops, largely located in the small scale and tiny sectors. Thus, with these units constituting a large chunk of informal activity in the industry, it becomes apparent that the process of informalisation in the leather industry is very closely linked to the nature of its export policies. The structure of the industry has been influenced heavily by both these aspects of government policy.

Besides these policies, the sector is subject to very little regulation as a whole, but lately, there have been moves to make the industry less polluting. Following a judgment by a Green Bench of the Supreme Court in 1996, a large number of tanneries were closed down in Tamil Nadu, as they were not complying with the requirements of effluent treatment and pollution control. In Kolkata, all tanneries are required to relocate themselves to a leather complex, on the outskirts of the city, where effective pollution control standards are to be mandatorily met.

These efforts to relocate polluting tanneries to a leather complex in Kolkata or to shut down tanneries that do not link up to common effluent treatment facilities in Tamil Nadu, have raised several issues that have serious implications for the

TABLE 2.8 : **India's export performance in leather and leather products (1975-76 to 1997-98)**

Year	Semi-finished Leather	Finished Leather	Leather Foot-wear	Footwear Components	Leather Goods	Leather Garments	Manf. of Sports Goods	Total
1975-76	144	55	19	1	8	1	4	232
1980-81	51	227	34	45	25	5	24	411
1985-86	68	334	41	224	59	28	25	779
1990-91	13	799	303	573	253	557	127	2625
1995-96	-	1241	1103	814	1013	1387	370	5928
1996-97	-	1059	1208	792	1244	1494	NA	5797
1997-98	-	1065	1062	853	1378	1547	NA	5905

Source: "Monthly Statistics of the Foreign Trade of India, Volume I - Exports and Re-Exports", March Issues of 1976 to 1995.

TABLE 2.9 : **Structure of Indian Leather Sector, 1998 (in Percentage of Production Capacity)**

Sr. No.	Product Sector	Cottage	Small Scale	Medium Scale	Large Units	Total
1.	Semi processed Leather	20	70	5	5	100
2.	Finished leather	5	25	40	30	100
3.	Footwear	40	35	20	--	100
4.	Garments	--	90	10	--	100
5.	Leather goods	30	65	5	--	100
6.	Saddlery and Harness	60	40	--	--	100

Source: A. Sahasranaman, 1998.

structure of the sector; to say the least, it may adversely affect the informal segments in the sector in a significant manner.

The promotional structure for the development of the leather industry is quite vast, with institutions set up for basic research on materials and processes (Central Leather Research Institute, Madras), for building a pool of technical manpower (leather technology colleges in different parts of the country), for training workers through training institutes (Footwear Design and Development Institute) and other such initiatives. There are also a large number of business associations, formed by entrepreneurs in different segments of the industry. However, several institutional and structural bottlenecks (which become clear subsequently) have prevented these structures, public or private, from providing a strong supporting infrastructure for the industry.

It is thus clear that the industry is characterized by a wide variety of organisational structures in terms of labour processes, employment patterns, size of production, technology-in-use, etc. Historical factors and government policies together have lent it a degree of informalisation within which sub-contracting seems to work well among diverse production groups. It is summarily because of this that our field work looked at specific kinds of activities of firms that either fall within the informal sector directly or whose production activities are closely linked with the informal sector. Before going on to the findings of the field study, we present a broad view of the two clusters where field work was done. This follows in Section 3.

3. Overview of the Madras and Kolkata Leather Clusters

Tiljala, Tangra and Topsia are the three areas that constitute the Kolkata leather cluster and are distinguished from each other in terms of the ethnic identity of the owners of the tannery units situated there. Tiljala houses traditional vegetable tanning units that undertake both bag tanning as well as pit tanning; these units are largely owned by Sikhs from Punjab who started these businesses more than 40 years ago. The workers all belong to the Chamar caste from Bihar and are referred to as 'rams'. Topsia contains tanneries owned mostly by North Indian Muslims whose families have been connected with leatherworking for generations, either through trade in raw hides or through possessing artisanal skills. Tangra, or 'Chinapara' (Chinatown in Bengali) houses tanneries owned by Chinese immigrants, many of whom originally owned shoe business in the city, or who arrived from China with traditional leatherworking skills and setup tanneries in the middle of the twentieth century. Product making units, however, are not necessarily characterized by ownership by any particular community.

Of these, the Tiljala tannery area has been in existence for 50-60 years, and the growth in the number of units in the other areas occurred only subsequent to the industry being declared a thrust area for exports in the sixties. This includes tanneries producing chrome, tanned leather as well as product making units. The latter are spread across various parts of the city, including the above three areas. While there are no direct estimates of the number of units or the size of employment, informal estimates, obtained from interviews with trade union activists and experts in the industry put the employment figures at 50,000, with tannery workers constituting nearly 20,000, the number of tanneries at about 600, and the numbers of product making units running into thousands[7].

[7] There is very little published material that provides the history of the cluster and almost no research on production organization in the cluster. The only concrete reference that we could find was Banerjee and Nihila (1995) and the rest of the information follows our discussion with industry experts and our field observations.

The leather industry in Tamil Nadu too has a long history going back to the middle of the nineteenth century[8]. The leather processing units are spread out in several clusters in many districts of the state, but are mainly concentrated in North Arcot District. The Chromepet- Pallavaram cluster, where we did some of our fieldwork, is situated some 15 kilometres away from the city's municipal limits. Chromepet, which was part of Pallavaram, acquired its identity from a large chrome factory which was set up there in the early part of the century. Today, Chromepet cluster has a distinct identity of its own. It consists of a large number of tanneries and some shoemaking units. What we have called the Madras cluster includes the areas of Chromepet-Pallavaram, as well as parts of the city where product making units have been set up.

Unlike in Kolkata, it was hard to identify any particular ethnic identity of owners in the Madras cluster. If we were to consider the whole of Tamil Nadu, however, the most important leather businesses are in the hands of muslim families, particularly in the North Arcot clusters.

There is an essential difference in the technology employed in Madras and Kolkata; Madras has a larger number of units using modern technology and employing trained technicians than Kolkata, although there is a proliferation of small units using very few machines and employing only unskilled informal labour in both clusters.

The Madras cluster is exclusively export oriented, with units either exporting directly, or fabricating for exporters, or are engaged in job-work for export production, or selling to exporters. In Kolkata, however, both tanning as well as product making units cater to both the domestic and the export markets. Tanneries here supply leather to local product making units, to domestic and exporting product making units in Agra and directly to exporting units in Madras.

The tannery segment in Kolkata consists of large numbers of units doing all processing from the raw to the finishing stage, but the tannery segment in Madras consists mainly of firms undertaking tanning only from the wet blue stage[9]. The tanneries in Madras are connected to a common effluent treatment plant, whereas no such facility exists in Kolkata. In product making, Kolkata is better known for producing bags, wallets, travel goods and shoes in the lower price ranges, whereas Madras is well known for its expensive shoes and leather garments.

---

[8] The leather industry in Tamil Nadu is a well researched area as far as aggregative as well as micro level information is concerned for the period preceding the 1980s, unlike in Kolkata.

[9] This is essentially because different parts of the tanning process have got split across different clusters in Tamil Nadu, with each cluster specializing in a particular segment. Because of the polluting nature of tanning operations from the raw to the semi-finished stage these have been gradually phased out in the Madras cluster, due to its proximity to the city.

3.1 Fieldwork methodology

As mentioned earlier, our fieldwork has gone into the activities of two sets of enterprises involved solely in tanning, one set of small enterprises in the product making segment, and a final set of larger establishments that do tanning or product making or both together, through some kind of an integrated process. All these units qualify as being part of the informal sector using one or more criteria. The samples that we have selected have been randomly decided upon and represent typical units in the diverse segments studied. The selection of these units was done in due consultation with people connected with the industry, who felt that looking at these units would provide the needed representative information.

The method that we used to gather information at the enterprise level was informal interviews with entrepreneurs and workers of the diverse types of units. We had separate questionnaires for entrepreneurs and workers and we used different channels to communicate with them. For example, we met the owners of several units in Madras through the office of the UNIDO in Madras which has an on-going anti-pollution project in the tannery area in Chromepet. In order to meet workers in the same units, we went through the Centre for Indian Trade Unions, which has the trade unions in these units affiliated to it. In Kolkata , we essentially went through the dominant trade union in the tannery area, the Tannery Mazdoor Union affiliated to the All India Trade Union Congress, in order to meet both entrepreneurs and workers.

We also interviewed trade union activists at the enterprise level and the central level, scientists and economists working in the Central Leather Research Institute, Madras, officials in various bodies such as the Council for Leather Exports, Indian Leather Products Organization, National Leather Development Programme, India Trade Promotion Organization, and so on, besides meeting many experts who have had a long association with the industry.

Sections 4-6 present the insights emerging out of the fieldwork conducted in Madras and Kolkata, between January and August 1999. The fieldwork attempted to document the activities of typical units that could either directly be classified as informal sector enterprises or could be said to be dependent on the informal sector for purposes of labour recruitment, credit availability, etc. In order to evaluate the degree of informalisation in the manufacturing part of the industry, we have used two criteria, one for the status of the unit of production and the other for the status of the labour force employed by the units directly as well as that linked indirectly to the activities of the different units. As part of the first criterion, what has been examined is whether the units have a legal standing in any sense, i.e, whether they have been registered in the records of the concerned authorities in the state. The second criterion looks at the status of workers in the units; whether they are recognized as regular workers by the units and are, therefore, required to be provided particular facilities/benefits and whether these benefits are actually available to them. Thus, a unit could be considered part of the informal sector directly if it does not enjoy any legal status in terms of its existence, and/or if its workers are largely unrecognized and do not enjoy a many of the benefits that are usually attached to a recognized work-force.

Finally, we have also examined to what degree credit has been available from the formal sector, government agencies, etc., and to what extent marketing channels of small enterprises are well established and work to their benefit.

4. Tannery Units in the Informal Sector

4.1 Introduction

From amongst the different categories of units that have been presented in Table 2.6, we studied the activities of two: traditional urban tanneries in Kolkata and job-work tanneries working on orders from larger units both in Madras and Kolkata. While the production process in both categories is very different from each other, both are highly informal in nature as far as access to credit, employment and working conditions are concerned.

Kolkata's cluster of traditional tanning units are housed in a specific area called Tiljala. The cluster has about 60 small units that undertake primitive vegetable tanning to produce heavy leather which is ultimately used to produce cycle seats and soles for chappals. The tanneries are housed in the midst of a densely populated area that consists of slums and an assorted group of other industrial units. Some of the units have been in existence for 50 years or so, much prior to the development of the leather industry in its present form all over the country. These units are not registered with any authority and have no legal status whatsoever.

Job-work tanneries that undertake chrome tanning, on the other hand, exist in all major leather clusters in India and their exact number is not known. Job-working as a phenomenon emerged in this sector from the late seventies, got consolidated during the eighties and is now a clear manifestation of the uncertain and volatile nature of demand that the industry faces. Job-work refers to the phenomenon where a unit undertakes to do a certain part of the production process in response to specific orders from a larger unit with which it has a subcontracting relationship, i.e., the larger unit contracts out jobs to these units. Only a certain part of the production process or some parts are undertaken by units doing job-work. Two types of job-work are possible, first, where a large unit rents out the use of specific machines to job-workers who perform specific operations on the basis of orders from other larger units, using their own workers, raw materials, chemicals etc; and second, where small sheds are erected with one or a few machines by small entrepreneurs, hiring some workers and doing specific tanning and finishing operations for larger units. When a large full tanning unit does job-work for others or lends out its machinery to others to undertake the same, it does so because it has idle capacity and does not have enough orders to utilize its entire capacity. On the other hand, exclusive job-work units depend on job-work for their very existence. In both Kolkata and Madras clusters, we found a proliferation of exclusive job-work units, engaged in different single/multiple tanning and finishing operations. We met workers and owners of 4 traditional tanneries in Kolkata and 6 exclusive job-work tanneries, 4 in Madras and 2 in Kolkata.

Physically, it is difficult to distinguish one traditional Tiljala tannery from the other. Each tannery consists of a series of pits and slushy flat areas where various production operations are done. Adjoining tanneries are separated from each other only by mud embankments and are, therefore, not easily distinguishable from one another. During the rainy season, which was incidentally on when we visited the units, embankments become slushy and the whole area becomes marshy with several pits separating the marshy areas. In both the clusters, the job-work tanneries, however, appear less cluttered and filthy than the traditional ones.

4.2 Production Process, Ownership, Technology and Employment

Traditional tanneries are owned mostly by scheduled caste Punjabis. They moved to Kolkata nearly fifty years ago to start the tanneries; incidentally, most of them still maintain social links with their families and relatives in Punjab, and economic links with agriculture in Punjab. On an average, each unit employs 10-12 workers. A typical tanning and/or finishing workshop is owned by a small-scale entrepreneur who hires between 5 and 20 workers to do various tanning and/or finishing operations. Unlike the traditional tanneries, no particular ethnic identity was observed among the owners of these units.

All the job-work units that we visited were proprietary concerns that were owned by single proprietors. Two of them were leather technologists. This is a phenomenon typically associated with job-work. Large number of technologists are produced each year by the colleges of leather technology all over the country. Very often, these graduates themselves go into actual production, although on a limited scale, through job working; a large number of such units owned by leather technologists have come up over the last decade or so.

The production process, degree of mechanization, and labour intensity of operations are very different for these two types of tanning enterprises. In the traditional tanneries, the main raw material that is processed consists of low grade, salted hide purchased from the local raw hide market or split hides obtained from the adjoining chrome tanning areas. Split hide consists of that part of the hide of a cow or buffalo that is towards the inside of the animals body and is 'split' from the outer side. It is both cheap as well as suitable for making heavy, rough leather. This raw material is purchased by the owners of the units themselves from the local market. The job-work tanneries, on the other hand, get their raw material (consisting of processed hides/skins) from the larger parent unit and is, therefore, not involved in its purchase.

Tanning operations in the traditional tanneries are all manual and extremely tedious. In the tanning process, the raw hide has to be transferred from one pit to another for processes referred to as liming, de-liming, tanning, drumming, etc. Each hide weighs 10-12 kilos and the process of transferring them from one pit to the other is fairly laborious. Apart from large drums, there are no machines used in most of the units, with the exception of a flattening machine (used to flatten the tanned hides) that is available only with a few units; often, this machine is rented out to other units. Thus the degree of capital intensity in these traditional tanneries is extremely low. The nature of work in these traditional tanneries clearly prompts us to guess that all is not well in respect of the working conditions and skill levels of workers in these units.

In the more modern chrome tanning units, including the job-work tanneries, operations are much more dependent on machines, though a large number of operations are still done by hand. The process of tanning consists of the following operations : first, raw hides are converted into semi-finished form, either by vegetable or chrome tanning and, second, the semi-finished leather is converted into finished leather. Some pre-tanning operations, such as soaking, liming, de-fleshing and de-liming are similar to those in the traditional tanneries, but the rest are done by workers with the help of machines.

Job work tanneries typically do one or two of the above processes. These units therefore have one or two machines or 3-4 drums. Pre-tanning operations such as soaking, liming, de-fleshing, de-hairing etc., are all done manually; regular cleaning of lime pits before liming operations are done is also done manually. The tanning operations are done by machines or in the drums, but typically the worker has to manually load the raw hide or skin on to the machines, or into the drums. In operations such as buffing, smoothening the wet blue tanned hide lets off fine blue chrome dust into the air that engulfs the entire workshops; the workers engaged in these operations, especially the neck and upper parts of their body, usually get covered with this harmful substance.

4.3 Labour Market, Division of Labour and Working Conditions

Both the traditional and job-work tanneries recruit labour entirely from the informal labour market. In Kolkata, this consists of a large number of workers belonging to the scheduled castes from Bihar, whereas in Madras, there is no such ethnic identity to the workforce. In Kolkata, the workers in the traditional tannery segment are distinct from those in the non-traditional segment in the sense that there is no mobility between the segments. Each traditional unit employs 10-12 workers in different pre-tanning and tanning operations. There is hardly any division of labour between them, with each one having to do all the filthy and tedious jobs involved in the operations. Apart from these, there are two other categories of workers: those who operate the flattening machine mentioned above and those who carry the raw, split and tanned hides between units for machine operations or to and from trucks, i.e., the head-load workers.

Since there are no official labour records, it is clear that there are no permanent workers in terms of benefits being available to them. All the same, we discovered some kind of a distinction between the so-called 'permanent workers' and 'casual workers'. Those who have worked for a period of 10-15 years in a unit consider themselves ' permanent' to the extent that usually they are not laid off even if there is a fall in demand. The 'casual' tanning workers who are also paid monthly salaries similar to the 'permanent' brethren do run the risk of being laid off; the piece rate workers are like daily wage earners, with no job security whatsoever. On an average, the minimum salary which is paid to a new entrant involved in tanning operations, in a traditional unit, is about Rs. 1200/- for an 8 hour working day, with a provision for overtime on piece rate basis. There is hardly any difference between 'Casual' and 'Permanent' workers in this regard. A worker, who had been working in a unit for 20 years or so, reported that he earned about Rs. 2000/- including over time, which means that hardly any rise in wages seems to have accrued to him over years. Piece rates are Rs. 0.70 or so for head load workers and machine operators; they reported that in the peak season (lasting for 2 to 3 months in a year), they earned about Rs. 1500 per month but, for the whole year, the average monthly earnings worked out to be Rs. 800 or so.

As far as the job-work units are concerned, they reported a peak employment of about 30 people when a large number of orders were forthcoming. Both in Madras and Kolkata clusters, we found that information regarding orders that any firm receives spreads through the area in a very short while and a large number of job-seeking persons turn up. Workers, whether in relatively long-term or completely casual employment, are paid exclusively through the piece-rate system in job-work units. With different rates prevailing for different operations, workers earn between Rs. 1500 and Rs. 2000 per month, which includes working overtime as well.

It is clear that work in chrome tanneries using machines involves higher levels of skills than in the traditional tanneries. However, average remuneration levels are roughly the same, or only marginally higher in the latter. These tanneries are part of a production chain that very often links them to the quality international market, but there is hardly any avenue for skill up-gradation or quality consciousness at the shop-floor level because of the informal nature of recruitment and the associated depressing wage levels.

Coming now to the working conditions, to a large extent, in both types of tanneries, work is extremely hazardous and also degrading. The pre-tanning operations that are done in pits involve the workers standing in waist-deep solutions to ensure adequate soaking of hides. There is a heavy stench that emanates from the pits due to the raw hides themselves and the solutions used, as also the fact that these pits have accumulated material that is as much as 40-50 years old in the case of traditional tanneries. Stitching, flattening and stretching operations are extremely tedious and involve hard physical labour, as does the transferring of heavy soaked hides from one pit to the other, or the transporting of hides by the head load workers. The workers complained of skin infections, tuberculosis and other respiratory disorders and also accidents at the flattening machine for which there is no provision of leave much less a medical allowance. In a study of female workers in the tanning industry in the Dindigul leather cluster in Tamil Nadu, Nihila (1999) found that while working conditions in tanneries are generally hazardous, those faced by women workers are particularly degrading and hazardous. For example, women workers who are brought into the industry entirely by contractors, are not recognized as legal workers in any sense of the term. They are made to do physically strenuous and debilitating work like cleaning lime pets, carrying heavy raw materials from one place to the other, drying hides and skins in hot chambers where they have to walk over burning charcoal to hook and unhook skins, and so on.

Both traditional and job-work tanneries do not provide any benefits, including health, to workers. Workers are permitted to go on leave for only ten days in a year in Kolkata, which is hardly ever followed by the employers, resulting in a high rate of turnover. A major reason for taking long vacation (a minimum of one month) by some workers is that they have to visit their families back in Bihar; hardly any of their families live in Kolkata. They themselves live in shacks close to the tanneries, paying rents of Rs.150-300 per month with each shack housing 8-10 workers. While the labour market is entirely informal and offers hardly any security, entry and exit is also tightly controlled by the workers themselves through the barrier of caste and region and this provides an implicit assurance that a job in some units will be available when they come back from vacations, and the actual difference in salary between a casual and permanent job is hardly anything.

As far as access to the credit market is concerned, the tiny traditional units in Madras and those in Kolkata (tiny and small ones) had no access to bank finance whereas units employing 15-20 workers in Madras (also the ones run by leather technologists) had access to bank finance from nationalized commercial banks. Raw materials are purchased from warehouses in the city, very often on credit from raw material traders who would be repaid after production and sales have taken place. In Madras, the units produce for the export market, i.e., produce for larger units with links to product-making and exporting units. In Kolkata, job-work units produce for larger tanneries that sell to both domestic as well as exporting product-making units. On an average, all units produce for 4-5 larger firms, under sub-contracts that last for fairly long intervals.

A large number of workers in the traditional as well as job-work units in Kolkata units are members of the Tannery Mazdoor Union, affiliated to the All India Trade Unions Congress; this union has been functioning since the 1960s. Collective bargaining in the entire tannery area in the Kolkata cluster consists of wage negotiations between the union representatives and tannery owners on the basis of the variable dearness allowance neutralization rate. According to this, for every percentage point increase in the consumer price index (CPI), published by the state government, an increase in monthly wages is demanded by Rs.1. After the CPI for the year 1998 was published, wages were revised by Rs.271 with effect from January 1999 on the basis of an increase of 271 percentage points in the CPI. However, for the traditional tanning units in Tiljala, the tannery owners argue that the wages paid in other parts of the cluster cannot be applicable to them because of their lower productivity, and as a result, inflation neutralization has always been lower, in this case about Rs. 240/- per month. No other demands of the trade union such as maintenance of labour records, making contract and piece-rate workers permanent, or provision of allowances such as PF and ESI have been taken seriously by tannery owners.

There is hardly any unionisation among tannery workers in Madras.

Having gone through various aspects of the informal tannery segment, the obvious question that arises is: what is the likelihood that these forms of organizations will continue to exist in their present forms? Is there an element of dynamism about these organizational forms which will help them survive as they are doing now, or will it warrant major changes at the sectoral and enterprise level? Answers to these questions are attempted in Section 7, but before that, a few points need to be underlined here.

As far as the traditional tanning units are concerned, while work methods and working conditions are primitive and they produce for the cheapest end of the market, it is clear that unlike many other types of informal sector activities (including household footwear production, examined in the next section) continuing to exist in the current form, these are extremely lucrative to the entrepreneurs. We made rough estimates of the costs and turnover of these units and calculated that profits alone could amount to

Rs. 2 lakhs or so per month[10]. There is no reason for the entrepreneurs to go in for more modern methods of production in the absence of this being articulated effectively by the trade union[11]. The external factor that will affect the prospects of this segment is the proposed clearing of the tannery area in Kolkata and its relocation to a leather complex on the outskirts of the city. Practically non-recognized by the prominent industry bodies and even the Supreme Court (in whose order to relocate tanneries there is no mention of these units), the clearing of the area will, in practical terms, involve the shutting down of all the traditional tanning units and unemployment of the entire work-force, with no alternative employment opportunities or compensation being in sight because of the informal nature of their employment. For entrepreneurs, the choice will be to wind up operations in the industry altogether or to go into chrome tanning and product-making as part of the leather complex, involving substantial investments.

Some of the more enterprising entrepreneurs have already gone into wet-chrome tanning with partial mechanization. They will probably convert their units to job-work tanneries in the eventuality that they will be forced to wind up their original operations.

As far as the job-work tanneries are concerned, they have come up in order to serve as feeder units, in a fairly long and wide subcontracting chain, to larger tanneries and finishing units. This system offers great advantages to the larger unit in terms of restricting the size of their workforce, reducing capital outlays and supervision costs, and cushioning them against the adverse impact of fluctuation in demand.

While there is a proliferation of job-working units both in Kolkata and Madras, and most of them are extremely small, there has been a dynamic aspect to the phenomenon. Many of the factory-type tanning and exporting units that will be analysed under Section 7 have grown from these small workshops doing exclusively job-work. This growth has come about most often by adding on processes and capacities without legal sanction and recruiting additional workforce without any legal standing. Thus, there

[10] Production	:	1000 heavy hides and 500 light hides
Sales turnover	:	Rs.1140000 (@ Rs.840 per heavy hide and Rs. 600 per light hide
Costs	:	Rs.900000, of which
Raw material (hides)	:	Rs . 600,000 - 700,000 for heavy hides and Rs. 120000-150000 for light hides.
Raw Material (lime, tanning material etc)	:	Rs. 35000 or so.
Labour costs	:	Rs 25000 or so
Profit per month	:	Rs. 214000 or so.

[11] The trade union leaders told us that in their own assessment, their demands had always been related only to wage increases or to the improvement in the status of the workers. With regard to the necessity of improvement in labour standards being linked up with productivity and technology up-gradation, in recent years, trade unions too were beginning to understand and articulate the link. Lately, according to these leaders, workers are becoming increasingly conscious of the need for such an up-gradation, for ensuring theirs and the enterprises' existence.

is a continuity in the production structure that is built upon informal production methods and informal labour processes. Since these units could be indirectly producing for the export market, there is every likelihood that they will continue to exist and in fact swell in numbers as the international market becomes more competitive and buoyant.

5. Informal Leather Product Making Units

5.1 Introduction

This section analyses the activities of a second category of informal sector units in the leather industry, that of fabricators of leather products and of units in the household sector. As in tanning, perhaps to a larger extent, product-making takes place through extensive subcontracting arrangements and the structure that obtains is a direct fallout of the volatile and segmented nature of demand for leather products. The informal segment in product making consists directly of fabricating units and household production units and indirectly (employing informal labour in spite of being part of the formal sector) of large factories producing and supplying to the domestic and international market.

Fabrication units are those that assemble entire bags, wallets, belts, etc. from components provided by a larger unit, using their own labour force and machinery. Units in the household sector consist of job-working workshops employing hired labour, where parts of production processes are performed, or of home-based units whose families do specific jobs without hired labour and are duly coordinated by an agent of a larger firm.

We interviewed the proprietors and workers of 5 footwear units in the household sector (2 household units and 3 household workshops), 3 leather garment fabrication units and 4 leather goods (bags, wallets, purses, belts etc.) fabrication units. Two footwear, leather garment and leather goods units each were examined in Madras and the remaining in Kolkata. We have, in addition, also looked at the results obtained by a survey of leather product units done by the Central Leather Research Institute in 1997.

5.2 Production Process, Ownership and Employment

All the footwear concerns that we visited were set up in the 1970s, in response to the boom in exports. They are all proprietary concerns and cater essentially to domestic demand. They produce four to five different types of footwear, from sandals and chappals to children's shoes to adult male shoes. Footwear production, with large variations, involves the following operations: pattern making, when a pattern is cut out on cardboard for each design; leather cutting, where finished leather is cut according to the pattern chosen; upper making, where the cut-out upper is embroidered or design stitched on to them; lasting, or the fixing of the upper on wooden or plastic shoe lasts to acquire the shape of a foot; fixing components such as buckles and laces; pasting and finishing of uppers; sole attachments and, finally packing. Footwear production is thus a highly skilled job even when there is hardly any mechanisation. The household workshop units that we visited used only traditional hand tools such as hammers, pincers, the three legged stand, knives, etc., which were purchased by the proprietors from local blacksmiths. The home-based units consisted of 2-3 women in each family engaged in sewing colourful plastic threads onto shoe uppers, both provided by a larger unit to be used for export production. In this case, obviously there were no machines used.

Out of the three proprietors of workshops that we interviewed, two belonged to the cheduled castes and one (in Kolkata) was a muslim gentleman. All women workers in the home-based units belong to the scheduled castes. The workshops hire between 6-10 workers for specific activities, in addition to using family members' own labour.

The leather garment and leather goods units that we visited are all fabrication units that came into existence after 1985, following the boom in exports of these products, and their production is exclusively geared to exports. In these units, no particular community background of the proprietors was evident and the workers, averaging between 7 and 10 , were all local people hired either for monthly wages or piece-rates. The units were all proprietary concerns with a single owner.

Both garment making and bag or wallet making hardly involves any big machines in such workshops except stitching and sewing machines. Among leather products, garments and small leather goods such as bags and wallets are amenable to production by fabricators because there are several advantages to it. First, unlike shoemaking in large factories, garment and small leather good manufacturing is not done by assembly line type operations even in large factories because the production process itself is different. With highly labour-intensive minute operations, it is easier to farm out operations to 'trusted' fabricators who are very often like employees of the larger firm. In most cases, the original pattern cutting is done in the parent unit. In fact, one of the leather garment fabricating units in Madras claimed to be a 'satellite' unit of one of India's largest leather garment exporters, Vantage India Ltd. The proprietor of this satellite unit was one of the master tailors in Vantage and was allowed to set up his own unit when Vantage encountered demand problems. Today, this proprietor supplies exclusively to Vantage, but bears the brunt of adjustment when demand goes down. This is the second advantage that fabrication allows larger units to have- that of contracting production with a fall in demand without generating idle capacity. Finally, it reduces the problem of having to manage a large work-force.

5.3 Labour Market, Division of Labour and Working Conditions

In all units, whether producing footwear, garments or leather goods, employment is entirely informal, in the sense that the workers are picked up from the informal labour market. However, there are wide differences in earning levels and working conditions.

In the footwear workshop units, the workers employed are made available through contractors who belong to the local area. They are employed on piece rates to do specific jobs such as cutting, which is an extremely skilled activity, sometimes for only a few hours a week, depending on seasonal demand. During the peak season, the hired workers too do a large number of jobs along with unpaid family labour, but when demand is slack, more household labour is used to adjust to the prevailing market instability. On an average, hired workers earn between Rs. 600 and Rs. 800 from each unit that they work in, giving them average earnings of about Rs. 1500-2000 per month. Workers in home-based units earn about Rs. 10 per day. They form the last link in a long subcontracting chain controlled by contractors and middlemen. These home-based units are huts with very little light and many of the women workers perform such jobs in addition to their household chores. Many of them suffer from eye strain and have worn-out hands and fingers due to the tedious stitching of colourful threads on to uppers.

In the garment and product making units, the situation is somewhat different. Even here, the workers are hired through a contractor. Each unit employs 8-10 workers out of which 3-4 are considered 'permanent' in the sense that they are not to be laid off during the slack season. In the garment making units, they are mostly master tailors who cut patterns and supervise stitching during the peak season, but have to do all types jobs during the slack season. These craftsmen can earn upto Rs. 5000 per month, while other hired workers' average monthly earning stays in the range of Rs. 1200-1500. In the case of women workers, average earning is about Rs. 600 per month. This is true in leather goods manufacturing units as well.

No benefits such as P.F. or E.S.I. coverage are available to any of the units in this category.

To sum up, a large proportion of product making in India takes place in small workshop type establishments that use traditional skills, or those that have come up in response to particular kinds of demand for the products. These units, existing at almost the bottom level of production in the long chain consisting of intermediaries or larger units, have come up to a large extent in the last couple of decades. It represents a significant aspect of the informalization of production.

Having examined the features of informal production in this significant segment of the leather industry, we focus again on the viability of these production and organisational structures. As in the case of job-work tanneries, product fabricators and home-based units form the last link in a complicated subcontracting chain that supplies to a highly volatile and segmented international as well as domestic market. With the nature of markets remaining the same, it is possible for these structures to continue to exist in their present form and in fact even increase in numbers. With competitive pressures mounting, it is possible that margins fall even more and exploitation worsens. While these organisational forms offer very little by means of income or security to workers, how lucrative they are to entrepreneurs is very difficult to establish. For the household workshops supplying the domestic market that essentially rely on artisanal skills, however, rough estimates show that they could not be earning more than Rs.6000 or so per month, which puts them in a very different category from that of informal units in the tannery segment[12]. In all fairness, these units would benefit greatly from support programmes specifically designed for the artisanal sector; to put them in the league of conventional entrepreneurs would be counter-productive to their own interests.

6. Units Bordering between Formal and Informal Sectors

6.1 Introduction

After having considered wholly informal units in the tannery and product making segments, a third category of units that we visited consisted of those which have been considered under the modern segment of the industry, employing about 100 odd workers, in reasonably large and mechanized and sometimes automated factories. There are both tanneries as well as product making units in this category and in both cases, either tanning or product-making constitute their main activity. In recent years, some of these tanneries have gone into product-making and exporting; however, this constitutes only a small proportion of their turnover. These units are, therefore, independent and operate only in one segment of the industry. Our study covered 4 product making units (2 in Madras and 2 in Kolkata) and 5 tanneries (2 in Madras and 3 in Kolkata).

6.2 Status of the Units, Ownership and Employment

All units covered have been registered with several agencies like the State Industries Department, Council for Leather Exports, Pollution Control Boards and so on. However, it was not clear whether information on their exact capacities, the dates on which additional capacities were added, or the operations they are involved in, was available; none of this is published in any comprehensive manner and the publications of various agencies did not contain any consistent information. It is, however, sure that in terms of the legality of their existence, all these enterprises fall strictly within the formal sector, although in terms of capital size, it is not clear whether all of them fall strictly within the small scale sector. Employment of 60-70

[12] A CLRI survey of product making units in 1995 found that a fairly large number of units in this category of household enterprises earned only about Rs. 45,000 or less per annum, with monthly earnings working out to be less than Rs. 4,000. Clearly, such enterprises are markedly different from those that we saw under Section 4 above.

workers was reported by most units. Finally, all units were partnership enterprises, each having two partners.

In Kolkata, very few tanning units have access to finance from the organized sector[13]. Borrowing is primarily from family or other informal sources within the community. The practice of getting raw material on credit from big hide and skin traders, to be repaid when sales have been effected, is also common. In Madras, however, credit is easily available from nationalized banks.

6.3 Employment and Wages

The structure of employment was different between enterprises located in Kolkata and those in Madras. In Madras, the tanneries and product making units employ a relatively permanent work-force that is provided facilities such as P.F., E.S.I. etc. and relatively clean working conditions, but are, on the average, paid low salaries that do not follow minimum wage norms. In fact, in Madras, while the average wages of male workers was reported to be around Rs. 1500, like in the two types of enterprises analysed above, that for female workers employed in product-making units was reported to be about Rs. 800-1000. Apart from this permanent work-force, records for which are submitted to the office of the Labour Commissioner, these units employ casual workers, but these do not constitute more than 10-15 per cent of the total work-force employed during the peak season. Thus, while various amenities are available, the entrepreneur/firm clearly cares only as much as the informal sector does for workers. In addition, firms are clearly benefiting due to the gender segregation in wages.

In Kolkata, in the tannery segment, more than 60 per cent of the work force is casual; consistent record of the permanent work force is not available either. Even the permanent work force is not provided any benefits that their more secure position could have entitled them to. Within the casual work force, most are paid piece-rates for different machine operations. The entrepreneurs are predominantly Chinese and some Muslim, whereas the workforce is mostly from among the scheduled castes from Bihar and, to a much lesser extent, from Nepal. In a sense, therefore, operations here are more socially entrenched than those of other kinds. Most of the units covered have come up from the tanning workshop type enterprises, covered under Section 4 above, where employing informal labour has clearly been a

[13] Entrepreneurs who were interviewed by us reported that the banks in Kolkata were biased against tanners due to traditional social prejudices and did not, therefore want to provide them credit. Some of the owners of larger units, however, felt that the tannery sector had a bad history of repayment and as a result, bankers shied away from lending to them in any significant manner. These large units did not find it difficult to get finance, whereas the ones that we are talking about found it difficult to obtain loans for working capital or funds for expansion.

source of accumulation. Also, in the product-making and exporting segment in Kolkata, almost the entire workforce is locally-recruited, temporary and piece-rated, marked by varying wage rates across different operations. A high degree of division of labour is discernible for manufacture of bags, travel goods and wallets. There is hardly any unionization among workers in product-making factories, whereas tannery workers, casual or permanent, are affiliated to one or the other central trade union. Nonetheless, the issues for collective bargaining are the same as in the tannery segment.

The product making units also get a significant proportion of output fabricated from workshops in the area. This, according to the owners, was to avoid directly recruiting a very large workforce which could create supervision problems. The workers who did the fabrication in this case would be employees of fabricators, as seen in an earlier section. In one case, however, we found an interesting phenomenon, where job workers worked under the same roof as the main factory workers and were being supervised by fabricators who were ostensibly independent and not employees of the larger firm. It seemed, therefore, that production taking place in the large factory premises, was by workers employed by the factory directly, as well as by small groups of workers working independently and doing job work for the large unit. Actually, this arrangement was neither a job-work nor fabrication by contract; it was part of the larger firm's own production process. By claiming that the small groups of people were job workers, the firm was understating the actual size of employment. In reality, it seemed as if the so-called supervisors were not independent fabricators, but were actually controlled by the larger unit. In the records of the larger firm, however, the workers doing the job work would not get recorded at all. This enables the larger firm to pay much lower wages to these workers as well.

To summarise the ground realities in this last category of enterprises, it is clear that even in leather and leather products manufacturing units that belong to the formal sector, in legal terms or in terms of capital size, informal labour recruitment procedures, working conditions and types and levels of remuneration are prevalent, to a very large extent. These larger units have grown from much smaller ones and, to a large extent, this growth has been 'facilitated' largely informal elements mentioned above. In other words, the informalisation of labour has played a major role in the growth of individual enterprises from small, unorganized units to larger, organized ones.

7. Major Constraints and Main Recommendations

7.1 Insights Emanating from the Field Study

Our inquiry into the working of the three categories of enterprises in the leather and leather products sector throws up a rich crop of insights which deserve to be recapitulated before concrete recommendations are framed. Here are the major ones.

1. Informalisation of production structures is pervasive across all categories of activities in the sector, beginning from carcass collection and flaying to production and export of fashionable products. While some typess of enterprises could be said to unambiguously belong to the informal sector, like the traditional tanning units in Kolkata and the job-work and fabrication workshops in the tanning and product making segments in Kolkata and Madras, some others which are considered part of the organized sector, such as the factory type small and medium scale tanneries as well as product-making units, are actively involved in informal operations as far as employment strategies and conditions, links to the credit market, etc. are concerned. Even large firms, whose direct production and employment are fairly organized and formal, are linked closely to the informal sector through extensive sub-contracting, job-working and fabrication.

2. What is striking about the pattern of informalisation of production structures is that these do not cater a demand for special or specified types of items, but to a wide range of products from the sector in both the domestic and international markets, ranging from rough cycle seats and soles to high fashion footwear, garments, bags, land so on. A combination of historical factors, the strong links that the sector has with the social structure, the segmented and volatile nature of demand for the sector's products, and government policy emphasizing more and more on producing cheaper and competitive products, have led to pervasive informalisation of production processes and relations. In addition, the evolution of important urban clusters of activity, combined with the decline of leather working activities in rural areas resulting in large-scale migration of artisans to these clusters and other urban areas, and the creation of a long chain of intermediaries involved in the marketing of products, have also contributed to the process of informalisation. In fact, informal production is built into the production chain in the leather and leather products industry and both its success in terms of providing lucrative opportunities as demonstrated by the margins involved for many categories of entrepreneurs, as well as its weaknesses, demonstrated by low levels of production, incomes, output, etc. are due to the pervasiveness of the informal economy.

3. The informal economy in this sector has not necessarily been the culmination of rural-urban migration, or as a residual phenomenon, but is part and parcel of the kind of development that the sector has seen. To a large extent, the kind of export policies pursued and the nature of the linkage among different layers of enterprises that have developed to cater to this demand have resulted in the

informalisation of production structures. Undoubtedly, a large part of the informal production structure has come into existence following the boom in export production.

7.2 Major Constraints and Salient Recommendations

We have seen how both in macro and micro terms, the informalisation of production structures (catering to both the domestic and international markets) has been an integral part of the development process itself in this sector. Hence, in terms of productive performance as well as labour welfare, the development of the sector, largely based on small-scale manufacturing, has resulted in what has often been referred to as the 'low road to flexible specialisation' or 'flexible casualisation' in the literature on alternative paths of small-scale sector development. The literature[14], taking cognizance of the differences among alternative models of small scale sector development, concludes that smallness of size and the flexibility imparted therein can be a great advantage for firms that function in clusters, if their production is characterized by inter-firm cooperation side by side with their respective specialisation, and that there are strong public institutions to provide supporting services for fostering this cooperation. However, the same smallness and flexibility can render them extremely vulnerable in terms of production performance and lead firms to pass the brunt of this to labour, as seems to be the case in the leather and leather products industry in India.

Whether the increase in demand for leather and leather products is going to be met by the sector getting more and more informalised in the way that we have looked at it, or whether a transformation towards a 'high road' type of model[15], characterized by successful productive performance, as well as high labour standards, can be envisaged, will depend on how the constraints that the sector faces are going to be dealt with.

This concluding sub-section attempts to outline the main constraints that are faced by the sector and the entities in the informal sector that are part of it, and also

---

[14] There is a large volume of literature on the possibilities of small scale enterprise development in the framework of the "flexible specialisation" paradigm. While Nadvi and Schmitz (1998) review the evidence on small scale enterprise clusters and the issues that they raise internationally, various articles in Bagchi (1995) look at the applicability of the concept in the Indian case, where the term flexible "casualisation" has been used to refer to the kind of informal employment and labour conditions that we have found in the leather sector.

[15] The specific terms "low road to flexible specialization" and "high road to flexible specialization" have been termed by Pyke and Sengenberger (1992) in referring to contrasts between small enterprise development that results in high productive performance as well as labour welfare, as seen in the case of the Third Italy, on the one hand, and the sweat shop conditions, as they exist in countries such India, on the other.

tries to make macro level as micro level recommendations on how to overcome these constraints.

The constraints have been grouped into three types: those that obtain at the macro level and affect the prospects of the sector as a whole; those that concern enterprises, particularly informal ones, and their productive performance; and those that concern labour, particularly informal labour. There is some overlap among these categories inasmuch as the constraints that affect the sector as a whole do also affect individual categories of enterprises in different ways, and these in turn affect the conditions of labour. The reverse is also true, with labour conditions affecting performance of enterprises, which in turn does not leave the total sector unaffected.

Before we go to elaborate the constraints, *it is necessary to reiterate the point regarding non-availability of reliable data on sectoral magnitudes as a whole and specifically that on the informal sector.* We noted in Section 2.1 that there are several problems with the available data sources such as National Sample Survey and the Annual Survey of Industries as a result of which we do not have reliable information even about the numbers of units, their output and employment, leave alone any more detailed magnitudes in this context. As a beginning towards overcoming this handicap, *it is necessary to have a sectoral all-India and state-wise enumeration of the numbers of types of enterprises that exist in the leather and leather products sector as well as the mumbers they employ and the output that they produce.* We recommend that this job should preferably be done by industry's own institutions, e.g., Central Leather Research Institute or any such institution in collaboration with the NSS and the ASI. It is impossible to seriously tackle many of the problems that the industry faces without this enumeration and collection of reliable statistics on basic magnitudes.

It is now time to come to the constraints faced by the sector as a whole, by enterprises and by labour that have been encapsulated in Table 7.1. As mentioned earlier, a major bottleneck relates to raw material availability because of the high price of raw hides and skins and its low quality. This, in turn, is due to backward practices of carcass recovery, flaying and preservation. Hardly any organized link exists between the meat and leather industries leading to a lot of wastage; long transportation time involved due to concentration of raw hide and skin markets in semi-urban and urban areas results in high costs and erosion in quality; in many areas, low incomes of traditional flayers lead to an exodus away from the occupation time to the low incomes and social stigma. To a large extent, this constraint can be dealt with if, as a first step, the shift in the leather sector completely away from the rural areas to the urban clusters is reversed partially. We recommend that this be done by establishing decentralized carcass recovery centres and, at the same time, by reviving rural tanning (vegetable- as well as chrome-tanning) at a cooperative

TABLE 7.1 : **Constraints and Recommendation**

Constraints	Recommendation
(I) Macro / Sectoral Constraint	
(IA) Sub-optimal raw material availability and poor quality	Establishment of decentralized carcass recovery centers and flaying-cum-tannnng cooperatives at village / taluka / district level to revive rural tanning
(IB) Insufficient technological upgradation and environmental safeguards.	Generation of large funds for technological upgradation by the government, provision of funds to individual units being subject to production efficiency as well as labour standards
(IC) Insufficient availability of skilled work force.	Availability of training centers for workers at cluster level.
(ID) Lack of Organised structure for markting.	Establishment of marketing consortia for the international market apart from the existing institutional setup.
(II) Constraints faced by enterprises in the informal segment.	
(IIA) Availability of raw material and components at reasonable prices	Establishment of centers supplying raw materials and components at reasonable prices in different clusters.
(IIB) Appropriate technology dissemination low	Setting up cluster level and decentralized technology dissemination centers.
(IIC) Credit availability for working capital, investment and technology upgradation meager.	Targeted programmes to provide credit to different kinds of units through public institutions, cooperative credit societies etc.
(IID) Marketing Problems	Active setting up of marketing cooperatives that guarantee off takes of products at reasonable prices.
(III) Constraints faced by labour	
(IIIA) Low wages and hardly any benefits in both formal and informal segments	Maintenance of labour records should be made mandatory and subject to supervision.
(IIIB) Very limited mobility	Minimum wage norms and associated benefits
(IIIC) Working conditions poor and many occupational and health hazard	should be enforced at cluster level through strict supervision by labour commissioner offices. Should be part of overall tannery modernization and technological upgradation programmes at cluster level.

level to take care of the leather needs of the local artisans. In fact, flaying cum tanning cooperatives should be set up at decentralized centers after working out minimum viable size of units. The technological package for the above has already been worked out by the CLRI, but its dissemination has been scanty. The carcass recovery centres can also be linked up to raw hide markets that supply raw material to the urban centres. With adequate technical help from the CLRI for flaying, preservation, tanning and effluent treatment, these decentralized centres could help stem the adverse terms of trade faced by rural artisans, provide employment to traditional workers in the sector, improve the overall quality of raw hides and skins, and also reduce the pollution load in the urban clusters, where all tanning activities get concentrated. Reduction in the pollution load would take place not because it gets dispersed but because it is easier to deal with small quantities of effluent effectively. State industries departments could take up the setting up of flayers' cooperatives-cum-tanning centres as a major promotional activity by providing cheap credit, disseminating technology and ensuring cooperative marketing systems. Establishment and effective functioning of these centres could also help deal with the very vulnerable position of the people involved in rural and urban areas in the informal sector, most pointedly in carcass recovery and flaying, and also provide them with additional and better employment opportunities.

At the enterprise level, the existing informal sector enterprises, operating in clusters, face the raw material constraint in terms of high prices, most essentially because small-batch buying is more expensive. Tanning enterprises have to buy raw hides and skins from traders in mandis through middlemen, while product-making units have to buy finished leather, mostly through middlemen, from markets that are invariably controlled by large tanneries; they have no suppliers who they can rely on by virtue of their small size. It is recommended that centres catering to the raw material need of small and informal enterprises be set up in different clusters that can supply it to them at reasonable prices. The same applies to the availability of components and accessories for product making units (zips, buckets, lasts, PVC soles, etc.) and of chemicals for tanning units. Small and informal sector enterprises have to be given centralized facilities where these can become available at reasonable prices.

A second major sectoral constraint is of inefficiency at enterprise level and at the sectoral level due to inadequate technological upgradation and non-adherence to environmental and anti-pollution norms. This constraint will result in an overall erosion of competitiveness as far as the sector as a whole is concerned, as also to the shutting down of polluting units in the tannery segment. While efforts such as the setting up of leather complex in Kolkata, where anti-pollution norms will have to be satisfied by individual units, are laudable in theory, in practice, pollution control and technological upgradation can come about only if large funds are raised, by respective governments, for setting up the facilities and their provision to individual units is subjected to production norms as well as adherence to labour standards. In an interview with a prominent tanner from Kolkata, who is also one of the office bearers of the Council for Leather Exports, we were told that a huge sum of Rs. 14,000 million that was being offered by Italy to India as a tannery modernisation fund did not finally make its way to India because the Indian policymakers delayed the procedures involved. Large-scale sectoral technological upgradation would need to be taken up very seriously by the government if significant improvement in productivity and efficiency are to be realized.

At the informal or semi-formal enterprise level, however, access to better technology, or to pollution-control mechanisms, would need to be provided by public institutions at cluster level. The reasons for low usage of common facility centres needs to be investigated and access to them improved through provision of information about them, locating them at convenient locations and providing the facilities, wherever enterprises need them.

A third major sectoral constraint is the low level of credit availability to the leather and leather products sector from the organized financial institutions. Whatever meager credit has been available, whether for addition of facilities, working capital, or technology upgradation, has been available mostly to the larger, formal enterprises. Our field-study found that almost all enterprises in the tannery segment in Kolkata, including larger ones, obtained credit from family and friends or the informal market, whereas institutional credit was more easily available to product making units, particularly those who export their output. Several tanners told us that this was because the tanning business is still considered an 'unclean' business due to notions of 'purity'. We were told that even in official circles, it is more 'respectable' to be an 'exporter' rather than a mere tanner, irrespective of profits made, because tanning is considered a dirty work. Further, those involved in tanning in Kolkata also belong to communities that have been isolated from others in a social sense as well as in a business sense. These are not Kolkata's traditional business communities and their involvement in what is otherwise an important industry in Kolkata is not considered important enough for major support by banks in the city. In addition, it is also true that the larger units and their owners, who invariably belonged to traditional leather manufacturing communities or to those who were involved in the raw hide business, wanted to maintain as much family control as possible and even in cases where bank credit was taken, they preferred to switch over to family funds as soon as possible. These facts present an interesting aspect of production in this sector; most notably, the fact that informal units in tanning as well as product making, where traditional social structures still prevail, find it difficult to get credit should hardly be surprising. This problem can be addressed only if credit that is tailored to the needs of specific enterprises is made available in sufficient quantities by public and/or cooperative institutions in specific clusters and it is made sure that people in charge of disbursing credit are free of social biases. This would need to be done with sufficient propaganda and through targeted programmes.

Another major problem that affects the sector as a whole is the poor availability of skilled workforce. As the description of the production processes in the various kinds of enterprises showed, a large part of the sector that is in the informal segment taps the informal market for labour and invests very little in them. However, many of the workers are from traditional leatherworking communities and possess innate artisanal skills, which has undoubtedly contributed to the growth of the sector in its own way. This does not, however, obliterate the shortage of skilled manpower as far as production operations in more modern enterprises are concerned. At the same time, enterprises are not willing to pay wages commensurate with skill and many tedious, actually skilled jobs such as embroidering of shoe uppers, actual stitching of bags, several tanning operations, are not even recognised as skilled jobs. It has to be made mandatory for enterprises of a certain size to invest in training of workers and skill upgradation and its use in production has to be rewarded in terms of enhanced wages/salaries. It is necessary to have a pool of skilled, trained manpower not only in areas such as leather technology (where colleges of leather technology produce large numbers of technologists each year), but also in more specific operations. The state and public institutions in the industry would have to take the responsibility and invest in training. This has to be a part of the decentralised development programmes where several facilities are provided in the clusters, as mentioned earlier.

Yet another major constraint that affects the sector as whole, particularly small, informal enterprises, is that of marketing. Marketing, however, affects different types of enterprises, at different levels. At the sectoral level, since demand for the sector's products is segmented and volatile, even large firms have to have several customers at an individual level at the same time in order to spread out risks. The diseconomies of such marketing have been overcome to a limited extent for some exporting units through the participation of individual units in international fairs. Even for such larger units, which are, in any case, not large enough in terms of their hold or participation in the international market, problems and costs of marketing could be brought down through consortium marketing. This would enable realization of better unit values in the international market and help a large number of small exporters who are forced, as individuals, to quote extremely low prices and pass the burden of price-adjustment down to labour.

As far as informal enterprises are concerned, cooperative marketing operations are a must and can be organised at cluster level as part of training on cluster development programmes. This has to be a part of decentralised development programmes where several facilities are provided in the clusters, as mentioned earlier.

In sum, a major restructuring of the sector is called for, firstly to redress the rural-urban imbalance, and secondly, to genuinely foster cooperation and collective action among firms in clusters, through the setting up of effective institutions to provide facilities that can help overcome diseconomies of small scale production. For this, the existing clusters will have to be revamped significantly and the role of public institutions in these clusters will have to be both supportive as well as regulatory.

Coming now to the constraints faced by labour, particularly informal labour, we have divided them into three broad categories : *low wages and few or no benefits; limited mobility of the workforce as a whole; and poor working conditions and occupational and health hazards.*

It is clear from our field work that average wages in the sector as a whole are extremely low across the industry. Minimum wage norms are not followed by enterprises both in Madras and Kolkata. Two points are noteworthy in this context: one, depending upon the types of informal enterprises that are formally registered with the formal sector, male workers in the leather industry earn roughly the same average wages per month, working out to be Rs. 1200-1500 or so. *The informal sector's employment norms seem, therefore, to set the standard for the whole industry.* Two, there is a gender aspect to employment in Madras where a large segment of the industry is concentrated, where large numbers of women are employed at extremely low wages, averaging Rs. 800 or so per month and where this phenomenon again is available in all forms of production organisations, ranging from high informal home-based and workshop production to factory production in the formal sector. As far as benefits go, many of the more formal units in Madras do provide provident fund and ESI facilities, but these are completely absent in Kolkata.

As regards the mobility of the workforce, we have seen how in the traditional tanning segment, the labour market is highly controlled through caste factors; it was difficult to imagine a marked improvement in their earnings as a general rule. In terms of upward mobility, with a large degree of casual and piece rated employment, the chances are obviously limited. For the women employed in the various units in Madras, the upward mobility is not an issue because mostly, only women in the age group of 18-30 are employed, and they leave after a few years when they get married. Thus, there is a very high rate of turnover. For the informal segment of the workforce, therefore, mobility is extremely restricted.

Finally, the poor working conditions and occupational and health hazards are most prominent in the tanning segments and in the home-based units stitching designs on to shoe uppers. In the latter, women workers suffer eye strain as well as worn-out hands and fingers. In the tanning segments, there are a large number of operations that are hazardous to health. In a study of women workers in the tannery sector in Tamil Nadu, Nihila (1999) found that prolonged contact with chemicals used in the leather industry could cause a variety of illnesses such as dermatitis, conjunctivitis, chest pain, ulcers, and so on. Among women workers, these have been known to cause menstrual disorders and problems related to pregnancy most notably still births. In addition, activities such as cleaning time pits, drying tanned hides in dark and hot chambers during the rainy season, and dyeing, also cause severe health and occupational hazards.

Coming now to our recommendations regarding labour welfare, at the macro level it must be recognized that the sweatshop conditions under which the entire industry seems to operate will have to be changed drastically to encompass all aspects of labour welfare. Enforcing minimum wage norms through strict supervision by labour welfare officials in the clusters is a must and be taken extremely seriously. All enterprises should be required to mandatorily submit records of different kinds of employment, the remuneration provided to the workers and the benefits provided. To ensure its effectiveness, this has to be part of an overall modernization progamme for the industry, monitored through cluster level institutions and coordinated at state and central levels. This programme should encompass tannery modernization, and upgradation of facilities in the product-making segments, along with occupational safety and environmental standards being maintained. In the informal segment, this modernization programme will have to be funded by government institutions through micro-credit or other such schemes; maintaining labour standards must also be made mandatory for upgradation of enterprises.

A complete restructuring of the leather and leather products sector as a whole is therefore warranted to effectively deal with the increasing informalisation of production structures that is taking place. Improving productivity and improving competitiveness cannot come merely through overcoming production constraints at the enterprise level, or modernizing selected segments in the industry, which is already taking place. Provision of 'decent work' is an absolutely essential condition not only for the welfare of the millions of people employed in the sector, but also from the point of view of production performance, in fact the survival itself, of the sector as a whole.

Bibliography

Administrative Staff College of India (1996). Proceedings of National Seminar on National and Industry Competitiveness in Leather and Leather Products, June, Hyderabad.

Bagchi, A.K. (1995). New Technology and the Workers' Response, Sage Publications, New Delhi.

Banerjee, N. and M. Nihila (1995). Business Organizations in the Leather Industries of Kolkata and Madras, Occasional Paper No. 148, Centre for Studies in Social Sciences, April, Kolkata.

Breman, Jan (1976) . " A Dualistic Labour System ? A Critique of the Informal Sector Concept, Part I", Economic and Political Weekly, December 4, pp 1870-76.

Cadene, P. and M. Holstrom(1998). Decentralised Production in India- Industrial Districts, Flexible Specialisation and Employment, French Institute of Pondicherry and Sage Publications, New Delhi.

Central Leather Research Institute(1987). Report of the All India Survey on Raw Hides and Skins, November, Madras.

____(1989). Report on Capacity Utilisation and Scope for Modernisation in Indian Tanneries, June, Madras.

____(1994). Indian Leather 2010 Technology, Industry and Trade Forecast, Madras.

____(1996). Women's Employment in Industry : The Case of Indian Footwear.

____(1997). Report of Nationwide Survey on Leather Product Units in India.

Central Statistical Organisation(1998). Annual Survey of Industries, Summary Results for the Factory Sector.

Central Statistical Organisation (1998). National Accounts Statistics.

International Labour Office(1972). Employment, Incomes and Inequality- A Strategy for Increasing Productive Employment in Kenya, Geneva.

Govt. of India (1998). 51st Round (July 1994-June 1995)- Unorganised Manufacturing Sector in India- Its Size, Employment and Key Estimates, NSSO.

____: (1990 and 1995). Report of the Working Group on Leather and Leather Products for the VIII and IX Five Year Plans.

Hart, K. (1971). "Informal Income Opportunities and Urban Employment in Ghana", Paper Presented at IDS Conference on Urban Unemployment in Africa, University of Sussex.

Knorringa, P. (1996). Economics of Collaboration-Shoe Makers between Market and Hierarchy, Sage publications, New Delhi.

Mead, D. and C. Morrison(1996).“The Informal Sector Elephant” World Development, Vol 24, No. 10, pp 1611-19.

Nihila, M. (1999). “Marginalisation of Women Workers : Leather Tanning Industry in Tamil Nadu ,” Economic and Political Weekly, Review of Women’s Studies, April 17-24.

Nadvi, K. and H. Schmitz(1998). “Industrial Clusters in Less Developed Countries” in Cadene, P. and M. Holstrom(eds.): Decentralised Production in India-Industrial Districts, Flexible Specialisation and Employment, French Institute of Pondicherry and Sage Publications, New Delhi.

Parthasarathy, G. (1996). “Unorganised Sector and Structural Adjustment”, Economic and Political Weekly, July.

Peattie, L. (1987). “An idea in Good Currency and How it Grew : The Informal Sector” World Development, Vol 15, No.7, pp 850-860.w

Pyke, F. and W. Sengenberger(eds.) (1992). Industrial Districts and Local Economic Regeneration, International Institute of Labour Studies, Geneva.

Rakowski, C.A. (1994). “Convergence and Divergence in the Informal Sector Debate : A focus on Latin America, 1984-92”, World Development.

Sahasranaman, A. (1998). A Survey of the Indian Leather Sector, (mimeo.).

Swiss Agency for Development and Cooperation (SDC) (1999). Leather and Leather Products - A Sub-Sector Profile.

Usha, P. (1984). Leather Industry of Tamil Nadu, A Study of Structural Change During 1960-80, Ph. D. Thesis (unpublished), Madras Institute of Development Studies, Madras.

Informal Sector in India: Case of Micro-Enterprises in I.T. Services Sector

Nagesh Kumar

1. Introduction

Recent trends and patterns of industrialization and development in developing countries like India in the era of liberalization have shown that employment generation in the organized sector has not kept pace with the rate of growth of industry (see for instance, Panchamukhi and Das, 1999). This has led to mounting levels of unemployment despite growth of aggregate incomes. Policy makers have now turned their attention to the informal sector to exploit its potential for generating new jobs. While in general the jobs created in informal sector activities might be characterized by low skills, low pay, and poor working conditions, some of the information technologies (IT) based services may provide opportunities for creation of better jobs, especially for the educated workforce and may provide opportunities for expanding the base for entrepreneurship because of their relatively low capital intensive and highly skill intensive nature.

Against that background, the present paper reviews the emerging patterns of informal sector activities in IT related services sector in India and examines the potential for creating 'decent' urban informal sector jobs in it.

The IT industry, especially the software services segment of it, attracts attention for several reasons. Apart from the phenomenal rate at which it has grown over the past several years, the sector's evolution is intimately connected with the informal sector. Some of the most successful software entrepreneurs of today have had their origin in the informal sector. The economies of scale are not so central to the industry; hence smaller enterprises may not face additional handicaps. It is essentially a service sector activity having applications into a whole range of value adding activities; hence valuable economies of scope exists. In addition to its versatility, the technology makes sub-contracting of different activities possible. It is highly dependent on tacit skills and is less capital requiring than most other industries. Hence, the sector provides enormous opportunities for generation of a pool of entrepreneurship and employment. Furthermore, globalization has important implications for the industry's growth in developing countries and a large part of its expansion in India has resulted from the trend of internationalization of value-adding activities in the industry by multinational enterprises, for instance, customization of software, back-office operations and software development. Accordingly, the growth rates achieved by the industry over the past decade are sustainable in the foreseeable future. The low level of usage of information technology in India, compared to more developed countries and, given the present thrust placed on increasing it, suggests that even the domestic market for the software and related services will continue to grow faster than the overall economy. Finally, the industry has some gender implications as well. Most jobs generated in the industry are desk jobs and physically less demanding than many other industrial jobs. Hence, they are also suitable for women. Besides, teleworking provides the flexibility of working from remote locations such as homes and hence could be found as a valuable source of creating work for women having other responsibilities such as those of doing household chores and bringing up small children.

The structure of the paper is as follows. Section 2 provides an overview of the industry at the macro-level. It will review the performance and evolution of the industry in the country in terms of growth rates, employment and exports, and discusses the emerging patterns and role of government policy and the future outlook for the industry. Section 3 presents the findings of a field survey undertaken in Delhi, Noida and Hyderabad to gather insights into the functioning of the informal sector activities and its potential for creation of jobs. Finally, Section 4 concludes the study with a number of policy recommendations with a view to facilitate creation of decent jobs in the sector.

2. India's Software Industry: An Introduction

One of the most remarkable developments of the past decade or so has been the rise of the software industry in India that has grown at an astonishing rate of 56 per cent over the past five years. Unlike any other industry in the country, the growth of software industry has been fuelled by external demand. Nearly 68 per cent of the industry's output was exported in 1998/99. The export turnover has recorded a compound annual growth rate of 61 per cent over the past five years ending March 1999 compared to 46 per cent for the domestic turnover (Table 1). As a result of this exponential growth, the ratio of software exports to India's merchandise exports has risen from a negligible level in 1990, to 1.8 per cent in 1994/95 and to as high as 8 per cent in 1999/2000. India's share in the US, the world's largest software market, has steadily gone up from 0.75 per cent in 1989/90 to 1.70 per cent 1994/95 (Heeks, 1996). Thus, Indian software exports, though still accounting for a marginal share of the US market, have been growing faster than the latter. Similarly, although the industry accounts for barely under one per cent of India's GDP, it contributes nearly seven per cent of its GDP growth.

TABLE 1 : **Growth of Indian Software Industry Revenues**

(US $ Million)

Year	Total	Domestic	Exports
1989/90	n.a.	n.a.	105.4
1994/95	835	350	4.85
1995/96	1224	490	734
1996/97	1755	670	1085
1997/98	2700	950	1750
1998/99	3900	1250	2650
1999/2000*	5700	1700	3900
Targets			
2000/01	8750	2450	6300
2008**	85000	35000	50000
Compound Annual Growth Rate			
1994/99	56.3%	46.05%	60.71%

**Estimated targets set by the National Taskforce on IT and Software Development, 1998.
Source: Author's compilation based on Hanna (1994) and NASSCOM (2000a and 2000b).

The impressive performance put up by the industry, especially in the exports markets, sustained over the longer term has raised a lot of optimism among policy makers, as reflected in rather ambitious targets of US $ 50 billion worth of software exports, and $ 35 billion of domestic revenues by the year 2008, set forth by the National Taskforce on Information Technology and Software Development (NTITSD), set up by the Prime Minister in 1998. However, some doubts have begun to be raised whether these targets could be considered realistic, given the slow-down trend of the US economy commencing towards the last quarter of 2000.

2.1 Globalization and the Indian Software Industry

The evolution of the Indian software industry is intimately linked to the trend of globalization of the value adding activities in large multinational enterprises (MNEs). It was Texas Instruments (TI), a US based corporation, which had set up a software development centre in Bangalore as far back as 1986, in order to tap the highly qualified workforce available in the vicinity (at the Indian Institute of Science, Bangalore, among many other institutions of excellence; see Kumar, 1999 for other illustrative cases). Although Tata Consultancy Services had also been exporting software since 1974, the entry of TI vividly testified to India's potential to outside MNEs. Subsequently, a number of other western corporations began to follow the footsteps of TI, for example, Citicorp Overseas Software Ltd. Seeing the potential, a number of Indian companies engaged in computer hardware started to spin-off their software divisions (Heeks, 1996). Nonetheless, despite the entry of most leading MNEs in India for software development, the industry is still dominated and driven by domestic companies and talent. The top 6 software companies in India, ranked either on the basis of overall sales or the overall turnover, are all domestically owned. Among the top 20 software companies too, no more than 5 to 6 are MNE affiliates or joint ventures.

The Indian software exporting companies themselves are sufficiently global in their outlook. As many as 212 Indian software companies have either subsidiaries or branch offices overseas (mostly in the US). Nearly 2000 of Indian software companies have obtained the International Standards Organization 9000 (ISO 9000) certification. As many as 32 Indian companies have received SEI-CMM (Software Engineering Institute, USA's Capability Maturity Model) Certification. Six of them have reached Level 5, a distinction which has been awarded only to 12 companies worldwide. Indian companies cater to the needs of large MNEs (203 of the Fortune 1000) in the developed countries which outsource their software requirements from India. Some of them e.g., Infosys and Satyam, have got listed on the Nasdaq stock exchange in the US and more are planning such moves. Hence, Indian software industry is very intimately linked to the emerging trend of globalization and outsourcing that is taking place worldwide. North America (mainly the US) continues to be the largest maket for Indian software, currently accounting for 61 per cent share, followed by Europe with a 23 per cent share. Japan (4 per cent), Southeast Asia (4 per cent), Australia - New Zealand (2 per cent) and West Asia (1.5 per cent) are the other markets (Kumar, 2000a).

2.2 Growing Competence

In the early years, the bulk of the software export activity of Indian enterprises consisted of lending their software professionals to their clients to deliver their services 'on-site'. The bulk of these services covered customization of software rather than export of software products or undertaking software projects. It was considered to be at a rather lower level of skill-intensity, compared to software product designing and development. The advantage of Indian enterprises in the on-site work emanated largely from the lower salaries of Indian software professionals compared to those prevailing in the developed economies. This has derogatively been termed as 'body-shopping' (Heeks, 1996). However, some Indian companies have progressively demonstrated their technological and project management skills by successfully completing turnkey projects for large companies (see, for example, Basrur and Chawla, 1999, for a case study of Tata Consultancy Services). As a result, the proportion of on-site exports has begun to come down in India's software exports from nearly 90 per cent in 1988 to 66 per cent in the mid-990s and 58 per cent in 1998/99 (NASSCOM 1999; Heeks, 1996). An increasing proportion of India's software is developed 'offshore' at the home bases of exporters in India and exported. The 'offshore' development, as it is called in the industry, currently accounts for 45 per cent of exports. This much rise in its proportion has been partly facilitated by the improved communication links in the Software Technology Parks (STPs) set up by the government that allow the teams of professionals, at vendor and clients' ends, to be in constant touch on real time basis, and by the growing visa restrictions in the US and Europe. It also turns out to be cheaper for the clients. Besides, the 10-11 hour time lag between India and the US virtually doubles the working time per day and hence cuts the development life cycle by half (Kumar, 2000b).

2.3 Employment and Job Potential

According to Nasscom Surveys, the software industry employed some 3,40,000 professionals on March 31, 2000, including software professionals working in software user organizations compared to 1,60,000 professionals in 1996. The software industry has thus created only about 1,80,000 jobs in three years. Nasscom expects 1,40,000 more jobs to come up in the next two years viz. 60,000 in 2000 and about 80,000 in 2001. Therefore, the industry generates about 60,000-70,000 more jobs every year and may have created so far no more than half a million jobs including ancillary jobs such as those of data entry operators despite so much rhetoric about its expansion and job potential. The compound annual growth of employment of 28.5 per cent recorded over the past three years, though impressive from the standards of growth of jobs in the national economy, is only half of the growth of the revenues in the industry. However, the potential of the industry to sustain its growth momentum does suggest its potential to emerge as a source of significant employment in Indian industry in times to come. The NTITSD projects that the software industry will employ 2.2 million workers by 2008. Half of these jobs, i.e. 1.1 million jobs, will be created by expansion of IT enabled services in the country by the year 2008 AD, compared to 23,000 only in 1998/99. Of these, nearly 5,60,000 jobs are expected to be in back office operations and in content development (compared to 15,200 jobs at present).

The other characteristics of the jobs created by the software industry can be seen from Table 2. The industry is creating job opportunities for highly qualified (majority with an engineering degree) young graduates with relatively short experience. The salary levels here are among the best across industries within the country and have been growing at a hefty rate of 16-21 per cent. In addition, the companies have begun to offer stock options to their employees. Given the high premia enjoyed by the software stocks, this is quite an incentive.

As many as 41 companies have reportedly offered stock options to their employees in 1998/99. Despite this, the attrition rate is quite high. The industry loses

TABLE 2 : **Key Characteristics of Employment in Software Industry**

Parameters	1996	1999	2000
Software Professionals (including those in non-commercial organization and user organizations)	1,60,000	2,80,000	3,40,000
Of which those engaged in :			
- Software Development (%)	70	67	63
- Marketing and Relationship Development (%)	10	11	14
Median Age (years)	28.4	26.2	25.7
Proportion of IT Degree Holders (%)	75	n.a.	n.a.
Proportion of those having 5 years Experience (%)	60	50	60
Rise in Basic Salary over Previous Year (%)	21	21 + ESO*	16 + ESO*
Attrition Rate (%)	17.2	16	14

* Supplemented by Employee Stock Options; 41 companies have offered ESOs to their employees.
Source: author's compilation based on the respective Nasscom Surveys.

quite a substantial proportion of its brightest professionals every year as they migrate to better paid jobs in other countries. This rate, though, has come down slightly over time.

Besides the organized segment of the software industry, employment opportunities are fast expanding in the smaller or the so-called informal or micro-enterprise segment in the software and services, e.g., software customization, data entry, and internet bureau to be growing in terms of numbers and size, at very fast pace. As a result, employment in these enterprises is expected to grow between 50-100 per cent per year. Although the salaries in these enterprises are relatively low to begin with but the sector provides opportunities for fast upwards mobility of personnel. While the larger and more organized enterprises are driven largely by the external demand, the informal establishments cater to rising demand of domestic industry, especially the small and medium enterprises (SMEs), for their office automation and customization needs. The sector also provides opportunities for self-employment for trained personnel who work as data entry operators at the lower end of the skill spectrum, to web page designers, and to software consultants at the upper end.

2.4 Gender Aspects of Employment

The jobs created in the software industry are generally physically less demanding than those in other manufacturing activities; these are white collared jobs. Hence, they are also well suited to women. NASSCOM surveys reveal that although the share of women among software professionals is low, it has gone up from 19 per cent to 27 per cent between 1996 and 1999. By 2001, it is expected to rise to 30 per cent. Earlier studies on the industry had reported an even higher domination of the industry by men with a share of women ranging between 5-10 per cent (Mitter and Pearson, 1992; Heeks, 1996). Compared to those estimates, the current proportion of 27 per cent represents a considerable advance. However, even the early surveys such as those conducted by Jayanthi and Madhavan in the mid-1980s (cited in Heeks, 1996) and another by Mitter in 1990 (cited by Mitter and Pearson, 1992) do not report any overt discrimination against women. Both these studies have reported that the industry offered a more relaxed and less discriminatory atmosphere than most other occupations and that women stand a better chance of reaching a position of seniority in this industry than in most others. The reasons for women's observed under-achievements, cited by those surveys, include a lack of international mobility because of family commitments, regulations against night work preventing companies from hiring them for round-the-clock contracts, and some international clients' reluctance to hire women consultants, especially in the Middle East. The declining dependence of the industry on on-site contracts may help remove some biases against women.

Furthermore, the IT enabled services that India is planning to enter into, in a significant manner, may offer more job avenues for women. The call centres and back-office services, especially data entry operations for instance, are predominantly staffed by women the world over. Quite a large part of these services can be delivered from home. For instance, a home -based worker answers a call from her home or enters data that are transmitted electronically to the client. These types of 'tele-working' opportunities, as they have begun to be called, are particularly well suited for self-employed women workers who wish to stay at home for family reasons (Hoon, Ng and Mitter, 1999).

2.5 Government Policy

In a large measure, the success of the Indian software industry has been attributed to the role played by the government in providing an enabling framework and infrastructure. Although the programme for promotion of software development, particularly for exports, was initiated way back in the early 1970s, it was only since the mid-1980s that a serious and sustained promotional effort began to be made (Heeks, 1996). The year 1984 saw the new Computer Policy that facilitated imports of thousands of personal computers into India by reducing tariff rate from 135 per cent to 60 per cent; this led to creation of a large number of software and computer maintenance companies. In 1986 a computer software policy was formulated, a Software Development Agency was set up, and entry into the computer software industry was de-licensed. In 1988, the Electronics and Computer Software Export Promotion Council was set up to provide marketing help to software companies in their exports. The government also initiated programmes to assist exporters with provision of export credit and insurance. The very same year, the industry re-organized itself and set up the NASSCOM (National Association for Software and Service Companies) as their apex body to lobby for their common cause with the government. From 1988 onwards, the government focused on providing telecommunication infrastructure, and its Software Technology Parks scheme began to evolve. Gradually, the Software Technology Parks of India Limited (STPI) has evolved into an autonomous organization, under the Department of Electronics, to provide an environment conducive to entrepreneurs operating under the STP scheme. STPs are located at Noida, Navi Mumbai, Pune, Gandhinagar, Hyderabad, Bangalore, Chennai, Bhubaneshwar, Jaipur, Mohali and Thiruvanathapuram. This scheme offers zero import duty on import of all capital goods, a special 10 year income tax holiday, provides infrastructural facilities like high speed data-communication links etc. Having recognized the potential of software industry for the country and to take steps to exploit the same, in May 1998, the government set up a National Taskforce on Information Technology and Software Development, under the chairmanship of the Deputy Chairman of the Planning Commission. The Taskforce submitted the Information Technology Action Plan comprising 108 recommendations in July 1998. All of these recommendations have since been accepted by the government through a Gazette Notification issued in July 1998 itself. The Action Plan includes opening of internet gateway access, encourage private STPs, zero duty on IT software, income tax exemption to software and services exports, encouragement to set up venture capital funds, a fund to handle the Y2K problem, 1-3 per cent of the budget of government departments earmarked for IT applications, networking of all universities and research institutions, allowing dollar linked stock options to employees of Indian software companies and new schemes to encourage access of students to computers, and so on.. As a follow-up of the Action Plan, a new Internet Policy has come into being and a large number of internet service providers have been licensed. Operation Knowledge has been launched for universalizing IT education and IT-based education, in a phased manner. A separate Ministry of Information Technology has been set up to coordinate the promotional role of the government in the industry.

The potential of the industry has also attracted the attention of state governments. A total of 14 states have announced IT policies in the recent months and seven more have set up IT taskforces or committees. NASSCOM, the industry body, seems quite satisfied with the role played by the government and explains the success of software industry in terms of an 'excellent teamwork by industry and government' (NASSCOM, 1999a).

2.6 Future Outlook

The apex body of the Indian software industry, NASSCOM, believes that it will be possible to sustain the frantic pace at which the domestic and export segments of the industry have been growing in the medium term, despite the quick drying up of the Y2K opportunities. This is so because, in the short-term, they are tapping the opportunities created by EURO solutions (involving adjustments in the computer systems required for transition of European businesses to a single currency). In the near and medium terms, the Indian companies hope to tap the expanding opportunities arising from internet or e-commerce, multi-media content development and services and in IT-enabled services. India is expected to emerge as a global hub for content development and e-commerce. Internet and e-commerce related software exports from India are expected to cross $ 340 million out of $ 3.9 billion of projected exports during 1999/2000 and are estimated to grow to $ 1 billion by the year 2002 AD.

NASSCOM sees a lot of potential for India in the large and expanding market of what is termed as IT-enabled services. These include several business activities of large corporations that can be relocated overseas, facilitated by the development of satellite communication links. These cover broadly the call centres, medical transcriptions, back-office operations such as accounting, processing of insurance claims, legal data-bases, content development/animation, payrolls and logistics management, and so on. Call centre services is already a large industry with global revenues of $ 200 billion and is growing at an annual rate of 23 per cent. Most companies in service industries such as finance and banking and transport among others, use call centres to provide an interface to clients on a 24-hour basis.

The back-office management and other IT-enabled services also add up to global revenues of $ 75 billion and are recording a 20 per cent growth rate per annum. India's large pool of English speaking computer-literate graduates could help her to tap a share of these service industries. The government has already begun to take note of the potential of these services and has taken steps to provide necessary communications infrastructure. Already a number of large MNEs, such as GE Capital, British Airways, Bechtel and Healthscribe, among others, have started setting up their call centres or back-office operations in India (NASSCOM, 1999b). There are, however, some who are not so optimistic about the prospects of mass scale relocation of call centres as companies may like to keep control of the client interface (Richardson, 1999). The other factors that may limit relocation are cultural, linguistic and those related to infrastructure. Hence, Richardson (1999) expects that outsourcing of call centre agents may be limited to about 10 per cent in the European context. Furthermore, given a rather low skill content in these jobs, they will be of foot-loose nature and may move to other destinations, as and when a competing cheaper location is available, as it did happen in the case of other low skill export-oriented manufacturing. Hence, the move from export-oriented manufacture to export-oriented services may not alter the basic pattern of the international division of labour for developing countries (Mitter and Efendioglu, 1999). Finally, these activities, having a rather low skill content, may provide limited scope for knowledge spillovers in the host country.

Despite the constraints outlined above, it is conceivable that the industry could sustain the rates of growth it has got used to in the past decade well into the coming decade, firstly because India has a long way to go to improve its share of global software and services market from its present very low level, and secondly, because it has established itself firmly as a possible location for software sourcing. The NTITSD has projected software and related revenues of $ 85 billion for 2008 AD of which $ 50 billion for exports and $ 35 billion for domestic market. The NTITSD has also projected creation of 11,00,000 jobs in the country by the year 2008 AD compared to 23,000 in 1998/99 from the expansion of IT enabled services.

3. Informal Sector Activities

The software and services industry in India, as overviewed above, presents a picture of a globalized, affluent, fast expanding, highly concentrated and organized segment of Indian industry. Although there are an estimated 1200 firms in the industry, 545 members of NASSCOM account for 95 per cent of all revenues. Of these, just top 20 firms account for 56 per cent of all exports. There is also a high degree of spatial agglomeration with 90 per cent of the activity being concentrated in metropolitan and urbanized centers; Mumbai, Bangalore and Delhi (along with sub-urban centres like Noida and Gurgaon) alone account for 60 per cent. Hydrabad, Chennai, Kolkata and Pune are other significant concentration centres.

From the above characterization, it may look difficult to conceive of a high potential for the informal sector activities in the industry. However, as will be seen below, rapid expansion of IT applications across a wide spectrum of industries and services in the economy has generated opportunities that have facilitated the growth of the informal segment in the industry. Given the largely skill intensive as against capital intensive nature of the industry, it may be argued that the scale of operations does not really matter for an enterprise's efficiency. Hence, the entry of new entrepreneurs to the sector should be fairly easy. Furthermore, some of today's most successful entrepreneurs of the industry have had their very modest beginning but they have been able to make it big in relatively short periods. This suggests that transition from small to large should be not too difficult either.

The informal segment in the sector has been defined to include largely unorganized and smaller enterprises or self-employed persons, who are not covered by government regulations concerning employment and work. These enterprises engage themselves in providing data entry, graphic designing and desk-top publishing services; they help their clients in customization of packaged software to their specific requirements, and provide network maintenance services to different enterprises.

In customization, the services of unorganized firms and the self-employed personnel are generally availed of especially by the small and medium enterprises (SMEs). Other increasingly popular activities are the e-mail and internet services to lay-public who do not have access to such facilities on their own. As a result of government's promotional policy to increase informalization of the economy and access to internet despite low telecom and computer density, cyber cafes are coming up in urban areas.

To understand and examine the nature of these activities, assess their potential in creation of employment opportunities for the large unemployed workforce and recommend policies for obviating any constraints on exploiting their potential, an exploratory field survey covering a sample of 141 agents in Delhi, Noida and Hyderabad was undertaken*.

Broadly speaking, the sample establishments were engaged in three types of activities:

1. Internet/email bureaus: Typically these bureaus are outgrowths of phone/fax bureaus that started to spring up in different parts of the cities. These bureaus provide various facilities such as e-mail/fax sending and receiving and internet access, often in addition to photocopying and similar services. Generally, the activities entail rather low level of skills than the other two types of activities.

2. Data entry and processing services: A number of firms and self-employed persons provide data and text entry services and desk top publishing services. In terms of skill intensity, they rank somewhere in between the other two. There might be patterns and layers of sub-contracting in the sense that larger firms are subcontracted the data entry work who might further subcontract to the self-employed or even smaller firms.

3. Software customization/content development and associated services: The third group of services covered in this survey includes a number of activities such as those of providing assistance in customizing packaged software to specific working environments, network maintenance, web page designing services, content development and specialized training services.

Three types of agents were interviewed: the employee, the self-employed and the employer. Sixty nine of the 141 agents (i.e. 49 per cent) interviewed were employers, 40 (28 per cent) were employees and 32 (23 per cent) were self-employed. The self-employed workers are generally home-based or part-time workers. Detailed structured questionnaires were supplemented by unstructured opinionaires. The questionnaire tried to elicit information on the education of the

* The field survey reported here was coordinated by Atul Mishra of Delhi University. For details see Mishra (1999).

agent (employee, employer or the self-employed), his training, income, work hours, past income, expected increase in income as well as employment and constraints on its growth; on the supply side, capital and skill availability and on the demand side on the size of the market. The preliminary work based on the study of *Yellow Pages* revealed that the firms in these activities cluster around commercial centres. These include Nehru Place, Bhikaji Kama Place and Okhla in Delhi and NOIDA in Uttar Pradesh. As with most surveys of this kind, there are gaps due to reluctance of interviewees to part with information (generally on income), their lack of knowledge for some aspects, and a host of other factors. Some of the information is necessarily of a qualitative nature.

The activity and location-wise break-up of the sample units is given in Table 3. It is evident that 36 per cent of the cases belong to the internet/ telecommunication segment of the activity; 16 per cent to data entry and 48 per cent to customization services. The Delhi sample has a greater concentration in customization services while Hyderabad's, in internet/telecom.

After controlling for the composition of activity, no significant differences across geographical locations were apparent. Hence, sample cases across locations were pooled together for the rest of the analysis. The data gathered from the questionnaires have been analyzed with the help of cross-tabulations to generate some patterns and expected causations. The patterns that emerge from these tabulations are summarized below:

TABLE 3 : **Activity and Location-wise Distribution of Sample Cases**

Type	Delhi	Noida	Hyderabad	Total
Internet/Telecom	29 (57)	10 (20)	12 (24)	51 (36.2)
Data Entry	15 (68)	3 (14)	4 (18)	22 (15.6)
Custimisation services	50 (74)	12 (18)	6 (9)	68 (48.2)
Total	94 (66.7)	25 (17.7)	22 (15.6)	141 (100)

Note: Figures in parentheses are percentages.

3.1 Nature of Activity, Employment, Set-up Costs and Earnings

The survey focussed on micro enterprises and self-employed professionals. As a result, their size in terms of employment as well as initial capital investments (set-up costs) is relatively small. However, the earnings derived from these activities are not so low.

The majority of sample establishments, nearly 70 per cent, employ no more than six workers. The modal class for internet and data entry operations is upto 3 employees, and for customization services between 4 to 6 employees (Table 4). However, 20 per cent of data entry establishments are larger scale enterprises, each with 16 or more employees.

TABLE 4 : **Industry Type by Number of Employees**

Number of Employees / Type	upto 3	4 to 6	7 to 10	11 to 15	16 and more	Total
Internet / Telecom	18 (44)	12 (29)	9 (22)	0 (0)	2 (5)	41 (100)
Data Entry	6 (40)	4 (27)	1 (7)	1 (7)	3 (20)	15 (100)
Custimization	12 (26)	19 (41)	8 (17)	4 (9)	3 (7)	46 (100)
Total	36 (35)	35 (34)	18 (18)	5 (5)	7 (7)	102 (100)

3.1.1 Initial Set-up costs

The modal set-up cost for data entry operations is between Rs 50,000 to 1,00,000, for internet/telecom bureaus, between Rs 2,00,000 to 5,00,000, and for the customization services, Rs 5,00,000 or more (Table 5). Data entry operations thus could be set up with relatively little initial capital investment while the other activities require considerably more investment in equipment and facilities.

TABLE 5 : **Distribution According to Set-up Costs**

Set-up Costs / Type	Upto Rs. 50,000	50,000-100,000	100,000-200,000	200,000-500,000	500,000-and more	Total
Internet / Telecom	6 (14)	3 (7)	6 (14)	16 (38)	11 (26)	42 (100)
Data Entry	5 (28)	6 (33)	0 (0)	4 (22)	3 (17)	18 (100)
Custimization	7 (12)	10 (17)	7 (12)	13 (22)	22 (37)	59 (100)
Total	18 (15)	19 (16)	13 (11)	33 (28)	36 (30)	119 (100)

3.1.2 Worker Salaries and Working Conditions

In the internet/telecom segment, the modal employee income was towards the lower end, viz. up to Rs. 2,000 although 25 per cent of employees figure in the

Rs. 6,000-7,000 range as well. For employees working in the data entry segment, the modal remuneration is in the range of Rs. 5,000- 7,000 and that accounts for nearly 50 per cent of the cases. The levels of remuneration are distributed more evenly in the case of customization services with a greater concentration in the higher salary range, namely Rs. 6,000-10,000 which accounts for 38 per cent of employees (Table 6). This pattern roughly corresponds to the perception that customization services entail more skill intensive work and internet/telecom, where the employees perform largely the attendant role, the least skill content.

TABLE 6 : **Current Monthly Remuneration of Employees**

(Rs.)

Monthly Salary / Type	Upto 2000	2000-2500	3000-3500	4000-4500	5000-5500	6000-7000	8000-10000	11000 and more	Total
Internet/Telecom	5 (31)	1 (6)	3 (19)	2 (13)	0 (0)	4 (25)	0 (0)	1 (6)	16 (100)
Data Entry	0 (0)	2 (33)	0 (0)	0 (0)	1 (17)	2 (33)	0 (0)	1 (17)	0 (100)
Customization services	3 (14)	1 (5)	1 (5)	4 (19)	2 (10)	4 (19)	4 (19)	2 (10)	21 (100)
Total	8 (19)	4 (9)	4 (9)	6 (14)	3 (7)	10 (23)	4 (9)	4 (9)	43 (100)

While employees in the majority of interviewed firms are paid a monthly salary, there is a small number of establishments which pay on piece rate basis. The rate varies according to the activity. In tune with the general worldwide pattern (Mitter and Pearson, 1992), employees working in data entry, desk top publishing (DTP) and web designing activity are often paid on piece rates (e.g., per page basis). Employee incomes in the informal sector segment of the software related services are generally lower compared to their organized sector counterparts and are often termed by the employees as exploitative. However, there is a very high turnover of employees and both employers and employees regard the low salary as stipends paid for apprenticeship. A number of employees use these jobs as means to support their further studies and training activities. A number of them were enrolled in a three-year diploma course while working in these data entry or customization outlets and take these jobs as intermediate steps towards a better future. Some of them also decide to be self-employed or become entrepreneurs after gaining requisite experience and training on the job, with almost exponential increase in income.

3.1.3 Employers' Income

The modal income for the employers was in the range Rs. 5,00,000-10,00,000 per annum in all categories of activities. However, in customization services, more people were placed in the higher earning brackets, i.e. Rs.5,00,000-1 million and more than either in data entry or telecom (Table 7). The modal range for the latter two activities is upto Rs. 1,00,000. This pattern is also in tune with the relatively greater skill orientation and hence earning potential of the customization services.

TABLE 7 : **Employers' Annual Income**

(Rs.)

Employers Income / Type	Upto 100,000	1-200,000	2-500,000	500,000 1,000,000	Over 1,000,000	Total
Internet / Telecom	5 (31)	2 (13)	2 (13)	4 (25)	3 (19)	16 (100)
Data Entry	2 (33)	1 (17)	1 (17)	1 (17)	1 (17)	6 (100)
Customization Services	2 (12)	3 (18)	1 (6)	6 (35)	5 (29)	17 (100)
Total	9 (23.1)	6 (15.4)	4 (10.3)	11 (28.2)	9 (23.1)	39 (100)

3.1.4 Self-employed Personnel's Income

The modal income here was in the range of upto Rs. 1,00,000 per annum (Table 8). However, there are more people in customization services earning an income in the higher end of upto Rs 5,00,000 per annum, than in telecom or data entry, as in the case of employers.

TABLE 8 : **Self-employed Personnel's Annual Income**

(Rs.)

Income / Type	Upto 100,000	1-500,000	more than 500,000	Total
Internet / Telecom	6 (75)	2 (25)	0 (0)	8 (100)
Data Entry	2 (40)	2 (40)	1 (20)	5 (100)
Customization Services	7 (54)	6 (46)	0 (0)	13 (100)
Total	15 (57.7)	10 (38.5)	1 (3.8)	26 (100)

Considering the low set-up costs and income levels prevailing in the country, the employers' and self-employed personnel's earnings are quite healthy. It suggests that software and related services offer rewarding opportunities for self-employment and for broadening the entrepreneurial base .

3.2 Sources of Initial Investments

The principal source of financing initial investment, among the sample establishments, has been house old savings for all three types of activities. As indicated in Table 9, over 40 per cent of establishments depended on household savings and another 19 per cent on a combination of household savings and bank loans. Loans from friends, family and relatives also formed an important source for initial capital. Only 14 per cent of establishments were set-up with bank loans providing the initial investments.

TABLE 9 : **Source of Financing of Initial Set-up Costs**

Source of Financing / Activity Type	Only Household Savings	Only Bank Loans	Household Savings and Bank Loans	In addition Equity Participation	In addition Loans from Family, Friends and Relatives	Total
Internet/Telecom	21 (48)	5 (11)	8 (18)	4 (9)	6 (14)	44 (100)
Data Entry	7 (39)	2 (11)	2 (11)	0 (0)	7 (39)	18 (100)
Customization Services	21 (36)	10 (17)	13 (22)	5 (8)	10 (17)	59 (100)
Total	49 (40.5)	17 (14)	23 (19)	9 (7.4)	23 (19)	121 (100)

The relative importance of different sources of financing can be expected to vary according to the size of investment. Household savings appeared as the most important source of financing a start-up enterprise for all size classes. They provided the set-up costs for the bulk of relatively smaller operations, viz., those with upto Rs.1,00,000 of initial investments. Loans from friends, family and relatives also formed an important source of capital, especially for the smaller size categories. This suggests that lack of capital availability from institutional sources prompts entrepreneurs to explore household and family sources. Equity participation is a relatively minor source of capital for these enterprises, even for larger among them. Bank loans were an important source of finance for set-up cost only for large investments, suggesting a bias against small loans in the bank lending. A small proportion of very small enterprises also reported receiving bank loans, presumably as a follow up of the recent government directive of granting loans up to Rs 2 lakhs to telecom bureau owners for installing internet/e-mail facilities. For others in the industry, for instance, for a self-employed professional, venturing to undertake customization services, seeking a bank loan, is rather difficult to succeed, since banks are generally unwilling to extend small loans to an activity that they are not familiar with. Furthermore, investigations revealed that banks insist on a collateral instead of hypothecation of the equipment, apparently due to high rates of obsolescence of computer equipment. This indeed shows a lack of flexibility and inability of banks to change with times. It is no wonder then that in this highly skill intensive activity, lack of credit, and not non-availability of skills, is reported by a majority of sample firms, as the major constraint for growth of entrepreneurship.

TABLE 10 : **Source of Financing of Initial Set-up Costs by Size of Set-up Costs**

Source of Financing / Set-Up Costs	Only Household Savings	Only Bank Loans	Household Savings and Bank Loans	In addition Equity Participation	In addition Loans from Family, Friends and Relatives	Total
10,000-50,000	10 (63)	3 (19)	0 (0)	0 (0)	3 (19)	16 (100)
50,000-1,00,000	10 (56)	1 (6)	2 (11)	0 (0)	5 (28)	18 (100)
1,00,000-2,00,000	5 (38)	1 (8)	2 (15)	2 (15)	3 (23)	13 (100)
2,00,000-5,00,000	11 (33)	1 (3)	11 (33)	2 (6)	8 (24)	33 (100)
5,00,000-	10 (28)	9 (25)	8 (22)	5 (14)	4 (11)	36 (100)
Column Total	46 (40)	15 (13)	23 (20)	9 (8)	23 (20)	116 (100)

3.3 Education, Training and Income Levels

Though in general, software and related services are skill intensive activities, there are considerable variations in skill levels across the three activities covered in this study. This is borne out by the educational and training profile of the agents. As many as 95 per cent of the employees, 82 per cent of the employers and 77 per cent of the self-employed personnel, engaged in the sample establishments, had at least a college degree or a higher qualification (Table 11). The majority (65, 59, and 58 per cent respectively) of them had a college or first degree. The customization services segment had a disproportionate share of university (post-graduate) graduates. Thus, it corroborates the expectation that customization services is relatively more sophisticated among the activities.

TABLE 11 : **Education Profile of Agents**

Level of Education	School	College	University	Professional Degree	Total
Employees					
Internet/Telecom	1 (9)	8 (73)	1 (9)	1 (9)	11 (100)
Data Entry	0 (0)	4 (67)	1 (17)	1 (17)	6 (100)
Customization Services	1 (5)	12 (60)	5 (25)	2 (10)	20 (100)
Total	2 (5.4)	24 (64.9)	7 (18.9)	4 (10.8)	37 (100)
Employers					
Internet/Telecom	5 (19)	16 (59)	5 (19)	1 (4)	27 (100)
Data Entry	3 (27)	5 (45)	1 (9)	2 (18)	11 (100)
Customization Services	4 (13)	19 (63)	6 (20)	1 (3)	30 (100)
Total	12 (17.6)	40 (58.8)	12 (17.6)	4 (5.9)	68 (100)
Self Employed Personnel					
Internet/Telecom	3 (27)	7 (64)	0 (0)	1 (9)	11 (100)
Data Entry	1 (20)	4 (80)	0 (0)	0 (0)	5 (100)
Customization Services	3 (20)	7 (47)	5 (33)	0 (0)	15 (100)
Total	7 (22.6)	18 (58.1)	5 (16.1)	1 (3.2)	31 (100)

Table 12 summarizes the training profile of the agents. The modal level of training across all types of agents and all types of activities is up to one year. However, over 50 per cent of the employers and the self-employed in the data entry and customization services have longer than one year training, with quite a few having even longer than two years training. On the other hand, bulk of the employers and self-employed in internet services have had up to one -year long training. That corroborates the relatively lower skill profile of the internet/telecom service bureaus compared to the other two activities. Very few employees have longer than two years of training. That is because the more highly trained personnel get absorbed in larger organized enterprises, given the general scarcity of the manpower in the sector.

TABLE 12 : **Training Profile of Agents Across Activities**

Length of Training	0-1 year	1-2 years	More than 2 years	Total
		Employers		
Internet/Telecom	17 (81)	4 (19)	0 (0)	21 (100)
Data Entry	5 (45)	4 (36)	2 (18)	11 (100)
Customization Services	12 (46)	9 (35)	5 (19)	26 (100)
Total	34 (58.6)	17 (29.3)	7 (10.3)	58 (100)
		Self - Employed Personnel		
Internet/Telecom	8 (73)	2 (18)	1 (9)	11 (100)
Data Entry	2 (40)	2 (40)	1 (20)	5 (100)
Customization Services	6 (50)	5 (42)	1 (8)	12 (100)
Total	16 (57.1)	9 (32.1)	3 (10.7)	28 (100)
		Employees		
Internet/Telecom	7 (64)	2 (18)	2 (18)	11 (100)
Data Entry	2 (33)	4 (67)	0 (0)	6 (100)
Customization Services	11 (61)	7 (39)	0 (0)	18 (100)
Total	20 (57.1)	13 (37.1)	2 (5.7)	35 (100)

Are levels of education and training of employees related to the levels of their earnings? Table 13 shows that higher educational qualification is associated with a higher monthly remuneration of employees. Bulk of the school pass-outs were in the monthly income bracket of Rs 2,000 or less, while the bulk of university graduates and professionally qualified personnel are concentrated in the upper end of the salary range, i.e., Rs. 6,000-10,000.

TABLE 13 : **Education Level by Current Salary of Employees**

Monthly Salary Education	Upto Rs. 2000	2000-2500	3000-3500	4000-4500	5000-5500	6000-7000	8000-10000	11000 and more	Total
School	3 (75)	0 (0)	0 (0)	1 (25)	0 (0)	0 (0)	0 (0)	0 (0)	4 (100)
College	3 (13)	3 (13)	3 (13)	4 (17)	2 (9)	4 (17)	1 (4)	3 (13)	23 (100)
University	1 (11)	1 (11)	0 (0)	1 (11)	0 (0)	4 (44)	1 (11)	1 (11)	9 (100)
Professional Degree	0 (0)	0 (0)	0 (0)	0 (0)	0 (0)	2 (67)	1 (33)	0 (0)	3 (100)
Total	7 (18)	4 (10)	3 (8)	6 (15)	2 (5)	10 (26)	3 (8)	4 (10)	39 (100)

A distribution of employees by the length of training acquired and earnings received is summarized in Table 14. In the lower end of the salary range, apparently it did not matter how many years of training the agent had obtained before taking up the current job. However, at the upper end, there was a clear sign of higher salaries being associated with higher levels of training.

TABLE 14 : **Duration of Training by Current Salary of Employees**

Monthly Salary	Upto Rs. 2000	2000-2500	3000-3500	4000-4500	5000-5500	6000-7000	8000-10000	11000 and more	Total
0-1 Year	4 (19)	2 (10)	3 (14)	4 (19)	1 (5)	6 (29)	1 (5)	0 (0)	21 (100)
1-2 Years	2 (15)	2 (15)	0 (0)	2 (15)	1 (8)	2 (15)	2 (15)	2 (15)	13 (100)
2-3 Years	1 (33)	0 (0)	0 (0)	0 (0)	0 (0)	1 (33)	0 (0)	1 (33)	3 (100)
Total	7 (19)	4 (11)	3 (8)	6 (16)	2 (5)	9 (24)	3 (8)	3 (8)	37 (100)

3.4 Education, Training and Entrepreneurial Success

How far do the levels of education and training contribute to the entrepreneurial success measured in terms of annual income? Table 15 shows that employers' earnings are distributed evenly across the different levels of their education and no dominant pattern is evident. Although, nearly 60 per cent of the employers were college (first) degree holders, the conventional college education is not particularly relevant for development of entrepreneurial abilities for this industry, as is evident from the examples of several successful employers in our sample who are college drop-outs (see Box 1).

However, the level of training does contribute to the entrepreneurial success in a more direct manner, as is evident from Table 16. As many as 56 per cent of the employers with up to one year of training were earning up to Rs 2,00,000 per annum. On the other hand, nearly 80 per cent of those with 2 years or more of training were earning Rs 5,00,000 - Rs 10,00,000 and more per annum. This suggests that the level of training rather than conventional education, is the key to entrepreneurial success in the software and related service industry. Because of the highly skill intensive nature of the industry, entrepreneurs' own training and skills become key assets for commercial success of the enterprise.

How far do educational attainment and levels of training contribute to the success of self-employed people in the industry in terms of earnings?

Table 16 shows that the bulk of self-employed personnel with school and college degrees concentrate in the lower end of the earning bracket, viz. up to Rs 1,00,000 per annum, while a bulk of those with university degree or professional qualification are in the higher earning brackets. Similarly, 82 per cent of the self-employed personnel with up to one year training are in the lowest earning class while a bulk of those with longer training fall in the higher income brackets. The levels of education and training both evidently contribute to the success of the self-employed personnel. The field-work results further suggest that the self-employed personnel are often home-based, usually working on part-time basis, to supplement income from their main occupation. It can, therefore, be inferred that a higher level of education and training enable them to better exploit the opportunities to supplement their income with part-time work from home.

3.5 Working Hours, Social Security, and Occupational Safety Practices

Table 17 summarizes the patterns according to working hours in the surveyed cases. Although the modal class is 8 hours per day, over a quarter of the cases work for 10 hours per day. A more detailed scrutiny, however, suggests that a bulk of the longer working hour cases are in the internet/telecom segment. As

TABLE 15 : **Educational and Training Levels and Employers' Annual Earnings**

Earnings	Upto Rs. 100,000	1-200,000	2-500,000	500,000 1,000,000	Over 1,000,000	Total
Education by Employers' Income						
School Pass	1	2	0	6	3	12
	(8)	(17)	(0)	(50)	(25)	(100)
College	3	4	4	4	5	20
	(15)	(20)	(20)	(20)	(25)	(100)
University	4	0	0	1	1	6
	(67)	(0)	(0)	(17)	(17)	(100)
Professional Degree	1	0	0	0	0	1
	(100)	(0)	(0)	(0)	(0)	(100)
Column Total	9	6	4	11	9	39
	(23.1)	(15.4)	(10.3)	(28.2)	(23.1)	(100)
Training By Employers' Income						
0-1 Year	7	6	1	5	4	23
	(30)	(26)	(4)	(22)	(17)	(100)
1-2 Years	2	0	2	3	1	8
	(25)	(0)	(25)	(38)	(13)	(100)
2-5 Years	0	0	1	2	2	5
	(0)	(0)	(20)	(40)	(40)	(100)
Total	9	6	4	10	7	36
	(25)	(17)	(11)	(28)	(19)	(100)

indicated earlier, the nature of the job in that segment is of attendant type, with a relatively lighter work load. Hence, they have a longer day. Most of the data entry and customization workers have a standard 8 hour work schedule.

Similar to informal sector elsewhere, there is absolutely no evidence of social security programmes covering the employees. Given the relatively young age profile of the employees (who are working for the first time in most cases) and a high rate of turnover, the lack of it is not yet seen as a major concern.

There is hardly any consciousness among the workers about occupational hazards posed by the technology they are working with. The work, being a desk job in most of cases, is considered a relatively safe from the point of view of occupational hazards. There is little awareness *regarding the repetitive strain injury, mental fatigue, eye strains,* etc. that have been found to be associated with long hours of work with key-boards and VDUs. Nor is there any awareness about the correct posture and other preventive steps to avoid these occupational hazards. Perhaps, the early phase of 'job sophistication' is not yet over.

TABLE 16 : **Education, Training and Income of Self-employed Personnel**

Earnings / Education and Training	Upto Rs. 100,000	1-500,000	500,000	Total
Education				
School Pass	3 (60)	1 (20)	1 (20)	5 (100)
College	10 (67)	5 (33)	0 (0)	15 (100)
University	2 (40)	3 (60)	0 (0)	5 (100)
Professional Degree	0 (0)	1 (100)	0 (0)	1 (100)
Total	15 (58)	10 (38)	1 (4)	26 (100)
Duration of Training				
0-1 Year	9 (82)	1 (9)	1 (9)	11 (100)
1-2 Years	4 (44)	5 (56)	0 (0)	9 (100)
2-3 Years	1 (33)	2 (67)	0 (0)	3 (100)
Total	14 (61)	8 (35)	1 (4)	23 (100)

TABLE 17 : **Industry Type by Working Hours**

Working Hours / Type	4	7 to 7.5	8	8.5 or 9	9.5 to 10	12 or more	Total
Internet/Telecom	0 (0)	0 (0)	8 24	4 (12)	15 (44)	7 (21)	34 (100)
Data Entry	2 (14)	0 (0)	7 (50)	1 (7)	2 (14)	2 (14)	14 (100)
Customization Services	2 (5)	2 (5)	20 (47)	9 (21)	8 (19)	2 (5)	43 (100)
Total	4 (4)	2 (2)	35 (38)	14 (15)	25 (27)	11 (12)	91 (100)

3.6 Gender Dimension of Employment

Not many firms provided information on the gender dimension of their workforce. On the whole, 72 per cent of the surveyed establishments did not employ women workers (Table 18). In 10 per cent of them, up to a quarter of employees were women and in another 17 per cent, between a quarter and a half of the workforce comprised of females. The customization services segment had a greater proportion of cases with women workers than the other two segments. In this segment, 32 per cent of the cases had women as a notable proportion of the work force and in 19 per cent cases, their proportion was greater than 25 per cent. The proportion of women in software industry in general, as seen earlier, is relatively small at 27 per cent; nonetheless, it seems to be steadily growing.

On the surface, no overt discrimination in terms of either the nature of jobs or remuneration is apparent. Detailed investigations, however, revealed a subtle gender bias both in the nature of jobs assigned to women as well as the compensation offered to them. Women are often employed as receptionists or in training sections in these firms and when they are actually given IT job, it is at the lower end of technology and salary/wage payment. One of the reasons for under-representation of women is the regulation that women cannot work after dark. This regulation reduces the flexibility that the employers may require for setting the work schedules and working hours. Some of the activities in the segments covered such as internet cafes work well after sunset.

There could be another explanation of under-representation of women in the smaller unorganized enterprises such as those covered in our sample. Larger organized firms employ women workers in routine and dead-end jobs, such as data entry, most ostensibly to avoid problems of unionization. Such an attraction is not relevant for smaller unorganized firms. Hence, they tend to employ more male workers.

TABLE 18 : **Patterns of Female Employment**

Proportion of Female Workers	0	0-25%	25-50%	50-75%	75-100%	Total
Internet/Telecom	31 (74)	3 (7)	7 (17)	0 (0)	1 (2)	42 (100)
Data Entry	11 (79)	1 (7)	2 (14)	0 (0)	0 (0)	14 (100)
Customization Services	31 (67)	6 (13)	8 (17)	1 (2)	0 (0)	46 (100)
Total	73 (72)	10 (10)	17 (18)	1 (1)	1 (1)	102 (100)

At another level, it is encouraging to note that the representation of women is higher in relatively more skill intensive segments, namely customization services, compared to the other two segments included in our sample. This shows that women are increasingly adopting a career in information technology, as is corroborated by the organized sector trends reported earlier in Table 2. We came across a few cases where highly qualified women had themselves become entrepreneurs, by starting up small ventures in customization services, web designing and similar activities. One woman entrepreneur we came across, for instance, has started a venture to provide computer training to school children in a Delhi's up-market neighborhood where the entire professional workforce comprises women, and men work only as support ing staff. Encouraged by the success of the venture, she now plans to set up similar centres in other locations. In general, therefore, the industry does provide opportunities for relatively better employment, both for men and women. The proportion of women in employment may go up in the future as the supply of well-trained women job aspirants rises.

3.7 Links with the Organized Sector

The links with the organized sector are nearly always vertical. Most of the customization and data entry firms interviewed are working directly for the end-user clients in the organized sector. These include public sector banks, corporate sector enterprises and even embassies. A few even work for outside (foreign) companies. For instance, a data entry firm directly gets jobs from a Canadian company (presumably through ethnic contacts). In the telecom/internet segment, the agents are dependent on service providers such as the VSNL and were directly serving individual customers. Very few sample firms sub-contract jobs from larger IT firms. The attraction of smaller firms such as these lies in their price competitiveness and more personalized services. Informal sector agents are communicated through advertisements in newspaper and yellow pages in telephone directories as well as through a word of mouth. The informal sector IT agents have good local networks and frequently share information with other agents, both on demand and supply. Therefore, as long as they can deliver quality services and ensure delivery schedules, the size of the establishment does not seem to matter in most parts of this industry. It is clear, therefore, that the so-called informal or unorganized segment of the software related services may be informal as far as the labour market is concerned, but in the product market, their presence is not informal, and they are expected to conduct their business as regular participants in the business.

3.8 Technology, Training and Quality Consciousness

Most of the entrepreneurs and self-employed persons are acutely aware of the importance of rapid technological changes in their field and of the need to keep pace with them to stay in the market. They are also aware of the importance of quality of service delivered for their survival, given the highly competitive nature of the market. The major source of information on technological developments in hardware and software industry magazines and other publications, vendors of hardware and software, advertisements and their peers.

Some entrepreneurs and self-employed persons do occasionally attend seminars and workshops organized by technology suppliers when a new generation of technologies is released. They specifically mention the need to have more such seminars from technology developers such as Microsoft and IBM. Some of them attend training courses abroad (Hong Kong was mentioned, for instance) on a regular basis. This, however, is restricted to entrepreneurs engaged in the relatively upper-end of skilled activity, such as customization services.

Box 1

Transition to Entrepreneurship: Some Illustrations

Mr A was a computer teacher earning Rs 7,000 per month. He has a college degree and has completed courses in web page designing, multimedia, etc. He started his venture in web page designing, financial accounting with TALLY in 1998 with an investment of Rs. 0.35 million raised from household savings and loan from a bank. Now, his venture employs 5 workers. He earns Rs. 1 million per annum and expects his earnings to go up to Rs 1.5 million within a year.

Mr B was an employee with a private company earning Rs 3,000-4,000 per month. He has completed school but has virtually no training to his credit. Yet he decided to set up a desk top publication, photocopy and laser printing venture in 1997 with an investment of Rs 0.35 million raised from household savings and a bank loan. Currently, he employs 8 workers. His current income from the venture is between Rs 2.0-2.5 million per annum.

Mr X was self-employed. He has a college degree earned through correspondence and has virtually no training. In 1997, he started an Internet Caf, in Noida with an investment of Rs 0.75 million raised from household savings and bank loans. Today, he employs 6 workers including two females. His own earnings from the venture are Rs. 0.8-0.9 million per annum and he expects a 50-60 per cent increase in it in the next year.

Mr Y, a college drop-out, was working in a private company with monthly emoluments of Rs 7,000-8,000 per month. In 1994, he started a telecom bureau with an investment of Rs 1,50,000 thousand raised from household savings and loans from friends and relatives. This venture was upgraded to provide internet and e-mail facilities subsequently. Now, he employs 6 workers. His current income from the venture is Rs 1.0 - 1.2 million per annum. He expects it to double within a year in view of the rising internet/ e-mail activity.

Source: The field survey.

3.9 Upward Mobility and Spread of Entrepreneurship

Most employees treat their jobs within the smaller and informal sector as a stop gap arrangement while they are still under training or studying. To be sure, this helps them to support their expensive training. Hence, most of the respondents report a very high turnover of employees. This situation does not provide cases of upward progression of workers in their jobs. However, the sample cases do provide a number of fascinating stories of transition of employees into entrepreneurs with sharp rise in incomes in a relatively short period. These include cases of people working as teachers in computer training institutions with relatively low salaries, later having become entrepreneurs and earning millions; a low ranking government official setting up his own internet/telecom venture; another one leaving a private company job to start his highly successful DTP venture, and so on (see Box 1). This suggests that the industry offers opportunity to expand the base of entrepreneurship in the country with relatively low 'entry barriers' as they are referred to in the literature on industrial organization (Kumar and Siddharthan, 1997).

3.10 Prospects of Employment and Income Expansion

The job potential in all the industry segments is strong. Most of the respondents believed that employment in the activities studied would grow in the next one year at an impressive rate of 50 to 100 per cent (Table 19). Most pointedly, 40 to 50 per cent of the cases in internet and customization services segments expect the jobs to grow at the rate of 50 to 100 per cent in the coming year. The growth potential of data entry segment does not appear that bright as 60 per cent of the respondents consider the growth rate to go up to 20 per cent only. It is interesting to note that the projections made by small enterprises, such as those in our sample, are broadly in tune with the rates applicable to the organized segments as discussed in the previous section.

A majority of the respondents (about 85 per cent) expect up to 20 per cent increase in the monthly salaries of workers (Table 20). This pattern holds good for all the three segments studied. It is interesting to note that salaries in the organized segment in the industry have also grown in the past year at about a similar rate, as was evident in Table 2. Therefore, the salaries in the unorganized sector firms in the industry seem to be somewhat related with those in the larger market, presumably because of relative short supply or scarcity of skilled/ trained personnel in the sector as a whole.

The future incomes of employers are expected to rise even faster than the workers' salaries. As many as 32 per cent of the respondents feel that employer earnings could rise at a rate ranging between 20 and 50 per cent (Table 21). In customization services and internet segments, the proportion of respondents

TABLE 19 : **Expected Increase in Employment**

Expected growth of employment	Nil	Up to 20 per cent	20-50 per cent	50-100 per cent	Total
Internet/Telecom	2 (20)	3 (30)	1 (10)	4 (40)	10 (100)
Data Entry	0 (0)	3 (60)	1 (20)	1 (20)	5 (100)
Customization Services	1 (6)	4 (22)	4 (22)	9 (50)	18 (100)
Total	3 (9)	10 (30)	6 (18)	14 (42)	33 (100)

TABLE 20 : **Expected Increase in Monthly Remuneration of Employees**

Expected Rise in salary	Internet/ Telecom	Data Entry	Customization Services	Total
Upto 20 per cent	11 (85)	5 (83)	17 (85)	33 (85)
20-50 per cent	1 (8)	1 (17)	1 (5)	3 (8)
50-100 per cent	1 (8)	0 (0)	2 (10)	3 (8)
All	13 (100)	6 (100)	20 (100)	39 (100)

predicting growth rates are distributed more evenly across extremes, with some predicting as high as 100-200 per cent growth rates. This tends to underline the optimism that the industry has generated among the entrepreneurs.

3.11 Role of Government Policy

In general, the interviewees feel that, being small, they are not much affected by the government policy directly. There seems to a general apathy towards dealing with the bureaucracy, primarily because of corruption. However, they do recognize the necessity as well as the signifinance of favourable policy measures such as availability of cheaper hardware, lower satellite connection rates, policy of giving loans to PCO owners to upgrade their establishments with internet facilities, and so on.

3.12 Constraints on Growth

The response to the question on constraints to growth was partly quantitative and partly qualitative. Major constraints identified related to the access to capital and skills.

TABLE 21 : **Expected Increase in Employers' Future Income**

Expected Rate of Growth	Internet/ Telecom	Data Entry	Customization Services	Total
0 - 20 per cent	2 (22)	1 (33)	3 (30)	6 (27)
20-50 per cent	3 (33)	1 (33)	3 (30)	7 (32)
50-100 per cent	2 (22)	1 (33)	1 (10)	4 (18)
100-200 per cent	2 (11)	0 (0)	2 (11)	4 (21)
200 per cent and more	0 (0)	0 (0)	1 (10)	1 (5)
All	9 (100)	3 (100)	10 (100)	22 (100)

3.12.1 Access to Capital

Access to capital was identified as a major constraint to growth by a majority (64 per cent overall) of the respondents across all the three segments (Table 22). This is not surprising keeping in view the earlier observation of the banks' bias against the small loanees and their insistence on collateral in preference to mortgage.

TABLE 22 : **Constraints on Growth**

Constraint	Internet/ Telecom	Data Entry	Customization Services	Total
Access to Capital	18 (86)	7 (64)	18 (51)	43 (64)
Access to Technology	2 (10)	0 (0)	7 (20)	9 (13)
Skilled Labour	1 (5)	0 (0)	7 (20)	8 (12)
Demand Limitation	0 (0)	4 (36)	3 (9)	7 (10)
Total	21 (100)	11 (100)	35 (100)	67 (100)

3.12.2 Skills and Technology

To some extent, the growth of customization segment has been limited by scarcity of skilled labour and access to technology, in the view of an equal proportion (20 per cent each) of respondents (Table 22). Evidence suggests that there is no shortage of personnel who have completed some short-term training courses, for the low-end section of the market. However, skilled personnel, especially those with 2-3 years of training are highly scarce. This is so for several reasons. First, there are fewer institutions providing longer duration training. Second, the supply of personnel with longer training tends to be limited because of exorbitant costs for students, given the high fees charged by the training institutes which are mostly in the private domain. Hence, very few opt to continue beyond the first year.

The respondents also complain about the too-much theoretical or conceptual content and limited practical application of the training courses offered by the private institutes such as NIIT and APTECH, which run biggest networks of training in the industry. Hence, new recruits need substantial 'on-the-job-training'. The poor quality of training in turn has been blamed on the shortage of qualified and competent teachers/trainers in these institutions. More often than not, these private institutions or training centres are staffed by under-qualified personnel which ultimately reflects on the poor quality of their instruction.

The expansion of training institutions' networks has led to rapid increase in the demand for trainers, that has never ever been matched by supply. This is because the brighter computer professionals with professional degrees who could have staffed these training institutes, generally prefer to join the organized industry. That is so because even though industrial jobs offer a lower starting salary, the career path, and hence the growth of emoluments offered by the industry, is much better compared to that in the training institutions.

It is curious that training institutions are not able to offer a matching career opportunity to software professionals, to be able to attract and retain competent faculty. This has some thing to do with the fact that these institutes operate in extremely oligopolistic markets. There is a rapidly rising demand for their courses, and their focus is on breadth rather than depth. They thus franchise outlets in every nook and corner of the country.

3.12.3 Demand and Competition

Most respondents thought that there is too much competition in their industry, but most also felt that they would survive it. The competition would increase, given the low barriers to entry in these market segments, as observed earlier. However, the demand seems to rise more than proportionately (only in the data entry segment, a significant proportion -36 per cent - of the respondents considered demand limitation also to be an important constraint on the growth). Hence, most of the entrants do not feel concerned about it.

3.12.4 Other Constraints

Other constraints/problems reported by the interviewees include:

- Frequent electricity failures; this being the activity highly dependent on electricity, creates problems for the smaller entrepreneurs by raising the capital cost because it necessitates investment in UPS systems.
- High cost of hardware and software was also mentioned as a problem although interviewees recognize that trade policy liberalization has brought down the prices considerably.
- High internet and ISDN charges for access to internet: hence they welcome the recent internet policy of the government to liberalize internet services.

4. Concluding Remarks and Policy Recommendations

The foregoing discussion suggests that there is much potential for creation of not only wage-paid jobs but also self-employment and entrepreneurship, waiting to be exploited in the software and related services in the informal sector activities, besides those in the fast growing organized sector. The organized segment's growth is primarily driven by external demand, given its high export-orientation. It has been helped by increasing activity in the industry world-wide and from the trend of efficiency-seeking internationalization of value adding activities in the MNEs. Hence, MNEs have begun to increasingly source their software requirements from countries like Ireland, India, Singapore, Mexico, Philippines, China, among others, which prove to be cheaper than getting the same in their home countries. However, the informal sector activities are mainly geared to domestic needs which may not keep pace with the growth of external demand. Yet, there are reasons to expect expansion of software and services activities in the domestic economy at a faster rate in the coming years. Given the present low levels of IT usage in the country and in view of the thrust placed on increasing it in the government policy as a part of IT Action Plan, it is expected that the domestic demand for software and related services may expand at an even higher rate. Our fieldwork also confirms that most of the activities would grow at an annual rate of 50-100 per cent in the coming years.

The jobs created in the informal sector activities may not be highly remunerative in the beginning and be at the lower end of the skill spectrum. But, as one grows in terms of either experience or training, the income levels grow rather fast. Given the general scarcity of highly trained people in the sector, they could actually be in demanding situations or could start on their own business. The per unit investment for creation of these jobs is also relatively small with high returns and hence with a relatively short pay-back period. In particular, barriers to the new entrants are low while returns are relatively high. Hence, the industry offers a big potential of expanding the domestic base of entrepreneurship. The media is full of profiles of a number of individuals who have exploited the emerging potential of internet-commerce or e-commerce opportunities and have made millions of rupees once their bright ideas are put into practice. But that kind of entrepreneurship falls in the upper end of the knowledge spectrum and hence does not allow a mass scale entry or follow-on. Nonetheless, our study clearly shows that even at the lower end of the skill continuum, there is a tremendous potential of expanding the base of entrepreneurship and creation of decent jobs for the unemployed educated, computer-literate youth, with relatively low capital investment. Furthermore, these opportunities are not concentrated only in the metropolitan centres but also in smaller cities and towns as well as suburban centres. There are also opportunities for self-employment and home-based work, which may be especially suitable for women with young children. In the near future, tele-working possibilities are expected to provide more such opportunities for women (Mitter, 1999).

Since demand does not appear to be a constraint for most part of the industry, concerted emphasis must necessarily be put on the supply side. For dealing with the supply side, the following steps may be considered to obviate some of the constraints faced by the informal sector enterprises and to improve their productivity.

4.1 Easing the Availability of Finance

By far the most severe handicap faced by the informal sector enterprises is the lack of initial capital. The banking system is not geared to dealing with small clients seeking small loans for buying equipment for starting a new business. For the larger enterprises, there are several term-lending institutions as well as the equity capital market. Venture capital funds too are coming up to finance individuals with bright ideas, in the implementation of their vision. Government of India has recently set up a Rs 1,000 million IT Venture Capital Fund to support such enterprises. However, for the young entrepreneurs having capital only in the form of a degree or diploma and wanting to start a new business of the type and scale described above, there do not seem to be many options other than to rely on personal savings or loans from relatives and friends, given the 'prejudice of the banking sector in dealing with young entrepreneurs in software activity', to quote an interviewee. There is a need for creating a micro-credit infrastructure in the country on the lines of Grameen Bank in Bangladesh. Easier availability of financing would also help in their expansion and eventually into their graduation and transition into joining the ranks of organized sector. The government has taken up steps to provide bank credit to telecom bureau owners for installation of internet/e-mail facilities and converting them into information kiosks. The Delhi Government also intends to convert 500 STD bureaus into internet kiosks in the city by providing loans through the Delhi Finance Corporation (*Times of India*, 21 December 1999). Similar credit facilities need to be created for smaller enterprises in software customization, content providers, data entry operators and DTP and graphic design shops.

4.2 Easing the Supply of Trained Personnel

The present system of training software professionals needs to be reformed. While entry of the private sector into software training in the early 1980s and its rapid expansion has contributed to the growth of industry by keeping up the supply of trained workforce, the present system now needs a rethinking. The high fees charged by them make their courses prohibitively expensive. For instance, the average revenue per student in 1998/99 received by private educational organizations in the industry was Rs 12,524 (*Dataquest, 1999*). This translates to more than a thousand rupees per month, on an average. For higher levels of training, it is much more. The high rates of fees charged, therefore, contribute to the 'exclusion' of underprivileged children from entry in this promising line. Secondly, the quality of their training and education seems to have been deteriorating with time. The focus seems to have moved to the breadth and market share with franchises practically in each locality of big cities. Many complaints have been received about the quality of teachers/ trainers employed in these institutions and the level of training imparted. Thirdly, while the number of institutions imparting such training seems to have grown, there is an evidence of a high degree of oligopolistic control in the market. The two top companies in the software education market, viz. NIIT and APTECH have a combined market share of 52 per cent (*Dataquest, 1999*). Although there are software training institutes in every nook and corner of cities and towns, they are franchisees of one or the other chains and are subject to the same fees structure. Such a high level of oligopolistic control over the vital supply link to the industry would require a look from an anti-trust perspective.

The Department of Electronics (DoE) has initiated a scheme of accreditation of informal sector training institutions. However, the DoE-accredited institutions cannot stand the competition with the established chains of NIIT/ APTECH type organizations because of their vast reach, advertising, vertical integration with the software generation activity and their contacts with the organized software industry. There is apparently a need for a look into the present system.

Since job opportunities for trained personnel in this sector are not a problem, loan facilities can be provided to children and adolescents from the underprivileged sections for meeting their training and education costs in software activities, besides providing subsidies and scholarships, and creating government aided institutions.

4.3 Reform of Educational System

Besides expanding training facilities in software, the conventional system of education needs a total overhaul to take note of the quiet IT revolution that is affecting all aspects of life, and all sections of the economy. The IT education should be integrated in school and college curricula and other traditional disciplines. A case in point is fine arts education that is still not integrated with the use of computers except in a few colleges. There is tremendous demand for artists trained in CAD, multimedia content development and design of web pages. The demand for artists proficient in CAD is likely to multiply with the expansion of e-commerce in the future. On the one hand, colleges and universities are producing conventional science and social science graduates who cannot find adequate job opportunities. On the other hand, there is an acute scarcity of computer trained and professional manpower. This mismatch needs to be corrected urgently. There is an immediate need for reform and re-engineering of educational system in the country, to be in tune with the changed requirements.

4.4 Social Security and Occupational Safety Schemes

The employees and self-employed workers in the informal sector, like in most other activities, are not covered under any social security scheme. The government can take steps to provide a framework for creating some coverage of social security to these workers. Besides, there is a need to increase awareness about the possible occupational hazards in working with the VDUs and key boards and preventive steps such as correct work-posturing. Public health authorities may bring out literature on these aspects and circulate it widely, besides advertising it through newspapers.

4.5 Infrastructural Facilities and Techno Parks

Creation of common facilities and infrastructure in the form of built-up office space equipped with communication facilities may facilitate the transition of knowledge workers to entrepreneurs, by reducing the start-up capital requirements for their ventures. Such Techno- Parks could be set up near major commercial centres because more often than not, the prospective small enterprises tend to cluster around such centres.

4.6 Self Help Groups

Smaller entrepreneurs in the activity could be encouraged to set up self-help groups that could help group members in keeping themselves updated with technical information, through organizing seminars and training programmes and taking up common problems with the concerned authorities. Here, valuable lessons could be learnt from the experiences of SEWA in Ahmedabad, which has gone to the extent of setting up a financial institution of its own to extend social security coverage and extending micro-credit to its members.

4.7 Learning from Experiences of Other Countries

International institutions like the ILO could use their international reach to bring out successful experiences on promotion and development of micro-enterprises in the software, IT and related services from different countries. In particular, experiences of countries such as the United States in promoting venture capital industry, which has facilitated the creation of new, skill-based entrepreneurs in the industry, need to be understood and debated; some features of these models may be useful to our industry. Furthermore, these organizations could help in evolving social security schemes for the unorganized workers in the industry by providing lessons from other countries' experiences. Finally, they may help in bringing experiences of other countries in reducing the gender gap in this area and in mitigating occupational hazards associated with some of these activities.

Bibliography

Basur, N.P. and Seema Chawla, (1999). "Trade in Software Services: From International Trade to Teletrade: The Case Study of Tata Consultancy Services in India", Europe and Developing Countries in the Globalised Information Economy, Routledge, London and New York.

Dataquest, (1999). The DQ Top 20 Giants, Vol. XVII, No. 13, July 15.

Freeman, C., Soete, L. and Efendioglu, U. (1995). "Diffusion and the Employment Effects of Information and Communication Technology", International Labour Review, Vol. 134(4-5).

Govt. of India, (1999). Economic Survey 1998-99, Ministry of Finance.

Hanna, Nagy, (1994). Exploring Information Technology for Development: A Case Study of India, World Bank Discussion Paper No. 246, Washington DC.

Heeks, R. (1996). India's Software Industry: State Policy, Liberalization and Industrial Development, Sage Publications, New Delhi.

Hoon Cheah Siew, Cecilia Ng and Swasti Mitter, (1999). Teleworking in Malaysia: A Primer, United Nations University (UNU/INTECH).

Huws, Ursula, (1999). 'Beyond Anecdotes: On Quantifying the globalization of Information Processing Work', in Europe and Developing Countries in the Globalised Information Economy, Routledge, London and New York.

ILO, (1998). ILO Declaration on Fundamental Principles and Rights at Work and its Follow-up, Geneva, 18 June, 1998.

Kumar, Nagesh, (1999). Multinational Enterprises, Overseas R&D Activity and Global Technological Order, RIS Occasional Paper No. 56,: Research and Information System, New Delhi.

____ and N. S. Siddharthan, (1997). Technology, Market Structure and Internationalization: Issues and Policies for Developing Countries, Routledge, London and New York.

____, (2000a). Developing Countries in International Division of Labour in Software and Service Industry: Lessons from Indian Experience, Background Paper for World Employment Report 2001, ILO, Geneva.

____, (2000b). National Innovation Systems and the Indian Software Industry Development, Background Paper for *World Industrial Development Report 2001*, UNIDO, Vienna.

Mishra, Atul, (1999). "A Report on the Field Survey of Informal Sector Activities in Software Services", (mimeo.), Shri Ram College of Commerce, Delhi.

Mitter, Swasti and Ruth Pearson, (1992). Global Information Processing: The Emergence of Software Services and Data Entry Jobs in Selected Developing Countries, ILO, Working Papers, SAP 4.14/WP.51 (rev.1).

____ and Maria-Ines Bastos (eds.), (1999). Europe and Developing Countries in the Globalised Information Economy, Routledge, London & New York.

____ and Umit Efendioglu, (1999). "Is Asia the Destination for `Runaway' Information Processing Work? Implications for Trade and Employment", in Europe and Developing Countries in the Globalised Information Economy, Routledge, London & New York.

____, (1999). "Telework, Teletrade and Sustainable Development: The Synthesis", Paper Presented at the Workshop on Telework, Teletrade and Sustainable Development: Indian Experience in a Global Context, Bombay, 15-16 November.

NASSCOM, (1999a). 'Indian Software Scenario', http://www.nasscom.org/indian.htm.

____, (1999b). 'It Enabled Services', http:// www.nasscom.org/html/IT%20Enabled.htm.

____, (2000a). Indian Software and Services Industry: A Strategic Review 2000, National Association for Software and Services Companies, New Delhi.

____, (2000b). 'Indian Software Export Grows by 57 per cent in 1999-2000: NASSCOM Report', 3 July, http://www.nasscom.org, Mumbai.

Panchamukhi, V.R. and Ram Upendra Das, (1999). Economic Reforms, Regional Integration and Labour Markets in the SAARC Region, SAAT-ILO Working Papers, ILO, June 1999.

Reardon, Geraldine, (1999). 'Telebanking: Breaking the Logic of Spatial and Work Organization' in Europe and Developing Countries in the Globalised Information Economy, Routledge.London and New York.

Rajeswari, A.R. (1995). 'Employment Characteristics of Software Personnel: Issues and Analysis' in Advanced Technology Assessment System: Information Technology for Development, Issue 10, New York and Geneva.

Richardson, Ranald, (1999). 'Call Centres and the Prospects for Export-Oriented Work in the Developing World: Evidence from Western Europe', in Europe and Developing Countries in the Globalised Information Economy, Routledge, London & New York.

Times of India, (1999). "Internet Kiosks in the National Capital City", December 21.

United Nations, (1995). Advanced Technology Assessment System: Information Technology for Development, Issue 10, New York and Geneva.

Informal Tourism Sector In India: A Study Of Two Cities

Surjit Singh

1. Introduction

Tourism has emerged as one of the fastest growing industries in the world. About 594 million people travel the world over every year and spend over $423 million (Sinclair 1998). Besides, every 9th person in the world is engaged in travel and tourism industry for earning livelihood (Tooman 1997). It is estimated that the world tourism directly employs 112 million persons, a majority of them being in the informal sector. The employment in this sector is relatively more prominent in the developing economies. In India, for instance, of the five million workers engaged in the tourism industry, only 2.1 per cent are in the formal sector (Sinclair 1998).

Tourism is favourably viewed as a clean industry as well as a labour intensive one, with the latter being a decidedly beneficial characteristic in economies largely of poorly educated or unskilled workers (Frederick 1993). Tourism's ability to generate employment not only in the formal but also in the informal sector is, therefore, especially advantageous for developing countries (Elkan, 1975). Employment conditions in the tourism sector are akin to those in the agricultural sector, because in both the sectors output varies seasonally (D'Souza 1993). The nature of tourism sector in developing countries is such that the activities may be in the formal sector but the labour market is largely informal. The work force invariably does not have a decent work environment. The present study is an attempt to understand the informal tourism sector in two important tourist centres of India, namely, Jaipur and Agra(1). More specifically, it provides insights into informal sector accommodation, board, escort and transport sectors. The study is based on the impressions gathered through unstructured primary survey conducted by us. More pointedly, an attempt is made to:

1) Describe the tourism sector in terms of demand pattern, business environment, growth, employment and working environment, policy/regulatory system and the role of government/other organizations;
2) Assess the current supply of, and access to, productive resources such as credit, raw materials, skills, information and the potential to enhance them;

3) Study the linkages of the informal with formal sector tourism and its impact on employment;
4) Determine the potential to raise productivity, incomes and employment;
5) Examine the working conditions and occupational hazards facedby workers, gender segregation and prevalence of child labour and to provide suggestions to remove the same;
6) To take stock of government policy and regulatory environment influencing the growth of the industry;
7) Suggest action plan for improving the working conditions in the context of decent work.

2. Toursim Sector: Policy and Growth

In India, both central and state governments have been playing a vital role for an effective development of the tourism industry; much of this becomes evident if we go through plan documents and policy statements. The government of India took notice of tourism industry's potential way back in the second five year plan (1956-61) although only a meagre sum of Rs.33.6 million was allocated to this sector; this constituted 0.07 per cent of total plan outlay. It was during the fourth five year plan only that the importance of tourism to Indian economy was fully realized and a plan outlay of Rs.360 million was made; this was the highest ever share of plan outlay (0.23 per cent) to tourism sector. Although the plan allocations were raised, by varying degree, during the next two plans, yet, till the end of sixth five year plan, the stress was on optimal use of existing capacity and substantial increase in the tourist accommodation in the public and private sectors. It was only during the Seventh Plan that a special thrust to the tourism sector became visible. Not only the investment outlay rose substantially but the plan set a target of 7 per cent growth in tourist arrivals through concerted improvement in the infrastructure, besides permitting some relaxation in the policies and procedures regarding the admittance of foreign tourists into the country. A major step was taken in 1989 to set up the Tourism Finance Corporation of India. The Eighth (1992-97) and the Ninth (1997-2000) Plans have carried forward the efforts made in the previous plans. The basic strategy during the Ninth plan is to establish effective coordination with all relevant agencies so as to achieve synergized development.

Recognizing the importance of tourism as a sector for economic development, a comprehensive tourism policy highlighting the objectives of tourism development in the country, was put forward by the Government in 1982. The policy envisaged the conversion of the many monuments/activities in India for tourism promotion through well planned, well defined and fully integrated national programmes. It specified the responsibility for tourism development as a common endeavour of all the agencies, directly and indirectly connected with tourism, at central and state levels including public and private sector enterprises: airlines, railways and road transport systems; municipal and local bodies as well as cultural and educational institutions. Further, it provided an action plan based on a **travel circuit** concept to maximize the benefits of tourism. The plan proposed to achieve intensive development of selected circuits, dispel the tendency of concentration in a few urban centres, encourage the diversification of tourist attractions and opening up economically backward areas, which otherwise hold many tourist attractions. Manpower development and training were also given due weightage to ensure efficient services and effective management of tourist facilities.

In continuation of the thrust unleashed by the 1982 tourism development policy, tourism was recognized as an industry in 1986. Consequently, it became eligible for several incentives and facilities including tax incentives, subsidies, priorities in sanctioning of loans by the state financial institutions and preferences in getting electricity and water connections. In 1991, tourism was also declared as a priority sector for foreign investment.

In spite these enunciations and policy supports, concrete results were not forthcoming. The tourist traffic has not increased compared to that in the South Asian Countries or even China. The Tourism Department has not been able to have coordination with other ministries. The road development has been poor even in the tourist attraction cities. Further, the Ministry of Tourism has not come out of its age-old policy of 'selling Indian culture', though stray efforts have been made to attract tourists to pleasure sites. Sight-seeing has somehow been the top most purpose of a major proportion of foreign tourists followed by **pleasure tourism,** while domestic tourists are more governed by pilgrimage and sight-seeing tourism.

The government has also not effectively intervened in the area of air links. The need is to review the visa policy in terms of waiving visa fee or the need to procure visa itself. The improvement in the existing poor sanitary conditions is still a distance dream. At none of the tourist centres, efforts are made to check unethical practices. Taj in Agra is a glaring example of turning a blind eye to the problem. There has been no effort to check the vending of poor quality food. The policy of high class tourism has not really let the government promote budget tourism accommodation. There is need for substantial improvement in the quality of accommodation. There is no doubt that upper class tourism fetches more revenue but some balance has to be struck among the expectations and requirements of different categories of tourists.

The tourist cities have no planned local transport system. Above all, the policy statements have ignored the informal sector tourist segment. At best, one discovers only a passing reference to budget accommodation and it is limited to provision of *yatri niwas*, tourist complexes, tourist lodges, tourist hostels/ homes at selected places. The hotel approval system is also not simple and it hinders the growth of informal sector hotel industry. The state level policies are also found wanting in many respects. They only indirectly try to help the informal sector tourism activities. The Tourism Ministry, through its Finance Corporation and State Finance Corporations, has a provision for providing finance to new entrepreneurs in the informal sector. The practice is, however, vastly different.

2.1 Tourist Arrivals

In 1951 the foreign tourist arrivals in India was 0.017 million, which stood at 5.53 million in 1998 a more than 300 times growth. In more recent times, the foreign tourist arrivals in India increased from 4.64 million in 1995 to 5.53 million in 1998; an jump of 19.2 per cent (Table 1). The domestic tourism too is on the rise. During 1995-98, the number of domestic tourists increased by 22.2 per cent while the total tourist number went up by 22.1 per cent. The domestic tourism has increased partly because, in recent years, more people have started visiting the religious places and the steady improvement in the income level of the middle class has prompted them to become mobile. There are regional variations in tourist movement firstly because of the highly uneven distribution of destinations of tourists' interest, and secondly because of the failure of some regions to exploit the potential. Most states in India, which traditionally received international tourists have observed a decline in share of foreign tourists, while new destinations have emerged in some other states.

TABLE 1 : **Tourist Arrivals in India (million)**

Tourists	1995	1996	1997	1998
Domestic	136.64	140.12	159.88	166.93
Foreign	4.64	5.03	5.50	5.53
Total	141.28	145.15	165.38	172.46

Source: GOI, Annual Report for various years, Ministry of Tourism, Delhi.

2.1.1 Regional Scenario

Since the study aims to examine the tourism sector in the cities of Jaipur and Agra, we briefly look at tourist arrivals in these two cities. In 1997, the city of Jaipur received 0.88 million tourists, of which 79.2 per cent were domestic and 20.8 per cent came from abroad (Table 2). The number of tourist arrivals in 1998 fell to 7.67 million, of whom, foreign tourists constituted 19.7 per cent. This means that in these two years, the proportion of domestic tourists increased. In Agra, of the 0.34 million tourists arriving in 1997, 63.9 per cent were domestic and 36.1 per cent were foreign tourists. In 1998, the tourist arrivals fell drastically to

0.12 million, of whom, domestic tourists were 58.8 per cent. The decline in tourist traffic was contributed both by domestic and foreign tourists.

TABLE 2 : **Tourist Arrivals in Jaipur and Agra (000')**

Area	Domestic		Foreign		Total	
	1997	1998	1997	1998	1997	1998
Jaipur	700	616	184	151	884	767
per cent	79.2	80.3	20.8	19.7	100.0	100.0
Agra	219	72	124	51	343	123
per cent	63.9	58.8	36.1	41.2	100.0	100.0

Source: Department of Tourism, Jaipur and Agra.

3. Sub-Sectoral Linkages

The tourism sector is an all-encompassing sector. All activities in the sector are interrelated and cater to the needs of a tourist. Moreover, the tourism sector, both formal and informal segments, has its linkages with other markets viz., labour, credit, inputs markets, and so on. The tourism sector's output is demand-induced by the distribution of tourist arrivals between the busy and slack seasons. Besides, the moments of production and of consumption are contemporaneous. Unlike in other sectors, the inventories cannot be accumulated or de-accumulated. The implications for employment are thus obvious. Consider the accommodation component. In 1998, the starred/approved hotels in the country stood at 1188, with 65,598 rooms. These hotels employ their work-force directly from training institutes either through advertisements or by visiting the training institutes. This work-force deals with the upper crust of tourists and is educated, skilled, better paid, organized; it works in shifts and for fixed working hours; it gets perks, and enjoys both social and job security. On the whole, the working conditions are fairly decent. Women too are employed in large numbers and there is no visible sex discrimination.

These hotels are linked with tour operators and travel agencies and formal sector credit market. The inputs required are also obtained from formal sector markets. Associated services like laundry, gardening, cleaning are done in-house. They also have restaurants of their own. The tourist guides/escorts cater to the customers of these hotels through travel operators/agencies. The customers use both formal and informal sector transport. To a large extent, there is a vertical integration among various activities in the formal sector. The non-starred/unapproved hotels have little or no link with their formal sector counterparts. These hotels have links with both formal and informal credit markets, informal labour market, informal service sector like laundry, etc. Practically, the whole lot of inputs are bought from the informal sector. The work force is temporary and employer often adjust, if not dictate, terms of employment including hours of work. Enterprises also lay-off workers during slack period. There is no social or job security of the workers. The wages here are much lower than those in the formal sector, for all categories of employees. The work-force is not employed through any formal advertisement or recruited from training institutes; recruitment is done informally. The work-force is generally unskilled or semi-skilled and poorly educated. Labour productivity is low. The worker turnover in these hotels is high. The workers are, however, not the first time jobbers or new entrants into the city. If the prospective worker has a contact, it helps in obtaining the job. The supply of labour is rather unlimited to these hotels. The employment is also governed by the occupancy rates.

It is in this category of hotels that the informal transport plays an important role in these two cities. The car taxis, auto-rickshaw drivers and cycle rickshaw pliers bring in customers to hotels and take them to tourist places within the cities. This relationship is of two types: one where no cost is attached for the hotel operator and the second where cost is attached. The cost is in terms of commission the hotel operator pays to the transport sector workers to attract customers. The hotels are also linked to tourist guides as they provide paid-assignments to guides (some hotels have tour desks and guides informally cultivate hotel owners). There is some link, albeit indirect, with outside eating places; most of the informal sector hotels do not have restaurants of their own. A few travel operators also directly send their clients to such hotels.

The informal sector eating places in Jaipur and Agra largely have strong links with the informal transport system since the latter send customers to eating places, both with commission and without. Both formal and informal credit markets are linked to restaurants, though the link with the latter is far more stronger.

Tourist guides have direct link with formal sector hotels and, to an extent, with informal sector hotels also. There are very few guides who are associated with restaurants, but they do suggest places to their clients. These guides hire informal sector transport to take tourists to intended destinations. In most cases, there is always an unwritten understanding between the operators of transport vehicles and guides. Further, formal sector training institutions train guides and these guides, in turn, get their business through travel agents/tour operators.

The major player in the tourism sector is the transport activity, both formal and informal. The formal sector transport deals largely with formal sector hotels, while the informal sector transport operators have an interface with all types of hotels (directly or indirectly) restaurants and guides. The informal transport sector has a labour market of its own, which is informal, though there may exist formal structure of ownership of vehicles. There are three main segments of the informal transport sector: car taxi, auto-rickshaw and cycle rickshaw. The most informal of these three is the cycle rickshaw. The cycle rickshaw plier may be an owner or may operate a hired vehicle. The entry is easy and entails very low cost. Migrant labourers form a major part of this segment. There are a few rich persons owning a thousand or so rickshaws and they rent them out, on a daily rent basis. Personal faith plays a role here; invariably no formal introduction is required to hire a rickshaw. In the auto-rickshaw segment, drivers may own the vehicle or operate a rented one. The entry is easy; only a driving license is required. The operators are mainly local and some may have experience of some other odd jobs in the informal sector. Some may also graduate from cycle rickshaw pulling to operating an auto-rickshaw. There is intense competition in these two segments. The taxi segment has both owner operating and drivers plying hired cars. Here, the job opportunities are limited compared to cycle and auto-rickshaw segments. There is competition between cars fleet owners and single car owners. The former are better equipped and more resourceful. These drivers have direct and indirect links with the shops/emporia in the cities. Most drivers are local and some may have graduated too, from the auto-rickshaw segment. The car fleet owners do have direct link with the formal sector hotels.

All activities connected with tourism are linked with government: national, state and local bodies. All have to follow policy guidelines, pay taxes, obtain licenses, and so on. We take stock of these details in the following sections.

4. The Study Method

Tourism is a composite product, involving transport, accommodation, catering, entertainment, natural resources and other facilities and services such as shops and currency exchange. It differs from other products in that it cannot be examined prior to purchase and it cannot be stored; it involves an element of travel (Sinclair 1998). It is, however, useful to examine it not as an industry *per se* but as a collection of interrelated industries and markets. For the purpose of the present study, the components of tourism sector covered are: accommodation: hotels; eating places: restaurants/dhabas; transport activities: taxis, autorickshaws and cycle rickshaws; and guides. To a significant extent, these activities are located in the informal sector. There is no fixed definition of an informal enterprise. Nonetheless, following Papola (1981), an establishment employing up to 20 workers has been taken as an informal enterprise in this study.

The transport sector comprises transporters who own and operate luxury, ordinary or mini buses, and cars, both for tourist and other purposes. Then, there are travel operators who own and operate varying combination of the three types of buses, and cars for tourist purposes. These operators are generally a part of the formal sector. In the informal sector, there are numerous operators who own one or more than one cars which may be owner operated or driven by fixed salary employed drivers. These owners may also rent out their cars on daily basis. The other city transport vehicles are autorickshaws and cycle rickshaws. A single person may own autorickshaws whose number may vary from one to a few hundreds; in the case of cycle-rickshaws, the number may simply go to a thousand. So, we have owner-operated auto- and cycle-rickshaws mingled with those who rent them out on daily basis. We have surveyed only the individual operators, whether owners or plying vehicles-on-rent.

The hotel sector has two types of establishments: starred/approved and non-starred/non-approved. The labour market in the non-starred/non-approved hotels is largely informal and in this study we have only considered non-starred/non-approved hotels. The restaurants/dhabas mostly have less than 20 workers or are family-run enterprises. Finally, tourist guides are individual operators and there are two categories of them in tourism business: approved and non-approved guides. We have considered only approved guides because they undergo some formal procedures/training to become guides.

Various methods were used for eliciting information from different categories of informants, structured questionnaires, unstructured interviews and group- and individual discussions with people in the industry, to name a few. These interviews included union leaders, government tourism officials, hoteliers and so on. For structured interviews, from the list provided by the hotel associations in both the cities, 26 hotels were randomly selected (12 in Jaipur and 14 in Agra) (2). In the case of restaurants/dhabas, a total of 35 were selected: 20 from Jaipur and 15 from Agra. In the case of taxi owners/drivers, 20 each in Jaipur and Agra were selected, while among auto-rickshaw drivers, 50 in Jaipur and 30 in Agra were interviewed. The number chosen from Jaipur is more because Jaipur has much larger number of registered auto-rickshaws. Fifty cycle-rickshaw pullers were interviewed in Jaipur and 30 in Agra. The effort was to cover all locations within the city. In Jaipur, both state level and regional level approved guides are 175 while in Agra their number is 98. From amongst these guides, we have selected 16 from Jaipur and 10 from Agra, for in-depth interviews. The selection of respondents has been random in all cases.

5. Accommodation: Hotels

The most vital component for tourism is provision of suitable accommodation for various categories of tourists. As tourists are not a homogeneous lot of people, accommodation ranging from budget and economy class to 5 star and resorts is under demand (3). Hotel accommodation is characterized by fixed capacity, associated fixed costs and economies of scale at the level of both individual establishment and hotel chain (Sinclair 1998). Perhaps, such economies could be reaped by hotels more effectively at the upper-end of the scale. The enterprises in the informal sector are largely individual outfits, having a weak integration between formal sector hotels and tour operators and travel agents.

5.1 Hotel Owners: Personal Features

In Jaipur and Agra, the informal sector hotels are mainly proprietary type of enterprises, and only in 4 cases in Jaipur, partnership was reported. The owners are largely middle aged individuals: the average age of hoteliers is 45 years (Table 3). The proprietors in Jaipur are relatively young, compared to those in Agra. The hotel industry is a male preserve only, as all but one hotel owner are males. The hotel industry in India has been traditionally a family affair and no need was ever felt for hoteliers to under-go hotel management training. Even the formal education in most cases is low. In Jaipur and Agra, this apparently is true as a majority of the hoteliers have graduation or lower level of education, and not much difference in education levels is noticed in these two cities. However, a minuscule number reportedly had obtained diplomas from the local universities in hotel- and tourism-management. This reinforces the argument that tourism, when operated by family or owner managed enterprises at small scale, requires relatively low levels of skills and entrepreneurship (Weiermair and Fuchs, 1998). In this sense, expansion of tourism helps in reducing unemployment, particularly unemployment of low-skilled youth and, at the same time, helps creation of self-employment.

TABLE 3 : **Age of Hotel Owners (Years)**

City	Mean Age	N	Minimum	Maximum
Total	45	26	25	72
Jaipur	40	12	26	55
Agra	49	14	25	72

Source: Own survey.

The father's occupation is considered an indicator of family background (Singh 1983). Table 4 shows that fathers of most hoteliers have been in some business activity (a higher proportion in Agra), followed by government/private service, agriculture and the same occupation as the respondent himself (a link in the hotel profession through the family). It may, however, be mentioned here that quite a few had been working in the hotel sector for a number of years before setting up their own establishment. A mingle of an outward mobility from parental occupations, and an upward shift from other occupations is thus in evidence.

TABLE 4 : **Number of Owners by Fathers' Occupation**

Fathers' Occupation	Jaipur	Agra	Total
Service	4	4	8
Agriculture	2	0	2
Business	5	9	14
Same	1	1	2
Total	12	14	26

Source: Own survey.

5.2 Nature of Hotels

The location of an enterprise is very important from a business point of view. It was ascertained as to what influenced the choice of location of the hotel. The choice of the hotel-site was influenced mainly by location of own land, availability of cheap land, posh area, hotel area in the city, nearness to tourist spot and nearness to bus stand or a railway station. Location is thus critical for better and regular business.

Since both the cities have their own distinct historical background, they have been receiving tourists for long, and therefore the hotel industry should be quite old in these cities. We find that the majority of hotels in both the cities are in operation for 5 or more years. However, in Agra, the proportion of older hotels is more than in Jaipur. The oldest hotel is 30 years old and the newest one is just 2 years old. This means that a fillip to hotel industry came only in recent years.

These small operators have not constructed the hotels in a single setting: the construction has been spread over a number of years. In both the cities, the earnings from the enterprise have been ploughed back for expansion. The hotel size varies significantly both within and between the two cities. The size of the hotel is measured in terms of the number of rooms available for occupancy. The combined number of rooms in these hotels is 444 rooms, the smallest hotel has 5 rooms and the biggest one has 40 rooms. The size of hotels in Agra is smaller than that in Jaipur. Of these 444 rooms, 114 are ordinary, 219 air-cooled and 111 are air- conditioned. These hotels have four types of rooms, viz., double, single, family and suites for different categories of customers. This categorization is necessary for these hotels because in the case of group-tourists, the demand for dormitories (family rooms) is fairly high because of lower tariff rates.

5.2.1 Occupancy Rates

The occupancy rates of these hotels range between 30 to 80 per cent (Table 5) and these are influenced by various factors viz., tourist traffic, seasonal rush, location, upkeep of rooms, nature of rooms, hotel service, weather conditions, nearness to Delhi and (in the case of Agra) closure of Taj at night, tariff rates, concessions offered, availability and quality of food, number of tourist sites to be visited (especially around Agra), package tours of Delhi, water and power availability, poor sanitation and cleanliness, more fast trains linking Delhi, law and order problem, extent of publicity, networking with travel agencies, existence of entertainment programmes and other attractions in these cities to hold back the tourists, airport facilities and international flights and finally, the budget of the tourist (4). The uncontrolled tourism mafia (touts) negatively affects the occupancy rate and its control would go a long way in enhancing the occupancy rates. It is stressed that lack of information about hotel sites with the clients also is partly responsible. There are no facilities available for outstation bookings, and above all, cut throat competition among hotels in this segment of hotel industry affects occupancy rates. These hoteliers pay commission to taxi, auto- and cycle-rickshaw pullers to bring customers (5).

TABLE 5 : **Occupancy Rates**

Occupancy Rates %	Jaipur	Agra	Total
30-50	8	13	21
50 plus	4	1	5
Total	12	14	26

Source: Own survey.

5.2.1.1 Marketing Strategies

What are the marketing processes of these hotels? These hoteliers adopt a variety of means to attract customers. It is reported that customers come direct to most of the hotels in both the cities. The reason for this is that foreign tourists use guide books and go to those hotels which are listed in the guide books. Domestic tourists either go direct to the hotels to avoid **touts** (it is always felt that if they go through touts,they may end up paying higher room rent) or the old customer of the hotel introduces the hotel to the new customer. Besides, in case of group tourists, for example Bengali or Gujaratis, the preference is for hotels which have family rooms and some facility for cooking, as they generally like to do their own cooking.

A small number of hotels also receive customers through travel agencies with advance booking. In this limited sense, there is a vertical integration of hotels with travel agencies/tour operators. These are invariably the new customers. This linkage needs to be strengthened. The touts - taxi, auto- and cycle- rickshaw pullers - are the major source through which these hotels get their customers. This is more so in Agra and relatively less in Jaipur due to locational advantage of hotels in Jaipur. The hotels in Jaipur are generally near the railway station or the bus stand. It is also a fact that no hotel turns back customers brought in through these individuals despite the fact that commission has to be paid; they know that if they do not take the customers in, the rivals would. The *modus operandi* is that these individuals take customers from one hotel to another till the customer settles in a room. Invariably 5- 6 hotels are visited. In most cases, these individuals do not charge the customer for taking them to various hotels. In other words, these do indirect marketing for the hotels. Ironically, all hoteliers do want an end to this practice while they are the ones to promote the same. It is also observed that these hoteliers hardly advertise except for putting up a sign board on the main road or putting in an advertisement in local daily. Most of these hotels are also do not figures in the guide books.

5.3 Income From Hotels

The nature of hotel industry is such that income flows to investment are not constant. There are fixed costs which are not divisible and at times work-force has to be hired in excess of the current requirement. It is also known that in this segment of the hotel industry, most hotels are price takers in the product market and there is a risk of losing the market. We have tried to ascertain what is the gross monthly incomes which informal sector hoteliers earn in both the cities (the figures quoted are indicative only). The gross monthly income as reported by these hoteliers range between Rs.10,000 to Rs.0.25 million (Table 6). It is found that, on an average, these hoteliers earn Rs.76,786 per month; income accruing to hoteliers in Jaipur is higher than those in Agra. What is the contribution of workers in this gross income i.e. per worker income generated? In these hotels, the per worker gross income is Rs.12,952 at the aggregate level, Rs.18,830 in Jaipur and Rs.5,278 in Agra. It simply means that the workers in Jaipur help generate higher incomes for the hoteliers compared to those in Agra.

TABLE 6 : **Gross Monthly Income from Hotels (Rs.)**

City	Mean Income	N	Min	Max
Total	76786	14	10000	250000
Jaipur	126429	7	35000	250000
Agra	27143	7	10000	50000

Source: Own survey.

5.4 Taxes and Union

The local bodies in these cities charge hotel license fee which has recently been hiked from a low of Rs.25 to Rs.2500 annually. In Jaipur, all hoteliers are members of the local hotel association. However, in Agra not all are members of the hotel associations. The common reason for becoming a member of a hotel association is that the it helps in fighting for the cause of hotel industry (6). The opinion among some hoteliers though is that most of the times the association serves largely the interests of the office bearers only.

5.5 Work Force and Wages

It is time now to analyze the nature of work-force and the conditions under which it works in the informal sector hotels. In this industry, the labour market is informal, although to an extent, the industry is formal as the owners are organized, and capital investment is much higher than with most of the informal sector enterprises. Moreover, due to seasonality in the output of this industry, employment and hours worked are adjusted by the employers. The labour market is more flexible in the sense that a hotel worker performs varied jobs like managing the counter, serving refreshments to customers and also managing commercial/marketing aspects. In what follows, we focus on some of these aspects and the information provided is only indicative due to small size of the sample. Nonetheless, the discussion does adequately reflect on the nature of the labour market in these hotels.

5.5.1 The Work Force

The informal hotel industry has basically two types of staff: managerial and non-managerial. The non-managerial staff is generally temporary and is mostly unskilled. The managerial staff is trusted by the hotelier and is given long term employment. Often, the educational level of the managerial staff is matriculation and above, while the non-managerial employees are either illiterate or have fairly low levels of formal education. A majority of non-managerial staff is from rural areas and in almost all cases, the present job is the second or the third one. It was also noticed that most of these employees are in the city without family members and so stay in the hotel premises itself. These individuals have obtained the present employment largely through contacts and some had to produce a reference for security. There is some screening of the employees and it is done by putting them on probation ranging from a few days to weeks.

Most of these hotels are proprietary managed, though quite a few (10 out of 26) appoint managers for a wage. In our sample, of the 40 persons managing the hotels, 30 are proprietors and 10 are hired managers. In Jaipur, a higher proportion of hotels hire managers on salary compared to those in Agra (Table 7). The total non-managerial staff in these hotels is 108, ranging from cooks to sweepers. The average number of non-managerial workers per hotel is 4.2 persons. In Jaipur, 12 hotels employ 55 non-managerial workers, with an average of 4.6 persons per hotel. In Agra, 14 hotels hire 53 non-managerial workers at an average of 3.8 persons per hotel. The workers per hotel, thus, are higher in Jaipur than in Agra, which means that the labour market is larger in Jaipur compared to Agra. The total number of persons employed (family and hired) in the selected hotels are 148, the average being 5.7 persons per hotel. In Jaipur, 12 hotels are operated by 79 persons (family and hired), with an average employment of 6.6 persons per hotel, while the total employment in Agra is of 69 workers giving an average of 4.9 persons per hotel.

TABLE 7 : **Employment in Hotels (No.)**

City	Managerial			Average No.	Non-Managerial		Total Work Force	Average No.
	Family	Hired	Total		Hired	Average No.		
Jaipur	16	8	24	2.0	55	4.6	79	6.6
Agra	14	2	16	1.1	53	3.8	69	4.9
Total	30	10	40	1.5	108	4.2	148	5.7

Source: Own survey.

Women are not employed at all in these hotels. This is because of the long and unspecified working hours besides a host of social reasons. Hoteliers also fear that in case of a mishap (say, a client getting involved with the female staff), the hotel gets a bad name. Children are also not employed in these hotels.

5.5.2 Wage Rates

At any point of time, for a typical hotel, the supply of labour is unlimited while the demand is fixed. This situation should reflect in low wages paid to the employees: these wages have to be lower than the market wages. There is no bargaining for a higher wage by the workers. However, an experienced hand in the same business is paid a higher wage. Family members are not paid any wages.

Hired managers are paid very low wages, ranging from a low of Rs.1500 to a high of Rs.6000 per month. The average wage paid to the managerial staff is Rs.2610. The average wage for managerial staff in Jaipur is higher than that in Agra (Table 8). The wages paid to non-managerial staff are lower than those paid to the managerial staff. The average wage rate ranges from Rs.900 to Rs.3000 per month. The per worker wage in Jaipur turns out to be Rs.1228 compared to Rs.1297 in Agra. For both together, the average wage is Rs.1261. This means that hotel industry workers in Jaipur get somewhat lower wages compared to those working in Agra. It may be pointed out here that the wage earned by this temporary work-force is not much different from casual workers in these cities, which in turn is closer to the prevalent minimum wage. These wages, it seems, are determined by prevalent wage rates in the market. The non-managerial employees are compensated by tips from the customers of the hotel. The employer also pays a part of the wages in kind generally in terms of free meals and a space to sleep in the hotel.

TABLE 8 : **Wages to Employees: Rs. per Month**

City	Wages/ Month		Non-managerial	
	Managerial	Non-managerial	Min	Max
Jaipur	2638	1228	900	2000
Agra	2500	1297	1000	3000
Total	2610	1261	900	3000

Source : Own survey.

5.6 Working Conditions

The working conditions are not so satisfactory in the informal hotel industry. The working hours are long for the hotel employees, normally extending beyond 12 hours. As most workers sleep in the hotel premises, their availability is assured for 24 hours. Most hotels do not provide extra room for its workers. The relationship with the employer is cordial, but the workers are always on their toes because wages are cut or job could be lost for mistakes committed. The employees are not provided with any uniform. Social security, medical benefits and insurance are conspicuous by their absence unlike in the case of the formal sector workers. This is despite the fact that the law requires provident fund provisioning for temporary employees too. The plea taken by the hoteliers is that if provident fund deductions are made then the employees' gross income would fall.

There are no unions of hotel workers either in Agra or Jaipur. A major reason for this is the insecurity and lack of contact with each other. The trade union leadership in these two cities is also not concerned because they feel that the number of employees in each enterprise is small and the enterprises are wide spread in the city. This makes it difficult to organize the work-force. To make matters worse, the employment is of short duration/temporary. There is a fairly high turn-over of employees in these hotels. Despite the fact that wages are low and other benefits are not available, these employees continue to work because the worker here is not taken to be unskilled manual labourers, which in itself carries some prestige.

6. Restaurants

After accommodation, the most important component of tourism industry are the eating and drinking places at the tourist sites. The tourist looks for safe and reasonably priced eating places. There are restaurants and dhabhas, which cater to different classes of customers. These are largely in the informal sector. The formal sector hotels have their own restaurants, but most of the informal sector hotels have none. The tourists too, in serach of variety, like to eat outside. In this section, we look at the restaurants and dhabas in the two cities. Here again, the discussion is in two parts: one regarding restaurants themselves and the second on the work-force employed in the same.

6.1 The Enterprises: Age, Location and Investment

In both the cities, the restaurants are proprietor-run enterprises. A majority of these enterprises have been in business for 10 or lesser number of years. The restaurants in Jaipur have been in existence for relatively longer durations: 18 years in Jaipur and 10 years in Agra (Table 9). Even in the case of restaurants, the location is important for business. The reasons for selecting the present site are: own land, vicinity to bus stand and railway station, nearness to tourist locations, availability of land at the present site within the budget and availability of government constructed accommodation.

6.1.1 Investment

The fixed capital investment in the informal sector originates usually from family sources or informal credit market (ILO 1991), while the working capital comes from the current income accruing from the enterprise. The fixed capital investment at the time of setting up the venture (reported by 14 of the 35 restaurant owners)

TABLE 9 : **Years Since Established: Restaurants**

City	Years of Establishment		Total	Mean
	Below 10	10 Plus		
Jaipur	9	11	20	17.6
Agra	12	3	15	10.3
Total	21	14	35	14.5

Source : Own survey.

is Rs.0.521 million, which translates to an average investment of Rs.37,179 per enterprise. In Jaipur, the average fixed capital investment is higher than that in Agra. The fixed investment depends on year of construction, location, size of the restaurant and nature of furniture, crockery and other fixtures. Here again, it is important to note that investment is not made at a time but staggered over a period of time. The earnings from the venture have been ploughed back into the business by most of the enterprises since their inception. There is a wide variation in investment among the chosen restaurants.

What are the sources of this investment? As stated earlier, investment in fixed assets is largely from own sources. Own funds accounted for around 62 per cent of total fixed investment; in Jaipur, the contribution is 53.0 per cent and in Agra all the investment is reported to be from own sources. Neither formal nor informal credit markets have played any role in the development of restaurants in these cities. Finance from the formal sector is limited because of lengthy procedures, reluctance on the part of the entrepreneurs to approach the banks, and low education levels of entrepreneurs deterring them from approaching the banks. On the other hand, high interest rates in the informal credit market are a major deterrent.

The working capital requirement of the informal enterprises is not very high and is met largely from daily earnings and sales.

6.2 The Owners: A Background

Who are the people who run these enterprises? All owners of restaurants originate from urban areas and are males. In general, very few women run the restaurants/dhabas in India. In this case too, there is only one widow running a restaurant in Jaipur; earlier, her husband used to run the enterprise. The age of the restaurants/dhabas owners ranges widely from as low as 21 years to as high as 70 years. The owners in Jaipur are relatively older than those in Agr, the average age being 39 years. Further, a majority of restaurants/dhabas owners are married, and presumably helped by their spouses, albeit indirectly, in their business.

The entrepreneurs possess the basic qualifications. Nonetheless, since most are young and have been in business for some time, the education level is expected to be low. We find that a majority of these entrepreneurs possesses 10 years or less of schooling, and only a minuscule proportion holds a graduate degree, in either of the cities.

For most of the respondents, the running of a restaurant/dhaba has been a part of the family's tradition of being in some kind of business; there is only one owner with diploma in hotel management. It is reinforced by the fact that fathers of 11 of the 34 selected restaurant/dhaba owners were running a restaurant

(Table 10). The fathers of another 18 restaurant/dhaba owners were in some business. For the rest, the father's occupation was agriculture or service. To some extent, therefore, our data exhibit inter-generational occupational mobility among the restaurant/ dhaba owners.

TABLE 10 : **Father's Occupation**

Father's Occupation	Jaipur	Agra	Total
Same	11	-	11
Service	2	1	3
Business	6	12	18
Agriculture	1	1	2
Total	20	14	34

Source: Own survey.

6.3 Clientele and Income

These informal sector restaurants get their clients directly; only one restaurant is reported to have advertised itself. The restaurants are frequented by local people, and lower and economy class tourists. In this sense, there are limited direct links with the travel agencies, guides etc. However, quite a few restaurants get clients also through travel agents and guides (perhaps touts also). This practice is prevalent more in Agra compared to Jaipur. The agents/touts would take the tourists only to fixed eating places in return for some commission often paid in terms of free meals or a token cash amount. The auto-rickshaw drivers and cycle-rickshaw pullers are also involved in this network, and often tourists who do not know their whereabouts in the city, end up getting guided by them. In Jaipur, the concentration of such restaurants is near the bus stand and railway station. Most hotels are situated within one sq. km area; as a result, customers are not taken for a ride by these intermediary elements.

In Jaipur, the reported gross monthly income varies between Rs.5,000 and Rs.40,000, while in Agra it ranges between Rs.9,000 and Rs.0.10 million (Table 11). The average income works out to be Rs.25,800 per month. In Jaipur, the total income accruing to 14 reporting enterprises is Rs.0.265 million or Rs.18,929 per restaurant per month, while in Agra, the gross income reported by 6 restaurants is Rs.0.251 million or Rs.41,833 per restaurant per month. This implies that, on an average, the restaurants generate higher income in Agra compared to Jaipur.

TABLE 11 : **Gross Monthly Income per Restaurant (Rs.)**

City	Mean	N	Min	Max
Total	25,800	20	5,000	1,00,000
Jaipur	18,929	14	5,000	40,000
Agra	41833	6	9000	1,00,000

Source: Own survey.

6.4 Food Type and Quality

These restaurants provide a variety of foods: North Indian, Rajasthani, Punjabi, South Indian and continental foods. However, the quality of food varies markedly across individual enterprises. In most restaurants, the cleanliness is far from the desired levels. The customer is not informed of what is the cooking medium and its quality; the waiters do not exhibit hygienic habits; the quality of water is usually contaminated; the crockery is invariably not properly cleaned and maintained, and so on (7). All restaurants do try to keep the surrounding clean every day, but the general cleanliness is found wanting. This is especially so in Agra.

6.5 Work Force and Wage Rates

The informal sector restaurants are mainly self-managed; the proportion of hired managers is rather negligible. The total number of persons employed in the interviewed restaurants was 199, of whom family members constituted 37 (Table 12). It comes to 5.6 persons per enterprise. In Jaipur, the average number per enterprise is 6.3 workers compared to 4.9 workers in Agra. Of the hired work-force, there is one manager and 160 non-managerial workers. The non-managerial helpers work as cooks and waiters; invariably, there is one cook in each of these restaurants though at times, the owner too performs this task. On an average, the restaurants in Jaipur employ a higher number of workers. As stated earlier, none of the restaurants has female workers. There are, though, 6 child workers employed in two enterprises; these children wash the dishes and clean the tables.

The workers are not first time migrants to the city. All have been engaged in some other activity earlier. The work-force is exclusively male, again because of long and stretched working hours and prevalent social practice. The workers are employed with little screening though, in some cases, having a contact is important. Some owners do ask for reference and previous work experience with some other restaurant.

TABLE 12 : **Employment in Restaurants (No.)**

City	Family Labour Managerial	Hired Labour Managerial	Others	Total Workers	Average Employment
Jaipur	22	-	103	125	6.3
Agra	15	1	58	74	4.9
Total	37	1	161	199	5.6

Source : Own survey.

6.5.1 Wage Rates

The supply of labour is elastic in this segment of the tourism sector, while the demand is limited. This situation keeps wages low. As the labour is mainly unskilled, this further pulls down the wage rate. The unskilled workers are paid a lower wage than the skilled worker. The wages are also influenced by market wage rate of casual labourers in the city. Other reasons for low wages are that these workers mostly eat and sleep in the restaurant premise and that they raise additional earnings from tips. These considerations too put a downward pressure on the wages.

The cash wage rate varies from a low of Rs.500 to a high of Rs.3,000 per month. The average wage paid to a restaurant worker in Jaipur ranges between a low of Rs.500 to a high of Rs.3,000 while in Agra, the minimum is Rs.1000 and the maximum is Rs.2,500. All the family members employed are not paid wages. Child workers are paid much lower wages, just about Rs.500 per month, despite the fact that working hours are the same as for their adult counterparts.

6.6 Work Conditions

In these enterprises, the work-force is temporary and nearly totally employed as casual workers. There is a high turnover of workers. Consequently, except for the cook, the other categories of workers are removed from the job even under a small pretext or damage. However, there are certain workers who continue to work for years together. Deductions from wages are made if damages are done and if the employee goes on leave, even if it is for medical reasons. There is no social security for the workers in the form of medical cover, insurance, leave, provident fund, etc. In most cases, workers are not provided with uniforms. In either city, there is no workers' union in these restaurants. The state is also indifferent to them; labour department invariably looks the other way whenever problems arise. Working hours are long: 18 hours a day. However, there is some respite from work in-between meals when customers are not around. On the whole, the working conditions are pretty poor, possibly as poor here as in most other wage-paid informal sector jobs.

No wonder, therefore, the workers having resigned to be at the receiving end of the labour market, enjoy 'a cordial relationship' with their employers.

6.7 Some Ratios

The informal sector enterprises are invariably labour intensive. The fixed capital per worker in these restaurants is estimated to be Rs.7,331; it is Rs.8,510 in Jaipur and Rs.4,524 in Agra. In Jaipur, the fixed capital per worker ranges between a low of Rs.500 to a high of Rs.22,757, while in Agra, the range is from Rs.3,333 and Rs.8,510. Sharp variability thus do exist within the informal sector. The ratio of gross income to fixed capital is estimated at 0.435 i.e. every rupee of fixed investment generates Rs.0.435 of income in Jaipur while in Agra it generates a much higher income of Rs.1.432. When gross income is taken to be a proxy for gross output, productivity per worker (income generated per person employed) works out to Rs.2,619 per month. In Jaipur, the corresponding productivity is Rs.2,090, while it is Rs.3480 in Agra. This is to say that work-force is more productive in Agra compared to that in Jaipur.

7. Transport Activities

This sector is another important segment of the tourism industry. Provision of road transport facilities within the country/city and from place to place is a necessary obligation of the host country/city. All tourists use road transport either for travel inside the cities they visit or for travelling to tourist destinations. Most of the transport used by tourists is provided by the private sector. Car taxis, auto- and cycle-rickshaws too play an important role in the tourism industry. They are mainly in the informal sector. They do not face serious handicaps in their business vis-a-vis the organized operators except that they face a lot of competition, both from within and without.

The labour market is highly unorganized, especially in auto- and cycle-rickshaw segments. There is a significant section of transport operators who drive hired vehicles. The entry is easy; investment levels are low; there are no fixed locations of operation; there is very limited dependence on the formal sector credit institutions; earnings are relatively unstable; and so on.

The nature of the job is also flexible and does not require much skill for entry. Lack of employment avenues in rural areas and limited opportunities in the cities drive individuals, especially those from the lower socio-economic strata into self-employed activities in the transport sector, invariably with the pulling of cycle-rickshaw to begin with. There is also very little problem in acquiring a driving license for a car and/or an auto-rickshaw. To understand what is really happening in this informal component of tourism sector, an attempt is to look at these three transport activities which, in their own way, contribute significantly to the tourism sector.

7.1 Area of Operation

Car taxis operate from railway station and from their assigned stands in the city, while the auto-and cycle-rickshaws operate from and to railway station, bus stand and various vintage points near the hotels, street corners and tourist spots. It is beneficial to operate from a fixed location as it is easy to get both business and parking space. The customer can also approach through telephone. There are no other fixed stands/locations for cycle rickshaws.

7.2 Who Are They?

Transport sector is primarily a male's preserve in India, Jaipur and Agra being no exception. All taxi owners/drivers, auto- and cycle-rickshaw pliers are males. This is because of social factors and also because of physically hard and highly demanding nature of work.

The average age of the taxi drivers is 36 years. The drivers in Agra are younger than those in Jaipur (Table 13). The auto-rickshaw drivers are relatively younger (average age 32 years); those in Agra are younger than in Jaipur. It is cheaper to hire a cycle-rickshaw. Since no license is required, one finds individuals of all ages plying cycle rickshaws, practically in all parts of the city. Most workers interviewed are married.

TABLE 13 : **Age of Transport Sector Operators (Years)**

City	Cycle-rickshaw		Auto-rickshaw		Car Taxis	
	Age	No	Age	No	Age	No
Jaipur	30.9	50	33.9	50	38.5	20
Agra	32.2	30	29.8	30	33.4	20
Total	31.4	80	32.4	80	35.9	40

Source: Own survey.

7.2.1 Skill Levels

People enter into these segments of the labour market at a relatively young age due to family stresses. As a result, their formal education level remains low. Our survey discovers that a majority of taxi drivers have schooling of 10 years or below (Table 14). There are illiterate taxi drivers too. The level of education of drivers is lower in Jaipur than in Agra. The education level of auto-rickshaw drivers compared to taxi drivers is even lower; only 8 per cent have had schooling beyond 10 years. In Jaipur, 16 per cent of auto-drivers are illiterate compared to 27 per cent in Agra. Up to 44 per cent auto-rickshaw drivers in Jaipur have received either no education or little education. This proportion is 47 per cent in Agra. The education levels of cycle rickshaw pullers are the lowest; only one driver possesses 10 or more years of schooling. In our sample, there are 44 per cent of cycle-rickshaw pullers in Jaipur who are illiterate compared to 57 per cent in Agra. Besides, 32 per cent of cycle-rickshaw pullers in Jaipur are primary or lower level educated, while one-fifth of cycle-rickshaw pullers in Agra fall in this category. This means that a significant proportion of cycle-rickshaw pullers in Jaipur and Agra have either no education or very low level of education.

TABLE 14 : **Education Level of Transport Sector Operators (Years)**

Education	Jaipur				Agra				Total			
	I	II	III	Total	I	II	III	Total	I	II	III	Total
Illiterate	22	8	2	32	17	8	4	29	39	16	6	61
Upto 5	16	18	7	41	6	6	1	13	22	24	8	54
6 to 10	11	23	6	40	7	11	10	28	18	34	16	68
Above 10	1	1	5	7	1	5	4	10	2	6	9	17
Total	50	50	20	120	30	30	20	80	80	80	40	200

Note : I- cycle-rickshaw, II- auto-rickshaw and III- car taxi.
Source: Own survey.

The above data clearly show that the transport sector is a source of employment for the less educated. The simpler and cheaper is the vehicle, lesser is the education of its driver. In India, the cycle- rickshaw plying is generally considered a low grade, menial job. Nevertheless, it is an activity that involves hard physical labour. Most of these drivers cannot speak English, at least not so easily, and it hinders their communication with non-hindi speaking tourists. The taxi- and auto-drivers, on the other hand, have motor driving skills; they also have knowledge of machines and are in a position to do minor repairs on their own.

7.2.2 Background of Drivers

We have observed that the education levels of most operators are low because of their family background. It is also noted that father's occupation in respect of most of these drivers is mainly agriculture, wage labour and service. The other occupations in which fathers' have been involved are artisan, cycle-rickshaw pulling and auto-rickshaw driving (Table 15). This again reveals that the background of most drivers is similar in both the cities minor variations notwithstanding. Another point that emerges here is that there is some inter-generational upward occupational mobility. Most individuals originally come from a poor socio-economic background and not much difference is discernible across the activities and cities.

The inter-city differences in the rural background of these drivers need to be underlined. In both the cities, most of the taxi operators and nearly the whole lot of auto-drivers are currently living in the city. However, a majority of cycle-rickshaw pullers in Jaipur are migrants from rural areas, other districts, other states and some even from Nepal (Table 16). This is not so in Agra where majority have been residents of the same city for a fairly long period; this is cent per cent so in the case of auto-rickshaw drivers. The major reason for migration to Jaipur city has been to look for better employment.

TABLE 15 : **Drivers by Fathers' Occupation**

Father's Occupation	Jaipur				Agra			
	I	II	III	Total	I	II	III	Total
Artisan	2	1	1	4	1	3		4
Shopkeeping	3	2	4	9	1	8	2	11
Wage labour	20	11	2	33	8	5	2	15
Agriculture	19	11	3	33	6	5	3	14
Service	5	19	6	30	9	7	10	26
Cycle rickshaw	1	4		5	5	1	1	7
Auto - drvier	-	2	4	6		1	2	3
Total	50	50	20	120	30	30	20	80

Note : I- cycle-rickshaw, II- auto-rickshaw and III- car-taxi.
Source: Own survey.

TABLE 16 : **Origin of Drivers**

Origin	Jaipur				Agra			
	I	II	III	Total	I	II	III	Total
Same City	11	50	17	78	20	30	17	67
Rural	4			4	3		1	4
Other Districts	11		3	14	2		2	4
Other States	23			23	5			5
Nepal	1			1				
Total	50	50	20	120	30	30	20	80

Note : I- cycle-rickshaw, II- auto-rickshaw and III- car-taxi.
Source: Own survey.

7.3 Ownership and Investment Pattern

To drive a self-owned vehicle gives added prestige. In the informal sector, the new entrants initially drive hired vehicles and subsequently purchase a vehicle either with own savings or through borrowing from informal or formal sector institutions. Our survey found that cars are mostly self-owned and operated; the proportion of drivers working on wage-paid basis, or of those who hire cars on a daily basis, is very small. There is an increasing tendency, however, to purchase the vehicle as finance is now becoming available through various formal sector channels. Auto-rickshaws are within the reach of many prospective drivers. In these cities, there are individuals who have auto-rickshaws in large numbers and they rent them out. In Jaipur, 56 per cent of sample auto-rickshaw drivers own the vehicle they drive. This proportion is 47 per cent in Agra. Others operate hired auto-rickshaws. Cycle-rickshaws too are plied by both, owners and those taking on rent. In Jaipur, 18 per cent of cycle-rickshaw pullers are owners of their vehicle; this proportion is 30 per cent in Agra. Others operate hired cycle rickshaws. This implies that costlier and more mechanical the vehicle is, higher is the possibility of it being owned; this cannot, however, be generalized unless hard data are available to support it. Finally, a strong rentier class exists in the formal sector, on which a continuing dependence of the informal sector operators is a hard and non-dismissible reality.

Of the three modes of transport, the cheapest is the cycle rickshaw followed by auto-rickshaw and cars, in that order. There is a tendency to purchase a second hand vehicle, at a fairly lower cost. The cycle rickshaws are locally assembled, while the auto-rickshaws are of two models: Bajaj and Lambretta. Cars are mainly Ambassadors, though a few new brands are also plying. There are very few air conditioned cars in operation in the informal sector. In general,the physical condition of auto-rickshaws and cycle-rickshaws is not good; the auto-rickshaws are particularly notorious from the point of view of pollution.

What is the source of investment? A majority borrows from varied sources (Table 17). There is no contribution from banks in the case of cycle rickshaws, though banks have financed auto-rickshaws and cars. Own funds are an important source in the case of cycle rickshaws (50 to 100 per cent share in total cost). This is slightly lower in the case of auto-rickshaws and cars. Relatives too are depended upon for extending loans. The role of non-institutional sources is vital in the case of cycle-rickshaws in the sense that either it is fully financed by owner/manufacturer or it is not financed at all. Contribution of the non-financial institutions (NFIs) in the case of auto- rickshaw ranges between 51 and 100 per cent and in the case of cars, from 25 to 100 per cent. The NFIs are dealers, manufacturers, and businessmen in the city, who regularly lend to informal sector entrepreneurs. These individuals charge high rates of interest (ranging between 24 to 36 per cent]. They become important if a second hand vehicle is to be purchased, which is the practice in many cases. This means that the credit linkages with both formal and informal credit markets do exist, with variations across the type of vehicles.

TABLE 17 : **Source of Finance**

Operator	Range of Finance [%]			
	Own	Bank	Relatives	NFIs
Cycle rickshaw	50-100	-	0-100	0-100
Autorickshaw	10-60	0-100	0-100	51-100
Car Taxi	10-100	71-100	33-67	25-100

Note : NFI : non-financial institutions.
Source: Own survey.

7.4 Work Environment

For most of the functionaries, the nature of work is such that it entails long working hours; in both the cities, these extend beyond 12 hours a day. However, the owner operator has the flexibility either to reduce his working hours or increase them. The hours worked has direct relationship with the income earned. In the case of taxi drivers, this depends on the client and the locations they visit, or else, sheer wait for a customer. In many cases, on many days, they idle around without any business: this is less so for auto rickshaws/cycle rickshaws and more so for four wheeler taxis. Despite the fact that the working hours are long, many of these workers do not get any working facility at the stands. The driver also eats differently than the tourists he carries; only in rare cases they may eat at the same place. These drivers lose lot of sleep. There are no wash or toilet facilities readily available to them. The state highways are also generally devoid of most of the needed facilities.

There is a limited vertical integration of the informal sector taxi drivers with travel agencies and hotels. All taxi operators are members of taxi association and likewise, a majority of the auto-rickshaw drivers are members of the auto-drivers association. There is no union of cycle rickshaw pullers in either of the cities.

7.5 Running Expenses and Incomes

Income accrues to these drivers only if the vehicle is hired. When the vehicle is running, expenses have to be incurred on petrol/diesel, rent for hiring the vehicle and maintenance, permit fees and personal expenses. A taxi is available on rent to a driver for Rs.100 per day. The daily rent for a auto-rickshaw varies from Rs.50 to Rs.100 (for a spell of 12 hours a day), while that of a cycle rickshaw varies from a low of Rs.7 to a high of Rs.35. The rent depends upon the condition of the vehicle; the older the vehicle, the lower is the rent. The cycle rickshaw, therefore, is relatively cheaper to hire than the auto-rickshaw, which in turn is cheaper than a car taxi.

The running cost of a taxi depends on the business and kilometer done by the vehicle. The average running cost of a taxi in Jaipur is Rs.3,820 per month, which includes the cost of fuel, maintenance and other expenses, while in Agra it is Rs.3,367 (Table 18). The lower running cost in Agra is due to relatively newer cars, cheaper fuel and lesser distance clocked. In Jaipur, the monthly running expense of auto-rickshaws, on an average, amounts to Rs.2,794; it is Rs.2,655 in Agra. In this expenditure, the major contribution is of fuel followed by maintenance and personal expenses. Another expense is annual permit fee for taxis and auto-rickshaws. The taxis operate with all-India and state permits which give them permission to operate in a specified areas (8). The auto rickshaw drivers have local city permits for driving the vehicle (9). All auto-rickshaw drivers operate within the city, though occasionally some go outside as well. The cycle rickshaws have local bodies' registration and all cycle rickshaws pullers operate within the city.

TABLE 18. **Average Monthly Running Expenses (Rs.)**

City	Cycle-rickshaw	Auto-rickshaw	Car Taxi
Total	84	2,742	3650
Jaipur	72	2,794	3820
Agra	104	2,655	3367

Source: Own survey.

7.5.1 Income Levels

In the informal sector, the income levels are mostly low. The evidence as to the effectiveness of self-employment in informal businesses as a source of livelihood is conflicting, because of the very diversity of activities which the term embraces. The fact that informal incomes are, in many places, higher than those available from formal employment, is not necessarily an indication that they are good incomes (Harper 1996). The average monthly earnings of taxi drivers range between Rs.3,000 and Rs.15,000. In Jaipur, this is Rs.7,276 compared to Rs.8,900 in Agra. The higher income levels in Agra are due to low running expenses, more brisk business, less local competition and higher tariff rates. The average income earned by auto-rickshaw drivers is Rs.6,355 per month in Jaipur, while it is Rs.4,655 in Agra (Table 19). The lower income levels in Agra is posssibly due to greater competition in that city. There is an intense competition in the cycle rickshaw segment and it affects the income of operators. The average monthly income is Rs.3,424 in Jaipur while it is Rs.3,095 in Agra. The off-season incomes are relatively lower in all the three segments in both the cities. The incomes earned are determined by tariff rates too (10). Moreover, as the vehicle becomes more mechanical, the income accruals too go up.

TABLE 19 : **Monthly Income in Rs.**

Income	Jaipur				Agra			
	I	II	III	Total	I	II	III	Total
<3000	30	1	3	34	22	9	1	32
3000-6000	20	33	9	62	8	18	3	29
>6000		16	8	24	--	3	16	19
Total	50	50	20	120	30	30	20	80
Mean Income	34	24	6355	--	3095	4955	8900	--

Note : I- cycle-rickshaw, II- auto-rickshaw and III- car taxi.
Source: Own survey.

7.6 Conditions of Transport Sector

The quality of internal transport services are not of international standard. The taxi service is limited to a few car makes and most are non-airconditioned. The condition of most cars and auto-rickshaws is also not too good. The fares are, however, reasonable. The sustenance is tough for most individuals. The upward mobility within the transport sector is not very strong either. The linkages of this sector are largely with the informal repair activities, or eating places (11) and low grade housing (slums). A large number of these individuals are addicts of liquor and drugs. Most cycle rickshaw pullers and auto-drivers do not take care of personal hygiene and this deters passengers at times. The labour market is open and competitive in lower segments of this sector. It is restricted only in taxi segment due to higher cost of vehicles. However, jobs are available for able and experienced drivers and some do succeed in graduating to formal sector jobs.

8. Tourist Guides

The foregoing discussion has revealed important features of major tourism activities. The analysis is incomplete without having a look at the tourist guides who are vital cog in the wheel of tourism sector. This section presents details on tourist guides in Jaipur and Agra.

The institution of guides is a very basic component of the tourist services, both for international and domestic tourists. There has been a continuous flow of international tourists into India. Also, as a result of increasing affluence, domestic tourist movement has also increased. To cater to this increasing demand, a 3-tier system of guides was introduced in February 1996 by the Tourism Department of India. These are regional guides, state level guides and local guides. The first category is trained by the Ministry of Tourism, Government of India through tourist offices or by the Indian Institute of Tourism and Travel Management or by Indian Institute of Hotel Management. The second category is trained by State Governments, while the third group is trained under the supervision of the state government/local administration.

8.1 Who Are They?

Like other segments of the tourism sector, this segment too is exclusively a male bastion. Both in Jaipur and Agra, all tourist guides are males. The major reasons for this are social factors, long working hours and working conditions that generally cannot go well with female job aspirants. The average age of guides in our sample is 34 years; the Jaipur guides are relatively older compared to those in Agra.

8.1.1 Education and Skills

A licensed guide is supposed to be a graduate, and like many individuals in India, a majority in this profession are also over educated. A significant number (17 of 26) are post-graduates (Table 20). There are more post-graduate guides in Jaipur than in Agra. The knowledge of a foreign language is vital for their better performance. Quite a few have knowledge of a foreign language (12) other than English. The foreign languages known by this group are German, French, Italian and Chinese.

TABLE 20 : **Education Level of Guides**

Education	Jaipur	Agra	Total
Graduates	6	3	9
Above Graduation	10	7	17
Total	16	10	26

Source: Own Survey.

As regards training/courses related to tourism, all the guides have obtained training either from the Department of Tourism, Government of India or the State Tourism Departments. The duration of these courses varies from one month to 18 months, and a majority of them did the course in Jaipur and Delhi. These courses helped them in their career as they learnt about Tourism, Art and Culture. Some guides reported skill enhancement after joining the profession, in terms of articulation, leadership, oratory skills, group handling and coordination.

8.1.2 A Background

The profession does not seem to have many takers and those who have opted for this profession must have done so due to parental background and influence.

These individuals were asked to report on fathers' occupation. We find that fathers of a majority of guides were in service (government or private), followed by business/ agriculture. This means that these individuals come from urban and literate families and have witnessed some occupational mobility in their own life time.

8.2 Reasons for Choosing the Profession

Why did these individuals choose this occupation? The reasons are varied such as wanted to be a free lancer and thus be liberal and independent, to avail of the opportunity to explain to others the culture and history of the country, have deep interest in such activities, freedom from written work unlike in other office jobs, glamour of the profession, chance to travel and meet new people and make career, to ward off unemployment.

8.3 The Labour Market

The labour market is restricted in the case of tourist guides. The entrants not only are required to have a minimum education and age and have to clear a written test followed by interview, but also need to procure a license. The licenses are issued by the Indian Tourism Development Corporation (ITDC), Department of Tourism of India, State Tourism Departments, and local palaces and museums. Some guides have licenses from more than one organization. Government of India does not charge any license fee whereas the State Governments levy only a token fee. However, in the case of local palaces and museums, the annual license fee varies from Rs.250 to Rs.1500. There is no problem in obtaining the license, provided the conditions set by Tourism Department of India are fulfilled (13). It is governed by requirement of guides at a time, and from time to time, the tourism department flashes advertisements for guides' training courses. This procedure is not approved by guides' unions; they have been contesting it from different forums under the plea that certificates distributed have no bearing on the level and nature of market demand.

A majority of tourist guides work independently in Jaipur and Agra but most do also get work through hotels and travel operators (14). The top and middle level hotels have travel desks which provide assignments to these guides; these assignments could be to accompany group tourists or individual tourists. In this sense, they have strong vertical links with the formal sector. The guides, however, have a continuing resentment against the travel operators/agencies as the latter do not make timely payments, on a regular basis. At times, guides get their payments after 6 months; this problem is more acute in Agra. Due to this problem, they do not want to be attached to a particular agency.

A majority of the guides intend to continue with the profession primarily because not many alternative opportunities are available with their qualifications and skills. However, a few are willing to change their profession because of uncertain future and insecurity that they face. It is also observed that there has been upward mobility among guides. There are individuals who have graduated from being simple guides to group escorts and the experience of the profession has led some to set up export business. This has been possible due to contacts they were able to establish. There are guides who were initially employed on menial jobs in hotels, subsequently learnt foreign languages and graduated themselves to become guides. This led to a big increase in their income. In this sense, the profession does provide added opportunities to grow if hard work is put in.

8.4 Monthly Earnings

What are the net monthly earnings of tourist guides? Of course, the earnings vary from peak to slack tourist season. In this part of India, the tourist season starts from October and lasts till March. The monthly income, during these months, varies between Rs.5,000 and Rs.10,000. Most in Agra earn this level of income, while relatively fewer guides, in Jaipur are able to earn this much. A fairly sizeable proportion of guides, particularly in Jaipur, earn Rs.5,000 or less. Nonetheless, even in Jaipur, there are some guides who are reported to have an income of Rs. 10,000 or more. Generally, they work as escorts to foreign groups. On an average, the seasonal monthly income for tourist guides is estimated to be Rs.7,000, it being Rs.6,500 in Jaipur and Rs.7,700 in Agra. The off-season income declines appreciably. The rate of remuneration for services rendered is fixed as per the Government of India norms (15). During outstation travels, wages are higher but the guides have to bargain for this. Competence of the guide matters too. At times, the rates are also set by the Guides Association.

8.5 Work Environment

The working hours of guides are long and invariably extend beyond 10 hours, even if there is no tangible work at hand. There are days when they have no assignments. The Tourist Guides' Association, however, assures its members that all of them will get one or the other assignment. In the busy season, some guides are required to stay away from their families for fairly long durations, at times, for 10 or more days in a month. There is an extensive competition in the profession, both from within and from the unauthorized lot of guides. The guides in Agra face *lapkas,* the customer snatchers (16). Most guides reported that the unscrupulous operation of lapkas has resulted in a steady decline in their incomes over the years. The competition has forced the number of working days to go down; some reported decline in working days per month from 28 to 18. The guides also reported nepotism practiced by travel agencies in the profession. Most guides do not have their own offices; only the few senior guides have offices at their homes, fitted with modern telecommunication equipment. However, the union office is available for all, but then, except for the union leaders, none else is allowed to use the telecommunication facilities. In essence, the union office works as a queuing place for seeking assignments, mostly on day-to-day basis.

Tourist guides face lots of hindrances in their operation. Police harassment, delayed wage payment, hawkers nuisance, no job guarantee, lean work availability, insecurity, exploitation by travel agents/agencies, lack of public utilities, beggar nuisance, etc. are the more obvious among them.

Licensed guides have associations in Jaipur and Agra. However, few members take active interest in the Association. Nevertheless, the Association does help in protecting the rights and often sorts out problems of wage rates and payments with travel agents/agencies. Finally, there is no social security worth mentioning that is available to guides.

9. What Could Be Done?

By and large, the work-force in the informal tourism sector is economically unprotected and does not have a decent work environment. Overall, the workers have low education level, low skills, low productivity, low wages and poor work conditions. The labour is employed largely on temporary basis, without social and job security. The working hours are long and competition is intense. There are few, if any, links with the formal sector. There is scope for upward mobility, but the opportunities are limited. In this situation, what could be done to improve productivity, income levels and work environment? As all the activities are inter-related, directly and indirectly, any improvement would require both macro and micro policy initiatives. The ultimate aim of these policies should be to increase the inflow of tourists. At the macro level, the governments, both Central and State, need to have a clear cut tourism policy which directly creates conditions that lead to increased tourist inflows. The necessary steps are:

(1) **Improvement in infrastructure:** There is need to plough back a share of earnings from Tourism Sector for development of a good road network (inter-state and inter-city roads). The public utilities need to be constructed and made functional. The inter-state transport system, power supply, drinking water system need attention. The airports should have better facilities, improved working standards and some of them should be able to receive international flights. All this could be created with proper pricing of the utilities.

(2) **Tax structure:** The tax structure of the local bodies has to be rationalized. There should not by any *ad hocism* in taxes. This would help the hotels and restaurants in Tourism Sector. Presently levies are raised without proper notices; this needs correction.

(3) **Land policy:** The land policy for hotels and restaurants should be made more effective so that prospective entrepreneurs can make full use of it. If land is available at a distance, then local transport system should be beefed up. The location of hotels and restaurants in residential areas be permitted provided the needed guidelines are followed and the local community faces no hassles and expresses no reservations.

(4) **Accommodation:** One stumbling block in setting up budget hotels is the high cost of land; it accounts for more than half the construction costs. It is simply not viable to have budget hotels on expensive lands in the cities. Therefore, special provisioning is needed for development of these hotels. The Urban Land Ceiling Act also acts as a deterrent to hotel projects; it has to be made friendly to Tourism Sector.

(5) **Measures to Attract** holiday tourists, who are high-spenders. This group has to be specially targeted.

(6) **Improvement in Law and Order and Political Stability:** These contribute to a marked improvement in hotel occupancy rate which, in turn, boosts up all other associated activities.

(7) **Project Clearance Policy:** This is the biggest deterrent to the development of budget hotels in the country. The rules have to be made easy and simple.

(8) **Improvement in Centre-State Relations:** There are centre-state tussles, which act as deterrent for implementation of tourism development policies.

(9) **Improved Services:** The services rendered by the Tourism Department need considerable improvements. The offices should be managed by trained staff, who have an aptitude to help tourists. The tourism sector should be under one regulatory body, which has representatives from all concerned agencies/sections.

(10) **Training Institutions:** There is need for training institutions, which can cater to the demand for human resources. It should be all encompassing institution.

(11) **Community Involvement:** There is need for involving the local communities in maintaining local facilities and tourist spots. It would help in reducing the adverse impact of tourism sector on the local areas and people.

(12) **Tourism Legislation:** A selective and discrete tourism legislation is needed as is prevalent in other states to regulate the travel trade and insulate the unsuspecting tourists from the clutches of unscrupulous traders, hawkers and beggars.

(13) **Exploring Overseas Market:** Aggressive overseas marketing of Indian destinations is needed to attract tourists from abroad; in particular, air services between important cities of India and rich countries, especially those which send out tourists every year in large numbers, must be brought to international standards.

(14) **Local Care-taking:** At each place of tourist interest, tourist police needs to be posted to control local mafia. Taj may be kept open at night as well. The water of Jamuna river should be cleaned and a barrage built so that tourists can see the reflection of Taj in the water. There should be strict control on polluting vehicles around Taj. At present, it is not happening. The forts and palaces should be maintained properly to preserve our rich heritage. The entry tickets need to be reasonably priced. Bar licenses may be given in the tourist cities provided rules are adhered too. Road maps with important locations in and around the city may be available to tourists just for asking. It should be binding on the hotels to display the brochures about the city. These cities should have regular entertainment programmes and fairs to attract and hold the tourists back.

These steps would go a long way to improve the tourist traffic and help in the growth of the tourism sector and improve the livelihood of the people involved. More specifically, the labour market in the informal tourism sector should be allowed to grow. In this regard, the effort should be to strictly enforce the labour laws in the hotels and restaurants. The trade union movement should take initiative in this regard. For social protection and guaranteeing certain fundamental rights to these workers (hotels and restaurants), the employers' organizations have to play a key role. Workers themselves have to forge suitable links with other organizations. For example, SEWA (Self-employed Women's Association) in Ahmedabad has women registered with it and when any organization needs workers/help, it is SEWA that supplies labour for a price. SEWA itself pays regular salaries to the workers. This model could be adopted, with some locally applicable variations. This takes care of social security and security of jobs. Such an organization could also help in skill up-gradation. At the state level, minimum wage enforcement is a must. The number of enterprises in a city is not so large that it cannot be accomplished. The wage structure has to be linked to a number of hours worked, more so in the case of the unskilled workers. All hotels and restaurants should provide uniforms, better sleeping/resting places and toilet facilities for workers. Above all, these workers need to have a union like the ones existing in more established hotels and restaurants. Also, no hotel or restaurant should be allowed to employ workers who are not registered with employment exchange or other such bodies that can register prospective workers (17). In regard to food, besides the government food departments, the community and local associations should take the initiative. There must be a procedure to blacklist the enterprise that is found to serve bad food.

In the transport sector, special efforts are needed for improving the education and communication skills of drivers, especially the taxi and auto drivers. Here, the adult education centres would be a great help. There should be strict enforcement of hiring rates and control over unlicensed drivers. If the tariff rates are properly fixed, well publicized and implemented, then the queue system for vehicles can be adopted. At the stands, the auto- rickshaw and taxis follow the queue system, which is imposed by drivers themselves. In this practice, unions can be involved. The pre-paid taxi system, that has not been a success so far, need to be made functional. There has to be an order at the airports, railway stations, and bus stands. There are no facilities at the taxi stands either for the drivers or for passengers. Night and day shelters should be constructed for drivers' rest. On the highways too, most of such facilities are lacking. The petrol pumps should be forced to implement the provision of free water, toilet and air facilities. The unions should be involved in running health centres for the workers of the tourism sector. One hardly finds taxi drivers and auto-rickshaw drivers in a uniform. A clean dress gives a good impression to a tourist. The condition of vehicles itself demands attention. There should be periodic review of the vehicles and unsafe and vehicles in poor condition should be put off the road. Attention has to be given to cycle rickshaw pullers as well. Except for the road-side tree shades, there is no resting place for them. The police harassment too should end. In a country like India, there is a need for having some drinking water facilities available on the road-side for these rickshaw pullers. They eat at pavement dhaba/eating places run by women. The food is cheap but the most unhygienic conditions under which it is served and eaten leaves much to be desired. The local administration should provide proper place to these food caterers and assure cleanliness.

In the case of tourist guides, the selection procedures have to be properly designed in which Guides Associations, the Hotel Industry and Restaurant Owners Associations should be involved. For effecting improvement in their working conditions, the local bodies have to play a major role. More specifically, there is a need for review of the 1996 policy of recruitment of guides. The poorly managed guides' courses need to be stopped. There is a requirement for better payment system of guides by the travel agencies. The rates need also to be rationalized, looking at the world-wide changing scenario of tourism. It should be mandatory for the tour operators to use the services of licensed guides. The tourist places should be cleared of unlicensed guides, beggars and hecklers. The composition of foreign tourists has been changing in particular and this requires knowledge of new foreign languages. There has to be language teaching institutions where the prospective tourist guides could get the needed training.

Finally, direct and indirect linkages of different activities within the tourism sector need to be strengthened and made operative to the satisfaction of the clients and for fostering growth of the industry. The formal and informal sector hotels have different types of clientele. However, a link could be established between the two by jointly advertising for different classes of tourists. This would improve the quality of services of informal sector hotels and better service technologies would be available to them. In the process, the work-force would gain. A link could also be established with restaurants and this would improve the quality and variety of food. Such linkages have to be accomplished by financial support from the formal sector establishments. The work-force could be commonly trained; as a result, the screening and work adjustment costs could go down in the informal sector. Already the formal sector hotels are themselves promoting budget hotels/restaurants. The informal sector hotels have linkages with the informal sector laundry.

The transport sector has implicit relationships with hotels and restaurants. The transport sector is also linked with the informal repair sector and it is mutually beneficial. The formal repair sector is small and beyond the reach of most. The credit market is increasingly getting linked now with all the activities, though informal credit market is much more closely linked. The formal sector has to develop mechanisms to help informal sector players. Guides are linked to hotels and travel agencies much more than the restaurants and transport sector. To develop greater cohesion between these activities, respective unions/associations need to have better coordination. A lot depends on how much cooperation could be generated among various actors.

NOTES

(1) The golden triangle comprising Delhi-Agra-Jaipur is important for Jaipur and Agra as in 1998, of the 5.532 million foreign tourists visiting India, 1.364 million (about 25 per cent) came to Delhi-Agra-Jaipur circuit alone.

(2) There are 123 unapproved hotels in Jaipur and 135 in Agra as per the hotel associations.

(3) In India, accommodation is very important for the tourism industry. In every forum, the lack of accommodation is raised as a major issue; this problem is more acute in the case of economy-budget tourists. A decent place of stay is vital at the lower end of hotel industry. There are 1188 approved hotels with 65598 rooms in India and of these 527 hotels are of 3 star or above category, with 52239 rooms (GOI 1998). This reflects poorly on tourism policy and a plain neglect of budget tourist whose number is increasing.

(4) The average number of nights a tourist spends in Agra is lower compared to Jaipur (Singh 1999). The starred and other approved hotels in India have an occupancy rate of 65 per cent (Monthly Commentary, August 1998).

(5) The auto-rickshaw driver charges at times 20 to 50 per cent commission on the one day room rent, while the cycle-rickshaw pullers gets 5 to 10 per cent commission. The commission is also influenced by the occupancy rates; lower the occupancy rate, higher the commission.

(6) For instance, in Jaipur, the hotel owners association has successfully convinced the government to exclude the bills on taxi, laundry and telephone from the purview of leviability of the luxury tax. The association has obtained a stay from a court on closure of hotels in residential areas. They have also pressurized the local municipal committee to postpone the heavy increase in license fee, and so on.

(7) In Agra, the discussions revealed that certain restaurant owners use unethical means with foreign tourists by adulterating food items and in connivance with local doctors corner insurance money of these clients.

(8) The permit fee of a taxi is Rs.1700 in Jaipur and Rs.2200 in Agra. The permits are issued by Regional Transport Offices [RTO].

(9) The annual permit fee is Rs.175 in Jaipur and Rs.350 in Agra. The cycle rickshaws have local bodies' registration number for which Rs.5 per year are charged.

(10) The taxis charge both fixed rates and also operate by kms. In Jaipur the Rajasthan Tourism Development Corporation (RTDC) has fixed the rates at Rs.4.40 per km. for a non-AC car, while it is Rs.6.50 for an AC car. The minimum running is 250 km. There are night charges at the rate of Rs.100. However the taxi union in Jaipur has fixed the rate at Rs.3 per km. for a non-AC car and Rs.5.50 for an AC car. The night halt charges are fixed at Rs.80 per night. Some taxis operate on pre-paid basis also. In Agra, the rates are higher by one rupee for both types. In the case of auto-rickshaws, for a given destination, however, the rates are fixed, but the whole day rates are charged by auto-rickshaw drivers, depending on the bargaining with the customer; invariably a lower limit is set by a auto-rickshaw stand. As the cycle-rickshaws are available in a large number and there is no union among them, a lot of bargaining is done by the customers. However, the rates are charged on the basis of distance. Cycle-rickshaw pullers rarely operate on a whole day basis.

(11) These individuals eat at informal food enterprises running on the pavements in the cities which operate under most unhygienic conditions. These enterprises are mainly run by women in groups. The rates are Rs.10 per meal. The clientele is more of cycle-rickshaw pullers and auto- rickshaw drivers.

(12) The foreign languages have been learnt from the local university, Language Institute in Pune, Alliance Frenchise, Pondicherry. There are very few non-university specialized language institutions in India.

(13) It is alleged that as licenses are not regularly issued, the applicants offer high bribe to concerned officials or their touts.

(14) The travel agencies on the scene are SITA, Mercury, TCI, Travel House, Pleasure Tours, Rajasthan Tours, Aravali and Safari, Heritage Tours, etc. The travel agencies are approved by the Tourism Department of India. The guide is assigned a task by the travel group operator. The guide buys entrance tickets to sites, takes the group around shopping and eating places. Some guides do dine with the group, stay in the same hotel, but invariably they are left to fend for themselves. The guides submit expense bills to the agencies after the group leaves which is honoured at times after 6 months. Some guides do get commission from shops where tourists are taken.

(15) If a guide works for four hours, the rate is Rs.345 and for 5 to 15 hours' work, the charges are Rs.460; beyond that, it is Rs.750. The foreign groups do occasionally tip the guides.

(16) These individuals operate with the full knowledge of the officials and the practice is rampant at the Taj in Agra. The unauthorized guides get commissions from the shops, showrooms, hotels, restaurants, etc. If caught, they occasionally bribe the police and officials. The attitude of the government is indifferent to this problem which gives bad name to the profession. These individuals are less informed and also work for small time travel agents. Such unauthorized individuals do not present a good picture of the Indian culture and often, provide a distorted view of the history.

(17) In India, there is a Migrant Worker Registration Act under which all migrant workers are supposed to register themselves, either in their home state or at the place of migration. Similar Acts should be put in place for informal sector workers.

Bibliography

D'Souza, Errol (1993). "Fluctuations and Employment Institutions in the Tourism Sector" Indian Journal of Labour Economics 36(4): 660-664.

Elkan, W. (1975). "The Relation Between Tourism and Employment in Kenya and Tanzania" Journal of Development Studies 11 (2): 123-130.

Frederick, Matha (1993). "Rural Tourism and Economic Development" Economic Development Quarterly 7: 215-224.

Govt. of India (1998). Annual Report: 1997-98 Ministry of Tourism, Delhi.

Harper, M. (1996). "Urban Planning and the Informal Sector" Regional Development Dialogue 17 (1): 97- 112.

ILO (1991). The Dilemma of the Informal Sector Report of the Director General, 78th Session, Geneva.

Monthly Commentary (1998). August, New Delhi.

Papola, T.S. (1981). Urban Informal Sector is an Developing Economy Vikas Publishing House, Delhi.

Sinclair, M. Thea (1998). "Tourism and Economic Development: A Survey" Journal of Development Studies 34(5): 1-51.

Singh, Surjit (1983). "Socio-economic Status, Human Capital and Earnings" Anvesak December.

Singh, Surjit (1999). "Tourism in Rajasthan and Its Impact on Livelihood" a paper prepared for Rajasthan Vision 2011 Project.

Tooman, L. Alex (1997). "Multipliers and Life Cycles: A Comparison of Methods for Evaluating Tourism and its Impacts" Journal of Economic Issues 31(4): 917-932.

Weiermair, Klaus and Matthias Fuchs (1998). "On the Use and Usefulness of Economics in Tourism: A Critical Survey" International Journal of Development Planning Literature 13(3): 225-273.

Labour Absorption in Urban Economy of Gujarat: Constraints and Policy Options

A.K. Pradhan

1. Introduction

A steady flight of rural population to urban areas in search of jobs and the failure of the urban modern sector to create matching number of job opportunities has given rise to the phenomenon of "urban labour force explosion"[1]. There have been models like those of Eckaus[2], Lewis[3] and Fei and Ranis[4] which attempt a rigorous analysis of the process of rural labour absorption in the urban modern sectors.

Todaro relates the decision to migrate to two principal factors viz., (a) the rural-urban real income differentials and (b) the probability of obtaining an urban job.[5] Despite fixing the minimum wages in the rural agricultural sector, the job opportunities there are dwindling on account of structural and technical changes. On the other hand, in the urban areas, with the rapid expansion of the government sector and the organised industrial sector, urban incomes are rising creating demand for basic needs like food, transport, day-to-day family requirements, and so on. These developments have promoted the growth of a diverse variety of economic activities which are conventionally put under the rubric of the traditional sector. In a large part of the urban traditional sector, the incomes may be higher than those in a large part of the rural economy. And what is more, this sector seems to have a large, if not infinite, capacity to absorb the migrants; for all practical purposes, there are no restrictions on entry into this sector.

---

1. Aziz, Abdul, Urban Poor and Urban Informal Sector, ISEC, Bangalore, 1984.
2. R S Eckaus, "The Factor Proportions Problem in Under-developed Areas", American Economic Review, Sept. 1955.
3. W A Lewis, "Economic Development with Unlimited Supplies of Labour", The Manchester School of Economic and Social Studies, 22, May 1954.
4. JCH Fei and G Ranis, Development of the Labour Surplus Economy: Theory and Policy, Richard B Irwin Inc. Homewood Illinois, 1964.
5. Michael P. Todaro, "A Model of Labour Migration and Urban Unemployment in Less Developed. Countries", American Economic Review, March 1969. Also John R Harris and Michael Todaro "Migration, Unemployment and Development: A Two-Sector Analysis", American Economic Review, March 1970.

The Indian Factories Act, 1948 is a good starting point for understanding the Indian situation. This Act defines establishments that need to be registered for being regulated by the State. According to this Act, all factories/establishments employing 10 or more workers with the use of power and those employing 20 or more workers without the use of power come under the State regulation. (Some hazardous industries, employing 5 or more persons, such as the brass-part foundries in Jamnagar City, also come under the Act). Under the Factory Act, the state regulates the working and employment conditions in the factories and this introduces an element of formality regarding the very attempt to start a factory and its functioning in terms of production, marketing, labour relations, etc. Therefore, as a first approximation, all those establishments which are formally registered and whose functioning is regulated by the state, may be said to be in the modern sector. In general, in such establishments, salaries and wages are high and are also subject to collective bargaining; modern technology and modern management techniques are employed; as a result, productivity is high. Production is carried on capitalistic principles so that the returns are expected to be maximised.

A word of caution here is necessary. In many small factories, collective bargaining may not be possible; likewise, minimum wages may not be observed in all cases. There may also be a high turnover of the labour force which, by itself, inhibits collective bargaining. On the other hand, labourers move from one establishment to the other in search of better salaries. These establishments thus display some characteristics of the urban traditional sector. This phenomenon is particularly observable in the diamond cutting industry in Surat, Bhavnagar, Ahmedabad and other cities of Gujarat.

The rest of the business units which are not formally registered and, by virtue of which, are not subject to state regulation, are in the urban traditional sector. These are small enterprises, mostly operated as proprietary form of business or on self-employment basis. The workers employed are mostly family members or relatives or those who work on a casual basis hardly ever coming under any trade union umbrella. Enterprises in this sector are an amalgam of a wide variety of service, trade and manufacturing activities. By virtue of their being small and a part of the traditional sector, they have to suffer exploitation, both in and outside the market.

Within the urban traditional sector, a further break-up into formal and informal segments is possible purely on the basis of the size of capital and labour employed, whether or not a fixed place of work/production is available, and so on. We will place the itinerant waste collectors, who use very little capital, practically no hired labour and operate in no fixed work-place, in the informal segment of the urban traditional sector. Their counterparts in other urban occupations are the street hawkers, shoe-shine boys, repair workers, manual transport workers, head loaders, and so on. The capital and labour-hiring entrepreneurs with a fixed work place like the waste collecting agents, bulk-buyers and manufacturers of our study can be placed in the formal segment of the urban traditional sector. Their counterparts in other urban occupations are the retail shops, vegetable vendors, fruit merchants, small workshop, repair and small manufacturers who have a fixed work place, use relatively large capital resources and hire outside labour in addition to using the services of family labour.

We may define the informal sector thus: it consists of small-scale units engaged in the production and distribution of goods and services with the primary objective of generating employment and incomes to their participants notwithstanding the constraints on capital, both human and physical, and know-how.

2. The Scenario in Gujarat

Gujarat has seen large scale rural to urban migration. This migration has resulted in urban poverty, growth of slums in a totally uncontrolled manner, poor living conditions and lack of even the basic amenities like housing and safe drinking water.

During the decade 1981-91, the rate of growth of urban population being 34.4 per cent was much higher than state's decadal growth rate of total population of 21.2 per cent Table 1). It may, however, be noticed that while the share of urban population in total population is rising, the rate of growth of urban population has slowed down. The projected share of urban population for 2001 and 2005 is 38.6 per cent and 40.5 per cent, respectively (Table 2).

Given the disparities between incomes in agricultural and non-agricultural activities, and between rural and urban areas, migration from rural to urban areas is not surprising. Notwithstanding advances in agricultural technology, the increasing pressure on land would seem to echo the Malthusian prediction of surplus population.

In Gujarat, growth in agricultural sector has also shown stagnation in recent years. The productivity index for all crops (base : biennium ending 1969-70 = 100) works out to 252.6 for 1997-98 compared to 244.3 for 1996.97. The growth rate is thus 3.4 per cent. Large areas of the state are semi-arid or receive low average rain-fall. Facilities for irrigation are limited; only 20 per cent of the agricultural area is under assured irrigation. Even after the Narmada Project is completed, only 39. per cent of state's agricultural area will come under assured irrigation through surface flow. The ground water potential is 25.5 per cent but, to a large extent, it depends on ground water recharge during rains. Agriculture in the rain-fed area is subject to the vagaries of the monsoons. Failure of rains results in disappearance of

TABLE 1 : **Growth of Urban and Total Population in Gujarat : 1961/1991**

Year	Total Population (in lakhs)	Urban Population (in lakhs)	% Urban Population	Decadal Growth Rate of Urban Population
1961	206.33	53.17	25.77	----------
1971	266.98	74.96	28.08	>41.0 %
1981	340.85	106.02	31.10	>42.42 %
1991	413.09	142.46	34.49	>34.38 %

Source: Census of India, 1991.

TABLE 2 : **Projected Urban Population in Gujarat : 1999, 2001 and 2005**

Year	Total Population (in lakhs)	Urban Population (in lakhs)	% of Urban to Total Population
1999	476.51	179.63	37.70
2001	491.62	189.71	38.59
2005	522.58	211.40	40.45

Source: Techincal Papers on Perspective Plan of Gujarat, 2005.

TABLE 3 : **Population Growth in Six Major Cities of Gujarat : 1971/1991**

City	1971	1981	%Growth	1991	% Growth
Ahmedabad U.A.	17,60,950	25,57,560	45.24	33,12,216	29.50
Vadodara U.A.	4,73,197	7,82,403	65.34	11,26,824	44.02
Surat U.A.	4,93,601	9,13,806	85.13	15,18,950	66.22
Rajkot	3,00,612	4,45,076	48.05	6,12,458	37.60
Bhavnagar U.A.	2,25,974	3,08,642	36.58	4,05,225	31.29
Junagadh U.A.	2,27,640	3,17,362	39.41	3,81,646	20.26

Source: Govt. of Gujarat, Population Characteristics of Gujarat 1991 (Urban Profile), Directorate of Economics and Statistics.

employment opportunities in the rural areas and consequently, a sizeable chunk of rural population seasonally migrates to urban areas.

The eastern belt of the state is inhabited by tribal population. The average land holding size is so small that, even during a good agricultural season, the landholding provides a very meager livelihood to the landholder. Hence, most of the land holders as well as agricultural labourers migrate to urban and semi-urban areas of the state, year after year. During a lean agricultural year, the migration may start very early and return of the migrating population may also be delayed.

Location of industries, expansion of government administration and concentration of opportunities for acquiring education and skill have also played an important role in attracting migrants to urban areas.

All this is reflected in the significantly higher growth rate of urban population compared to the growth rate of the state's population as a whole (Table 1).

2.1 Population and Work-force

Changes in the concept used for the measurement of working population from census to census make comparisons difficult. However, the proportion of main workers and marginal workers by sex and area is given in Table 4. It is observed from the above table that the proportion of the main workers, both in rural and urban areas, has shown an increasing trend during 1961-91, both for males and females.

It is observed from the above table that the proportion of main workers, both in rural and urban areas, has shown an increasing trend during 1961-91, for each sex of persons.

The proportion of cultivators, agricultural labourers, household industries and other workers to main workers in Gujarat (1961-91) is given Table 5. The proportion of cultivators has declined from 48.33 per cent in 1961 to 33.37 per cent in 1991. The proportion of those working mainly as agricultural labourers has increased marginally from 21.94 per cent to 22.92 per cent during 1961-91. The proportion of main workers in household industries in the state has shown a decline from 2.96 per cent in 1961 to 1.40 per cent in 1991. However, the proportion of other workers to main workers increased from 26.77 per cent in 1961 to 42.30 per cent in 1991.

Around mid-1990s, the unemployment rate among the youth (15 to 29 years of age) was 2 per cent in rural areas and 8.1 per cent in urban areas. Thus, the rate of open unemployment among the urban youth is many times higher compared with their rural counterparts. However, unemployment rate among both males and females and both rural and urban areas has been significantly lower than at the all-India level which is 4.4 per cent for the rural youth and 12.4 per cent for their urban brethren. However, unemployment rates among the educated persons (15 plus age) were similar between rural and urban areas of Gujarat and India, being 4.4 per cent for the former and 3.9 per cent for the latter.

2.2 Employment in the Unorganized Sector

According to the 1991 census, out of the total population of 413.10 lakhs, 140.96 lakhs (34.12 per cent) were main workers and 25.25 lakhs (6.11 per cent) were marginal workers. Out of the main workers, only 16.19 lakhs (11.5 per cent) workers were in the organized sector. The total number of workers increased to 167.88 lakhs in 1998. The organized sector however, grew to 17.62 lakhs or by

TABLE 4 : **Proportions of Main Workers by Sex and Rural and Urban Break-up for 1961-91 : Gujarat**

Area	Sex	1961	1971	1981	1991
(1)	(2)	(3)	(4)	(5)	(6)
Rural	Persons	31.61	32.96	34.18	36.76
	Males	52.59	52.83	53.07	54.36
	Females	9.64	12.06	14.49	18.25
Urban	Persons	26.52	27.57	28.46	29.50
	Males	45.61	47.30	48.96	50.62
	Females	5.21	5.48	5.80	6.26
State	Persons	30.29	31.45	32.23	34.37
	Males	50.75	51.25	51.77	53.06
	Females	8.53	10.26	11.85	14.09

Source: Technical Papers on Perspective Plan of Gujarat, 2005, p. 77.

TABLE 5 : **Sectoral Break-up of Main Workers in Gujarat : 1961/1991**

Category of Main Workers	1961 (Estimated)	1971	1981	1991
(1)	(2)	(3)	(4)	(5)
1.Cultivators	48.33	43.12	37.76	33.77
2.Agricultural Labourers	21.94	22.48	22.88	22.92
3.Household Industriess	2.96	2.82	2.71	1.40
4.Other workers	26.77	31.58	36.71	42.30

Source: Technical Papers on Perspective Plan of Gujarat, 2005, p. 78.

TABLE 6 : **Employment Status of Gujarat's Working Population**

Rural / Urban	Proportion of Workers		
	Self Employed	Regular Jobs	Casual Workers
Rural	52.2	6.8	43.0
Urban	38.3	40.9	20.8

For Gujarat, the percentage distribution of usually employed persons, area-wise, is given in Table 6; self employment continues to be important, both in rural and urban areas.

about 25,000 jobs per year during the period 1991-1998 as against an average annual increase of 3.75 lakhs workers in the unorganized sector. Accordingly, the percentage share of the organized sector employment came down to 10.5 per cent in 1998 against 11.49 per cent in 1991. As per the data available with the Director of Employment and Training, Gujarat, the organized sector employment further declined to 17.27 lakhs in 1999. *This brings into sharp focus the importance of the informal sector in absorbing the expanding army of surplus labour.*

From 1991 to 1999 (estimated), the urban population has gone up from 142.46 lakh to 179.63 i.e. an increase of 27.17 lakh persons. If we assume a labour-force participation rate of 29.50 per cent for urban areas, it has meant an addition of about 8 lakh job seekers in urban areas during the period 1991- 999 (8 years).

Table 7 gives sector-wise percentage share of employment in the urban organized sector, for the period 1980 to 1999. It is more than evident that, by and large, employment in the organized sector as a whole has been rather stagnating since mid-1990s. The stagnation is particularly manifest in the major sectors of the

TABLE 7 : **Employment in the Formal Sector of Gujarat's Urban Economy by Broad Production Sectors : 1980/1999**

Sr. No.	Industrial Classification	No. of Persons Employed as on 30th June						
		1980	1990	1995	1996	1997	1998	1999
1	**2**	**3**	**4**	**5**	**6**	**7**	**8**	**9**
1	Agriculture, Hunting, Forestry and Fishing	17	25	24	20	20	18	18
2	Mining and Quarrying	16	22	23	21	21	20	20
3	Manufacturing	502	592	616	645	699	688	669
4	Electric, Gas and Water	29	45	44	44	45	46	46
5	Construction	72	70	70	71	76	86	79
6	Wholesale and Retail Trade and Restaurants	17	27	24	25	26	26	26
7	Transport, Storage and Communication	165	181	189	185	186	185	183
8	Financing, Insurance, Real	61	94	104	108	106	107	107
	Estate and Business Services							
9	Community, Social and Personal Servics.	431	563	596	595	592	596	579
	Total	1310	1619	1690	1714	1771	1762	1727

Source : Directorate of Employment and Training, Gujarat State, Gandhinagar.

urban economy, such as manufacturing, transport-storage-communication and community-social-personal services. To bank upon the urban organized sector as a major source of future employment expansion is clearly an unwise strategy . The main burden has thus to be borne by the informal sector.

2.3 Emerging Economic Environment

With the accelerating pace of globalization and an increasing degree of openness of the Indian economy, states would also face new and much more difficult economic environments under which the nature of state intervention in economic matters would be substantially different and reduced, most ostensibly through winding up of public sector enterprises and voluntary retirement schemes clamped on public servants, controls would be dismantled and more reliance would have to be put on market processes, and so on.

The labour market cannot remain unaffected. Perhaps, the following effects have already started surfacing, in varying form and combination, in states, including Gujarat:

(1) A tendency towards downgrading of regular jobs in favour of contracted jobs;

(2) Outsourcing of operations/processes being resorted to, especially in areas of troubled labour relations and high export stakes; and

(3) Increasing contractualisation and actualization of labor force.

In consequence, there is a shrinkage of jobs in the organized sector. The corporate sector is talking of rationalization and downsizing which, in other words, means retrenchment and displacement of work-force.

Major industries such as engineering, textiles, chemicals, etc. are in the grip of recessionary trends. These industries find that their operations are becoming uncompetitive in the face of imports from China and other countries. Another problem being faced by the industry is the lack of job flexibility in the labour force. The industry in Gujarat has employed a high proportion of unorganized workers and no concerted efforts have been made for up-gradation of skills of the existing lot of workers. There is thus a redundancy of skills combined with redundancy of jobs. The tendency of protecting employment in existing jobs, especially in view of a variety of judicial restrictions, has only resulted in inefficiency in productive works. The system of job security that the formal/organized sector confers on the existing stock of workers/ employees would also prevent the entry of low paid informal/unorganized sector workers into the formal sector. Insistence on job security without corresponding efforts to improve productive quality of manpower forces many enterprises in the organized sector to resort to job redundancy or outsourcing or sub-contracting, and so on. All these developments breed expansion of the urban informal sector.

2.4 Number and Types of Urban Enterprises: Provisional Results of the 1998 Economic Census

A quick perusal of the provisional results, based on quick manual tabulation (QMT) of the Fourth Economic Census, 1998 for Gujarat, throws up many important features.

2.4.1 Enterprises

In Table 8, the information on percentage distribution of enterprises by location and by their important characteristics (like agricultural and non-agricultural, own-account enterprises and establishments, having premises, energy used in operation, type of operation and type of ownership) is given. In 1998, there were around 19.15 lakh enterprises in Gujarat; nearly 43.0 per cent of them were located in urban areas. Further, out of 19.15 lakh total enterprises of the state, 31.42 per cent were engaged in non-crop type of agricultural activities (e.g., livestock production, hunting, trapping and game propagation, forestry and logging and fishing) while the remaining 68.58 per cent were of non-agricultural type. Around three fourth (14.43 lakh) of the total enterprises were own-account enterprises (run entirely by self-employing household members and/or other unpaid workers only) and the remaining 25 per cent were establishments (i.e. enterprises engaging at least one hired worker, on a fairly regular basis).

A large proportion of state's total agricultural enterprises (95 per cent) and state's total own-account enterprises (62.4 per cent) were located in rural areas whereas nearly 61 per cent of non-agricultural enterprises and 63 per cent of establishments, were in urban areas. As is to be expected, around 95 per cent of the urban enterprises were associated with non-agricultural activities.

Out of 19.15 lakh enterprises of the state, 14.18 per cent were working without premises. 79 per cent were operated without using power/fuel, 95.73 per cent were perennial in nature and 96.7 per cent were privately owned entities.

2.4.2 Employment

Table 9 shows that around 52.8 lakh persons were usually working on a fairly regular basis in 19.15 lakh enterprises of the state, giving the average number of persons per enterprise to be 2.76. Out of the total of 52.8 lakh persons employed, nearly 80.0 per cent were engaged in non-agricultural activities; again, of the total workers, 55.5 per cent were engaged on wage/salary basis.

3. Employment and Income in the Informal Sector: The Case of Ahmedabad Urban Area

Information on trends in employment and income generation in a city will be useful in understanding the role of the informal sector. A study of the informal sector in Ahmedabad was carried on by Papola in the 1970s (Papola, 1981). A further study was conducted by Gujarat Institute of Development Research (GIDR)

TABLE 8(a) : **Number and Types of Enterprises in Rural / Urban Gujarat : 1998**

Sr. No.	Characteristics of Enterprises	Distribution	Rural	Urban	Total
(1)	(2)	(3)	(4)	(5)	(6)
1	Agriculture	% Nos	95.22 572837	4.78 28762	100.00 601599
2	Non-Agricultural	% Nos	38.97 571605	61.03 801472	100.00 1312977
3	All Enterprises	% Nos	56.64 1084442	43.36 830134	100.00 1914576
4	Own - Account Enterprises	% Nos	62.39 921649	37.61 555626	100.00 1477275
5	Establishments	% Nos	37.23 162793	62.77 274508	100.00 437301

Source: Fourth Economic Census, Gujarat, 1998.

TABLE 8(b) : **Enterprises with and without Premises, Perennial and Seasonal Enterprises and those under Private Ownership : Gujarat State 1998**

Sr. No.	Characteristics of Enterprises	Distribution	Rural	Urban	Total
(1)	(2)	(3)	(4)	(5)	(6)
1	Agriculture	% Nos	56.64 1084442	43.36 830134	100 1914576
2	Non-Agricultural	% Nos	14.89 161459	13.25 109962	14.18 271421
3	All Enterprises	% Nos	84.68 918341	71.48 593421	78.96 1511762
4	Own - Account Enterprises	% Nos	94.49 1024721	97.35 808120	95.73 1832841
5	Establishments	% Nos	95.51 1035778	98.27 815795	96.71 1851573

Source: Fourth Economic Census, Gujarat, 1998.

in 1997-98 (Unni and Rani 2000). We extensively draw upon these studies, especially the latter one, for writing this section.

TABLE 8(c) : **Agriculture and Non-agriculture Enterprises by Size of Employment (Own Account Enterprises and Establishments) Categories : Gujarat State 1998**

Sr. No.	Characteristics of Enterprises	Distribution	Rural	Urban	Total
(1)	**(2)**	**(3)**	**(4)**	**(5)**	**(6)**
1	Agriculture	% Nos	52.82 572837	3.46 28762	31.42 601599
2	Non-Agricultural	% Nos	52.71 511605	96.54 801372	68.58 1312977
3	All Enterprises	% Nos	47.18 1084442	43.36 830134	100 1914576
4	Own - Account	% Nos	84.99 921649	66.93 555626	77.16 1477275
5	Establishments	% Nos	15.01 162793	33.07 274508	22.84 437301

Source: Fourth Economic Census, Gujarat, 1998.

TABLE 9 : **Employment in Rural/Urban Enterprises by Type of Enterprise and Paid/Unpaid Work : Gujarat 1998**

Employment Type	Distribution	Rural	Urban	Total
(1)	**(2)**	**(3)**	**(4)**	**(5)**
(A) All Workers (paid + unpaid)				
(1) Agriculture	% Nos	44.86 1054812	2.25 65931	21.2 1120743
(2) Non-Agriculture	% Nos	55.14 1296301	97.75 2862866	78.8 4159167
(3) All Enterprises	% Nos	100.00 2351113	100.00 2928797	100.00 5279910
(B) Hired Workers				
as % of Total Workers in all Enterprises	% Nos	35.41 832478	71.69 2099602	55.5 2932080

Source: Results of fourth Economic Census (1998), Gujarat).

3.1 Employment Growth in Ahmedabad's Economy

Ahmedabad is a metropolitan city located in the highly industrialized and urbanized Indian state of Gujarat. The city economy of Ahmedabad was on an upswing since 1861, when the first modern textile mill was located in the city. Since then, the growth of textile mills continued and it also led to migration of labour, mostly the working class, into the city. The global recession of the 1930s, and the communal riots of 1940s, slowed down economic growth of the city, as it saw the closure of a number of textile mills. However, the textile mills revived after the recession and have continued to flourish ever thereafter.

The city economy has grown spatially from 108.24 sq. km. in 1971 to 190.85 sq. km. in 1991. The population has grown from 0.9 million in 1951 to 3.31 million in 1991, at a decadal growth rate of 35.6 per cent in 1951-61, 40.8 per cent in 1971-81 and 30.0 per cent in 1981-91, indicating an absolute decline during the last decade. While the population in the municipal area outside the fort walls grew rapidly during the sixties, the seventies saw the growth shifting to the peripheries which continues even today. The large-scale construction of residential housing in the city's outskirts is a visible sign of increasing urban spread since the late 1980s.

The economic structure of the city witnessed a considerable change since the sixties, with a substantial degree of diversification of industrial activity into a number of chemicals, petrochemicals and other engineering industries, in the eastern and western peripheries. However, the dominant and dynamic textile industry stagnated during this period, practically marked by no growth in employment. In Table 10, a closer look at the economic structure of the city identifies the major trends.

Employment in Ahmedabad city grew at the rate of 2.8 per cent over the three decades 1961-91. The fastest growing sector was construction, followed by trade and commerce and transport, storage and communications. Interestingly, the decade-wise overall growth has been the same for each of the three decades. However, wide variations in sector-wise growth are clearly discernible for each of the three decades since 1961.

TABLE 10 : **Employment Trends in Ahmedabad City (Growth Rates)**

Production Sector	61-71	71-81	81-91	61-91
Agriculture	1.55	-5.87	4.12	2.04
Manufacturing	2.29	3.21	0.39	1.97
Construction	4.69	2.56	7.00	4.75
Trade and Commerce	5.1	3.00	4.87	4.30
Transport, Storage and Communication	5.29	4.24	3.09	4.21
Other Services	2.10	2.26	3.79	3.31
Total	3.00	2.80	2.70	2.80

TABLE 11 : **Sectoral Shares of Employment in Ahmedabad**

Sector	1961	1971	1981	1991
Agriculture	5.0	4.3	1.8	2.1
Manufacturing	47.1	43.9	45.9	36.4
Construction	2.6	3.1	3.1	4.7
Trade & Commerce	16.1	19.8	20.2	25.1
Transport, Storage and Communication	6.1	7.6	8.8	9.2
Services	23.1	21.1	20.1	22.4
Total	100.0	100.0	100.0	100.0

Employment in Ahmedabad's manufacturing sector grew by about 2.3 per cent per annum from 1961 to 1971. The seventies saw a slight increase in the growth rate of employment, to 3.2 per cent. However, there was a sharp decline of manufacturing sector growth to 0.4 per cent per annum during 1981-91. The almost stagnant employment situation during 1981-91 testifies to the seriousness of the situation in the urban economy of Ahmedabad. The city's growth rate of employment in the construction sector rose tremendously during 1981-91. This could be the result of urbanization and industrialization where construction work absorbs a large proportion of labour. Growth rate of employment in the city witnessed a consistent improvement in other services also over the three decades.

The share of employment in the manufacturing sector witnessed a sizeable decline between 1961 and 1991 (Table 11). The importance of the tertiary sector increased since the sixties. The share of trade and commerce rose gradually from 16 per cent in 1961 to 25 per cent in 1991, while that of transport, storage and communication rose from 6 to 9 per cent during the same period. The proportion of other services, which covers administration, education, health etc., remained more or less steady over the period.

3.2 Informal Sector Employment in Ahmedabad

It is important to see how is growth of employment distributed between the formal and informal sector of the city's economy. Growth rates of employment, in the two sectors, during the period 1976-77 to 1997-98 are presented in Table 12.

Employment is computed only for non-agricultural sectors of the city, since the agricultural sector constitutes an insignificant proportion of employment in Ahmedabad's economy. The overall growth rate of employment for the period 1976-1998, that is, using the estimate of employment in the two city studies, was 4.3 per cent. Growth rate of employment between 1980-90 was 2.5 per cent, corresponds

TABLE 12 : **Employment Growth in Formal and Informal Sectors in Ahmedabad - 1976 / 1998**

Period Covered	Formal	Informal	Total
1976-77 to 1980	-11.44	2.57	-5.29
1980 to 1990	2.26	2.78	2.52
1990 to 1997-98	2.44	16.40	11.20
1976-77 to 1997-98	2.57	7.61	4.30

fairly closely to 2.7 per cent based on the Population Census data for the city of Ahmedabad. Employment in the informal sector grew faster at 7.6 per cent, compared to only 2.6 per cent in the formal sector. During 1976-77 to 1980, there was an absolute decline in employment; it grew slowly at 2.5 per cent during 1980-90 and then rapidly, at 11.2 per cent, during 1990 to 1997-98. These swings in employment growth could partly be due to the differences in the methodologies used to collect data on employment in the different sources.

The informal sector has grown by about 2.8 per cent and the formal sector by about 2.3 per cent during 1980-90. During the nineties, there was a faster growth of employment in the informal sector, 16.4 per cent compared with 2.4 per cent only in the formal sector. As suggested above, this could reflect the additional efforts made in the city study to capture employment in this sector which often remains invisible to the official data collection machinery. In any case, *irrespective of the data sources, all time periods showed a larger growth rate of employment in the informal sector, compared with that in the formal sector.*

It is equally important to underline that a sizable proportion of the city's workforce was engaged in manufacturing, both in the formal and informal sectors, in each of the sub-periods covered between 1976-77 and 1997-98 (Table 13).

The share of the manufacturing sector, however, declined continuously from 47.2 per cent in 1976-77 to 36.8 in 1990 and finally to 36.3 per cent in 1997-98. The closing down of the textile mills in the late seventies and the early eighties contributed substantially to this process. Community and other services and trade, hotels and restaurants are the other sectors with high shares in employment, though these show a slight decline in 1997-98. Transport and construction sectors have shown a substantial increase in their respective share of employment in the recent year.

The share of the informal sector in total employment has increased consistently since mid-1970s rising from 37 per cent in 1976-77 to about 50 per cent in 1990 (Economic Census estimates) to 74.2 per cent in 1997-98 (GIDR's latest city study). Perhaps, a word of caution is in order, at this stage. While the Economic Census is likely to have left out a large proportion of the invisible informal sector

TABLE 13 : **Industrial Distribution and Share of the Informal Sector in Non-Agriculture, Ahmedabad**

Sector	Industrial Distribution				Share of the Informal Sector			
	1976-77	1980	1990	1997-98	1976-77	1980	1990	1997-98
Manufacturing	47.2	43.4	36.8	36.3	29.3	39.5	34.9	67.4
Electricity, Gas, Water	1.1	0.9	0.1	0.8	0	11.3	34.1	0
Construction	3.3	0.5	0.6	9.5	100.00	77.8	71.8	69.6
Trade, Hotels & Restaurants	14.8	20.1	27.8	19.5	100.00	94.7	84.7	90.5
Transport	6.3	4.4	2.7	13.0	79.1	68.2	75.1	91.5
Storage	0.6	0.8	1.6	0.1	0	68.8	69.1	0
Communication, Banking & Insurance	5.1	6.6	7.8	4.0	0	26.4	26.5	0
Commercial & other Services	21.5	23.2	22.5	16.8	100.00	29.9	36.2	81.5
All	100.0	100.0	100.0	100.0	37.0	49.1	50.3	74.2

activities, the city study estimate could tend to overestimate the informal sector. The Economic Census of 1980 and 1990 showed a decline in the share of the informal sector manufacturing industry (Table 13). This could be due to the following. One, the decline in sub-contracting work as a result of the closure of a large number of mills. Two, it is possible that the data fails to capture a large proportion of own account enterprises, small sized units and home based workers in the informal sector. Three, a genuine shift of informal economic activity from manufacturing to the tertiary sector such as, transport, community and other services, might have occurred.

The city study of 1997-98 succeeded in capturing a large proportion of home-based workers and small manufacturing units, so that the informal sector share was 67 per cent of the manufacturing sector. The informal sector share also grew substantially in the transport and service sectors during 1980 to 1997-98.

Table 14 presents the distribution of income and employment estimates for the unorganized sector for Ahmedabad city, based on the state sample of the NSS Unorganized Sector Survey in 1994-95. The unorganized sector, according to this official data source, employed 1.01 lakh workers and generated an income of about Rs. 4401 million. The average value added per worker thus came to about Rs. 44,000, which may be an over- estimate.

The GIDR-SEWA Survey succeeded in capturing the lowest segment of the manufacturing sector consisting of a whole range of households units, which are

TABLE 14 : **Income Generation from Unorganized Manufacturing Sector in Ahmedabad City, 1994.**

Codes	Industry Group	Total workers %	Gross Value Added %
20	Food products	4.1	2.3
22	Tobacco products	1.1	0.3
23	Cotton Textiles	5.6	5.4
24	Other Textiles	2.0	12.5
26	Textile products	5.0	1.2
27	Wood	5.5	4.1
28	Paper	3.4	2.2
29	Leather Products	0.6	0.5
30	Rubber, Plastic, Petrochem	5.2	4.1
31	Chemical Product	5.6	6.4
32	Non-metallic product	1.2	0.3
33	Basic Metal and Alloys	3.6	11.5
34	Metal products	12.2	12.8
35	Machinery & Equipment	17.4	19.9
37	Transport equipment & parts	0.5	2.5
38	Other manufacturing	13.1	7.9
39	Repair of capital goods	2.1	0.9
97	Repair services	11.7	4.9
	Total	100	100
	Estimates	101220(Nos.)	Rs. 440.1 Crores

probably left out by the official unorganized sector survey. The informal sector survey showed that about 2.57 lakh persons were engaged in various manufacturing activities and they generated an income of about Rs. 4235 million (Table 15). We found that manufacture of paper products, in this case the kite makers, followed by textile products or garment making, formed a major chunk of the workers. About 27.3 per cent of workers in the informal sector were engaged in the manufacturing of paper products and they generated about 7.1 per cent of income. The garment industry employed 14.5 per cent and generated about 3.6 per cent of income. Other sectors such as food which basically included making pickles, papads and other food items, engaged about 5.3 per cent of workers and generated about 3.9 per cent of income. In the case of beedi-making, about 4.2 per cent of workers engaged in this activity could contribute just about 1.4 per cent to income.

The value added per workers for the informal manufacturing sector was Rs. 16,424, which was very low, compared to the organized and unorganized components of the manufacturing sector (Table 15). The value added per worker was particularly low in tobacco, textile and paper products. The reason for low labour productivity in these branches of manufacturing could be that a large proportion of workers are engaged as home-based workers, who undertake this activity on a contract basis, often work for part of the day primarily to supplement the household income which come mainly from other sources.

The plight of the garment makers in the home-based industry has been highlighted in studies by Self-Employed Women's Association (SEWA). These poor workers, mostly ladies, work for sub-minimum wages, without any guarantee of continued employment, and at the caprices of and exploitation by the contractors. Usually, they have no health cover or insurance. That SEWA has organized them for contributory medical insurance, and is fighting the workers' cause for minimum wages, is, however, a different matter.

3.3 A Comparative Estimate of Income and Employment in Ahmedabad City

The GIDR study has also worked out employment and income estimates under different sectors of Ahmedabad's economy, the error margins in some sectors and activities notwithstanding (Unni and Rani, 2000). Nonetheless, these income and employment estimates do give us some rough idea about the state of affairs in the city's economy. These estimates are sketched out in Table 16.

TABLE 15 : **Income and Employment from Manufacturing Sector, 1997-98**

Sectors	Persons employed (Percentage)	Net value added (Percentage)	Value added per worker (in rupees)
1. Organised Sector	32.6	56.9	71658
2. Unorganised sector	19.0	23.7	51353
OAME	5.7	3.8	27219
NDME	6.0	5.6	38101
DME	7.2	14.4	81531
3. Informal Sector	48.4	19.4	16424
Food	2.6	0.8	11901
Tobacco	2.0	0.3	5404
Cotton Textiles	1.0	0.3	12690
Textile products	7.0	0.7	4082
Paper	13.2	1.4	4269
Other Manufacture	22.6	15.9	29053
Total (1+2+3)	100	100	41073
Estimates	532861 (Nos.)	2062 (Nos.)	–

TABLE 16 : **Formal and Informal Sector Employment, Income and Productivity in Ahmedabad City, 1997-98**

Production Sector	Employment		Income		Labour Productivity		
	Total	Informal[1]	Total	Informal[1]	Formal	Informal	Total
Agriculture	1.9	70.9	0.7	80.8	9076	15651	13740
Manufacturing	35.3	67.4	36.4	43.1	68953	24051	38694
Electricity	0.8	0	2.3	0	110728	0	110728
Construction	9.2	69.6	3.6	68.4	15989	15177	15424
Transport	12.7	91.5	11.7	80.5	84501	32272	36693
Storage	0.1	0	0.2	0	100563	0	100563
Trade, Hotels and Restaurants	18.9	90.5	18.9	63.1	155485	27733	39809
Communications, Banking and Insurance	3.9	0	192.5	0	126489	0	126489
Services	16.4	81.5	11.6	48.9	64454	16989	24056
Rentals	-	-	2.2	-	-	-	-
Total	100	74.2	100	45.7	91540	23520	39066

Note : 1. Percentage share of the informal sector in each industry group.
Source: Unni and Rani 2000.

The productivity per person in the city was found to be Rs. 39,066. As expected, it was much too higher (Rs. 91,540) in the formal sector than that in the informal sector (Rs. 23,520). Among the individual sectors, the productivity gaps between the formal and informal segments are more pronounced among manufacturing in the secondary sector, and, trade-hotels-restaurants and services among the tertiary sector. The lagging position of the informal sector is most evident from the hiatus between its share in employment and that in income. At the aggregate level, for example, the informal sector employs nearly three-fourth of workers in Ahemadbad's economy and yet, it has to rest content with only about 45.7 of income generated. The employment-income gap is discernible, in varying form and degree, practically in each segment of the city's economy.

3.4 Conclusion

The employment scenario in Gujarat showed a shift from the manufacturing sector to other sectors of the state economy; the shift seems to have been accelerated by structural reforms or the liberalization process underway in the state. The manufacturing sector showed buoyant growth during the decade 1971-81, but declined thereafter.

It is evident that even within the manufacturing sector, it was the organized manufacturing sector which performed better in terms of increasing growth rates in enterprises, employment, value added and fixed assets, especially during the post-liberalization period. The unorganized manufacturing segment, however, showed a decline in the rate of growth in the post liberalization period. It appears that the new policies support industries and units with greater productivity, better technology and capital intensity, which are in the organized sector. However, it needs to be mentioned that the employment in the unorganized manufacturing sector grew at 5.9 per cent per annum over the three decades and that in the organized segment only at 0.6 per cent, which, in a sense, clearly shows that employment is being created, 'almost dutifully', in the unorganized sector. Thus, there exists a large pool of workers, the 'informal sector workers' or 'invisible workers', who obtain work on contract basis, not only from the organized and unorganized manufacturing sectors but also from the trading sector.

The services sector continues to be buoyant in employment growth, specially the construction sector. Another sector which shows high potential for growth is Information Technology (I.T.) Enabled Services.

The existence of the big pool of informal sector workers was evident from the employment scenario in Ahmedabad city, where 74 per cent of workers, employed in the informal sector, generated only about 46 per cent of income in the city economy. The sectors in which the informal activities dominate are trade, hotels and restaurants, transport and the manufacturing sector. The existence of such a large proportion of informal sector activities in a city economy, and its substantial contribution in terms of employment and income to the city, raises the question of the lack or inadequacy of policy concern that has been accorded to this sector.

Papola's study (though dated) revealed that specific activities in which a sizeable number of independent workers is found are retail trade in vegetables, fruits, fish, eggs etc., laundry services, transporting by man and hand cart, pedal rickshaw and motor vehicles; building repairs; retail trade in beverages, tobacco products and foodstuffs; shoe repair; and hair dressing, each claiming over five per cent of the sampled workers. In all likelihood, the position has not changed much since then.

In Papola's study, the average number of workers per establishment was 3.84. The study was for Ahmedabad city with a negligible component of agricultural sector. The results of the Fourth Economic Census of 1998 for Gujarat reveals that there were 8,30,134 non-agricultural establishments in urban areas employing 28,62,866 workers or an average of 3.45 workers per establishment. This tends to indicate that the average size of establishments has gone down. This could have been due to an upward shift in the technology frontier, or an increase in the proportion of self-employed persons; the latter seems to be the more probable cause.

4. Waste Recycling Industry in Ahmedabad

Interestingly, the informal sector not only relies heavily on the use of local resources, but also plays a significant role in recuperating and recycling materials that are otherwise wasted. In this way, the informal sector provides not only cheap inputs but also cheaper wage goods for a big majority of workers in the formal sector.

A systematic study about the waste recycling industry in Bangalore was carried out by Aziz (1984). An important reason for choosing waste recycling industry was, in his own words, that it would provide a key to our understanding of the mechanism of poverty among the urban workers. The Bangalore study revealed that, on an average, one enterprise in this industry provides 615 mandays of work which is equivalent of employing two persons almost for the whole year. Ahmedabad's Gujari Bazar is also a waste recycling market and its study should thus be of great value both for understanding an important segment of a city's economy and for looking deeply into the employment, earnings and other associated details about the urban poor[6]. Section 4 throws up many valuable insights about the Gujari Bazar of Ahmedabad[7].

Ahmedabad's Gujari Bazar (hereafter Bazaar) was established during Ahmed Shah's rule. Since then, it has been shifted from one place to the other, before reaching its present location in Victoria Garden area of the city. It consists of 900 members a majority of whom belong to the Muslim Community; Marwadi, Waghri, Baniya, Bhil and the rest are from other communities. The Bazaar has a 10-member executive committee with a President who is nominated by turn. The annual membership fee is Rs. 5 plus Rs. 21 donation paid to the association. The association employs a total of 18 staff members which include 4 watchmen, 4 fund collectors, 2 munims (account clerks), 1 sweeper, 1 mike operator, and so on. Drinking water is provided free to the customers at four points in the Bazaar. The accounts of the association are audited every year. All disputes among the members are settled by the association.

The Bazaar functions every Sunday from 7.00 a.m. to 7.00 p.m. During the rest of the days, members of the association work at different jobs, as casual labors, hawkers, and do other miscellaneous things for their regular livelihood. Some members manufacture goods for the Bazaar itself. A permanent place (stall) is

---

6. The study was carried out with the help of Dr. Harshida Dave in November, 1999.
7. Markets selling recycled wastes orsecond hand goods are found in most big cities in India. Chandni Chowk in Delhi, Sahar Road in Mumbai, Surat's Chowk Bazar and Ahmedabad's Victoria Garden are well known.

allotted to each member and they organize their shops and bring the goods in cart and sell it. A nominal fee is charged for the allotted space. The Bazaar functions round the year for 52 weeks and occasionally; it remains closed only during communal disturbance and rainy season.

All types of goods like wooden furniture, electronic goods, old books and clothes, crockery, musical tools and cassettes, automobile spare parts, tube and tyres, utensils, steel furniture, and numerous other items are sold at rates which are considerably lower than the those prevailing in the regular markets. Nearly one lakh people visit this Bazaar for purchasing items of daily use to the household. The earning per participant varies between Rs. 500 to Rs. 2000; this earning is in addition to the income that accrues to them in their normal economic activity or source of employment.

Commercial and cooperative banks advance loans to the members of the association. These vary from Rs. 5,000 to Rs. 10,000; a 14 per cent rate of interest is charged. The loan is advanced on the authority of a certificate issued by the association. The association issues identity cards to its members which help them in establishing their identity during disturbed law and order situations, against police harassment, and in dealing with lending institutions and agencies. As is reported from many other areas, the city police in Ahmedabad too harasses the vendors in many different ways, at times by throwing out their goods, beating them on false pretexts, and almost regularly by extracting a 'weekly gratification (the so-called 'hafta') from each vendor. The police is especially harsh with the vendors in areas around (but outside) the Bazaar (e.g., Bhadra, Italian Bakery, Akhandanand Hospital, I.P.Mission School, etc.).

Our study of the Bazaar is based on the information obtained from 50 weekly market-respondents. The main results of the study are as under:

4.1 Economic Activity

In the Bazaar, a wide variety of items are sold; sale of cloth and garments, old books, furniture and fixture, utensil, electronic goods, glass items and crockery, automobile tools and parts, etc. are the major items traded upon. Thanks to the steadily rising pace of urbanization, and the changing composition of the urban population, the Bazaar has also been adding new activities to its list. Apart from their business activities in the Sunday Bazaar, the vendors are engaged in various other activities during the other six days of the week; details follow later.

4.2 Housing

Most of the respondents have their own houses. All houses have semi-pucca and pucca construction. The respondents mostly reside in different parts of the city (e.g., Jamalpur, Shahpur, Astodia, Maninagar, Isanpur, etc); only 10 per cent live nearby the Bazaar. Most of the respondents have 3-4 room houses; only a few have 1-2 room houses, with the needed civic facilities available inside the house.

4.3 Age of the Respondents

Nearly two-third of the respondents are young, in the age groups 21 to 30 and 31 to 40 years. Hardly 5-6 per cent of them are below the age of 20 years, and very few (10 per cent) are old, say, 51 years and above. The pattern of young and middle-aged persons dominating among the sample respondents is discernible both among the males and females, especially among the latter. That women too are actively involved, in a big way, in the informal activities of the Bazaar is a clear signal of the fact that it is the poverty of the household that drives them to carry out additional, but low paying, activities in places such as the Gujari Bazaar of Ahmedabad city.

4.4 Other Occupations

The head of the family as well as other members of the household are engaged in a host of activities, in addition to what they do at Bazaar. Table 17 gives the broad details.

As Table 17 shows, the responding households are involved practically in all types of activities listed in the table. The number is fairly evenly spread over different occupations. The involvement of persons is, however, not so even among different occupations. Casual labour is the family activity of a very large number of persons. This at once shows that it is the inadequacy of the household earning from the main occupation that prompts some members to do their additional bit in the Gujari Bazaar. In any case, in most of the other occupations too, most markedly Lari Galla (driving of hand carts), hawking, job works, petty business, etc., the yearly earnings of the

TABLE 17 : **Economic Activities of the Households**

S. No.	Type of Occupation	No. of Families	Male	Female	Total
(1)	Casual Labour	6	27	30	57
(2)	Business	7	18	4	22
(3)	Job Works	7	10	2	12
(4)	Manufacturing Goods	9	20	5	25
(5)	Automobile Garage	4	5	-	5
(6)	Lari Galla	8	10	8	18
(7)	Hawker	5	12	3	15
(8)	Others	4	10	8	18
	Total	50	112	60	172

households are not sufficient to provide two square meals. Involvement of some members of such households in the Gujari Bazaar activities is essentially a part of the survival strategy that the family sets for itself.

4.5 Education of the Respondents

Table 18 gives a highly disparate picture on the educational background of the respondents. Although a majority of them are either illiterate or have had schooling up to seventh standards, yet quite a few of them did secondary level schooling; some of them are even graduates and nearly 10 per cent of them did obtain technical or vocational education as well. The case of Ahmedabad's Gujari Bazaar clearly show that the informal labour market is not the exclusive preserve of the illiterate or the uneducated lot of job seekers. A substantial number of them involved in diverse types of the informal sector activities are educated but have not been able to gain entry into the formal job market; hence, no choice but to fall back upon the informal sector as long as 'the sun refuses to shine directly over their head'.

TABLE 18 : **Educational Background of the Respondents**

Level of Education	No.	Percentage
Illiterate	10	20
Primary upto VII Std.	19	38
Secondary & HSC	8	16
Graduate	8	16
Other	5	10
Total	50	100

A very high proportion of female respondents were illiterates. This suggests that the state sponsored literacy programmes have not made any noticeable impact so far. In any case, the Bazaar pattern of female education reconfirms the general neglect of women's education that comes up, again and again, in varying form and content, in all parts of our society. To the extent that many among the fe male Gujari Bazaar respondents are migrants from the rural areas, their low level of education is a natural fallout of the social moorings under which they spent their teens and adolescence.

4.6 Education of the Family Members

Table 19 gives the educational background of the family members of the responding households. Compared with men, a much higher proportion of women are illiterates. On the other hand, a much higher proportion of men are educated, say, secondary and higher level of schooling. In total terms, men are much better off in terms of their educational accomplishments than their female counterparts. This is indeed in conformity with the male:female educational differentials that one comes across, practically in all parts of our society in general, including the urban areas.

TABLE 19 : **Educational Standards of Family Members**

Level of Education	Male	Female	Total	%
Illiterate	30	65	95	27
Primary upto VII Std.	65	45	110	31
Secondary and HSC	60	40	100	28
Graduate	10	5	15	4
Other	18	18	36	10
Total	183	173	356	100

It is nonetheless important to note that in spite of their relative educational backwardness compared with the males, women belonging to lower sections of the urban society do also attach premium to education; among our sample households, a fairly sizeable number of them have had a secondary and higher level of education to their credit; perhaps, a slightly higher proportion of them have acquired technical and professional education as well. Thus, the impact of the urban society in bridging the male:female educational gaps seems to be at work; perhaps, it is a slow process but, in sharp contrast to the rural socio-cultural milieu, the females in the open and less orthodox urban environment, seem to be catching up with their male counterparts.

4.7 Household Income

Net Income of the families from regular occupational sources (i.e., all sources other than the Gujari Bazaar) is given below:

It seems, a majority of the sample households have monthly income between Rs. 1000 to 5000 per month. Thus 16 per cent of the families had income below Rs. 1000 per month. By any objective reckoning, the income levels from their regular occupations seem to be low for ensuring a minimum standard of living. In some cases, even survival may be at stake. It is natural, therefore, for most of these households to venture into some additional sources of earnings. The urban informal sector is thus the natural economic refuge, and for our respondents, the Gujari Bazaar

TABLE 20 : **Household Income from Regular Occupations**

Income Per Month	Nos.	%
Upto Rs. 1000	10	20
Rs. 1001 to Rs. 3000	15	30
Rs. 3001 to Rs. 5000	20	40
Rs. 5001 to Rs. 7000	3	6
Rs. 7001 to Rs. 10000	2	4
Total	50	100

turned out to the final choice. Any additional income earned by our respondents from the Bazaar helps them in sustaining their families.

The additional income earned from their Gujari Bazaar activities is sketched out in Table 21. More than two-third of the households earn up to Rs. 1,000 or less from their Bazaar activities. This may appear to be a ridiculously small amount, but then, this is largely the outcome of a once-a-week engagement. From the view point of the survival of the family, even a small supplementary earning goes them a long way. And, this indeed is the triggering factor behind a wide range of the informal sector activities, most ostensibly because, for the people involved here, no better alternatives are available.

TABLE 21 : **Income Earned from the Gujari Bazaar Activities**

Income Group	Nos.	%
Upto Rs. 500	17	34
Rs. 501 to Rs. 1000	17	34
Rs. 1001 to Rs. 2000	6	12
More than Rs. 2000	10	20
Total	50	100

4.8 Borrowings

On account of low income, the respondents have often to incur loans (Table 22). It is not a very happy scenario that only 10 out of 50 respondents could secure loans from Cooperative Banks. The case of Gujari Bazaar authenticates the general impression that institutional credit generally bypasses the informal sector enterprises. Nonetheless, Table 22 also shows that very few respondents fall back upon money lenders and, friends and relatives. It seems, there is very little demand for credit among the Gujari Bazaar respondents presumably because they are involved in activities with extremely low capital stakes, or the fact of borrowing from money lenders and relatives is not disclosed, or the unhelpful procedures of the institutional agencies keep many of them away. In spite of such infirmities, the amount of loan advanced by a cooperative banks is substantially higher than that borrowed from private sources. This has implications, both on the demand and supply sides of the institutional credit market.

TABLE 22 : **Borrowings by Sample Respondents by Source of Lending**

Source of Loan	No.	Amount of loan
Money lender	1	Rs. 3000/-
Friends and Relatives	4	Rs. 1000 to Rs. 2000/-
Cooperative Banks	10	Rs. 5000 to Rs. 10000/-

4.9 Summing Up:

Informal markets are the nerve centres of economic, social and cultural activities; they also serve as a contact point with the regular market channel. Informal labour market plays an important role in sustaining people who cannot obtain productive employment elsewhere in the economy and whose only alternative is destitution. Section 4 clearly shows that the waste recycling industry supplements the incomes of a large number of persons engaged in the informal sector.

Some *suggestions,* made by our sample respondents, to improve their conditions, are that:

(1) the land should be maintained and could be used for other purposes except Sunday;

(2) members of the Association should be given equal land for marketing;.

(3) unnecessary encroachments should be removed either by police department or by the Ahmedabad Municipal Corporation; the police should strictly keep in check anti-social elements;

(4) folding sheds for marketing should be provided to vendors in Gujari Bazar, so that they can carry on their business better even under adverse weather conditions;

(5) small shops should be constructed and provided to the members on license and lease base;

(6) a Government agency should encourage members by providing them loan and marketing their goods so that they get out of the clutches of the big manufacturers;

(7) basic civic facilities such as electricity, water and toilets etc. should be provided near the Bazaar; and

(8) women should be encouraged to undertake manufacturing of goods and helped in setting up small units of their own.

The study reveals some of the problems faced by the informal sector and should be useful in deciding policies which can give it the necessary fillip so that it can provide opportunities for employment to a large number of persons who cannot find entry into the formal sector.

5. Supportive Action for Informal Sector

Various studies have now established that the segment of the informal sector which holds a definitive potential for making significant contribution to generation of employment and incomes consists of small establishments. Independent workers were doing well in terms of earning a livelihood, but not generating much investible surpluses. Hotels and restaurants have grown faster and their employment:turnover ratio is also the highest, but their growth is highly dependent upon the whole gamut of economic activities in the city.

Papola's study about informal sector activity in Ahmedabad showed that for manufacturing establishments, labour productivity was found comparable to formal sector counterparts, specially in metal products, machinery and transport equipment. The capital intensity was, however, only one half of that in the formal sector. They were also at ease in the matter of raw materials availability. However, in their attempt to continue to be exempt from provisions of certain labour legislation, they may try to minimize the use of labour and overcapitalize, thus leading to a decline in employment potential on the one hand, and sub-optimal utilization of capital on the other. Secondly, this may further depress the earnings and working conditions of workers in this sector, although labour productivity may go on increasing. There is lesser attention paid to worker safety, to save on costs. The degree of exploitation of workers is certainly higher in this sector than in the formal sector. Hours of work are not regulated effectively, and therefore a sizeable proportion of workers have to work for 10 to 12 hours a day. Wages in the manufacturing sector are less than one half of those in the organized sector although labour productivity is almost at par. Most importantly, the informal sector activities which have shown better performance are the ones which are linked to the formal sector in terms of market and technology; their growth is, therefore, highly dependent on the growth of the formal sector.

In traditional economic theory, non-regular jobs and petty self-employment which together constitute the informal sector, were considered a transitory phenomenon. However, it is now clear that it is far from being a temporary phase. The pressure on the informal sector to absorb surplus labour will continue to grow. If so, how do we support such activities so as to create more and sustainable jobs, especially self-employment opportunities.

In order to arrive at some realistic solution, it is necessary to recapitulate some basic facts. The informal sector (IS) for the city economy of Ahmedabad provides employment to 74.2 per cent of the work-force. If we look into IS employment in non-agriculture sector alone, 57.7 per cent is in trade, transport, hotels, storage and communications and other services; another 4.7 per cent is in the construction sector. The productive labour absorption in these activities will depend on the growth and value added in these activities. This in turn will depend on the growth of commodity producing sectors which are agriculture and manufacturing. There is thus an increasing realization among the state policy makers that much greater emphasis is required to be given to agriculture in future planning for the state's economic development.

Promotion of agricultural growth, by spread of technological innovation including bio-technology, to more crops and more regions, is expected to result in dispersed regional growth which, by its very nature, will mesh with the dispersed character of I.S. itself. It is in this context that support to export orientation of agro-based products is needed. Public investment in supporting agriculture related research and development and transmission of new technologies to fields, and protection and utilisation of indigenous genetic resources, should be increased. It is increasingly felt that, in years to come, it is this kind of strategy more than the conventional wisdom of making greater public investment in irrigation, that will accelerate development and employment generation, on an enduring basis.

5.1 Upgradation of Technology

As regards manufacturing, the dividing line between informal and formal enterprises is in terms of either investment or number of persons employed. The dividing line itself has been changing, and there is, therefore, no fixed definition. In fact, the relatively better off segment of the informal manufacturing sector, i.e. SSIs appropriate to itself most of the benefits from the Government sponsored policies. Nonetheless, there are several innovative technology options for urban informal sector in food processing, leather and animal waste based technology, building material, drinking water, environment and sanitation, artisans skill development, and so on. These technologies are developed by a host of R&D organizations in India which include CSIR, ICAR, Indian Institutes of Technology, Universities, KVIC, and in Gujarat, by the Rural Technology Institute RTI). The R.T.I. has developed several innovative and cost effective machines like Pearl dwelling machine, leather tanning drum, carcass lifting device, leaf cup making machines, modified potters wheel, and so on. What is missing is the extension mechanism, which should be developed as a top priority. Further, while we contemplate upgradation of technology, care has to be taken that the scale of production does not make the enterprise unviable in the local context.

5.2 Provision of Finance

Informal sector enterprises have emerged out of necessity to create one's own employment in spite of lack of investment resources. Most of the enterprises do not have access to formal bank credit, but depend primarily on own savings, borrowings from friends and relatives, usually at usurious rates of interest.

Capital shortages lead to sub-optimal level of productivity and employment. Unable to buy in sufficient quantities, small enterprises may have to depend upon middlemen rather than original sources and end up paying higher prices. Hence I.S. has to be provided access to formal sources of capital at reasonable rates of interest. A liberal policy of sanctioning institutional loans and government grants is advocated. However, this might increase the default rate in repayment of loans, thereby increasing the burden on the public exchequer. Despite this risk, provision of financing for small enterprises is a high priority for the State Government. This issue is being emphasized in State Level Banker's Committee meetings as well as District Level Banker's Committees for review of the Self-Employment Schemes directed to IS enterprises, among others.

5.3 Self-Employment Schemes

There are many self-employment generating schemes, launched by State and Central Governments, including those expressly directed to the educated youth.

Among these, *Vajpayee Swarojgar Yojana and Prime Minister Rojgar Yojana* are the centrally sponsored schemes and have been working with a varying degree of success. *Din Dayal Upadhyaya Sankalit Swavalamban Yojana* is a state sponsored scheme that aims at creating self-employment opportunities for educated youth in 51 backward taluka of Gujarat. In 1998, the total number of the youth in live registers was 45,460 in these talukas. The programme included counseling, helping them in preparing projects and applications for bank loans, meeting their training needs and establishing backward and forward linkages. Out of the 45,460 candidates on live registers, 21728 actually expressed their readiness for taking up self-employment projects. Of these, 4,280 actually succeeded in settling themselves in one or the other type of some self-employment ventures. This scheme has thus helped, in a limited way, in creating self-employment.

5.4 Education and Labour Force

In the year 1997-98, 6.19 lakhs students appeared in the Secondary School Certificate Examination. Of these, 2.11 lakhs passed. Thus 4.08 lakhs actually remained as drop-outs, even after two trials. Added to this is the fact that 6.67 lakh students were on rolls in Standard VIII and only 4.14 lakh could reach Standard X, leaving an additional 2.2 lakhs as drop-outs between StandardVIII and X. Thus, a total drop-out of adolescents are nearly 6.33 lakhs per year. The options before such drop-outs are limited. It could be the search for work, mainly as unskilled or semiskilled literate workers, in the small scale industry, shops and commercial establishments or in the service sector. If failed in this search, they probably end up as helpers or home-based workers or simply as farm labourers. But then, a sizeable number of them do not find even such menial types of work opportunities. The result is that nearly half of them become 'nowhere children', neither at school nor at work, and become susceptible to all types of socially unacceptable activities or they just lumpenize around. The State is making a concerted effort for bringing the drop-outs back to the school as well as on giving them vocational skills.

Upgradation of skills of the informal sector workers has long been contemplated as a means of making the youth fit for self-employment. The TRYSEM programme has had a limited success in the State for facilitating transition from training to the successful quarrying of enterprises in the line of business for which skill was imparted. The State has laid great emphasis on vocational training, with 34,000 candidates having been trained so far, for N.C.V.T. approved regular as well as short term courses. Further, with the opening up of employment opportunities in Information Technology Enabled Services, the State plans to train 1 lakh youth in short-term computer courses over the next two years.

5.5 Home Based Workers

Within the informal sector, the home-based workers constitute an important category not only because of the sheer number involved but also because they are mainly women who are vulnerable to exploitation due to low bargaining power. A recent estimate made by SEWA Ahmedabad about their number in Gujarat places it at 19 lakhs. Table 23 provides activity-wise break-up of such workers.

The low bargaining power arises due to over crowding in home-based activities and from their multiple responsibilities as workers, wives, mothers and so on. Moreover, they are piece rate workers, usually with no relationship between human effort put and earning. The piece rate per unit of work is fixed at a low level due to their low bargaining power.

Further, availability of work depends on the supply of raw material provided by the employer while their efficiency depends on the quality of raw material, skill and working and living conditions. Hence, the growth of opportunities even for home-based work depends on the growth of the associated activities.

The issue of employer-employee relationship in the home-based work has been debated for long. The criteria such as supervision and control, power to reject products and of late, test of economic reality, have been used by the courts of law.

TABLE 23 : **Activity-wise Break-up of Home-based Workers in Gujarat : SEWA Estimates**

Activity	Total Workers	Males (%)	Females (%)
1. Beedi-making	1,50,000	3,000(2)	1,47,000(98)
2. Cloth-making	4,00,000	1,60,000(40)	2,40,000(60)
3. Agarbatti-making	50,000	3,500(7)	46,500(93)
4. Papad and Food Processing	3,00,000	1,20,000(40)	1,80,000(60)
5. Embroidery	10,00,000	1,0,000(10)	9,00,000(90)

The International Labour Organization has also recently passed a convention that seeks to regulate conditions of work and welfare of home-based workers.

The common problems in the home-based work, such as stitching garments, food-processing, beedi- and agarbatti-making, tin-smithy and paper and bamboo work are (1) low wages, (2) low bargaining power, especially the absence of an organizational support to secure better economic deal, (3) absence of diversification and skill upgradation, and (4) lack of social security and health support system:

Given the depressing working conditions of the home-based workers, most essentially because of the predominance of women workers among them, a suggestion has been made in various fora, particularly in the report of National Commission on Women Self- Employed Persons, to establish Tripartite Boards in major urban centers which have a pronounced concentration of home-based workers in particular activities. Such Boards could be on the pattern of Mathadi Workers Board in Maharashtra or Kapad Bazar Kamadar Board in Gujarat. Such a Board is expected to take up mainly welfare schemes, the finance for which can be raised through tripartite contributions. In setting up a Tripartite Board, due emphasis has to be put on the relation between a group of employers and a group of workers in a given activity, rather than on individual relationship between the workers and the employer. These Boards can undertake welfare and social security initiatives such as fixation of piece rate wages, implement social insurance schemes such as life insurance, health insurance, maternity benefit schemes, provident fund scheme.

5.6 National Renewal Fund and Re-deployment of Displaced Workers

Gujarat faced the problem of almost a lakh of textile workers losing their jobs due to the closure of composite textile mills. The concept of National Renewal Fund (NRF) was announced by Government of India as a part of its new Industrial Policy of July 1991, to protect the interests of workers who may be affected by technological upgradation and modernization in Indian Industry.

The NRF scheme of retraining and redeployment is applicable to those workers who have been displaced after 24th July, 1991. An age-limit of 55 years is imposed for those who require vocational training. Under the present programme, training is given for 50 working days, and for each day of training, the workers are paid a stipend of Rs. 60.00 in Ahmedabad and Rs. 50.00 in other centers; as many as 43 trades have been identified for training in selected training centres.

However, the number of displaced workers who have shown interest in retraining has been small; presumably, they have either found some workable alternative or have preferred to live retired life due to age. A total of 11,787 workers have been surveyed in the last five years and provided counseling for prudent investment of their compensation money, if any, and on available alternative avenues of their self-employment or jobs with or without retraining. Of these, 7,590 workers have been imparted retraining in a variety of vocational skills. After training and counseling, 2,111 workers were found to be gainfully redeployed in the activities for which retraining was given. About 60 per cent among the redeployed workers were self-employed, the rest had got wage employment.

A survey of 1,729 displaced textile workers in Ahmedabad carried out by the Mahatma Gandhi Labour Institute in 1995-96 showed that, on an average, a self-employed worker was found earning Rs. 837/- per month while a wage-paid worker was earning Rs. 870/- per month. Among the self-employed, the income was relatively high in transportation and of those who were engaged in the distribution of gas, water, power, etc. Among the wage-paid workers also, the monthly wage was relatively high in transportation and in the distribution of gas, water, etc. What is however striking is that there is no significant difference between the monthly income of the self-employed and the casual workers. The overall environment for financial prudence and discipline is vitiated and hence, there are general problems of low recovery, channelising finance to non-target group, distortion of the purpose of utilising finance and even under-financing.

Given this context, the role of NGOs to provide finance for such petty entrepreneurs have been considered crucial. SEWA-Ahmedabad Bank partnership has shown very good success in this regard. Loans at commercial rate of interest without subsidy and more than 90 per cent recovery, through their informal organisational channels, have shown the innovative path of how to provide finance to such petty producers. However, even in the case of NGOs, the real cost of credit is likely to be high because, in reality, they have low cost funds and the complete absence of imputed costs including that of manpower deployed, makes all the difference. Even so, we need to promote informal credit unions by involving associations of each category of home-based workers.

5.7 Handloom Sector

Special reference is required to be made of the handloom sector as a source of self- employment. There are about 38,500 handloom weavers in the State. Of these 20,178 are members of cooperative societies, 8,626 are registered with the State Handloom Development Corporation and another 9,800 with the State Khadi Board. However, the handloom sector has been showing a consistently downward trend over the past 7-8 years. Production has come down to half the level of 1990-91 and as many as 23,500 of the 38,500 handloom weavers are idle. The reason can be attributed to rise in the price of yarn due to export, rise in the cost of dyes and chemicals, and unequal competition with power-looms and textile mills. The policy of structural readjustment looks on protection, reservation and subsidies with disfavour. However, production in such unorganized and vulnerable sectors through subsidy support, input quotas and reservation, is necessary because of their handicaps in the product, input and credit markets.

5.8 Issues of Urban Environment and Policy

Although slum dwellers and workers in the I.S. are not synonymous, there is a large degree of overlap all the same. The urban I.S. has myriad activities, but a fairly large part of the service sector consists of vendors of goods, fruits and vegetables, domestic servants, service provides like shoe-shine boys, makers of toys, statue handicrafts etc. Serious problems exit both at the place of their business and residence.

Municipal authorities carry out periodic demolition of stalls, confiscation of hand carts and chasing away street vendors. This drive at improving the city environment does not have any permanent effect, as these persons have nowhere else to go. Regulation thus results only in harassment, loss of goods and income and further economic deprivation; extortion of money by police and municipal enforcement staff then becomes a routine affair. A solution, often suggested and debated upon, is to provide the I.S. workers a permanent place of work, but this should not be given free. The I.S. workers should be asked to pay lease rental according to the economic value of the allotted place. Patronage in any form should be scrupulously avoided; it is invariably cornered by a few unscrupulous persons while the needy and deserving are left out.

The second problem concerns the growing slum population. The six major urban centres of Gujarat (Ahmedabad, Surat, Vadodara, Rajkot, Bhavnagar and Jamnagar) each have a slum population of around 30 to 40 per cent of their total urban population. The State has consistently tried to upgrade the slums wherever these exist, and also give titles to squatters, but constraints of space make this task onerous. Many slum dwellers are also not amenable to multi-story dwellings. For instance, the makers of religious idols (say, Ganesh murtis) in Ahmedabad want space for their work, and also to maintain their goats and poultry which provide them supplementary income and/or nutrition, and hence insist on ground floor dwellings. We have to find satisfactory solutions to these problems within the overall content of urban development.

6. Labour Standards in the Informal Sector

As yet, there is no proper alignment of industrial relations policies with the industrialisation strategies being currently pursued in India. A majority of the work-force is outside the purview of formal industrial relations system. The labour policy, legal framework and labour administration have not yet fully perceived and internalized the concerns and challenges facing or rather inhibiting the work-force at large. The changing times call for a radical rethinking on the form and content of labour policies. It should move away from restriction and regulation to facilitation, from reaction to pro-action and dispute resolution to the creation of sound and harmonious, relations conducive to economic and social development. There should be a decisive shift towards proactive labour market interventions with a major thrust towards development of skills, attitudes, approaches and insights to build a cohesive and productive work culture. Labour policies must be more closely aligned to changes in industrial and other policies; they should provide stimulus rather than supplant job creation. Labour market flexibility is an important ingredient of employment intensive growth strategy. Right mechanisms should, therefore, be devised for sustaining flexible labour market.

Industrial relations in the informal sector cannot be subjected to the same legal and institutional framework as in the formal sector. This is on account of (1) absence of clear employer-employee contractual relationship, (2) lack of stability and durability of employment, (3) low level of literacy, awareness and capability of both the proprietor and the worker, (4) time and cost involved in the usually long drawn out civil and adjudication proceedings, an luxury neither the employer nor the worker can afford. Such problems are already experienced in the case of home workers, in particular with regard to beedi-, agarbati- and garment-making and food processing industry in Gujarat. The contractors supply raw materials to home workers and collect finished products from them against piece rate payment; they also have the right of supervision over the quality of the finished product including right of rejecting the product which does not conform to their standards.

Actually, this practice has been adopted purely to avoid employer-employee relationship. The workers are thus deprived of minimum wages and other benefits like provident fund and gratuity. On the other hand, forcing the employees into a formal relationship with home-based workers may result in shrinkage or disappearance of the informal sector job opportunities.

Papola's study of the informal sector at Ahmedabad also indicated that the degree of exploitation of workers is much higher in this sector than in the formal sector. The hours of work are also not regulated and a sizeable proportion of workers have to work for over 10 hours a day. Wages in the manufacturing establishments in the informal sector are also around one-half of those in the organised sector. All these could be considered as an effect of over-crowded labour market and lack of job opportunities in the formal sector. An improvement in this condition can come about partly through increase in productivity and profitability of the informal sector by providing them finance and other support. Purely legal solutions are not likely to work this situation.

Instead of subjecting such establishment to the rigours of conciliation, arbitration and adjudication, which are time consuming and expensive, alternate systems and procedures will have to be thought out; perhaps, this may an appropriate issue for reference to the Second Labour Inquiry Commission.

7. Social Security for the Unorganized Sector Workers

Social Security has to be seen in the contest of the overall need of the urorganized sector. It is a measure to increase and maintain the productivity of the workers in times of distress so as to make them viable economically and increase their economic security at other times. This security can be provided through various types of insurance. Although insurance market in India is rapidly growing, most insurance companies are not looking to the unorganized sector as a possible market. Insurance companies tend to see this sector as unable or unwilling to participate in insurance schemes. This however, may be a misplaced perception which results in the unorganized sector not being offered insurance policies which meet their needs. Crises are a recurrent fact in the life of the unorganized sector; every time a crisis occurs, the sector becomes weaker and more vulnerable. Thus, it is usually a crisis, personal, social or natural that drives a family into the downward cycle and finally into destitution. However, if the facility of insurance was available to them, they would be able to spread the risk over a longer period, so that they could pay for it during the very time of their earning. In other words, insurance would offer them the facility of spreading risk and vulnerability over a period of time.

The Life Insurance Corporation has a Janata Policy Scheme which offers coverage for life insurance at a premium of Rs. 10.00 for every thousand rupees of insurance benefit. The coverage under this scheme is not however very wide among the unorganized workers. The Government of Gujarat has, however, a scheme of its own which covers 73 lakh unorganized workers (i.e. all those not covered under the Employees State Insurance Scheme). The coverage is of Rs. 20,000.00 for accidental death or complete disability and Rs. 10,000.00 for partial disability. At present, the scheme is wholly government financed. We have to make the scheme participatory; the workers may also be induced to have life insurance coverage through their own token participation.

Here, it may be appropriate to refer to the successful SEWA Bank linked insurance scheme which links insurance with workers' savings and promotes trade union approach in the sector. The details of the insurance coverage are set out in Table 24. At present, the scheme covers about 30,000 workers. It throws up many lessons; most essentially, it reminds us that (1) the unorganized workers are willing to pay, whatever is possible within their capacity, a premium for insurance coverage, and (2) providing insurance to the unorganized sector requires institutional mechanisms which offer services that are usually accessible to workers in the organized sector.

Government of India too has implemented a scheme of housing subsidy for beedi workers and hamals in big cities under which a subsidy of Rs. 1,000.00 per house is available. The Gujarat Government is proposing a further subsidy of Rs. 10,000.00 in addition to the subsidy of Rs. 10,000.00 provided by the Government of India. These schemes are, however, at a nascent stage, and the coverage is very limited. As the unorganised sector comprises 74 per cent of the total labour force, much greater effort has to be put in to provide them with reasonable housing and social security.

TABLE 24 : **Details of Insurance Coverage under SEWA Bank Linked Scheme**

Type of Coverage Premium	Amount of Coverage Rs.	Annual Rs.
1. Sickness (Health Insurance)	1,000	15.00
2. Accidental Death and Partial Disablement	10,000	3.50
3. Accidental Death and Partial Disablement of Spouse	10,000	3.50
4. Loss during Flood, Fire, Theft, etc.		
-- Loss of Work Implements -- Loss to Hut/House	2,000 3,000	8.00 15.00
5. Natural Death of Person or Spouse	3,000	15.00
6. Maternity	300	On use of FD linked insurance
7. Total Annual Premium	–	45.00

Bibliography

Aziz, Abdul, Urban Poor and Urban Informal Sector, ISEC, Bangalore, 1984.

Eckaus, R.S. "The Factor Proportions Problem in Under-developed Areas", American Economic Review, September 1955.

Fei JCH and Ranis G. Development of the Labour Surplus Economy: Theory and Policy, Richard B. Irwin Inc. Homewood Illinois, 1964.

Govt. of Gujarat, Technical Papers on Perspective Plan of Gujarat, 2005. Planning Department.

____, Population Characteristics of Gujarat 1991 (Urban Profile), Directorate of Economics and Statistics.

____, Results of Fourth Economic Census, Gujarat State, 1998. Directorate of Economics and Statistics.

____, Primary Census Abstract: General Population, Part II-B(i), Directorate of Census Operations, Gujarat.

Harris John R. and Todaro Michael P. "Migration, Unemployment and Development: A Two-Sector Analysis", American Economic Review, March 1970.

Lewis, W.A. "Economic Development with Unlimited Supplies of Labour", The Manchester School of Economic and Social Studies, 22, May 1954.

Papola T.S. Informal Sector in an Urban Economy: A Study in Ahmedabad, Giri Institute of Development Studies, 1979.

Unni Jeemol and Rani Usha, Employment and Income in the Informal Sector: The Case of Ahmedabad, GIDR-SEWA, 2000.

Todaro, Michael P. "A Model of Labour Migration and Urban Unemployment in Less Developed Countries", American Economic Review, March 1969.

Informal Sector in Urban Economy of Uttar Pradesh: Issues and Policy Concerns

A.P. Verma and Arvind Mohan

1. Introduction

In Uttar Pradesh (UP), a major part of the economy consists of small and tiny production organisations, run on self-employment basis. This segment has been variously described as the informal, the unorganised, or the traditional sector. In UP, the development trends since the 1980s reveal that the employment generation capacity in the formal segments of the two major sectors, viz. agriculture and industry, has declined. Naturally, much of the growing labour force is finding employment outside these sectors. Since entry into the informal sector is largely driven by one's own choices, and alternatives to the expanding army of the semi-literate, unskilled and capital-poor employment seekers are generally absent, it has emerged as a major employer in the state. It is, however, observed that during the 1990s, the absorptive capacity of this sector has generally tended to decline, throwing up serious challenges for policy makers in the country. This paper seeks to develop a macro economic perspective on the working of the urban informal sector in the state. Despite data limitations, the paper attempts to delineate the broad trends and dimensions of this sector in the most populous Indian state of Uttar Pradesh.

The formal and informal sector dichotomy was first attempted by Keith Hart, in a study of Urban Ghana. The ILO-UNDP mission in Kenya adopted the term 'informal sector' to analyse the employment situation and to work out a strategy for employment generation in Kenya. Easy entry for new enterprises, reliance on indigenous resources, family ownership, small scale operation, unregulated but competitive markets, labour intensive technology, and informally acquired skills of workers, were widely accepted as the main characteristics of this sector.

John Weeks, in his definition, suggests that the distinction between the formal and informal sectors, depends on the *"organisational characteristics of exchange relationship and the position of economic activity vis-a-vis the state"*. The nature of exchange relationship is primarily a consequence of *economic insecurity of operation in the informal sector*. This, in turn, is a direct consequence of the *latter's limited access to all types of resources*. The formal sector has the benefit of the protection of the state in the form of restrictions on competition and reduction in risk and uncertainty through tariff and quota protection, tax rebates and holidays, low interest rates, etc. Restricted competition and privileged access to resources such as foreign technology, foreign exchange, etc. provide disproportionately high rewards from operating in this sector. It must be mentioned that some of the characteristics proposed above are mainly appropriate to Kenya but may not be equally applicable to a state like U.P.

In the context of Uttar Pradesh, the characteristics such as *easy entry for new enterprises, small scale of operation, unregulated but competitive markets, labour intensive technology, informally acquired skills of workers,* etc. do have absolute relevance. However, other characteristics such as indigenous resources, availability of foreign technology and foreign capital are not the features that can distinguish the state's informal sector from the formal sector.

Nonetheless, some other important characteristics typical of UP, for that matter any other big and populous state of India, are:

(1) the informal sector is not a homogenous category. It can be easily classified into three distinguishable segments, namely (a) micro enterprises, (b) subcontracting type units, and (c) others;

(2) unprotected labour market;

(3) rural continuum built into its very operation;

(4) role of family tradition;

(5) social stratification on caste and religious lines;

(6) imputed wages of women workers;

(7) importance of price competition absence of product differentiation; and

(8) absence of entrepreneurial return in subcontracting type units.

It is thus clear that the primary distinction between these two sectors lie in the *market structure, barrier to entry, technology, unprotected labour market, social stratification and relationship with the government.* In the context of UP's urban economy, we are, therefore, strongly advised to treat dichotomies like the formal and informal and organised and unorganised sectors as interchangeable entities. This is what we do in the rest of the paper.

In order to develop a macro perspective regarding the nature, structure and the process involved in this sector, the paper looks into many of its features that are germane in the UP's context. The size, organization and the functioning of the urban informal sector, especially the process of informalisation that pervades all over the sector, labour market infirmities including the specific problems of women workers that are typical of it, the income and wage levels, the near-absence of social protection, etc. are analyzed to the extent that the available data permit.

Despite data limitations, the entire informal sector of the state has been taken as the universe of the study. Available secondary data has been used extensively to generate a macro picture of the sector. The 1990 Economic Census of UP, the Census of Small Scale Industries (UP, 1988), the Fourth Economic Census of UP 1998, studies by Directorate of Industries (GOUP), Technical Studies by Department of Labour;, and Arvind Mohan's studies on the informal sector and small scale industries (SSIs) of UP, have been some of the important secondary references used in this study besides drawing upon ILO's published work and other individual writings.

To sharpen our understanding of the sector, especially to throw bare the grass-roots realities as succinctly as possible, micro-level case studies and success stories have also been used extensively. to generate a general understanding about the working of the informal sector in UP. Some field information has been generated through canvassing of questionnaires and interviews. Due care has been exercised to generate data from different locations of UP, spread over as wide a range of industries as possible. Leather, hand-loom and power-loom, tourism, brassware, silk weaving, carpet-, lock-, and biscuit making are the major industries that provide source material for portraying the informal sector realities.

2. Informal Sector in Urban U.P.

As in any other big and populous state, the urban informal sector in U.P. has many facets, peculiarities and internal heterogeneities that may be difficult for a single paper to accurately caricaturize. Nonetheless, in Section 2, some kind of a profile of this sector is built, on the strength of whatever data was available to us.

2.1 Informalisation Process and Market Mechanism

The study of UP's informal sector testifies to the existence of the *informalisation process* in numerous activities dotting the sector. A typical economy has a large number of buyers dispersed all around. On the other hand, it has a large number of producers too. The producers have to know what and how much they have to produce, for whom do they have to produce, and so on. The answers to these questions lie with the consumers. What is needed is a communication mechanism, which informs the producers. The market mechanism emerges as the finest communication mechanism ever devised by mankind. *Information dissemination* is, therefore, the first important function of the market. It informs the producers what, how, how much and for whom they should produce. At the same time, it also informs the consumers how they can satisfy their demands/wants.

The second important function of the market is resource allocation. Consumers have unlimited wants and producers want to satisfy all of them. However, resources are limited on either side, and all the demands cannot be satisfied. It is, therefore, necessary to prioritise. The market mechanism emerges as the most efficient barometer of *resource* allocation. It allocates resources to those sectors and individuals who need it the most (highest bidder). Under normal circumstances, if the market mechanism functions appropriately, there is no need to segmentize the economy *into formal and informal sectors.* Also, there is no possibility of unemployment and underemployment or low wage employment in the informal sector happening. However, in reality, all these elements are found to be operative, in varying form and combination. We have unemployment, under employment and inflation and we also have a large unorganised/informal sector with low returns and low wages. It is very obvious that all this is the result of market imperfections and market failures.

We are of the view that information dissemination and resource allocation that is happening as a consequence of the working of the price mechanism is distorted. *It seems that the economy is not functioning as one integrated system rather it is divided into circuits.* The requirements of those who have "effective demand" get communicated to the organised/formal segment and resources get allocated to the producers of this sector so that they are able to meet those demands. The rest of the economy, which can be termed as the area of ignorance (of the market mechanism), remains outside the domain of reasonable information dissemination. *Even where effective demand exists and the information is disseminated to the informal sector also, the resources are not automatically allocated to this sector.* This is a clear case of breakdown of the market mechanism. It is more or less clear that the economy is functioning in response to false price signals.

The problem must also be evaluated in the context of *"price adjustment and quantity adjustment"* framework. It appears that the imperfect market is not in a position to cater to the needs of the entire population. The formal segment works in a manner that the cost structures are such that large-scale demands are not converted into effective demands and consequently, they are not provided for. One important reason for the emergence of the informal sector is the existence of this contrived kind of a market. It is understandable, therefore, that a tiny sector emerges which readies itself to operate on low margins, using traditional and obsolete technology. Looked at this way, it is clear that the *informal sector emerges to fill the gap left by the formal segment.*

This sector is *designated as informal plainly because it lies outside the formal market mechanism.* It is a new circuit altogether, which is in the shadow of the market mechanism. Naturally, some of the practices and methods have to be different from those in the organized segment. Much of the resources used in this segment do not flow within the broad confines of a money market exchange relationship. It is, therefore, not difficult to appreciate how the credit which flows into this segment normally does not flow against collateral security. Rather, it flows on the basis of inter-personal relationships. Often, credit and capital flow show some kind of a barter relationship. For example, in the credit-induced 'SEWA'[1] experiment, around 8000 women get employment. The turnover runs into crores and a number of production centres are at work. The production centre owners and the independent artisans are all self-employed people. However, the raw material and other associated pre-requisites are purchased by the SEWA management and the same is sent to the artisans sitting at home or at their respective production centres. Once the work is completed, the product is taken back and wages and other services paid for. Understandably, the credit needs of the artisans and other functionaries are taken care of. Under normal circumstances, the small artisans would have been required to generate their own resources. In the absence of any collateral security, these artisans would not have survived in the formal sector.

In the case of Kalpi handloom workers, much of the working capital and fixed investment come from family and friends. As far as technology is concerned, certainly the lower end technology is used in this segment and it becomes economically viable only when a variety of innovations are put through. In a handloom sector case study[2] Arvind Mohan found that the micro enterprise was producing and selling teri-cot shirt lengths at a rate of Rs. 16 per meter (1996). These are the rates at which the formal sector cannot produce, much less sell. Such low rates are the result of adaptation of traditional technology to modern circumstances. It involves innovations of the highest order. Interestingly, however, such prices have not brought the tiny sector in direct competition with the formal sector[3]. It is observed that *the informal sector is operating in a 'low level circuit', where the area of overlap with the larger circuit is very limited.* It appears that in the formal sector circuit, *product competition* is more important than the *price competition* and that, in turn, creates barriers to entry. *'Two-circuit'* existence is essentially a result of difference in the nature of competition. *Price competition* is the defining feature of the informal sector, whereas *product differentiation* defines the formal sector. We are of the opinion that the standard dichotomous classification may better read as *'Informal Circuit'* and *'Formal Circuit'*.

Given the 'two-circuit' theory, and the nature of growth of the informal sector in UP, the authors are convinced that its existence does not appear to be transitory. Equally

---

1 SEWA Lucknow is a kind of a co-operative of the informal units.

2 "Notes on the Informal Sector" by Arvind Mohan (mimeo).

3 ibid.

important is to note that the informal sector is catering to the needs of all those who have been ignored by the market mechanism. On the one hand, it is catering mostly to the demand of the under-privileged and, on the other, it is ensuring employment and survival to a vast majority of the population. *Market imperfection and failure have serious implications for resource allocation and distribution. In Uttar Pradesh, which has abundance of labour supply, labour emerges as the most affected resource. The distortions would, therefore, take the form of low wages, underemployment and the near-absence of imputed wages for family women workers, on one extreme, and unhygienic working and living conditions, on the other.* Time has come when research on the informal sector should move away from a mere analysis of the structure to the dynamic realm of *quantity adjustment* and *transmission mechanism.* The informal sector is not merely an area of welfare but it also involves policy implications regarding growth, choice of technique, equity and justice.

2.2. Organization of the Micro Enterprise Sector

A sizeable segment of the informal sector actually consists of micro enterprises, which have a linkage with the organized industry segment. For example, the carpet industry is divided into several processes and a large number of these processes like clippering, washing, etc. are jobs which are handled by the informal sector micro units. Again, in the brassware industry too, there are several processes or sub-activities, which are performed by the informal sector micro units; examples can be multiplied. In other words, the informal micro units are actually working as a peripheral constituent of a larger organized sector unit. These micro enterprises are very small in size. Often, there is a self-employed person who, in turn, employs another one or two persons. It deserves to be emphasized here that, for all practical purposes, informal sector enterprises of this kind, exist only as a 'group of wage earners' or sheer labourers. The payments made to the units are only sufficient enough to cover the wage cost of all the labour force involved. Perhaps, in some cases, they also cover expenditure made on hiring of premises.

Although an informal sector micro enterprise is critically linked to the larger organized sector industry, the *self-employed person or sub-contractor is not paid for his entrepreneurial function.* This is a critical dimension of exploitation and this appears to be structural rather than incidental. The micro enterprise makes significant contribution to the over-all profits of the organized industry. However, the entrepreneur in these micro units does not get any share in these profits. The normal logic of economic distribution suggests that wages should be received for the skills and profits for organizational contribution and uncertainty bearing. The entrepreneurs in this sector are getting only wages for the skills that they posses, plainly on the basis of piece wage rates for the work performed; they are not receiving any kind of entrepreneurial returns.

Amongst the 'sub-contracting units', there is no opportunity for generating price advantage because this sector is not actually competing with the formal sector but is working with it, in a regime of 'unequal exchange'. Either the middlemen or the larger formal sector entity enjoy all profits and a very small fraction of it is passed on to the micro enterprise. It is true that the informal sector produces at very cheap rates and these products are passed on to the next stage of production or to the middlemen. This however, does not lead to low prices for the consumer for the simple reason that in between, large profit margins are taken away by the formal sector enterprise and the middlemen.

The independent micro sector enterprises, which are not involved in some kind of sub-contracting relationship with the formal sector, show certain special characteristics of their own. They seem to have grown on the strength of their advantage in producing commodities at cheaper rates. They also seem to be having an advantage in terms of *access* to far-flung rural and remote area markets. Their marketing methods are traditional but time tested. The entrepreneurs in these units have to take care of a variety of functions such as design development, arranging working capital, managing official rules and procedures, and marketing. They put in extraordinarily *long hours of work,* operate on *low margins* and end up with very low returns. The labor intensity in these industries is found to be much higher than the formal sector. If long hours of work are taken into account, *labor intensity* is found to be even *higher* in this sector.

The full potential of the enterprise is not realized because, in most cases, *when some production is generated, the entrepreneur himself has to switch over from production to marketing and as a result, machines and everything else remain idle for that period. Only when the product is sold and some cash flow is generated that the raw material is bought and production restarts.* It appears *(a) the requirement of credit, particularly working capital, (b) design development, (c) technology, (d) marketing strategy, (e) skill upgradation, etc.* are the missing links in making this segment successful and self-sustaining.

The informal sector is in a position to generate price competition. It tries to compensate for its numerous disadvantages through very hard work, sometimes bordering on self-imposed sub-human working conditions, and extraordinary innovations. This is how it produces goods at prices, which are phenomenally lower than those in the formal sector. Unfortunately, however, the defining feature of the formal sector competition is product competition. The informal sector is thoroughly ill-equipped to position itself against the formal sector entity. The resourcelessness and the tininess of each individual operator in this sector is the root cause of this problem. Given the nature of the problem, it is felt that the state has the responsibility of ensuring that the informal sector at least gets an opportunity of competing in the domain of product competition.

It is interesting to note that the case for public sector is usually built on the argument of market failures. A plethora of literature exists on the theory of social goods. There is a world-wide understanding that there are goods which, because of their very nature, cannot be entrusted to the private sector; it is in larger public interest that production of such goods is entrusted to the care of the public sector. Unfortunately, however, similar attention has not been given to the informal sector and to the 'public interest outfit of the informal goods'. Here is a sector, which comes into existence as a consequence of the market failures. It is also the sector that provides employment to an overwhelming majority of the work-force and accounts for a very big chunk of urban production. It is difficult to understand how this critical entity of the national economy has not received due attention although we profess to be a welfare state. So far we have confined our attention to competition and fairness of competition within the formal sector. Time has come when at least the efforts of the government should not leave out the informal sector when dealing with issues like justice, equity and fair play; surely, something more concrete needs to be said about the unfair and unequal competition between the formal and the informal sectors.

2.3 Size of the Urban Informal Sector in U.P.

As per the 1998 Economic Census, there were 30.43 lakh enterprises in UP. Of these 4.4 per cent (or 1.33 lakh units) were agricultural enterprises and 29.1 lakh (95.6 per cent) were non-agricultural enterprises. In terms of location, 15.64 lakh units (51.4 per cent) were located in urban areas. Out of the urban units, 75.5 per cent were own account enterprises (OAEs) and 24.5 per cent were establishments. Further, 1.20 lakh OAEs were agricultural while the remaining 21.79 lakh were non-agricultural. Forty seven per cent (10.82 lakh) of the OAEs were located in urban areas. In 1998, there were 7.44 lakh establishments in Uttar Pradesh, 64.8 per cent of them being located in urban areas. The total number of enterprises grew by 15.6 per cent during 1990-98, at an annual growth rate 1.8 per cent. In the urban areas, the annual growth rate of these enterprises was 1.9 per cent. The highest number of enterprises were found in Lucknow followed by Kanpur.

In all, 74.80 lakh workers were employed in these enterprises; 32.32 lakh (43.2 per cent) in rural and 42.48 lakh (56.8 per cent) in urban areas. Hired labour accounted for 34.37 lakh (45.9 per cent) workers. Around 37.7 per cent of the hired workers were in the rural areas. In other words, 62.3 per cent of the hired hands worked in the urban area. During 1990-98, the total number of workers grew by 8.3 per cent, giving an annual growth rate of around 1.0 per cent. In the urban areas, this growth rate works out to around 7.3 per cent. This was lower than the growth rate recorded in the rural areas. As a matter of fact, *employment of hired workers actually recorded a negative growth rate in the urban areas; it declined by 1.3 per cent during 1990-98.*

2.4 Informal Sector Labour Market in U.P.

The informal sector labor market in UP reflects a number of unique features/characteristics, that need to be underlined.First, the labor force shows strong tendencies of urban-rural continuum. Interestingly, the migrant population is estimated to be accounting for a relatively small fraction of this labor force[4]. Although much of the urban labor is local, yet the present of the rural-urban continuum cannot be denied. The migrant labour, working in the urban economy, mostly come from the landless labour, marginal and small farming or displaced artisan families.

Second, caste and religious stratification (on rural lines) is present in the informal sector of U.P. In the *leather industry,* leather workers socially belong to low caste communities. Muslims, who had no social taboo, and were engaged in the slaughter business, also moved into flaying and tanning. After this initial entry, Muslims have done well in this sector. A significant upward mobility is seen in this group. At present, they are the entrepreneurs who have seized the opportunity created by the growth in the leather sector. The low caste workers, because of socio-religious resistance as well as their original poverty, continue to be the workers rather than the owners in the leather industry.

In the silk weaving industry, the weavers and Gristas are mostly Ansari (Muslims); the Mahajans/Gaddidars have mostly been Hindus. However, in recent decades, some large Gristas from among the Ansaris have also moved up; apparently there is place for only a few at the top.

Third, as some studies show, entry into the formal sector labour market is restricted by artificially raised hiring standards, norms and procedures. In the case of U.P., however, it is very obvious that the most important barrier to entry is created through the working of the mechanism of product differentiation in the formal sector, as outlined earlier in Section 2.1.

Fourth, labor in the informal sector shows a tendency of high degree of absenteeism. The element of professionalism is missing. Some kind of a work/leisure trade-off seems to be playing a significant role in the informal sector of the state.

Fifth, most of the labor families are large. In slums, suburban areas and villages around Lucknow, it is found that a majority of worker families have very large number of children.[5] In a number of cases, the number of children was more than ten. Interestingly, the Muslim labour families have a larger number of children in comparison to other religious groups.

---

[4] Around 20 per cent.

[5] Notes on the informal sector - Arvind Mohan.

Sixth, kinship and village relationship have played a significant role in the development of urban settlements and in the localization of labor in terms of residence.

Seventh, on the whole labour lacks mobility. Rigidity in movement is a contributory factor in the persistence of low wages and poor living conditions. It seems, the 'large families and kinship based concentration' have contributed to the lack of mobility. This, in turn, has resulted in low wages and low living conditions.

Eighth, workers enjoy informal relationship with the employers. In a way, this contributes to a healthy industrial relationship, most significantly marked by a near-absence of strikes and other dilatory tactics. This, however, also means that there are no formal working hours. Workers in the informal sector work much more than the stipulated/generally accepted 48 hours per week norm. It must also be mentioned that when wages are measured in this sector, often this aspect of longer working hours is not taken into account. If this facet is considered, the wage differential between the formal and informal sectors would emerge to be much sharper. The pecuniary benefits like maternity leave; pension, provident fund & gratuity etc are altogether absent.

Finally, the labour in this segment is absolutely unorganised. Most of the units are very small in size. Consequently, the number of labour units is also very small. This does not afford them an opportunity to organize themselves into any meaningful pressure group. The nature and composition of the informal sector circuit is such that even the units are not homogenous in terms of their activity. This also acts as a *barrier to the possibility of becoming organised.* Thus, labour in this sector is not merely faced with barriers to entry into the formal sector, they are also subjected to face barriers in regard to the formation of trade unions. This naturally weakens their position vis-a-vis their counterparts in the formal sector.

2.5 Wages and Income

Wages and income in this sector are lower than those in the formal sector. Table 1 shows the prevalent wage situation in some of the relevant industries. Barring certain exceptional cases, it is very clear that wages which are being paid to the skilled, semi- skilled and unskilled labourers are too meager for a decent existence. In the table above, the wages are shown on the basis of 26 days of work per month. In a large number of cases, the worker and entrepreneur are not able to get work for 26 days every month. In fact, the employees actually earn much less than what Table 1 shows. It is clear that the wage structure does not conform to the norms and conditions laid down by the Minimum Wages Act.

In the other, non-micro enterprise segment, the work scenario is found to be even worse. Table 2 brings out the monthly earnings, job security and working hours in this segment. In a majority of cases, it is found that monthly wages vary

TABLE 1 : **Wage Structure in Some Selected Informal Sector Industries**

Sr. No.	Industry	Return per Month	Wages (Skilled)	Wages (Semi-Skilled)	Wages (Un-Skilled)	Remarks
1.	Brassware	7800-8200*	3120-5200*	2340	1560	
2.	Brassware (Turning)		1560			All the earnings go to labour as wages.*
3.	Bangle		1000-1900	800		All the earnings go to labour as wages.*
4.	Carpet (Washing)			1600-1870		All the earnings go to labour as wages.*
5.	Carpet (Clippering Process)			1560		All the earnings go to labour as wages.
6.	Carpet (Binding Process)			1450		All the earnings go to labour as wages.*
7.	Carpet (Imposing Process)			1400		All the earnings go to labour as wages.*
8.	Leather		1800	1200		

Source: 1. Technical Reports, Dept. Of Labour GOUP- 1999.
2. Director of Industries GOUP-2000.

* Most of the Micro enterprises don't generate enough returns for the entrepreneur. The entrepreneur actually ends up earning returns for his functions as a labour. The entrepreneurial functions like uncertainty bearing and organisations don't seem to generate any returns.

between Rs. 800 to Rs. 1600. The wage levels are naturally much lower than the requirement of the Minimum Wages Act. Similarly, *lack of job security is another very serious problem.* The worker always remains uncertain about his future earning options. In a number of cases, the loss of job is sudden and highly demoralizing. A much bigger problem is the possibility of such an eventuality happening rather than its actual occurrence. It is this vulnerability or threat, which affects a much larger proportion of employees in this segment. This is even true for the workers in the micro enterprise segment. In a large number of cases, it is found that the workers are forced to *work for 12 hours or more every day, for all the 7 days of the week. In some cases, the wage-paid work is available only for 12-15 days per month.*

TABLE 2 : **Wage Situation in Non-micro Enterprise Sector**

Occupation	Monthly Earning (per month)	Job Security	Working Hours per Day	Work Availability (Days per Week/Month)
Peon	800	Medium	10-12	7 / Week
Cook	1400 - 1600	Medium	10	7 / Week
Mason	2200 - 1800	Low	9	15 - 18 / Month
Daily Labourer	800 - 1000	Very Low	9	12 - 15 / Month
Maid	800 - 1000	Medium	10	7 / Week
Plumber	3000 - 4000	High	8-9	20-22 / Month
Magazine Boy	3000	High	8	6 / Week

Source: Arvind Mohan, 1998-99.

2.6 Employment of Women

A large number of women find employment in the informal sector. Such employment can be classified into two distinguishable entities. The first category consists of the *hired women workers.* They are found in significant numbers in construction sites, leather industry, weaving sector and so on. The other category consists of *self-employing family labor* where a large number of women workers are involved literally in every possible segment of the informal sector.

A 1997 study by the Leather Research Institute found that, on an average, 43 per cent of women workers are employed in the footwear industry in Tamil Nadu. The percentage of women workers in the total leather industry work force was found to be as high as 85-90 per cent. *In U.P. however, this percentage is much lower.* A survey conducted by the Directorate of Industries, Government of U.P. found that *women accounted for only 10 per cent of the work force in Kanpur and Agra leather industry.* It found that women workers get much lower salaries compared with their male counterparts. It must, however, be noted that a number of government sponsored programmes like SIFPSA etc. are trying to make a mark in the field of health, mother- and child-care, family planning, etc. The NGOs are also playing a critical role in improving both the life and working environment in different parts of UP. We also found that in areas like Jajmau in Kanpur district, Chirgaon and Moth in Jhansi district and Brahmapur in Gorakhpur district, the informal sector women workers were getting benefited from the work of NGOs. It appears that a strong NGO movement is building up in U.P. although, for the time being, in most of the cases, their interventions are not directed towards the informal sector workers. Nonetheless, these workers, constituting as they do one of the major groups, is getting some benefits through such interventions.

It is painful to note, however, that *much of the contribution made by women, whether as an entrepreneur in the home-based enterprises or as wage-labour under unwholesome circumstances, largely goes unnoticed;* it gets no recognition at all. In the case of family labor, the wages are never paid; these are not even measured or taken into account in the accounting exercise of the micro enterprises.

2.7 Social Security

Going by the definition of social protection used by 'EUROSTAT', the following aspects are considered to understand the prevalence or absence of social security among the workers engaged in the informal sector enterprises:

- health care support;
- income maintenance and social support in case of sickness, disability, old age, death of a family member, family circumstances (pregnancy, childbirth, care for children and other family members) and un-employment;
- help towards the cost of housing;
- support against social exclusion.

2.7.1 Health Care

In UP, a system of health insurance coverage, with a provision for reimbursement, does not exist in much of the informal sector. In the leather industry, silk weaving, and other industries, such a social support for health is found to be non-existent. On the basis of detailed studies on many industries, it can be safely presumed that in a major part of the informal sector, such a support is conspicuous by its absence. However, most of the workers of the urban informal sector are actually slum dwellers. The State Urban Development Agency (SUDA) co-ordinates the 'Swarn Jayanti ' employment scheme under which a provision is made for the health check-up of the poor families. As per the directives of the Central Government, one fifth of the expenditure incurred during the check-up is borne by the slum dwellers themselves while the rest is borne by SUDA.

It needs to be mentioned that some elaborate state sponsored health and education initiatives are in existence. However, their efficacy remain suspect. The PERFORM Survey (1995) suggests that, for every population of 5000 persons, a public sector health facility exists. However, *only 9 per cent of the people actually make use of it; in other words, more than 90 per cent of the intended beneficiaries remain dependent upon private sources.* It is also found that people living in the rural areas and wage earners in the informal sector remain dependent on Indian System of Medicine (ISM). Most of the ISM practitioners lack in quality training. Consequently, the quality of health services available to the informal sector people also remains low.and unacceptable.

In an 1995-96 NSSO survey, the cost of hospitalization for the poorest two quintiles of population was estimated to be over 60 per cent of the actual mean household expenses in U.P. The richest quintiles paid 107 per cent of annual average expenses for hospitalization. The poor do not have the family income, savings, or other asset of the rich. To pay for medical care, the poor are more likely to depend on loans and sales of assets. Table 3 shows how different income groups meet expenses of a debilitating illness. The richest group meets 92 per cent of such expenses from their accumulated savings. The poor households often have to turn to unsecured loans, sale or mortgage of land and other assets for meeting such expenditures. Although provision of free health services to a majority of the state's population is a major social welfare responsibility of the state, the reality is quite different. *Health care expenditures* continue to be a common cause of rural impoverishment (World Bank Report, 2000). A base-line survey for UP Health Systems Development Project (Mohan, 2000) reveals that the financial burden of providing such a health-care is not fully borne by the government agencies, that there is lack of cleanliness in facilities and that the behavior and attitude of the staff is not very pleasing. These findings are also supported by other surveys and studies, notably the World Bank Study of District Level Health Assessment.

It is also found that in small towns, suburbs and rural areas, *child and maternal care* is pathetic. At the time of childbirth, *over 60 per cent of mothers are not attended by any trained medical person, including trained dais.*[6] In a sector where wage earning is not enough to make even two ends meet such a weak social security network compromises and degrades the quality of life. It also reflects rather poorly on the claims of the Uttar Pradesh government about the provision of *decent work environment* in the urban informal sector of the state.

TABLE 3 : **Pattern of Financing Illness Related Expenditure by Quintile Group**

Source of Financing/ Expenditure Class	%age of Expenditure Financed by Each Source					
	Poorest Group	Consumption Quintile			Richest Group	Overall
		2nd	3rd	4th		
Savings	68	69	77	82	92	77
Sale of Assets	5	2	2	2	1	3
Unsecured Loans	23	23	19	14	7	18
Mortgage or Assistance	3	6	2	2	1	3
Total	100	100	100	100	100	100

Source: 1. World Bank Report. 2. U.P./Bihar survey of living conditions, 1998.

[6] The situation is slightly better in the urban areas.

In the field of education, the state remains committed to universalisation of primary education. In urban Lucknow alone, as many as 154 of government aided schools exist. However, a study by CII has found that many of these schools, particularly those in the city periphery, are being run in sub-human conditions due to paucity of funds.

The special circumstances of the informal sector workers are such that *a very small proportion of the children actually goes to school.* A good number of them are involved in their own family business and some as wage earners. Consequently, these children do not go to school at all. In the weaving industry and the handloom sector, the child actually enters the industry as an apprentice, even at the tender age of 5-6 years and grows to become an adult weaver, in due course of time. Even where the children are actually going to schools, the drop-out rate is found to be very high. In total terms, because of the special circumstances of such industries, methods of imparting primary education should also be designed in conformity with its functioning.

2.7.2 Income Maintenance and Social Support

In spite of the difficult circumstances of the informal sector enterprises, special efforts are being made to improve the quality of life of the people. As regards income protection, 65 types of industrial activities are covered under the *Minimum Wages Act* wherein minimum wages for five categories of workers are fixed, on monthly basis. The state also provides for old age and widow pension. Broadly, there are programmes for social support in the case of sickness, disability, old age, death of a family member, family circumstances (pregnancy, childbirth, care for children and other family members). However, the base line survey of UP clearly points out that these programmes need much to be desired.

Besides the government, a number of NGOs and other formal and informal structures are operating in different areas of Uttar Pradesh. Several NGOs, such as *The Hunger Project, Disha, Shramik Bharti Sakhi* and many more, are making interventions, ranging from health to thrift and income generation. The Hunger Project (operating on a more significant scale in rural areas) and Shramik Bharti have been able to launch a very significant micro credit programme for the families of low-income people. A large chunk of them actually belong to the informal sector. This actually is a thrift programme where the members of the group can avail of small lending facility and meet their working capital, and even fixed capital, requirements. The loans are also available for consumption purposes. While the Shramik Bharti is supported by "Rashtriya Mahila Kosh" programme in this endeavour, The Hunger Project operates mostly with its own resources.

In the Jajmau area, which is inhabited by the informal sector leather industry workers and a sizeable number of self-employed men and women, SIFPSA (State

Innovations in Family Planning Project Services Agency) has launched a major health improvement initiative for these workers with the help of NGOs such as Shramik Bharti and Sakhi, etc. In some of the areas, even the toilets have been constructed by the NGOs which are primarily involved in the micro credit programmes. SUDA (State Urban Development Agency) and DUDA (District Urban Development Agency) are also running a variety of programmes aiming at improving the quality of life of people living in urban slums.

SUDA runs a credit and thrift programme for the slum dwellers through DUDA. Under this programme, the women members of these groups and their husbands are provided an insurance coverage of Rs 25,000.00. The amount is payable if casualty or disability occurs due to accident. Insurance cover of Rs 25000.00 is also provided to a girl child born after 1997 and the coverage remains available till the age of 18. In the case of the death of mother or father, the amount becomes available to the girl.

3. Policy Initiatives: Looking Back and Forth

In most other states, many policy initiatives have been undertaken, from time to time, in UP also, and there is scope for many more of them, partly because of the fast changing circumstances occasioned by pressure of lobbying at home and partly because of the open trade regime that has intensified itself in recent years. A few important policy initiatives may better be delineated, especially from the perspective of the urban informal sector enterprises.

3.1 Capital Flow and Credit Availability

A sizeable chunk of the informal sector in Uttar Pradesh lies outside the scope of institutional credit. Most of the commercial banks are normally unwilling to provide credit to this sector. For certain specific activities, the government has designed some schemes that are expected to ensure a smooth flow of finance to micro enterprises in the informal sector. For a number of production areas and activities, loans are available through the commercial banking sector, at subsidized interest rates ranging from 4 per cent to 12 per cent, under one or the other government scheme. The subsidized credit schemes do not work as happily as these are supposed to do. It is confirmed by many studies that it is the availability of credit, rather than the rate of interest at which it is available, that works as a much more crucial ingredient for the growth of this sector. And, there are other studies to show that among those who seek financial accommodation from these sources, due benefits do not percolate to many of the targeted beneficiaries in the informal sector, especially the small artisans. This is particularly so because a preponderant majority of credit seekers in the informal sector have no collateral security to pledge and have consequently to remain devoid of any such facility A study by Arvind Mohan reveals that a large number of micro enterprises prefer to borrow from traders and moneylenders. Often, the rate of interest in such borrowings is found to be as high as 5 per cent per month or 60 per cent per annum. It looks intriguing that in spite of such high interest rates, the artisans and other petty entrepreneurs in the informal sector prefer to borrow from moneylenders; interestingly, *most of the successful entrepreneurs were actually those who borrowed from trade intermediaries and other non-institutional sources, and not from the banks.* This clearly suggests that institutional credit agencies must change their *modus operandi* if the informal sector enterprises have to gain an effective access to them.

The methods adopted by the traders are simple, even *collateral security is not asked for. In addition, the borrowing from traders also ensures a very strong market linkage.* This kind of an integration of activities and merger of credit and product suppliers, where the traders perform the function of lenders as well as the market, has made very significant contribution to the process of development of independent micro enterprises. Moreover, those micro enterprises which are working closely with the organized sector units or are related to traders, *their credit requirements are often met through such linkages.* In a major study, entitled "SSIs in Uttar Pradesh: A Perspective for Restructuring"[7], it was found that traders often provide raw material, design and working capital to micro enterprise units. It is, however, a different, although a serious, matter that credit through this contrived production-trade regime, is made available at highly exploitative rate of interest that works to the detriment of the informal sector enterprises.

Similarly, in such informal sector enterprises as carpet and brassware industries, designs/specifications and often credit is made available by the organized sector parent unit. The interesting fact is that the organized sector entity or the trader often borrows from the commercial banks. The rate of interest which they are required to pay to the commercial banks is often close to 18 per cent per annum. However, when the same credit is passed on to these micro enterprises, they are forced to pay exorbitantly high rate of interest, often 60 per cent per annum. In other words, *bank credit actually travels to these micro units, through a contrived mechanism, at interest rates which are far too above those that exist on paper.* The banks prefer to lend to the intermediaries, perhaps fully aware of the fact that some of this credit actually travels over to the micro units who were denied credit on the ground of lack of collateral security. *Non-availability of credit thus becomes a major reason for keeping the activities of petty entrepreneurs, artisans and other functionaries in the informal sector cost ineffective, that contributes both to their low growth and non-decent work environment, and perpetuation of their poverty.*

---

[7] "SSIs in UP: A Perspective for Restructuring" by Arvind Mohan (mimeo).

In sum, time has come to re-design credit policies which ensure availability of credit. As said earlier, *it is perhaps in the interest of the micro enterprises themselves that credit is made available at market rates rather than at subsidized rates.* The need is to ensure that the credit actually reaches the needy enterprises and the possibility of leakage is substantially reduced. Even today, a majority of the enterprises are getting credit at interest rates as high as 60 per cent per annum. *If credit becomes available at the market rates, i.e. 18 per cent or so, it will reduce cost of production of the micro enterprises, lend them an enhanced degree of competitiveness; these improvements, in turn, will ensure a much better work and earning conditions, both for the self-employed and the wage-paid workers engaged in UP's urban informal sector.*

3.2 Technology and Change

Technology plays a very significant role in all sector. For the informal sector, technology has wider implications that encompass the growth prospects of the sector itself, its environmental-friendly capacity to proliferate further in the urban areas, its employment potential, working and living condition of workers, and so on. Equally important is its implication for organizational structure and social protection.

In the leather industry, change in technology led to a large-scale concentration of the informal sector entities in the urban areas. Some time back, a new technology was introduced in this industry, which necessitated tanning through the use of synthetic chemical. This automatically led to centralization. Large tanning centres emerged in some parts of the state; Kanpur is a classic example of the same. The entire areas of Jajmau, along river Ganga, developed as a settlement of informal sector tannery workers. This had significant implications for urban informal sector, the most significant being slum like unhygienic and sub-human living conditions.

Secondly, tanning at the primary village level using vegetable dyes declined. A large-scale exodus of job-seekers to urban areas led to growth of slums over there. Caracas collection, which was happening earlier, on a large scale, at the village level, witnessed a drastic decline[8]. This decline also meant loss of jobs in the rural areas. This contributed further to the urban-ward exodus of rural people and the ultimate emergence of large-scale urban settlements of informal sector leather workers. As a result, urban industry found itself overburdened with over-supply of labour.

Like in any other state, there was a given technological dualism in the industrial structure of UP. The formal sector industry showed features of rigid production function. *The informal sector leather industry has had a relatively more malleable production function. This naturally meant a high degree of labor absorption and lower wages in the informal sector.* A study[9] of the informal sector leather industry reveals that a

[8] Study of the Directorate of Industries, Govt. of U.P.

[9] ibid.

typical skilled worker is getting around Rs. 1800.00 and a semi-skilled one only Rs. 1200.00 per month. Undoubtedly, these wages are much lower than the minimum wages; in contrast, the wage scenario in the formal sector is much better.

The third important implication of the technology change was the increasing role of capital in the whole process. Large clusters developed and markets sprung up around these clusters. In these markets, capital tended to play a dominant role. *Labor and the self-employed in the informal sector were increasingly marginalised.*

Another example of technology change is found in the handloom sector. A study[10] of the Kalpi handloom industry reported that, not very long back, 700 handlooms were in existence in Kalpi, Jalaun. In order to make a positive intervention, the government decided to support the technological switch-over from hand-looms to power-looms. A large number of the handloom workers were lured into switching over to the powerloom. The end result has been that today 600 of the looms have already closed down and the remaining 100 are on the verge of closure. *A large number of the self employed and wage earning hand-loom workers have been rendered jobless.* The reasons for this impact are not difficult to find. As a result of these interventions, the working capital requirement went up. The loom owners had already exhausted their resources in the switch-over bid. Secondly with higher production, an enlarged market was needed or a new strategy for marketing was needed, which was hardly forthcoming in and around Kalpi. Thirdly, in a place like Kalpi, power supply remained very erratic. While government took care to ensure a smooth switch-over to power-loom operation, they failed to design a policy or a programme which could have taken care of problems like availability of working capital, power supply, marketing and design support. The Kalpi case study persuades us to infer that *the intervention should be more holistic in nature and should take care of all possible consequences and related issues.*

Another contrasting feature pointed out by the Kalpi study[11] is that, while 600 of the 700 looms went out of operation, some of the micro industries not only did succeed in surviving but have actually thrived. One of the major reasons was their capacity to adopt to the changing circumstances, including the needed changes in technology. One major factor, which contributed to this success story, was the fact that the entrepreneurs started purchasing second-quality yarn from Surat. This yarn was brought to Kalpi where *family women workers of all age groups started using some traditional kind of charkha to convert this second-quality yarn into usable yarn.* After this process was over, this yarn was loaded on the power-loom and cloth for terricot shirts and pants was prepared. Using this method, the entrepreneurs were

---

[10] "SSI in U.P. : A Perspective for Restructuring" - Arvind Mohan (mimeo).

[11] A perspective for restructuring - Arvind Mohan.

able to sell terricot shirt pieces at a very cheap price of around Rs. 16.00 a meter. Their capacity to produce at cheaper rates, despite change in technology and rising cost, enabled them to thrive in their craft. What needs to be underlined is that *the traditional talent and craftsmanship of women workers and their capacity to adopt to changes and introduce innovations, in the face of changing technology and trade circumstances, have been the key elements behind this success story.* Perhaps, at the present juncture of expanding globalization, and the multi-lateral free trade regime, lessons of adaptability need to be learnt more seriously now than ever before.

3.3 Government Schemes

The informal sector has never been a major policy focus of the government in Uttar Pradesh. However, a number of programmes have been devised for the tiny segment of the micro industrial sector, as also the rural sector. There are some other programmes, which are meant for all kinds of industries like tiny, small and medium scale enterprises. It must be appreciated that most of the programmes mentioned here are not exclusively designed for the informal sector. In most of the cases, the informal sector is also intended to be one of the beneficiaries. It seems that the handloom, village and cottage industries are the only segment in the informal sector, which has received some exclusive attention from the government in Uttar Pradesh.

Nonetheless, several schemes of the state and central governments are facilitating the informal sector of the state in multifarious ways. The interventions include training and consultancy, credit and finance, technology and testing, marketing support, and so on. Broadly, leather and footwear, hand-loom and power-loom, brassware, silk weaving, carpet-, lock- and biscuit-making and tourism come under the umbrella of state support and intervention. A number of state and central government institutions are directly responsible for training, skill-upgradation and technology development; other autonomous agencies (such as the Central and State Khadi Boards, Handloom Corporation, cooperative agencies, etc.) are also at work; a few state and central government supported welfare programmes (e.g., weavers welfare fund, health package scheme, work-shed and housing scheme for weavers, group insurance scheme, old-age and widow pension, etc.) are also in vogue. It must, however, be mentioned that the interventions, howsoever variegated they may seem and whatever be their intended coverage, have been rather sketchy, ad hoc and un-coordinated. Most crucially, they lack in terms of necessary focus and orientation. Naturally, these programmes have failed to provide the necessary support which was needed for the growth and healthy development of this sector.

A thorough review of these programmes is, therefore, called for. There is a need for an **Informal Sector Policy** for its needed development. For too long, the informal sector remained out of focus. The consequences are evident. It must be remembered that this is the biggest employer and the largest producer in the state's urban economy. During the past 20 years, the absorptive capacity of the organized industry and agriculture has declined. This throws up serious challenges in terms of employment generation. The informal sector, which is marked by a malleable production function, could have provided a reasonable alternative for employment generation. The truth, however, is that during 1990-98, the absorptive capacity of urban informal sector has actually declined by 1.3 per cent per annum. With growing liberalization of the economy and a determined move towards dis-investment, the challenge of unemployment is going to become increasingly serious. The informal sector probably holds the key to a reasonable response to this challenge. This may provide an opportunity for 'reforms with human face'. Reasonable capacity building and policy framework for this sector is a necessity. Retraining and redeployment of people displaced because of the reforms process must form an essential part of such a policy framework.

The support structure for this sector should be designed keeping in mind quality, access and demand. From the point of view of productive efficiency, it will mean :

1. enhanced access to institutional and supportive credit facilities. Absence of collateral security is the most important barrier to the availability of institutional credit to this sector. The *modus operandi* of the lending institutions needs to be drastically changed in favour of the urban informal sector.

   Financial innovations are the need of the hour. Our own experience suggests that innovations like 'kisan credit cards' and 'self help and thrift groups', which stipulate no backing in the form of collateral security, have been immensely successful. As a matter of fact, the recovery rate for self-help groups is reported to be above 95 per cent; perhaps, this is better than the recovery rate for any other type of bank lending. Schemes of this kind have created a high degree of confidence of the banking system towards lending to the informal sector groups; credit flow has witnessed a considerable expansion. *There is reason to believe that innovative solutions of this kind for fulfilling the credit needs of the informal sector is possible and should, therefore, be attempted.* Equally important is the fact that availability of institutional credit (direct) will bring down the cost of credit for a large chunk of producers. This is likely to enhance the viability of many of them. Also, the cost of production will naturally fall, improving the competitiveness of many of these units.

2. The size of the informal sector and the nature of its organization is at the root of this sector's inability to stand up against the formal sector when it comes to product competition. It needs to be mentioned that barriers to entry and practices which restrict the operation of the informal sector are macro-economic in nature. These are substantially the result of the process of informalisation. It is felt that government should look at this sector as a development initiative. *Interventions like marketing*

where a large number of OAEs may be represented under one brand name should certainly be attempted. Such interventions should naturally be accompanied by quality testing/assurance and advertisement. This will allow the informal sector to position itself against the formal sector, perhaps with an added degree of confidence and a greater possibility of success.

3. Many of the case studies, reviewed in this paper, suggest that *innovations and pooling of talent and resources* have led to worthwhile success stories. It will be useful to understand the elements which have led to such successes. These elements should then be replicated and, if possible, institutionalized.

   Some of the case studies stoutly suggest that behind the success of many units lie the interventions that *substituted commodity flow for credit flow.* In such cases, some kind of cooperative structures have come into existence which have ensured both the functioning of a commodity flow mechanism and availability of a centralized marketing and procuring unit, ensuring a better bargaining power. Perhaps, the experiences of this kind deserve to be replicated in other activities.

4. In certain cases, the *choice of product* (e.g., herbal products) has contributed to the success of the enterprise. The uniqueness of the product by itself ensured low competition from the formal sector. It will be worthwhile creating some product identification project appraisal facility for this sector. Equally relevant will be setting up of facilities like venture funds for the informal sector.

5. Other areas where the institutional support needs to be strengthened are (a) design development and support, (b) marketing, (c) technology improvement, and (c) uninterrupted flow of working capital.

It is very obvious that the informal sector is not a transient stage in economic development of the state; in fact, like many other states, it is the defining feature of U.P.'s under-development. More enduring solutions have to be found just as more analytical understanding of the functioning of the sector has to be developed. In the context of the two-circuit existence, it is clear that the constraining factors behind underdevelopment of the informal circuit are the contrived nature of the existing market structures, barriers to entry into the formal circuit, technological backwardness of the informal sector, unprotected labour market, social stratification and less-than-serious relationship with the government. The policy regime, naturally, has to look into these issues. It needs no special emphasis that the informal sector represents a ticklish mingle of social and economic problems. On our part, we have tried to focus attention on many of these dimensions and the policy issues at stake. The informal sector must get due recognition, and the policy makers must spare a more focused attention for this sector in order to ensure its growth and a decent living conditions for the millions involved in it.

Bibliography

Arvind Mohan, SSIs : A Perspective for Restructuring (A Study and Presentation for Confederation of Indian Industry, North India) .

Arvind Mohan, Notes on Informal Sector (Unpublished), 1998-99.

Arvind Mohan, 2000. Health Profile of Uttar Pradesh (A Sub-study for Uttar Pradesh Human Development Report 2000-20001).

Central Leather Research Institute, Report of Nationwide Survey on Leather Product Units in India, Madras, 1997.

Dre'ze, J. and Sen, A. 1991. "Public Action for Social Security: Foundation and Strategy", in E. Ahmad, J. Dre'ze, J. Hills and A. Sen (eds): Social Security in Developing Countries, Oxford, Clarendon Press.

Govt. of India, Status Report of Leather based Industry: Action Plan 1998-99. Ministry of Industry, Department of Small Scale Industries, Agro & Rural Industries GoI.

____, Census of India 1991. Primary Census Abstract: General Population', Part II-B (i) Series 25, Directorate of Census Operations, Uttar Pradesh.

____, Census of India 1991. Final Population Totals, Paper-1 of 1992 Vol. I Series 1, Registrar General and Census commissioner, India.

____, Food Processing Industries - Outline of Assistance under Schemes of 9th Plan: 1997-2002, History of Food Processing Industries.

____, 2000. Non-agricultural Enterprises in the Informal Sector in India, 1919-2000, NSS 55th Round, July 1999-2000, N.S.S.O.

Govt. of Uttar Pradesh, Urban Food Policy and Agro based and Food Processing Industries, Department of Horticulture and Food Processing, Uttar Pradesh.

Hart, K. (1971). "Informal Income Opportunities and Urban Employment in Ghana", Paper Presented at IDS Conference on Urban Unemployment in Africa, University of Sussex.

ILO, 1999. Report of Director - General : Decent Work, International Labour Conference, 87th Session, Geneva, June.

ILO, Employment, 1972. Income and Equality: Strategy for Increasing Productive Employment in Kenya, Geneva.

John Weeks, 1975. "Policies for Expanding Employment in the Informal Urban Sector of Developing Economies", International Labour Review, January.

M Vijay Jagannathan and Animesh Haldhar, 1988. "A Case Study of Pavement Dwellers in Calcutta: Occupation, Mobility and Rural-Urban Linkages", Economic and Political Weekly, December 3, 1988.

Navneet Sehgal, Write-up on SUDA Activities in UP, SUDA, Lucknow.

Rao M. Koteshwar and M. Prasad Rao, 1994. "Socio-economic characteristics of labour in urban informal sector", in M Koteshwar Rao (ed.) : Growth of Urban Informal Sector and Economic Development, Vol. II, Kanishka Publishers.

Sethuraman, S.V. 1995. The Urban Informal Sector in Asia : Policies and Strategies ILO, Geneva 1995.

T.S.Papola, 1982. "Informal Sector : Concept & Policy", Economic and Political Weekly, Volume 15 Issue No. 18.

T.S.Papola, 1979. Informal Sector in an Urban Economy : A Study in Ahmedabad, GIDS, (mimeo.).

World Bank, 2000. World Development Report, Washington, D.C.

Govt. of Uttar Pradesh, Aligarh stith tala udyog me niyojit matranupati shramikon per takniki adhyan report, Office of Labour Commissioner, Kanpur, U.P.

____, Moradabad stith peetal udyog me niyojit maatranupati shramikon per takniki adhyan report, Office of Labour Commissioner, Kanpur, U.P.

____, Sant ravidas (Bhadohi)stith kaaleen udyog me niyojit matranupati shramikon per takniki adhyan report, Office of Labour Commissioner, Kanpur, U.P.

____, Saharanpur stith wood carving udyog me niyojit matranupati shramikon per takniki adhyan report, Office of Labour Commissioner, Kanpur, U.P.

____, Kanpur stith biscuit udyog me niyojit matranupati shramikon per takniki adhyan report, Office of Labour Commissioner, Kanpur, U.P.

____, Firozabad stith choodi udyog me niyojit matranupati shramikon per takniki adhyan report, Office of Labour Commissioner, Kanpur U.P.

____, Chaturth Arthik gadna Uttar Pradesh 1998, arth avam sankhya prabhag rajya niyojan sansthan, Uttar Pradesh.

Trends in Job Creation in Urban Informal Sector in West Bengal

V. Subramanian

1. The Concept of Informal Sector

In most cases, an attempt to study the informal sector at best succeeds in identifying the symptoms and practices in the economy rather than analyzing the characteristics and finding ways of protecting those operating in the sector, both as employers and employees. Till recently, the informal sector was described as the one that comprises economic activities not officially registered, recognized or taxed. It was also believed that the growth in the informal sector was a necessary process of transition from an agrarian society to an economy in which people would be predominantly employed in the modern sector. It was widely believed that units in the informal sector would be necessarily small, non-lucrative and precarious and would progressively disappear with development. It was also assumed that the pace of disappearance or decline of this sector would be fast if the pace of economic development were speedy. If there were evidences to the contrary, such slowness of decline of the informal sector was attributed to population pressures, unfavourable terms of trade and investment, inefficient public administration and unsupportive external environment. Untaxed and unregistered economic activities prevail in every economy - developed, developing or undeveloped - the extent of the same varying depending upon the state of the economy. It is a fact grudgingly admitted even in the developed world that informal sector could account for as much as 30 - 4 cent of the national income.

Very often, the informal sector is understood to be signifying very small units producing and distributing goods and services comprising a large number of independent and self- employed producers or providers of services in urban areas of the developing economies. Many such units deliver goods and services produced by their own labour, a few hired hands and in a few cases, with the help of family labour. The level of investment and technology is mostly low and these units operate at a low level of efficiency. They are also not capable of having access to organised markets and credit institutions. These activities, usually being unregistered, unrecognized, and unregulated, face a great deal of risk, which adversely affects both the producer and the workers. The inherent risk component drives the owner-entrepreneur to minimize the adverse effects of risk by trying to ensure low level of wages for those who are wage-paid workers. The low visibility of workers in such sectors also prevents application of the laws for protection of employment, decent living wages and social security benefits. As a result, they are also beyond the scope of action by the trade unions.

A fact, that one has to reconcile with, is that the informal sector exists and thrives basically because there is a demand for the goods and services offered by this sector. By their enterprise and work, the stakeholders in this sector fulfill some needs of the society which the formal sector is not in a position to meet or because the terms of the formal sector are inefficient or costly in those branches of production and servicing.

There could be an argument that the sector does not fulfill quite a few legal requirements. Some of these aspects may relate to tax laws, statutory regulations and labour legislations. Perhaps, there could be a case for a re-look at the existing laws to ascertain whether the laws have themselves caused the reluctance of this sector from coming into the mainstream. The new era of competition and market economy, that ostensibly ensued since July 1991, would make some of the existing activities to be costlier, thus forcing these activities to fall into the lap of informal sector. Moreover, the informal sector does not exist in isolation. In a large number of cases, it plays an essential role of fulfilling the needs of the formal sector itself.

1.1 Stakeholders

For understanding the problems of the stakeholders in the informal sector, one has to understand various terms being used to describe the sector. Terms like organized and unorganized sectors, formal and informal sector, organized and unorganized labour, self- and wage-employed workers, are used by various persons and groups. The meanings of these terms cannot be understood unless one is aware of the interest group the persons are representing, the intentions of the persons using these terms and the context in which these are used. In the absence of a clear consensus on the concept of the informal sector, especially from the point of view of production, productivity and contribution of this sector to the economy, any discussion on the creation of jobs in the informal sector has its limitations.

'Labour in the informal sector' is a term differently defined all over the world. The definitions are very nebulous and depend a lot on the person's or organization's perception of the sector itself. We may try to assume broadly that the labour in small and tiny enterprises, often with minimum resources and with no legal provisions and encompassing a wide range of jobs, occupations, activities and services is said to be the labour employed in informal sector.

The National Conference of the International Labour Organisation attempted to describe the characteristics of the informal activity. They are a combination of factors such as ease of entry, reliance on indigenous resources, family ownership of enterprises, small scale operations, working in temporary or semi-permanent structures, work in variable locations, deployment of skills acquired in non-formal education systems, operation in unregulated but highly competitive markets etc. Insecurity and unemployment characterize the labour market in the informal sector. The general neglect of the informal sector by the national governments has led to neglect of the workers engaged in it. The priorities of the governments and the political leadership normally tilt towards labour in the organized sector who have the advantage of articulation of their points of view through associations and unions.

Of late, the concept of 'employment' has also come to mean wage-paid employment in the organized sector. This has led to excessive emphasis on creation of new jobs in the organized sector rather than on the issues relating to protection of labour and provision of decent wages in the informal sector. Workers beyond the formal labour market who are underpaid or work in a system of unregulated wages, self-employed and those who work at home, remain neglected and outside the purview of most legislative and administrative initiatives.

1.2 Positive Side of the Informal Sector

The pre conceived notion that the informal sector is necessarily exploitative of labour has also led to motivated interpretation of data. The concern about informal sector so far has been mostly from labour's point of view. Though there are clear factors in favour of bringing the identifiable activities within the purview of registration, regulation and taxation, many of these activities have been left untouched because of political reasons. The sector as a whole has remained isolated from the ambit of economic policy framework as a result of which the full potential of the sector in turning professional has remained untapped and the labour force deprived of many pecuniary and other benefits. Since the reach of the organised trade unions is limited, to a large extent, to the organized sector, often a perception is created that the informal sector has no role and justification to exist and that the sector is necessarily evil and exploitative. While it should be admitted that workers in the organized sector are better off from the point of view of job protection and relatively reasonable wages, there appears to be no reason to presume the opposite across the entire informal sector. If the full employment potential of the informal sector is to be tapped, a major change is called for in the attitude of the policy makers.

The basis assumptions relating to informal sector need to be changed drastically in order to redirect the approach towards solutions to the problems. It may be worth looking at the basis and positive aspects so that perceptions are in right focus.

a. Informal sector is large, complex and heterogeneous;

b. Informal sector also has virtues - economic, social and cultural;

c. Informal sector has also an important role in the economy;

d. Informal sector is bound to grow and thrive in a system of production which is appropriate to factor and resource endowments in labour surplus and developing countries;

e. Informal sector is also a reservoir of entrepreneurship and innovation at the micro level;

f. Informal sector uses the resources in a manner that is efficient, competitive and optimum;

g. Informal sector has generated a great deal of employment both in the urban and rural areas and its potential to create further employment is huge;

h. Informal sector is generally shy of expansion of activities due to stringent regulations on registration and labour protection;

i. Informal sector activities in a few areas, have been created and they survive as a direct result of the activities of the formal sector;

j. Informal sector is an effective adjunct to the formal sector in the matter of providing services;

k. Informal sector's productivity index should be far greater than that of the formal sector if it could be worked out on a realistic basis;

l. Informal sector has been neglected in the policy framework and environment;

m. Informal sector is not necessarily exploitative of labour;

n. Informal sector has suffered differently due to excessive attention to the organised sector and this suffering has been passed on to the workforce in this sector;

o. Informal sector chooses to remain outside the purview of the mainstream of the economy mainly due to excessive controls and regulations by the Governments;

p. Informal sector activities are not necessarily illegal;

q. Informal sector is contributing a great deal to the creation of wealth in the newly emerging areas of computers, information technology, etc.

1.3 Policy Support Matters

In the ultimate analysis, the government's approach and the society's attitude to the working and living conditions of millions of people engaged in the informal sector are of considerable significance. This is especially so because the informal sector is not organised into lobbying groups and associations like the organized sector into chambers of commerce, industry associations etc; these people are deprived of the opportunity of voicing their anxieties and concerns and being heard in the right fora. Admittedly, it is not at all possible to step into each activity and attempt to convert low productivity and low status jobs into 'decent work activities', yet there is a vast scope for lending support to a multitude of jobs. Perhaps, a few illustrations are in order.

1.3.1 Development Efforts of the Government

For example, construction of a link road and bridge over a river, to connect a group of villages, would lead to increased earnings for the farmers in view of the accessibility to markets in the nearby urban areas. The need to reach the produce to the markets would also lead to creation of employment for a whole lot of new persons offering transport facilities for the purpose. The persons who take the initiative to purchase carts, rickshaws and trucks will not only get themselves gainfully employed but also offer such employment to a new set of persons to drive and maintain transport equipment. At the same time, the persons who were engaged in operating boats to ferry passengers, goods and animals, will stand to lose their livelihood as a result of the construction of a link road and a bridge. Essentially, this developmental effort should be looked at as one, which is detrimental to the interest of the boatmen who are now thrown out of their employment. In other words, a new set of employment opportunities is created in the informal sector to replace another set of existing occupations in the same sector. In fact, a few jobs may be created even in the organized sector by way of bus services which were hitherto non-existent in the local economy.

1.3.2 Credit Availability

The availability of finance at reasonable interest rates and at appropriate points of time is crucial to the survival of many an industry. Non- availability of timely working capital has led to the activities of industries being curbed and leading to eventual closure. The informal activities in the financial sector take care of the requirements outside the formal sector.

1.3.3 Legal framework for labour issues

The present legal framework, governing labour relations, being excessively stringent in matters relating to retrenchment, lay-off and closure with powers of permission with the Governments, many industries find it easier and cheaper to declare a lockout leading to ultimate closure rather than follow the laws. In fact, there is an indirect but substantial benefit to an industry if they seek to circumvent the law by keeping their units beyond the purview of law.

1.3.4 Urbanisation

The demand for new services in areas that are being urbanised lead to new opportunities for the locals as well as those in the neighbouring areas. Similarly, the increased demand for existing services may result in improving the quality of services due to competition among the existing and new operators.

2. Employment Growth in India and West Bengal

Employment in the Indian economy has grown quite sizably over the past five decades. However, the growth has been much more in the informal (or unorganized) than in the formal (organized) sector; here, we do not go into the definitional subtleties or operational differences between the informal and the unorganized sector (Table 1). For nearly two decades now, the share of employment in the organised sector have been around 8 to 10 per cent of the total employment. In fact, in recent years, the share of employment in the organised sector has been coming down. In any case, bulk of the growth in employment has been in the unorganised sector.

TABLE 1 : **Growth of Employment in Different Sectors of the Indian Economy**

Year	Employment (Million Persons)			
	Organised	Unorganised	Total	Organised Sector's Share (%)
1973	18.8	217.5	236.3	8.0
1978	21.2	249.5	270.7	7.9
1983	24.0	278.7	302.7	7.9
1988	25.7	296.3	322.0	8.0
1991	26.7	315.2	341.9	7.8
1994	27.4	344.6	372.0	7.4
1997	28.2	379.8	408.0	6.9

(Organized Sector means all the establishments in the public sector and those non-agricultural establishments in the private sector employing 10 or more workers. Figues are based on the data published by the NSSO, (various rounds) and the Economic Survey, 1998-99)

It would be worthwhile looking at the employment figures. in the organized sector, in the entire country before analyzing the employment scenario in West Bengal. The organized sources of employment may be conveniently divided as the Union Government, State Governments, Public Sector and the Private Sector. A study of Table 2 indicates very clearly that there has been growth in employment in absolute terms, practically under each source. However, the share of employment under State Governments and public sector has been growing steadily whereas the share of the private sector and that of the union government has been stagnant in the nineties - the years of economic liberalization.

In West Bengal, public sector accounts for around 65 per cent of the employment in the organised sector (Table 3). However, in recent years, total employment in the organized sector has witnessed a steady decline which was contributed both by the private as well as the public sectors. In relative terms, the decline in the private sector employment has been a more worrisome episode in as much as, during the years of economic liberalization, market forces are expected to contribute far more towards employment expansion rather than the other way round. It seems, West Bengal's experience with the organized sector employment runs counter to that of most other states, and it needs to be understood and interpreted in its own right.

If one looks at the figures of employment in the factory sector alone, the picture from West Bengal does not offer cheers (Table 4). The recent past has been rather stagnant. Although the figures do not take into account the number of factory workers out of employment due to closures, strikes and lock-outs, yet it is more than evident that the average number of workers employed per factory has remained the same over the last five years. The number of factories has also not shown a significant increase either. The disturbing signals from the state once again corroborate the thesis that a major part of the burden of employment squeeze in the formal sector has to be borne by the informal sector.

TABLE 2 : **Employment in the Organised Sector of the Indian Economy by Source of Employment**

(Figures in Millions)

Year (31st. March)	Union Govt.	% Share	State Govt.	% Share	Public Sector	% Share	Private Sector	% Share	Total
1961	2.09	17.3	3.01	24.9	0.77	6.4	5.04	41.7	12.09
1971	2.77	15.9	4.15	23.8	1.93	11.0	6.74	38.6	17.47
1981	3.20	14.0	5.68	24.8	4.58	20.0	7.40	32.3	22.88
1991	3.41	12.8	7.11	26.6	6.22	23.3	7.68	28.7	26.74
1992	3.43	12.7	7.19	26.6	6.39	23.6	7.85	29.0	27.06
1993	3.38	12.4	7.29	26.8	6.49	23.9	7.85	28.9	27.18
1994	3.39	12.4	7.34	26.8	6.51	23.8	7.93	29.0	27.38
1995	3.39	12.3	7.36	26.7	6.52	23.7	8.06	29.3	27.53

Note: Figures are rounded off.
Source. Statistical Outline of India, 1997-98, Tata Services Ltd.

As is the case with most other states, in West Bengal too, the contribution of the services sector to the State Domestic Produce has been going up year after year, it is also seen that the rate of growth has been the highest in the services sector (Table 5). This is one sector, which has been growing without any deliberate or express support from the governments. Very often, there has been a great deal of debate about the incentives to be offered to this sector to enable it to grow at a rate faster than the present rate. But the fact remains that this sector has grown largely in an informal manner without any specific encouragement from the State.

TABLE 3 : **Distribution of Total Employment in the Organised Sector of the West Bengal Economy**

Year	Public Sector	Private Sector	Total
1994	1541000	858000	2399000
1995	1524000	774000	2298000
1996	1499000	780000	2279000
1997	1493000	798000	2292000
1998	1493000	798000	2291000

Source: Govt. of West Bengal, 1998.

TABLE 4 : **Employment in Registered Factories in West Bengal in Recent Years**

Year	Number of Factories (Public and Private)	Total Employment
1995	10730	947338
1996	11047	925503
1997	11238	889857
1998	11230	900577

Source: Govt. of West Bengal, 1998.

TABLE 5 : **Share and Rate of Growth of Various Sectors in State Domestic Product of West Bengal : 1998-99**

Sector	% Share in SDP	Rate of Growth
Agriculture	30.66	1.77
Industry	25.54	6.79
Services	43.80	9.47

Source: Economic Review 1998-99, Govt. of West Bengal.

A set of figures available on the share of household income derived through different types of economic activities reveals that a small part of it is derived from activities which are not outside the purview of the organized sector (Table 6). For example, salaried employment, the ultimate source of livelihood in the formal sector, accounts for only 18.6 per cent of the household income in the state. On the contrary, a major share of household income in West Bengal is derived from activities which can be typically defined only as a part and parcel of the informal sector.

3. Urban Unemployment in West Bengal

Another set of figures, often quoted to highlight the extent of unemployment, relates to the registration of job seekers with the employment exchanges. Given the limited reach of the employment exchanges, that too only to a few establishments even with the public sector, the figures convey no definite trend; in fact, these are not adequate enough to provide us a base for a meaningful analysis. Nonetheless, going by the available statistics, we find that in West Bengal, as on 31st December, 1998, there were 56,48,780 candidates registered with the employment exchanges in West Bengal. Of these, 24.80 lakh persons were illiterates or semi-literates having gone through some schooling. Another 17.66 lakh registrants had studied upto class X. Those who had passed upto class XII, were 6.92 lakhs. Another 6.47 lakh registrants were those who had completed graduation or post-graduation. Considering that the placements offered by employment exchanges over the previous three years was around 8000 to 10000 each year, there is no hope, whatsoever of all these registrants finding jobs in the foreseeable future. If this is the reality, one has reasons to assume that many of the registrants have employed themselves in the informal sector, and, at the same time, have registered themselves with the employment exchanges under the hope that they would find jobs in the formal sector, in the foreseeable future. If figures of employment, in the formal and informal sectors, and of the employment exchange registrants were studied together, it would be evident that we cannot place completely rely on data pertaining to registration with employment exchanges.

TABLE 6 : **Analysis of Household Income in West Bengal**

Activity Description	Average Annual Income per Household (Rs.)	Percentage Distribution
Agriculture and Allied Activities	11692	36.7
Artisans and Other Industry Related Work	10372	4.0
Petty Traders and Small Businesses	13617	18.7
Organised Trade/Business	19601	3.3
Salaried Employment	19110	18.6
Qualified Professional	12204	0.8
Rent, Interest and Dividend	4453	0.2
Agricultural Wage	6278	12.2
Non-Agricultural Wage	4354	12.2
Other Sources	6750	1.2
Total from all Sources	18113	100

Source: NCAER, Human Development Report : 1999.

4. The Urban Informal Sector in West Bengal

Despite the use of the figures quoted above, the major problem in focusing attention on the informal sector is the lack of reliable and comprehensive data on the activities in this sector. Except for the broad assessment that this sector employs no less than 90 per cent of the labour force, there has been no data relating the various activities and services and the number of people engaged in them. The non-availability of data makes the task of understanding the magnitude and complexities of this sector's problem very difficult.

For example, the shops and establishments that are regulated by a statute, should give us a good idea of the number of people engaged in this sector. Unfortunately, even here, the information that is thrown up does not lead to a very accurate assessment. For example, at the end of 1998, in West Bengal, 5,83,575 shops and establishments were covered under the relevant Act. These shops and establishments employed only 5,98,780 persons on the same date. Going by these statistics, it would mean that the average employment in this sector is just about one person per shop/establishment. If that indeed is the case, the Act does not apply to the urban areas of the whole state. It is, however, a common knowledge that this position is not correct, primarily because there is a significant under-reporting of persons employed by the owners, for a variety of reasons.

The situation in West Bengal is not very much different from other States in the country as far as creation of employment is concerned. An analysis of the available data, collection of new data, appreciation of the factors leading to creation of new opportunities would probably help us to devise an appropriate strategy to ensure the sustenance of the employment that is created and socially protect those who are employed in this sector. The data base in the country as a whole and West Bengal in particular lays excessive emphasis on the employment in the organised sector. The data is collated entirely on the basis of returns submitted by the factories and establishments under the Factories Act and the Compulsory Notification of Vacancies Act. The data thus collected is just collated without any system of verification and checking. Any attempt to inspect the records and ascertain the accuracy of the figures is looked down upon by the employers. The data collected represent only a part of the organised sector and it is not correct to assume that the entire organised sector is covered under the process.

When one starts discussing about the informal sector and employment therein, one is immediately led to think of thousands of persons who work on daily wages, which are low, and employment, which is insecure. At the same time, one has also to look at those informal sector jobs where wage levels are reasonable and can be improved upon and some kind of continuance ensured by marginal changes in the approach, from one of security in employment to social security. As a matter of fact, one can see two distinct trends that have been coming up in the growth of employment in the informal sector. The first is the growth of jobs in very many activities where services are not available in the formal sector. The second is to push the formal sector jobs into the informal sector either deliberately (say, as a matter of strategy of cost saving) or due to the desire to avoid enforcement of the provisions of law specially relating to contract labour.

For example, the growth in the automobile sector has led to a significant increase the sales of cars. In Kolkata city alone, an average of ten thousand new cars per year are being sold and registered. These cars are only those which are registered as personal ownership vehicles and excludes trucks, taxis, two wheelers, auto-rickshaws and the light commercial vehicles. Most of these cars are net addition to the fleet of cars on road, since there is no replacement market for cars in the economy as yet. Assuming, there exists a replacement demand of say 10 per cent, it is a net addition of more than 63,000 cars out of the 70,000 sold during the last seven years. Again assuming that only about 50 per cent of the new buyers would choose to drive the cars themselves, we are left with 35,000 cars which have to be driven by those who are not the owners. This effectively means that about 35,000 persons have got employed as drivers of these private cars with the owners. It is seen that the wage levels are not low for these drivers and they are often in a position to bargain for and achieve more than decent wages - but this bargain is based on skills and reliability and not on the basis of collective bargaining. These are the persons who would not have found jobs, had not the production of automobiles increased. Also, the growth in the sale of automobiles has led to other jobs in new shops and service stations for supplying spares, components, fuels etc. While such growth, to some extent, has been in the organized sector, bulk of new jobs have been created for the mechanics, cleaners and drivers in the informal sector. This is but just one example of the growth in the formal economy creating a variety of new jobs in the informal sector.

On the other hand, there is a distinct trend of jobs being reduced in the organized sector, say, through rationalization measures, voluntary retirement schemes, etc., in order to cope with improved technology that usually calls for less of manpower or to cope with the competition that calls for reduction of cost including labour cost; these are deliberate attempts on the part of management to reduce the workforce. There have been instances of the management being forced to reduce the overhead costs and also avoid the possible complications of strict application of laws with regard to contract labour. As an example, one could cite the instance of the companies, which were providing lunchroom facilities for their senior executives and tea, snacks and lunch for their staff. Traditionally, the facilities were extended to them by a system of contracts whereby the nominated contractor engaged workmen to deliver the service served the executives and the staff in their workplace. The demand to treat such workmen as regular employees of the company also led to problems. Unionization of the employees of the contractors who had some sort of job security and their demand to be treated as regular employees started a trend of doing away with the services which were being made available to the officers and staff. This was conveniently substituted by a system of lunch or tiffin allowance to be paid in cash to their regular employees. This in effect meant a move away from a system where there was some kind of organised employment to one where the informal arrangement was encouraged. The officers and staff were happy with the extra cash that they received. The management reduced its cost and also the problems of providing the facilities. In the process, the workmen who had certain amount of security of jobs and some decent wages lost out. The extra cash, even if it was utilized for the same purpose, was spent on food shops on the pavements, which are basically in the informal sector. We have thus a typical example of a formal sector rationalization policy giving rise to informal sector jobs.

4.1 Informal Sector in Kolkata

Some surveys have been conducted, now and then, to assess the economic content and the functioning of the informal activities and the people employed therein. However, they have been of limited use in the long run. One such survey in the recent past was commissioned by the Indian Chamber of Commerce to estimate the number of jobs in the urban services sector (Source: Survey, ICC, Kolkata, 1995). The main findings of this survey were as follows:

- On a particular day in 1995, 2794 vendors were present in the three wards of Kolkata viz. Dalhousie, Gariahat and Shyambazaar. They employed, in turn, directly or indirectly, 6,597 persons;
- The total employment in the three wards was 9321 persons that includes the vendors and their employees;
- The survey was confined to 22 areas of activities such as fruit and fruit juice marketing, preparation and sale of foodstuff, sale of cigarettes, beedi and pan, newspaper selling, shoe polishing, sale of vegetables, sale of readymade garments on the pavements, hair cutting, sale of pictures and picture postcards, and so on;
- The total monthly income of the 9321 persons was around Rs.231 lakhs;
- Of this, an amount of approximately Rs.71 lakhs accrued to the vendors - entrepreneurs cum employers and Rs.162 lakhs was earned by the employees;

- The average monthly income of the vendors and their employees was Rs.2488 approximately, which gives an average annual income of Rs.29000;
- The average monthly income of each person works out to be slightly over Rs.2000 under the assumption that, on an average, a minimum of 2000 persons are employed as vendors or as their employees;
- Each of the wards of the city of Kolkata;
- The total employment in all the 141 wards of the city in the unorganised sector would be around 2,82,000, confined to the activities that were covered under the survey;
- The estimate of employment limited to a few activities amounts to only around 10 per cent of the non-organized sector population of 29 lakhs as per the 1991 census report;
- The total monthly income of this section alone is around Rs.55 crores.

Another study, confined only to a few wards of the Corporation limits of Kolkata, excluding the suburbs and the other urban areas, testifies that the informal sector is fairly vibrant inasmuch as it provides employment to millions in and around Kolkata.

Urbanization and expansion of urban areas lead to a demand for new services and increase in the existing services. Since these services are not usually extended by the formal sector or because the reach and ability of the formal sector are limited, new entrepreneurs step in to provide such services. The absence of proper public transport system leads to such facilities being offered by taxis, rickshaws and other modes of transport. Though such services are to be regulated by the authorities, services need not necessarily wait for legal procedures to be put in operation. Almost all the suburbs of Kolkata, where new habitations have come up including those that were sheltered under a planned resettlement programme, have such unauthorized and unregulated transport services in place.

The increase in the number of middle class families, in and around Kolkata, has led to a spurt in the demand for domestic help. In response to such increases in demand, a number of women have shifted from the rural areas, and have added to the numerical strength of the urban informal service sector workers. Also, a large number of maids daily commute from their villages, largely by local trains, to render services in households. They arrive in the morning, work in various households and return in the evening. It is roughly estimated that as many as 50,000 women commute everyday to work in households in Kolkata.

The increased tempo of construction activities has also called for a large shift of rural labour into urban areas as construction labour. Practically, the whole of employment in the construction industry is in the informal sector including those falling in the skilled categories. Still further, the increased demand for bricks under the construction industry, has led to large number of labourers being brought into the State as contract labourers.

The daily needs of the increasing urban population are met by small shops, vendors and self- employed skilled functionaries. Almost all these activities are unregistered and unregulated. They come into existence to meet the needs and demands of the society and they survive and thrive, as long it is economical for them. Very often, the efforts to remove the vendors from the pavements and unauthorized places have failed not only because of their determination but also because of the support of the society they serve.

5. Paradigm must Shift

In order to bring the informal sector into the mainstream of the economy and also protect the interest of labour, a paradigm shift is called for in the approach and policies of the governments especially in the area of labour.

i) Labour policy should be more holistic and focus more on the entire labour force rather than on concentrating on the labour in the organised sector;

ii) Labour policy should change to one of facilitating social security from that of regulation in the area of job protection;

iii) The system of outsourcing of products, raw material, consumables, spares and most importantly "services" by the organised sector units needs to be recognized in realistic and enforceable legal terms;

iv) A clear recognition of the need to outsource services by way of contracts in areas, which are not core to the industry or business in the formal sector, is called for. A conscious appreciation of the fact that the ability to render specific services could also become the strength and competence of many units in the formal sector, would enable these outsourcing endeavours;

v) Necessary changes in the legislation relating to contract labour abolition and regulation or, if needed, replacement of the Act itself, to confer legitimacy and recognition of the contract services, should be carried out immediately. A positive approach to the system of contract services to the organised sector would provide a stimulus to job creation in the unorganised sector rather than supplant it;

vi) An effective system of combining social security and labour market flexibility would slowly shift the service providers to the formal sector and professionalise them. Such an approach would also improve the bargaining power of workers in the informal sector;

vii) At present, there exists a centrally operated system of provident fund under the Employees Provident Fund Organisation and medical benefits under the Employees State Insurance corporation which cover the employees in the organised sector in which the worker does not have a feel of involvement or commitment. This could be replaced by an enabling legislation to provide such social security benefits at the local level to be managed by the stakeholders themselves;

viii) Necessary changes in the policy are called for to convert the role of the Government from one of a regulator to that of a facilitator would help in growth of jobs in the informal sector; and

ix) There is a compelling need to facilitate the growth of a system of unemployment insurance to take care of the periods of unemployment with contributions from the employees and employers in the informal sector.

Informal sector, as such, is not illegal or unethical. If it survives, thrives, expands and persists, it is because of a need. The need is created by the inability of the other sectors of the economy to provide employment opportunities and adequate levels of income. Attempts should be made to correct the distortions rather than to do away with this sector which can be only at a heavy cost to the labour, the constituency we seek to protect. This sector has come to stay and stay as a universal phenomenon. The present state of labour in the informal sector has come about by deliberate non-recognition of their role, harmful regulations and excessive protection of the organised sector - both of the entrepreneur and the labour. The strategy now should be one of integrating the informal sector with the formal and enhancing the capacity of this sector to generate employment and reasonable incomes for large numbers of people.

Given the present rate of growth of employment in the organised sector in West Bengal, the strategy should be one of encouraging growth of the informal sector. One of the essential components of such a strategy would be to get the labour benefited by welfare schemes so that they are protected by fair wages and social security benefits. Training and skill development of the potential employees in the informal sector would also enable them to bargain for fair wages and social security benefits based on skills and competence rather than on collective bargaining, the scope for which in the informal sector is highly restricted.

Bibliography

Govt. of India, 1999. Economic Survey, 1998-99, Ministry of Finance.

____, Reports on Employment and Unemployment (various rounds), NSSO.

Govt. of West Bengal, 1998. Labour in West Bengal: 1998, Dept. of Labour and Employment.

____, 1999. Economic Review 1998-99, Directorate of Economics and Statistics.

Indian Chambers of Commerce, 1995. An Estimate of the Number of Jobs in the Urban Services Sector.

NCAER, 1999. Human Development Report, India, 1999.

Tata Services Ltd., 1999. Statistical Outline of India, 1997-98.

Strategic Approach to Job Creation in Urban Informal Sector in Assam

N.C. Barooah

1. Introduction

As per the 1991 Population Census, the total working population in Assam was 8.09 million, which constituted 36.09 per cent of the state's population. Of this workforce, 7.32 million were in the rural areas. Thus, only 0.77 million, or less than 10.0 per cent of the workforce, was in the urban areas. Finally, more than 50 per cent of the urban work force was concentrated in some five major towns of Assam.

1.1 Growth of Population and Labour Force

While up-to-date figures for the growth of labour force in Assam have yet to become available, a few distinct characteristics of the employment scenario may better be underlined. Till the beginning of the nineties, population growth in Assam has been quite rapid, averaging a little higher than the national average. The decennial growth in population of Assam, from 1951 onwards, is given in Table 1.

TABLE 1 : **Decadal Growth Rate of Population in Assam**

Decade	Decadal Growth Rate of Population (%)
1951-61	35
1961-71	35
1971-81	26
1981-91	27
1991-2001	19

** The 1981 Census could not be held in Assam.

1981 figures have been computed by interpolation.

Although there is a perceptible decline in the growth of population during the 1990s, yet, among the Indian states, most markedly among the eastern states, Assam has witnessed a fairly high growth of its population, from one decade to the other. Very largely, this has been due to the influx from other states of India as well as from the neighbouring countries. A very sizeable proportion of the migrants consists of workers, or work-seekers, mostly in the informal sector. In addition, in the past decades, migration from the rural to the urban areas of the state has also been of a substantial order. Taking all these factors into account, it can be conjectured that, at present, the working population in urban Assam would exceed one million. Given the nature, and the limited base, of its urban economy, it is not an easy task to locate decent jobs for the people who keep on thronging the urban labour market.

1.2 Employment Scenario

Every year, a part of the population attains adulthood and joins the labour market, in search of one or the other employment avenue. When the rise in population is high, the pressure for employment generation is also very heavy. It is generally accepted that it is the organized sector which catalyses employment generation. Unfortunately, due to the sluggish growth in Assam's economy, there has been stagnancy in the development of the state's organized sector. One can think of various economical, historical and geographical explanations for the tardy growth of Assam's economy in general, and its urban segment, in particular; these need not be dwelt here. The crucial fact to underline is that because of this stagnating growth scenario, employment generation in the state's organized sector has been declining; in one single year between 1996 and 1997, employment in the organized sector in Assam fell by 7 per cent, from 1.18 million to 1.10 million. Undoubtedly, the urban informal sector has to step in to absorb the pressure of the expanding army of job seekers.

Table 2 indicates the pattern of employment generation in the public and private sectors in Assam in the last few years.

TABLE 2 : **Employment Generation in Public and Private Sectors in Assam**

(Million Persons)

Year	Total Employment (Public + Private Sectors)
1991	1.05
1992	1.08
1993	1.05
1994	1.16
1995	1.11
1996	1.18
1997	1.10

Source: Directorate of Employment Craftsman Training, Assam.

Even though the statistics provided by the Employment Exchanges may not be completely accurate, yet the data thrown up by them may be considered as indicative of the trend of unemployment in Assam. The total number of applicants seeking jobs has increased at a very fast rate from year to year. For example, the total number of job-seekers in the Live Registers of the Employment Exchange shot up from 3,60,343 in May 1981 to 8,32,426 in May 1987, a rise of 131 per cent! This phenomenal increase of the backlog of people seeking jobs in the formal sector clearly shows that, in the interim period, a very high proportion of the new additions to the workforce are engaged in the informal sector.

Another striking feature of Assam's employment scenario is the rapid increase of educated job-seekers. The number of educated unemployed in the Live Register of the Employment Exchange rose from 1,49,799 in 1981 to 4,51,938 in 1987, a rise of 201 per cent! The total number of educated job-seekers, as per the same live Register, stood at 1.00 million at the end of 1997, as against 0.85 million at the end of 1996. The educated job-seekers constituted 96 per cent of the total job-seekers in the Live Register in 1997. Of these, nearly 50 per cent were matriculates, 36 per cent had higher secondary schooling, 9 per cent were graduates while the rest were having technical and professional qualifications. Most of these educated job-seekers would be in the urban areas and some of them may be already employed in the informal sector.

1.3 The Urban Informal Sector

Agriculture productivity is generally low in Assam. Non-agricultural activities have also not substantially expanded. As a consequence, there has been considerable influx of rural population into the urban areas. While most of these would be in the unskilled sector, it has also been observed that with the spread of literacy and education, migration of educated rural population to urban areas has also been very heavy. Nevertheless, bulk of the state's population continues to live in the rural areas.

While reliable and uptodate statistics may not be available, the Economic Census of 1990 indicated that of the 0.54 million workers in the urban sector in Assam, 0.39 million (72.3 per cent) were engaged in their own enterprises, which forms a substantial part of the informal sector. Of these 0.39 million workers, 50.82 per cent were concentrated in the four districts of Kamrup (28.76 per cent), Nagaon (7.69 per cent), Dibrugarh (7.00 per cent) and Tinsukia (7.37 per cent), out of the 23 districts in Assam. The details are given in Tables 3-A and 3-B. This trend is not expected to have undergone much change in the last decade. We can safely assume that the concentration of the informal sector in the above four districts continues to be as much pronounced today as it was a decade ago.

A Survey conducted by the Town and Country Planning Organisation of Assam in the eighties indicated that the annual opportunity in commerce is increasing at the rate of 5 per cent per year. In the absence of the growth of the industrial sector, the commercial sector has grown tremendously in recent years. Most of this growth would be in the informal sector and in the urban areas.

No formal and in-depth study has been undertaken about the structure of the informal sector in the urban areas in Assam. However, it is generally assumed that informal sector employment consists of three categories:

1. Workers in small establishments like shops, service stations, small cottage industrial/establishments, etc;
2. Self-employed or 'independent' workers producing goods or providing services in their individual capacity for sale to different types of consumers; and
3. persons working for households mainly providing services like domestic servants, drivers, gardeners, etc.

On the basis of the patterns in other towns and the general characteristics of the towns in Assam, it is assumed that of those employed in the urban informal sector, 60 per cent are engaged in the first of the three categories given above. About 20 per cent of employment is forthcoming in each of the other two categories.

1.4 Policy Thrusts

The Government of Assam has recognised that employment generation through expansion of economic activities, especially in the urban areas, has not been commensurate with the inflow of skilled, semi-skilled and unskilled persons into the employable categories. The result has been an ever increasing size of the unemployed, both educated and uneducated.

The Government, therefore, recognizes that the thrust of the employment policy should be on generation of self-employment. With the high level of educated unemployed, the Government believes that opportunities for self-employment exist in almost every sector of the economy. Most of this type of employment generation would be in the informal sector. However, the task of generating self-employment is very challenging, especially in an environment where the basic culture does not encourage deviation from the status quo.

The Das Committee, appointed by the state government, to suggest ways and means for employment expansion, advocated the promotion of self-employment as the main way out for the employment stalemate. It was of the view that the basic requirement in development of self-employment is development of entrepreneurship. Most of the indigenous population lacked entrepreneurial spirit and motivation. Hence, the Government has to take intensive measures to motivate the unemployed to undertake self-employment and refrain from running after jobs, even of low quality, in the organised sector.

TABLE 3-A : **Number of Own Account Enterprises and Establishments and Number of Hired Persons Usually Working in Urban Assam**

District	Enterprises			Hired Persons Usually Working		
	Total	Own Account	Establishments	Total	Male	Female
1. Dhubri	9740	6632	3108	14358	13227	1131
2. Kokrajhar	3299	1712	1587	7981	7143	838
3. Bongaigaon	4077	2452	1625	7065	6621	444
4. Goalpara	2889	1591	1293	6812	6067	745
5. Barpeta	5849	3245	2604	11105	10295	810
6. Nalbari	2436	1026	1410	5981	5476	505
7. Kamrup	31426	13525	17901	112218	100846	11372
8. Darrang	5012	3001	2008	9164	8434	730
9. Sonitpur	8426	4790	3636	17638	16143	1495
10. Lakhimpur	4181	2457	1724	9109	7913	1196
11. Dhemaji	933	588	345	1690	1539	151
12. Morigaon	2201	1173	1028	7228	6724	504
13. Nagaon	15509	9002	6507	29996	27437	2559
14. Golaghat	4182	2342	1840	9831	8824	1007
15. Jorhat	6435	3362	3073	19352	17477	1875
16. Sibsagar	5697	3203	2494	14500	13455	1045
17. Dibrugarh	8335	4079	4256	27320	24775	2545
18. Tinsukia	9570	4663	4907	28767	26773	1994
19. Karbi-Anglong	4094	1981	2113	11721	10547	1174
20. NC Hills	1950	1061	889	6524	5469	1055
21. Karimganj	4253	2667	1586	10775	9657	1118
22. Hailakandi	2296	1534	762	4144	3651	493
23. Cachar	6994	4083	2911	16909	14988	1921
Total	149784	80172	69612	390188	353481	36707

Source: Govt. of Assam, Third Economic Census : Assam, 1990, Directorate of Economics and Statistics.

The industrial policies enunciated by the Government of Assam from time to time have also emphasized the need for self-employment. The policies have liberalized the procedures for loans, assistance and subsidies to the informal sector so that this sector can contribute to the growth and development of the state. The Government has also encouraged various governmental agencies such as public works department, public health and other similar departments to assign small works and jobs to local registered youths. In addition, the Government proposes to set up agencies to assist such entrepreneurs in marketing, raising working capital and availing of various other services, which, in the absence of a well-defined institutional support, may be time-consuming and difficult to obtain.

TABLE 3-B : **Percentage Distribution of Own Account Enterprises and Establishments and Number of Hired Persons Working in Urban Assam**

District	Enterprises			Hired Persons Usually Working		
	Total	Own Account	Establishments	Total	Male	Female
1. Dhubri	6.50	8.27	4.47	3.68	3.74	3.08
2. Kokrajhar	2.20	2.14	2.28	2.05	2.02	2.28
3. Bongaigaon	2.72	3.06	2.33	1.81	1.87	1.21
4. Goalpara	1.93	1.98	1.86	1.75	1.72	2.03
5. Barpeta	3.91	4.05	3.74	2.85	2.891	2.21
6. Nalbari	1.63	1.28	2.03	1.53	1.55	1.38
7. Kamrup	20.98	16.87	25.72	28.76	28.53	30.98
8. Darrang	3.35	3.75	2.88	2.35	2.39	1.99
9. Sonitpur	5.63	5.98	5.22	4.52	4.57	4.07
10. Lakhimpur	2.79	3.06	2.48	2.34	2.24	3.26
11. Dhemaji	0.62	0.73	0.50	0.43	0.44	0.41
12. Morigaon	1.47	1.46	1.48	1.85	1.90	1.37
13. Nagaon	10.35	11.23	9.35	7.69	7.76	6.97
14. Golaghat	2.79	2.92	2.64	2.52	2.50	2.74
15. Jorhat	4.30	4.19	4.41	4.96	4.94	5.11
16. Sibsagar	3.80	4.00	3.58	3.72	3.81	2.85
17. Dibrugarh	5.57	5.09	6.11	7.00	7.01	6.93
18. Tinsukia	6.39	5.82	7.05	7.37	7.57	5.43
19. Karbi-Anglong	2.73	2.47	3.04	3.00	2.98	3.20
20. NC Hills	1.30	1.32	1.28	1.67	1.55	2.88
21. Karimganj	2.84	3.33	2.28	2.76	2.73	3.05
22. Hailakandi	1.53	1.91	1.09	1.06	1.03	1.34
23. Cachar	4.67	5.09	4.18	4.33	4.24	5.23
Total	100.00	100.00	100.00	100.00	100.00	100.00

Source: Calculation based on figues in Table 3-A.

Various government organizations have undertaken entrepreneurship development and promotion as one of their activities. An institute that has been set up specifically to develop entrepreneurship in the north eastern region of India is the Indian Institute of Entrepreneurship (IIE). The Hyderabad-based Central Government's National Institute of Small Industries Extension and Training (NISIET) set up a regional office in Guwahati in 1981. The activities of the regional office multiplied as the need for self-employment in the region developed. Consequently, the Government of Assam converted the regional office of the NISIET into a national entrepreneurship development institute, and named it IIE.

The institute has played multifarious roles in development of entrepreneurship in the region. The IIE's activities start from motivating youngsters, even at the school level to the identification of potential entrepreneurs, hand-holding them from identification of projects to going through the various procedures and finally implementing the same. In addition, the IIE also conducts functional programmes and gives thrust into different sectors of the industry. Table 4 gives some idea of the activities undertaken by the IIE in different fields.

TABLE 4 : **Development Programmes Conducted by Indian Institute of Entrepreneurship**

Sr. No.	Type of Programme	No. of Programmes		No. of Participants	
		1997-98	1998-99	1997-98	1998-99
1.	PNE	15	23	357	506
2.	GEE	8	6	165	102
3.	CFB	1	2	23	53
4.	CEE	6	6	86	103
5.	S&W	-	6	-	321
	Total	39	59	857	1556

Note: PNE : Promotion of New Entrepreneurs.
GEE : Growth of Existing Entrepreneurs.
CFB : Continuity of Family Business.
CEE : Creation of Environment for Entrepreneurship.
EE : Entrepreneurial Education.
S&W : Seminars and Workshops.

Source : IIE, Annual Reports for 1997-98 and 1998-99.

The State Government has formed various sectoral corporations like the Development Corporations for SC/ST, Minorities, etc. which give loans on easy terms to people in these categories, largely for promoting self-employment. Many of the success stories in self-employment in the urban sector are attributable to the loan availed of by prospective entrepreneur from such corporations.

Other organisations like the National Small Industry Corporation, the District Industries Centre, NEITCO, SISI, etc., have also played important roles in promoting and development of entrepreneurship. The North Eastern Council (NEC), the IDBI, the SIDBI, the IFCI etc., have also funded numerous such programmes. Most of these organisations are located in the urban areas and thus the benefits have mainly been availed of by those engaged in the urban informal sector.

Some selected results of the efforts made by the IIE in the direction of promoting self-employment are given in Table 5.

TABLE 5 : **Results of NEC-IDBI-SIDBI Sponsored Programmes (1998-99)**

Particulars	General EDP	Women EDP
No. of parcipants in the Entrepreneurship Development Programme	74	25 of which
Project Selected (No.)	72	23 of which
Project Reports Prepared	63	19 of which
Applied for Loan from Appropriate Agencies	45	12
Units Started	22	4

The above results could be termed as highly encouraging, especially in the context of the fact that most of the participants in the programme have no family or social background of self-employment or ever have been entrepreneurs.

Many NGOs have also embarked into the field of self-employment generation. Organisations like the North Eastern Women Entgrepreneurs' Association, and Association of Small Industries, have pioneered entrepreneurship development. They have networked with various sister organisations as well as governmental bodies to promote entrepreneurship. Organisations like the Shanti Sadhana Ashram, Bosco Reach-out, Rotary Clubs, Lions Club etc., have also undertaken motivation and training initiatives. The Institute of Electronics and Telecommunications Engineering of India (IETEI) has conducted various training programmes, in collaboration with the Norwegian Aid Agency (NORAD) to impart computer training amongst women to enable them to set them up self-employing enterprieses in the field of computer operations and maintenance.

1.5 The ILO Initiative

The 1990s witnessed some of the most drastic upheavals in the economy of the world. With the advent of economic liberalisation, globalisation took roots and market forces have become the most dominating factor. The impact of these on the social environment has been tremendous. Employment patterns have undergone drastic changes and there has been a clamour to give a 'more human face to the global economy'. It became imperative for the ILO to have a fresh look at its own mandate.

The ILO proposes to move away from its traditional approach towards labour by defining four strategic objectives: fundamental principles and rights at work, employment, social protection and social dialogue. In this drive, the ILO is concerned not only with employment generation, but also in 'creating jobs of acceptable quality'.

It proposes to strive for what it terms as 'Decent Work'. The ILO's emphasis in this particular case is towards the urban informal sector. In such a situation, growth of the urban informal sector has to be the main recourse.

As stated above, the informal sector in the urban economy has been identified with entrepreneurship development. Of course, the spectrum of the urban informal sector is very wide. However, it may not be possible to encompass all the diversities inherent in this sector. It has also to be borne in mind that there is considerable underemployment in the urban informal sector, as is also the case with the rural sector. This underemployed sector would cover those engaged in part-time work, casual engagements, contract workers, etc.

It has been stated above that there has been some recognition of the fact that the informal sector exists in the urban regions and the massive employment generation required has to come from this sector only. Some steps have also been taken. However, the results of these efforts have been haphazard and have lacked focus. It has also not been possible to take into cognizance the ILO objectives. The conditions in the urban informal sector have not been satisfactory. The urban sector is socially very sensitive and the high level of unemployment, especially amongst the educated job-seekers, is not a healthy phenomenon. Therefore, there is a need to tackle the situation in an urgent and time-bound manner. The potential for development in this sector may be high. A concerted, focussed and well-directed strategy can play a positive and contributory role.

2. Experiential Learning

Before developing a strategy for the viable growth of the urban informal sector, it may be useful to study the working of some informal sector so that the strengths, weaknesses and opportunities open to the informal sector are thrown bare in a reasonably reliable manner. We conducted five case studies, all engaged in different types of the informal sector activity, located in different parts of the city of Guwahati. The case studies reflect a wide array of diversities: some involve persons who were adequately educated but failed to secure employment which made them go for self-employment in the informal sector, while for others, it was acute poverty that forced them to seek self-employment avenues.

Practically, in all the five cases, the entrepreneurs were able to identify potential sources of livelihood by meeting some very important requirements of society, whether providing fast and hygienic food to people who are in a hurry, supplying essential requirements or meeting a growing service need. Thus, they were able to adequately cover the marketing aspect of their businesses. Micro-credit was available to one of the five cases which helped in establishing himself much faster and provide still better service. If micro-credit could have been made available to the other cases also, they could have established more vibrant enterprises and/or expanded themselves much further. One reason why entrepreneurial efforts flounder in Assam is the lack of adequate financial resources. It is heartening to note that the North Eastern Development Financial Corporation (NEDFC) has initiated a scheme to extend micro-credits to such sectors.

What would be common in all the five case studies is that all the persons concerned were driven by an intense desire to be self-employed, had perseverance and determination, are hard-working and frugal in habits and have, what in today's parlance, is termed as 'customer orientation'. These are basic qualities and are essential if one is to succeed as an entrepreneur. At the same time, it has to be realised that these success stories are very few in numbers.

While the whole issue is being studied at the macro level, there is a need to examine the sector at the micro level to remove any bottlenecks or impediments that may act as constraints in actual implementation of the proposals. For example, many governmental schemes fail to deliver because of cumbersome procedures and irritants. Lack of clarity in procedures, non-uniform interpretation of statutes, corruption etc., are other factors that may act as deterrents to success of many schemes. Studying some existing units and learning from their experiences may, therefore, be very useful to identify some of the removable irritants.

The scope of self-employment is quite high in the informal sector. There are many needs of the urban population that have not been met adequately. Some of the needs are individual in nature while in some cases even the societal needs have remained unfulfilled. In the case of the individual needs, we may cite the example of need for properly trained service personnel to repair and maintain consumer durable items in the households like TV, refrigerators. Similarly, there is also an unfulfilled need of various trades like plumbers, paints-men, masons, carpenters, etc. who would do odd jobs. Domestic helps like drivers, gardeners, watchmen, part-time domestic servants, are also in demand in the urban areas. At present, persons who are not adequately trained meet these demands in the informal sector with the result that the services are not rendered in a satisfactory manner, and future demand expansion always remains a question mark.

Again, the urban society is also in need of proper sanitary and cleaning services. Co-operative housing colonies have also started coming up in the urban areas where collective security, sanitation, and supply services are required. All these requirements can be made only through the informal sector. There is scope to organise the informal sector to meet these requirements.

It would, therefore, be useful if some structured, in-depth exercises are carried out to examine the various needs of the society that can be met through the informal sector. It may be construed that these needs are growing rapidly as the urbanisation process catches up. However, the deterioration in the urban sector, both on the social and hygienical sides, indicates that the needs have not been properly met. It would, therefore, be useful to study what have been the constraints that have inhibited the growth of the urban informal sectors in the region.

Such diagnostic studies would not only identify the problems, but also suggest appropriate action plans. The state of various governmental agencies, which have been set up with similar objectives, need also be examined. At the same time, there is also a need to examine the sector at the micro-level to remove any bottlenecks or impediments that may act as constraints in actual implementation of the proposals. The available experience warns that, in some cases, many well-intentioned proposals fail at the implementation stage because of minor bottlenecks at the micro-level.

3. The Development Strategy

What is clear from the above is that there is a gross mismatch between the societal needs and the means available to fulfill them. The level of unemployment in the urban sector has started assuming serious proportions. Yet, there is a vast scope in the urban informal sector, which can be met by the urban unemployed. Thus, there is a need to develop an employment generation strategy that seeks employment generation in the urban informal sector. The emphasis of this strategy would be to meet the unfulfilled needs of the urban society through the informal sector. The strategy suggests a focussed approach, so that efforts are not spread too thin. We suggest below a number of sector strategies that, in our opinion, should work well in augmenting the employment opportunities to the urban job aspirants, especially the educated youth of Assam. As should be evident to a discerning reader, the ILO imperatives are duly taken note of while venturing employment promotion schemes.

It needs to be emphasized, at the very outset, that it is only through entrepreneurship development that meaningful employment generation is possible under the present developmental scenario. This would require motivating young people towards entrepreneurship and guiding them in project selection and hand-holding. In Assam, a casual scan of the environment would indicate that there are quite a few sectors that have potential for further growth and development, and these are the sectors where entrepreneurship could be promoted in a big way. The sectors that hold special promise are (1) food processing, (2) handloom/handicrafts, (3) tourism, (4) information technology, and (5) equipment servicing and maintenance.

3.1 Food Processing

The North Eastern region grows abundant quantity of fruit and vegetables, like pineapples, tomatoes, oranges, etc. There are specific belts in the region where such perishable commodities are grown in plenty. However, during the peak harvest seasons, a fairly large amount of the perishable items get destroyed due to poor storage and transport facilities. Farmers are often required to make distress sale of their produce.

Efforts have been made in the past to develop the food processing industry in the region. However, food processing industry requires, apart from heavy capital investment, certain infrastructure support most notably a reliable electric power supply, proper transport system, flexible storage capacity, etc. Assam is rather poor in infrastructure. To set up a modern food-processing industry, apart from raw materials, there are a large variety of other inputs like modern packaging materials, food preservation items, etc that are equally important. While the raw material may be available locally, the other requirements proposed industry have to be met from outside the state. This renders the prospects of setting up a modern food processing unit in the state economically unviable. Economy of scale, high operational and transportation costs and marketing are the problems this sector faces in Assam. That is why, the organised food-processing sector has not been able to achieve the desired results in Assam and meet the competition from large-scale units located outside the state.

Taking the realities into account, a new strategy needs to be adopted. The established processed food industry in India basically caters to the premium segment of the society. Here, the value addition and the operating margins are high. However, taking into account the high costs involved in food processing, it is proposed that Assam invests in low technology in the food processing sector and go for retail marketing of raw food items like vegetables, fruits etc. in an intense manner. Investment may be made for immediate off-take of the produce from the farmers and their distribution in the markets through individual sellers. In this way, wastage would be reduced and farmers would also be ensured of getting decent prices for their produce.

Another strategy to meet the competition from established brands might be based on price, by keeping the cost of production down and catering to the lower end of the market. For example, this region is very suitable for mushroom cultivation. Some amount of mushrooms is sold, packed in tins. These are costly and cater to a microscopic segment of the total mushroom market. Mushroom is easy to grow and cultivate. After harvesting, mushrooms can be sun-dried and sold raw in the open market directly to consumers like any other vegetable. Bulk supply of such mushrooms can also be made to large commercial food producers who may out-source the supply of quality mushrooms. Thus, mushroom has the potential of substantial employment generation in the informal sector. Mushroom is a rich food and its use could also be propagated so that the demand increases in due course of time.

Once the lower end of the food market is identified as the potential thrust area, production of processed pea-nuts, potato-chips, banana chips etc., can also be taken up in an intense way. There is already a big unbranded market in these products. In addition, traditional food stuff like rice power, puffed rice as well as condiments etc. are areas where the informal sector can play a positive role. If the informal sector is developed and the people involved are trained adequately, there is a possibility that many branded manufacturer would outsource their requirements from this sector. Of late, ethnic food has caught people's fancy. There is also an export market for such foods.

3.2 Handloom/Handicrafts

Assam is rich in its traditional craftsmanship. With the growth in ethnic concepts and its impact in the fashion market, handloom and handicraft sectors have potential to develop on a global basis. A large number of Assamese people are adept in various handloom and handicraft skills. In the field of sericulture, Assam has some unique advantages, which are not available to others. For example, Muga silk is available only in Assam. The scope to exploit this uniqueness is tremendous. Similarly, Assam has a multi ethnic base. Each ethnic group has their distinct characteristics, most ostensibly reflected in their crafts. Their traditions could be marketed on a global basis, with imagination and creativity. At the same time, one has to bear in mind that this sector has a big advantage in that it is a non-polluting sector and its proliferation would also be beneficial to society in general.

The growth and development of the handloom and handicraft sectors has not been satisfactory in Assam. This is because of an unsatisfactory raw material supply, inadequate skill development, obsolete techniques, non-development of contemporary designs to meet modern tastes, and so on. The basic weakness is lack of market orientation and sticking to traditional methods and systems. This sector too has a tremendous scope to grow even internationally and can easily subscribe to what the ILO terms as 'Decent Work'.

Thus, the basic requirement in this sector is to give it a market orientation. What the market actually seeks in handloom and handicrafts should be meticulously identified. This would involve carrying out market research, both on national and international basis. Research and developmental work has to be undertaken in design and execution of products. Since fashion designs keep on changing very fast, a system has to be evolved so that emerging trends are identified and product and design changes are incorporated instantaneously to meet changing tastes.

Next, there has to be a sincere effort to upgrade skills and techniques. Many countries have stringent craftsmanship rules that require high level of skills. The local artisans and craftsmen must be able to upgrade their skills to such levels. This involves intense training to the crafts people. So far, we have been rather complacent in assuming that our crafts people are highly skilled. The fact is that they are traditionally skilled, but their skill levels could be enhanced through proper training. More skilled our crafts people are, the higher would be the value added, which, in turn, gives enhanced returns to investment and human effort. The challenge and responsibility of the public sector institutions (e.g., handloom and handicrafts boards/ agencies at the local and state levels) in fostering the needed technological up-gradation, and to educate/inform the local crafts people to feel the pulse of the changing demand patterns are thus obvious.

The handloom and handicrafts sectors could be developed as cottage industries, even in the urban sector. There is a considerable scope to introduce micro-credit to purchase equipment and raw materials and develop proper supply and distribution chains through which regular flow of materials could be maintained.

3.3 Tourism

Tourism is another sector in Assam, which has remained inadequately explored. Already, a large number of domestic tourists come to Assam because of one single attraction: the Kamakhya Temple in Guwahati. Similarly, most of the foreign tourists to Assam come just to visit the Kaziranga National Park. However, the tourism potential of Assam remains grossly under-exploited. There is a tremendous scope to be innovative in developing the tourism potential of Assam. For example, apart from wild-life tourism, there is a vast unexplored scope for developing eco-tourism, hiking, angling, bird-watching, nostalgic tourism, ethnic tourism. Since tourism has emerged as one of the fastest growing industries in the world, there is absolutely no doubt that, given adequate emphasis, this sector can develop in Assam also.

The growth of tourism normally depends on small tour operators. This is a field where the scope for entrepreneurship development is very high. Young persons could be trained to be tour operators, tourist guides, etc. They may be given certificates, which would establish their credentials and help them to get business. They may be assisted in developing contacts and networking with major national and international tour operators so that marketing efforts at their own level get substantially reduced, and more time and attention is spared for rendering better tourist services. The Government can assist by promoting the state as a tourist destination and leave the actual operations to these small operators.

Already eco-tourism has been developed in the Nameri Wild-life Park near Tezpur in Assam. This is a brilliant example of various agencies coming together. Here, an NGO and the Forest Department have got together to develop an eco-camp in the middle of the forest with scope for angling and normal wild-life tourism. This can be taken as a model and other such parks could be developed in different parts of Assam, and in other states.

3.4 Information Technology

Common with the experience of some other states, a large number of Assamese youth have gone outside the state, even abroad, and have taken up very successful careers in the field of information technology. This is mainly because they do not have adequate scope in Assam, even though they have the training and skill. One of the problems that the IT sector faces in Assam is the lack of adequate infrastructure. There is inadequacy in training facilities with the result that most people have to go outside for training. Uninterrupted power supply and lack of ease of connectivity are the two other problems inhibiting the growth of the IT sector in Assam.

In Assam, there is a potential to set up public e-mail and web-surfing facilities. Already a few such units have been set up in Guwahati and it is seen that they have been very successful. This shows that the demand for such services has been latent so far. It is still not possible for many people in Assam to have their own computers at home. For such people, a public e-mail and surfing facility would be a big boon. The potential for job creation, in the informal sector, can be easily imagined on this account.

A Software technology park is also being set-up soon at Guwahati. It is expected that this park would help the state to network with the main software markets of India and the world. Once the park develops fully, there would be scope for the informal sector to grow to meet its various needs. Individual entrepreneurs would be able to provide outsourcing facilities to the operators of the park.

A crucial pre-requisite for facilitating such outsourcing outfits is to standardize the training needs of the IT sector. There is every reason to believe that the IT sector is the emerging sector of tomorrow. Hence, there is a race to hitch oneself to this bandwagon. The result is that numerous IT training centers have mushroomed in the state. The training imparted in these centres is of questionable standard. It is recommended that a set curriculum be developed for such training institutes. Also, the government lays down the basic infrastructural and human resource requirements for such centres to operate. An evaluation and monitoring agency is formed which would constantly watch these training centres so that proper training is imparted. This would ensure that a genuinely trained cadre of trained people is created in the state to meet the emerging needs of this field.

3.5 Equipment Servicing and Maintenance

Manufacturers of white goods and other consumer durables often comment that the consumers of the North Eastern Region are generally early adapters of most convenient products. Thus, the sale of such items is relatively high in this region. When the number of consumers of consumer-durable items increase, there is a corresponding rise in demand for their servicing and maintenance. In Assam, servicing and maintenance of such goods and equipment have never been satisfactory. Even today, in the urban areas, there is a dearth of properly trained service engineers and other specialists, who could repair and maintain items like TVs, Audio-video equipment, computer hardware, washing machines, automobiles etc. This is mainly because most dealers do not give adequate emphasis on after-sales service in the region.

To meet this requirement, again the informal sector can play a big role. Standard training programmes could be developed to train the educated job-seekers in the region in the field of equipment maintenance. Formal training programmes could be developed, with appropriate evaluation of the trained personnel. A standard accreditation body may also be created that would certify the skills of such trained persons. These trained personnel could then set themselves up as service entrepreneurs. If they are certified by a credible accreditation agency, obviously, public would not hesitate to avail of their services. Thus, a big need of society could be met in the most satisfactory manner, and, at the same time, many new and remunerative self-employing jobs can come up in the urban informal sector.

It should be borne in mind that the above few sectors are not the only sectors where the scope for development of the informal sector exists. These are just a few examples. There are many sectors where development so far has been rather negligible, but scope for expansion may emerge in the long run. For example, with an increase in life span, the demographic profile of the population is changing. There are now more old people in the population who need continuous care. At the same time, with the gradual break-up of joint family system, and employment mobility facilitated by numerous factors, it is not possible for the off-springs of such old persons to always look after their parents. In the long run, old age homes would come up in large numbers in Guwahati and other towns in Assam. There would be a demand for people from the informal sector who would be engaged in caring for the old inmates of such homes. At present, this concept is at a very nascent stage of development. Probably, it would catch on well in due course. Once that happens, the demand on the informal sector would be substantial. There are many other such fields where there is potential demand that would emerge gradually.

It can, therefore, be safely assumed that the informal sector has tremendous potential for growth in Assam. There are many individual and societal needs that are not yet fulfilled. With innovation and creativity, the informal sector could meet these needs. Once that happens, the informal sector can play a big role in ameliorating the employment situation in the state.

4. Proposed Thrust

One conclusion that can be drawn from the above is that a concerted effort is required, on part of the government, to develop the urban informal sector. At the same time, it has to be ensured that the efforts do not get diffused and lose their focus. As the first step, it is, therefore, proposed that the initial thrust towards employment generation may be restricted to the main towns of five districts of Assam. By limiting the thrust to specific focussed areas, it would be possible to have proper monitoring of the proposed developmental efforts. At the implementation stage, quick feed-backs, and actions on such feed-backs, would be crucial. By limiting the efforts to specific areas and specific dimensions in each area, such immediate response would be possible. Furthermore, such an effort would go more like a pilot study, which would give the scope to learn from experiences and make changes wherever required. To reiterate, the five districts selected are Kamrup, Nagaon, Tinsukia, Dibrugarh and Cachar.

While the first four districts cover almost 50 per cent of the total urban informal sector in Assam, Cachar district is included to ensure that South Assam is included in order to maintain some kind of regional balance. It is proposed that the initial efforts are restricted to these five districts so that there is proper identification, implementation and monitoring of efforts. The learning experiences from these five districts could be utilized in spreading the efforts to other urban areas, as well as in developing additional manpower towards these efforts.

The strategy proposed to be adopted by government in these districts would be to:

1. give adequate publicity to various government schemes for promotion of entrepreneurship ;
2. intensify the activities of organizations such as IIE, DICs, etc. so that the potential entrepreneurs are identified, motivated, and trained to undertake self-employment of their choice ;
3. simplify procedures and methods for availing of government schemes and programmes so that potential entrepreneurs do not get entangled in red-tape and other procedural hassles ;
4. set up institutions that would give standardized training in equipment servicing and maintenance as well as in skill development. The government may also set up accreditation agencies that would certify to the technical capabilities of such trained personnel and monitor their performance and skill up-gradation on a continuous basis ; and
5. take appropriate measures to develop the infrastructure base, which sustains the informal sector. This may also include promoting the state of Assam in terms of its potential in various sectors, making the international consumers aware about its products and services and basically becoming the link for the informal sector with the outside world.

Bibliography

EPW Research Foundation, 2001. "Population in India", Economic and Political Weekly, XXXVI/6, April 21-27.

Govt. of India, Population Census Reports for Assam (various decades).

Govt. of Assam, Employment Situation in Assam (various issues), Directorate of Employment and Craftsmen Training.

————, Third Economic Census: Assam, 1990, Directorate of Economics and Statistics.

Indian Institute of Entrepreneuship, Annual Reports for 1997-98 and 1998-99, Guwahati.

Training and Work in the Informal Sector: Issues and Good Practice

Fred Fluitman

1. The Why, What and How of Training

Among several other complex problems, many developing countries are faced with an employment problem that has massive proportions. Their economies are characterized by various imbalances in the labour market, by serious under-employment and by ample scope for improving performance at work. There are, by far, not enough wage-jobs for all those who want one and, pending efforts at structural adjustment and promoting economic growth, there are few in store. A large majority of the labour force is, therefore, engaged in rural subsistence and urban informal sector activities. People make ends meet in micro-enterprises, by doing whatever seems reasonable in the circumstances. There are some who perform relatively well and others who barely survive. Very few can afford to do no work at all.

As poverty is largely an outcome of what people do for a living and how well they do it, skills of all sorts come to mind early as something they need in order to be more productive, to do things differently or to do different things. Training is, therefore, commonly considered to be one of the missing pieces in the development puzzle; and training is usually one of the first things proposed, once governments have come around to improving informal sector conditions.

Unfortunately, training systems almost every where, it seems, are insufficiently demand-driven or problem-oriented. There is a tendency in the world of training, natural enough in the light of uncertainty and when decisions are left to trainers whose perspectives are partial, to go by the book; to do more of the same; to decide, on behalf or in spite of the 'client', what skills are on offer and how they should be delivered.

The sort of vocational training currently available, especially the one from the government-run or government-sponsored institutions in countries with a significant informal sector, is not always very relevant. Rather than reflecting the realities of the labour market, one may find that scarce resources are primarily devoted to providing for a limited number of young school-leavers, mostly male, with training of questionable quality, for jobs which, in the end, either do not exist, or do not materialize, if at all they exist. At the same time, most training institutions are unwilling, or in any case unable, to reach out to people who work in the informal sector and who might have some use for a skill or two.

Haphazard targeting of trainees is a sure way of wasting resources. For training to have an impact, it is essential, before even thinking of implementation, to have established precisely who is to benefit and how, and perhaps to have asked why one is to benefit and not another. A crucial choice in this regard, with far reaching consequences for subsequent choices, is between training for school leavers who are bound to end up in the informal sector, and training for people who already work in micro-enterprises. The accumulated experience suggests that training for work in the informal sector has been the most effective, if aimed, in limited doses, at established micro-entrepreneurs and their apprentices. Moreover, survey after survey confirms that people at work in the informal sector demand such training and are usually prepared to pay for it. In the case of the unemployed youth, on the other hand, training has not been shown to do away with their problem. It keeps them off the streets for a while but it does not automatically get them jobs. They are more likely to benefit from other, less expensive, measures, including additional schooling, if possible with some emphasis on self-employment. It is indeed widely recognized that ensuring a solid basic education for all will yield ample results, including trainability throughout a career, even if it is an informal sector career.

Re-orientating training systems, away from an almost exclusive focus on preparing young people for wage-employment in the formal sector, towards paying more attention to the skills of people at work in informal sector enterprises, is easier said than done, however. A case must be made so as to convince those who decide on these things; and once policy decisions have been taken, they should be implemented. As in any process of policy development, or policy reform, a point of departure (the status quo) and a destination (realistic aspirations) should be agreed to before it is decided how to get from the one to the other. Only when it is clear what the problem is, need solutions be spelt out and pondered over, in the light of factors such as what it would take to administer a remedy.

The informal sector operators are, typically, burdened by a variety of complex problems. The common ones concern access to markets for inputs and outputs, access to credit, technology, and useful information, the efficient use of inputs and the quality of outputs. Good policy would acknowledge that, among multiple problems, only some will squarely qualify for a training solution. For example, training may help in improving product quality or in reducing accidents at work; it may be a conduit for product diversification or for the adoption of more appropriate technologies. In other instances, training may represent only part of a solution, meaning that it is of no use unless complementary measures are in position and are duly available to those in need. And then, there are plenty of problems which call for solutions other than training. Learning how to apply for, or how to manage, credit is without consequence where there is no credit to be had; learning to negotiate with suppliers does not really help when they are monopolists; learning to operate a new machine is of no immediate use if the operator is unable to buy one; and so on. A critical element in the diagnostic process is, therefore, to determine whether the people one has targeted, are having problems for which the sort of training one is able to provide, would bring a solution; or, even where problems are not so evident, whether opportunities exist, through training, to improve their performance or working conditions. In other words, it is important to argue the case for intervention in terms of what difference the training would make.

The informal sector is notoriously heterogeneous. Men and women, young and old, educated or illiterate, are involved in a wide range of economic activities, with a varying degree of success. Many are on their own, or working with a partner, in micro-enterprises; there are others who employ a few wage-workers, unpaid family helpers, or apprentices. Some are ambitious and eager to learn, while others are less convinced that new skills will make a difference. Not all are perfectly trainable. And not all have equal amounts of time on their hands. All of these variables, and the particular context in which they come to play, should be expected to impact on training needs, if any, on demand for training and, on ways and means of meeting such demand.

If training is contemplated as a measure of informal sector support, it is furthermore important to consider, upfront, in some depth, and without prejudging the issue, what sort of skills are currently being used in the concerned micro-enterprises, how people working there have acquired these skills and what, if anything, might be wrong in the circumstances, with either the skills or the way in which they were acquired. It is important, because one should want to acknowledge the merits of relatively unexplored pathways of learning, and protect these, as necessary, from being supplanted with something less effective.

Recommending training where it will make a difference is one thing, providing the training is another. Training aimed at more than a few informal sector operators in poor countries, must obviously be affordable and mechanisms should exist for delivering the necessary skills in a convenient and efficient manner. Conventional training institutions may find it difficult to cater to a new clientele, particularly when large numbers of trainees are to be involved for short periods. Indeed, new mechanisms or alternative providers may have to be thought of. In this context, reference may be made to efforts in some countries at protecting and improving traditional apprenticeship arrangements. Rather than legislating away a system which, however, imperfect, has long transferred useful skills to large numbers of young people, steps may be taken, including skills upgrading for both masters and apprentices, to build on its strengths while addressing its weaknesses. Alternatively, or in addition, it may be possible through incentives or direct support to improve the coverage and quality of *'back street colleges'* and other private providers whose contribution is not usually taken seriously by the *'people in the ministry'*. Other avenues include the establishment of micro-enterprise extension facilities or small business advisory services which address training needs in an integrated manner; these may be perceived as a new window for existing training institutions or result from offering a variety of already available, but dispersed services in a *'one-stop-shop'*.

Re-orientating training systems towards improving conditions in the informal sector enterprises may be done in many ways. As circumstances and aims vary considerably, over time and space, there are no standard recipes and there is ample scope for experimentation. That being said, general lessons may be drawn from experience in a variety of countries, in particular as regards the sort of ingredients and instruments that have been known to give rise to an appropriate strategy.

2. Good Practice in Developing a Training Strategy

Governments interested in re-orientating or reforming their national training system, so that it would more readily respond to training needs and opportunities in informal sector enterprises, would seem well advised to develop a comprehensive strategy rather than engage in marginal tinkering. As a matter of course, they should get hold of the facts that are necessary to grasp the status quo, then set achievable aims and objectives, and finally propose how these should be met.

Developing a training strategy for the informal sector should, therefore, begin with an analysis of the national labour market and with an inquiry into the peculiar situation of those who are considered informal sector workers. In trying to understand why things are the way they are, the analysis should then be extended to the training system itself and bring out its strengths and weaknesses. One should establish why indeed the system does not target informal sector workers and what it would take to correct the situation. Only a sharp picture of both the demand and supply side of the training system will allow one to formulate precise reasons for intervening, to set priorities, such as based on equity considerations, to quantify objectives, and to specify resource implications.

Drawn from good practice in countries where pertinent reforms have been implemented, the following suggestions may be useful in re-orientating training systems towards improving conditions in informal sector enterprises :

(1) Training for employment should be conceived broadly, meaning well beyond what happens in the typical, government-sponsored, two or three year programmes aimed at preparing school leavers for their first jobs in the formal sector, related concepts, notably that of trainee and trainer, should be defined accordingly;

(2) It is important, before developing a training strategy for informal sector enterprises, to reach a c onsensus about the merits of improving conditions for large numbers of people who work at very low levels of productivity and income, possibly at the expense of some other worthy cause;

(3) For reasons of feasibility, and on equity grounds, training measures to improve, little by little, conditions in large numbers of informal sector enterprises, may be favoured over measures aimed at 'picking a few winners' instead of offering full-fledged training courses, one could think of administering distinct 'shots of skill' aimed at the most obvious weaknesses in enterprise performance; ways and means of persuading and motivating private training providers, including micro-entrepreneurs who might qualify as master craftsmen, to get involved in implementing a modular approach of the sort, should be explored;

(4) It makes sense in conditions of uncertainty, for example, about future skill requirements, to try and make training systems and their product more flexible than what is usually the case; it should be acknowledged, however, that such flexibility is easily compromised by an undue infatuation, common among bureaucrats, with regulation, such as concerning minimum entry qualifications, or in respect of training standards, testing and certification, or as regards conditions to be met by private sector training providers;

(5) While aiming at early results, the basic approach to systemic reform should be to pursue gradual changes in existing structures and procedures; policy-makers, after all, may make mistakes, or run behind new developments, or under-estimate resistance to top-down approaches; there should be ample opportunity for evaluation and for appropriate adjustments;

(6) It is crucial to convince training managers, trainers and others concerned, of the need for change, to involve them in the design of alternative policies, and to provide them with training and incentives as necessary to ensure smooth implementation;

(7) The effectiveness of training increases as and when clients are somehow involved in making decisions which affect them; the merits of decentralizing public provision should, therefore, be explored, including the devolution of control over budgets to training managers; in any event, programme implementers should have room for manoeuvre and be allowed, within limits, to experiment, for example, as regards training contexts and methodology;

(8) Major changes, even if implemented gradually, are likely to require substantial resources; rather than claim additional government funds, existing ones should be re-budgeted and made better use of, while alternative means, including

external resources, are being explored; likewise, it is recommended to rely as much as possible on existing institutions, be they public or private, adapted or regrouped, as necessary for meeting new purposes;

(9) Training for work in micro-enterprises should, as necessary, be complemented by before- and after-training services, such as vocational guidance and trouble-shooting in respect of credit or markets or access to technology;

(10) Targeting trainees from groups designated as disadvantaged, one should not be led to believe that their training will do away with the root cause of their disadvantage.

Re-orientating training systems towards improving conditions in informal sector enterprises is now increasingly included in government agenda and endorsed by donor agencies. While being discussed and tried out, the impression is, nonetheless, that there is a long way to go before informal sector training may count on the kind of government resources currently devoted to *'regular vocational training'*, however limited these may be. Meanwhile, non-governmental organizations, some of them with support from external sources, and private-for-profit training providers, contribute along different tracks, with a varying degree of success, to the development of skills among some of the many informal sector workers in the developing world. An overwhelming majority of these workers still acquire their know-how by trial and error, perhaps a respectable but inefficient and narrow path of learning, to make much headway.

India's Urban Informal Sector and Workers: Role of Social Partners

Amarjeet Kaur

1. The Inside of the Informal Sector

Would the process of development, modernization and technological upgradation bring better working and living conditions for the working masses who are the major tools for creating wealth and advance of civilization. It very much depends on who are the people at the helms of affairs making decisions for those development models in changing paradigms. The key factor that decides the final outcome or impact of any policy is who, in the mind of the policy makers and implementing agencies, is the target group, and for whose benefit the whole processes are to take place.

It needs to be recognized that the fast changing world, in the context of globalization, liberalization and privatization, is bringing shocks for millions of working masses, with rise in unemployment, job insecurity, poverty and destitution, as accepted recently in certain reports even by the propagandists and promoters of the whole philosophy of free-market economy. The Structural Adjustment Programmes are causing increasing informalisation and casualisation of the labour force. Thus, the trend of rise in the informal sector is a reality. To address this scenario, and to provide decent work and working conditions to the workforce, as proclaimed by the present Director General of the ILO, it is necessary first to look into the prevailing conditions of work in this sector; it will assure us of a better appraisal and a more purposeful presentation of future projects for looking after the interests of the vast army of people engaged in this growing sector.

From the trade union point of view, the key objective should be decent work with rights of collective bargaining, minimum wage/earning to live with dignity and to meet basic necessities of life, social security benefits, applications of equal remuneration act for gender justice, occupational safety and health for all categories of workers, and conducive, safe and secured working environment for women.

The Indian Constitution enjoins upon the State to secure, by suitable legislation, economic organization or in any other way, to all workers, agricultural, industrial or others, work for earning a decent wage that ensures a reasonable standard of life, and social and cultural opportunities.

Since labour occurs in the concurrent list of distribution of powers, both central and state governments have been empowered to enact labour laws. Consequently, uptil now, as many as 150 legislations, the largest in any country in the world, stand enacted in both the states and the centre. Nonetheless, the process of law enforcement has been such that the laws invariably have been used against the poor. The poor, therefore, feels that the laws are meant to be used against him/her and the rich, affluent and the powerful are above the law. Several pronouncements of the High Courts and the Supreme Court, especially those in response to public interest litigations, in favour of workers in the sweated and the unorganized sectors, including bonded labourers, contract and migrant workers, clearly point to sad state of affairs. The directions of the courts are for the very same enforcement machinery whose indifference and insensitivity had led to recourse to public interest litigations, in the very first instance. Hence, one needs to look into the improvement of enforcement mechanisms and also to look for alternatives.

Presently, most of the conditions as desired by the constitution makers and reiterated by the judiciary, are absent in the informal sector. Let us face the truth that workers are not paid the minimum wages. It is a hard struggle to get a wage hike for the workforce of this sector in response to the rise in cost of living. Generally speaking, the women in this sector do not get equal pay for equal work or similar work; in most cases, no attention is paid to safety and health questions; no system of maternity benefit coverage exists in a majority cases due to casualisation, contractualisation and home-based work on piece-rate. There is no job-security; there is no work guarantee at all. There is no coverage of a vast majority of them in any health scheme. There is no access to market mechanism for a majority of self-producing entities. There is no limitation on hours of work; interval for rest and system of leave or holidays are nearly totally absent.

2. Women Workers in the Informal Sector

Let us have a brief look at the plight of women workers in general and their counterparts in the informal sector in particular.

The irony is that while working women bear a double burden of doing domestic work as well as income/waged work, patriarchal perceptions reducing the importance of their economic role result in women being considered a secondary labour force whose income is simply a complement to the family unit. Women's work remains under-recognized, their capacities and talents as a human resource remain under-utilized and our society is yet to recognize them as economic participants and contributors, equal to their male counterparts, if not more.

There is a tendency to segregate women in particular industries and occupations through notionally reserving certain types of work mainly for them. For example, a large number of women are employed as nurses, health workers, teachers, clerks, stenographers and sweepers in the organized sector, and as assembling, packing and processing workers in the industrial units. Telephone, electronics, food processing, plantations etc. are the industries employing more number of women workers in the formal sector.

Women usually face a double work day. On an average, they normally work for 4 to 5 hours a day at home, fulfilling their traditional domestic responsibilities in addition to their economic activity. This leads to an unequal sharing of workload between the sexes; it also imposes, *ceteris paribus*, limitations on the ability of women to compete on equal terms with men in the labour market.

Except in women-preferred industries and jobs, employers are often reluctant to employ women. Not only are they not prepared to incur the expenses of crèches and maternity benefits, they are often prejudiced and feel that women are less efficient and productive than men. Employers ignore the family responsibilities and double burden that women have to deal with.

Social security schemes are non-existent or, when they exist, are insignificant, ill-conceived, delayed or simply not implemented for the unorganized sector women workers. In spite of this, most women in the informal sector, and quite a sizeable proportion of them in the formal sector, are not organized in trade unions. In the informal sector, it is plainly the insecurity of their tenure and their total dependence on their jobs that makes them wary of trade union activities. Sexual exploitation of women by employers, contractors, middle-men is another serious issue related to working women.

With a growing number of single women joining the workforce, one of the major problems in the metropolitan cities is the shortage of safe accommodation near their place of work. Very few establishments in the cities provide quarters to their employees. A very big majority of working women have to depend on rented accommodation or on working women's hostels, usually located far away from their work place and highly inadequate in number. The problem is more acute for those who come to the city for work from villages and from other regions.

For those who may be married and have children, the lack of sufficient day care centres, creches etc. is another major problem. In many cases, women workers have to give up their jobs for want of child care facilities.

The pittance that women earn in the informal sector perpetuates the image of their being only 'supplementary' earners. Thus, even as women are increasingly emerging as the main breadwinners or heads of households, policy-makers continue to uphold notions which blots out the reality. Effectively, this results in no efforts at training and skill-development for women with the result that they continue to suffer discrimination at all levels of entry to the labour market; the tendency perpetuates itself practically over the whole working career of women workers.

Assets are rarely owned by women. Also, they have limited access to credit facilities. Banks and other credit institutions hesitate to give loans to women without sufficient security or without the signatures of men. As a result, most women have to depend on money-lenders or contractors or middle-men.

Unfortunately, there are no specific and reliable figures available for urban households. Visible trends would suggest that the number is very large and growing. This means that there is an ever-growing number of the poor women who are forced into whatever employment they can find, and whatever levels of wages are paid. Many single women support their natal families.

Women workers are the first to be affected by increasing mechanization and automation in all sectors of production. In general, the concentration of women is usually at the low-skilled, lower level of employment. As modern capital intensive technology is introduced, either new technology renders human hands redundant or because of the skills involved, women are replaced by men. Since women lack access to training, the chance of their being employed to work on sophisticated machinery are bleak. In the past, rationalization policies have cost women their jobs in the textile, coal and jute industries, among others. In today's world of sophisticated industries, women find jobs only in packing, labeling and other low-skilled, and low-paid jobs.

Another aspect to be noted is that liberalization has also intensified stratification among women workers themselves. While at one end of the spectrum are some very visible women, earning high wages in executive positions or in jobs in the beauty and glamorous sectors or in high-tech offices, at the other are the growing numbers of increasingly underpaid, over-worked, poor women who lack any job security or legal protection.

Overall, the implications of the structural adjustment programmes have been typically negative, in terms of reduced real incomes and standard of living for most women, along with a greater burden of unpaid work. A growing proportion of women is, therefore, living in poverty; by cutting into the existing public provision of 'safety nets', SAPs, *inter alia,* readily exasperate the poverty syndrome, especially among the women.

Credit for self-employment, designed to benefit the poorest of the poor, often does not reach the intended beneficiaries, through conventional channels such as commercial banks, farmers' banks or rural cooperative credit societies. For poor women, gender and poverty interact to make these structures virtually inaccessible.

Most organizations develop centralized bureaucracies and are too inflexible to care for the needs and priorities of the poor women. On their part, commercial banks and financial institutions prefer to concentrate on large loans because of economies in transaction costs. Also, in the absence of collateral securities, the poor are not perceived to be creditworthy.

Those working at the level of a factor, agency or institution do not always get covered by the benefits of various labour laws because of the limit of employment fixed by various statutes. The unscrupulous employers would keep the employment marginally below the prescribed limit in order to dodge implementation of the law. As a result, these workers do not get any benefit of provident fund, gratuity, ESI, leave facility, limitation of hours of work, and retirement benefits. They are deprived of even retrenchment compensation since under the prevailing labour market conditions, they can be thrown out of job at any moment at the sweet will of the employer. In the case of all those units which could be termed as formal and are covered under factory act and various other acts, the laws are violated by the employers, denying all benefits that should routinely accrue to workers.

An overwhelming majority of workers are engaged in the informal sector; this is all the more true of women workers. This workforce is organized at a very low level. The other area of the unorganized labour force is in the small scale formal sector, where all the laws are flouted and employment of migrant, contract and casual labour is a common feature. The unionization in this sector is also very low as there is strong resistance from the employers who simply throw workers out of job if efforts are made to organize unions at the factory unit/agency level. The third area where the workforce is organized, yet again at an extremely low level, is home-based work; it is a growing sector where 90 per cent of the workforce is women and exploitation is intense. The entire infrastructure costs, such as electricity, work site, sometimes even part of the raw materials, are provided by the workers. Often, the whole family, including children, is involved in the work for long hours but the payment received for their combined effort is a mere pittance. No labour legislation applies to this sector; so, there is no provision for minimum wages, no fixed hours of work, and no provision for leave, rest, social security coverage, and so on.

The degree of statistical accuracy and precision, that operates in the organized sector, has been absent in the informal sector; consequently, an adequate and reliable data base is still a distant dream. The number is over-whelming, range and complexity of problems are very large which largely remain un-attended to. For improving data base, the unorganized labour should be categorized broadly in terms of occupation, nature of employment, specially distress categories and in terms of service categories.

Another serious problem which goes against the interest of labour force in the unorganized sector is that this sector suffers from cycles of seasonal unemployment, the usual absence of employer-employee relationship, scattered work in different habitations, and so on. The fact that most of the workers in the urban informal sector are indebted at the time of migrating from rural areas, land them up in bondage which is the worst form of denial of human freedom and life of dignity. A large part of this sector continues with primitive production technologies and feudal production relations that do not permit or encourage the workers to imbibe and assimilate higher technologies and better production relations. Being illiterate and ignorant of their new environment, as also being deeply entrenched in myths and superstitions, the workers in this sector have less exposure to the goings on in the outside world and so there is poor absorption of new ideas.

3. Minimum Wages

After a prolonged battle and outcry by the trade unions, the Minimum Wages Act was promulgated in 1948, expressly to protect and safe guard the interests of workers in the unorganized and sweated sectors. It was said that the minimum wage is subsistence/ living wage below which no employer can go, since it is not related to the industry's capacity to pay; in fact, the capacity is presumed to be inherent. In a special leave petition No. 15680 of 1990, the Supreme Court of India had ruled that an industry which cannot assure payment of minimum wages has no right to exist.

Contrary to what the Supreme Court of India ruled, many sectors are not yet covered by the Act itself, the minimum wages announced for the scheduled employment are not paid, the wages fixed several years ago have not been reviewed or revised even within the existing statutory period of five years. Moreover, in the absence of specific norms for fixation of minimum wages under the Act, the wages fixed by the statutory wage fixation machinery are extremely low and, more distressingly, are not revised periodically.

The ILO Convention concerning fixation of National Minimum Wage has not yet been ratified by Government of India, with the result that the employers are still free to pay extremely low rate of wages to these employees. The failure of the government to fix a national minimum wage to workers not covered by schedule of employment is primarily responsible for their present plight.

The emergence of contract labour system provides a fertile ground for continuation of the unjust working conditions for the unorganized workers. Despite passing of the Contract Labour (Regulation and Abolition) Act, these workers failed to get any material protection; ironically, even in permanent and perennial jobs, the system continues to operate non-challantly.

In the wake of liberalization, certain new market forces have been unleashed in the name of linking the national economy with the global economy; this is furthering the process of contractualisation and casualisation of the workforce. The guiding spirit of the law is to employ workers on a regular basis in jobs which are regular and perennial and to employ workers on contract/casual basis where the nature of employment is casual, sporadic or intermittent. Unluckily, the grass-roots experience shows that regular jobs are being off-loaded increasingly in favour of contract and casual workers. These workers being unskilled/semi-skilled, illiterate and ignorant become easily vulnerable to the manipulative and fraudulent practices adopted by contractors and sub-contractors.

The unorganised sector is thus allowed to expand rapidly even within the organised sector of the Indian economy, mainly with the purpose of exploiting the unorganised workers as a source of cheap labour. When the jobs are prohibited for contract labour, the workers working on them are thrown out of jobs and outsiders are recruited for the job; in plain terms, the provision of exemption of undertaking from the provision of the Act is largely misused.

4. Migrant Workers

The participation of migrant workers in the urban informal sector is very substantial and the trend does not show any arrest to this phenomenon.

Migration of human beings in pursuit of better employment, better wages and better quality of life is a welcome phenomenon as there is apparently nothing wrong in migration per se; it is a well accepted social and economic phenomenon. However, migration leading to exploitation and culminating in human misery and deprivation of the irreducible barest minimum to which every worker as a human being is entitled to, definitely needs to be looked at with a critical eye. The exploitative mechanisms of unscrupulous employers/contractors need to be checked in order to save the workers from indignity, injustice and inhuman behaviour.

The plight of women and young girls who migrate is extremely tragic. The fate of women and children accompanying migrant workers is deplorable. In the absence of any worthwhile accommodation, they have to put up in make-shift structures. Men, women and children living in such accommodation can be termed as animals living in hovels. No safe drinking water is available; sanitation facilities are totally absent, leading to their falling victim to water born diseases, on the one hand, and rise in vulnerability of women in all spheres, on the other hand.

Distress and subsistence-induced migration, which is usually the case with migrant workers engaged in the informal sector, puts them at the mercy of principal employer. The contractors/subcontractors, as also their middlemen, make them vulnerable to exploitation, especially when no organizational support is around to protect their interests. The migrant workers contribute into the economic prosperity of the state to which they migrate but the recipient states have generally been insensitive to their problems. There is a common feature that many cases of injuries caused due to accidents, sometimes even resulting in death or disablement, are not reported and workmen's compensation in case of those accidents is not deposited and paid. In the case of the inte-rstate migrant workmen and their family members, it is extremely difficult to deal with the problems they face because of distance from their origin and place of work, unfamiliarity with local language, customs, geography, topography, land above, local court procedures. In the absence of their unionization, the protection of their rights and safeguarding of their interests become very difficult. Their children are deprived of access to educational opportunities on account of absence of educational infrastructure, and language problems and, in many cases, local schools not accepting them. Driven by acute poverty, and the critical need to add to the meager earning of the household, the parents often subject their children to work, much against their wish.

In spite of the initiative taken and effort made by different national and international agencies, including the ILO, the working conditions in the new export promotion zones in seafood processing, hosiery and other sectors has not brought better life for the workers, a majority of them being migrant workers, with a sizeable presence of young females among them. Different studies have revealed and. Guided by our regular contact with those women, we can state, with first hand information, that this work force is denied free-movement, minimum wages, social security benefits, and so on. And, there is no dearth of independent studies to corroborate our understanding. The work environment in many of these units does not at all meet occupational safety and health requirements. The case of physical and mental harassment of women are common. One should rather say that they are living under conditions of bonded labour. The work conditions creates several gynecological problems including impotency.

5. Child Labour

It is to be noted that the child labour is also a common phenomenon of the informal sector. For keeping the cost of production at low levels, contract/casual or child labour, is the best choice of the employers; child labour is not only cheap but is highly malleable and docile also. We are in unison with all sections of our society, including the government and non-government agencies, that oppose any linkages between trade and labour standards. We strongly feel that the issue of labour standards lies in the purview of ILO and not with trade norms. Nevertheless, we would like to assert in our own right that exploitation of children and adult labour force, especially the women, must stop. Various labour laws, rules, and regulations have to be faithfully implemented and the onus for this should lie with the employers and the administration.

6. Living Conditions

Under the new economic dispensations, unleashed by the liberalizing and free trade policies, the tiny and small scale industry may gradually be denied the kind of assistance and support that it used to get from government and financial institutions. Competition from the big industry at home, and Multinational Corporations from outside, is making the going more and more difficult for such enterprises. 'Lack of security for survival', as a threat to small scale industry and no automatic guarantee of outlet and markets, would have serious consequences for the owners of such tiny and small enterprises, but many times more, for the workforce that may reach starvation stage with no work and no earning. This truth is being witnessed with every day reports of the starvation deaths and of suicides of workers who lost their jobs due to closures and no work. When we argue for the workforce, let us be understood in proper light that we look at the health and security of work force in consonance with a desire for the better health and security of the industry they are engaged in; the workers earn their bread while producing wealth for the nation. They are justified in asking for their share in decent human existence.

The living conditions, the transportation, and basic civic amenities are another area where the informal sector work force is discriminated against. The pressure on sèrvice sector and resources in the urban areas is ever on a rise, due to the continuous inflow of labour-force migration, with no matching efforts by the administration. This is a very vital sector to be kept in mind when we talk of creation of job opportunities in the urban informal sector.

Those works which were shifted to homes more for consideration of keeping cost of production low, due to piece-rate nature of work, without having any obligation under various statutes, need to be looked at closely. The fast changing economic activities are resulting in a pronounced shift towards home-based sector. We are all aware of the unwholesome working conditions and deplorably low levels of earnings of these workers, a vast majority of whom are women. It is these very reasons that push their children too into work. Living in small houses hardly sufficient to accommodate the whole family and then to convert the same into a living-cum-working place has its own implications which, in many situations, could be extremely dangerous for children. There are practically no laws to protect this sector. Happily, therefore, the ILO convention on home-based work has come at a right time; perhaps, it gets some relief to the home-based workforce.

7. Setting an Agenda for Action

Having stated all this, we need to enter into serious deliberations with a realistic and holistic approach towards creation of job opportunities in the urban informal sector. So, it is necessary that all partners take a sober view of the whole situation and address the issue squarely.

- The rapid growth in productivity helps in the quality of employment, but it is not enough to create the right kind of employment opportunities only. What is more important is to provide the people with human capital by which they can take advantage of these opportunities. It is necessary to provide opportunities and access for education and skill development. Here lies the first and foremost requirement of free and compulsory elementary education, supported by mid-day meal programmes in the school. Special efforts for developing skills and technological levels that can open up new channels for people engaged in traditional occupations, are therefore, the high priority areas of public policy.
- As regards the migrant labour, apart from effecting the needed amendments in the Regulation of Employment Conditions of Service Act 1979, the issue needs to be addressed in two other ways. The government of the originating state should create and intensify avenues of public works so that the migrant population could get assured employment for more days in the home state itself. At the point of destination, the migrant worker could be protected by provisions of journey allowance, dislocation allowance, protective clothing during winters, housing accommodation, payment of minimum wages in time, no deduction by way of commission to the middlemen and safe repatriation to the state of origin.
- Let us recognize that organization of workers is a very important aspect to ensure amendments and implementation of the existing laws. It is important to enumerate the groups of the unorganized workers in different avocations, to organize women work-force, especially to ensure their enhanced participation in general organizations of workers, to identify the constraints of forming organizations in such groups and to attempt to remove the same, to create awareness among the mass of workers, to identify basic needs of the group under consideration at a time for suitable activities, to have legal centres to aid, protect and safeguard the rights of the worker, and so on.
- Technology is another important area that needs to be addressed. There should be clear-cut government support for skill training in the context of shift of activities from organized manufacturing to small scale service sector. Technology must be appropriate, relevant, affordable and easily adaptable as well as easily replicable. The training must be designed, keeping in view that there is low-levels of literacy and awareness among these workers who are at the lowest rung of the ladder of development. The training need be conducted in non-conventional and unorthodox manner with a lot of in-built flexibility so that it is at once acceptable to the intended beneficiaries.

- There is a need of national minimum wage fixation criteria along with a sector-wise regional wage parity. In other words, departing from the present practice, we must work for the linkage of the minimum wage with price index.
- Amendment to the Minimum Wages Act providing norms for fixation of wages, obligatory payment of dearness allowance, deletion of powers of the government to exempt units from the purview of the Act, periodic revision of wages and compulsory punishment of imprisonment to employers for violating the Act.
- Provision of eight hours of work a day, weekly off and holidays with wages for all the unorganised workers and payment of double over-time for extra work.
- Legal provision against arbitrary dismissal and termination of services of the unorganized workers, ensuring a minimum degree of job security for them.
- Government sponsored housing schemes for all the unorganized workers.
- Abolition of contract labour system and regularization of all the contract labour in a time bound programme without reference through employment exchange, pending which, payment of wages to contract workers at par with regular workers. Courts should be given judicial powers to decide wages for similar nature of job.
- All casual, NMR, daily rated, work charged and temporary workers to be made permanent after 150 days of work, including breaks imposed by employers in permanent and perennial jobs.
- There is a need to expand concepts of social security and to create new structures, flexible approaches, with universal characteristics, in defining and implementing all provisions, to cover all types of workers (local or migrant, regular, contract/casual or home-based) ostensibly because each category is working and producing wealth for the nation.
- The wages so fixed and social security so finalized should be properly implemented so as to reach those for whom it is meant.
- That the economic commuting between home and workplace with availability of cheap transportation be ensured.
- That the ILO convention on home-based work be ratified and the relevant law be enacted to cover the problems of the home-based workforce.
- That the minimum basic civic amenities are assured for proper living. Access to safe drinking water, sanitation, schools for children for health care etc. is a must.

- No excuse whatsoever to employ child labour, directly or indirectly, in home- based activities and outside, be entertained.
- That there be a national scheme to cover all women in the maternity benefit.
- That provision of universal child care services be the national agenda and the prime responsibility for providing these facilities to all working women should lie with the centre and state governments.
- That free and compulsory elementary education for all children be made a legal obligation of the governments.
- That the right to unionisation and free-movement is to be respected as a fundamental right of workers.
- That those in the home-based sector and very small level co-operative activities be given protection and market mechanism for their survival, sustenance and growth.
- Financial help to various enterprises/institutions/individuals for development of urban informal sector has to be combined with honest commitment for implementation of the minimum basic conditions in favour of work force.
- That women entrepreneurs get sufficient attention for their initiatives through an adequate flow of micro-credit and other facilities.
- Flexibility in approach is the need of the time; rigid baskets, especially at the implementation stage, usually defeat the very purpose for which schemes are floated. This caution is very much in order because such has been the experience of people for whom the schemes are prepared and put into operation.

Job Creation in the Urban Informal Sector: Agenda for Action by the Employers

C.P. Thakur

1. Introduction

The world of work has become extremely complex all over. There is a considerable turbulence in labour markets and more so in labour surplus economies like India. Awareness as well as concern in this regard are growing. For the ILO, concern for all workers, employed and unemployed, is quite high on their agenda. The recent document on decent work recognizes the significance of improving the situation of human beings in the world of work. The manifest need for finding sustainable opportunities for decent work has been emphasized. This is the "converging focus" of its four strategic objectives: (a) employment, (b) promotion of rights at work, (c) social protection, and (d) social dialogue. There is a growing realization of the need to integrate human rights with sustainable human development. Issues relating to (a) human rights, (b) human development, (c) right to life and (d) right to livelihood occupy centre stage in the objectives and agenda for development. But then, the massive 'failure of implementation' of these objectives is highly embarrassing. This is particularly true on the employment front.

1.1 Indian Perspective on Employment

Employment is central to decent human existence. It inextricably blends economic as well as non-economic dimensions of human life. It is also the most-potent source of one's happiness. It brings disposable income, and in the process, a welcome state of economic security.

Constitutional directives, judicial pronouncement and development strategy in India have all emphasized the value of and the need for maximizing the productive use of economically active work force. The Directive Principles of the State Policy require the state to direct its policy towards securing the right to an adequate means of livelihood, equally for men and women. Within the limits of its economic capacity, Article 41 of the Constitution requires the state 'to make effective provision for securing the right to work, to education, and to public assistance in case of unemployment.' The highest echelon of India's judiciary too has expressed its position firmly. In its view, the right to life includes the right to livelihood. It observed that any person deprived of his right to livelihood, except according to just and fair procedure established by law, can challenge the deprivation as offending the right to life conferred by Article 21 of the Constitution.

Nevertheless, the right to life and the right to livelihood cannot be defended without earnest efforts toward promotion of opportunities for work itself. This, in turn, is dependent on the pace and pattern of development. Despite efforts over the last several decades, the pace of development has not been fast enough to eliminate unemployment. Whatever development that has occurred is not evenly distributed across regions, sectors and work organizations. Indian development planning has all along emphasized the crucial significance of a balanced regional development. Yet, glaring inter-regional inequalities are an unpleasant reality of today, perhaps no less than what they were many decades back. Labour surplus regions have markedly lagged behind in development. This has further exasperated the unemployment situation, and consequently, social restiveness is throwing discomforting symptoms all over the country. Professional opinion on indicators of development is converging on the fact that priority to employment over and above GNP and per capita income growth must guide our national strategy in the times ahead.

The outgoing century has witnessed phases of contrasting trends such as (a) employment friendly, (b) employment neutral, and (c) employment unfriendly development. Development debate has, therefore, acquired divisiveness. Uneasy questions are being raised : (a) is growth eliminating more jobs than the work opportunities that it is adding?; (b) is technology, a powerful tool in development process, now inadvertently turning out to be an agent of human suffering, as it were?; and (c) whether there is a quest for decent work, on the one hand, and new jobs are turning inferior in terms of security and rewards, on the other? There are no settled answers to these questions; surely, they vary from region to region inside a developing economy, just as they vary from country to country. Happily, at the global level, the end of work scenario seems unfounded; we have had fairly respectable rates of net additions to jobs despite massive technological transformation and spread. And proportionately, more jobs have been better in quality, too. Unluckily, the Indian reality has been far different in this regard.

The present paper focuses on the urban informal sector in India with particular reference to its current state and the scope for its future contribution to job creation. It first takes stock of the Indian labour situation on supply as well as demand sides. This is followed by an overview of the current picture of India's urban informal sector and its characteristics. A discussion on the strategy and agenda for future job creation and the scope for its healthy contribution to the Indian economy as a whole, comes at the end.

2. Labour Absorption in the Economy

For labour absorption in the Indian economy, its basic factor endowment emerges as the primary reference point. The massive population base, its age structure, and particularly the rate of growth of labour force together bring immense pressure on the supply side of the labour market. A billion plus population is now expected to register deceleration in its growth. But the total workforce in the economy grew from 227 million in 1971 to 268 million in 1978 and further to 360 million at the dawn of the new millennium. It is projected to grow to about to 643 million in 2021.

Nearly 50 per cent of the population in 1997 was in the economically active age group of 15-59 years. It is projected to move up to 60 per cent in 2000. The urban labour force is projected to increase from 70 million in 1991 to 191 million in 2021. The annual increment in urban labour force during 1991-2001 is projected at 3.5 million while during 2011-21, it would grow at the rate of 4.2 million. During the Ninth Five Year Plan, with a projected 6.2 per cent growth of GDP, nearly 47 million jobs are likely to be created. It is indeed far short of the corresponding 53 million net addition to the labour force during the same period (Govt. of India, 1999).

The incidence of open unemployment would touch 6 million. If the projected rate of growth turns out to be slower, the picture on unemployment would become gloomier. There are positive symptoms of recovery in the economy but they are not strong enough. Post 2001-2002 budget developments, after the initial optimism, have set in an air of depression. Imponderables on the political scene, and the stock market imbalance, are unlikely to encourage investors, whether domestic or foreign. There is no guaranty, therefore, that in the absence of vigorous efforts to eliminate numerous bottlenecks on the one hand and to accelerate investment on the other, the increase in unemployment would at all be arrested. And, in addition to open unemployment, a high level of underemployment would also be there, as usual.

Certain distinct features of the employment scene need to be noted. First, there is a persisting imbalance in the supply of and demand for labour. Second, the rate of growth of labour force in the near future is projected to be higher than the likely net additions to jobs. Third, there are growing backlogs of the unemployed over five year plan periods. Fourth, the recent shift in development strategy, comprising liberalisation, privatisation and globalisation is creating the new phenomenon of surplus labour and the need for downsizing. The labour market is characterised by voluntary retirement schemes, retrenchments, substitution of capital for labour both in (a) new investment projects as well as in (b) restructuring industries and enterprises. Fifth, a growing incidence of sickness and closure is further adding to the problem of unemployment. Together, these features are creating a discouraging outlook on the labour absorptive capability, particularly that of the organised manufacturing sector.

Agriculture (and its associated activities) still provides substantial job opportunities. In absolute terms, it would continue to be a dominant source of employment. Despite several decades of development, the expected transfer of labour force from agriculture to non-agricultural sector has not been strong enough; in fact, there is some evidence of a reversal of the trend during the nineties. The surplus and retrenched workers from the organized sector are relocating themselves in other sectors and activities. Within agriculture too, even with the projected (*albeit* highly ambitious, and probably non-achievable) growth rate of 4.5 per cent, not more than a million jobs would be created. In total terms, therefore, the main brunt of absorbing the expanding army of job seekers is naturally to be borne by the informal sector. In the urban economy, there is hardly any choice.

Nonetheless, even within the precincts of the stipulated growth strategy, if there were (a) increase in the weightage to tradable component of products, and (b) greater success in export penetration, the suspected deterioration on the employment front can be arrested, to some extent.

3. Sectoral Employment Elasticity

Thanks to the differences in the nature and composition of production, significant differences in employment elasticity always exist across different sectors of the economy. The familiar dualism of the organized and the unorganized sectors has to be noted in particular. Table 1 gives the profile of employment elasticities in the organized and the unorganized sectors, and Table 2 gives the same for different segments of the unorganized sector alone, for the period 1980-81/1993-94.

TABLE 1 : **Employment Elasticity in the Organized/Unorganised Sectors**[1]

Time Period	Organised	Unorganised
1980-81 to 1984-85	0.22	0.31
1985-86 to 1990-91	0.18	1.34
1991-92 to 1993-94	0.08	0.47

TABLE 2 : **Employment Elasticity in Unorganised Sector - Industrywise**[2]

	Agr.	Mfg.	Constn.	Trade	Transport	Services
80-81/84-85	0.08	0.46	-ve	0.60	2.23	0.44
85-86/90-91	-ve	0.92	3.48	1.25	0.59	2.03
91-92/93-94	0.48	0.23	0.06	0.51	0.50	1.05

From the above tables, it is evident that with some variation, the employment elasticity in the unorganized sector has been higher. The labour absorptive capacity of the organized sector is far less than unity. Its share is employment in 1987-88 was only 8 per cent, and it fell to around 7 per cent in the 1993-94. The rate of growth of

[1] Govt. of India, 1999; RBI, 2000; Bhalla, 1994; Mishra, R.K. et al., 1993.

[2] Mishra, *ibid,* 1993.

output in the organized sector has been greater than the rate of growth in employment. The possibility of net addition to employment in this sector is rather dim, therefore.

Public enterprises and public services account for a dominant share of employment in the organized sector. Both of these are undergoing massive transformation. Pressure of acquiring competitive edge in a liberalizing economy is forcing public enterprises to switch over to superior technology and other cost cutting and productivity promoting measures. Further, the missing budgetary support for investment as well as growing exposure to capital market, through debt or equity manipulation, bring their own pressure on retention of employment in some sectors and its expansion in others. Resource crunch and growing demand of higher levels of wage, salaries and benefits are forcing shrinkage in public services jobs too. Vacancies are not being filled, and the existing jobs are planned to be reduced by sizeable margins in central government. This is bound to have cascading effects on the state and the local government too. There may be resistance as well as delay, but the trend seems irreversible. Pressure to reduce the cost of public services, to bring greater efficiency and quicker results would require adoption of modern technology as well as major reforms in delivery systems and procedures. The net impact on employment in public services is likely to be negative in the intermediate perspective.

TABLE 3 : **Employment in the Informal Sector**[3]

1.	Total	364 Million
2.	Non - Agriculture	107 Million
3.	Manufacturing	38 Million
4.	Trade	26 Million
5.	Commercial Service	14 Million
6.	Construction	11 Million
7.	Transport	7 Million

The policy makers are accordingly reconciled to the fact that much of current and future employment has to be in the unorganized sector. Its recent picture is set out in Table 3.

Variation in employment elasticity was evident earlier from Tables 1 and 2. A further disaggregated picture has been presented in a recent study (Kulshrestha and Singh, 1999) Within the unorganized sector, agriculture holds a highly dominating position. On the other hand, within the non-agricultural sector, the share varies significantly across sub-sectors of the economy. Nonetheless, manufacturing dominates among them, followed by trade, commercial services, construction and transport, in that order.

[3] Kulshresta and Singh, 1999.

TABLE 4 : **Per Worker Productivity in the Urban Unorganized Manufacturing : 1994-95[4] (Value in Rs.)**

NIC 1987	Group	OAME	NDME	DME	Unregistered SSI
20-21	Food Products	12425	18754	23595	38982
22	Beverages, tobacco, etc.	6152	18069	11071	38062
23	Cotton	5007	15957	18564	28612
24	Silk, Wool	6735	16960	18139	119774
25	Jute	3858	15980	6162	57437
26	Cotton Cloth	6410	13903	20303	35945
27	Wood, Furniture etc.	8380	23782	24520	61875
28	Paper printing etc.	9464	18492	23130	48523
29	Leather and fur products	12692	13388	18346	65234
30	Basic chemicals, etc.	4705	15168	24904	73885
31	Rubber, Plastic, etc.	11475	23546	25717	44507
32	Non-metallic products	6240	11851	11986	20001
33	Basic metals and alloys	17215	19381	33181	67497
34	Metal products	12056	18660	23369	56692
35	Machinery (non-elec.)	15925	22123	30669	40673
36	Electrical Machinery	10132	20822	43617	70505
37	Transport equipment	10877	29239	26621	40740
38	Other manufacturing	14108	16240	25336	57736
39	Repair of capital goods	14144	14277	43961	8514

Source: Govt. of India, Unorganized Manufacturing Sector in India : Its Size, Employment and Some Key Estimates, Report No. 433, NSSO, 8/1998.

3.1 Labour Productivity in the Unorganized Sector

Apart from employment, it is essential to present the estimates of value added per worker in the unorganized sector. Table 4 gives the 1994-95 picture on per worker productivity, for each of the three segments of the urban unorganized manufacturing.

Table 4 boldly indicates the low rates of value addition for several groups. This calls for adopting productivity improvement and cost cutting measures in many branches of the urban unorganized manufacturing sector. The picture with regard to value addition per worker in the rural segment of the unorganized manufacturing is much less satisfactory (Chadha, 1999). The mismatch between a high rate of labour absorption and the low levels of value addition per worker requires policy and managerial correctives.

[4] Kulshreshta, *ibid,* 1999.

4. Urban Sector Employment

Although India is predominantly a rural economy, yet urban India has a significant presence. During the decade of independence urbanisation trend increased moving from 17 per cent to 25.7 per cent in 1991. The projected urban population is Likely to be 31.0 per cent in 1996-97 and 38.0 per cent in 2006-07. Roughly 5-6 million of rural people move to urban India every year. With one of the largest urban sector, India would have 40 metro cities in 2001, compared to 23 in 1991 with a population of 269 million and 2176 million respectively. Within the overall decline in the rate of urbanization in recent years, there is a growing concentration of urban population in larger towns. Apart from pressure on basic infrastructure, employment issue in urban economy acquires urgency.

There is variation in the incidence of urbanisation across States; so is the case with regard to employment in the urban informal sector. Data collected from economic census 1990 and population census 1991 present some interesting picture on informal sector employment in relation to urbanization (Table 5). States with

TABLE 5 : **Urbanisation and Informal Sector Employment**[5]

Proportion of Workers Engaged in Informal Sector (1990)					
Level of Urbanization in 1991	Less than 50	50-54-59	55-59-99	60-64-99	65 and above
10.00-14.9		Assam		Bihar	Orissa
15.00-19.99					U.P.
20.00-24.99			Haryana		Madhya Pradesh, Rajasthan
25.00-29.99			Punjab	Andhra, Kerala, W.B., Karnataka	
30.00-34.99	Gujarat			Tamil Nadu	
Above 35.00	Maharashtra				

levels of urbanization lower than the national average have higher levels of informal sector employment. On the other hand, informal sector employment has higher incidence in states with lower level of urbanization. It appears, there is an inverse relationship between urbanization and informal sector employment, as it were.

As Table 6 shows, the distribution of main workers, engaged in different sectors of India's urban economy, has also tended to change sizeably between 1980 and 1990.

---

[5] Mitra, 1998.

TABLE 6 : **Percentage Distribution of Main Workers in Urban India**[6]

Sector	Male		Female	
	1981	1991	1981	1991
Cultivators	5.2	4.9	4.6	5.1
Agril. Labourers	4.7	5.4	16.7	15.6
Forestry, Fishing etc.	1.8	1.7	1.8	1.5
Mining & Quarrying	1.1	1.2	0.7	0.7
Hh Manufacturing	4.2	2.5	10.4	7.5
Nh Manufacturing	26.0	23.2	14.6	14.1
Construction	4.3	5.3	3.1	3.3
Trade & Commerce	21.3	23.7	8.9	10.3
Transport	10.0	9.2	2.2	1.9
Other Services	21.4	22.8	37.0	40.1

TABLE 7 : **Units and Workers in Manufacturing and Repair Activities in the Unorganised Sector**[7]

(Persons in Million)

Source of Data		Units		Workers	
A. Population Census 1981		Urban	Total	Urban	Total
Primary Census Abstract				2.40	7.9
Economic Census 1980	(1)	1.36	4.65	2.40	8.11
	(2)	1.91	5.58	3.97	10.57
	(3)	2.14	5.97	10.23	20.10
B. Population Census 1991					
Primary Census Abstract				2.00	6.08
Econmic Census 1990	(1)	1.02	3.80	1.93	7.01
	(2)	1.91	5.35	10.81	21.82
C. NSS 45th round 1989-90	(1)	2.82	13.10	4.98	24.51
	(2)	3.71	15.79	7.91	29.61

Manufacturing base of urban India has weakened during the seventies and eighties. The share of the non-household sector has fallen from 26.0 per cent in 1981 to 23.2 per cent in 1991 for males; for female workers, there was hardly any change. NSS data, gathered over different rounds, also confirm this trend.

The situation with regard to the unorganised urban sector is not different either. During the eighties, both the numbers of units as well as the number of workers in the urban unorganised manufacturing have registered a declining trend (Table 7).

[6] Kundu and Lalitha, 1998.

[7] Kundu, *ibid,* 1998.

The number of workers as well as units in the unorganised manufacturing has declined during the decade 1981-91. The Primary Census data indicate a decline of workers from 2.4 million 1981 to 2 million in 1991. Even the Economic Census data suggest a similar trend with regard to the number of manufacturing units.

There is variation over time in the increase or decrease of the number of units and the workers employed in the unorganised sector. Between 1978-79 and 1984-85, the number of units (OAME) more than doubled, but during 1984-85 and 1989-90, it decreased by 23 per cent. As a result, the corresponding employment figures indicate an increase by 122 per cent, and a fall by 6.2 per cent, during the two sub-periods, respectively. This trend is supported by other data sources as well. This had its effect on the number of workers per enterprise as well. which decreased from 1.65 to 1.46, between 1978-79 to 1984-85, and later moved up to 1.77 between 1984-85 to 1989-90.

In overall terms, the share of manufacturing in the urban unorganised sector has witnessed a declining trend. This is, *inter alia,* a result of the falling share of total manufacturing employment itself in the urban economy.

5. Employment in Services

As the economy moves up on the growth path, there is a secular trend towards increase in the share of services in employment and GDP. The tertiary sector's contribution to the GDP has been much faster. In fact, it has been more than twice compared to the primary sector and at par with the secondary sector. Nonetheless, the overall sectoral distribution of workforce has remained practically unchanged.

TABLE 8 : **Sectoral Distribution of Employment in Own Account Enterprises :1990**[8]

Sector	Employment
Mining	0.26
Manufacturing	31.27
Electricity	0.04
Construction	0.96
Wholesale Trade	1.94
Retail Trade	38.35
Hotels-Restaurants	4.83
Transport	1.95
Storage	0.50
Communication	0.02
Financial Services	1.26
Community Service	18.59

[8] Mitra, *op.cit,* 1998.

Because of these inter-sectoral variations, value addition per worker in the tertiary sector has been moving up. We cannot, however, ignore the fact that the shift of workforce from the primary to the secondary and tertiary sectors has been rather inadequate. Structural imbalance in workforce deployment is evident, therefore.

Table 8 indicates the dominance of services in the share of employment. With 38.35 per cent share, retail trade has a higher share than that of manufacturing at 31.27 per cent. Community services with a share of 18.59 per cent is the third largest employer, followed by hotels-restaurants at 4.83 per cent. The rest of the sectors account for only a marginal share each. However, it is likely that with the growing pace of urbanization, the demand for services of (a) old, (b) new, and (c) complementary kinds would influence its share in employment. With higher growth in per capita income, employment in 'new' forms of services would grow. It is expected that employment in the 'complementary' category of services would register impressive growth as the economy gets further industrialized and further urbanized. New category of services comprising administrative matters, transport, communications, entertainments and recreations, professional services including banking and insurance, hold a substantial promise of expansion. Non-farm activities in rural economy too have a major role as modernization of the economy gathers momentum; by implication, some of the urban-ward exodus may get halted.

6. Government Schemes for Employment Promotion

Several government programmes for employment promotion directed towards self-employment as well as wage-employment have been launched from time to time. On balance, there is a greater weightage to self-employment than wage-employment. In concrete terms, success in term of promoting sustainable employment has not been outstanding. Some jobs are continuing, but are low paying and less productive. Usually, the rewards that such jobs carry are lower; they are not welcome to job seekers. Casualisation of workers has also been increasing. A fairly large number of jobs are in the nature of relief operation, particularly in rural areas. They may be providing income but are neither sustainable nor productive.

Resource inadequacy, irrational uniformity for administrative convenience and complex rules and procedures have not facilitated their effective implementation. Occasional reviews and evaluations have led to revisions, modifications and, in some cases, restructuring of the schemes. Currently, the major employment promotion programmes for the urban areas include *Prime Minister Rojgar Yojna, Nehru Rojgar Yojna* for micro enterprises, *Prime Minister Integrated Urban Poverty Eradication Programme,* and *Swarn Jayanti Shahri Rojgar Yojna.* For greater success, they need (a) differentiation rather than uniformity, (b) more integrated package for promotion, (c) administrative/managerial innovations, and (d) commitment for good results.

Bureaucratic indifference, unfavorable attitude of financial institutions, poor planning in developing viable projects, inadequate entrepreneurial capability and missing complementary skills are the sources of inadequate or poor results. However, this need not encourage pessimism on the role of the urban informal sector in promoting employment and income opportunity. The revised and modified versions of the schemes indicate awareness of these gaps, and the schemes should, therefore, hold better promise in term of results. But then, it is for sure that additional efforts are required at a massive scale.

Earlier neglect of and ambivalence with regard to the informal sector have adversely affected the clarity on its characteristics. Attempts to define and caricaturize the sector by several scholars over the years have helped in bringing some clarity[9]. Even the data base on its size, the number of units, the number of employees and its contribution to GDP, has much to be desired. Nonetheless, the researchers have marshalled information from several available sources to bring some 'neatness' in our understanding of the sector. The Population Census, Economic Census and NSS data, etc. have been a great help. Yet, more updatedness in data availability and more neatness in analysis are of extreme value.

Notwithstanding the 'definitional quicksand', three broad categories have been identified within the informal sector: (1) establishment based; (2) foot-loose; and (3) home-based outfits. The first category includes manufacturing, repair shops, wholesale and retail trade, personal services and other non-manufacturing services. Activities under the second category activities are not so easy to identify, largely because they are non-establishment based. They fall in the own account unit group, and most of them pay some kind of tax to local authorities. Their employees are largely transient in nature, and are not easily traceable. The last category, home-based informal activities, is expanding. With employment and family work combined, usually within the household premises, its visibility is indeed not so evident. An important feature of this component is that it is dominated by female family members. Their operation is pretty loose, their income meagre and they are totally dependent on fluctuating work order, from one or several sources. Nature of work order for product and services could vary with variation in market demand from the side of end-users. This adds enormously to uncertainty and insecurity of employment and earnings.

7. Some Dilemmas

Employment promotion is a priority-issue. How to deal with it is always a challenge. Although there is a rising trend in the growth of informal sector no doubt, yet the quality of jobs in it has been declining. Moreover, in terms of the variety of jobs, the sector is as much variegated as one can imagine. Casualisation, contractualisation and non-continuity of jobs, inter alia, are the features that throw

[9] Papola 1980; Kundu, *op.cit.,* 1998, Mitra, *op.cit.,* 1998.

up the possibility of high degree of exploitation of workers, including, in some cases, the self-exploitation of the entrepreneurs themselves. Most notably, the informal sector employment is dominated by women. As a matter of fact, the paid women are increasingly taking over jobs from child labour, at any rate, in the urban sector.

These elements plainly point towards the vulnerable status of a big majority of our working population who are poor in spite of being employed. Their number is declining yet they are 3.5 times the number of those who are un- and under-employed. About 50 per cent of the casual workers fall below the poverty line, with 57 per cent of them being located in urban segment of the informal sector. It is thus natural that the problem of the urban informal sector has attracted several schemes for promoting wage- as well as self-employment.

The challenges of (a) increasing job opportunity, (b) improving the quality of jobs in terms of wages and security/continuity of job, (c) promoting productivity, (d) reducing the possible exploitation of weaker sections like women, children, unskilled workers, and (e) retaining relative cost advantage, are indeed complex with no easy choices. Decisions and actions, on a balanced consideration of advantages and implications, are needed to be put through.

Within the informal sector, there are broadly two categories (a) modern and (b) traditional, each having its own typical features. The units in the modern segment have a greater chance of sustainability as also a greater economic viability. In some cases, they are more efficient and compete, with well-founded advantages, with

TABLE 9 : **Operative Features of Modern and Traditional Segments of the Informal Sector**

MODERN	TRADITIONAL
Capital intentive	Low capital base
Large size	Small/Tiny size
Dynamic technology	Poor and static technology
Better linkage with the Organised Sector	Poor or no linkage with the organised sector
More skilled workforce	Low skilled workforce
High labour productivity	Poor Labour Productivity
High entrepreneurial income	Low enterprenuerial capability and income
Serving higher income groups	Serving low income group
Producing modern goods and Services	Producing traditional goods and services
Greater stability and Sustainability	Prone to Sickness
Greater potential of employment and income generation	With high entry and exit rates, it serves as a sponge to absorb those left out of the formal sector

the organized sector. Nonetheless, they do need better linkage with the latter. On the other hand, the traditional component of the informal sector has more serious problems. They lack stability, and face high incidence of quick entry, sickness and demise and yet, they absorb a large number of workers, with lower wage and skills. Poverty, uncertainty, insecurity as well as exploitation are pronouncedly concentrated here. Any worthwhile package of poverty eradication must necessarily focus on this category, on a priority basis.

8. Empirical Realities in the Informal Sector

The urban informal sector employment is very widely spread across industries and services. The extensive variety in manufacturing and services need to be underlined in particular. Most jobs are visible, but some are invisible and are not easily tractable. Table 10 provides some hints in this regard.

TABLE 10 : **Variety of Jobs/Activities in the Informal Manufacturing and Services**

Manufacturing Industries	Services
1. Light Engineering	1. Auto Repair
2. Ceramics	2. Transportation
3. Textiles, Garments, Hosiery etc.	3. Restaurants/Dhabas
4. Handicrafts	4. Retail Trade
5. Surgical Instruments	5. Hawking
6. Coir and Jute Craft	6. Scrap Collection
7. Sandal Making	7. Recreation
8. Shoe Making	8. Personal Care/Beauty Parlours
9. Carpentry	9. Tourism
10.Food Processing	10. Communication including IT Services, Cyber Cafe/Telecom Booth, Secretarial Services

Among the above, some have clustered location. But their thin spread is to be found all over, with varying concentration. With a rise in the intensity of forward and backward linkages between the organized and the unorganized sectors, corresponding shifts and variations in the working of the latter come up as well. Among the services, most are continuous, but some have strong seasonality like tourism. Similarly, festival or seasonality linked handicrafts experience shifts in work orders with its impact on employment and earnings. It would appear, therefore, that a mingle of continuous, intermittent and seasonal nature of employment and income is a familiar and continuing feature of the urban informal sector.

We come across yet another marked distinction, say, between registered and unregistered units or establishments. All home based work on a putting out pattern is unregistered. The same is true for hawkers, scrap collectors, rag pickers and those in tourism and its related services. Among the establishment-based informal employment too, there is a heavy concentration of the unregistered units. They are dominant in small and medium towns and in non-conforming areas of large towns and metropolises. Registration involves cost and brings certain obligations on employment conditions and emoluments, apart from other accountabilities. Employers want to avoid them. Among the registered establishments too, a fairly good number of workers have an informal status. They get no appointment letter, terms of employment like wages, hours of work, period of employment, leave and holidays, etc. are based purely on verbal understanding. The relative bargaining power based on labour market situation becomes the final determinant. But there is a high degree of job insecurity; wages are poor, and other service benefits are nearly totally absent.

8.1 Wages and Earnings

Informal sector workers have hardly any access to legal or regulatory arrangement for their wage setting and payment. Even under the statutory Minimum Wage Act, there is no universal coverage for all workers. In fact, only the workers employed in designated trades and industries, notified from time to time, can hope to benefit. But this too is dependent on effective enforcement by labour administration. Trade union as well as market forces separately or in conjunction can help in obtaining a modicum of wage/earning security.

Piece rate based payment is pervasive in the informal sector. Average daily earning is invariably lower than the normal factory wages. Quality and quantity control by employers leaves scope for underpayment. Female workers get still lower wages, particularly in the unregistered units.

There could be variation in the levels of earnings, based on regular, intermittent or casual nature of employment. Some among the regular employees could even look forward to certain non-wage benefits. Under-reporting of the number of regular employees, even among the registered establishments, is not unknown. The principal consideration behind under-reporting is to avoid the payment of non-wage benefits, on the one hand, and to acquire relative comparative labour cost advantage, on the other.

The worst sufferers are those employed in the unregistered units, located in dispersed urban slums, particularly the women workers. The rates of wages are low, the mode of payment is piece rate, the number of days in employment irregular and fluctuating and invariably beyond the vigilant eyes of law enforcers or the helping-hand of trade unions. However, with low levels of skills, and inferior technology, productivity of workers is not high either. Hence, low wages are natural to follow.

8.2 Empowerment and Support

Unlike employees in civil services, public enterprises and unionized organized private enterprises, workers in the informal sector have hardly any voice. They are exposed to different forms and sources of exploitation as well as victimization. Employers, civic authorities, police, landlords, money lenders, and shop keepers, are all agents of victimization, in varying degree and form. Women, children and unskilled ones are the most vulnerable in this regard.

Casual and other informal sector workers need to be empowered. One obvious, but not necessarily easy, method is to mobilize efforts towards organizing them. Undoubtedly, with weakening base of trade unionism, even in the organized sector, organizing informal sector worker is indeed a daunting task. And yet, it is not beyond the scope of feasibility. A typical initiative taken by the National Labour Institute speaks a lot in favour of such a possibility. An NLI observer penetrates the workers' community, identifies workers' potential for articulation, and assertion and encourages them towards some action. A realization that some form of collectivity provides a ray of hope for the solution of their plight encourages them. Low wage workers as well as petty commodity producers in the informal economy appear to have demonstrated some success in this regard.

SEWA is another organization that successfully arouses some enthusiasm among the under-privileged women workers engaged in numerous types of informal sector activities. Its efforts have paid off in organizing (a) home-based workers, (b) petty traders, and (c) manual workers. It must be noted that SEWA organized them more as a cooperative than as a trade union in its conventional outfit. This organizational variant has proved far more promising; SEWA, as an NGO, has earned tremendous respect, both at home and abroad.

The state government aided Beedi Cooperative in Kerala is yet another success story. A strategic alliance of government and trade unions helped in this endeavour in Kerala. A distinguishing feature of beedi workers' cooperative is its uniqueness in extending the organization both on the production as well as the market side. Likewise, the fishermen of Kerala are also well organized.

Even the established trade union centres have been realizing the need for and value of organizing the informal sector markets. However, their efforts have been meagre and have yielded poor results so far. The informal sector workers need a new and innovative strategy in organizing themselves. The market they work in is not uniform, and their employers oppose any countervailing power, most ostensibly in the form of a union. Their highly dispersed location imposes serious constraints Yet, there are instances to show that state efforts, alliance with trade unions, and a two-pronged strategy to combine cooperative and trade union formation have borne fruits. Their replication and further innovation can promote the process of empowerment.

8.3 Training for Skills

Another, and perhaps more enduring and easier, instrument of empowerment is support in acquisition of relevant marketable skills. Most informal sectcr workers enter job market at the lowest end with no education or training. Through a long process of on-the-job informal working, with exploitatively low wage, they move up in scale of skills, earnings and even in occupational status. With better education and training, the value addition from workers would be added. Individual employers' cannot internalize the cost of training. They cannot provide the needed infrastructure for initial skill formation or their renewal under conditions of obsolescence.

The government-run craftsmen training institutions are the principal agencies for imparting a variety of skills, on the top of some formal education of the apprentices. With most of these training institutions, there is the statutory Apprenticeship Scheme that covers a wide range of skills. Unluckily, however, the total intake through these channels is insufficient; even the quality of acquired skills is often poor. New generation skills and diversified occupational needs are only marginally covered within their curricula. Employers invariably have low preference for the product of these streams. They prefer on-the-job trainees instead. There is no choice to continuous updating of supply end of skill streams. For this updating, demand profile for existing and emerging skills is equally essential. Data base on labour market operation could serve as a sound basis for decisions in this regard. Employers, and their associations, are indeed better equipped to move in this direction for improving their competitive efficiency based on workers' skills.

Lately many private training institutions have come up. But their number, in-take capacity, location and curriculum have left much to be desired. The quality and numbers coming out of these streams do not match the demand. Employers associations on their own can provide and augment such infrastructure for the benefit of all, either collectively or in partnership with government or international agencies. There is some awareness on this issue, but much progress is not discernible. Even an NGO or a self- help group could be encouraged to undertake such efforts.

9. Summary and Overview

Constitutional directives, judicial decisions and the relevant development strategy increasingly emphasize the concern for human and social dimensions in economic decision-making. This requires promoting gainful jobs and income generating opportunities. Both macro-economic policy and corporate management strategy have a significant role to play and specific responsibilities to shoulder.

9.1 Multi-pronged Initiatives Needed

Persisting greater supply over demand for labour is exasperating the unemployment problem. Recent strategy for liberalizing and modernizing the economy is forcing steps for acquiring competitive capability at all levels. Labour saving and capital-intensive investment decisions are reducing the labour absorptive capacity in the private organized sector, public enterprises and public services. This trend is likely to intensify itself in the near future, and the scope for additional job opportunities may decline further among such employers. The informal sector has, therefore, a significant role to play in the lives and living of a fairly sizeable chunk of our population, both in the rural and urban areas.

In a sense, it is redeeming to see that the informal sector is no more perceived as a residual or transient component of the economy. It is growing and has strong characteristics of enduring presence. Happily again, it is characterized by its own internal dynamism, demonstrating a variety of changes over time, across industries, locations, product lines and services streams. Again, it is refreshing that development planners are getting persuaded to provide it a respectable place. For example, the felt need for commodity balance in the development process requires production of wage goods and delivery of low cost services with speed; considerations of regional balance emphasize the case for maximum spatial dispersal of goods and services producing activities with economic viability with its inherent content for growth and expansion of the informal sector; the anti-poverty concern requires maximizing, in the shortest space of time, employment producing and income generating opportunities, in the country. The informal sector acquires a persuasive and credible case for its role on all these counts. Mass production for scale economies is necessary, but the value of production by masses through small and tiny units cannot be overlooked in a labour surplus economy.

Environment lobby and city planners have a strong case against the proliferation of the informal sector in urban centers, based on their concern regarding pollution, traffic congestion and increasing pressure on limited social and physical infrastructure. But then, the incidence of poverty and unemployment in urban India is an equally serious cause for worry. The push from rural poverty and pull of urban promises will intensify migration to urban centres, at any rate, to mega cities. Extended efforts from the supply end of infrastructure to meet the challenge opens this sector for added initiative and efforts from the government as well as larger corporate enterprises. Artificial fetters on the demand side is neither administratively feasible nor socio-economically desirable.

Better technology for healthy, cleaner and socially congenial urban habitat should be the agenda of city planners and urban services providers. There is considerable scope for shift in planning and managerial strategy in this regard. This also opens up considerable scope for creative public-private sector partnership. Services of NGOs in selected sectors, on a planned basis, can also be a source of relief.

Larger corporate enterprises for relative locational cost advantage have historically concentrated in large urban centres. The relative cost advantages are now encouraging shift to new non-urban locations. Counter magnate city programme, de-industrializing strategy of major city planners as well as the availability of and choice in favour of non-polluting industries together will reduce the organized sector hostility towards its unorganized counterpart.

A segment of the informal sector, both in goods producing as well as in service providing activities, does not have to compete with its organized counterpart. As a matter of fact, in such activities, there is much scope for cooperation and complementariness.

The relative cost advantage in tradable goods and services (garments, jems and jewellary, software, etc.) with the help of informal sector brings out a strong case in its favour. Much of the current and growing exports in a fast opening world economy is expanding the opportunity of gains through the contribution of the urban informal sector.

Wholly owned subsidaries, out-sourcing, contracting out, and growth of home-based economic activity are the symptoms of spurt in the informal sector. These developments are likely to gather further momentum.

The organized sector has a strong supportive role in (1) providing inputs, (2) technology improvement, (3) lending managerial expertise, (4) extending access to finance and market, and (5) in building social infrastructure. Units and activities in the informal sector are non-viable, un-economical and vulnerable, practically in each of these areas. Their struggle is for mere survival at low margin and against intense competition. Their sickness, demise or switch-over to new locations and activities indicate these. In plain words, the informal sector cannot stand on its own just as the formal sector cannot be entrusted with all development and social responsibilities, most ostensibly the provision of employment to the expanding army of the urban labour force.

Employers organizations have formidable potential to persuade for changes in public policies. They campaign, on a massive scale, and on a continuing basis. Part of it could be mobilized in support of the informal sector growth and its sustainability. Problems of the working poor and the vulnerable have attracted major initiative for aid from the organized corporate sector in many developed countries. Associations of larger corporate employers have massive resource base, managerial competence and a vision for development. They are corporate citizens interested in their own survival and growth. Government support is sought for and obtained in various forms. Their self- interest goals would acquire greater credibility if it is blended with a mission of concern for the unemployed and the working poor before the public policy planners. Employment and income generation programmes provide a constructive arena for a healthy strategic partnership between the two. Also, there is need to eliminate the area of hostility and conflict between them.

Entrepreneurs in the two sectors, and their associations, have different priorities. This is an unfortunate feature of our economic life; to a great extent, it is avoidable. The recent decision to do away with the quantitative restrictions on imports and continuing pressure for de-reservation for the SSI units have portents for further conflict. A strategy has to be worked out to blend the two for national gains, on a complementary, rather than mutually antagonistic basis.

Clearly, three areas can be visualized where the informal sector needs priority support.These are access to finance, access to market, and technology improvement.

Adequate, timely and relatively less costly financing is required for purchasing raw material, and meeting other day-to-day production expenses, and for upgrading technology and equipments through lease or outright purchase. There is, however, a continuing dilemma between adequate and easy delivery and recovery and fear of default. On balance the credibility of the informal sector units is relatively better, the growing incidence of sickness and closure among them notwithstanding. Yet, they face casual, hostile and non-cooperative attitude from financing agencies as well as government. The total allocation for this sector is never exhausted in terms of disbursement. The flow of credit often gets dry when the entrepreneurs need it the most. The requirement of collateral in terms of land, etc. emerges as a major deterrent even in schemes where collateral is not required; in PMIR, banks are fighting shy in marking credit available. Policy and system changes with regard to micro enterprises are required. The ILO and its counterpart agencies could give priority to this aspect in promoting adequacy and timeliness of finance.

Marketing remains the most critical area of challenge. Those linked with the organized sector and functioning as a vibrant and growing sector have an easy and viable existence. Evidences of exploitative relationship are known, yet they are better off than their counterpart. Encouragement in this field is needed on a tangible basis.

Even the units serving multiple buyers can also do extremely well if their product choice, market proximity as well as quality and cost advantage favour them.

There is need to identify and extend promotional support to this segment. Development agencies, appropriate government departments as well as dedicated NGOs with competence and commitment, can help in this area. The ILO and other multilateral agencies could have a major role here, both as promoters and supporters.

Improved technology is the most effective aid for ensuring economic survival and competitive advantage. Its identification and timely incorporation are critical. There are choices in buying, leasing or renting in this regard. No uniform policy is possible. But a well-organized clustered infrastructure for technological aid could be a dependable way- out. This again opens the scope for government, corporate enterprises, their association as well as international agencies. The initial technological support is necessary, but for ensuring its sufficiency on an enduring basis, there is the continuing challenge of updating and renewal. This has not been easy under conditions of fast technological obsolescence, high cost and intensifying competition for units in this sector.

Much of the value addition in the formal and more so in the informal sectors comes from quality manpower. The latter, at any rate a major segment of it, is not endowed with better educated and superior skilled manpower. They need vigorous, continuous and updated skill development inputs. This is not possible through their internal financing. Acquiring skilled manpower from market erodes their labour cost advantage. The transient character of their operation encourages labour turnover and high replacement cost. Here clustered and externally supported training facility, at a reasonable cost, could help considerably. Government, corporate sector and their association and international agency could re-examine their current strategy, commitment and resource allocation policy for greater relevance and effectiveness. Again NGOs can serve as delivery vehicles with necessary resource support from all or one of the possible sources.

New and changing consumer choices, growing emergence of sectors like information, entertainment, tourism, etc. are opening up new and fast growing opportunities for employment. But then, relevant and high level complementary skills are necessary. The existing policies, programmes and institutions have yet to show dynamism and resilience. This gap has to be filled with speed and innovativeness. For obvious reasons, initiatives for effecting such changes have to come from outside the informal sector.

Sufficient and good quality social infrastructure is of equally great value. Housing, sanitary facilities and social protection are desperately needed by the economically weaker, socially vulnerable and transient mass of workers, particularly young working women engaged in menial errands for earning their livelihood. Slum lords, exploitative contractors, agents of socially unacceptable activities find them as easy prey. Choice of support in this area is known. The will, commitment and the resources needed to intervene effectively are missing; so are the dedicated agencies.

In the ultimate analysis, the required initiative rests with the employers and the government. The former has the obligation, expertise and even scope for gains, while the latter has the ultimate responsibility. With prompting and support from international agencies like the ILO, much that is needed can become a reality too.

The search for decent work has begun at the right-time and with refreshing candour. The ILO initiative is commendable. However, by itself alone, it has handicaps. In collaboration with the employers and their collective body, the scope for creative, constructive and highly desirable contribution is open ended.

Fighting poverty is a combination of economic, social, human and politically rewarding activity. Informal sector is large and dominated by high incidence of poverty, too. It also holds the promise of improving the lot of the poor and the uncared, in leveling up their quality of life and living.

Shedding hostility, if one still persists, promoting innovative and appropriate strategy, creating and nurturing relevant institution and delivery systems, etc. provide considerable scope for the well-meaning section of any society. Let us hope there would be visible progress on the path ahead. Any effort in this regard need not be constructed as mere altruism. It is in fact an investment in collective self-survival.

Growth in employment promotes disposable income and expands market price for products and services. Any progress in this regard relieves the demand constraint pressure in the domestic market. In addition, export promotion with relative cost advantage becomes more feasible.

Finally, employment growth, and improvement in its quality brings social harmony necessary for healthy investment climate.

9.2 Agenda for Employers

As suggested above, much responsibility devolves on the employers just as the government has to do a lot for the sector. An agenda for action awaits them as well.

In our opinion, let the employers :

1. build consensus on the need to promote employment and improve the performance of those employed; examine their collective capacity in directly creating employment or extending support to efforts in this regard; and,

delineate their agenda for action nationally, sectorally as well as industry-, location- and unit-wise;

2. agree to allocate resources: finance, managerial and lobbying power, collectively for this; allocation methods may often need a differentiated approach;
3. encourage promotion of credible data base of successful cases, whether autonomous or sponsored, where the informal sector has contributed to employment growth without compromise to economic viability;
4. support studies on determining the qualitative characterisitics of such cases in urban, sub-urban and rural segments; discovering differences and uniqueness in such case would help enormously;
5. undertake pro-actively the task of promoting backward and forward linkages between the organized and the informal sectors, both in production and service activities; there is a considerable scope for complementarity;
6. build or extend support to infra-structure facilities for the use of informal sector agents; this could cover a wide range of supports, e.g., technology, input bank, finance market access , training and retraining, and social security, etc;
7. mount moral pressure on government agencies for extended support in partnership with employers and their association;
8. explore the possibilities of involving NGOs in this task; they could be entrusted with the task as supporting agents or even emerge as direct vehicle of delivery in such areas as micro finance, marketing and training;
9. wherever necessary, new institutions or NGOs should be floated and nurtured; self-help groups have demonstrated healthy capacity and strong will in this regard;
10. encourage multilateral agencies with innovative and constructive agenda for their consideration; also, respond pro-actively to their initiative and undertake direct responsibility as delivery agents; and
11. never ignore the scope and need for timely course correction and modification; action agenda must cover the unemployed, particularly the youth and educated, women and the less-endowed, in terms of human capital and other assets.

Bibliography

Bhalla, Sheila, "Globalisation, Growth and Employment", in G.S. Bhalla and Manmohan Agarwal (eds), World Economy in Transition: An Indian Perspective, Har-Anand Publications, New Delhi, 1994.

Chadha, G.K. " Trade, Technology and Employment: Some Missing Links in India's Rural Economy", Indian Journal of Labour Economics , 42/4, 1999.

Govt. of India, Unorganized Manufacturing Sector in India: Its Size, Employment and Some Key Estimates, Report No. 433, NSSO, August 1998.

————, Ninth Five Year Plan 1997-2002, Vol. I: Thematic Issues and Sectoral Programmes , Planning Commission, 1999.

Kulshreshta A.C. and Singh Gulab, "Gross Domestic Product and Employment in the Informal Sector of the Indian Economy", Indian Journal of Labour Economics, 42/2, 1999.

Mitra, Arup, "Employment in the Informal Sector", Indian Journal of Labour Economics , 41/3, 1998.

Kundu, Amitabh and Lalitha, N. "Informal Manufacturing Sector in Urban India: Sectoral Trends and Interdependencies", Indian Journal of Labour Economics, 41/3, 1998.

Papola, T.S. "Informal Sector: Concept and Policy", Economic and Political Weekly, XV, No. 18, 1980.

Mishra, R.K. Nandagopal, R. and Mohammad, A. "Sale of Public Enterprise Shares: Fritting Away Nation's Wealth", Economic and Political Weekly , XXVIII, No. 48, November 27, 1993.

RBI, Handbook of Statistics on Indian Economy , Reserve Bank of India, 2000.

Decent Employment in the Urban Informal Economy: A Perspective

Samir Radwan

1. Introduction

What kind of a strategic approach could India devise to achieve a breakthrough in its informal sector which, for reasons given by Director General Juan Somavia, I may better call the informal economy? (By the way, a Nigerian colleague calls it now the popular economy, because it has the majority of the people working in it). In my view, such a strategic approach should have two components. The first component is that we really need a coherent policy framework. In a typical developing economy, usually we have many policies. Whether these policies lead to a smooth and fast growth of the informal economy depends on whether these policies are internally consistent. If one policy is pulling in one direction and the other in another, the informal economy hardly gathers a growth impetus. So, we need a very hard-nosed look at the whole gamut of macro economic public policies, having direct and indirect bearing on the informal economy; land rights, registration and licensing laws, water rates, etc. are one set of public policies, and credit flow, institutional help for technology up-gradation, training and skill formation, etc. are another set of policies. It is of crucial significance that we critically examine those policies, and evaluate them in terms of the present needs of the informal economy and its need to grow.

Since we are talking of the bulk of the Indian economy, my first proposal is that the policy package addressed to it, should be highly nuanced and highly differentiated because of the different nature of the various components of the informal economy. I would imagine, a working group focuses on developing this coherent policy framework. A number of policy issues have to be answered. For example, what would be the contribution of the urban informal economy if the envisaged overall growth rate of 7-8 per cent is duly realized. What would be the role of the most dominant informal sector, namely, agriculture, in the growth process, and how can we maintain the contribution of the informal economy, and, if possible, streamline its functioning in tandem with its formal counterpart? What are the policies required, for achieving each of these objectives? I am sure, the Indian policy makers and other public analysts are capable of finding the right answers to all these questions. The right answers would serve not only India's own national and regional interests but would be doing favour to other developing countries. So, we have to look at the rate of growth, and the pattern of growth with ramifications for sectoral or regional balances. The extremely crucial role of agriculture needs to be underlined in particular.

China could register a remarkable breakthrough in its rural non-farm sector primarily on the strength of fast growing agricultural incomes that became a reality soon after the 1978 economic reforms took roots. The east Asian economies too, especially Malaysia, realized tremendous gains of a very rapid growth in agriculture, and in agricultural productivity; it created a very good market for the non-formal sector which, in turn, led to a tremendous change in the Malaysian countryside. These are just two examples of dynamic experiences; there are others also. So these are the sort of the building blocks of a policy framework that targets the informal economy.

2. Action Programme

The second component of my proposal is a package, a kind of action programme, and there, the policy makers have to be very modest, and very strategic at the same time. For the package to be effective, it must have four elements. These are credit, training and skill development, social protection and organization. The idea is to try and target a region over a sector or an activity and have some pilot experience there, and it might generate formidable triggering and multiplier effects. We are told that the history of transformation of the informal sector in England is, in fact, the history of the electric plug. Electricity, a little building and other pre-requisites were made available to cottage industry, in the form of a viable package, and that created history of its own kind. Could we try some thing like that, in developing economies in general, and India in particular?

What I am trying to say here is that we need a package that has all those components. My feeling is that all those components are being tried, but probably they are tried separately, and selectively. The objective usually is to target only the twenty five per cent productive part of the informal economy. But then, the seventy five per cent is not to be neglected; perhaps, it needs a different policy intervention. A very high proportion of people involved in this bigger segment of the informal economy are poor; for them, it is the anti-poverty package that should be the focus of policy attention, while productivity improvement should be the core of development strategy for the smaller segment. Through this kind of differentiated and selective approach, if we target the twenty five per cent segment and declare that the activities, currently being pursued by it, would emerge as viable small scale enterprises, through organizations and through cooperatives, by a specified year, it is most likely to register a very high degree of success. A package, howsoever attractive and well-meaning, uniformly foisted upon the whole of the informal economy, is bound to bring a limited degree of success.

How do we implement these ideas and approaches? I propose an informal sectoral strategy group, ISSG. This ISSG should be tripartite. Such a group should bring all concerned actors together, to reflect on those proposals, and that would bring in the donor community too, in due course. Here, it is in the fitness of things to add a word on the whole issue of development assistance. I believe, since last year in particular or the year before (1998), the DAC (Development Assistance Committee) of the OECD has come up with an extremely important piece of work, where they, as a result of tremendous research, let us fix the objective of halving poverty by the year 2015; they worked out the rates of growth necessary for achieving that, and the finance necessary for supporting that. And from my contacts with the members of the DAC, I know that there is hard thinking of abandoning the traditional technical corporation approaches by donors into new modalities; the new modalities are to hedge against uncertainties, vulnerability, and doggedly try to reach that objective of halving world poverty. And I think, the ISSG should really target this new thinking by the donors and should go for it. Of course, the ILO has its share of effort to contribute. The very fact that the ILO Director General, Mr. Juan Somavia, chose to come to this crucial workshop, and Mr. Fred Fluitman from ILO's Turin Centre, Ms. Anreasin from ILO headquarters, practically the whole of New Delhi Regional Office and the ILO-SAAT, are involved, in varying capacity, in the deliberations of the workshop, testifies to the seriousness that the ILO attaches to this policy areas.

The primary goal of the ILO today is to help the national governments promote employment opportunities, especially for women, and to obtain decent and productive working conditions that would have freedom, equity, security, and human dignity built into them. I must admit, we were a little apprehensive about the concept of decent work, perhaps for no other reason that it was tending to become a new fashion and a new clich,, as far as the 'decent work' paradigm is concerned. However, our apprehension was soon over and we decided to accept the challenge of how to give concrete operational content to the concept. Let me, therefore, begin by explaining what does the concept of decent work mean to the ILO. Is it one of those fluffy slogans? We cannot shy away from the basic premise that when the processes of globalisation and liberalization get more and more firmly entrenched, impact on domestic work force is bound to be felt, in varying form and content; we cannot stop the change. But, it must also be admitted that these processes are asymmetrical in the sense that they will have different impacts in terms of income distribution, both between countries, and within countries, among different groups of people. Perhaps, that is how we see the phenomenon of the expanding informal economy in the developing economies not much differently from the one in the developed countries. The transition economies too share the same fate where the informal (variously described as 'underground' or 'black') economy is getting widespread. So, all policy attempts for devising innovative coping mechanisms under the pressures of globalisation and liberalization, are steps towards improving employment base of all categories of economies, and are aimed at lessening human misery at large.

3. Concept of Decent Work

Amartya Sen, in his June 1999 lecture at the annual labour conference, carried the concept of decent work a bit further and said that for anybody who is dealing with the issue of employment and well-being, working people should be taken as one. And the trouble with our thinking about employment problems has been that we have been focusing only on the 8-10 per cent of the work force that constitutes the formal economy, to the exclusion of the preponderant majority of workers. And, for an organization like the ILO and for anybody who cares for employment, all types of work is important and should be seriously taken note of. How can Sen's concept of decent work be put into an operational framework? In my view, it translates itself into three concrete elements.

The first is that the work done should be *productive* and *remunerative*; unluckily, the core feature of the informal sector is that the work is neither highly productive nor highly remunerative. The second element is that the work done should receive due *recognition*. The work may take different forms, and may be pursued under different organizational outfits; thanks to the information and communication technology that is permeating into all types of economies, and all layers of production and service regimes, the differentials in the quality of work done are getting sharper by the day. The increasing productivity gaps between the formal and the informal sectors need to be noted in particular. Lest the policy makers are too much swayed by high productivity standards of the formal sector enterprises, the need for recognizing the economic content of the low productivity work in the formal sector is no less important. The third aspect of decent work is that the process of structural adjustment and change must be accompanied by adequate safeguards and social protection against the vulnerabilities. That the informal sector already suffers from numerous vulnerabilities, and that these should not multiply as a consequence of trade liberalization, needs hardly be emphasized.

4. Up-scaling the Informal Sector

Now I come to my final, and a somewhat vexatious, point. It is about up-scaling of the informal sector, especially the issue of financing. In this regard, we need to confront four sets of issues. The first issue is to mount attempts for reversing the basic characteristic of the informal sector, which is low productivity. If this is the major sector of the economy that involves the majority of the labour force but its contribution to GDP is low, by definition, it is a low productivity sector. Indeed, the informal sector is enmeshed in a low productivity trap which can be broken through multiple policy initiatives. We have to think of new and more promising activities for the informal sector, new linkages that it can foster with the formal sector, new production and management skills, expressly germane to the requirement of the informal sector, and so on. This is going to be the dividing edge in competitiveness and the distribution of gains from globalization in the future.

The second issue is about the dilemma of the informal sector. The informal sector exists, and survives, because it is a low cost sector. If we insist on applying social security and social protection obligations, it might crowd the sector out of its existence. Are there innovative ways of striking a sensitive and difficult balance between the two requirements? It is a very practical issue that can best be resolved by practitioners including employers and workers' organizations. I have one experience from my own country where the Alexandria Businessmen Association, a very active business organization, introduced a scheme under which all support is given to upgrade those members of the informal sector who are sub-contracted with the Association. They are given better technology and the needed marketing outlets, and the scheme has proved to be extremely successful. So, there are ways of resolving the dilemma.

The third issue relates to public policy. One of the most difficult aspects of public policy is to harmonize the relative movement of factor shares, as the economy grows. Let us recall Hans Singer's risk of the Kenyan report; it was called *'free distribution with growth'*. The process of growth has also to carry with it mechanisms for continuous wage distribution. All that happened in Europe after the Second World War, and in the Tigers of Asia before their recent financial crisis, has crucial policy import for most of the developing world, including India. A part of the increase in productivity went to maintaining real wages or real returns to labour, at a steadily increasing rate but less than the rate of increase in productivity; the difference went to capital accumulation. The policy lesson is that the process of capital accumulation has to be stepped up, especially when the informal sector faces competition both from within and without.

The final, and really the most difficult, is the issue of organization. Here, the employers and the workers' organizations have a real task to perform. There are numerous experiences the world over, e.g., Vancouver Experience, mandated workers' outfits in Chile and Brazil, where the employers and workers' organizations have extended their helping hand to the informal sector. Others can follow suit.

5. Open Trade and the Informal Sector

Let me now briefly turn to the likely impact that the open trade regime would have on the informal sector. The classical economics teaches us that free trade leads to an increase in total welfare. Globalization became a living phenomenon only during the nineteenth century, and the documented experience of trade during this century shows that gains from sale are highly asymmetrical and unequal, for reasons which are well known and well accepted. One does not have to elaborate on that account. The trouble with the process of globalization is that it does not create a single, and unidirectional, process of exchange and adjustment. Three major processes can be readily pointed out. The first is trade liberalization, the second is the information technology revolution which includes revolution of communication, and the third is the capital flows; perhaps, the third one could be highly dangerous from the point of view of trade and employment interest of the developing world. The loose and foot-lose capital exchanges hands almost every day. We would do ourselves a service if we analyze the impact of each of these processes very precisely.

We have done as many as twelve studies on trade liberalization. The preliminary results show that the impact depends critically on what a particular country liberalizes. Further, the impact differs markedly between an economy that uses skilled labour for the tradable part of its production compared with the one that makes do with the unskilled or semi- skilled labour. In any case, a sophisticated and in-depth study is needed to work out the whole process of globalization and its impact on different aspects of domestic economy, most especially on employment in the informal sector.

Globalization and liberalization usually result in greater insecurities which, in turn, generate increased inequalities. The problem with policy makers in the past, especially during the structural adjustment period, is that safety nets as an essential tag-on of the liberalization process, came only as an after-thought. It almost amounts to looking for an ambulance when our own decisions or choices inflict an injury upon us. Luckily, the thinking process is now undergoing a remarkable change the world over; even the World Bank people now realize that the so-called safety nets have to be a part and parcel of economic and social policy. In plain terms, when a developing economy is designing its economic and social policy, if it does not take the distribution factor into account, it is bound to get troubles later.

Before I conclude, let me sound a note of caution. Let us not be under an illusion that the informal sector is a panacea. I do not know of any country in the world that has developed through the informal sector. But I know of many experiences in economic history where a transformed informal sector proved to be a vehicle of progress. The ILO's mandate is to see a radical transformation of the informal sector in the developing world; all social partners have to contribute to this process.

Welcome Address

by

Ms. Mary Johnson

Director, ILO Area Office

I express my great happiness on the presence of the Director-General, ILO, Mr. Juan Somavia, who has kindly agreed to give the keynote address. I am equally happy that Dr. Manmohan Singh, the author of Economic Reforms in India, is presiding over the Inaugural Session. I extend special welcome to Mr. S.S. Dhindsa, Union Minister of Urban Employment and Poverty Alleviation and Mr. Rolf Thusing, Vice Chairman of the ILO Governing Body.

I take the opportunity to express my thanks to all members of the Steering Committee, particularly Mr. I.P. Anand, Chairman of the Steering Committee for his untiring and committed leadership, Dr. L. Mishra, a friend and a guide, and other collaborators - Ministry of Labour and IFCI/ILD, Mr. Narasimhan in particular, who have collaborated from the outset and contributed generously along with SIDBI. I thank Haryana State Government for the great support, and welcome Chief Secretary, Mr. R.S. Varma and other senior officials for creating the pleasant atmosphere for the workshop. The hard work and intellectual contribution of all the consultants and ILO-SAAT colleagues for making a lasting contribution to the understanding of the Urban Informal Sector deserve to be commended.

After the deliberations of the workshop are over and the fine intellect gathered have critiqued and dissected the preparatory studies, it is proposed to produce a significant publication as one of the outcomes of the workshop. The number and quality of participants who have travelled from far and near, with different backgrounds and having different work experiences, are the best testimony of the timely choice and topicality of the subject.

With these words of welcome, I request Dr. L. Mishra, Union Secretary, Labour for his words of welcome and also to read the message from the Minister of Labour, who is held up on account of a cabinet meeting.

Welcome Address

by

Dr. L.D. Mishra

Secretary, Ministry of Labour, Govt. of India

Mr. S.S. Dhindsa, Ministry of Urban Employment and Poverty Alleviation, Mr. Juan Somavia, Director General of ILO, Dr. Manmohan Singh, former Finance Minister and former Secretary General of the South South Commission, Geneva, Mr. I.P. Anand, Member ILO Governing Body, and Chairman of the Workshop Steering Committee and the guardian angel, and the voice behind this prestigious event, Mr. R. Thusing, President, International Organisation of Employers, Shri R.S. Varma, Chief Secretary, Government of Haryana, Mr. P.V. Narasingham, Chairman, IFCI and ILD, distinguished members of the Steering Committee, distinguished delegates to the ILO-ILD National Workshop, ladies and gentlemen.

On behalf of the Ministry of Labour, Government of India, and on my own, it gives me great pleasure to join Madam Mary Johnson to welcome Mr. Juan Somavia, Director General, ILO, all the distinguished dignitaries and delegates to the ILO, ILD Workshop for job creation in the urban informal sector this morning. This is the first visit of Mr. Juan Somavia to India after he was elected to the position of Director General of the oldest international organisation in March 1998. It is quite appropriate and is of symbolic significance that the visit of Mr. Juan Somavia to this august assembly comes in the wake of a brief visit to Raj Ghat the Samadhi of Bapu. Mr. Somavia, in his life time, has symbolized and continues to symbolize the very same values, ideas and principles which Bapu represented in his life and for which Bapu sacrificed his life on 30th of January 1948. The values and principles being fight against dictatorship, against authoritarianism, colonialism, and against imperialism. Mr. Somavia has been a sane voice of humanity, representing the concerns resting on voluntarism, consensus moderation, and restraint and yet, a firm and uncompromising fight for justice, equity, and fair play, all key attributes of democracy. It is extremely gracious on his part to have graced this function soon after his arrival in Delhi. The depth and intensity of the commitment demonstrated by him towards the problems and concerns of the developing countries in general, and towards the problems of men, women and children at work in unorganized and informal sector has been a source of great inspiration and strength for the three social partners ever since he assumed the office of the DG, ILO. This commitment has manifested itself in a series of statements made by him, both before and after he was elected as DG, ILO with a massive mandate and with total solidarity and support from the three constituents of the Indian delegation, the employers, workers and government.

The urban informal sector in India has been a mind boggling issue in terms of magnitude of the problem, complexity and peculiarity of operations and immensity of deprivation and suffering of the workers and their family members who are engaged in this sector. These problems are further compounded on account of the gradual shrinkage of jobs in the regular and organized sector, recourse to rationalization, retrenchment and displacement of labour, lack of stability and durability of employment, necessitating migration of millions of households from one part of India to another. Existence of a network of ma l - and dys-functional middlemen who are out to appropriate unmerited benefits at the cost of others, exasperates the problem. Absence of basic facilities and amenities in terms of housing, drinking water, primary health care, primary education for children, hygiene and environmental sanitation for the workers in the sector, is a reality to which most of us seem to have become moot spectators. Pervasive contractualization and casualisation, lack of adequate physical and human infrastructure and inadequate investment in the process of skill formation and skill up-gradation resulting in deprivation and exploitation of workers, routinely occurring in more ways than one. It is in this context that a national workshop is timely and appropriate and the organizers deserve to be congratulated for this initiative.

The workshop has been extremely well structured, and all the basic issues associated with strategies for job creation in the urban informal sector have been correctly identified for an in-depth discussion. Association of a large number of planners, administrators and management experts, trade unions and NGOs in the area of employment and skill training has converted this workshop into a rich reservoir of creative forces and energies. We, in the Ministry of Labour, have no doubt that the outcome of the workshop will provide rich inputs to the government of India and the Planning Commission in planning an appropriate strategy for job creation in a manner which will take us nearer the goal of full, freely chosen and productive employment which was adopted at the end of the world summit on social development at Copenhagen in March, 1995 of which Mr. Somavia was the chief architect. And in which, Prof. S.R. Hashim and Shri K.R. Venugopal as members of the Indian delegation, had played a key role, particularly in drafting the declaration. This would all the more be quite handy for the task force headed by Dr. Montek Singh Ahluwalia, Member Planning Commission, which is in the process of completing the exercise of drawing up a strategy for creation of a hundred million jobs in the coming ten years in pursuance of the announcement made by the Prime Minister of India on 15th August, 1998. With these words I would like to extend to Mr. Juan Somavia, to all the distinguished dignitaries and to all of you a very warm and cordial welcome.

Opening Speech

of

Shri I.P. Anand

As a curtain raiser to this Workshop, I need to confine myself to the subject. I may, however, in view of the spirit of friendship and consideration our distinguished guest, the Director General of ILO has always shown to me and to my various observations in Geneva, join the earlier speakers in conveying my greetings on his first visit to this country. This Workshop is a modest attempt to implement and spread the basic message of "Decent Work" Report through ILO cooperation.

The ILO's basic mission is to improve the situation of human beings in the World of Work. Even though a lot more may be required yet to be done in the organized sector in developing societies, the informal sector where the potential lies has so far regarded the ILO as a caretaker and custodian of interests of ivory towers in the organized sector only. However, lately, SMEs and informal sectors have been the recipient of much vocal concern as well. Lacking a constituency support and a forum this sector has been like an orphan. The message of Decent Work, as it is, has to be defined and articulated within this sector. Much needed, deeper and sustained action oriented supportive attention through technical and financial cooperation at the international level and resources allocations at the national level is called for. And specific projects aiming at accelerated job opportunities need to be rejuvenated and implemented in the urban informal sector which is expanding at a rapid pace.

The participation of the informal sector in Latin America has crossed 60 per cent of its total employment. In Africa over 90 per cent of the new urban jobs during the past decade have been provided by the informal economy. In terms of human development, South Asia, of which India is a major component, despite employment pattern changes in the last decade, much more needs to be done. Consequent to unabated population pressure, persisting unemployment continues to be a threat to internal law and order and provides a fertile ground both for crimelinked and mercenary motivated terrorism. This phenomenon threatens the foundations of work-devoted societies who believe in healthy, democratic, civic and social structures. Decent Work approach and policy pursuit, therefore, has aroused a lot of HOPE which must be accomplished into REALITY before it becomes too late.

The Workshop design conceived and structured by SAAT experts with assistance of outside experts, workers and employers representatives and State

Administrators, who have provided the rich material in the studies is worthy of examination. State and sectoral studies were undertaken both on representative and job potential basis so as to carve out opportunity multiplication. The outcome of debates and discussions here should certainly provide a high quality feedstock both for regional action and ILO technical cooperation policies.

In the Steering Group we have assumed the relevance of a "social floor" which is indeed essential for stability of socio-economic super structure contemplated in open economics in the globalished societies. And the new century's social floor should not be a thin layered one based on minimum wages and secured jobs but should also cover the wider dimensions of four strategic objectives accepted by the 1999 International Labour Conference. In physical terms, there should be wholesome contributive elements to vibrant and viable small and medium enterprises. Thus, the Director General's crusade against widespread unemployment and for poverty eradication should get further momentum through a series of follow-up initiatives all over. His message to the Workshop, this morning will surely inspire all those engaged in the field of job creation in the informal sector.

I am grateful to Mr. Samir Radwan, Senior Policy Adviser in the ILO Employment Sector and his team at the Geneva headquarters for the inspiration, support and guidelines under which the workshop scope has been determined. Relevant documentation has been professionally researched and finalized accordingly. I must acknowledge his personal commitment to the cause and his offer to guide and steer the discussion here to purposeful and implementable conclusions.

Our invitation to Union Ministers, Dr. Jatiya and Sardar Sukhdev Singh Dhindsa was reciprocated by both of them with warmth. Dr. Jatiya being the Head of the national tripartite structure has played a key role in adjustment of confrontationist past into cooperative future so as to ensure well integrated social coherence. He has already initiated some basic foundational steps, but we are yet stuck at door steps. I hope, he will act with more speed. Sardar Dhindsa has a common cause with us in ensuring an incentive prone infrastructure for attainment of common goal. We do look forward to their sustained support in evolving a transparent, robust and small enterprise and informal sector.

I am glad Dr. Manmohan Singh Ji has found time to encourage us notwithstanding other pressures from his newly adopted pursuits. A distinguished son of India, internationally recognized Economist as he is, he countenances economic liberalization which sustains a buoyant human face. And his vision and approach in this regard is an equivalent variable of the concept of Decent Work. The Steering Group and the participants deeply value his presence this morning and look forward to his wise counsel. This would not be based now on his academic and intellectual capabilities only. Lately, as we know, he has acquired a deep link up with field action. He is no longer one of those who "go around and then come back having visited ministries, bureaucracies and the official counterparts". He is one of those who "see the people for whom we are trying to do something". I am obliged to him for his joining us today.

Before I close, may I take liberty to echo what the Director General expressed at 1999 "Enterprise Forum" in Geneva as a last thought. And I quote: "We need to develop a sensitive approach to the other - other languages, other cultures, other races, other religions, other realities; in sum, a capacity to be a multicultural person". Humbly I submit, my country of which, along with many others of my generation, I am proud, had in past millennia the requisite sensitivity. Since Alexendar's invasion on India and thereafter, following series of military and cultural intrusions from the North and the Western World during various periods of history, India has, in fact, absorbed and accepted other languages, cultures, races, religions and realities to be the embodiment of "multiculturism" of his vision. Consequently, our composite and multicultural heritage and value system have emboldened us to stand up till date for the vision ILO and the Director General stand for.

My response as above is with reference to the standing, distinctive tripartite character and supremacy of ILO among other UN organs in regard to human and social issues vis-a-vis trade links on which India has been firm, transparent and outspoken. However, Seattle incidents and Davos debates and aggressive postures of well-entrenched elements and powers around ILO cause us worry as to the future. We are convinced that real and lasting answer to comparative disparities which disturb some developed nations lies in quicker economic growth and social progress in the unorganized, informal and rural sectors and not in coercive or imposed regulatory instruments or through sinister and divisive techniques so as to dull or isolate our voice. These tactics have neither succeeded in the past nor it would be so in the future in this increasingly awakened world.

We have absorbed, during the outgoing eight decades, all constructive elements ILO had sponsored and have trained ourselves to sustain a progressive and scientific outlook notwithstanding centuries long external domination and internal persisting poverty. This land, therefore, continues to be fertile both for new and progressive ideas and small and medium enterprise promotion and is capable of achieving his vision expressed at the Forum and widely shared by our people here. Therein would be the corner stone of Decent Work. The Director General is, therefore, at home with us in exploring a common approach and, pilot exercise to which this first National Workshop has been dedicated viz. Evolution of an effective strategic approach to job creation in the informal sector.

Thank you for your patience.

Address

by

Mr. S.S. Dhindsa

Union Minister of Urban Employment and Poverty Alleviation

Mr. Juan Somavia, Director General, ILO, Dr. Manmohan Singhji, Shri I.P. Anand, Dr. Mishra, Mrs. Marcy Johnson, Mr. Narasimha, Mr. Burman and Mr. Thusing, distinguished guests and friends and participants. I am extremely happy to be with you today to participate in this national workshop on job creation in the urban informal sector. More than hundred million live below the poverty line in India today. My immediate concern is the welfare of these people. The informal sector which we are to discuss today is one of the main areas which can provide employment to the urban poor. The problem of urban poverty is becoming more acute due to the migration of rural poor to the urban areas in search of employment. By and large this migrant population is accommodated in formal urban settlements which we popularly call slums. It has been estimated that more than fifty million people live in slums in India, in conditions lacking in basic amenities such as water supply and sanitation. The areas also lack healthcare, proper shelter, and have high crime rates. The Ministry of Urban Employment and Poverty Alleviation is entrusted with the task of creating avenues for the employment of these people. Employment or under-employment in rural areas has a direct relation to agriculture. This is not the case in urban areas. In fact, even among the poorest of the urban poor, there is no such thing as complete unemployment. Almost everybody in every poor urban family does some work. The problem is more of under-employment or disguised unemployment. Long hours, poor wages and indifferent working conditions characterise urban poverty. It is not possible for any government to provide or facilitate one job for every poor person. However, it can create an environment, which increases job opportunities. It can ensure flow of capital towards the poor and above all it can train and upgrade the skill of the poor so that they can utilise these opportunities.

My Ministry is implementing a programme called the Swarna Jayanta Shahri Rozgar Yojana. The programme has three main components, namely the urban self-employment programme which attempts to provide low cost subsidised capital to the urban poor for setting up micro enterprises. The urban wage employment programme which seeks to generate man-hours of work for urban labour and the training for capacity building programme which seems to upgrade the capacities and the skills of the urban poor. After viewing these programmes I have come to the conclusion that far too little emphasis has been placed on training and self-upgradation. Under my direction, therefore, this Ministry is busy recasting the guidelines of the programme so that more emphasis is laid on the training and skill upgradation, thereby arming the urban poor with the capacity to rise above poverty.

The performance of urban self-employment programmes can largely be termed disappointing due to the failure of financial institutions to provide credit to the urban poor. It is my view that higher government subsidy will not encourage banks to lend. Confidence can be created in financial institutions if we are able to create a reservoir of skills among the urban poor. I am sure that if we do this, there are unlimited opportunities for the urban poor. In areas such as the construction sector, services sector, and skill professions like carpentry, plumbing, motor mechanics etc., the possibilities are endless. However, it is essential to have a reliable data on job opportunities, particularly in the informal sector and to match our training and capacity building programmes to these requirements. The Ministry of Labour and my Ministry can form a useful partnership and match job opportunities with such training programmes.

I would also like to stress the need for convergence among various government programmes. I have noted that there are large number of programmes directly or indirectly benefiting the urban poor being implemented by various ministries. The Ministry of small scale industries implements Prime Minister's Rozgar Yojana. The programmes implemented by Rashtriya Yuva Kosh, certain schemes run by the Ministry of Social Justice and Empowerment also come readily to my mind. I believe that an overview is lacking. A compartmentalised approach has given an impression of bad resources. Though the urban sector may be comparatively neglected in terms of budgetary provisions we must keep in mind that the urban environment is far more vigorous economically instead of moaning over lack of resources. The various departments of government must get together and maximise the benefits of their programmes through mutual cooperation. Inter-departmental coordination is also lacking at the policy making and planning levels. The Ministry of Labour, the Planning Commission and the Ministry of Urban Employment and Poverty Alleviation are the three key agencies which monitor and plan employment generation for the poor. I find that other than in work relating to the Parliament, there is little interaction. My Ministry does interact with Planning Commission from time to time. Our interaction with the Ministry of Labour needs to be improved.

The honourable Prime Minister has shown the importance that the NDA government places on solving the problem of urban poverty by creating a separate Ministry namely the Ministry of Urban Employment and Poverty Alleviation to look after the welfare of the urban poor. I intend to fully utilise this opportunity and with the cooperation of sister ministries like the Ministry of Labour, give urban poverty programmes a focus which they hitherto were lacking. I assure that the urban informal sector will also receive my intention. I find from the agenda that this workshop is looking at the importance and dynamic sectors like leather and leather goods, food processing industries, the khadi industries sectors, software etc. I shall be happy to receive inputs as to how my Ministry can contribute in making the urban informal sector a tool for upliftment of the urban poor. I would be particularly happy if this workshop emphasises the need to make life long provisions for those especially vulnerable sections among the poor, namely the aged, the physically challenged, women and children. May I also suggest that this workshop be followed by a series of workshops in important urban centres so that the awareness can be generated in the shortest possible time. I congratulate the ILO and the Ministry of Labour for their initiative in this Workshop.

Address

by

Dr. S.N. Jatiya,

Labour Minister, Govt. of India

(read by Dr. L.D. Mishra, Labour Secretary, Govt. of India)

I am very happy to be associated with this National Workshop on "Strategic Approach to Job Creation in The Urban Informal Sector In India". We appreciate the initiative taken by International Labour Organisation (ILO) to organise such a conference when India has recently taken steps to liberalize its economy. The presence of Director General, ILO amidst us in this workshop shows his concern about the unemployment situation and generally unsatisfactory conditions in the informal sector. The global employment situation remains unfavourable and is a matter of great concern. In India, there are an estimated 10 million fully unemployed and around 23 million under-employed persons. Of more serious concern is the large section of our work force who is working at low levels of productivity and income.

The formal sector of the Indian economy constitutes only about 8 per cent of the work force. In relation to the total work force, it is showing a decreasing trend. According to the latest 1999-2000 estimates, a little more than a quarter of our population is also below the poverty line. Thus, the conditions of work of the people working in the informal sector is a matter of concern for us in this country. The emphasis on 'decent work' by Mr. Juan Somavia, the present DG of ILO, is both timely and important for India.

Globalization of the economy has resulted in competition with other countries which have experienced faster technological changes. Certain adverse consequences follow to this process. There could be many difficulties in ensuring sustainable employability to large segments of India's labour force. The level and quality of skills which the labour force possesses would not be in tune with the emerging demand patterns. Rapid technological transformation and transition entails certain social costs by way of rationalization and displacement. India, like many other developing countries, does not yet have a comprehensive and satisfactory mechanism for minimizing the adverse consequences of globalozation on labour. The new millennium will witness continuing pursuit of new knowledge, information and skills which are of direct interest and relevance to the globalization process and technological changes. To a significant extent, the utilization of labour force will thus become dependent on the knowledge and the access of labour force to information technology.

Globalization and rapid technological change also bring, in their wake, alteration of the normal employment relations, pervasive contractualisation, casualisation and shrinkage of jobs in the organised sector with more and more people being forced to enter into the informal sector. This will make the workers scattered and fragmented; they will find it more difficult to demand and get their due. Due to a number of reasons, trade unions also appear to be losing their strength. Therefore, there is an urgent need for action by national governments and the ILO. It is also important that India and the ILO collaborate in improving skill training, retraining and improving labour market information. I am indeed hopeful that the visit of DG, ILO will make a significant improvement in these areas by direct collaboration between Ministry of Labour and ILO.

We will have to think of extending social security effectively to the unorganized sector. Employers also need to play more attention to updating of training and overall development of their human resources. They must also proactively share with their labour force their concepts on restructuring. Restructuring is quite similar to a development project. The cost of restructuring is indeed a part of the overall project cost. Employers must, therefore, take more responsibility for this process.

India is the second most populous country in the world with a population of about one billion. Human resource development plays an important role in the national economic development. A part of the unemployment problem emanates from a mismatch between the skill requirement of employment opportunities and the skill base of the job seekers. The mismatch is likely to become more acute in the process of rapid structural changes in the economy. It is also necessary for government, therefore, to reorient the educational and training systems towards improving their capabilities to supply the requisite skills in the medium and long run and introduce greater flexibility in the training system so as to enable it to quickly respond to labour market changes in the short run. Besides, the system should also be in a position to impart suitable training to the large mass of workers engaged as self-employed and wage earners in the informal sector for up-gradation of their skills as an effective means for raising their productivity and income level.

The informal sector in rural areas is primarily dominated by agricultural activities. The urban informal sector is becoming important in manufacturing, construction, wholesale and retail trade, hotels and restaurants, transport, storage and communication, finance and insurance, real estate, and community, social and personnel services. These secondary and tertiary sector activities are growing and will continue to grow in the years to come. Setting up of micro enterprises, small-scale industries, household industries in these sectors are to be encouraged. For this, a proper linkage between government, industry, financial institutions and other organizations, especially for dealing with marketing problems, will have to be established. Multi-skilling will be of prime importance since such micro level enterprises cannot afford to hire separate persons for various types of jobs.

Entrepreneurship has to be developed among prospective employers. The proper linkage between organized and informal sectors will also go a long way in developing the informal sector activities in the urban areas. When the informal sector was initially studied by the ILO, it was felt that those employed operated at low levels of skill, capital and technology. I think that the way forward is to improve access in all these three areas. It is now becoming increasingly evident that the informal sector does not always consist of self-employed persons or micro-enterprises with freedom of action. Quite frequently, these informal sector activities tend to disguise pervasive contractualisation. Access to working capital and marketing are also subject to serious bottlenecks. There is a need for more regional and local level studies in these areas.

I hope that this workshop will deliberate on all these aspects and come out with suggestions as to how we should go about for creating jobs in the informal sector, with humane conditions. We should not forget that, in India and a large part of the developing world, the informal sector is crucial not only for employment but also for their contribution to gross domestic product.

While concluding, I wish to express satisfaction of my government for the visit of DG, ILO, and its timeliness. I am hopeful that he and his team will be able to visit at least some parts of the country and experience its rich heritage and cultural diversity. We have been encouraged by the DG's genuine concern for the conditions of work of the majority of labour force. We are looking forward to a new era under his stewardship of ILO, where this great organisation will act both independently and innovatively to assert its basic mandate.

Keynote Address

by

Mr. Juan Somavia

Director-General, International Labour Organization

Thank you all for being here today. Job creation in the informal economy is the key issue for the future of many of our countries and I truly wanted to have this opportunity of being present with you at the moment of launching this meeting.

This is my first time to be back in India in my capacity as Director General of ILO. So, it is a very symbolic moment for me and that is why I want to thank you, very particularly Mr. I.P. Anand, who had a lot to do with my being present here today. He is a great friend of mine; I admire him enormously and I want to thank him for the role he has played to make sure that I would be in India today. Minister Dhindsa, I want to thank you for your presence here in representation of the Government together with the Secretary of the Ministry of Labour, Dr. Mishra, who plays such an important role in our Governing Body.

It is a particular pleasure for me that Dr. Manmohan Singh is chairing this session. All of you, of course, know his role in the intellectual and political life of India. I also have to say that he is a symbol of the contribution that India has made to the international community in so many different spheres. And, I am very proud that he is here with us today. Mr. Thusing is Employer Vice-Chairperson of our Governing Body and his presence is also very important. I also want to thank Mr. Narsimham and all the authorities from Haryana State who are also with us.

India, over the years, has been central to both my thinking and my world of action. As I stand here today, the images of different 'Indias' across the ages pass in front of me. The India of Tagore which, for a Chilean, is very important because he was a very good friend of Pablo Neruda, the famous Chilean poet who was also a Nobel Prize winner. The India of Gandhi whose resting place I visited today. When you see the list of seven sins that Gandhi formulated in 1925 and then you look at the world of globalization today and you go through them one by one, you see that every single one of these sins is the right question to pose today. A certain world is being created, people have a right to ask what is this world and even how should you be responding to the seven questions that Gandhi posed way back in 1925. Then, the India of Nehru and the search for Independence and identity after colonialism; the fight for that and for the country that was going to become the biggest democracy in the world. These are the things that make India what it is and these are the reasons why you are such an extraordinary country and the reason for which I am so happy that I am here with you today.

India has also played a key role in the ILO, almost from its inception. In 1928, the ILO opened its branch office in New Delhi. The ILO field office for Asia was set up in Bangalore in 1949 from where the ILO covered all of Asia for many years. This may be seen as an acknowledgement of the leadership of the Indian Government, the Employers' and Workers' representatives and their contribution to the ILO's technical and substantive work throughout the last century. For these and many other reasons, it is a privilege to be able to join you in opening this important workshop on Job Creation in the Urban Informal Sector of India.

Let me turn to the issue that has gathered us together today. This is a key subject which demonstrates the relationship between the ILO and India. Many of you no doubt know that the term 'Informal Sector' was launched by the ILO in 1972. Just to refer to a little bit of history, when my friend, Prof. Hans Singer led the Employment Strategy Mission to Kenya in 1972, he was struck by a phenomenon that did not fit into the traditional economic analysis, and this is what was then called the informal sector. He reported that the informal sector provided income earning opportunities for a large number of people, though it is often regarded as unproductive and stagnant. He saw it as providing a wide range of low cost labour-intensive, competitive goods and services. Continuing to quote from his report: "a most important consequence of low income was the primacy of risk and uncertainty. We, therefore, advocate a positive attitude on the part of the Government for the promotion of the informal sector".

Since 1972, the informal sector has grown in developing, transition, and developed economies and continues to attract tremendous attention. Statistics vary. According to one estimate, the informal sector represented 43 per cent of non-agricultural workers in North Africa in the beginning of the last decade, 74 per cent in Sub-Saharan Africa, 57 per cent in Latin America, 63 per cent in Asia and 88 per cent in India. But this is not the whole story. What is now being observed is the growth of a wider informal sector and I think we do need to move to a new concept, that of the informal economy, which permeates all countries and represents up to 15 per cent of GDP in developed countries, according to some data. One could and should research further these numbers, because there are many different ways of measuring the informal economy. But the fact remains that the informal economy is large and increasing, particularly in times of economic downturn. This has been the case during the Asian crisis under the pressure of deregulation of labour markets. In 1999, virtually all new jobs generated were in informal activity in Latin America. In Africa, the informal sector accounts for 60 per cent of the urban labour force, and 80 per cent of its growth, while formal employment is declining.

The conclusion that I would like to draw from this is that we have, on the one hand, as a result of the global economy now being shaped, the growth of a knowledge economy, the network society, the information technology revolution that is driving many of the changes that occur in the world, and on the other hand, and at the same time, the growth of the informal economy in all sectors of production. And this is probably one of the biggest dangers in front of us - the digital divide which is expressed by this new duality of the knowledge economy, of financial services, entertainment, the media, the things that we see in the press every day.

When you look at the television, you are accustomed to hearing a lot about market fundamentals. But, you sometimes feel that people are forgetting about the fundamentals in people's lives. We have to be able to make the market work for everybody. We have to link market fundamentals to the fundamental needs of people. This is probably the biggest challenge that we have in front of us. Probably, the way in which this tension is most clearly expressed, reflecting the fact that markets and globalization are not reaching enough people, is the growth of the informal economy. This is the biggest analytical, intellectual, and I would say, political challenge. How can we marry the potential, the creativeness, the richness, the entrepreneurship of the new economy with the fraction of our societies that are not part of it, but that should be part of it if we want to ensure stability in the future. One of the areas about which, I believe, we have to think, concerns small enterprises, because they may provide the link. The small enterprise lives in a world that hovers between the informal economy and the more formal economy. I believe that this is a vast challenge for the ILO.

The strength of the ILO is precisely the presence of the three constituents, the employers, the workers and governments and I want to salute all representatives of employers and trade union organisations that are here today because they confirm an essential dimension of what the ILO is about. Their vision, and the way they perceive the scenario, is very important. Why? Because the whole informal economy is precisely an area in which employers' organisations and workers' organisations are present, whereas governments have a big problem in reaching into it. Within the informal economy, there are many people who are working on their own, isolated, and generating a means of survival and no more. We have to be able to transform that basic instinct of survival from something that belongs, into something that is inclusive, into something that happens in the context of the society and not on the margins of society. This is, I think, the great challenge of your meeting today.

How can we make that happen? I believe that from an ILO point of view, we must zero in on small enterprises. I am talking about a range that goes from self-employment and micro-enterprises, through different forms of sustainable livelihood into more and more organised and structured forms of enterprises; so it is a very wide spectrum that I am referring to. Look at what happens in the real world. It is probably more difficult to create a small enterprise than a big enterprise in the world today. It is ridiculous but that is the way it is. And the reason is because the small entrepreneur, to begin with, does not have a credit record; so the banker says 'sorry, I cannot lend to you because, what would happen if you go broke'. And this goes on, and on. The large enterprise benefits from a number of externalities, as a result of ownership of capital, of the knowledge factor, etc. But individual small entrepreneurs do not have these advantages. I think, from an ILO perspective, the single instrument that can make a difference in the future is that we succeed in taking out the small enterprise from the margin of the political economy at home and from the margin of the global economy, and putting it at the centre-stage.

If we put the small enterprise at the centre of the future, we are going to be able to begin solving the problem of meeting people's aspirations for employment and jobs. Large enterprises, large transnational and multinational corporations may be the providers of trade, technologies, finance and other things that are part of the economy, but they will not provide large numbers of jobs. So, we need to interrogate the global economy of today, and ask who will be the providers of jobs. From where will the employment needs of our societies be met? The answer is that it is essentially in small enterprises that jobs are being created today.

I believe that we have an enormous interest in trying to make small enterprises the source of jobs that are needed, but for that, we have to develop radically different attitudes. If you look at the government side, there is no single government that does not have a Small Enterprise Department, but the fact is that this is not an issue that can be properly tackled by government alone. If you look at banks, they usually do have a window for small enterprises, but it is always a small window for small enterprises; it is not a big window. Regarding organization, I ran into a very surprising situation in a particular developing country. I was invited to meet with the trade unions, and people began to introduce themselves. Sitting in the meeting was the Head of the Association of Small Enterprises of that country. Of course, I was surprised seeing that person sitting there, but he said, 'look, you may be surprised to see me here, perhaps feeling comfortable, but for this country, small enterprises have more interests in common with the trade unions than with the big enterprises'. I am just reflecting on things I have seen, and they may or may not be typical, but clearly, there is a question of representation which needs to be looked at carefully.

So, there is a need and a potential for a new and different look at this area. I would very much like to make the ILO the centre of world reflection on the process of creating small enterprises, and consequently, of creating jobs, the decent jobs that our countries need. And, I think, we have the potential to do this because it also brings together, very strongly, the employers' interest, the trade unions' interest and the governments' interest in generating employment. The ILO is well placed to help in building consensus among its tripartite partners. Indeed, we are already doing a number of things in this field, and in particular, have just launched a new major programme on boosting employment in small enterprises.

I think, employment and workers' rights go hand in hand. Probably one of the biggest enemies of workers' rights is unemployment. If you do not have work, on the whole, you do not benefit from workers' rights, and at the same time, any increase in the pool of the unemployed, diminishes the capacity for negotiations of those who are employed. So, employment is fundamental for workers' rights. You sometimes hear comments such as, "it is better for people to have their noses above the water than to be drowning, so let us not care too much about the working conditions provided there is employment". That may be true for a moment, but, in the long run, we all know that this is not sustainable. So, if we are talking about the informal economy, right from the start, we have to have the perspective, even if it is not immediate, of making it a part of the formal economy, in order to defend rights and assure protection. How can we make sure it moves in the right direction, even if there is first a period of time in which it stays at a certain level? The only sustainable process would be one in which the working conditions and the processes in small and informal enterprises become part of a much wider framework of economic growth, social stability and recognition of social protection.

Something that worries me is that we have a big debate in the world about social protection focussed on whether it should be public or private, whether individuals should be responsible for their own security or whether the state should intervene, whether the money is going to be there to pay for the benefits of increasing numbers of older people, and so on. The ILO is following these debates and contributes with analysis and views, but here, we are faced with a different problem. It is that a majority of people in the world do not have social protection of any kind. That is the reality and let us not confuse ourselves as to the nature of the problem. On one side, there is a discussion as to the best way of ensuring relatively decent forms of social protection, and on the other,there is none.

So, these are the questions that I believe ILO has to pose in a constructive way, in a creative way, in a consensus building way, acknowledging the problems, without attributing fault to one side or the other. Everyone has something to contribute to solve the problem. And what I feel is my responsibility is to obtain from everyone the willingness to put something on the table in order to solve the problem, rather than thinking that 'I am going to lose by sitting down at the table'. It is this sort of a social dialogue which I would encourage at the national level and which it is ILO's responsibility to promote - and of course, it is also a shared responsibility of the employer, worker and government representatives within the country, to promote the idea of sitting together to try to reach solutions in the same way as when we sit down in Geneva.

Let me finish by saying that possibly two things cut across all of this. In a seminar on the urban informal sector, we are inevitably talking about women, about the situation of women in the whole productive sector, whether working in enterprises at home or elsewhere. One of the things that strikes me when I travel in Latin America is the large number of women, who when asked, 'do you work?', say 'no, I do not work', but in reality, they are working 15-16 hours a day; only that they are not in formal employment, but are engaged in informal work, care-work and work in the home. In your discussions, the work of women is absolutely important and key to understanding informal work, and if we do not get that equation right, and we just use more traditional conceptions of employment, a lot of the action is going to be missing.

The other thing that we need to talk about is entrepreneurship. There is an incredible amount of entrepreneurship in the world. Information technology, for instance, people decided to do it and they did it. That is extraordinary. A couple of kids began working in a part of their house, and there was Bill Gates. Somehow, they have done this incredible thing. A company that started only about ten years back grows to the point where it can go out and buy the biggest entertainment business on the market. So, obviously entrepreneurship is out there, strong and alive and quite extraordinary.

The other side of the picture, I believe, is that the biggest entrepreneurs in the world of today are the poor people that have the guts to subsist. It is those people who were born into conditions that would condemn them, and yet they subsist, struggle, and live through them. For them, it is a day to day existence; they do not have a long term perspective. It is today and tomorrow, and then tomorrow again. And, it is this entrepreneurship, will to live and their commitment to life that we have the responsibility to back. It is their belief that, in the end, it is worthwhile for them to strive to have that energy. How can we look away when those kinds of things are happening? Is it not our responsibility to be absolutely beside that person and help him or her work out how, and in which way, one work strategy rather than the other, will give him the needed energy to transform himself and his situation towards a life in which his family will be better off? So, when we talk about entrepreneurship, let us not forget that such a type of entrepreneurship is probably the single most important energy in this world.

One of the things that worries me most is that when we discuss policy, we often do not make connections; we do not realise that the unemployed person means a very unhappy family. A family that does not have a regular income is a family in which there are more possibilities for violence, violence against women or children, or for linkage with drugs or for petty crime or for all the other things that add up to what are sometimes called 'dysfunctional' families. But how can you call a family dysfunctional if it is so because a person was not able to find a decent job, and loses his dignity as a human being. Can we say, well, it is that person's fault, he was not up to it, he was incompetent, incapable? This is what one sometimes hears, from those who put too much emphasis on individual responsibility. I agree that personal responsibility is important; it is the key in order to move forward, and it makes a major contribution to economic and social progress. But, it is only a part of the story, and the society too has major responsibilities to shoulder; society has to be present to support those who are disadvantaged and to be with the people who want to fight and who have that energy to do that.

So, I want to end with that notion. Every time, we talk about a policy option, we are talking about life options, every policy has its impact on the life of people and we cannot disassociate policies from people and simply say, this is going to be very hard and stop there. We have to say, this is going to be very hard but this is the way we ought to deal with the harshness of it. Both things go together. The need is to combine economic efficiency and social efficiency and this, I believe, is the essence of resolving the policy tensions that we have in front of us. We have to make economic efficiency and social efficiency operate at the same time and not separately.

Thank you so much for the opportunity of opening this session and I want to say that I look forward to your conclusions, to different things that are going to be said here. This is a key moment in your country, a key moment worldwide for the issues we are going to discuss today. You can be absolutely sure that your conclusions and the policy lines or ideas and the sensitivities that emerge in your debate will leave a very strong influence on the work that we do in the ILO.

Thank you so much again.

Presidential Address

by

Dr. Manmohan Singh

Former Secretary General, The South Commission, Geneva

My esteemed friend and Director General of the ILO, Dr. Somavia, Sardar S.S. Dhindsa Sahib, Shri I.P. Anand Sahib, Dr. Mishra, Shri Verma, Mr. Thusing, distinguished ladies and gentlemen, I am very happy to be present on this occasion when you are discussing a subject which touches the lives of millions of people. People who in their quest for a life of dignity and self-respect are struggling all over the world and as my esteemed friend, Dr. Somavia pointed out, the challenge before our times is to find a judicious blend of economic efficiency and social efficiency. Change is the law of life, and we are living in a time of unprecedented technological, social and economic change. And we cannot reverse that process and, therefore, the real challenge before the world community is the orderly management of this change. How do we manage change in a manner that it does not disrupt the rhythm of peaceful living, and does not create disturbances which had tremendous social political and economic costs. And together with that, we must also accept that in a world of unprecedented change there are also risks as well as opportunities. Today, as never before, in the human history, modern science and technology have made it possible that chronic poverty does not have to be the inevitable lot of a majority of human kind. It is the task of all those who are involved in social engineering, to design policies and programmes to make it realizable what is possible. And therefore, from all these angles, great importance attaches to the work that lies ahead of your workshop in the next two or three days.

When we talk of the so-called informal sector, or as Dr. Somavia said, the informal economy, we are not talking about a small segment of the humanity. In our own country, as some papers under consideration at the workshop show, we are talking about ninety to ninety two per cent of our working population. We are talking about that segment of our population which contributes nearly sixty per cent to our gross national product. Therefore, we are dealing with the great mass of our people and if economics is about any thing, it is about enabling people to lead a life of dignity and self-respect. And, I am very happy, therefore, that on an occasion like this, when you are discussing the role of the informal sector in generating new jobs, you have the august presence of Dr. Somavia. I think in his previous capacities, he has been a resolute fighter for the cause of social justice. For an equitable international order, he and I have taken part in numerous international meetings in the last thirty years to see that the world economy and the world economic and social order respect imperatives of reconciling social cohesion with economic efficiency. That a person of his eminence is heading the ILO, I think, is something of tremendous significance and I sincerely hope and trust that during his distinguished tenure-ship of the Director General's post, the ILO will scale new heights in enabling all the people of the world to live that life of dignity and self respect about which I have talked a moment ago.

I am very happy that the honourable Minister for Urban Poverty and Unemployment is with us. He has sketched the landscape, and he has pointed out the dilemmas that he faces, and the type of policy coordination he seeks to tackle the problem of urban unemployment and poverty. And, I do hope that your seminar will come up with some concrete suggestions on how to realize that goal. Shri I.P. Anand is a very dear old friend of mine and, in his opening remarks, he has touched upon the key issues that we face in the development of that segment of our economy which the Director General has just now described as the informal economy.

Having been associated with processes of public policy formulation for nearly thirty years in our country, I do feel that the time has come when we ought to undertake a fresh look at what we have been doing. The first thing that I do want to say to this distinguished audience is that, in a world where the only constant is change, you cannot solve the problems of unemployment, whether in the formal sector or in the informal sector, by stopping the process of change. And, when people talk about employment issues divorced from macro economic issues of stabilization and structural change, I am afraid, they are likely to lose sight of what is really realizable on the ground.

Poverty cannot be abolished by having reckless inflation; poverty cannot be removed by having unsustainable fiscal deficits. No country has the option to live beyond its means unless you happen to be the United States, because Japan and many other countries are willing to lend you resources. But no other country, least of all poor countries, have the option to live beyond their means. So, we have to control our fiscal systems. We have to control the inflation, because in many ways, inflation is the worst enemy of the poorest segments of our population. We have to control the balance of payments deficits; no grand mother is available to finance unsustainable deficits. So, all economies have perforce to find ways and means of living within their means. Hence the quest for fiscal deficit, the quest for macro management which will contain balance of payments deficits within limits of tolerance. Now all these can be done in many ways and some ways are better than others, in terms of their impact on social justice, income distributions, and on employment. And the challenge before the intellectual communities, both at the national and at international levels, is to design the context of stabilisation and structural programmes in a manner that they protect the most vulnerable sections of our population. That they avoid unnecessary changes in patterns of income distribution, that right through the beginning they build into their structures the needed social safety nets which will ensure that the costs of change are not put on the weakest shoulders, that is the challenge which the world community, as far as the national economies, and those who formulate economic policies, must face and face securely.

The second thing that I do want to say is that we must also accept that, in the world that we live in, no country can live in isolation; the world economy has become interdependent in a manner which was unthinkable, even two decades ago. The scientific revolution, the resolution in transport and communications, the dismantling of tariff walls have brought about an integration of the world economy which was unthinkable until recently and which is also probably irreversible. So, the real question before us is not that we can wish away this growing interdependence of the world economy; the real question is how to manage this growing inter-dependence purposefully, in the interest of all countries, poor and rich. I think, a real challenge before the world community is to counter the false hope that the processes of globalisation can be rolled back. Again, the real challenge is how do we manage, in an equitable fashion, the growing global inter-dependence of peoples in all countries in a manner that protects the interests of the poor and the rich alike. I think, this is the perspective that should guide all our designs of policy making, both at the national and international levels.

Now, coming to the urban informal economy, first and foremost, what I would like to say is that you cannot find meaningful solutions to the problems of this sector or problems of poverty in a stagnant economy. We need a strong resurgent economy which is growing fast enough to find meaningful solutions to problems, both on employment and poverty. In our own country, we find that, at present estimations, the employment elasticity of income is about 0.40. So, in an economy where labour force is increasing at a rate, say, 2.4 per cent, we need a minimum growth of about 6 per cent to ensure that we do create, in the process of development, enough job opportunities to absorb all the entrants to the labour force. And therefore, all that will go to produce a resurgent economy is fundamental, not only for macro economic management but also for dealing with the problems of poverty and the informal sector. In this seminar, you are dealing with the problems of the informal urban sector.

But then, the magnitude of the problem in the urban informal sector would be more manageable if there is not a premature rush of poor people from the rural areas to the urban sector. That way, in any integrated society, or a scheme of development, if you are trying to solve the problem of cities and urban areas, you must pay due attention to the problems of villagers, of agriculture, of creating more jobs within agriculture, and to create more jobs in the rural non-farm sector. Experience in our own country shows that when agricultural economy grows at a healthy rate, opportunities do arise for creating jobs in the non-farm sector close to the rural areas. We have to ensure that this process continues. And, there is a danger that this process may be disserved or may be hurt by the onward march of more competition. With the improvement of the means of transport and communications, many micro and small enterprises, particularly manufacturing enterprises, and also with the spread of television, the ability of large enterprises to advertise throughout the country, this process can hurt the growth of the so- called non-formal sector, whether it is in rural or in urban areas. So, we have to find counter magnets to neutralise these factors, which in a liberalised economy, can hurt the growth of the informal sector irrespective of its rural or urban locale.

So, if you really want to ensure that the problems of urban informal sector really remain manageable, then we must pay a lot more attention to problems of creating more jobs in rural areas, in agriculture and in the rural non-farm sectors. I have a vision that we have a re-look at the whole strategy of agriculture and industrial development. The classical type of industrialisation that was typical of the West European economies, is somehow not producing the results in terms of employment opportunities in our country, and in other developing countries, for many reasons. First of all, the policy mix which has guided the process of industrialisation whether in Latin America, India or in Africa, with its excessive emphasis on import substitution, neglect of export opportunities, excessive subsidies to capital, repressed interest rate regimes, licensing system which placed a premium on creation of excess capacity, and the labour market rigidities, have all moved together to create a situation where the process of industrialisation in the developing countries is not creating that many jobs as it did during industrial revolution in England and Western Europe. And therefore, there is the need for economic reforms. We must ensure that industrialisation in future, even in the formal sector is freed of such bottlenecks which stand in the way of employment creation; that more drastic policy changes are needed for the informal sector needs hardly to be emphasized.

Important though it is, you will not be able to find meaningful solutions to the problems that we face in this sector unless you are also simultaneously tackling the problems of agriculture and rural development and also to deal with those distortions which restrict the amount of employment creation in the formal sector of the economy. Hence, the need for economic reforms so that the latent potential of industrialization to create more jobs for the benefit of the people can be realized. Within the urban informal sector, there are several schemes dealing with supply bottlenecks, imperfections of the capital market, credit support measures, imperfections in markets and in human resource development strategies, etc. that need to be re-looked upon. However, if the governments of the developing countries are excessively preoccupied with the problems of the ten per cent of the population, I don't think we will find administrative, financial or physical resources to deal with the problems of the informal sector. When we are talking about the informal sector, we are talking about the majority of our people. And yet, when you read newspapers, all the emphasis on policies, programmes, and thrusts deal with the welfare of ten per cent of the population. I think we need to change that mindset.

When I launched India on to the path of liberalization in 1991, there were many pressing reasons. We were faced with tremendous macro economic tensions; we were faced with financial bankruptcy and so we had to do certain things. But my idea was that by economic reforms, by deregulation we would free the government's administrative and financial resources to concentrate on the problems of the poor, and of social development. Unfortunately, that is not happening. And if this is not happening, liberalization by itself cannot solve the problems of poverty, nor can it deal with the problems of equitable distribution of benefits that accrue to us in the process of development. So, while pursuing the task of economic reforms, we must not lose sight of the fact that an economy in the final analysis is not an end in itself. The economy is only a means to enable our people to lead a life of dignity and self-respect.

We must also not forget that markets are very important. We are poor economies, so we cannot afford inefficient functioning of our economic enterprises whether in the public or the private sector. That certainly is true. But we must also never forget that markets benefit those who are part of the market system. When millions and millions of people live on the edge of subsistence, market signals cannot mean very much for them. Therefore, we need extra market measures to deal with the problems of the poor who are at the bottom rung of the ladder. That is why the need for massive investments in social development in general, and health and education in particular. The problems of the informal sector cannot be solved if we cannot deal with the mass illiteracy that prevails among vast segments of our population. Universalisation of access to elementary education has to be a prime lever in which you can give people a hope of getting a decent job in their lives. We cannot replicate the western systems of social security. These are proving to be expensive even in the western countries. But we need to think of new measures to provide social securities for the poor and to those who live in the informal sector. I think, Shrimati Ila Bhatt's very creative work in Self-Employed Women' Organization has shown the way that, even at very low levels of income and acute poverty, it is possible to devise programmes of health care and other social services, which can reach even the poorest of the poor.

So, it is necessary for us to have a fresh look at all instrumentalities of dealing with the backlog of our hope of providing decent work or jobs for the urban poor. I do believe it can be done. Social protection of the classical type, excessive regimentation, excessive regulation through state bureaucracies, I think, will be counter-productive. There is, therefore, a need for creating thinking on the part of other actors in the civil societies, the non-governmental organizations such as the one which has been set up by Shrimati Ila Bhatt in Ahmedabad and surrounding areas to deal with problems of social protection, health care, and basic education for the poor and the down-trodden. That is an essential pre-requisite to give these workers the skills, which they must have if they have ever to get the chance of earning a decent living at levels of productivity and efficiency which will ensure that their jobs are truly sustainable and do not remain sweat shop jobs only.

Coming to the economy, we will have to look at the mechanisms which can improve the productivity of the people engaged in the informal sector. First and foremost is the tremendous shortage of capital. I think, Dr. Somavia and other speakers have mentioned, and we all know that the organized banking system is often unwilling and unable to meet the credit requirements of the poor people. When I talked about the programme of banking sector reforms, it was my hope that in five or six years' time, we would have created a situation where bankers would run after customers, rather than customers running after the banks. Unfortunately however, that vision has not become a reality because, in the mean while, government deficits have grown to an unsustainable levels, so that the banks are quite happy investing in government securities rather than doing their primary function of seeking customers in the productive sectors.

So, we have a major problem. How do we deal with the problem of providing or meeting the credit needs of the people in the informal sector. In our country, Small Industries Development Bank (SIDBI), NABARD, and IDBI have thought of many innovative programmes. But, it would be right to conclude that these programmes have touched only a fringe of the problem. And here also, I do feel, learning from the experience of Gramin Bank in Bangladesh or Self-Help Credit Groups in various other parts of our country, we need to think of other viable alternatives to meet the credit needs of the poor.

It is widely acknowledged that in all informal sector activities, the private moneylender happens to be the most important source of supplying the credit needs. Perhaps, the time has come when we must think of ways and means of linking the unorganised money lender or money market to the organized banking system so that the credit needs of the informal sector can be met more effectively. I hope, this is a subject which will figure in your discussions. In the same way, Dr. Somavia has drawn our attention to the need for developing entrepreneurship, and I do not have to dwell upon that. It needs to be emphasized nevertheless that skill upgradation must be an integral part of the process of giving people a ray of hope, particularly in a world that is witnessing technological changes at such a fast pace. So, for promoting vocationalisation of secondary education, there is a need for setting up top quality industrial training institute for medium type of skills, and I think, this has to be given a lot more priority than has been the case thus far. In our own country, experiences show that while manufacturing sector is ceasing to be the most important source of generating employment, whether in the formal or the informal sector, it is the services sector which offers the greatest potential. Now, the services sector, whether in terms of its importance for creation of employment, or its contribution to the growth of the economy as a whole, its potential is great but that potential is not reflected in the policy mix that has been devised. Services sectors are discriminated against when it comes to giving bank credit, and when it comes to dealing with the problems of government bureaucracy. So, I think, we have to look much more intensively on the needs of a vibrant services sectors which can create more productive jobs in the informal sectors.

The third thing that I do want to say is the marketing support. In a more liberalized economy, the informal sector activities will often be at a disadvantage, with the lowering of the transport costs; rural or urban non-farm enterprises cannot easily compete with products of large-scale enterprises. With the ability of large scale enterprise to advertise massively through multimedia, I suppose, the ability of the informal sector enterprises to stand up to the rigour of competition is also going to be affected. Hence, we need to devise counter strategies to neutralize the advantage of the so-called large-scale sector. I do feel that not all enterprises will be able to flourish in the new liberalized environment. More so, if import liberalization is taking place along with removal of barriers to domestic competition, we must identify sectors which have the potential of standing up to this new threat of competition.

In total terms, you have a fruitful agenda for research for identifying sectors and activities in the informal sector which have the potential of becoming viable, given suitable promotional measures on the part of the state. It is also possible that when all is said and done, many activities in the informal sector will not remain viable in the long run. But that does not mean that they should be allowed to wither away in a disorderly manner. Take the case of khadi and village industries: I do believe that, in a situation when jobs opportunities are not increasing at a fast pace, we cannot willfully talk of throwing people out of work. And also, in a country where institutions of social security are also so underdeveloped, I firmly believe, extra care has to be taken to ensure that problems of transition, especially of small though potentially viable enterprises, are handled with a human touch. That the implicit cost of the process of transition to a more dynamic economy has to be borne much more by the poor and the deprived need not be elaborated here. Accordingly, suitable mechanisms must be created for providing explicit protection to certain activities in the stage of transition such as, for example, insisting that some government departments must provide an assured market for the products of khadi and village industries. I do believe, they continue to have a role even when we talk of a more liberalized economy being on the horizon.

I have listed out all these issues not because I know all the answers to tackle the problems of the informal sector. I have talked about these which will receive in-depth examination and analysis. You have had a very good start with the Director General of the ILO himself having come down from Geneva to give his blessings, his powerful support and his interest in the very important area of our national work and the international communities' work. With these words, I wish your deliberations god's speed, and all success.

Discussion at the Workshop: Major Highlights

G.K. Chadha

The three-day long workshop was spread over 6 technical sessions, one special luncheon session, 4 working-group sessions besides the inaugural and the concluding sessions. In each session, issues were raised, opinions were shared and suggestions were offered, as freely and enthusiastically from the floor as one could imagine, followed by lively discussions, including those emanating through question-answer exercises. On the whole, the workshop threw up a large number of issues, questions and recommendations that have bearing on the functioning of the urban informal sector in general, and its job creating capabilities in particular.

Following the discussion in the four working-group sessions and the six technical sessions, some major highlights of the workshop are briefly discussed under the four broad areas:

1. Policy and Regulatory Environment ;
2. Business Development Services ;
3. Improving Conditions of Work ; and
4. Technology, Productivity and Skill Development.

1. Policy and Regulatory Environment

Given the fact that the sector consists of a multitude of diverse and tiny economic activities, which are often not organized and which generally go unrepresented in policy making, it was strongly felt that there must be a friendly institutional framework for monitoring the overall policy and regulatory environment faced by the sector. The legal and regulatory framework should be transparent and simple; the access to information should be easy and free; market discrimination against the informal sector should stop, and a level playing field should become a rule for all categories of economic activities. In sum, the policy environment should work in a way that the informal sector work is made a decent work. In the context of policy environment, the major points highlighted were as follows.

1.1 The existence and importance of the informal sector need to be recognized by all sections of the society, including the formal sector, so that activities carried on in the sector gain due legitimacy in the eyes of law. Unless this is done, the sector cannot avail of the incentives offered to it, cannot have any legal basis for lodging claims; in brief, all policy interventions would have very low appeal among the intended beneficiaries themselves. The present attitude of the formal sector, and often the government too, to recognize the existence of the informal sector for some purposes, and denying the same otherwise, will automatically disappear when recognition is accorded, and the linkages between the formal and the informal sectors would grow. The official recognition of the sector would also generate congruence of perspectives among all social partners: government, employers, employees, formal sector, ILO; the bureaucratic apathy, that usually mark the informal sector's relationship with the government, especially at the municipal level, would get considerably subdued, if not eliminated.

1.2 The informal sector must engage government's attention at national, state and municipal levels. There is a need for a national policy, that will provide a framework within which, at the state and then at the municipal levels, the authorities and the actors would be able to fill in details that fit into their own local circumstances. In other words, while the central government's attention may largely be fixed on policy front, at the municipal level, it is the programme front that needs to be strengthened. It was also suggested that government should not pay 'too much attention' and involve itself in too many things; to be sure, its interventionists and regulatory approaches must be confined to those areas where these are inescapable.

1.3 The existing registration system needs considerable improvement. The informal sector enterprises are clearly divided between those registered with municipal authorities and those which do not do so due to lack of transparency regarding observance of rules, the fear of taxation, or simply lack of information. The latter usually find themselves vulnerable to legal action or harassment from the law-enforcing agencies, besides denying themselves access to institutional support, be it for credit, extension services, grant of business license, allotment of land, redressal of business grievances, and so on. For this group of operators, there is clearly a case for a sensitization campaign in favour of registration. Perhaps, a two-pronged action, simplification of registration procedures and the peer group pressure, may help.

For the registered units, the major problems are of empowering them vis-a-vis the government machinery at the grass-roots level, on the one hand, and, subjecting them to observe labour laws, on the other. Although self-employment dominate employment in this sector, yet the proportion of hired labourers is quite sizeable in some segments; and in terms of their working conditions and earnings, they are one of the worst off sections of the urban labour force, although, admittedly, many of their employers too are living close to the poverty line. For the wage-paid workers in the sector, the need to enforce labour laws dealing with the payment of minimum wages, regulating work intensity, equal pay for equal work, minimum acceptable safety standards and hygienic conditions at the work place, compensation and insurance against accidents, etc., was repeatedly emphasized.

1.4 Once the society recognizes the significance of the informal sector, and the public authorities register it as a legal entity, empowerment of the sector follows and the people engaged in it get their right of advocacy before the local urban authorities. Many things automatically fall in place, and the case for facilitating the activities carried out by the sector gains due strength. In that event, the need is to make the policy and regulatory environment perfectly transparent and simple so that the people involved in the informal sector understand it and it is no more fearful for them to approach the public authorities and for the latter to unwillingly or indifferently deal with their day to day problems. Most of the facilitating ingredients, e.g., easy access to information, a license to launch an enterprise, credit, raw materials, etc. would then follow smoothly. Usually, one window service is very helpful for micro enterprises so that they do not have to go to various agencies to carry out their work.

1.5 It is well known that a very big majority of the informal sector enterprises have no legitimate access to land; most of them operate in unauthorized spaces. Their work sites are temporary, usually without proper structures. Many among them operate in the open space and carry out manufacturing and other activities in corridors of shops. Although, the basic mandate of the urban development and municipal authorities is to provide clean and hassle-free civic amenities to the citizens which, in many cases, are interpreted to be threatened by the expanding presence of the informal sector enterprises, yet the time has come to emphasize that, because of the sheer size of its employment and its role in containing human misery, the informal sector must feature as an important element in a socially purposeful urban planning exercise.

The provision of authorized work sites, with due regard to proximity to the demand centers for the goods and services provided by the informal sector, may become an integral part of urban planning. The Chandigarh model of allotting space for Rehri markets, and the Hisar model of localizing auto markets in allotted space, are good examples that can be considered for replication elsewhere.

1.6 Improvements in the urban informal sector must not be sought in urban areas only; rural development which has the potential of reducing the unbridled urban-ward movement of people to the already inflated urban informal sector can be a great help. Many studies reveal that it is the rural poverty, occasioned by low productivity of agriculture, and lack of non-farm avenues of employment, that pushes out many a poor and unemployed rural people to the urban informal sector. The need is to develop expanded avenues of non-farm employment in rural areas themselves so that the process of rural poverty getting transferred to urban slums is kept under check. In other words, rural poverty and the urban informal sector must be seen together for effective policy solutions. The Chinese strategy to 'let people leave land but not the country-side' has some lessons for India.

1.7 There is tremendous scope for improving the data base on the informal sector. Firstly, gaps, anomalies and discrepancies are very common; population census, economic census and NSS data suffer from many infirmities. Inter-temporal comparisons are always risky. Secondly, the national-level quinquennial NSS surveys on the informal sector are highly inadequate and outdated; in 2001, we have information on the unorganized manufacturing for 1994-95 only, and on the unorganized trade, for 1997 only, and so on. The data gaps are more glaring when one goes down to three- or four-digit classification of economic activities; a few activities are just bypassed. Thirdly, very little information is available for occupational categories; it is for sure that even the most regular and efficient data gathering agency would not know how many masons, electricians, carpenters, plumbers, motor mechanics, maid servants, vegetable vendors, etc., are languishing in the urban informal sector! Fourthly, evaluation reports, periodically brought out on specific activities or segments of the informal sector, remain only a paper exercise; they usually stay outside public domain. Strengthening data base is thus as much important as other policy issues.

2. Business Development Services

Discussion on business development services included the working of different institutions vis-a-vis the informal sector enterprises, micro finance, marketing assistance, critical networking of tiny and small enterprises. In terms of their direct significance, for up-scaling of the informal sector enterprises at the grass-roots level, the suggestions/ recommendations in this section constitute the most crucial component of the workshop deliberations. The main highlights were as follows.

2.1 The most critical input for setting up and smooth expansion of an informal sector enterprise is credit. Commercial banks and other associated credit agencies are the two institutional players while money lenders, traders, friends and relatives constitute the informal sources of credit. An impression, overwhelmingly endorsed by the workshop, is that, by and large, the informal sector has gained no significant access to institutional sources of finance, for fixed capital and perhaps, much more for working capital. This is largely because the banks usually shy away from providing collateral-free credit. Moreover, for a number of reasons, the banks have a tendency to pay a second fiddle to small account holders; this keeps many of the informal sector entrepreneurs away from the banks. They are thus obliged to fall back upon the informal sources of finance. The nexus between the informal sector enterprises and the informal credit agencies has been highly detrimental to the former; a link with the formal credit institutions must, therefore, be built. There are other problems also.

The problem of credit needs to be tackled from different angles. First, from the bankers' angle, an attitudinal change in their modus operandi is a must so that they perceive the needs and difficulties of the informal sector as a 'respectable client', and do their own bit for promoting the best practices required for the purpose. The bankers should be ready to take more risks especially because the repayment profile of the informal sector borrowers has been highly satisfying. Second, the group lending approach, which has already fostered, albeit in selected areas, a rapport between the informal sector borrowers and the banking sector, deserves to be extended to more areas and more production groups. Group lending drastically cuts down transaction costs; it also cuts down on borrowers' costs like collateral, registration, transportation costs, etc. By entailing a joint liability, it reduces the risk of default and also does away with the requirement of physical collateral.

There are a number of international and national successful experiences of group lending that need to be drawn upon. The Grameen Bank Scheme of Bangladesh, the Bank for Agriculture and Agricultural Cooperatives in Thailand, the Unit Desa Programme of the Bank Rakyat in Indonesia, ACCION International Solidarity Landing Programme, etc. are examples of the former, and the successful functioning of NGOs such as Self-Help Groups run by SEWA in Gujarat, MYRADA in Karnataka, the Working Women's Forum in Tamil Nadu, PRADAN in Bihar and Tamil Nadu, Rashtriya Mahila Kosh, and Girijan Cooperative Corporation of Andhra Pradesh, and so on, are examples of domestic initiatives. Many of the NGOs in India have benefited by linking existing thrift and credit groups to banks through the Self-Help Group scheme, originally initiated by NABARD in 1992, and later adapted by other agencies. Besides an assured flow of credit, interest rate charged on such loans usually does not exceed 12 per cent per annum. Incidentally, India's experience of providing loans to micro enterprises, at subsidized interest rates, has not been very successful and has only discouraged banks from lending to such enterprises. Perhaps, the Group Lending Scheme does promote the philosophy of working under good rather than bad risks.

Government must also seriously consider some credit-guarantee schemes. Some such schemes are already under discussion in the Planning Commission. Venture capital too needs to be addressed. The Planning Commission has already chosen 15 clusters of the informal sector enterprises where a variety of schemes on small and medium enterprise development have been launched, on pilot project basis. This pilot project should have a demonstrative effect for other areas.

2.2 In some cases, especially when an illiterate or a semi-literate person succeeds in obtaining loan for mounting a tiny enterprise, mentor support may become essential. How is such a person to find a place to set up his enterprise, how, and on what terms, is he to relate to his neighbours, how quickly is he able to steer through the local municipal paper work, etc. are the evolutionary problems he may not be able to resolve on his own. The District Urban Development Agencies can help from the government side, and NGOs such as Bharatiya Yuva Shakti Trust and SEWA-Ahmedabad can step in from the non-government side.

2.3 To the extent possible, networking of small enterprises needs to be encouraged. The available experience testifies that such networks spread culture of self- help; the net cumulative benefits from the total stock of experiences of successes and failures are much more than when enterprises plough their lonely furrows. Again, the available experience shows that networking works much more satisfactorily when the informal sector is operating in clusters rather than as scattered and itinerant ventures. To what extent, the networking can be promoted through internet facilities, cannot be satisfactorily answered primarily because digital status differs from region to region, and within a region, from one urban centre to the other.

It was suggested that NGOs should also network so as to share mutual experiences of successes and failures. The successful experiences need to be promoted for capacity building of the actors involved in the field, who may come from the NGOs themselves, the corporate houses, banks, government agencies and institutions (e.g., I.T.I., polytechnics), etc. The manner of networking can vary from region to region.

2.4 It is time that entrepreneurs in the informal sector, especially the young educated and trained urban debutants, are encouraged to get into new production and service ventures. In the coming years, the scope for expanding the network of the urban informal sector activities is likely to improve, firstly, because the domestic economy is poised to throw up newer production relations and inter-industry and inter-sector linkages, and secondly, because the level and nature of demand for services is likely to change drastically in favour of skill- and education-intensive activities as the Indian economy gets more and more globalized.

The anticipated increase in tourist traffic, both from within the country and from abroad, an accelerated pace of the likely expansion of communications and I.T. network, increasing demand for entertainment goods and cultural activities, newer construction of building, roads and other commercial establishments, etc. are a few examples of new areas where the informal sector entrepreneurs can make bold to enter. A long chain of food processing industries awaits to be explored. There is also a tremendous scope for improving the handicrafts and ready-made garments sectors, especially the export-linked segments; regional specializations in handicrafts have yet to prove their commercial strength, especially in the international market. Yet again, the informal sector can expand its employment base, and improve its quality, if the limited production and marketing links with the formal sector that have been cultivated so far, are promoted on a large scale, formally through sub-contracting or ancillarization or putting-out and outsourcing systems.

2.5 An important element of an enabling environment for the informal sector activities is physical infrastructure, e.g., roads, transport, utilities, communications, etc. While improved infrastructure is an indispensable pre-requisite for the growth of any economic activity, some of the infrastructure creation activities can themselves lead to the emergence of the informal sector activities through diverse linkage effects. Increased public investment in infrastructure is thus an important aspect of policies for promoting economic development in general, and the informal sector in particular. An assured accessibility of basic utilities such as gas, electricity and water, and above all, proper and authorized work sites, can substantially improve the working efficiency of the informal sector enterprises.

In many situations, the number and quality of jobs in the informal sector also depend upon the level and pattern of investment in social infrastructure made by public or private agencies, or both. For example, if government establishes a college or a technical institute, many informal sector activities (e.g., restaurants, hotels, photography and stationery shops, photo-copying and telephone booths) come up around it. Similar multiplier effects can be visualized for private investment in social assets, say, a temple complex built by an industrial house. Interpreted from a slightly different perspective, it is thus clear that, in such situations, it is the investment by the formal sector that promotes employment in the informal sector; the formal sector here includes government also.

3. Improving Conditions of Work

Discussion here included improvement in the working conditions and provision of social protection to workers, gender issues, child labour, organization of workers and the role of social partners. Extensive comments were made about the poor quality of employment that included total job insecurity, unwholesome physical working conditions on the one hand, and, pitiable economic conditions reflected by low earnings/wages for a sizeable proportion of the work force, on the other. Anguish against the nearly complete absence of legal provisions for protecting workers in this sector against occupational diseases and injuries, exploitation of child and women workers was voiced with equal vehemence. The non-compliance of the informal sector with labour legislation and core labour standards is of particular concern to the ILO. Action is required in several areas. For example:

3.1 There is a need to develop a national consensus on the problems of the informal sector. This would provide the framework for developing more specific policies at the state and local municipality levels. Recognizing the internal heterogeneity of the sector, policies need to be tailored to specific sub-sectors, and activity groups.

3.2 With regard to social protection, the Kerala Welfare Fund obviously provides a model that has demonstrated a considerable degree of success in extending the scope of social security beyond the traditional frontiers. The model cuts across the boundary between the public and private sectors, and offers an effective mechanism through which the government at the state level is able to address the issues and reach a much wider sections of the work force than has been possible in most of the smaller initiatives which are wide spread throughout the country. The Beedi Workers' Welfare Fund is another national example of success. Then, the group insurance schemes, particularly those offered by the Life Insurance Corporation of India, which provide health care and health benefits to its members and SEWA Insurance Scheme, offer their own bunch of strong points. Finally, the Maharashtra Contract Labour (Mathadi Workers') Boards and Tamil Nadu Welfare schemes for unorganized workers, especially for the construction workers, may also be looked at.

3.3 Particular attention ought to be given to the question of financing of social welfare provisions; this is extremely crucial from the point of view of long run sustainability of such welfare measures. Undoubtedly, the state has a big role to play which has to go much beyond making a formal budget provision. Another mechanism that deserves a serious consideration is the possibility of levying a cess on the output of particular industries, which can be used to build up a fund in the same way as is done with the Beedi Workers Welfare Fund.

3.4 The existing laws need to be more rigorously implemented. It is often the case that the legal provisions, most pointedly in respect of wage rates, compensations, work intensity, working conditions, etc., are dodged not only by the informal sector employers but by the formal sector in its dealings with the informal sector, and by government itself, in its dealing with contract, sub-contract and casual labour.

The inability of the informal sector to comply with certain aspects of labour legislation is not necessarily an indication of defects in the legislation itself; in most cases, it is a reflection of the highly unsatisfactory conditions in which the informal sector has to operate. Deregulation of the labour market would do little, if anything, to improve those conditions. The general approach should therefore be to regard the basic standards and provisions of labour legislations as non-negotiable goals to be attained progressively in the informal sector - and to establish the needed institutions to promote their attainment rather than to regard the precarious and unregulated nature of work in the informal sector as the norm for the rest of the society.

But then, the progressive application of labour standards does not necessarily have to wait until the informal sector starts "catching up" with the formal sector. For example, observance of certain core standards, such as fundamental human rights at work (freedom of association, abolition of forced labour and child labour, non-discrimination in occupation and employment) cannot be the exclusive obligation of the formal sector alone. In the case of child labour, high priority needs to be given to eliminating the worst forms of child labour, such as their involvement in hazardous work. Law enforcement must be accompanied by measures to extend and improve facilities for education - formal and non-formal. Occupational safety and health are other priority areas. Understandably, the informal sector cannot comply with the full range of government safety and health regulations, yet, there is no reason why they should not benefit from information and guidance on the often simple and inexpensive measures that can be taken to reduce risks or from occupational health and safety counselling provided through community-based programmes, perhaps supported by NGOs.

The extension of social security schemes to the informal sector has to be carefully planned and selectively implemented. To begin with, the well-established schemes could be extended to the more developed micro-enterprises in the informal sector. The Union Government should strengthen the national social security institutions, and, hopefully, the public's confidence in them. It should also encourage, and where possible, assist the state governments to strengthen locally-based institutions. The involvement of groups from civil society is essential in order to reach out to widely-spread workers in the informal sector. Group-based solidarity schemes, though usually small in scale and coverage, are often attractive to informal sector workers. Some such schemes could be directly governed by associations or organisations of the informal sector workers themselves (e.g. producer and employers' organisations, cooperatives and credit associations), or they could use intermediate carriers such as trade unions and non-governmental organisations. Once again, the Kerala Welfare Fund, the Maharashtra Mathadi Workers' Boards, the Tamil Nadu Construction Workers Welfare schemes, etc. stand out as good examples. Similarly, the successful schemes developed by NGOs such as Annapoorna Mahila Mandal, Self-Employed Womens' Association, Asian Centre for Organisation, Research and Development (ACORD), etc., for providing at least basic social security benefits at the "grassroots" level, deserve to be documented and replicated.

3.5 It was emphatically suggested that it is only through their own organised efforts and group solidarity that the informal sector workers and producers will achieve lasting improvements in their situation. In the past, it has been the internal heterogeneity of the informal sector, characterized by very diverse interests, priorities and involvements, on the one hand, and competition within these groups for small markets, on the other, that have stood in the way of group solidarity. It is largely because of the absence of pressure from within the informal sector that the various discriminatory policies and practices against the sector have endured themselves for so long. Those working in the informal sector continue to be harassed and exploited, and enjoy little or no protection at all. This must change.

It is encouraging to note that some small local organisations have already been created within the informal sector. Most of the hawkers on the streets of Mumbai, Kolkata and many other cities have formed their own trade unions or associations. In certain cities of Gujarat, they are members of trade associations. Practically, in each big city, taxi drivers, rickshaw pullers, auto-rickshaw operators and truck operators have formed loose federations that protect their interests. Two remarkably successful and very well-known women's movements in India - the Working Women's Forum (WWF) and the Self-employed Women's Association (SEWA) - which started out as cooperative-type movements have succeeded in developing numerous services for an ever-growing number of members. These are now registered as trade unions. Generally, however, such organisations have a highly localised range of their operation, and with their inadequate resources, may not be able to do much in changing the overall environment in which the informal sector operates.

There is also a change in the perception and approach of trade unions towards the informal sector workers. It is now increasingly realized that the trade union movement has to adopt a longer term perspective, and that, organising the informal sector is critical if the movement is to acquire added capability to protect all kinds of workers. It is also increasingly realised that a "community-based" approach to organising, in conjunction with other proven "shop-floor" organising methods, might be more effective in reaching workers in informal activities, particularly when organisers, howsoever determined they may be, are denied access to the workplace or cannot locate the workplace, as is often the case with home-based workers or domestic workers.

A comparable challenge is to foster the informal sector producers' organizations. The informal sector micro enterprises should not always see themselves in antagonistic relationship with the formal sector, but rather as potential partners whose growth could result in more dynamic interchanges between the formal and the informal sectors from which all could benefit. The informal sector, if it had the opportunity to develop, could become a far more important market for the goods produced by the modern sector and at the same time, a more efficient source of a broader range of high-quality inputs required by the modern sector. The informal sector employers' organisations have therefore a critical role to play in promoting self-employment through spreading entrepreneurial culture and assisting it to rise above its marginalized existence in the economy. They could act as a pressure group for the removal of many of the constraints which at present impede the growth of the informal sector. They could also provide the informal sector with access to improved technology and with the improved skills necessary to operate that technology. And they could help small entrepreneurs by educating them about simple management concepts of successfully running an enterprise.

3.6 In specified product, service and trade lines, e.g., computer software and maintenance services, machine parts manufacturing, leather processing and leather products, garment manufacturing, vegetable and fruit selling shops, it may be advisable to have clusters of such activities, located in specified urban pockets. Such clusters automatically result in better working conditions since they provide a useful platform for public intervention, most notably a better enforcement of labour laws and social protection measures, through more frequent inspections of work sites and control over work intensity, wage payments, and so on.

4. Technology, Productivity, Skill Development and Training

Numerous crucial issues were touched upon in this session. The more prominent among these were development and access to technologies, improving quality of work force, the role of basic education, sensitization of formal institutions to the problems of the informal sector, skill development and the role of the vocational training and apprenticeship, the employability of the trained people, the role of cooperatives and industrial estates, fostering partnership with the formal sector in technology up-gradation and productivity improvement, and so on. A number of suggestions were made :

4.1 Access to technology must improve. Several participants mentioned that India has a tradition of creating excellence in the institution of higher learning and research. But the benefits of these brilliant efforts have largely gone to the formal sector; except for sporadic successes, one has yet to come by technology policies and technology development, specifically tailored to the needs of the small and micro enterprises. It was, therefore, vociferously suggested that public institutions and policies should be oriented to provide the expertise of these institutions to the small and micro enterprises as well.

The crucial question is how these institutions can be reoriented and sensitized towards the informal sector. What could be the effective vehicle that would allow dissemination and technology transfer? It is not advisable to create new institutions; instead, the focus should be on building partnership between the formal research agencies and technology imparting institutions and the informal sector; perhaps, NGOs and producers' cooperatives, wherever they exist, can facilitate such partnerships.

Access to technology can be considerably enhanced if technologies are relatively simple, and information on their use and maintenance is easily accessible and user-friendly. Moreover, the technologies on offer should be cheap, relevant and appropriate to the production requirement of the informal sector enterprises. The availability of local resources, ceteris paribus, should guide the technology development choices; if local skills and resources are used judiciously, and dissemination of technology is well targeted, an all-round improvement of the informal sector is pre-assured.

At the policy level, it would be useful to categorize sections of users, each with its own relatively homogenous demand for technology application and related skills. In this regard, separate targeting of entrepreneurs, self-employed and workers can be rewarding. The technology diffusion activities of the Khadi and Village Industries Commission, in respect of specified village industries, could be useful to look at.

4.2 The quality of work force must improve. Among other things, productivity performance and earning capabilities critically depend upon the education, skill and training background of the people at work in the informal sector. It is well known that a sizeable part of the informal sector is occupied by illiterate workers or school drop-outs; the situation is far worse in the case of women workers. A sizeable proportion of the entrepreneurs themselves are no better; lack of technical, managerial and marketing skills is a very common feature with them.

For on-the-job workers, the existing training providers, be they schools, technical training institutes or higher echelons in the educational hierarchy, usually have no schemes to reach them, even those who would like to have a part-time training; whatever knowledge of the trade such workers begin with, and accumulate over time, gets outdated, and consequently, they remain stuck at the lower end of the workers' hierarchy. Training and re-training are thus essential pre-requisites for improving the employment conditions and earnings of the people involved in the informal sector. Perhaps, it would be unrealistic to believe that, in the large and heterogeneous labyrinth of the informal sector, training is relevant for some, say the upper crust of the sector, and not for the vast majority of those operating at the very bottom.

For workers, skill development through vocational training and apprenticeship, as well as through short-term 'hands-on' experience, can be a useful method of imparting training to the workers. There is a need for certification and standardization in the vocational training system. For the micro entrepreneurs in the informal sector, there is a critical need to provide training in basic techniques of book-keeping, marketing, production organization, costing, pricing, etc. Without such knowledge, they will always remain at a disadvantage vis-...-vis their competitors in the formal sector. It is worthwhile to look at the initiatives taken by NGOs such as Resource and Support Centre, Mumbai and Development Alternatives, New Delhi. Provision of training in local polytechnics, in the evenings or on public holidays, could also be given a trial.

It deserves to be emphasized that the informal sector possesses remarkable ingenuity and capacity to innovate; in fact, such an ingenuity is the result of years of learning how to survive in a hostile economic environment. It is important, therefore, that whatever approach is followed for training and technology development for the informal sector, it should build on, and not smother, these inherent qualities of the informal sector.

4.3 In absolute terms, educational facilities have registered a phenomenal expansion during the preceding decades, especially during the 1980s and 1990s, yet, a sizeable proportion of India's children, including those in the urban areas, do not attend any educational institution, even at present. It is children of today who will join the urban labour market, say, after 5 or 10 years. Understandably, in the fiercely competitive labour market, lack of education would prove to be their Achilles' heel; unless the situation on the educational front get quickly rectified, the urban India is bound to watch further expansion of the informal sector's vast pool of low-paid jobs, side by side with the growth of a very small pool of high-paid jobs. More concerted attention, therefore, needs to be paid to basic education.

The need for enhancing basic education is being emphasised by most public fora and academic circles. Perhaps, public investment in the impending Tenth Plan may tilt in favour of social sectors, notably education and health, yet the issue cannot be left at a slightly higher allocation of funds. Looking at the globalization and liberalization contexts, basic education should no more be the same as it was, say, twenty years ago. One of its aims should be to make people trainable so that they are more apt at absorbing skills and knowledge attitudes that are needed in their work. This way, the employability of the trained people would increase, and the ugly situation of the mis-match between what the market needs and what the trained persons are capable of doing, would get considerably reduced. Education followed by training should henceforth be seen as two inseparable elements of human resource development.

4.4 There is also a need to learn from good experiences and set up documentation of best practices. Based on such experiences, tools could be developed and disseminated across the board. It may be a good idea to prepare, for each state, a list of specialized urban training centers where groups of the informal sector workers come for higher training, from within the state or from the neighbouring areas. Panipat, Ambala and Yamuna Nagar in Haryana, Khurja, Aligarh, and Meerut in Uttar Pradesh, etc. are good examples of such centers.

4.5 Organization of small scale and micro enterprises may facilitate better targeting for policy makers and training institutions. Being organized, the demand for skill development and training can be created by workers themselves; perhaps, they can also train themselves. SEWA-Ahmedabad fully supports this line of thinking.

Overall, the workshop participants evinced considerable optimism on the growth potential of the informal sector if appropriate policy environment and institutions are put in place. Most of the suggestions and recommendations set out in this concluding note, and those sketched out in individual papers in this volume, are worthy of a serious consideration, by all concerned stake holders. If some follow-up ensues, 'decent work conditions' in the informal sector, which must necessarily include expanding avenues of productive and secure employment, would no more be a distant dream.

National Workshop on Strategic Approach to Job Creation in the Urban Informal Sector

17-19 February 2000, Surajkund

List of Participants

Government

Mr. K.G. Varma
Financial Commissioner &
Secretary to Govt. of Haryana
Labour & Employment Dept.
Haryana Civil Secretariat
Chandigarh-160 019

Mr. S.C. Sharma
Ministry of Urban Employment
& Poverty Alleviation
Room No. 238 "C"
Nirman Bhawan
New Delhi-110 001

Dr. K.R.S. Krishnan
Ministry of Science & Technology
Dept. of Science & Technology
Technology Bhavan
New Mehrauli Road
New Delhi-110 016

Mr. S. Agarwal
Joint Secretary
Ministry of Industry
Dept. of Small Scale Industries &
Agro and Rural Industries
Udyog Bhawan
New Delhi-110 011

Mr. Sat Paul
Director
Ministry of Industry
Dept. of small Scale Industries &
Agro and Rural Industries
Udyog Bhawan
New Delhi-110 011

Mr. B.B. Mohanty
Labour Commissioner
Office of the Labour Commissioner
Govt. of Rajasthan
Jalebi Chowk
Jaipur-302001

Mr. S. K. Das
Director General Labour Welfare
Ministry of Labour
Shram Shakti Bhavan
New Delhi-110 001

Mr. S. Rao
Director, DGE&T
Ministry of Labour
Shram Shakti Bhavan
New Delhi-110 001

Mr. D.K. Sharma
Director, DGE&T
Ministry of Labour
Shram Shakti Bhavan
New Delhi-110 001

Ms. A. Sarvaria
Director
DGE&T
Ministry of Labour
Shram Shakti Bhavan
New Delhi-110 001

Ms. V. Kumar
Director
Ministry of Labour
Shram Shakti Bhavan
New Delhi-110 001

Ms. U. Goswami
S.O. DGLW
Ministry of Labour
Shram Shakti Bhavan
New Delhi-110 001

Mr. C.A. Bhaskaran
Deputy Secretary
Ministry of Labour
Shram Shakti Bhavan
New Delhi-110 001

Mr. V. Parameswaran
Joint Director
Ministry of Labour
Shram Shakti Bhavan
New Delhi-110 001

Mr. O.P. Dahiya
Deputy Director
Ministry of Labour
Shram Shakti Bhavan
New Delhi-110 001

Mr. C.R.V. Rao
Deputy Director General
Ministry of Tourism (G.O.I.)
Transport Bhavan, Parliament Street
New Delhi - 110 001

Ms. Padmja Mehta
Dy. Advisor (Employment)
Planning Commission
Yojna Bhavan, New Delhi-110 001

Mr. C.S. Prasad
Addl. Dev. Commissioner
Office of the Development Commissioner
Small Scale Industries
Ministry of Industry, Govt. of India
Nirman Bhawan (South Wing), 7th floor
Maulana Azad Road, New Delhi-110001

Mr. Ramesh Surwade
Managing Director
Leather Industries Devp. Corpo. Ltd.
Bombay Life Building, 5th floor
45, Veer Nariman Road
Mumbai - 400 001

Mr. Bias P.B.,
Dy. Director
Employment & Self Employment
Guidance Bureau
Old Govt. Aswani Barac No. 12
Opp. Commissioner (Revenue Office)
Nashik Road, Nashik-422101

Shailendra Sharma
Adviser (LEM)
Planning Commission Room No. 115
Yojna Bhavan, Sansad Marg
New Delhi-110 001

Mr. N. Sharan
Sr. Research Officer
Room No. 531
Planning Commission
Yojna Bhavan, Sansad Marg
New Delhi-110 001

Mr. Lukose Vallatharal
Commissioner of Labour, Karnataka
VSL House, J.C. Road
Bangalore-560002

Mr. S.K. Gupta
General Manager
DIC, Udyog Bhavan
Jaipur-302 001

Mr. Sarvesh Vyas
Dy. Director
Dept. of Employment
Govt. of Rajasthan
Jaipur-302 001

Mr. Ishwar Singh
Under Secretary
Ministry of Commerce
Udyog Bhavan, New Delhi-110 001

Employers

Mr. Vineet Virmani
Managing Director
S P Virmani & Sons Pvt Ltd
15 Golf Links, New Delhi 110 003

Dr. (Ms.) N. Hamsa
Additional Secretary
FICCI
Federation House
Tansen Marg
New Delhi-110 001

Mr. G.P. Srivastava
General Manager (P & HR)
Pawan Hans Helicopters Limited
Corporate Office
Safdarjung Airport
New Delhi-110 003

Mr. G.D. Maheshwari
Dy. Secretary General
PHD Chamber of Commerce & Industry
PHD House
Khel Gaon Marg, New Delhi-110 016

Mr. Michael Dias
Secretary
The Employers Association, Delhi
13/16 W.E.A.
Karol Bagh
New Delhi-110 005

Mr. S.K. Sood
Adviser
Employers Federation of India
Army & Navy Building
148 Mahatma Gandi Road
Mumbai-400 001

Mr. T. Tewari
Director (Personnel)
Steel Authority of India Ltd
Ispat Bhavan
Lodi Road
New Delhi-110 003

Mr. C.M. Krishna, Adviser
PHD Chamber of Commerce & Industry
186 Mandakini Enclave
Alakananda
Kalkaji
New Delhi-110 019

Mr. Rajiv Gupta
Dy. General Manager
Dalmia Industries Ltd.
8-A Atmaram House
1 Tolstoy Marg
New Delhi-110 001

Mr. V.N.L. Rao
Hon. Adviser
Employers Association of Rajasthan
231 Bhag Singh Ka Chowk, Adarsh Nagar
Jaipur 302 004

Mr. N.B. Mathur
Adviser
Confederation of Indian Industry
23, Institutional Area
Lodi Road
New Delhi-110 003

Trade Unions

Mr. Shyam Singh Chauhan
President
Haryana State Branch of INTUC
Workshop Road, Yamunanagar
Haryana

Mr. Ashok Singh, President
Uttar Pradesh State Branch of INTUC
3/435, Viswas Khand III Gomati Nagar
Lucknow, U.P.

Mr. K.J. Thakkar
Vice President
Bharatiya Mazdoor Sangh
Shastri Pole
Vadodara-390 001

Mr. W.R. Varadarajan
Secretary
Centre of Indian Trade Unions
AE 113, 10th Main Road
Annanagar
Chennai

Mr. Kunal Rawat
Secretary
Rajasthan State Committee of AITUC
Swami Kumuranand Smarak
Near Hathroi Qila
Jaipur-302001

Mr. Harbhajan Singh Sidhu
General Secretary
Hind Mazdoor Sabha
Delhi State Council
12-Chelmsford Road
New Delhi-110055

Institutions / Academicians / NGOs

Mr. R.S. Antil
Executive Director
Institute of Labour Development
Prakash Deep, 3rd floor
Station Road
Jaipur-302 001

Mr. Alak N. Sharma
Institute for Human Development
IAMR Building (3rd floor)
I.P. Estate, Mahatma Gandhi Marg
New Delhi-110 002

Mr. J.L. Choudhury
Dy. Chief Executive Officer (Khadi/Adm)
Khadi and Village Industries
Commission
Gramodaya, 3, Irla Road
Vile Parle (West)
Mumbai

Mr. Vasant Gupte
Director (Affiliated with HMS)
Maniben Kara Institute
Shrama-Sashana, 57 D, Pradhan Road
Hindu Colony
Dadar (East)
Mumbai-400 014

Ms. J. Andharia
Tata Institute of Social Sciences
Devnar, Sion
Trombay Road
Mumbai-400 088

Ms. R. Sudarshan
NCAER
Bhai Sheila Bhawan
I.P. Estate
New Delhi-110 002

Prof. T.C.A. Anant
Delhi School of Economics
University of Delhi
University Enclave
New Delhi - 110 007

Dr. Keshab Das
Faculty Member
Gujarat Institute of Development Research
Gota, Ahmedabad-380 060

Ms. Neetha N.
Associate Fellow
V.V. Giri National Labour Institute
Post Box No. 68
Sector-24, NOIDA-201 301

Mr. C.P. Gupta
Director (SIPS)
National Productivity Council
5-6 Institutional Area
Lodi Road
New Delhi-110 003

Mr. V.K. Dhar,
Associate Professor
National Institute of Urban Affairs
I&II Floor, Core 4-B
India Habitat Centre
Lodhi Road, New Delhi-110 003

Dr. Arup Mitra
Institute of Economic Growth
Delhi School of Economics
University Enclave, Morris Nagar
Delhi-110 007

Mr. M.S. Ramanujam
Adviser
Institute of Applied Manpower Research
I.P. Estate
Mahatma Gandhi Marg
New Delhi-110 002

Dr. Praveen Sinha
Friedrich Ebert Stiftung
K-70B Hauz Khas
New Delhi-110 016

Mr. M.V. Patro
Deputy General Manager
National Bank for Agriculture and Rural Development
DPD NFF,Samruddin Bldg.,
MIDC Central, Andheri East Road
Bombay-400093

Dr. V.S. Krishna
National Centre for Human Settlements and Environment
E-5/A Girish Kunj
Arera colony
Bhopal-462016

Mr. D.D. Bhuptani
Chairman & Executive Director
International Centre for Entrepreneurship and Career Development
E-1/41, Sterling City
Bopal-380 058
Ahmedabad

Ms. Preet Rustagi
Junior Fellow
Centre for Women Development Studies
25 Bhai Vir Singh Marg
New Delhi-110 001

Donors

Mrs. Gabriele Ramm
Programme Director, GTZ / SHPAP
SHPAP Office
21 Jor Bagh
New Delhi-110003

Mr. M. Gulati
Focal Point Manager
UNIDO
A-445 Lower Ground Floor
Defence Colony
New Delhi-110 024

Mr. N.K. Maini
General Manager
Small Scale Industries Development
Bank of India
1 Jai Singh Road
YMCA Cultural Centre
New Delhi -110 001

Dr. Landa Ruth
MF&ED Advisor
Department for International Development (DFID)
B2/16 Vasant Vihar
New Delhi-110 057

Chairpersons / Resource Persons / Consultants

Dr. Manmohan Singh, M.P.
Former Secretary General
The South Commission, Geneva & Former Union Finance Minister
19 Safdarjung Road
New Delhi-110 001

Mr. S.S. Dhindsa
Union Minister of Urban Employment & Poverty Alleviation
Government of India
Nirman Bhavan
New Delhi-110 001

Dr. S.N. Jatiya
Labour Minister
Government of India
New Delhi - 110 001

Dr. L.D. Mishra
Secretary
Ministry of Labour
Government of India
Shram Shakti Bhavan
New Delhi-110 001

Mr. I.P. Anand
Member ILO Governing Body & Chairman
Workshop Steering Committee
16 Nizamuddin East
New Delhi-110 013

Mr. P.V. Narasimham
Chairman
Institute of Labour Development
C/o The Industrial Finance Corpn. of India Ltd.
IFCI Tower
61 Nehru Place
New Delhi-110 019

Mr. R.S. Varma
Chief Secretary, Haryana
Haryana Civil Secretariat
Chandigarh-160 019

Mr. A.K. Pradhan
Principal Secretary (Labour and Employment)
Government of Gujarat
Block No. 5, New Sachivalaya
Gandhinagar-382010

Mr. N.C. Barooah
Labour Secretary
Government of Assam
Dispur-781006
ASSAM

Mr. A.P. Verma
Principal Secretary Industries
Govt. of Uttar Pradesh
Sachivalaya
Lucknow - 226 001

Dr. Arvind Mohan
Director
Development Planning Board
Lucknow University, Lucknow

Ms. Amarjit Kaur
Secretary
All India Trade Union Congress (AITUC)
24 Canning Lane, New Delhi-110 001

Dr. C.P. Thakur
34, National Media Centre
Gurgaon-122 001 (Haryana)

Mr. C. Subramanian
Principal Secretary
Dept. of Health and Family Welfare
Writers' Building
Govt. of West Bengal
Kolkata-700 001

Prof. G.K. Chadha
School of Social Science
Jawahar Lal Nehru University
New Delhi-110 067

Dr. Ritu Dewan
Dept. of Economics
University of Mumbai (Kalina Campus)
Mumbai

Ms. Sumangala Damodaran
Lady Shri Ram College for Women
Delhi University
Delhi-110 007

Dr. Nagesh Kumar
Senior Fellow
Research and Information System for the the Non-aligned and other Developing Countries
Zone IV, Fourth Floor
India Habitat Centre
New Delhi-110 003

Prof. A. Kundu
School of Social Sciences
Jawahar Lal Nehru University
New Delhi-110 067

Prof. Surjit Singh
Institute of Development Studies
8-B Jhalana Institutional Area
Jaipur-302004

Mr. M. P. Kapoor
Director
Thapar Institute of Engineering & Technology
Thapar Technical Campus
Post Box No. 32
Patiala (Punjab)

Prof. L.K. Deshpande
Flat No. 8, Chaitraban
Hanuman Ex Road No. 1
Ville Parle
Bombay-400 057

Mr. S.L. Kapur
C/o PHD House
Opp. Asian Games Village
New Delhi-110 016

Mr. D.N. Davar
B-5/82 Safdarjung Extension Area
New Delhi-110 029

Mr. S. Krishnan
Jt. Secretary Ministry of Labour & DGE&T
Shram Shakti Bhavan
New Delhi-110 001

Ms. Indira Mishra
Principal Secretary Labour
Govt. of Madhya Pradesh
Vallabh Bhawan
Bhopal (M.P.)

Ms. Navraj Sandhu
Labour Commissioner Haryana
30 Bays Building, Sector 17
Chandigarh-160 019

Dr. S.P. Gupta
Member Planning Commission
Yojna Bhavan
Parliament Street
New Delhi-110 001

Mr.S.S. Chattopadhyay
Secretary to Govt. of India
Ministry of Urban Employment & Poverty Alleviation
Nirman Bhavan
New Delhi-110 001

Mr. B.M. Agarwal
Vice Chairman
Institute of Labour Development
C/o The Industrial Finance Corp of India Ltd.
IFCI Tower, 61 Nehru Place
New Delhi-110 019

Dr. T.S. Papola
Head, Mountain Enterprises & Infrastructure Division
International Centre for Integrated Mountain Development
Jawalakhel, Lalitpur
P.O. Box 3228
Nepal

Ms.Renana Jhabvala
National Co-ordinator
Self Employed Women's Association (SEWA)
Sewa Reception Centre
Opp. Victoria Garden
Bhadra, Ahmedabad-380001

Mr. V.P. Sawhney
3/4 Sarvapriya Vihar
New Delhi-110016

ILO, Geneva

Mr. Juan Somavia
Director-General
ILO, Geneva

Mr. P. Gopinath
Counsellor to DG
ILO, Geneva

Mr. Gerry Rodgers
Executive Director, Cabinet
ILO, Geneva

Mr. Samir Radwan
Senior Policy Adviser
ILO, Geneva

Ms. Andrea Singh
Job Creation and Enterprise Development Dept.
ILO, Geneva

ILO, Turin

Mr. F. Fluitman
Manager
Employment and Skill Development Programme
International Training Centre of the ILO
TURIN

ILO, New Delhi

Ms. Mary Johnson
Director
ILO Office, New Delhi

Mr. A.S. Oberai
Director
ILO-SAAT, New Delhi

Mr. G. Sandi
Deputy Director
ILO Office, New Delhi

Mr. G.Joshi
Senior Specialist
Small Enterprise & Management Development
ILO-SAAT, New Delhi

Ms. J. Tuladhar
Senior Specialist
Gender & Women Workers' Issues
ILO-SAAT, New Delhi

Mr. J. Woodall
Senior Specialist
Social Security
ILO-SAAT, New Delhi

Mr. S. Acharya
Senior Specialist
Labour Market
ILO-SAAT, New Delhi

Mr. D.P. A. Naidu
Senior Specialist
Workers' Activities
ILO-SAAT, New Delhi

Ms. S. Rothboeck
Associate Expert
ILO-SAAT, New Delhi

Ms. C. Hakansta
Associate Expert
ILO-SAAT, New Delhi

Ms. H. Junger
Programme Officer
ILO Office, New Delhi

Ms. Madhu Dhawan
ILO-SAAT, New Delhi

Mr. P. Gopi Krishna
ILO-SAAT, New Delhi

Ms. Kusum Chand
ILO Office, New Delhi

Mr. K. Nair
ILO Office, New Delhi

Mr. M.L. Nandrajog
ILO Consultant -Workshop Co-ordinator

www.ingramcontent.com/pod-product-compliance
Ingram Content Group UK Ltd.
Pitfield, Milton Keynes, MK11 3LW, UK
UKHW020225290926
15470UKWH00001B/381

9 789221 119043